Investment
Volume 2: Tax Policy
and the Cost of Capital

Investment
Volume 2: Tax Policy
and the Cost of Capital

Dale W. Jorgenson

The MIT Press
Cambridge, Massachusetts
London, England

This book was printed and bound in the United States of America.

Library of Congress Cataloging-in-Publication Data

Jorgenson, Dale Weldeau, 1933–
    Investment / Dale W. Jorgenson.
        p. cm.
    Includes bibliographical references and index.
    Contents: v. 1. Capital theory and investment behavior — v. 2. Tax policy and the cost of capital.
    ISBN 0–262–10056–8 (v. 1: alk. paper). — ISBN 0–262–10057–6 (v. 2: alk. paper)
    1. Capital investments — United States. 2. Capital costs—United States.
3. Income tax—United States. 4. Corporations—United States—Taxation.
I. Title.
HG4028.C4J67   1996   95–45426
332.6—dc20   CIP

Contents

List of Tables

Preface

Dale W. Jorgenson

This is the second of two volumes containing my empirical studies of investment behavior and is devoted to the cost of capital approach to tax policy. The first volume, entitled *Capital Theory and Investment Behavior,* focuses on the cost of capital as a determinant of investment expenditures. The unifying framework for the two volumes is a model of capital as a factor of production that I introduced in 1963.

The cost of capital approach has supplied an important intellectual impetus for reforms of capital income taxation in the United States and around the world. The early 1980s continued the shift from income to consumption as a base for taxation that had characterized the postwar period. Earlier, three landmark reports in Sweden, the United Kingdom, and the United States had proposed taking these developments to their logical conclusion by completely replacing income by consumption as a tax base.[1]

Initially, inventives for investment were enhanced by allowing more rapid write offs of investment outlays. An alternative policy was to offset tax liabilities by subsidies for investment. In the United States an investment tax credit was introduced for this purpose in 1962. The ultimate incentive would be to treat investment expenditures symmetrically with outlays on current account, thereby removing investment from the tax base and shifting the base to consumption.[2]

To stimulate saving, individuals were allowed to establish tax favored accounts. In the United States these took the form of pension funds for corporate and noncorporate businesses and Individual Retirement Accounts. Contributions were excluded from income for tax purposes and earnings were not taxed until withdrawn, so that saving through these accounts was removed from the tax base. By allowing unlimited contributions to the accounts the tax base could be shifted from income to consumption.

When the Administration of President Ronald Reagan took office in

January 1981, there was widespread concern about the slowdown of U.S. economic growth. Tax reform received overwhelming support from the Congress with the enactment of the Economic Recovery Tax Act of 1981. The 1981 Tax Act combined substantial reductions in tax rates with sizable enhancements in incentives for saving and investment.

Beginning with the introduction of accelerated depreciation in 1954 and the investment tax credit in 1962, U.S. tax policy had incorporated progressively more elaborate tax preferences for specific forms of capital income. The 1981 Tax Act brought these developments to their highest point with adoption of the Accelerated Cost Recovery System and a 10 percent investment tax credit. These tax provisions severed the connection between capital cost recovery and the economic concept of income.

The tax reforms of the early 1980s substantially reduced the burden of taxation on capital income. However, these policies also heightened discrepancies among burdens on different types of capital. This gave rise to concerns in the Congress about distortions in the allocation of capital. In the State of the Union Address in January 1984 President Reagan announced that he had requested a plan for further reform from the Treasury, initiating a lengthy debate that eventuated in the Tax Reform Act of 1986.[3]

The 1986 Tax Act abruptly reversed the direction of U.S. tax policy. The tax base was broadened by wholesale elimination of tax preferences for both individuals and corporations. The investment tax credit was repealed for property placed in service after December 31, 1985. Capital consumption allowances were brought into line with economic depreciation. Revenues generated by base broadening were used to finance sharp reductions in tax rates at corporate and individual levels.

The 1986 Tax Act reflected a new conceptual framework for the analysis of capital income taxation. This framework had its origins in two concepts introduced in the 1960s—the effective tax rate, pioneered by Arnold C. Harberger (1962, 1966), and the cost of capital, originated in my papers of 1963 and 1965. These papers are reprinted in the companion volume, *Capital Theory and Investment Behavior*. The cost of capital and the effective tax rate were combined in the concept of the marginal effective tax rate introduced in my 1980 paper with Alan J. Auerbach, reprinted as chapter 8 below.

Marginal effective tax rates must be carefully distinguished from the average effective tax rates introduced by Harberger (1962, 1966). Marginal and average tax rates differ substantially, since changes in tax laws usually apply only to new assets. In the model of capital as a factor of production that I introduced in 1963, new and existing assets are perfect substitutes in production, so that marginal rather than average tax rates are relevant for measuring distortions in the allocation of capital.

The average effective tax rates presented by Harberger (1962) included corporate income taxes and property taxes, but not individual taxes on corporate distributions. Harberger (1966) incorporated individual taxes on dividends as well as taxes on capital gains realized on corporate equity.[4] Martin S. Feldstein and Lawrence H. Summers (1979) presented average effective tax rates for the U.S. corporate sector that included individual as well as corporate tax liabilities.

Widespread applications of the cost of capital and the marginal effective tax rate are due to the fact that these concepts facilitate the representation of economically relevant features of complex tax statutes in a highly succinct form. The cost of capital summarizes the information about the future consequences of investment essential for current decisions. The marginal effective tax rate characterizes the tax consequences of these decisions and greatly enhances the transparency of tax rules.

My testimony before the Committee on Finance of the U.S. Senate on October 22, 1979, and the Committee on Ways and Means of the U.S. House of Representatives on November 14, 1979, provided the initial impetus for using marginal effective tax rates in reforming the taxation of income from capital. This testimony applied marginal effective tax rates based on my work with Auerbach to quantify differences in the tax treatment of different types of capital. Although the cost of capital approach had no effect on the 1981 Tax Act, this approach spread rapidly among tax policy analysts, both inside and outside the government.

An important milestone in diffusion of the cost of capital approach was the Conference on Depreciation, Inflation, and the Taxation of Income from Capital, held at the Urban Institute in Washington, D.C., on December 1, 1980. The participants in this conference included tax analysts from universities, research institutions, the U.S. Department of the Treasury, and the staff of the U.S. Congress. I presented marginal effective tax rates for all types of assets and all industries in my paper with Martin A. Sullivan, reprinted as chapter 9 below.

The publication of the conference proceedings in 1981 was followed quickly by the first official estimates of marginal effective tax rates by the President's Council of Economic Advisers in early 1982. Subsequently, marginal effective tax rates helped to frame the alternative proposals that led to the Tax Reform Act of 1986. An important objective of this legislation was to "level the playing field" by equalizing marginal effective tax rates on different types of capital income.[5]

The literature on the cost of capital approach developed at an explosive pace during the 1980s, leading to the presentation of the Treasury proposal, requested by President Reagan, in November 1984.[6] This proposal was accompanied by marginal effective tax rates for different types of assets. An important objective was to equalize these rates. A second objective was to insulate the definition of capital income from the impact of inflation. The cost of capital provided the analytical framework for achieving both of these objectives.

Many of the important issues in implementing marginal effective tax rates have been debated for nearly three decades following introduction of the cost of capital in my 1963 paper, reprinted in the companion volume, *Capital Theory and Investment Behavior*. Statutory tax rates and the definition of taxable income provide only part of the information required. In addition, estimates of economic depreciation are necessary to assess the need for capital cost recovery. Since the income tax base is not insulated from inflation, rates of inflation must also be taken into account.

The first empirical issue in measuring the cost of capital is the description of capital cost recovery. The cost of capital formula introduced in my 1963 paper allowed for differences between tax and economic depreciation. The modeling of provisions for capital cost recovery as the present value of deductions from income was the crucial innovation in my 1967 and 1971 papers with Robert E. Hall, reprinted as chapters 1 and 2 below. This formulation of capital cost recovery has been adopted in almost all subsequent studies.

My 1967 paper with Hall was the first application of the cost of capital approach to the analysis of tax policy. We modeled the introduction of accelerated depreciation in 1954 and new guidelines for asset lifetimes in 1962. We considered the impact of the investment tax credit, also introduced in 1962. Finally, we analyzed the impact of a hypothetical tax reform, treating investment expenditures in the same way as expenditures on current account, thereby shifting the tax base from income to consumption.

My 1971 paper with Hall analyzed all of the tax policies considered in our 1967 paper. In addition to adoption of the investment tax credit in 1962 we analyzed the 1964 repeal of the Long Amendment, which had reduced the base for depreciation by the amount of the credit. We also considered reduction in the corporate income tax rate in 1964 and suspension of the investment tax credit in 1966.

The model for taxation of corporate capital income I developed with Hall was also used in implementing the concept of capital as a factor of production in my 1973 paper on postwar U.S. economic growth with Laurits R. Christensen, reprinted in my 1995 book, *Productivity, volume 1: Postwar U.S. Economic Growth.* Christensen and I extended this model to noncorporate and household capital incomes. This enabled us to include differences in returns due to taxation in our measure of the growth of capital input.

Christensen and I imbedded estimates of the cost of capital into a complete system of U.S. national accounts. The critical innovation in this accounting system was the construction of internally consistent accounts for income, product, and wealth. We distinguished two approaches to the analysis of economic growth. We used data on inputs and outputs from the production account to allocate the sources of economic growth between investment and productivity. We divided the uses of economic growth between consumption and saving by means of data from the income and expenditure account.

In the Christensen-Jorgenson accounting system saving was linked to the asset side of the wealth account through capital accumulation equations. These equations provided a perpetual inventory of assets of different vintages. Prices for these different vintages were linked to rental prices of capital inputs through a parallel set of capital asset pricing equations. The complete system of vintage accounts contained stocks of assets of each vintage and their prices. Stocks were cumulated to obtain asset quantities, while prices were used to derive the cost of capital for each asset.

My initial modeling of tax provisions for capital cost recovery was based on the plausible assumption that taxpayers choose among alternative provisions to minimize their tax liabilities. This assumption was used, for example, in my papers with Hall and my paper with Christensen. Sullivan and I presented a detailed study of actual practices for capital cost recovery in our 1981 paper, chapter 9 below. This description has been employed in many subsequent studies, including my 1986 paper with Kun-Young Yun, reprinted as chapter 11, and our 1991 book, *Tax Reform and The Cost of Capital.*

The second empirical issue in measuring the cost of capital is inflation in asset prices. A comparison of alternative treatments of inflation in measures of the cost of capital was included in my 1968 papers with Calvin D. Siebert, reprinted in the companion volume, *Capital Theory and Investment Behavior*. The assumption of perfect foresight or rational expectations of inflation emerged as the most appropriate formulation and has been used in most subsequent studies.

The third empirical issue in implementing the cost of capital is measuring economic depreciation. This was the focus of my 1974 paper, "The Economic Theory of Replacement and Depreciation," reprinted as chapter 5 below. This paper presented a theory of replacement investment and a dual theory of economic depreciation. The theory of depreciation was originally introduced by Harold S. Hotelling (1925) and subsequently developed by Kenneth J. Arrow (1964) and Hall (1968). My paper also surveyed the empirical literature and concluded that depreciation at a constant geometric rate provides a satisfactory approximation for measuring the cost of capital.

Charles R. Hulten and Frank C. Wykoff (1981a) developed an econometric methodology for measuring economic depreciation. Hall (1971a) had modeled prices of assets as functions of age and asset characteristics. The important innovation by Hulten and Wykoff was to allow for "censoring" asset prices by retirements. They demonstrated that a geometric decline in efficiency of assets with age provides a satisfactory approximation to the actual decline.[7]

Hulten, James W. Robertson, and Wykoff (1989, p. 255) carefully documented the stability of efficiency decline in the face of changes in tax policy and sharp increases in energy prices during the 1970s. They concluded that " the use of a single number of characterize the process of economic depreciation (of a given type of capital asset) seems justified in light of the results of this chapter." Constant depreciation rates greatly simplify the model of capital as a factor of production in chapter 5. Replacement is proportional to the stock of capital, while depreciation is proportional to the asset price.

Constant geometric depreciation rates based on those of Hulten and Wykoff (1981a) were incorporated into estimates of marginal effective tax rates in my papers with Sullivan and Yun, reprinted as chapters 9 and 11, my 1991 book with Yun, and the international comparisons I given in my 1993 book, edited with Ralph Landau. The Hulten-Wykoff depreciation rates were also employed in measuring capital input my 1987 book with Frank Gollop and Barbara Fraumeni, *Productivity and U.S. Economic Growth*. The results are summarized in my 1988 paper on growth of the U.S. economy, reprinted in my 1995 volume, *Productivity, volume 1: Postwar U.S. Economic Growth.*

The marginal effective tax rates introduced in my 1980 paper with Auerbach included corporate taxes. Marginal effective tax rates for corporate source income including both corporate and personal taxes provided the basis for detailed comparisons of taxes in Germany, Sweden, the U.K., and the U.S. for 1980 by Mervyn A. King and Don Fullerton (1984). Fullerton (1987) and Fullerton, Robert Gillette, and James Mackie (1987) provided comparisons among tax rates for corporate, noncorporate, and housing sectors of the U.S.

The tax base for corporate income depends on provisions for capital cost recovery, while the tax base for personal income depends on the treatment of corporate distributions—dividends, interest, and capital gains. To analyze the impact of tax incentives for investment the corporate income tax is the focus. Incentives to save are reflected in the personal income tax. Of course, both levels of taxation are required in assessing the impact of the corporate income tax.

My 1993 paper presented international comparisons of tax reforms for capital income over the period 1980-1990 in the G7 countries—Canada, France, Germany, Italy, Japan, the United Kingdom, and the United States—together with Australia and Sweden. These comparisons were based on marginal effective tax rates for different types of capital income in all nine countries for the years 1980, 1985, and 1990. These tax rates were constructed by nine teams, one from each country, using a common methodology incorporating that of King and Fullerton (1984).

My international comparison of marginal effective tax rates revealed widespread changes in the taxation of income from capital, similar to those in the U.S. Base broadening through elimination of investment and saving incentives and reductions in tax rates were nearly universal. This resulted in considerable "leveling of the playing field" among different assets. However, wide gaps among effective tax rates remained in all nine countries, so that important opportunities for tax reform still exist.

The incorporation of personal taxes into the corporate cost of capital raised a host of new issues.[8] In the "new" view proposed by King (1977) the corporation retains earnings sufficient to finance the equity portion of investment and dividends are determined by the residual cash flow. The marginal source of equity funds is retained earnings, so that the tax rate on dividends does not affect the price of capital services or the effective tax rate on corporate income.

Under the new view of corporate finance and taxation, the most attractive investment available to the corporation is to liquidate its assets and repurchase its outstanding shares. Each dollar of assets liquidated enhances the value of the remaining shares. Repurchasing the firm's outstanding shares is ruled out by assumption, so that equity is "trapped" in the firm. Accordingly, this view of corporate taxation has been characterized as the "trapped equity" approach.

In chapter 11 Yun and I presented an alternative model of the cost of capital in the corporate sector. This is the "traditional" view of corporate finance and taxation employed, for example, by Harberger (1966), Feldstein and Summers (1979), and James Poterba and Summers (1983). In the traditional view the marginal source of funds for the equity portion of the firm's investments is new share issues, since dividends are fixed by assumption. An additional dollar of new share issues adds precisely one dollar to the value of the firm's assets.

It is important to underline the critical role of the assumption that dividends are a fixed proportion of corporate income. If the firm were to reduce dividends by one dollar to finance an additional dollar of investment, stockholders would avoid personal taxes on the dividends. The addition to investment would produce a capital gain that is taxed at a lower rate and shareholders would experience an increase in wealth. It is always in the interest of shareholders for the firm to finance investment from retained earnings rather than new issues of equity.

As Sinn (1991) has emphasized, both the traditional and the new view of corporate taxation depend crucially on assumptions about financial policy of the firm. The traditional view depends on the assumption that dividends are a fixed proportion of corporate income, so that the marginal source of funds for financing investment is new issues. The new view depends on the assumption that new issues of equity (or repurchases) are fixed, so that the marginal source of funds is retained earnings.

In fact, firms use both sources of equity finance, sometimes simultaneously. The King-Fullerton framework employed in my international comparisons of 1993 is based on the actual distribution of new equity finance from new issues and retained earnings. Since retained earnings greatly predominate over new issues, this approach turns out to be empirically equivalent to adopting the new view. Sinn (1991) suggests choosing new issues and retained earnings to minimize the cost of equity finance. This is also equivalent empirically to the new view for most countries.

The second set of issues raised by the introduction of personal taxes into the corporate cost of capital relates to the treatment of debt and equity in the corporate tax structure. In chapter 11 Yun and I assumed that debt-equity ratios are the same for all assets within the corporate sector. This assumption was also employed by King and Fullerton (1984). However, Roger H. Gordon, James R. Hines, and Summers (1987) argued that different types of assets should be associated with different debt-equity ratios.

The inclusion of personal taxes on corporate distributions to equity holders also raises more specific issues on the impact of inflation in asset prices. A comprehensive treatment of these issues is provided by Feldstein (1983). Since nominal interest expenses are deductible at the corporate level, while nominal interest payments are taxable at the individual level, an important issue is the impact of inflation on nominal interest rates. Feldstein and Summers (1979) assumed that Fisher's Law holds, namely, that a change in inflation is reflected point for point in changes in nominal interest rates. Summers (1983) provided empirical support for this assumption.

The cost of capital has become an indispensable analytical tool for studies of the economic impact of tax policies. These studies have taken two forms. First, the cost of capital has been incorporated into investment functions in macroeconometric models. These models are useful primarily in modeling the short run dynamics of responses to changes in tax policy. More recently, the cost of capital has been incorporated into applied general equilibrium models that focus on the impact of tax policy on the allocation of capital. These models are essential for capturing the long run effects of tax reforms.

Investment functions incorporating the cost of capital were proposed for the Brookings quarterly macroeconometric model of the U.S. in my 1965 paper, reprinted in the companion volume, *Capital Theory and Investment Behavior*. I also constructed more detailed investment functions in papers I published with James A. Stephenson in 1967 and 1969 and Sidney S. Handel in 1971, also reprinted in that volume. This work is summarized in my 1971 survey paper, reprinted there.

At the beginning of the debate over the Economic Recovery Tax Act of 1981 the investment equations for all major forecasting models for the U.S. economy had incorporated the cost of capital.[9] Simulations of alternative tax policies had become the staple fare of debates over the economic impacts of specific tax proposals. Illustrations of this type of simulation study are provided by my 1971 paper, reprinted as chapter 4 below, and my 1976 paper with Gordon, reprinted as chapter 7. Both papers employed modifications of the DRI quarterly macroeconometric model of the U.S.

My 1971 paper replaced the investment functions in the DRI quarterly model with alternative functions like those in my 1971 paper with Hall, chapter 2. The specific focus of this paper was the economic impact of a new system of depreciation tax rules–the Asset Depreciation Range (ADR) System announced by President Richard M. Nixon on January 11, 1971. I simulated the U.S. economy for the five year period 1971-5 with and without this policy change. I also compared the impact of the ADR System with that of re-institution of the investment tax credit, which had been suspended in 1969.

The economic impacts of the tax policy changes analyzed in my papers with Hall, chapters 1 and 2, were limited to simulations of investment expenditures and capital stocks. We modeled the short-run dynamics of investment by holding prices and interest rates as well as the level of economic activity constant. By incorporating our investment functions into the DRI quarterly model, I was able to project impacts on employment and economic activity, prices and interest rates, and government deficits. All of these variables were determined endogenously by the DRI model.

The focus of chapter 7 with Gordon was a proposal to employ the investment tax credit as an instrument of counter-cyclical policy. Under this proposal a tax credit would apply during recessions, but would be eliminated during booms. We simulated the impact of the credit, including its introduction in 1962, its enhancement with repeal of the Long Amendment in 1964, the suspension of the credit in 1966-7, repeal in 1969, and, finally, re-institution in 1971. We again employed the DRI model in these simulations.

The conclusion of my work with Gordon was that the use of the investment tax credit as an instrument of counter-cyclical policy had been highly detrimental to economic stability. Of the five major changes in the tax credit since its introduction in 1962, three were badly mistimed and two were in the wrong direction. We concluded that growth, rather than stabilization, should be the primary criterion for selecting the tax credit rate.

One of the important innovations in the econometric model of investment that I introduced in 1963 was the use of an explicit model of production. This generated a sizable literature that is summarized and evaluated in chapter 6. In this chapter I focus on the assumptions that the production function is Cobb-Douglas with elasticity of substitution equal to unity and constant returns to scale. I showed that both of these assumptions were consistent with a broad range of empirical evidence from both cross section and time series studies of production. They have become the standard assumptions for much subsequent work on investment behavior, including that reported in chapters 1, 2, 4 and 7 and the work of Andrew B. Abel (1981).

Another important issue in this type of application, emphasized by Robert E. Lucas (1976) in his critique of econometric methods for policy evaluation, is modeling expectations about future prices of investment goods. This is required in measuring the cost of capital and simulating the impact of changes in tax policy. Since my 1968 papers with Siebert, future prices have been modeled by means of perfect foresight or rational expectations. However, macroeconometric models, such as the DRI model, did not incorporate rational expectations into simulations of alternative policies.

The model of capital as a factor of production, introduced in my 1963 paper and described in much greater detail in chapter 5, contains two dynamic relationships. The first is an accumulation equation, expressing capital stock as a weighted sum of past investments. The second is a capital asset pricing equation, expressing the price of investment goods as the present value of future rentals of capital services. Both relationships should be incorporated into simulations of the effects of changes in tax policy. Macroeconometric models have incorporated the backward-looking equation for capital stock, but have omitted the forward-looking equation for the price of investment goods.

The omission of the capital asset pricing equation from macro-econometric models was due to the lack of simulation techniques appropriate for perfect foresight or rational expectations.[10] To evaluate the economic impact of the 1981 tax reforms, I constructed a dynamic general equilibrium model with Yun that incorporated both the backward-looking equation for capital stock and the forward-looking equation for asset pricing. This model is presented in our 1986 paper, "The Efficiency of Capital Allocation," reprinted as chapter 10.

In the model presented in chapter 10 equilibrium is characterized by an intertemporal price system that clears markets for labor and capital services and consumption and investment goods. This equilibrium links the past and the future through markets for investment goods and capital services. Assets are accumulated through investments, while asset prices equal the present values of future services. Consumption must satisfy conditions for intertemporal optimality of the household sector under perfect foresight. Similarly, investment must satisfy requirements for asset accumulation.

In collaboration with Lawrence Lau, Christensen and I constructed an econometric model of producer behavior based on the translog production possibility frontier. This is presented in our 1973 paper, reprinted in the companion volume, *Econometrics and Producer Behavior*. We estimated this model from data on inputs and outputs in the production account of the Christensen-Jorgenson accounting system. Yun and I incorporated this production model into the model of U.S. economic growth presented in chapter 10.

An important feature of the model of chapter 10 is the representation costs of adjustment. The production possibility frontier captures the demand for capital services and costs of adjusting this demand through the supply of investment goods. The production of investment goods entails foregoing the opportunity to produce consumption goods. The costs of adjusting capital services through investment are external rather than internal and are reflected in the market price of investment goods.

By contrast my 1973 paper, reprinted in chapter 3, presented a model of investment behavior with internal adjustment costs and irreversibility.[11] Internal adjustment costs are reflected in the loss of capital services that must be devoted to the installation of capital rather than the production of marketable output. The cost of capital in these models is a shadow price that reflects both the market price of investment and the shadow value of installation. The model of external adjustment costs in chapter 10 has the decisive advantage that the cost of capital depends only on the market price of investment.

In 1975 Christensen, Lau, and I constructed an econometric model of consumer behavior based on the translog indirect utility function. Our 1975 paper is reprinted in the companion volume, *Modeling Consumer Behavior*. We estimated this model from data in the income and expenditure account of Christensen-Jorgenson accounting system. Yun and I incorporated this model of consumer behavior into the model presented in chapter 10.

My paper with Yun, "Tax Policy and Capital Allocation," reprinted as chapter 11 below, employed our model to simulate the economic impact of the 1981 Tax Act. We found that this tax reform increased potential U.S. economic welfare by 3.5 to 4 percent of the U.S. private national wealth in 1980. We also considered alternative tax reforms, including a shift from income to consumption as the base for taxation. We found that the replacement of corporate and personal income taxes by a consumption tax would have produced dramatic gains in welfare, amounting to 26 to 27 percent of private national wealth.

Yun and I also evaluated the economic impact of the 1986 tax reform, using a new version of our dynamic general equilibrium model of the U.S. economy in our 1990 paper, reprinted as chapter 12. We summarized the 1986 reform in terms of changes in tax rates, the treatment of deductions from income, the availability of tax credits, and provisions for indexing. We also summarized reform proposals that figured prominently in the debate leading up to the 1986 Tax Act. For this purpose we utilized marginal effective tax rates and tax wedges, defined in terms of differences in tax burdens imposed on different types of capital.

My 1990 paper with Yun evaluated the effects of changes in tax policy on economic efficiency by measuring the corresponding changes in potential economic welfare. The reference level of welfare, which served as the basis of comparison among alternative tax policies, was the level attainable under U.S. tax law prior to 1986. Finally, we analyzed losses in efficiency associated with different tax wedges.

We found that much of the potential gain in welfare from the 1986 reform was dissipated through failure to index the income tax base for inflation. At rates of inflation near zero the loss is not substantial. However, at moderate rates of inflation, like those prevailing in the mid-1980s, the loss is significant. Second, the greatest welfare gains would have resulted from equalizing effective tax rates on household and business assets. The potential welfare gains from an income-based tax system, reconstructed along these lines, would have exceeded those from an consumption-based system.

Effective tax rates or tax wedges do not complete the analysis of distortionary effects of capital income taxes. These effects also depend on substitutability among assets. As an example, consider the allocation of capital between short-lived and long-lived depreciable assets in the corporate sector. Even if the interasset difference in tax treatment were large, the distortion of capital allocation could be small if services of the two types of assets were not substitutable. Similarly, the distortion in resource allocation over time could be small if intertemporal substitutability in consumption were small.

In my 1991 article with Kun-Young Yun, reprinted as chapter 13, efficiency losses due to taxation were assessed by means of the concept of the excess burden of taxation. We measured this burden by comparing the growth of the U.S. economy under the actual tax system with growth under a purely hypothetical "lump sum" system. Under the alternative system taxes are levied as a lump sum deduction from wealth, rather than as a proportion of transactions in outputs and factor services. Taxes on these transactions insert tax wedges between demand and supply prices and produce losses in efficiency.

In chapter 13 we evaluated alternative tax policies in terms of the welfare of a representative consumer. For this purpose we employed an intertemporal expenditure function. This gives the wealth required to achieve the level of welfare produced by each tax policy at prices associated with a reference tax policy. We measured the excess burden for the U.S. tax system before and after the Tax Reform Act of 1986.

We summarized our comparisons of alternative tax policies in terms of average and marginal excess burdens per dollar of tax revenue raised. The average excess burden is the cost per dollar if the tax is wholly replaced by a lump sum tax. The marginal excess burden is the cost of replacing only the first dollar of revenue raised by the tax. Marginal excess burdens are relevant for reform. We find that the marginal excess burden of taxation after the 1986 Tax Act was 39.1 cents per dollar of revenue raised, while this burden was 47.2 cents per dollar before the reform.

While the 1986 Tax Act reduced the excess burden of taxation, this legislation did not successfully address the imbalances of the U.S. tax system. After the reform the marginal excess burden of sales taxes was only 26.2 cents per dollar of revenue raised, while the cost of property taxes was even lower at 17.6 cents per dollar. By contrast the cost of income taxes was 49.7 cents per dollar. Substantial imbalances among different income tax programs also remained. The marginal efficiency cost of corporate income taxes was 44.8 cents per dollar. The cost of labor income taxes was 37.6 cents, while the cost of individual taxes on capital income was $1.02 for every dollar of revenue raised!

The analysis of the economic impact of tax policy requires the integration of the cost of capital into macroeconometric models and applied general equilibrium models. The economic impact of the Tax Reform Act of 1986 has been analyzed by means of models of both types. In the simulations of tax policies presented in chapters 11 and

12, each policy was associated with an intertemporal equilibrium, including markets for different types of capital. The disaggregation of capital exposed all the margins for substitution affected by the 1981 and 1986 changes in tax policy.

Shortly after the passage of the Tax Reform Act of 1986, the Department of the Treasury (1987) published a study by Fullerton, Gillette, and Mackie (1987) of the effect of the new legislation on marginal effective tax rates. The results were incorporated into an applied general equilibrium model by Fullerton, Yolanda K. Henderson, and Mackie (1987) and used to estimate the economic impact. Fullerton (1987) presented a closely related study of marginal effective tax rates, while Fullerton and Henderson (1989a, 1989b) conducted a parallel simulation study.[12]

My final objective is to evaluate the cost of capital as a practical guide to tax reform. The primary focus is U.S. tax policy, since the cost of capital has been used much more extensively in the U.S. than other countries. Auerbach and I introduced the key concept, the marginal effective tax rate, early in the debate over the U.S. Economic Recovery Tax Act of 1981. We showed that the tax policy changes of the early 1980s, especially the 1981 Tax Act, would increase barriers to efficient allocation of capital.

By contrast the Tax Reform Act of 1986 substantially reduced barriers to efficiency. The erosion of the income tax base to provide incentives for investment and saving was arrested through vigorous and far-reaching reforms. Incentives were sharply curtailed and efforts were made to equalize marginal effective tax rates among assets. The shift toward expenditure and away from income as a tax base was reversed. My international comparisons of 1993 showed that these reforms had important parallels in other industrialized countries.

The cost of capital approach has also proved its usefulness in pointing the direction for future tax reforms. The initial focus was the allocation of capital within the corporate sector, as in my papers with Auerbach and Sullivan, chapters 8 and 9, and the important extensions by Fullerton and King (1984). My 1990 paper with Yun, chapter 12, revealed that important discrepancies remain between effective tax rates on owner-occupied housing and business capital, so that opportunities still exist for improvements in efficiency.

My international comparisons of 1993 showed that equalizing the tax burdens on housing and business capital has proved to be extraordinarily difficult within the framework of the income tax. An alternative approach would be to revive proposals to convert the tax base from income to consumption. However, taxation of owner-occupied housing as an expenditure involves precisely the same difficulties as taxation on the basis of income, since expenditure and income on this housing are identical.

In the United States proposals to replace income by consumption as a tax base include the "flat tax" of Hall and Rabushka (1983), a European-style consumption-based value added tax, and a comprehensive retail sales tax on consumption. My papers of 1986 and 1990 with Yun, reprinted as chapters 11 and 12, demonstrated that a consumption tax would have been markedly superior to the tax reforms that took place in 1981 and 1986. However, we also showed that an income-based tax that "levels the playing field" among all assets is superior to a consumption tax.

My overall conclusion is that the cost of capital and the closely related concept of the marginal effective tax rate have provided an important intellectual impetus for tax reform. Effective tax rates at both corporate and personal levels are now available for many countries around the world. International comparisons of tax reforms have provided extensive illustrations of successful applications of the cost of capital approach. My hope is that these illustrations will serve as an inspiration and a guide for policy makers who share my goal of making the allocation of capital within a market economy more efficient.

I would like to thank June Wynn of the Department of Economics at Harvard University for her excellent work in assembling the manuscripts for this volume in machine-readable form. Renate D'Arcangelo of the Editorial Office of Division of Applied Sciences at Harvard edited the manuscripts and proofread the machine-readable versions. Warren Hrung, then a senior at Harvard College, checked the references and proofread successive version of the typescript. Gary Bisbee of Chiron Inc. prepared the manuscripts for typesetting, typeset the volume, and provided the camera-ready copy for publication. The staff of The MIT Press, especially Terry Vaughn, Ann Sochi, and Michael Sims, has been very helpful at every stage of the project. I am also grateful to William Richardson and his associates for providing the index. Financial support from the Program on Technology and Economy Policy of the Kennedy School of Government, Harvard University, is gratefully acknowledged. As always, the author retains sole responsibility for any remaining deficiencies in the volume.

Notes

1. See Sven-Olof Lodin (1978), James E. Meade, *et al.* (1978), and U.S. Treasury (1977).

2. Robert E. Hall and Alvin Rabushka (1983) and David F. Bradford (1986) presented detailed proposals for a consumption-based tax in the United States. These were rejected in favor of an income-based approach by the U.S. Treasury (1984).

3. An illuminating account for the tax debate preceding the 1986 Tax Act has been given by Jeffrey H. Birnbaum and Alan S. Murray (1987).

4. Harberger's (1966) estimates were subsequently revised and corrected by John Shoven (1976).

5. The objectives of the 1986 tax reform are discussed by Charles E. McLure and George R. Zodrow (1987).

6. See U.S. Treasury (1984).

7. See, especially, Hulten and Wykoff (1981a), p. 387.

8. Summaries of the alternative views of taxation and corporate finance are given by Anthony B. Atkinson and Joseph E. Stiglitz (1980), esp. pp. 128–159, Auerbach (1983), and Hans-Werner Sinn (1991).

9. See, for example, Robert S. Chirinko and Robert Eisner (1983) and Jane G. Gravelle (1984).

10. These techniques were introduced by David Lipton, Poterba, Jeffrey Sachs, and Summers (1982) and Ray C. Fair and John B. Taylor (1983) long after the methodology for constructing and simulating macroeconometric forecasting models had crystallized.

11. This model combined features of models originated by Arrow (1968) and Lucas (1967a).

12. Henderson (1991) surveys six studies of the economic impact of the 1986 Tax Act by means of applied general equilibrium models. Except for my model with Yun, these models did not include the capital asset pricing equation and are subject to the "Lucas critique."

List of Sources

1. Robert E. Hall and Dale W. Jorgenson 1967. Tax Policy and Investment Behavior. *American Economic Review,* 57, No. 3 (June): 391–414. Reprinted with permission.

2. Robert E. Hall and Dale W. Jorgenson 1971. Application of the Theory of Optimum Capital Accumulation. In *Tax Incentives and Capital Spending,* ed. G. Fromm, 9–60. Washington, DC: The Brookings Institution. Reprinted with permission.

3. Dale W. Jorgenson 1973. Technology and Decision Rules in the Theory of Investment Behavior. *Quarterly Journal of Economics,* 86, No. 4 (November): 523–543. Reprinted with permission.

4. Dale W. Jorgenson 1971. The Economic Impact of Investment Incentives. In Joint Economic Committee, *Long-Term Implications of Current Tax and Spending Proposals.* Washington, DC: Ninety-second Congress, First Session, 176–192. Reprinted in *Readings in Macroeconomics,* eds. W. E. Mitchell, J. H. Hand, and I. Walter. New York, NY: McGraw-Hill, 1974.

5. Dale W. Jorgenson 1973. The Economic Theory of Replacement and Depreciation. In *Econometrics and Economic Theory,* ed. W. Sellekaerts, 189–221. New York, NY: MacMillan. Reprinted with permission.

6. Dale W. Jorgenson 1974. Investment and Production: A Review. In *Frontiers of Quantitative Economics,* Vol 2, eds. M. Intriligator and D. Kendrick, 341–366. Amsterdam: North-Holland. Reprinted with permission of Elsevier Science Publishers B.V.

7. Roger H. Gordon and Dale W. Jorgenson 1976. The Investment Tax Credit and Counter-Cyclical Policy. In *Parameters and Policies in the U.S. Economy,* ed. Otto Eckstein, 275–314. Amsterdam: North-Holland. Reprinted with permission of Elsevier Science Publishers B.V.

8. Alan J. Auerbach and Dale W. Jorgenson 1980. Inflation-proof Depreciation of Assets. *Harvard Business Review* 58, No. 5 (September-October): 113–118. Reprinted with permission of the Harvard Business Review. Copyright 1980 by President and Fellows of Harvard College; all rights reserved.

9. Dale W. Jorgenson and Martin A. Sullivan 1981. Inflation and Corporate Capital Recovery. In *Depreciation, Inflation, and the Taxation of Income from Capital,* ed. C. R. Hulten, 171–238, 311–313. Washington, DC: The Urban Institute Press. Reprinted with permission of The Urban Institute Press.

10. Dale W. Jorgenson and Kun-Young Yun 1986. The Efficiency of Capital Allocation. *Scandinavian Journal of Economics* 88, No. 1, 85–107. Reprinted with permission.

11. Dale W. Jorgenson and Kun-Young Yun 1986. Tax Policy and Capital Allocation. *Scandinavian Journal of Economics* 88, No. 2, 355–377. Reprinted with permission.

12. Dale W. Jorgenson and Kun-Young Yun 1990. Tax Reform and U.S. Economic Growth. *Journal of Political Economy* 98, No. 5, Part 2 (October), 151–193. Reprinted with permission of the University of Chicago Press.

13. Dale W. Jorgenson and Kun-Young Yun 1991. The Excess Burden of Taxation in the U.S. *Journal of Accounting, Auditing, and Finance* 6, No. 4 (Fall): 487–509. A Greenwood Subscription Publication.

Investment
Volume 2: Tax Policy
and the Cost of Capital

1

Tax Policy and Investment Behavior

Robert E. Hall and
Dale W. Jorgenson

The effectiveness of tax policy in altering investment behavior is an article of faith among both policy makers and economists. Whatever the grounds for this belief, its influence on postwar tax policy in the United States has been enormous. In 1954 and again in 1962 amortization of capital expenditures was liberalized by providing for faster writeoffs. Since 1962 a tax credit for expenditure on equipment has been in force. Nor is tax policy in the United States atypical. As Otto Eckstein (1962) has pointed out,

Tax devices to stimulate investment have certainly been the greatest fad in economic policy in the past ten years. In a period when the trends in the use of policy instruments were in the direction of more general, less selective devices, all sorts of liberalized depreciation schemes, investment allowances, and tax exemptions were embraced with enthusiasm all over the non-Communist world.[1]

The customary justification for the belief in the efficacy of tax stimulus does not rely on empirical evidence. Rather, the belief is based on the plausible argument that businessmen in pursuit of gain will find the purchase of capital goods more attractive if they cost less.[2] In view of the policy implications of this theoretical argument, it is surprising that no attempt has been made to estimate the magnitude of tax effects on investment. Previous studies have been limited to calculations of the effects of tax policy on the cost of capital services.[3] The relation between these changes in the cost of capital and actual investment expenditures has not been studied empirically. As a result, the most important questions for economic policy—How much investment will result from a given policy measure? When will it occur?—have been left unanswered.

The purpose of this paper is to study the relationship between tax policy and investment expenditures using the neoclassical theory of optimal capital accumulation.[4] First, we measure the cost to the business firm of employing fixed assets. This cost depends on the rate of return, the price of investment goods, and the tax treatment of business income. Second, we determine empirically the relation between the cost of employing capital equipment and the level of investment expenditures. This relationship is a straightforward generalization of the familiar flexible accelerator theory of investment. We first obtain an estimate of the distribution over time of the investment expenditures resulting from a given increment in the desired level of capital services; then we estimate both the amount of investment resulting from a change in tax policy and its distribution over time. We consider the effects of: (1) the adoption of accelerated methods for computing depreciation for tax purposes in 1954, (2) the investment tax credit of 1962, and (3) the depreciation guidelines of 1962. As an illustration we consider the hypothetical effects of (4) adoption of first-year writeoff in 1954 in place of less drastic accelerated depreciation.

Our basic conclusion is that tax policy is highly effective in changing the level and timing of investment expenditures. In addition we find that tax policy has had important effects on the composition of investment. According to our estimates, the liberalization of depreciation rules in 1954 resulted in a substantial shift from equipment to structures. On the other hand, the investment tax credit and depreciation guidelines of 1962 caused a shift toward equipment.

1.1   Tax Policy and the Cost of Capital Services

The neoclassical theory of optimal capital accumulation may be formulated in two alternative and equivalent ways. First, the firm may be treated as accumulating assets in order to supply capital services to itself. The objective of the firm is to maximize its value, subject to its technology. Alternatively, the firm may be treated as renting assets in order to obtain capital services; the firm may rent assets from itself or from another firm. In this case, the objective of the firm is to maximize its current profit, defined as gross revenue less the cost of current inputs and less the rental value of capital inputs. The rental can be calculated from the basic relationship between the price of a new capital good and the discounted value of all the future services derived from this capital good.[5] In the absence of direct taxation this relationship takes the form:

$$q(t) = \int_t^\infty e^{-r(s-t)} c(s) e^{-\delta(8-t)} ds, \tag{1.1}$$

where r is the discount rate, q the price of capital goods, c the cost of capital services, and δ the rate of replacement; in this formulation t is the time of acquisition of the capital goods and s the time at which capital services are supplied. Differentiating this relationship with respect to time of acquisition we obtain:

$$c = q(r + \delta) - \dot{q}, \tag{1.2}$$

which is the rental of capital services supplied by the firm to itself. Under static expectations about the price of investment goods, the rental reduces to:

$$c = q(r + \delta). \tag{1.3}$$

Expression (1.3) derived above for the cost of capital services may be extended to take account of a proportional tax on business income. We assume that the tax authorities prescribe a depreciation formula $D(s)$ which gives the proportion of the original cost of an asset of age s that may be deducted from income for tax purposes. Further, we assume that a tax credit at rate k is allowed on investment expenditure and that the depreciation base is reduced by the amount of tax credit.[6] If the tax rate is constant over time at rate u, the equality between the price of investment goods and the discounted value of capital services is:

$$q(t) = \int_t^\infty e^{-r(s-t)} [(1-u)c(s)e^{-\delta(s-t)} + u(1-k)q(t)D(s)] ds + kq(t). \tag{1.4}$$

Denoting by z the present value of the depreciation deduction on one dollar's investment (after the tax credit),

$$z = \int_0^\infty e^{-rs} D(s) ds. \tag{1.5}$$

The implicit rental value of capital services under static expectations then becomes:

$$c = q(r + \delta) \frac{(1-k)(1-uz)}{1-u}. \tag{1.6}$$

Under the Internal Revenue Code of 1954 at least three depreciation formulas could be employed for tax purposes: straight-line, sum of the years' digits, and double declining balance. To obtain the appropriate cost of capital services for each formula, it is necessary to calculate the present value of the depreciation deduction for each one. Throughout we assume that the asset has no salvage value.

For straight-line depreciation, the deduction is constant over a period of length τ, the lifetime for tax purposes:

$$D(s) = \begin{cases} \dfrac{1}{\tau} & \text{for } 0 \leqq s \leqq \tau, \\ \\ 0 & \text{otherwise}. \end{cases}$$

The present value of the deduction is:

$$z = \int_0^\tau \frac{e^{-rs}}{\tau}\, ds\,,$$
$$= \frac{1}{r\tau}(1 - e^{-r\tau})\,. \tag{1.7}$$

For sum of the years' digits, the deduction declines linearly over the lifetime for tax purposes:

$$D(s) = \begin{cases} \dfrac{2(\tau - s)}{\tau^2} & \text{for } 0 \leqq s \leqq \tau, \\ \\ 0 & \text{otherwise}. \end{cases}$$

The present value of the deduction is:

$$z = \int_0^\tau e^{-rs}\, \frac{2(\tau - s)}{\tau^2}\, ds\,,$$
$$= \frac{2}{r\tau}\left[1 - \frac{1}{r\tau}(1 - e^{-r\tau}) \right]. \tag{1.8}$$

Tax provisions for double declining balance depreciation are more complicated. A firm may switch to straight-line depreciation at any time. If the switchover point is denoted τ^+, the double declining balance depreciation formula is:

$$D(s) = \begin{cases} \dfrac{2}{\tau}\, e^{-(2/\tau)s} & \text{for } 0 \leqq s \leqq \tau^+, \\ \\ \dfrac{1 - e^{-(2/\tau)\tau^+}}{\tau - \tau^+} & \text{for } \tau^+ \leqq s \leqq \tau, \\ \\ 0 & \text{otherwise}. \end{cases}$$

The present value of the deduction is:

$$z = \frac{2}{\tau} \int_0^{\tau^+} e^{-(r+(2/\tau))s}\,ds + \frac{1 - e^{-(2/r)\tau^+}}{\tau - \tau^+} \int_{\tau^+}^{\tau} e^{-rs}\,ds,$$

$$= \frac{\frac{2}{\tau}}{r + \frac{2}{\tau}} [1 - e^{-(r+(2/\tau))\tau^+}] + \frac{1 - e^{-(2/\tau)\tau^+}}{r(\tau - \tau^+)} (e^{-r\tau} - e^{-r\tau}). \qquad (1.9)$$

The switchover point which maximizes z is $\tau^+ = \tau/2$.

Representative values of the present value of the deduction for each of the three methods are given in table 1.1.[7] From this table it is clear that the sum of the years' digits depreciation formula dominates the double declining balance and straight-line formulas in the range of discount rate and lifetimes with which we are concerned. For this reason we have represented the 1954 tax revision as a change from straight-line to sum of the years' digits depreciation formulas.[8] Under static expectations the formulas for the rental value of capital services for these two methods of depreciation are:
straight-line:

$$c = \frac{1-k}{1-u} q(r + \delta)\left[1 - \frac{u}{r\tau}(1 - e^{-r\tau})\right]; \qquad (1.10)$$

sum of the years' digits:

$$c = \frac{1-k}{1-u} q(r + \delta)\left[1 - u\frac{2}{r\tau}\left(1 - \frac{1}{r\tau}\{1 - e^{r\tau}\}\right)\right]. \qquad (1.11)$$

Table 1.1
Present value of depreciation deduction

Lifetime	Interest rate	Straight-line	Sum of the years' digits	Double declining balance
5	.06	.864	.907	.888
5	.12	.752	.827	.795
10	.06	.752	.827	.795
10	.12	.582	.696	.651
25	.06	.518	.643	.594
25	.12	.317	.456	.410
40	.06	.379	.518	.469
40	.12	.207	.331	.297

Under the assumption that firms behave so as to maximize profit and that the markets for their output are perfectly competitive, a firm's desired level of capital can be derived from the condition that the value of the marginal product of capital should be equal to the rental price of capital. For a Cobb-Douglas production function, the desired level of capital K^+ is:

$$K^+ = \alpha \, \frac{pQ}{c} \, , \tag{1.12}$$

where p is the price of output, Q its quantity, c the rental price of capital, and α the elasticity of output with respect to capital. We assume that the flow of capital services is proportional to capital stock. This completes the determination of desired capital.[9]

To complete the theory of investment behavior it is necessary to specify the relationship between changes in desired capital and actual investment expenditures. After a change in the desired level of assets, plans must be formulated, funds appropriated, orders and contracts let, and so one. We assume that subsequent to a change in desired capital, a certain proportion of the resulting investment expenditure takes place over each interval of time. This proportion may vary by class of asset but is independent of calendar time.[10]

Second, we must specify the theory of replacement investment. We assume that subsequent to an investment a certain proportion is replaced over each interval of time. Again, we allow this proportion to vary by class of asset, but assume it to be independent of calendar time. Under our earlier assumption of a constant rate of replacement, investment for replacement is proportional to capital stock. This assumption implies an exponential survival curve for capital goods.[11]

Under these assumptions the theory of investment behavior takes the form of a distributed lag function; in discrete form this function may be written:

$$I_t = \sum_{s=0}^{\infty} \mu_s \, \Delta K_{t-s}^+ + \delta K_t \, . \tag{1.13}$$

Gross investment in period t, I_t, is the sum of a weighted average of past changes in desired capital and replacement investment. The change in desired capital in period $t - s$ is ΔK_{t-s}^+; the parameter μ_s is the proportion of the change in desired capital in period $t - s$ that results in investment expenditures in period t. Replacement investment is proportional to capital stock K_t; the constant of proportionality is δ, the rate of replacement. An alternative and equivalent form of the distributed lag function gives net investment N_t as a weighted average of past changes in desired capital stock:

$$N_t = I_t - \delta K_t, \tag{1.14}$$

$$= \sum_{s=0}^{\infty} \mu_s \Delta K_{t-s}^+ .$$

To estimate the parameters of the distributed lag function, it is necessary to impose further restrictions on the sequence of coefficients $\{\mu_s\}$. We have taken the first two coefficients of this sequence to be arbitrary with the remaining coefficients declining in a geometric series. The final form of the resulting distributed lag function is:

$$N_t = \gamma_0 \Delta K_t^+ + \gamma_1 \Delta K_{t-1}^+ - \omega N_{t-1}, \tag{1.15}$$

where γ_0, γ_1, and ω are parameters that characterize the sequence $\{\mu_s\}$. Adding an independently and identically distributed random term ε_t to the final form, we obtain the regression function:

$$N_t = \alpha \gamma_0 \Delta \frac{p_t Q_t}{c_t} + \alpha \gamma_1 \Delta \frac{p_{t-1} Q_{t-1}}{c_{t-1}} - \omega N_{t-1} + \varepsilon_t, \tag{1.16}$$

where α is the elasticity of output with respect to capital. The parameters γ_0, γ_1, ω and α are unknown and must be estimated.[12] This investment function provides the basis for the statistical results reported in the following section.

To summarize, investment in period t depends on the capital stock at the beginning of the period and changes in the desired level of capital stock in previous periods. The form of the relationship depends on the parameters of the distributed lag function and the rate of replacement. Desired capital depends in turn on the value of output, the rental value of capital input, and the elasticity of output with respect to capital input.

The effects of tax policy on investment behavior enter the investment function through the rental value of capital input. A change in tax policy changes the rental value of capital input. This results in a change in the desired level of capital stock. A change in desired capital stock results in net investment (or disinvestment), bringing capital stock up (or down) to its new desired level. If there are no further changes in tax policy or in the other determinants of desired capital stock, net investment eventually drops to zero. The change in tax policy continues to affect gross investment through replacement of a permanently larger (or smaller) capital stock.

Our procedure is, first, to estimate the investment functions under the tax policies that actually prevailed. The results are given in the following section. Second, we employ the estimated investment functions to calculate the investment resulting from alternative tax policies. These calculations are given in section 1.3. We then analyze the results in order to assess the effectiveness of tax policy in changing the level and timing of investment expenditures. We also study the effects of tax policy on the distribution of investment between plant and equipment.

1.2   Estimates of the Parameters of the Investment Function

To implement the theory of investment behavior outlined in the preceding section, we have fitted the corresponding econometric model to data on investment expenditures from the Capital Goods Study of the Office of Business Economics (OBE).[13] Data are available for structures and equipment separately and for both manufacturing and nonfarm, nonmanufacturing sectors of the U.S. economy for the years 1929–1963. These data are derived by allocating the commodity flow data on gross private domestic investment from the national product accounts among sectors of destination.

Estimates of capital stock at the beginning of each period K_t, were obtained by applying the following recursion relation to the investment data described above:

$$K_t = I_{t-1} + \delta K_{t-1},\qquad\qquad(1.17)$$

where I_t is investment in current prices deflated by an investment goods price index and δ is the rate of replacement, taken to be 2.5 times the inverse of the Bulletin F (U.S. Department of Treasury, 1942) lifetime. The following values were used for δ:

manufacturing equipment	0.1471
manufacturing structures	0.0625
nonfarm, nonmanufacturing equipment	0.1923
nonfarm, nonmanufacturing structures	0.0694

Initial values for capital stock were estimated by cumulating net investment over the whole period for which data are available for each asset.

Published price indexes for gross private domestic investment are biased because to a considerable extent they measure the price of inputs to the capital goods industries rather than the price of output. To overcome this bias, we used price indexes based on output prices that are close substitutes in production for producers' durables and business structures—the implicit deflator for consumers' durables from the national product accounts and the Bureau of Public Roads price index for structures.[14] For the years before these indexes are available we used the indexes implicit in the OBE Capital Goods Study, adjusted for bias in the rate of growth. The biases were estimated by regression which yielded the following values: 0.00651 per year for equipment and 0.0183 per year for structures.

The effects of tax policy enter the investment function through the desired level of capital stock. To estimate the desired level we used value added at factor cost as a measure of output $p_t Q_t$. We calculated value added for manufacturing and nonmanufacturing, nonfarm sectors by adding estimates of capital consumption allowances to national income originating in each sector.[15]

The desired level of capital stock also depends on the rental value of capital input c_t. Through 1953 the appropriate rental value of capital services corresponds to straight-line depreciation. Since 1954 the appropriate rental value corresponds to sum of the years' digits depreciation. Until 1962 the investment tax credit k is equal to zero. For 1962 and 1963 this credit is 7 percent of the value of investment goods. In the formulas for the rental value of capital goods, the tax rate u, the aftertax rate of return r, the investment goods price q, and the lifetime of capital goods allowable for tax purposes τ are variables. The rate of replacement δ is a fixed parameter. The values of this parameter are the same as those employed in calculating capital stock.

We took the corporate tax rate to be the statutory rate prevailing during most of the year. We did not attempt to allow for excess profits taxes during the middle thirties or the Korean War. For the discount rate before taxes we used the figure of .14 throughout the period. Although there is little evidence that this rate varies over the period of fit, except for cyclical fluctuations, this rate appears to be somewhat conservative.[16] Estimates of lifetimes of assets allowable for tax purposes were obtained separately for assets acquired before 1954 and during and after 1954 from a special Treasury study (1959). The change between the two periods was divided equally between 1954–55 and 1955–56. For 1962 and 1963 the proportional change for the new guidelines relative to existing practice as estimated by the Treasury (Office of Tax Analysis, 1962) was applied to the 1961 lifetimes for equipment. Lifetimes assumed were as follows:

Period	Equipment	Structures
1929–1954	17.5	27.8
1955	16.3	25.3
1956–1961	15.1	22.8
1962–1963	13.1	22.8

Investment functions for equipment and structures for both manufacturing and nonfarm, nonmanufacturing sectors of the U.S. economy for the years 1931–41 and 1950–1963[17] are presented in table 1.2. The coefficients associated with $\Delta(p_t Q_t)/c_t$ and $\Delta(p_{t-1}Q_{t-1})/c_{t-1}$, respectively, are estimates of the $\alpha\gamma_0$ and $\alpha\gamma_1$. The coefficient associated with lagged net investment, N_{t-1}, is an estimate of $-\omega$. Using the fact that the coefficients of the distributed lag function sum to unity, an estimate of the elasticity of output with respect to capital may be obtained. This estimate, $\hat{\alpha}$, is also presented in table 1.2.

Second, the average lag between changes in desired capital and actual investment expenditure as derived from the coefficients of the distributed lag function is presented in table 1.2. Finally, table 1.2 contains measures of the goodness of fit of the regression—R_I^2, R_N^2, and d, the Durbin-Watson ratio. Goodness of fit is measured in two ways: the ratio of the explained sum of squares to the total sum of squares for gross investment, R_I^2; the ratio of the explained sum of squares to the total sum of squares in net investment, R_N^2. Of course, gross investment is the variable of interest for policy considerations.

Estimates of the coefficients of the distributed lag function $\{\mu_s\}$ may be calculated from estimates of the parameters γ_0, γ_1, and ω by the usual recursion formula.[18] The first fifteen terms of the sequence $\{\mu_s\}$ derived by this technique are presented in figure 1.1. The general shape of the distributed lag functions coincides with previous results based on quarterly data. A substantial part of the investment takes place during the year in which the change in desired capital occurs. However, even more occurs in the following year. By assumption the proportions of investment that result from a given change in desired capital decline geometrically in subsequent years. The average lag for

Table 1.2
Investment functions for manufacturing and nonfarm, nonmanufacturing equipment and structures for 1931–1941, 1950–1963

	$\Delta(pQ/c)_t$	$\Delta(pQ/c)_{t-1}$	N_{t-1}	α	Mean lag	R_N^2	R_I^2	d
Manufacturing equipment	.01419 (.00372)	.01242 (.00442)	.6152 (.1001)	.0691 (.0156)	2.065 (.258)	.7219	.9566	2.036
Manufacturing structures	.00396 (.00131)	.00526 (.00145)	.7658 (.0790)	.0394 (.0126)	3.840 (.343)	.8475	.9208	2.474
Nonfarm, nonmanufacturing equipment	.02452 (.00844)	.01460 (.01038)	.4692 (.1342)	.0737 (.0141)	1.257 (.261)	.6899	.9616	1.738
Nonfarm, nonmanufacturing structures	.01296 (.00197)	.00227 (.00223)	.8801 (.0322)	.1269 (.0250)	7.488 (.239)	.9830	.9908	1.435

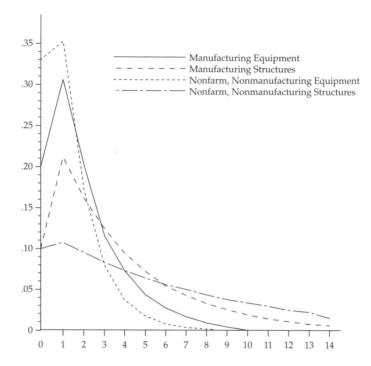

Figure 1.1
Time form of lagged response

investment in equipment is approximately 2 years for manufacturing and about 1.3 years for nonmanufacturing. The average lag for structures is considerably longer, ranging from 3.8 years in manufacturing to 7.5 years in nonmanufacturing.

To give a better notion of the degree of conformity between fitted values of investment and the actual observations, fitted gross investment is plotted against actual gross investment in figures 1.2a–d. Net investment is calculated from the fitted regression; replacement investment, taken as a given datum, is then added to obtain the fitted value of gross investment. Data on replacement investment are also plotted in figures 1.2a–d. Despite the wide variability in levels of gross investment during the periods 1931 and 1963, the fitted investment functions provide an accurate representation of actual investment behavior. In almost every series the largest observation is at least ten times the smallest, so that the goodness of fit of the investment functions provides much stronger confirmation for the under-

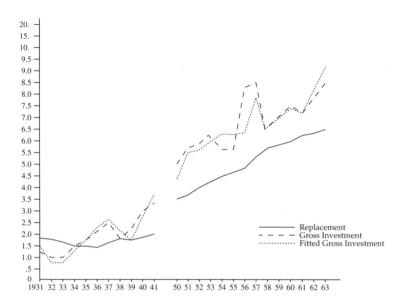

Figure 1.2a
Manufacturing equipment

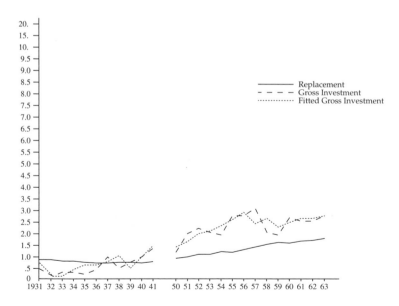

Figure 1.2b
Manufacturing structures

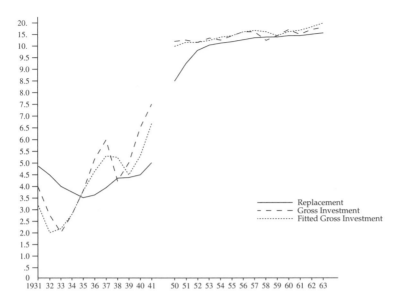

Figure 1.2c
Nonfarm, nonmanufacturing equipment

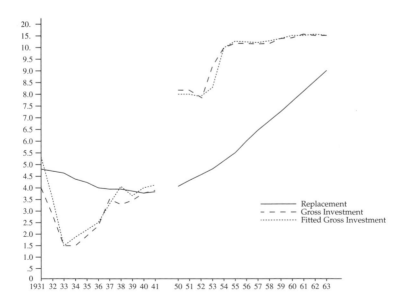

Figure 1.2d
Nonfarm, nonmanufacturing structures

lying theory of investment behavior than functions fitted to postwar data alone.

1.3   The Effects of Tax Policy on Investment Behavior

The effects of a change in tax policy are: (1) an initial burst of net investment which brings the capital stock up to the new desired capital stock, (2) a permanent increase in gross investment resulting from replacement of a larger capital stock, and (3) a proportionate increase in net and gross investment caused by changes in other determinants of desired capital stock. To calculate the magnitudes of these effects for various alternative policies, we have assumed that tax policy has no effect on the before-tax rate of return or on the price of capital goods.

We present results for three actual changes and for one hypothetical change in tax policy: (1) the adoption of accelerated methods for computing depreciation for tax purposes in 1954, (2) the shortening of lifetimes for tax purposes allowed for equipment by the depreciation guidelines of 1962, (3) the investment tax credit of 1962, and (4) the hypothetical adoption of first-year writeoff in 1954. For each of the actual changes in tax policy our procedure is to calculate the rental price of capital on the assumption that the change in policy did not take place. We then calculate the changes in desired capital and investment for the resulting rental price of capital. Desired capital and investment depend on the parameters of the investment function; in our calculations, these parameters are replaced by the estimates given in table 1.2 above. For the hypothetical first-year writeoff of investment expenditures beginning in 1954 our procedure is to calculate the rental price of capital under this policy. We then calculate the resulting changes in desired capital and investment from the fitted investment functions, as before.

The reductions in the rental on capital goods brought about in 1954 as a result of accelerated depreciation were as follows:

	Before change	After change
Manufacturing equipment	.310	.284
Manufacturing structures	.207	.188
Nonfarm, nonmanufacturing equipment	.375	.344
Nonfarm, nonmanufacturing structures	.218	.198

Our estimates of the increase in net investment, gross investment, and capital stock resulting from this change are given in table 1.3. For comparison the actual levels of net investment, gross investment, and capital stock are given in table 1.4.

The effects of the switch to accelerated methods for computing depreciation are quite dramatic. For each of the four classes of assets, the change in depreciation rules results in a substantial increase in desired capital stock. The effects of this increase depend on the time lag between changes in desired capital stock and the resulting net investment.

Although essentially the same pattern prevails for all four classes of assets, it is useful to trace out the effects of tax policy on net investment, gross investment, and capital stock for each class. The peak effect on net investment for manufacturing equipment is attained in 1955 with a level of $.680 billion (in constant 1954 dollars) or 70.8 percent of net investment in that year. By 1961, the increase in net investment has fallen to $.089 billion. Over the whole period 16.9 percent of the net investment in manufacturing equipment may be attributed to the change in depreciation rules. Similarly, the peak effect for nonfarm, nonmanufacturing equipment is $1.214 billion in 1955, or 39.7 percent of the net investment that took place in that year. Over the 1954–1963 period 19.1 percent of the net investment in nonfarm, nonmanufacturing equipment may be attributed to the change in depreciation rules. By 1961, the increase in net investment has fallen to $.193 billion.

The pattern of net investment for structures is similar to that for equipment. For manufacturing structures the peak effect on net investment occurs in 1955 with $.434 billion or 28.9 percent of the net investment that took place in that year. The decline of net investment in structures is more gradual. By the end of the 1954–1963 period the increase in net investment in manufacturing structures due to the change in depreciation rules in 1954 is still $.125 billion. Over the whole period 20.8 percent of net investment may be attributed to the change in depreciation policy. For nonfarm, nonmanufacturing structures the peak effect on net investment is in 1955 with $1.246 billion or 17.5 percent of the net investment that took place. This level falls off to $.765 billion by 1963, the end of the ten-year period, 1954–1963. Over the whole period 15.7 percent of the net investment in nonfarm, nonmanufacturing structures may be attributed to the change in depreciation rules.

Table 1.3
Change in net investment, gross investment, and capital stock resulting from accelerated depreciation, 1954–1963 (billions of 1954 dollars)

Year	Manufacturing equipment			Manufacturing structures			Nonfarm nonmanufacturing equipment			Nonfarm nonmanufacturing structures		
	N	I	K	N	I	K	N	I	K	N	I	K
1954	.418	.418	0	.189	.189	0	1.059	1.059	0	1.045	1.045	0
1955	.680	.742	.418	.434	.446	.189	1.214	1.417	1.059	1.246	1.319	1.045
1956	.480	.641	1.098	.367	.406	.623	.683	1.120	2.273	1.076	1.236	2.291
1957	.305	.537	1.579	.258	.320	.990	.386	.954	2.957	.955	1.189	3.368
1958	.154	.431	1.884	.186	.264	1.249	.220	.863	3.343	.896	1.196	4.324
1959	.124	.423	2.038	.169	.259	1.436	.202	.887	3.564	.954	1.316	5.220
1960	.133	.451	2.162	.190	.290	1.605	.201	.926	3.766	.959	1.388	6.175
1961	.089	.427	2.296	.154	.266	1.796	.193	.956	3.968	.904	1.399	7.134
1962	.127	.478	2.385	.127	.249	1.950	.274	1.074	4.161	.833	1.391	8.038
1963	.179	.549	2.513	.125	.255	2.078	.288	1.141	4.435	.765	1.381	8.872

Table 1.4
Actual levels of net investment, gross investment, and capital stock, 1950–1963 (billions of 1954 dollars)

Year	Manufacturing equipment			Manufacturing structures			Nonfarm nonmanufacturing equipment			Nonfarm nonmanufacturing structures		
	N	I	K	N	I	K	N	I	K	N	I	K
1950	1.522	4.917	23.081	.257	1.240	15.726	3.579	12.086	44.238	4.172	8.141	57.189
1951	1.985	5.604	24.603	1.101	2.100	15.983	3.301	12.496	47.817	3.925	8.183	61.361
1952	1.839	5.750	26.588	1.093	2.161	17.084	2.499	12.329	51.119	3.345	7.876	65.287
1953	1.914	6.096	28.428	.974	2.110	18.178	3.041	13.352	53.618	4.539	9.302	68.633
1954	1.148	5.612	30.342	.841	2.039	19.152	1.692	12.588	56.659	5.589	10.668	73.172
1955	.961	5.593	31.491	1.504	2.754	19.994	3.061	14.282	58.352	7.135	12.601	78.761
1956	3.398	8.171	32.452	1.478	2.822	21.499	4.633	16.443	61.413	6.041	12.002	85.897
1957	3.159	8.432	35.850	1.682	3.119	22.978	3.829	16.530	66.047	5.739	12.119	91.938
1958	.672	6.410	39.009	.593	2.134	24.661	.614	12.822	69.876	5.340	12.119	97.677
1959	1.013	6.850	39.682	.391	1.969	25.255	1.396	14.715	69.261	6.047	13.196	103.010
1960	1.314	7.301	40.695	1.141	2.744	25.646	2.723	16.311	70.658	6.911	14.480	109.060
1961	.921	7.101	42.010	.980	2.654	26.788	.840	14.951	73.382	6.585	14.634	115.970
1962	1.428	7.744	42.931	.900	2.635	27.768	2.790	17.063	74.222	6.242	14.748	122.560
1963	1.935	8.461	44.360	1.057	2.849	28.668	3.172	17.982	77.012	5.878	14.817	128.800

Since capital stock is simply a cumulation of net investment, the pattern of its behavior may be deduced from that for net investment. For both manufacturing and nonfarm, nonmanufacturing equipment capital stock rises rapidly over the levels that would have prevailed during the first few years following the adoption of accelerated depreciation methods. More than half of the increase over the period, 1954–1963, had already occurred for manufacturing by 1957 and for nonfarm, nonmanufacturing by 1956. The rise in capital stock for structures is more gradual. Half of the total increase had occurred for manufacturing by 1958 and for nonfarm, nonmanufacturing by 1959.

Turning to the effects of accelerated depreciation on gross investment, we recall that gross investment is simply the sum of net investment and replacement and that replacement rises in proportion to capital stock. Replacement becomes the dominant component of gross investment in equipment by 1958 for manufacturing and by 1957 for nonfarm, nonmanufacturing. In both sectors gross investment rises to a peak in 1955 with net investment predominating. As net investment declines, replacement investment rises so that gross investment remains nearly stationary at levels somewhat below the 1955 peak. In manufacturing the increase in gross investment due to accelerated depreciation is $.549 billion in 1963, which may be compared with the peak level of $.742 billion in 1955. Similarly, in the nonfarm, nonmanufacturing sector the increase in gross investment due to accelerated depreciation is $1.141 billion in 1963, compared with a peak of $1.417 billion in 1955. The pattern in manufacturing structures is similar to that for equipment. The peak level of investment of $.446 billion is attained in 1955; the 1963 level is $.255 billion. For nonfarm, nonmanufacturing structures net investment continues at a high level throughout the period so that gross investment is roughly constant from 1959 to 1963, when the level is $1.381 billion. This level may be compared with the relative peak of $1.319 billion in 1955.

The effect of accelerated depreciation on gross investment during the 1954–1963 period may be seen by calculating investment resulting from accelerated depreciation as a proportion of the total investment that took place. For equipment 7.1 percent of gross investment in manufacturing and 6.8 percent of the gross investment in nonfarm, nonmanufacturing may be attributed to accelerated depreciation over the period, 1954–1963. For structures the percentages are 11.4 for manufacturing and 9.8 for nonfarm, nonmanufacturing. Another perspective on the effect of the depreciation rules may be obtained by calculating the proportion of gross investment resulting from the change to total investment at the end of the period. For manufacturing equipment 6.5 percent of gross investment in 1963 is a result of accelerated depreciation; the corresponding percentage for nonfarm, nonmanufacturing equipment is 6.3 percent. The effects of the change are more significant in structures. In 1963, 9.0 percent of gross investment in manufacturing structures could be attributed to accelerated depreciation; similarly, in nonfarm, nonmanufacturing structures 9.3 percent of gross investment could be attributed to the change in depreciation rules.

In 1962 new guidelines for the determination of lifetimes allowable for tax purposes were issued (U.S. Department of Treasury, 1959). These guidelines involved a substantial reduction in equipment lifetimes allowable for tax purposes. The reductions in the rental on capital goods which the change in guidelines brought about in 1962 were as follows:

	Before change	After change
Manufacturing equipment	.273	.267
Nonfarm, nonmanufacturing equipment	.331	.323

We have calculated the effects on net investment, gross investment, and capital stock resulting from the depreciation guidelines of 1962. These calculations give the increase in equipment investment over the levels that would have prevailed had lifetimes remained at their 1961 levels. The results are given in table 1.5.

The impact of the revised guidelines is substantial, though not as dramatic as the shift to accelerated methods of depreciation in the Internal Revenue Code of 1954. The impact is limited to equipment, whereas the effects of accelerated depreciation were much greater for structures than for equipment. The peak response to the new guidelines, occurring in 1963, is less than half the peak response of investment in equipment to the switch to accelerated depreciation. In percentage terms 14.8 percent of the net investment in manufacturing equipment in 1963 is due to the change in guidelines; 17.6 percent of the net investment in nonfarm, nonmanufacturing equipment is due to the change. The impact on gross investment is proportionately smaller. In 1963 only 3.7 percent of gross investment in manufacturing equipment is due to the new guidelines; 3.6 percent of investment

Table 1.5
Change in net investment, gross investment, and capital stock resulting from 1962 depreciation guidelines and the investment tax credit, 1962–1963 (billions of 1954 dollars)

Year	1962 Depreciation guidelines					
	Manufacturing equipment			Manufacturing structures		
	N	I	K	N	I	K
1962	.185	.185	0	.504	.504	0
1963	.287	.315	.185	.559	.656	.504

Year	Investment tax credit					
	Nonfarm nonmanufacturing equipment			Nonfarm nonmanufacturing structures		
	N	I	K	N	I	K
1962	.509	.509	0	1.388	1.388	0
1963	.792	.867	.509	1.541	1.808	1.388

in nonfarm, nonmanufacturing equipment could be attributed to the revised lifetimes.

A second change in tax policy during 1962 was the adoption of a seven percent investment tax credit for machinery and equipment in the Revenue Act of 1962.[19] Seven percent of the value of purchases of new plant and equipment is a credit against tax liability. The depreciation base is reduced by the amount of the tax credit. The remaining 93 percent is then amortized over the lifetime of the equipment. The reductions in the rental on capital goods which the investment tax credit brought about in 1962 were as follows:

	Before change	After change
Manufacturing equipment	.286	.267
Nonfarm, nonmanufacturing equipment	.346	.323

To isolate the effects of the investment tax credit, we have calculated the resulting net investment, gross investment, and capital stock. These calculations give the increase in investment over levels that would have prevailed in the absence of the investment tax credit. This increase is given in table 1.5.

The effects of a 7 percent investment tax credit are quite startling. Although the impact is limited to equipment, the peak response of net investment to the tax credit, occurring in 1963, is greater for both manufacturing and nonfarm, nonmanufacturing than the response to accelerated methods of depreciation. Fully 40.9 percent of the net investment in manufacturing equipment in 1963 can be attributed to the investment tax credit. The corresponding percentage for nonfarm, nonmanufacturing equipment is 48.6 percent. Of course, the impact of the investment tax credit on gross investment is less startling, but this impact is also quite dramatic. Of the total of $8.461 billion of investment in manufacturing equipment in 1963, 10.2 percent can be traced to the effects of the investment tax credit. Similarly, of $17.982 billion of investment in nonfarm, nonmanufacturing equipment in the same year, 10.1 percent can be attributed to the investment tax credit. There can be little doubt that an investment tax credit is a potent stimulus to investment expenditure.

The progressive liberalization of depreciation for tax purposes since 1954 has had an important impact on investment behavior. The investment booms of 1955–1957 and beginning in 1962 reflect, in part, the response of investment behavior to the changes in tax policy that took place in 1954 and 1962. According to our calculations, the adoption of accelerated depreciation in the Interval Revenue Code of 1954 resulted in a shift in the composition of investment from equipment to structures. Similarly, the adoption in 1962 of new guidelines and the investment tax credit resulted in a shift of investment from structures to equipment. This shift was especially dramatic for the response to the investment tax credit.

The magnitude of the past response to liberalization of depreciation suggests an investigation of the response to further liberalization. To take an extreme assumption we can investigate the pattern of investment that would result from complete "expensing" or first-year write-off of investment. Under such a tax policy expenditures on capital account would be treated in the same way as expenditures on current account. As Vernon Smith (1963) has demonstrated, the effects of this policy are the same as the effects of no taxation of business income.[20] The reductions in the rental on capital goods which first-year writeoff would have brought about in 1954 are as follows:

	Before change	After change
Manufacturing equipment	.284	.214
Manufacturing structures	.188	.130
Nonfarm, nonmanufacturing equipment	.344	.260
Nonfarm, nonmanufacturing structures	.198	.137

We have calculated the effects on net investment, gross investment, and capital stock resulting from the hypothetical adoption of first-year writeoff in 1954. The changes represent the increment in investment and capital stock over the levels that resulted from accelerated depreciation. The increases in net investment, gross investment, and capital stock are presented in table 1.6.

The adoption of first-year writeoff for investment expenditures in 1954 would have resulted in a sharp rise in desired capital for all four classes of assets. The effect of this rise on investment is relatively rapid for equipment; for manufacturing net investment in equipment for 1955 would have been over twice as large as a result of first-year writeoff. The relative increase in equipment investment in the non-farm, nonmanufacturing sector would have been somewhat smaller. The increase in net investment in equipment for both sectors would have returned to relatively moderate levels by the beginning of the 1960s. The response is much more gradual for structures than for equipment. The increase in net investment in structures would have remained at substantial levels throughout the 1950s and 1960s. The effects of adoption of first-year writeoff in 1954 on gross investment in both equipment and structures would have been substantial throughout the period 1954–1963. By the end of the period the chief effect of this policy would have been an increased level of replacement investment.

1.4   Conclusion

We have calculated the effects of changes in tax policy on investment behavior for three major tax revisions in the postwar period: (1) the adoption of accelerated methods for calculating depreciation in the Internal Revenue Code of 1954; (2) the reduction of lifetimes used for calculating depreciation on equipment and machinery in 1962; (3) the investment tax credit for equipment and machinery in the Revenue Act of 1962. The effects of accelerated depreciation are very substan-

Table 1.6
Change in net investment, gross investment and capital stock resulting from hypothetical adoption of first-year writeoff of investment expenditures, 1954–1963 (billions of 1954 dollars)

Year	Manufacturing equipment			Manufacturing structures			Nonfarm nonmanufacturing equipment			Nonfarm nonmanufacturing structures		
	N	I	K	N	I	K	N	I	K	N	I	K
1954	1.606	1.606	0	.937	.937	0	4.071	4.071	0	5.168	5.168	0
1955	2.555	2.791	1.606	2.085	2.144	.937	4.519	5.302	4.071	5.842	6.201	5.168
1956	1.692	2.304	4.161	1.633	1.822	3.023	2.310	3.962	8.591	4.691	5.455	11.011
1957	1.023	1.884	5.853	1.072	1.363	4.657	1.233	3.329	10.901	4.106	5.196	15.702
1958	.508	1.520	6.877	.769	1.127	5.730	.719	3.053	12.134	3.858	5.233	19.809
1959	.417	1.504	7.385	.706	1.112	6.499	.691	3.163	12.854	4.126	5.768	23.668
1960	.463	1.611	7.803	.807	1.258	7.205	.708	3.313	13.546	4.157	6.086	27.794
1961	.311	1.527	8.267	.656	1.157	8.013	.685	3.426	14.254	3.921	6.138	31.952
1962	.328	1.590	8.578	.544	1.086	8.670	.642	3.515	14.940	3.617	6.107	35.873
1963	.447	1.757	8.906	.538	1.114	9.214	.656	3.652	15.582	3.325	6.066	39.491

tial, especially for investment in structures. The effects of the depreciation guidelines of 1962 are significant, but these effects are confined to investment in equipment. The effects of the investment tax credit of 1962 are quite dramatic and leave little room for doubt about the efficacy of tax policy in influencing investment behavior. These three tax policies represent a progressive liberalization of depreciation for tax purposes. To get some idea of the effects of further liberalization we have calculated the impact of the adoption of first-year writeoff of investment expenditures beginning in 1954. This tax policy represents the ultimate liberalization since it is equivalent to treating capital expenditures in the same way as current expenditures for tax purposes. The effects of such a policy on investment expenditure would have been very substantial throughout the period, 1954–1963.

Notes

1. See Eckstein (1962, p. 351); an excellent comparison of U.S. and European tax policy, including depreciation policy and investment tax credits, is given in Eckstein (1964).

2. The effects of tax policy on investment behavior are analyzed from this point of view by N. B. Ture (1963, esp. pp. 341–345); by S. B. Chase, Jr. (1962); and by R. A. Musgrave (1963, pp. 53–54, 117–129). Many other references could be given.

3. See, for example: E. C. Brown (1955) and Chase (1962, pp. 46–52).

4. This model has been studied previously by D. W. Jorgenson (1963, 1965).

5. The equivalence of these two formulations is discussed by D. W. Jorgenson (1967).

6. This assumption is valid for 1962 and 1963. For 1964 and later years the depreciation base was not reduced by the amount of the tax credit.

7. The results presented in table 1.1 may be compared with those of Sidney Davidson and D. F. Drake (1961); see also: Davidson and Drake (1964).

8. The adoption of accelerated methods for computing depreciation in 1954 involved a change from straight-line depreciation to either sum of the years' digits or double declining balance formulas. Since sum of the years' digits offers a slight advantage over double declining balance, we have assumed that accelerated depreciation was taken in the form of the sum of the years' digits. Further, we have assumed that accelerated methods were adopted immediately after they were made available. In fact, approximately 50 percent (of new assets) were depreciated on an accelerated basis the first year and a similar percentage of the uncovered balance was added in subsequent years. For firms that had negotiated shorter lifetimes than those allowed beginning 1954, there was some incentive to continue using straight-line methods in order to meet the "reserve ratio test," now effectively abandoned. The shorter lifetimes may be approximated by accelerated depreciation.

9. A more detailed derivation of desired capital stock is given in "Anticipations and Investment Behavior," (Jorgenson, 1965, pp. 43–53).

10. This theory of investment is discussed in more detail in "Anticipations and Investment Behavior," (Jorgenson, 1965, pp. 46–50).

11. See "Anticipations and Investment Behavior," (Jorgenson, 1965, p. 51).

12. Methods of estimation for such a distributed lag function are discussed by D. W. Jorgenson (1966).

13. The OBE Capital Goods Study is reported by George Jaszi, Robert Wasson, and L. Grose (1962). More recent data were kindly supplied by Mr. Robert Wasson of the OBE.
14. The implicit deflators for structures from the U.S. national accounts are primarily indexes of the cost of input rather than the price of output. The Bureau of Public Roads index for structures is based on the price of output; D. C. Dacy (1964) has derived price indexes for road construction based on input and output prices. His index for the price of output grows from 80.5 to 98.2 from 1949 through 1959 while the price of input grows from 61.5 to 102.4 in the same period, both on a base of 100.0 in 1958. The implicit deflator for new construction in the national accounts grows from 51.3 to 103.0 in the same period. Although there is no real alternative to the Bureau of Public Roads index as an output price for structures, it is reassuring to find that the corresponding input price behaves in a manner very similar to that of the input price for all of new construction.

The price indexes for equipment from the U.S. national accounts are based on data from the wholesale price index of the Bureau of Labor Statistics. Since expenditures in the wholesale price index are less than those on the consumer's price index, adjustments for quality change are less frequent and less detailed. Some notion of the resulting bias in the growth of the implicit deflator for producers' durables can be obtained by comparing this index with the implicit deflator for consumers' durables. The producers' durables deflator increased from 64.6 in 1947 to 102.0 in 1959. Over this same period the deflator for consumers' durables increased from 82.7 to 101.4. Both indexes are computed relative to a base of 100.0 in 1958. A direct comparison of the durables components of the wholesale and consumers' price indexes reveals essentially the same relationship.

For further discussion, see Zvi Griliches and D. W. Jorgenson (1966).
15. All data are from the U.S. national accounts; see: U.S. Department of Commerce (1958) and *Survey of Current Business* (1959).
16. A figure suggested by the results of Griliches and Jorgenson (1966) is 20 percent before taxes. This figure excludes capital gains whether realized or unrealized.
17. The years 1942–1947 are eliminated from the regressions because of the widespread use of nonprice allocation of capital goods during these years.
18. This formula is given in D. W. Jorgenson (1966).
19. Actually, limitations making the tax credit inapplicable to very short-lived assets reduce its effective rate to about 6.6 percent. In 1964 its effective rate was raised to around ten percent by allowing depreciation to be taken on the cost before rather than after the tax credit.
20. See also R. A. Musgrave (1959).

2 Application of the Theory of Optimum Capital Accumulation

Robert E. Hall and
Dale W. Jorgenson

Tax measures for controlling investment expenditures by providing incentives or disincentives through tax credits and accelerated depreciation are now a permanent part of the fiscal policies of the United States and many other countries. The quantitative study of tax incentives, however, has lagged far behind the study of policies that operate directly upon income. For example, the multiplier effect of the tax cut of 1964 has been estimated with some care; much less is known about the quantitative effect of the investment tax credit of 1962. In view of the many current proposals to apply the tax incentive system in other sectors, notably low-cost housing, policies of this kind clearly call for extensive empirical study.

The effectiveness of tax policy in altering investment expenditures has been established in a qualitative sense by a number of authors; their argument can be stated in its essence as follows: If capital services cost less as a result of tax incentives, businessmen will employ more of them.[1] This view is not free of ambiguities even at the qualitative level. For example, a reduction in the tax rate would appear to reduce the burden of the corporate income tax and to act as a stimulus to investment. But as Samuelson has demonstrated, a reduction in the tax rate may make assets more attractive, less attractive, or equally attractive to the investor, depending on depreciation allowances for tax purposes.[2] At a further remove, a change in the tax rate may increase, decrease, or leave unchanged the prevailing cost of money.[3] The effect of a reduction in taxes depends on the responsiveness of saving, as well as that of investment, to the proposed change.[4]

Even where the qualitative implications of a tax change are clear and unambiguous, no answers are given to the important questions for economic policy: How much investment? When will it occur? A stimulus to investment may have large or small effects. The resulting investment expenditures may take place immediately or over a considerable period of time. To determine the effects precisely, a quantitative analysis of investment behavior is required. In two previous papers we have presented an econometric model designed specifically to study the effects of tax policy on investment behavior.[5] We have estimated the unknown parameters of this model from annual data on investment expenditures for the nonfarm sector of the United States beginning with 1929. Given the empirical results, we have calculated the effects of tax policy on investment behavior in the postwar period. Specifically, we have studied the effects of the adoption of accelerated depreciation in 1954, new lifetimes for depreciation in 1962, the investment tax credit in 1962 and its modification in 1964, and suspension of the investment tax credit in 1966–1967.

The purpose of this study is similar to that of our previous work. We first reestimate our econometric model of investment behavior, taking into account data that have become available since our earlier work. We have revised our econometric technique to take advantage of recently developed methods of estimation. With these changes we obtain a new set of investment functions for the nonfarm sector of the United States, which we employ to characterize the effects of the various measures adopted between 1954 and 1967. We calculate both the impact of the suspension of the tax credit actually in effect from October 1966 to March 1967 and the hypothetical results of the originally proposed suspension through December 1967.

The evolution of tax policies during the postwar period provides a broad range of experience for a quantitative study of their effects on investment behavior. On the basis of our analysis, we conclude that tax policy has been highly effective in changing the level and timing of investment expenditures. It has also affected the composition of investment expenditures in the nonfarm sector. The adoption of accelerated methods for depreciation and the reduction in depreciation lifetimes for tax purposes increased investment expenditures substantially. They also resulted in a shift in the composition of investment away from equipment toward structures. Limited to equipment, the investment tax credit has been a potent stimulus to the level of investment; it has also shifted the composition of investment toward equipment.

An econometric model of investment behavior has a decisive advantage over a purely qualitative analysis of the effects of tax policy as a basis for policy making. At the same time our study has significant limitations that must be made explicit at the outset. Our calculations are based on a partial equilibrium analysis of investment behavior. A general equilibrium analysis would be required to determine the full effects of a change in tax policy. We calculate the effects of tax policy on investment behavior given the prices of investment goods, the cost of financial capital, and the level and price of output. Obviously, the results derived from a complete econometric model—incorporating our econometric model of investment and an explanation of the prices of investment goods, the cost of financial capital, and the level and price of output—could differ substantially. Since no econometric model of this scope is currently available, such a general equilibrium analysis of tax policy, however desirable, is not now feasible. For quantitative analysis we are forced to choose between an econometric model of investment behavior that adequately reflects the direct effects of tax policy on investment and general equilibrium analysis based on the more traditional *ad hoc* explanations of investment behavior. This important gap in the study of macroeconometric models could be remedied by combining our model of investment behavior with an explanation of the supply of investment goods, the supply of and demand for consumer goods, and the supply of saving.

2.1 Theory of Investment Behavior

Our econometric model of investment behavior is based on the theory of optimal capital accumulation. This theory can be approached from two alternative and equivalent points of view.[6] In the first, the objective of the firm may be taken as the maximization of its market value. Given a recursive description of technology—output depending on the flow of current input and of capital services, and capital depending on the level of investment and the past value of capital—maximization of the market value of the firm implies that the marginal product of each current input is equal to its real price and the marginal product of each capital service is equal to its real rental. In the second approach, the objective of the firm is maximization of profit, defined as the difference between current revenue and current outlay less the rental value of capital services. The rental price of capital services is determined from the condition of market equilibrium that equates the value of an asset and the sum of discounted values of all capital services from that asset. These two approaches lead to the same theory of the firm. In this study, the maximization of profit is taken as the objective of the firm and an appropriate price of capital services determined from the price of capital assets. Tax policy affects investment behavior through the price of capital services.

There are, however, two objections to the theory of optimal capital accumulation as a basis for an econometric model of investment behavior. First, a substantial body of survey data suggests that "marginalist" considerations such as the cost of capital and tax policy are irrelevant to business decisions to invest. This evidence has, however, been carefully analyzed by William H. White, who concludes that the survey data are defective even by the standards of noneconometric empirical work and that no reliance can be placed on conclusions drawn from them.[7] A second objection is that previous attempts to analyze investment behavior on the basis of neoclassical theory have not been successful. This objection is valid so far as the first such attempts are concerned. Negative results have been reported by Jan Tinbergen, Charles Roos, and Lawrence Klein for models incorporating marginalist considerations.[8] However, an econometric model based on current formulations of the neoclassical theory provides a better explanation of investment expenditures than its competitors, the flexible accelerator model studied intensively by Robert Eisner, and the models containing combinations of capacity utilization, liquidity, and the rate of interest studied by Locke Anderson and by John Meyer and Robert Glauber.[9] Further, the predictive performance of the neoclassical model is as satisfactory as that of models based on alternative theories of investment behavior.[10]

In addition to the direct support for the neoclassical theory from econometric studies of investment behavior, indirect support overwhelmingly favorable to it is provided by econometric studies of cost and production functions.[11] Current empirical research emphasizes such technical questions as the appropriate form for the production function and the statistical specification of econometric models of production. As an example, Nerlove has recently surveyed the literature, running to more than forty references, devoted solely to estimation of the elasticity of substitution.[12] In it, the neoclassical theory of the firm mistaken as a point of departure. The purpose of the empirical research reviewed by Nerlove is to give more precise results within the framework provided by neoclassical theory.

2.1.1   Rental Price of Capital

To be noted first in this detailed analysis of the relationship between tax policy and investment behavior is that the objective of the firm is to maximize profit. Profit Z_B' is defined in a special sense as the difference between current revenue and current outlay less the rental value of capital services:

$$Z_B' = pQ - wL - cK,$$ (2.1)

where:

p = the price of output
Q = the quantity of output
w = the price of labor input
L = the quantity of labor input
c = the rental price of capital
K = the quantity of capital.

Profit is maximized at each point of time subject to a production function,

$$Q = \Phi(L, K).$$ (2.2)

Investment I is the sum of changes in capital stock $\dot{K}$ and of replacement. We assume that replacement is proportional to capital so that investment may be determined from the relationship,

$$I = \dot{K} + \delta K,$$ (2.3)

where δ is the rate of replacement.

Necessary conditions for profit maximization are that the marginal product of current input is equal to its real price,

$$\partial \Phi / \partial L = w/p;$$ (2.4)

similarly, the marginal product of capital input is equal to its real rental,

$$\partial \Phi / \partial K = c/p.$$ (2.5)

Second, the price of new capital goods q must equal the present value of future rentals.[13] In the absence of direct taxation this relationship takes the form

$$q(t) = \int_t^\infty e^{-r(s-t)} c(s) e^{-\delta(s-t)} ds , \tag{2.6}$$

where

r = the rate of return
c = the rental price of capital input
$e^{-\delta(s-t)}$ = the quantity of capital input at time s resulting from the purchase of one unit of the capital asset at time t.

If prices of new investment goods are expected to remain stationary,[14]

$$c = q(r + \delta) . \tag{2.7}$$

For the nonfarm sector of the U.S. economy, taxes are imposed on current revenue less outlay on current input and less certain deductions on capital account. As an approximation, taxation is represented in the nonfarm sector by the corporate income tax. It is assumed that business income is taxed at a constant marginal rate with deductions allowed for interest payments and for depreciation on capital assets. In addition a tax credit is allowed on the acquisition of new investment goods. Where the before-tax rate of return ρ reflects deductions of interest allowed for tax purposes, the relationship between the price of new capital goods and the present value of all future rentals and tax deductions becomes

$$q(t) = \int_t^\infty e^{-(1-u)\rho(s-t)} [e^{-\delta(s-t)}(1-u)c(s) + uq(t)D(s-t)]ds + kq(t) . \tag{2.8}$$

The rental value of capital services after taxes is $(1 - u)c$, where u is the tax rate. The depreciation formula $D(s - t)$ gives the depreciation allowance per dollar of initial investment for tax purposes at time t on an asset of age $(s - t)$. Note that depreciation allowances depend on the price at which the asset is acquired $q(t)$, not the price of assets at the time depreciation is allowed as a charge against income q(s). Finally, the tax credit is $kq(t)$, where k is the proportion of the value of the asset allowable as a credit against taxes; the tax credit is not deducted from the amount of depreciation to be claimed. This formulation is inappropriate to the tax credit for the years 1962 and 1963, during the period the Long amendment was in effect. Under this amendment the tax credit was deducted from allowable depreciation so that

$$q(t) = \int_t^{\infty} e^{-(1-u)\rho(s-t)}[e^{-\delta(s-t)}(1-u)c(s)$$

$$+ uq(t)(1-k)D(s-t)]ds + kq(t).$$ (2.9)

As before, it is assumed that the prices of new investment goods (and the rate of the investment tax credit) are expected to remain stationary. The relationship between the price of capital services c and the price of capital assets q after repeal of the Long amendment was

$$c = q[(1-u)\rho + \delta](1-k-uz)/(1-u).$$ (2.10)

where

$$z = \int_t^{\infty} e^{-(1-u)\rho(s-t)}D(s-t)\,ds$$ (2.11)

may be interpreted as the present value of depreciation deductions totaling one dollar over the lifetime of the investment. Before repeal of the Long amendment, when the tax credit was deducted from the allowable depreciation base, the relationship was

$$c = q[(1-u)\rho + \delta](1-k)(1-uz)/(1-u).$$ (2.12)

Considering the impact of changes in the tax structure on the price of capital services, an increase in the investment tax credit k will always reduce the price of capital services. Where the investment tax credit is deducted from the allowable depreciation, this credit has precisely the effect of a direct subsidy to the purchase of investment goods.[15] Second, an increase in the present value of depreciation deductions z, resulting from a reduction in lifetimes of investment goods allowable for tax purposes or from the use of accelerated depreciation formulas, reduces the price of capital services.

The effect of a change in the tax rate u on the price of capital services depends on the effect of such a change on the rate of return. If the before-tax rate of return ρ is held constant, a change in the tax rate is neutral in its effects on the price of capital services if the combined value of depreciation allowances and the investment tax credit is equal to the value of "economic" depreciation, where economic depreciation corresponds to

$$D(s-t) = \delta e^{-\delta(s-t)}.$$ (2.13)

The present value of economic depreciation z^* is

$$z^* = \int_t^\infty e^{-(1-u)\rho(s-t)}\delta e^{-\delta(s-t)}\, ds, \tag{2.14}$$

$$= \delta/(1-u)\rho + \delta.$$

Provided that

$$k + uz = uz^*,$$

then

$$c = q(\rho + \delta),$$

so that the price of capital services is unaffected by changes in the tax rate.[16] On the other hand, if the after-tax rate of return $r = (1-u)\rho$ is held constant, a change in the tax rate is neutral if the combined value of depreciation allowances and the investment tax credit is equal to the value of immediate expensing of assets. Provided that

$$k + uz = u,$$

then

$$c = q(r + \delta),$$

thus the price of capital services is unaffected by changes in the tax rate.[17]

Therefore, if the before-tax cost of capital is fixed, changes in the tax rate have no effect on the price of capital services when the combined effect of the investment tax credit and depreciation allowances for tax purposes is equivalent to economic depreciation. Second, if the after-tax cost of capital is fixed, changes in the tax rate are neutral when the combined effect is equivalent to immediate expensing of assets. Thus the neutrality of changes in the tax rate depends on whether the burden of the tax is borne by the firm (before-tax cost of capital constant) or shifted (after-tax cost of capital constant). To resolve the controversy surrounding the incidence of the corporate income tax requires a general equilibrium analysis based on an econometric model including saving as well as investment.[18] Here it is assumed that the burden of the tax is borne by the firm, that is, that the before-tax rate of return is unaffected by changes in the tax rate.

2.1.2   Depreciation Formulas

Straight Line. Prior to the Revenue Act of 1954, essentially the only depreciation formula permitted for tax purposes was the straight-line formula, with a constant stream of depreciation over the lifetime of the asset. This formula can be expressed

$$D(\tau) = 1/T, \qquad 0 \leq \tau \leq T, \tag{2.15}$$

where T is the lifetime and $\tau = s - t$ is the age of the asset. The present value of depreciation deductions under the straight-line formula is

$$z = [1/(1 - \mu)\rho T][1 - e^{-(1 - \mu)\rho T}]. \tag{2.16}$$

Under the Revenue Act of 1954, three depreciation formulas were allowed for tax purposes. As alternatives to the straight-line formula, taxpayers were permitted to employ the sum-of-the-years-digits and declining-balance formulas. These two formulas are known as accelerated methods of depreciation because for a given lifetime and cost of capital they result in higher present values of depreciation deductions than the straight-line method.

Sum-of-the-Years-Digits. In the sum-of-the-years-digits method the deduction for depreciation declines linearly over the lifetime of the asset, starting at twice the corresponding straight-line rate; the depreciation formula is[19]

$$D(\tau) = 2(T - \tau)/T^2 \qquad 0 \leq \tau \leq T. \tag{2.17}$$

The present value of depreciation deductions under this formula is[20]

$$z = [2/(1 - u)\rho T]\{1 - [1 - e^{-(1-u)\rho T}]/[(1 - u)\rho T]\}. \tag{2.18}$$

Declining Balance. In the declining-balance method of depreciation, the deduction drops exponentially over the lifetime of the asset starting at a fixed proportion of the straight-line rate. If this proportion θ is 2, the method is referred to as double declining balance; if the proportion is 1.5 the method is called 150 percent declining balance. Tax provisions permit taxpayers to switch from the declining-balance to straight-line depreciation at any point during the lifetime of the asset. Obviously, the switchover point that maximizes the present value of the depreciation deduction T^* occurs where the flow of declining-balance depreciation equals the flow of straight-line depreciation after the switch. The declining-balance depreciation formula is

$$D(\tau) = \begin{cases} (\theta/T)e^{-(\theta/T)\tau}, & 0 \leq \tau \leq T^*, \\[2ex] \dfrac{e^{-(\theta/T)T^*}}{T - T^*}, & T^* \leq \tau \leq T. \end{cases} \qquad (2.19)$$

When (2.19) is solved for the optimal switchover point,

$$T^* = T[1 - (1/\theta)]. \qquad (2.20)$$

The present value of depreciation under the declining-balance method is[21]

$$z = \frac{\theta/T}{(1 - u)\rho + (\theta/T)} [1 - e^{-[(1 - u)\rho + (\theta/T)]T^*}]$$

$$+ \frac{e^{-(\theta/T)T^*}}{(1 - u)\rho(T - T^*)} [e^{-(1 - u)\rho T^*} - e^{-(1 - u)\rho T}]. \qquad (2.21)$$

2.1.3   Production Functions

Econometric implementation of a theory of investment behavior based on the neoclassical theory of optimal capital accumulation requires an appropriate form for the production function. The choice of the form has been the subject of much empirical research, which is currently focused on the choice of an appropriate value for the elasticity of substitution. Summarizing his recent survey of this research, Zvi Griliches finds that "the studies based on cross-sectional data yield estimates which are on the whole not significantly different from unity. The time series studies report, on the average, substantially lower estimates."[22]

In an attempt to reconcile this basic conflict between the estimates based on time series and on cross-sectional data, Griliches modifies in three ways the regression of output per employee on the real wage (both in logarithms) employed by Arrow, Chenery, Minhas, and Solow:[23] (1) measure of labor quality are introduced into the regression; (2) regional dummy variables are introduced to take account of possible differentials in price of output and labor quality by region; and (3) allowance is made for the possibility of serial correlation in the error term due to persistence of omitted variables.[24] The resulting cross-sectional estimates of the elasticity of substitution are similar to previous estimates. Only one (out of seventeen) of these estimates of the elasticity of substitution is significantly different from unity, and that one is above unity.[25] Allowing for serial correlation of the errors in successive years, Griliches obtains estimates for successive cross section that he characterizes as "... not ... very different from unity, the significant deviations if anything occurring above unity rather than below it."[26] "I do not intend to argue," Griliches concludes from these and additional estimates of the elasticity of substitution, "that these results prove that the Cobb-Douglas [elasticity of substitution equal to unity] is the right form for the manufacturing production function, only that there is no strong evidence against it. Until better evidence appears, there is no reason to give it up as the maintained hypothesis."[27] On the basis of the results presented by Griliches and the work that both he and Nerlove surveyed,[28] we adopt the Cobb-Douglas production function for our theory of investment behavior. This form was used in our earlier studies.[29]

2.1.4   Capital Accumulation

If there is no lag in the completion of investment projects, the level of investment appropriate for optimal capital accumulation may be determined from the conditions necessary for maximization of profit. In the theory of investment behavior described below, the assumption is that the actual level of capital stock may differ from the optimal level. More specifically, given capital stock, the levels of output and current input are assumed to be determined from the production function and the marginal productivity condition for current input. The desired level of capital is determined from the actual level of output, given the marginal productivity condition for capital input, while the actual level of capital is determined by past investment. Finally, time is required for the completion of new investment projects. Projects are initiated at every point in time so that the actual level of capital plus the backlog of uncompleted projects is equal to the desired level of capital.

If the production function has the Cobb-Douglas form, the marginal productivity condition for capital input may be written

$$\alpha(Q/K^{*}) = (c/p),$$ (2.22)

where α is the elasticity of output with respect to capital input and K^* is the desired level of capital. To solve for desired capital,

$$K^* = \alpha(pQ/c).\tag{2.23}$$

To represent the theory of investment, the proportion of investment projects initiated in time t and completed in period $(t + \tau)$ was designated μ_τ. It is assumed that the sequence of proportions μ_τ depends only on the time elapsed between initiation of a project and its completion. New projects are held to be initiated in each period until the backlog of uncompleted projects is equal to the difference between desired and actual capital. Under this assumption new investment orders in each period are equal to the change in desired capital stock. In every period the level of actual net investment is a weighted average of projects initiated in previous periods,

$$I_t - \delta K_{t-1} = \mu_0[K_t^* - K_{t-1}^*] + \mu_1[K_{t-1}^* - K_{t-2}^*] + \ldots,\tag{2.24}$$

where I_t is gross investment and δK_{t-1} is replacement investment.

To make the notation more concise, it is useful to use the lag operator S, defined as:

$$Sx_t = x_{t-1},$$

for any sequence x_t. With this notation, the expression for the level of net investment given above may be written more compactly as

$$I_t - \delta K_{t-1} = \mu(S)[K_t^* - K_{t-1}^*],\tag{2.25}$$

where

$$\mu(S) = \mu_0 + \mu_1 S + \ldots,\tag{2.26}$$

is a power series in the lag operator.

2.1.5   Summary

To summarize, investment in period t depends on the capital stock at the beginning of the period and changes in the desired level of capital in previous periods. The form of the relationship depends on the form of the distributed lag function and the rate of replacement. The desired level of capital depends on the level of output, the price of output, and the rental price of capital input. Tax policy affects investment behavior through the rental price of capital input. This price depends on the price of investment goods, the cost of capital, the tax rate, the formulas for calculating depreciation allowances for tax purposes, and the level of the investment tax credit. A change in tax policy changes the rental price of capital input and consequently the desired level of capital stock. An increase in desired capital stock generates net investment; if the price of capital input and the other determinants of desired capital remain constant, net investment declines to zero as capital stock approaches its desired level. The change in tax policy continues to affect gross investment through replacement requirements for a permanently larger capital stock.

2.2   Econometrics of Investment Behavior

Our theory of investment behavior implies a distributed lag relationship between net investment and changes in the desired level of capital. If this theory is to be implemented econometrically, restrictions must be imposed on the sequence of μ_τ coefficients. In previous studies we have employed the restriction that this sequence has a rational generating function. With this restriction the power series $\mu(S)$ may be represented as the ratio of two polynomials in the lag operator, that is, a rational function of the lag operator,

$$\mu(S) = \gamma(S)/\omega(S). \tag{2.27}$$

The resulting rational distributed lag function may be written as a mixed moving average and autoregressive scheme in changes in the desired level of capital and net investment.[30] Second, a random component ε_t must be added to the distributed lag function,

$$\omega(S)[I_t - \delta K_{t-1}] = \gamma(S)[K_t^* - K_{t-1}^*] + \varepsilon_t. \tag{2.28}$$

Finally, an appropriate specification must be chosen for the stochastic component ε_t. In previous studies we have assumed that the random component is distributed independently and identically over time, a feature that we retain here. In addition we employ further restrictions on the sequence of coefficients μ_t in order to economize on the number of parameters to be estimated.

The first assumption is that the distributed lag function may be represented as a finite moving average with an autoregressive error, that is

$$I_t - \delta K_{t-1} = \beta(S)[K_t^* - K_{t-1}^*] + v_t, \tag{2.29}$$

where $\beta(S)$ is a polynomial in the lag operator and v_t is an autoregressive error. It is assumed that v_t is generated by an autoregressive scheme,

$$\omega(S)v_t = \varepsilon_t, \tag{2.30}$$

where $\omega(S)$ is a polynomial in the lag operator and ε_t is distributed independently and identically over time. Multiplication of both sides of the distributed lag function by the polynomial $\omega(S)$ results in an alternative form of the distributed lag function,

$$\begin{aligned}
\omega(S)[I_t - \delta K_{t-1}] &= \omega(S)\beta(S)[K_t^* - K_{t-1}^*] + \omega(S)v_t \\
&= \omega(S)\beta(S)[K_t^* - K_{t-1}^*] + \varepsilon_t, \tag{2.31}
\end{aligned}$$

which is a rational distributed lag function with independently and identically distributed error term, the specification employed in our earlier studies.

With the representation of the power series $\mu(S)$ as the ratio of two polynomials in the lag operator, it is possible to write

$$\omega(S) = \omega(S),$$
$$\gamma(S) = \omega(S)\beta(S).$$

The rational distributed lag function employed in our earlier studies is now further restricted in that the polynomial $\gamma(S)$ is the product of two polynomials, one of them $\omega(S)$, the denominator of the original representation of the power series $\mu(S)$. If this restriction is valid, it may be used to reduce the number of parameters to be estimated. Further, the implied estimator of the power series $\mu(S)$ reduces to an estimator of the polynomial $\beta(S)$, since

$$\mu(S) = \frac{\gamma(S)}{\omega(S)} = \frac{\omega(S)\beta(S)}{\omega(S)} = \beta(S).$$

This restriction overcomes a possible objection to an unconstrained estimator of the parameters of the power series $\mu(S)$ for a rational distributed lag function. In some circumstances relatively small variations in the coefficients of the numerator of the power series may give rise to large variations in the coefficients of the power series itself, as Griliches has suggested.[31] Under the restrictions proposed here, the estimator of the coefficients of the power series $\mu(S)$ is independent of the estimator of the coefficients of the numerator $\omega(S)$.

As an example, if there are five terms in the original polynomial in the lag operator $\beta(S)$, the distributed lag function becomes

$$I_t - \delta K_{t-1} = \sum_{\tau=0}^{4} \beta_\tau [K^*_{t-\tau} - K^*_{t-\tau-1}] + v_t. \tag{2.32}$$

If, further, the order of the polynomial $\omega(S)$ is unity, that is, the distur-bance has only first-order autocorrelation, both sides of the distributed lag function may be multiplied by $\omega(S) = 1 + \omega_1 S$ to obtain

$$[I_t - \delta K_{t-1}] + \omega_1 [I_{t-1} - \delta K_{t-2}] = \beta_0 [K^*_t - K^*_{t-1}]$$

$$+ \sum_{\tau=0}^{3} [\omega_1 \beta_\tau + \beta_{t+1}][K^*_{t-\tau-1} - K^*_{t-\tau-2}]$$

$$+ \omega_1 \beta_4 [K^*_{t-5} - K^*_{t-6}] + \varepsilon_t$$

$$= \sum_{\tau=0}^{5} \gamma_\tau [K^*_{t-\tau} - K^*_{t-\tau-1}] + \varepsilon_t. \tag{2.33}$$

Satisfactory specifications of the distributed lag function between net investment and changes in the desired level of capital have been obtained using polynomials $\omega(S)$ of low order. However, as many as five terms in the polynomial $\beta(S)$ have been required to obtain a satis-factory specification. In order to economize further on the number of parameters to be estimated, we have employed an approximation pro-posed by Shirley Almon.[32] This method assumes that the polynomial in the lag operator $\beta(S)$ has coefficients generated by a polynomial in the lag itself:

$$\beta_\tau = \pi_0 + \pi_1 \tau + \cdots + \pi_\kappa \tau^\kappa. \tag{2.34}$$

To make this an approximation at all, of course, the order of the approximating polynomial must be less than the order of the polyno-mial in the lag operator.

If the order of the approximating polynomial is two and there are five terms in the original polynomial in the lag operator $\beta(S)$, the dis-tributed lag function becomes

$$I_t - \delta K_{t-1} = \sum_{\tau=0}^{4} \beta_\tau [K^*_{t-\tau} - K^*_{t-\tau-1}] + v_t,$$

$$= \sum_{\tau=0}^{4} [\pi_0 + \pi_1\tau + \pi_2\tau^2][K^*_{t-\tau} - K^*_{t-\tau-1}] + v_t,$$

$$= \sum_{i=0}^{2} \pi_i \sum_{\tau=0}^{4} \tau^i [K^*_{t-\tau} - K^*_{t-\tau-1}] + v_t. \tag{2.35}$$

On transformation this function becomes

$$[I_t - \delta K_{t-1}] + \omega_1 [I_{t-1} - \delta K_{t-2}] = \sum_{i=0}^{2} \pi_i \sum_{\tau=0}^{4} \tau^i [K^*_{t-\tau} - K^*_{t-\tau-1}]$$

$$+ \omega_1 \sum_{i=0}^{2} \pi_i \sum_{\tau=0}^{4} \tau^i [K^*_{t-\tau-1} - K^*_{t-\tau-2}] + \varepsilon_t. \tag{2.36}$$

In this distributed lag function there are only four unknown parameters: π_0, π_1, π_2, and ω_1.

Ordinary least squares may be employed to estimate the unknown parameters of a rational distributed lag function with independently and identically distributed error term ε_t. The resulting estimator is consistent; its asymptotic distribution may be characterized in precisely the same way as in our previous studies.[33]

Estimating Procedure

Provided that the restrictions on the coefficients we have proposed are valid, it is useful to take them into account in estimating the unknown parameters of the distributed lag function. First, approximation of the coefficients of the polynomial in the lag operator $\beta(S)$ by a polynomial in the lag itself results in restrictions that are linear in the unknown parameters β_τ. These restrictions are used to eliminate the parameters β_τ and express the distributed lag function in terms of the parameters π_i. The constrained distributed lag function is still linear in the unknown parameters so that ordinary least squares may be applied directly. Secondly, generation of a rational distributed lag function by autoregressive transformation of a finite moving average results in a distributed lag function that is nonlinear in its parameters. To estimate such a function, Durbin's two stage least squares is employed.[34] It begins with application of an ordinary least squares estimator to the unconstrained rational distributed lag function, and continues with estimation of the parameters of the moving average β_τ by applying least squares to the dependent and independent variables transformed in accord with the original autoregressive scheme. Parameters of the scheme ω_τ are set equal to their first-round estimates. The procedure results in estimates of the parameters β_τ, ω_τ that are asymptotically efficient.[35] It is easily seen to converge on successive iterations to the maximum likelihood estimator of the distributed lag function.

Durbin's two-stage procedure may be characterized as follows: First, the parameters of the rational distributed lag function equation (2.33) are estimated with constraints—ω_1, $\gamma_0 \cdots \gamma_5$—by ordinary least squares. Second, least squares are applied to the relationship

$$[I_t - \delta K_{t-1}] + \hat{\omega}_1 [I_{t-1} - \delta K_{t-2}] = \sum_{i=0}^{2} \pi_i \sum_{\tau=0}^{4} \tau^i \{ [K_{t-\tau}^* - K_{t-\tau-1}^*]$$
$$+ \hat{\omega}_1 [K_{t-\tau-1}^* - K_{t-\tau-2}^*] \} + \hat{\varepsilon}_t , \qquad (2.37)$$

where

$\hat{\omega}_1$ = the first-round estimator of the autocorrelation parameter

$\hat{\varepsilon}_t$ = the error in the distributed lag function plus the error in the first stage estimator $\hat{\omega}_1$, times the corresponding variables and parameters.

Since the first stage estimator is consistent, the error in it does not affect the asymptotic properties of the estimator of the remaining parameters π_0, π_1, and π_2.

To test the validity of the two constraints we have proposed, we begin with the unconstrained least squares estimator of the unknown parameters of the distributed lag function. This is the first stage in Durbin's two-stage estimator. We then impose the constraints, obtaining an estimator satisfying the restrictions that $\gamma(S) = \omega(S)\beta(S)$ and that $\beta(S)$ has coefficients that may be approximated by a polynomial in the lag itself. A test statistic $\mathcal{F}$ that is asymptotically equivalent to a likelihood ratio test is:

$$\mathcal{F} = \frac{(\hat{\varepsilon}'_0 \hat{\varepsilon}_0 - \hat{\varepsilon}'_1 \hat{\varepsilon}_1)/(m_1 - m_0)}{\hat{\varepsilon}'_1 \varepsilon_1/(m_2 - m_1)} , \qquad (2.38)$$

where

$\hat{\varepsilon}_0 \hat{\varepsilon}'_0$ = the constrained estimators

$\hat{\varepsilon}'_1 \hat{\varepsilon}_1$ = the unconstrained estimators

m_1 = the number of parameters to be estimated without constraints

m_0 = the number of parameters to be estimated with constraints taken into account

m_2 = the number of observations.

This statistic is asymptotically equivalent to the statistic associated with the likelihood ratio test of this hypothesis. In the example above there are seven unknown parameters in the unconstrained distributed lag function so that $m_1 = 7$. In the constrained estimator there are only four, so that $m_0 = 4$. It should be noted that acceptance of the null hypothesis at conventional levels of significance is not in itself justification for imposing the constraints; it is merely an indication that there is no strong evidence contradicting the constraints.

2.3   Estimates of the Parameters of the Investment Functions

2.3.1   Data Sources

The econometric model of investment behavior outlined in previous sections has been fitted to data on investment expenditures based on the 1966 capital goods study of the Office of Business Economics (OBE).[36] Data are available for structures and equipment separately for both the manufacturing and nonfarm nonmanufacturing sectors of the U.S. economy for the years 1929–1965. The data are derived by allocating commodity flow data on gross private domestic investment from the national product accounts among sectors of destination. The investment data used in this study differ from those employed in our earlier studies in two ways: (1) They reflect revisions in commodity flow estimates of gross private domestic investment resulting from revisions of the U.S. national income and product accounts,[37] and (2) they incorporate estimates of government-owned capital used in private production and some other minor adjustments made by Gordon.[38]

Published price indexes for gross private domestic investment are biased because they are based in part on the price of inputs to the capital goods industries rather than the price of output. To overcome this bias we used the Bureau of Public Roads price index for structures in our previous studies. Here we use an index constructed by Gordon, based on price indexes for the output of structures from the 1966 capital goods study. In our previous study we replaced the implicit deflator for producers' durables by a deflator for consumers' durables. To avoid a possible bias resulting from differences in the cyclical behavior of consumers' and producers' price indexes, it was decided not to attempt to correct the bias in the producers' durables price index, which, in any case, is not very substantial.[39] Accordingly, the implicit deflator for producers' durables from the national product accounts is employed in this study. All price indexes have a 1965 base.

Capital stock for equipment and structures in both industry groupings is obtained from the recursive relationship,

$$K_t = I_t + (1 - \delta)K_{t-1},$$

where I_t is investment in period t, derived as outlined above, and δ is the rate of replacement, taken to be 2.5 times the inverse of the Bureau of Internal Revenue's *Bulletin F* lifetime.[40] Similar rates of replacement were used by the Office of Business Economics in its 1966 capital goods study. The values of δ are the same as those employed in our previous studies:

Manufacturing equipment	0.1471
Manufacturing structures	0.0625
Nonfarm nonmanufacturing equipment	0.1923
Nonfarm nonmanufacturing structures	0.0694

Initial values for capital stock in 1929 were estimated by cumulating net investment over the whole period for which data are available for each asset.

The desired level of capital stock depends on the value of output. As a measure of output and prices pQ, we have used gross value added at factor cost, in current dollars, defined as gross product originating in each industry less indirect business taxes. For the years 1929 to 1946 these data are identical to those of our previous studies. For the years 1947 to 1965 data were obtained from the OBE study of gross product originating in each sector.[41]

The desired level of capital also depends on the rental price for capital services. Through 1953 the rental price is that appropriate to straight-line depreciation. Since 1954 the rental price is that appropriate to sum-of-the-years-digits depreciation.[42] From October 1966 to March 1967 the appropriate rental price for structures is that for 150-percent-declining-balance depreciation.

The investment tax credit was introduced in 1962 at a rate nominally equal to 7 percent of the value of investment in equipment. In practice certain limitations on the applicability of the investment tax credit reduce its effective rate to 6 percent for manufacturing equipment and 5.8 percent for nonfarm nonmanufacturing equipment.[43] For 1962 and 1963, under the Long amendment, the base for depreciation was reduced by the amount of the tax credit; after 1964, with the repeal of the amendment, the base for depreciation is not reduced by the amount of the credit. From October 1966 to March 1967, the investment tax credit was suspended.

The rental price of capital services also depends on the tax rate u, the after-tax rate of return r, the investment goods price q, the rate of replacement δ, and the lifetime of capital goods allowable for tax purposes. We took the tax rate to be the statutory rate prevailing during most of each year. We did not allow for excess profits taxes during the middle thirties or the Korean war. For all years we took the rate of return before taxes ρ to be constant at 20 percent. This value is higher than the value of 14 percent used in our previous studies, but it is consistent with the results of Jorgenson and Griliches.[44] Under the assumption of a constant before-tax rate of return, the after-tax rate $r = (1 - u)\rho$ varies with the tax rate.

The investment goods price is the same as that used to deflate investment expenditures in current prices and the rate of replacement is the same as that used to calculate capital stock. Estimates of lifetimes of assets allowable for tax purposes were based on a special Treasury study,[45] and are the same as those employed in our previous studies:

	Asset lifetimes (years)	
Period	Equipment	Structures
1929–54	17.5	27.8
1955	16.3	25.3
1956–61	15.1	22.8
1962–65	13.1	22.8

2.3.2 Equation Estimates

The previous section described a statistical technique for fitting our econometric model to data on investment expenditures. In summary this technique is based on the application of least squares in two stages. First, an unconstrained rational distributed lag function is fitted to data on net investment and changes in the desired level of capital for each class asset for each sector. The independent variables include lagged values of net investment and current and lagged changes in the desired level of capital. We have designated the lag operators $\beta(S)$ and $\omega(S)$ as fourth- and first-order polynomials, respectively, so that one lagged value of net investment and current and five lagged changes in desired capital are included among the independent variables. The results of the first stage regressions, of the form of equation (2.33), for the periods 1935–1940 and 1954–1965 are presented in table 2.1. The coefficient $-\hat{\omega}_1$ is associated with lagged values of net investment and is an estimate of the autocorrelation of the disturbances. The coefficients $\hat{\alpha}\hat{\gamma}_0 \cdots \hat{\alpha}\hat{\gamma}_5$ are associated with changes in the ratio of the value of output to the rental price of capital services.

Measures of goodness of fit of the first stage regressions are also given in table 2.1. Goodness of fit is measured in two ways: (1) the ratio of the explained sum of squares to the total sum of squares for gross investment, R_I^2, and (2) the ratio of the explained sum of squares to the total sum of squares for net investment, R_N^2. Neither ratio is corrected for degrees of freedom. While net investment is the dependent variable in the regression, gross investment is the variable of primary interest for policy considerations. The standard error of estimate S_e, corrected for degrees of freedom, is also presented for each of the regressions. The standard error is the same for gross and net investment. Autocorrelation of errors has already been taken into account in the generation of the distributed lag function underlying our econometric model. A test for autocorrelation may be performed by combining first and second stage results. For completeness the Durbin-Watson ratio DW is presented for each regression. The usual test for autocorrelation based on this ratio is, of course, biased toward randomness.[46]

Actual and fitted values of net investment from the first stage regressions are plotted in figures 2.1–2.4. The overall goodness of fit is superior to that of our previous investment functions for 1931–1941 and 1950–1963, except for manufacturing structures. This improvement is mainly due to the change in time period and to revisions of the basic investment data; however, it is also due partly to the change in specification of the distributed lag function. The addition of three lagged changes in desired capital improves the result to some extent.

The second stage of our statistical procedure is to transform all variables in accord with the estimated autoregressive scheme of the errors from the first stage. We approximate the polynomial in the lag operator $\beta(S)$ by a polynomial in the lag itself. We have chosen a

Table 2.1
Fitted investment functions for equipment and structures, by industrial sector, 1935–1940 and 1954–1965, first stage regressions

Sector and asset class	$\hat{\omega}_1$	$\hat{\alpha\gamma}_0$	$\hat{\alpha\gamma}_1$	$\hat{\alpha\gamma}_2$	$\hat{\alpha\gamma}_3$	$\hat{\alpha\gamma}_4$	$\hat{\alpha\gamma}_5$	R_N^2	R_I^2	S_e	DW
Manufacturing											
Equipment	−0.4753 (0.2276)	0.0123 (0.0052)	0.0190 (0.0058)	0.0071 (0.0079)	0.0034 (0.0075)	0.0001 (0.0069)	0.0015 (0.0057)	0.801	0.969	0.658	2.277
Structures	−0.6109 (0.3255)	0.0036 (0.0042)	0.0055 (0.0040)	0.0030 (0.0045)	0.0035 (0.0048)	0.0015 (0.0046)	0.0001 (0.0043)	0.524	0.815	0.585	1.447
Nonfarm, nonmanufacturing											
Equipment	0.0916 (0.3319)	0.0317 (0.0117)	0.0389 (0.0198)	0.0229 (0.0163)	0.0143 (0.0138)	0.0054 (0.0132)	0.0202 (0.0133)	0.820	0.965	1.255	1.837
Structures	−1.0065 (0.0953)	0.0057 (0.0037)	0.0082 (0.0040)	−0.0010 (0.0044)	−0.0025 (0.0039)	−0.0029 (0.0039)	−0.0046 (0.0038)	0.987	0.967	0.531	1.931

Source: Equation (2.33).
Note: t statistics are shown in parentheses.

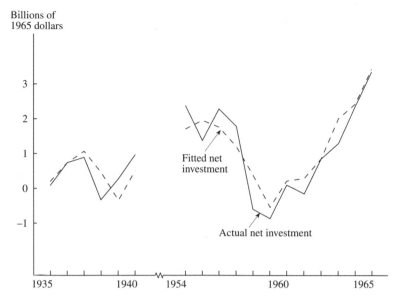

Figure 2.1
Net investment in manufacturing equipment, 1935–1940 and 1954–1965, first stage regressions

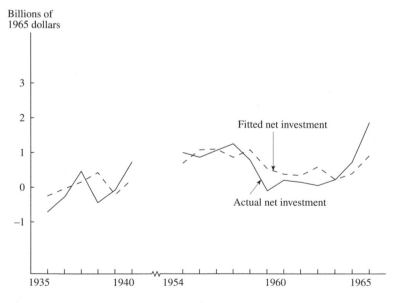

Figure 2.2
Net investment in manufacturing structures, 1935–1940 and 1954–1965, first stage regressions

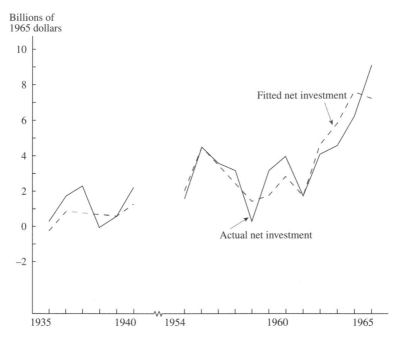

Figure 2.3
Net investment in nonfarm nonmanufacturing equipment, 1935–1940 and 1954–1965, first stage regressions

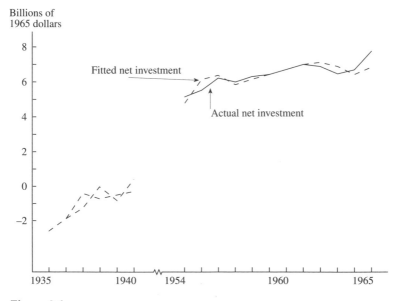

Figure 2.4
Net investment in nonfarm nonmanufacturing structures, 1935–1940 and 1954–1965, first stage regressions

second-order polynomial for this purpose so the lag function is a parabola. The dependent variable is now net investment plus $\hat{\omega}_1$ multiplied by lagged net investment, while the independent variables are weighted sums of changes in desired capital plus $\hat{\omega}$ multiplied by the corresponding lagged value. The weights depend on the lags. The derived estimates of the parameters $\alpha\beta_0 \cdots \alpha\beta_4$ are presented in table 2.2. Measures of goodness of fit similar to those presented for the unconstrained distributed lag functions are also given in table 2.2. It should be noted that R^2 for those regressions is a measure of the degree of explanation of the autoregressively transformed values of net investment. The only measure of goodness of fit comparable to those in table 2.1 is the standard error of estimate S_e for each of the regressions. This standard error is uniformly lower for all regressions, reflecting the fact that loss in explanatory power due to reduction in the number of parameters to be estimated is more than compensated for by the reduction in the number of degrees of freedom required for estimation. Actual and fitted values of net investment from the second stages regressions are plotted in figures 2.5–2.8. The actual values in these plots are net investment, not the transformed net investment series that served as the left-hand variable in the second stage. The fitted values were calculated by substituting the parameter estimates from the second stage into the first stage regression equation. It would not be meaningful to plot the actual and fitted values directly from the second stage because of the autoregressive transformation.

We have generated the distributed lag function for our econometric model of investment behavior by using two restrictions: (1) The distributed lag is finite (that is, the error is autoregressive); and (2) the coefficients of the polynomial $\beta(S)$ lie along a second degree polynomial in the lag itself. The statistic derived above, based on sums of squared residuals with and without constraints, is used to test the validity of these restrictions. The resulting test statistic $\mathcal{F}$ is presented in the first column of table 2.3. When the very low values of this statistic are compared with the critical value of the $\mathcal{F}$-ratio at the 0.05 level, 3.59, the null hypothesis is easily accepted for all regressions. We conclude that the distributed lag is finite and that the coefficients of $\beta(S)$ lie along a second degree polynomial. Accordingly, we employ the second stage regressions for further analysis of the distributed lag function.

Table 2.2
Fitted investment functions for equipment and structures, by industrial sector, 1935–1940 and 1954–1965, second stage regressions

Sector and asset class	$\hat{\alpha\beta}_0$	$\hat{\alpha\beta}_1$	$\hat{\alpha\beta}_2$	$\hat{\alpha\beta}_3$	$\hat{\alpha\beta}_4$	R^2	S_e	DW
Manufacturing								
Equipment	0.0130 (0.0047)	0.0200 (0.0034)	0.0208 (0.0040)	0.0153 (0.0040)	0.0036 (0.0053)	0.602	0.620	2.099
Structures	0.0041 (0.0033)	0.0082 (0.0030)	0.0093 (0.0035)	0.0073 (0.0032)	0.0024 (0.0034)	0.186	0.513	1.304
Nonfarm, nonmanufacturing								
Equipment	0.0374 (0.0083)	0.0282 (0.0038)	0.0211 (0.0063)	0.0160 (0.0047)	0.0129 (0.0090)	0.800	1.190	1.724
Structures	0.0059 (0.0034)	0.0105 (0.0032)	0.0118 (0.0035)	0.0098 (0.0031)	0.0046 (0.0029)	0.169	0.506	1.825

Source: Equation (2.37)

Note: t statistics are shown in parentheses.

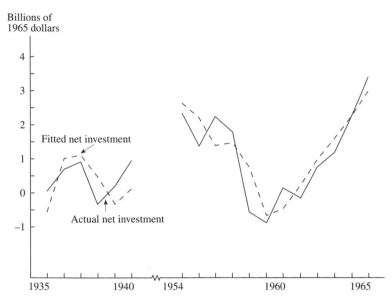

Figure 2.5
Net investment in manufacturing equipment, 1935–1940 and 1954–1965, second stage regressions

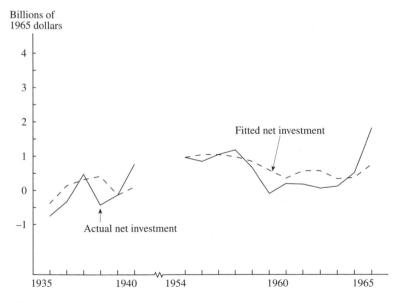

Figure 2.6
Net investment in manufacturing structures, 1935–1940 and 1954–1965, second stage regressions

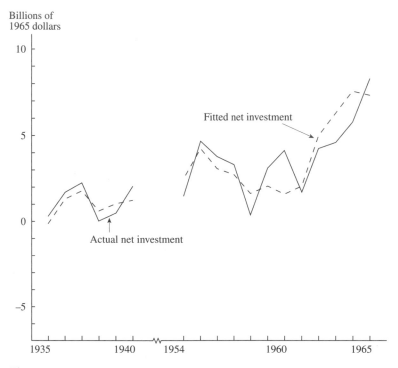

Figure 2.7
Net investment in nonfarm nonmanufacturing equipment, 1935–1940 and
1954–1965, second stage regressions

Also presented in table 2.3 (column 2) are the results of testing the
null hypothesis of no autocorrelation in the finite parabolic distributed
lag model. The $\mathcal{F}$-statistic for this test is

$$\mathcal{F} = 14(\hat{\varepsilon}'_0\hat{\varepsilon}_0 - \hat{\varepsilon}'_1\hat{\varepsilon}_1)/(\hat{\varepsilon}'_1\hat{\varepsilon}_1),$$

where 14 is the number of degrees of freedom in the unconstrained
regression, $\hat{\varepsilon}'_1\hat{\varepsilon}_1$ is the sum of squared residuals in that regression, and
$\hat{\varepsilon}'_0\hat{\varepsilon}_0$ is the sum of squared residuals in the constrained regression.
The unconstrained regressions are those reported in table 2.2. The
constrained regressions are of precisely the same form as those in table
2.2 except that the variables have not been subjected to the autoregressive transformation. As can be seen, there is evidence of autocorrelation in all sectors except nonmanufacturing equipment. The null
hypothesis is rejected in both equations for structures. These results
are exactly in accord with the regression results for the first stage
regressions reported in table 2.1. The very high autocorrelation in the

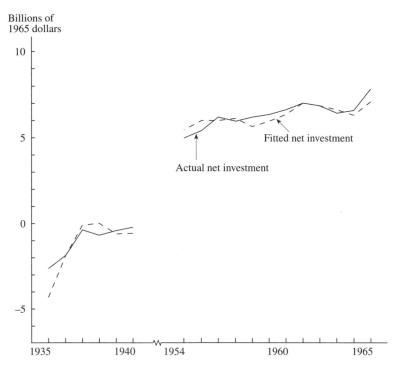

Figure 2.8
Net investment in nonfarm nonmanufacturing structures, 1935–1940 and
1954–1965, second stage regressions

Table 2.3
Fitted investment functions for equipment and structures, by industrial sector,
1935–1940 and 1954–1965, derived results

Sector and asset class	$\mathcal{F}_1$[a]	$\mathcal{F}_2$[b]	$\hat{\alpha}$[c]	Mean lag (years)
Manufacturing				
Equipment	0.577	3.912	0.0727	1.67
Structures	0.138	4.764	0.0312	1.86
Nonfarm, nonmanufacturing				
Equipment	0.623	0.004	0.1160	1.47
Structures	0.655	156.681	0.0426	1.92

[a] $\mathcal{F}$-statistic for the null hypothesis that the distributed lag is finite and has a parabolic shape. The critical value of $\mathcal{F}$ with 3 and 11 degrees of freedom is 3.59 at the 0.05 level.

[b] $\mathcal{F}$-statistic for the null hypothesis that there is no autocorrelation. The critical value of $\mathcal{F}$ with 1 and 14 degrees of freedom is 4.60 at the 0.05 level.

[c] Estimate of the elasticity of output with respect to the capital input.

equation for nonmanufacturing structures suggests the possibility of specification error.

2.3.3   Distributed Lags

The parameters of the distributed lag function μ_τ may be estimated by employing the constraint that the sum of the coefficients of this function must be unity to estimate the parameter $\hat{\alpha}$.[47] The resulting estimates are given in table 2.3. The derived estimates of the parameters of the distributed lag function are plotted in figures 2.9–2.12. The mean lag for each function is also given in table 2.3. When these mean lags are compared with estimates from our earlier studies, the new estimates are found to be very similar for investment in equipment. The mean lag is now estimated to be slightly lower for manufacturing equipment and slightly higher for nonfarm nonmanufacturing equipment. For structures, however, the new estimates differ substantially from the old. The old estimate of the mean lag for manufacturing structures was 3.84 years, whereas the new estimate is 1.86; the old estimate of the mean lag for nonfarm nonmanufacturing structures was 7.49 years, while the new estimate is 1.92. For both sets of results the lags are estimated to be longer for structures than for equipment.

A disturbing feature of our earlier results is that the lag pattern fails to agree with the substantial body of evidence from studies by Jorgenson and Stephenson at the level of two-digit industries and by Jorgenson and Siebert at the level of the individual firm.[48] For manufacturing, Jorgenson and Stephenson estimate the average lag at about

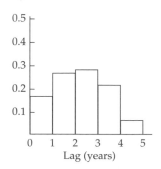

Figure 2.9
Estimated lag function β_τ, for manufacturing equipment

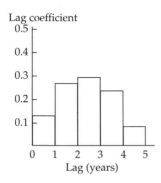

Figure 2.10
Estimated lag function β_τ, for manufacturing structures

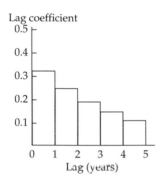

Figure 2.11
Estimated lag function β_τ, for nonfarm, nonmanufacturing equipment

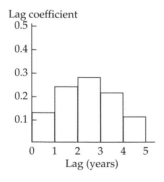

Figure 2.12
Estimated lag function β_τ, for nonfarm, nonmanufacturing structures

two years, while results from individual industries range from six to eleven quarters and cluster in the neighborhood of the overall average. The results for individual firms are characterized by more variability than the results for industries, as would be expected. The average lags estimated by Jorgenson and Siebert range from less than a year to over three years, with values between one and two years predominating. Based on a survey he made, Mayer's estimate of the average lag from the decision to undertake investment to the completion of the project for manufacturing is seven quarters.[49] We conclude that our new estimates agree closely with Mayer's results and with estimates derived from investment functions for industry groups and for individual firms. Our previous estimates of the average lags for structures are evidently biased by specification errors in the underlying distributed lag functions and should be replaced by our new estimates.

2.4 Impact of Tax Policy on Investment Behavior

If desired capital stock is increased by a change in tax policy, through a consequent change in the rental price of capital services, additional net investment is generated; if the determinants of investment then remain at stationary levels, this net investment eventually brings actual capital stock up to the new desired level. The initial burst of net investment increases gross investment at first, but this effect gradually declines to zero as the gap between desired and actual capital stock is eliminated. However, gross investment is permanently increased by the higher levels of replacement associated with higher levels of capital stock. If desired capital stock is decreased by tax policy, these effects are precisely reversed.

The qualitative features of the response of investment to a change in tax policy are essentially the same for all changes. To evaluate the effects of particular tax measures, it is useful to assess the response of investment quantitatively. Accordingly, we calculate the effects of changes in tax policy that have taken place in the United States in the postwar period. The calculations are based on a partial equilibrium analysis of investment behavior. All determinants of investment expenditures except tax policy are held equal to their actual values. We then measure the impact of tax policy by substituting into our investment functions parameters of the tax structure—tax rate, depreciation formulas, tax credit, and depreciation lifetimes—appropriate to alternative tax policies. The difference between investment resulting from actual tax policy and investment that would have resulted from alternative tax policies is our measure of the impact of tax policy.

We present estimates of the impact of the adoption of accelerated depreciation in 1954 and of new lifetimes for depreciation of equipment and the investment tax credit in 1962, the tax cut of 1964, and the suspension of the tax credit for equipment and restriction of the use of accelerated depreciation for structures in 1966–1967. The tax measure of 1964 reduced the corporate tax rate from 52 percent to 48 percent and also restored the tax credit to the depreciation base for tax purposes. In our earlier studies we presented calculations of the effects of all these changes in tax policy. In view of the substantial revisions in the underlying investment data and the alternations in our specification of the investment functions, we provide a complete set of estimates based on our new results.

In the new calculations both investment and capital stock are measured in 1965 prices. We estimate the impact of all changes in tax policy through 1970. In order to make these estimates, we employed a rough set of projections of the determinants of investment. No great precision was required in these projections, since the estimates of the differential impacts of alternative policies are not at all sensitive to the assumed level of investment. The projected levels of gross value added and the price deflators for investment goods are shown in table 2.4.[50] Although the projections of gross value added are in current dollars and are likely to be serious underestimates because of the relatively rapid rate of inflation that has developed recently, this will not affect the results, since only the ratio of gross value added and the investment deflator enter the calculations. Finally, all tax variables were assumed to stay at their 1965 values, except for the brief suspension of the investment tax credit and accelerated depreciation in 1966–1967; the treatment of this suspension is described in detail below.

As a basis for comparison with alternative tax policies, table 2.5 presents data on the actual levels of gross investment, net investment, and capital stock, for 1950–1965. Also included are extrapolated values calculated from the fitted investment functions for 1966–1970 for plant and equipment, for both the manufacturing and nonfarm nonmanufacturing sectors.

Table 2.4
Projected levels of gross value added and price deflators for
manufacturing and nonfarm, nonmanufacturing, 1966–1970

	Gross value added (billions of current dollars)	
Year	Manufacturing	Nonfarm, non-manufacturing
1966	198.4	363.6
1967	209.1	383.2
1968	221.6	406.2
1969	234.9	430.6
1970	249.0	456.4

	Price deflators (1965 = 1.000)		
Year	Manufacturing equipment	Nonfarm, non-manufacturing equipment	Structures, both sectors
1966	1.031	1.031	1.043
1967	1.068	1.068	1.079
1968	1.103	1.095	1.100
1969	1.142	1.121	1.121
1970	1.183	1.150	1.144

Source: See text, p. 61.

2.4.1 Accelerated Depreciation, 1954

The first change in tax policy we attempt to evaluate is the adoption of
accelerated methods of depreciation for tax purposes in 1954. As an
alternative policy we suppose that only the straight-line formula was
permitted from 1954 to 1970 and that all other determinants of investment are unchanged. The levels of the annual rental price of capital
services, and the reduction brought about in 1955 (the first full year)
through the adoption of accelerated methods of depreciation, were:

	Without accelerated depreciation	With accelerated depreciation	Percentage decrease
Manufacturing equipment	0.293	0.267	8.9
Manufacturing structures	0.229	0.208	9.2
Nonfarm, nonmanufacturing equipment	0.375	0.341	9.1
Nonfarm, nonmanufacturing structures	0.239	0.217	9.2

Table 2.5
Gross investment, net investment, and capital stock in equipment and structures, by industrial sector, actual, 1950–1965 and projected, 1966–1970 (in billions of 1965 dollars)

	Manufacturing					
	Equipment			Structures		
	Investment		Capital stock	Investment		Capital stock
Year	Gross	Net		Gross	Net	
Actual						
1950	5.553	0.627	33.488	1.949	−0.252	35.220
1951	7.265	2.247	34.115	2.776	0.591	34.968
1952	8.291	2.942	36.362	2.888	0.666	35.558
1953	8.578	2.796	39.304	3.091	0.827	36.224
1954	8.544	2.351	42.100	3.276	0.960	37.051
1955	7.927	1.388	44.451	3.222	0.846	38.011
1956	9.034	2.291	45.840	3.526	1.097	38.858
1957	8.875	1.795	48.131	3.751	1.254	39.955
1958	6.726	−0.618	49.926	3.321	0.745	41.209
1959	6.423	−0.830	49.308	2.490	−0.132	41.954
1960	7.299	0.168	48.477	2.821	0.207	41.822
1961	7.067	−0.089	48.645	2.786	0.159	42.029
1962	8.040	0.897	48.557	2.681	0.044	42.188
1963	8.550	1.275	49.454	2.836	0.196	42.233
1964	9.941	2.479	50.729	3.353	0.701	42.429
1965	11.333	3.506	53.208	4.659	1.963	43.130
Projected						
1966	11.434	3.092	56.714	4.462	1.644	45.093
1967	11.259	2.462	59.806	4.306	1.385	46.737
1968	11.138	1.978	62.268	4.216	1.208	48.122
1969	11.044	1.593	64.246	4.165	1.082	49.330
1970	11.104	1.419	65.839	4.222	1.071	50.412

Table 2.5
(continued)

	Nonfarm, nonmanufacturing					
	Equipment			Structures		
	Investment		Capital	Investment		Capital
Year	Gross	Net	stock	Gross	Net	stock
Actual						
1950	14.469	4.079	54.028	9.323	3.986	76.903
1951	14.659	3.485	58.107	8.895	3.281	80.889
1952	14.421	2.577	61.592	8.775	2.934	84.170
1953	15.020	2.680	64.169	10.348	4.303	87.104
1954	14.327	1.472	66.849	11.345	5.001	91.407
1955	17.699	4.561	68.321	12.195	5.504	96.408
1956	17.714	3.699	72.882	13.264	6.191	101.912
1957	17.973	3.246	76.581	13.445	5.943	108.104
1958	15.595	0.244	79.827	14.125	6.210	114.046
1959	18.671	3.273	80.072	14.740	6.394	120.256
1960	20.090	4.063	83.345	15.459	6.669	126.651
1961	18.617	1.809	87.408	16.190	6.937	133.320
1962	21.475	4.319	89.216	16.563	6.829	140.258
1963	22.641	4.654	93.535	16.582	6.374	147.087
1964	25.175	6.293	98.189	17.251	6.601	153.461
1965	29.323	9.231	104.482	18.977	7.869	160.061
Projected						
1966	28.337	6.470	113.713	19.557	7.903	167.930
1967	28.149	5.038	120.183	20.127	7.924	175.833
1968	29.198	5.118	125.221	20.841	8.088	183.757
1969	29.598	4.534	130.339	21.610	8.296	191.845
1970	30.243	4.307	134.873	22.446	8.556	200.141

Source: Unpublished data from the 1966 capital goods study of the U.S. Department of Commerce, Office of Business Economics. The capital stock figures are derived from unrounded data and will not necessarily equal the sum of the preceding year's capital stock and net investment.

Estimates of the increase in gross investment, net investment, and capital stock resulting from the adoption of accelerated depreciation in 1954 are given in table 2.6.

The effects of the adoption of accelerated depreciation are very substantial. Although the same pattern prevails in all four classes of assets, it is useful to trace out the quantitative impact of tax policy on net investment, gross investment, and capital stock for each class. The peak effect on net investment for manufacturing equipment is attained in 1956 with a level of $744 million, or 32 percent of net investment in that year. By 1959 the effect is essentially nil; however, the adoption in 1962 of new equipment lifetimes for tax purposes and of the investment tax credit provides an additional stimulus from the use of accelerated methods of depreciation. We estimate that 17.5 percent of the net investment in manufacturing equipment over the period 1954–1970 may be attributed to the change in methods for calculating depreciation. Similarly, the peak effect for nonfarm non-

Table 2.6
Estimated changes in gross and net investment in equipment and structures, and in capital stock, resulting from accelerated depreciation, 1954–1970 (in millions of 1965 dollars)

	Manufacturing					
	Equipment			Structures		
	Investment		Capital	Investment		Capital
Year	Gross	Net	stock	Gross	Net	stock
1954	209	209	0	79	79	0
1955	627	596	209	280	275	79
1956	862	744	805	432	410	354
1957	878	650	1,549	450	402	764
1958	621	298	2,199	323	250	1,166
1959	395	27	2,497	181	92	1,416
1960	369	− 2	2,524	153	59	1,508
1961	406	35	2,522	169	71	1,567
1962	487	111	2,557	180	78	1,638
1963	545	152	2,668	172	65	1,706
1964	660	245	2,820	165	53	1,771
1965	733	282	3,065	159	45	1,824
1966	727	235	3,347	93	− 24	1,869
1967	696	170	3,582	41	− 74	1,845
1968	682	131	3,752	97	− 14	1,771
1969	702	131	3,883	193	83	1,757
1970	728	138	4,014	287	172	1,840

Table 2.6
(continued)

	Nonfarm, nonmanufacturing					
	Equipment			Structures		
	Investment		Capital	Investment		Capital
Year	Gross	Net	stock	Gross	Net	stock
1954	847	847	0	204	204	0
1955	1,871	1,708	847	649	635	204
1956	1,756	1,265	2,555	944	886	839
1957	1,723	988	3,820	1,023	903	1,725
1958	1,662	737	4,808	867	684	2,628
1959	1,519	453	5,545	584	354	3,312
1960	1,294	141	5,998	448	194	3,666
1961	1,386	205	6,139	478	214	3,810
1962	1,573	353	6,344	430	201	4,024
1963	1,779	491	6,697	473	178	4,225
1964	2,090	708	7,188	440	134	4,403
1965	2,049	531	7,896	384	70	4,537
1966	2,067	446	8,427	206	−114	4,607
1967	2,068	362	8,873	113	−205	4,593
1968	2,213	437	9,235	258	− 46	4,388
1969	2,214	354	9,672	471	169	4,342
1970	2,309	377	10,049	675	362	4,511

manufacturing equipment is $1.708 billion in 1955, or 37.4 percent of the net investment that took place in that year. Over the seventeen-year period, 15.4 percent of the net investment in nonfarm non-manufacturing equipment may be attributed to the change in depreciation rules in 1954.

Although the average lag in response of investment is longer for structures than for equipment, the effects of accelerated depreciation are broadly similar. For manufacturing structures the peak effect on net investment occurs in 1956 with $410 million, or 37.3 percent of the net investment that took place in that year. For the 1954–1970 period the increase in net investment in manufacturing structures due to accelerated depreciation is estimated at 15.0 percent of the total. For nonfarm nonmanufacturing structures, the peak effect on investment occurs in 1957 with $903 million, or 15.2 percent of the net investment that took place in that year. Over the whole period, 4.5 percent of the net investment in nonfarm nonmanufacturing structures may be attributed to the adoption of accelerated methods for depreciation in 1954.

Capital stock is a cumulation of net investment so that its behavior is implied by that of net investment. For both manufacturing and nonfarm nonmanufacturing equipment, two phases in the response of capital stock can be distinguished. First, the immediate impact of adoption of accelerated depreciation was to raise desired capital substantially above actual capital. By 1957 more than half the gap resulting from accelerated depreciation was eliminated; by 1959 none remained. Second, adoption of accelerated depreciation in 1954 resulted in additional stimulus from subsequent changes in lifetimes for tax purposes and from adoption of the investment tax credit. Half the total rise in the stock of manufacturing equipment from 1954 to 1970 took place by 1958, while half the rise in nonfarm nonmanufacturing equipment took place by 1959. The patterns for structures in both the manufacturing and nonfarm nonmanufacturing sectors are qualitatively similar to those for equipment but without a clear demarcation between successive phases. As in equipment, half the total rise in the stock of manufacturing structures over the period as a whole took place by 1958, while half the rise in nonfarm nonmanufacturing structures took place by 1959.

Gross investment is the sum of net investment and replacement; further, replacement rises in proportion to capital stock. By 1958 replacement had become the dominant component in the response of gross investment in equipment to the adoption of accelerated depreciation for both the manufacturing and nonfarm nonmanufacturing sectors. For manufacturing the peak response of gross investment occurred in 1957 with a change of $878 million. By 1970, added replacement requirements are expected to maintain gross investment at near-peak levels of $728 million. Similarly, gross investment in nonfarm nonmanufacturing equipment reached a peak of $1.871 billion in 1955, declined for several years, and will rise to a new peak of $2.309 billion by 1970, propelled by rising replacement requirements. For manufacturing structures the high of $450 million was attained in 1957; by 1970 it is estimated the level will reach $288 million. The general pattern of response for investment in nonfarm nonmanufacturing structures is similar in timing but different in magnitude. The largest response of gross investment was $1.023 billion in 1957; the level in 1970 is estimated at $672 million.

The total effect of the adoption of accelerated depreciation in 1954 on gross investment during the whole period from 1954 to 1970 may be assessed by comparing investment resulting from the new methods of depreciation with investment that would have taken place under the old methods. For equipment, 6.7 percent of gross investment in manufacturing and 8.0 percent of the gross investment in nonfarm nonmanufacturing may be attributed to accelerated depreciation over the period in question. For structures, the percentages are 5.7 for manufacturing and 3.0 for nonfarm nonmanufacturing. By 1970 we estimate that 6.6 percent of gross investment in manufacturing equipment, and 7.7 percent of gross investment in nonfarm nonmanufacturing equipment, will be due to the adoption of accelerated depreciation in 1954. The corresponding percentages for structures are 6.8 for manufacturing and 3.0 for nonfarm nonmanufacturing.

2.4.2   Depreciation Life Guidelines, 1962

The adoption of new guidelines for the determination of lifetimes allowable for tax purposes in 1962[51] affected only equipment lifetimes. The levels of the annual rental price of capital services, and the reductions brought about through the adoption of the 1962 depreciation guidelines, were:

	Without guidelines	With guidelines	Percentage decrease
Manufacturing equipment	0.315	0.307	2.5
Nonfarm, nonmanufacturing equipment	0.384	0.374	2.6

Estimates of the increase in gross investment, net investment, and capital stock in equipment resulting from adoption of the new guidelines are given in table 2.7.

2.4.3   Investment Tax Credit and Long Amendment, 1962

A second change in tax policy during 1962 was the adoption of an investment tax credit of 7 percent for equipment in the Revenue Act of 1962. As has been noted, various limitations on the applicability of the tax credit reduce the effective rate to 6 percent for manufacturing and 5.8 percent for nonfarm nonmanufacturing. Furthermore, the imposition and subsequent repeal of the Long amendment first eliminated the tax credit from the depreciation base in 1962 and 1963 and then restored it in 1964 and subsequent years. The levels of the annual rental price of capital services for 1963, and the reductions brought about by adoption of the tax credit with the Long amendment, were:

Table 2.7
Estimated changes in gross and net investment in equipment, and in capital stock, resulting from 1962 depreciation guidelines and investment tax credit, by industrial sector, 1962–1970 (in millions of 1965 dollars)

	Depreciation guidelines					
	Manufacturing equipment			Nonfarm, nonmanufacturing equipment		
	Investment		Capital	Investment		Capital
Year	Gross	Net	stock	Gross	Net	stock
1962	165	165	0	743	743	0
1963	292	268	165	770	627	743
1964	375	311	433	845	582	1,370
1965	369	260	744	816	441	1,952
1966	260	112	1,004	828	368	2,393
1967	215	51	1,116	641	110	2,761
1968	211	39	1,167	687	135	2,871
1969	218	41	1,206	687	109	3,006
1970	226	43	1,247	716	117	3,115

	Investment tax credit					
	Manufacturing equipment			Nonfarm, nonmanufacturing equipment		
	Investment		Capital	Investment		Capital
Year	Gross	Net	stock	Gross	Net	stock
1962	185	185	0	804	804	0
1963	527	500	185	1,711	1,556	804
1964	992	891	685	2,773	2,319	2,360
1965	1,229	997	1,576	2,726	1,826	4,679
1966	1,015	637	2,573	2,069	818	6,505
1967	724	252	3,210	2,017	609	7,323
1968	635	126	3,462	2,516	991	7,932
1969	723	195	3,588	2,283	567	8,923
1970	884	328	3,783	2,330	505	9,490

	Without credit	With credit	Percentage decrease
Manufacturing equipment	0.316	0.297	6.0
Nonfarm, nonmanufacturing equipment	0.383	0.361	5.7

Estimates of the increase in gross investment, net investment, and capital stock in equipment resulting from the investment tax credit are given in table 2.7. The impact of both of these policies is substantial, although the effect of the investment credit is several times larger than that of the depreciation guidelines. For the guidelines, the peak response in manufacturing industries of net investment in equipment took place in 1964, when they accounted for 12.5 percent of total net investment. The peak response to the investment credit took place a year later in 1965; in that year it accounted for 28.4 percent of net investment in equipment in the manufacturing sector. In non-manufacturing industries, both peak responses took place earlier—17.2 percent for the guidelines in 1962 and 36.8 percent for the investment credit in 1964—reflecting the shorter lag in equipment investment in that sector.

The responses to the investment credit in both sectors show a dip resulting from its suspension in 1966–1967. A smaller dip appears in the estimated effect of the depreciation guidelines during the same period, especially in the nonmanufacturing sector. This is explained by the fact that after the repeal of the Long amendment, investment credit and depreciation policies enhanced each other's effect. Thus the depreciation guidelines had a smaller impact during the period of the suspension of the investment credit for equipment.

2.4.4   Corporate Tax Cut, 1964

In analyzing the effect of the reduction from 52 percent to 48 percent in the corporate tax rate in 1964, we assume that the before-tax rate of return was left unchanged. Under this condition the effect of a change in the tax rate on the rental price of capital services is neutral provided that depreciation for tax purposes is equal to economic depreciation.[52] Under the conditions actually prevailing in 1964, depreciation for tax purposes was in excess of economic depreciation for both plant and equipment in the manufacturing and nonfarm nonmanufacturing sectors. Accordingly, the rental price of capital services resulting from the tax cut was actually greater than the rental price before the cut. Following are the results for the annual rental prices for 1965, the first full year of the tax cut:

	Without tax cut	With tax cut	Percentage decrease
Manufacturing equipment	0.296	0.299	1.0
Manufacturing structures	0.237	0.240	1.3
Nonfarm, nonmanufacturing equipment	0.352	0.355	0.9
Nonfarm, nonmanufacturing structures	0.247	0.250	1.2

Our estimates of the change in gross investment, net investment, and capital stock resulting from this change are given in table 2.8. In gen-

Table 2.8
Estimated changes in gross and net investment in equipment and structures, and in capital stock, resulting from the tax cut of 1964, by industrial sector, 1964–1970 (in millions of 1965 dollars)

	Manufacturing					
	Equipment			Structures		
	Investment		Capital	Investment		Capital
Year	Gross	Net	stock	Gross	Net	stock
1964	− 49	− 49	0	−20	−20	0
1965	−136	−129	− 49	−62	−61	− 20
1966	−181	−155	−178	−88	−83	− 81
1967	−186	−137	−333	−87	−77	−164
1968	−155	− 86	−470	−66	−51	−241
1969	−120	− 38	−556	−43	−25	−292
1970	−119	−32	−594	−43	−23	−317

	Nonfarm, nonmanufacturing					
	Equipment			Structures		
	Investment		Capital	Investment		Capital
Year	Gross	Net	stock	Gross	Net	stock
1964	−135	−135	0	− 44	− 44	0
1965	−267	−241	−135	−125	−123	− 44
1966	−217	−145	−376	−167	−155	−167
1967	−223	−123	−521	−168	−146	−322
1968	−274	−150	−644	−142	−110	−468
1969	−245	− 92	−794	− 99	− 59	−578
1970	−213	− 43	−886	− 88	− 44	−637

eral, the effects of the rate reduction are small and negative. It should be emphasized that these estimates depend on the level of output actually resulting from the tax cut; quite clearly the overall effect of the tax cut was to stimulate investment by increasing output.

2.4.5   Repeal of Long Amendment, 1964

A second, little-noticed change in tax policy in 1964 was the repeal of the Long amendment, which restored the tax credit to the depreciation base for tax purposes. Under the amendment, the effective rate of the tax credit was approximately 6 percent; repeal raised it to almost 10 percent. The levels of the annual rental price of capital services, and the resulting reductions, are:

	With Long amendment	Without Long amendment	Percentage decrease
Manufacturing equipment	0.302	0.293	3.0
Nonfarm, nonmanufacturing equipment	0.363	0.352	3.0

Estimates of the increase in gross investment, net investment, and capital stock resulting from this change are given in table 2.9.

These increases are quite substantial. The peak effect for manufacturing equipment took place in 1965, when the net investment in equipment attributable to the repeal was 10.4 percent of total net

Table 2.9
Estimated changes in gross and net investment in equipment and structures, and in capital stock, resulting from repeal of the Long Amendment, 1964–1970 (in millions of 1965 dollars)

	Manufacturing			Nonfarm, nonmanufacturing		
	Investment		Capital stock	Investment		Capital stock
Year	Gross	Net		Gross	Net	
1964	238	238	0	1,042	1,042	0
1965	400	365	238	958	758	1,042
1966	412	329	567	706	360	1,800
1967	349	217	896	750	335	2,160
1968	229	67	1,113	1,021	541	2,495
1969	236	64	1,180	761	177	3,036
1970	297	115	1,244	792	174	3,213

investment. In nonfarm nonmanufacturing, the peak effect for equipment came in 1964, accounting for over $1 billion and 16.6 percent of net investment in that sector. Once again, he diminution of the impact of this policy change can be seen in 1966 and one or two years after, resulting from the suspension of the investment credit. The lag structure in the nonmanufacturing sector makes the dip much more noticeable there than in the manufacturing sector.

2.4.6   Investment Credit Suspension, 1966

In 1966 an important objective of economic policy was to restrain investment. After a number of alternative changes in tax policy were considered and rejected,[53] the investment tax credit for equipment was suspended beginning October 10, 1966; at the same time accelerated depreciation for structures was replaced by 150 percent declining-balance depreciation. Originally, the suspension was to remain in effect until the end of 1967, or almost fifteen months, but it was lifted on March 9, 1967, so that the period was a little less than five months. The effects of the suspension on the annual rental price of capital in 1967 were the following:

	Without suspension	With suspension	Percentage increase
Manufacturing equipment	0.320	0.351	9.7
Manufacturing structures	0.259	0.276	6.6
Nonfarm, nonmanufacturing equipment	0.379	0.414	9.2
Nonfarm, nonmanufacturing structures	0.270	0.287	6.3

Our estimates of the effects of the suspension on gross investment, net investment, and capital stock are given in table 2.10.

For all categories of assets, the suspension had a restraining effect on the level of investment in 1967, which we estimate continued into 1968 except for nonfarm nonmanufacturing equipment. For both sectors the restoration of the original tax credit for equipment and accelerated depreciation for structures will result in a stimulus to investment in 1969 and 1970. For no class of assets is the level of capital stock as high at the end of 1970 as it would have been in the absence of the suspension. The total gross investment for the five-year period 1966–1970 is considerably lower than it would have been in the absence of the five-month suspension.

Table 2.10
Estimated changes in gross and net investment in equipment and structures, and in capital stock, resulting from suspension of the investment tax credit for equipment and accelerated depreciation for structures from October 10, 1966, through March 8, 1967, 1966–1970 (in millions of 1965 dollars)

	Manufacturing					
	Equipment			Structures		
	Investment		Capital	Investment		Capital
Year	Gross	Net	stock	Gross	Net	stock
1966	−177	−177	0	−46	−46	0
1967	−271	−245	−177	−89	−86	−46
1968	−153	−91	−422	−60	−52	−132
1969	−9	66	−513	−11	−12	−184
1970	157	223	−447	74	75	−172

	Nonfarm, nonmanufacturing					
	Equipment			Structures		
	Investment		Capital	Investment		Capital
Year	Gross	Net	stock	Gross	Net	stock
1966	−762	−762	0	−119	−119	0
1967	−599	−452	−762	−200	−192	−119
1968	69	303	−1,214	−126	−104	−311
1969	51	226	−911	−11	−18	−415
1970	18	150	−685	111	139	−397

If the suspension of the investment tax credit for equipment and accelerated depreciation for structures had continued for fifteen months, the impact on the level of investment would have been much more substantial, as our estimates in table 2.11 reveal. For investment in structures the restraining effect of the suspension would have continued into 1969 in both sectors, although the impact would have been very slight in that year. For investment in equipment, as well as in structures, the magnitude of the impact would have been much greater. As a result, the stimulus from restoration of the tax credit and accelerated depreciation would have been correspondingly increased.

Table 2.11
Estimated changes in gross and net investment in equipment and structures, and in capital stock, resulting from hypothetical suspension of the investment tax credit for equipment and accelerated depreciation for structures from October 10, 1966, through December 31, 1967, by industrial sector, 1966–1970 (in millions of 1965 dollars)

	Manufacturing					
	Equipment			Structures		
	Investment		Capital	Investment		Capital
Year	Gross	Net	stock	Gross	Net	stock
1966	−177	−177	0	− 46	− 46	0
1967	−872	−846	− 177	−250	−247	− 46
1968	−567	−416	−1,023	−234	−216	−293
1969	−181	31	−1,439	− 63	− 32	−509
1970	270	477	−1,408	117	152	−541

	Nonfarm, nonmanufacturing					
	Equipment			Structures		
	Investment		Capital	Investment		Capital
Year	Gross	Net	stock	Gross	Net	stock
1966	− 762	− 762	0	−119	−119	0
1967	−3,190	−3,043	762	−614	−606	− 119
1968	208	940	−3,805	−475	−425	− 725
1969	171	722	−2,865	−154	− 74	−1,150
1970	093	505	−2,143	193	278	−1,224

2.5   Conclusion

The objective of this study is to assess the effects of tax policy on investment behavior. For this purpose we have presented an econometric model of investment behavior based on the neoclassical theory of optimal capital accumulation. This model differs from a version used in two earlier studies[54] mainly in the imposition of further restrictions on the parameters of the underlying distributed lag function. These restrictions enable us to improve our specification of the lag structure and to economize on the number of parameters to be estimated. The resulting numerical estimates of the unknown parameters of our econometric model reflect the alterations in our statistical technique and incorporate data that have become available since our earlier studies. The lag structure derived from our new estimates suggests that the average lag between changes in the determinants of investment and actual expenditures for structures is shorter than that derived from our previous estimates. The new results are in much better agreement with evidence on the lag structure from sample surveys and from econometric models of investment fitted to data for industry groups for individual firms.

Our overall conclusion is the same as that in our previous studies: Tax policy can be highly effective in changing the level and timing of investment expenditures. Qualitatively speaking a change in tax policy that reduces the rental price of capital services will increase the desired level of capital stock. This increase will generate net investment that eventually brings actual capital up to the new desired level. Gross investment follows the course of net investment at first, but gradually replacement requirements resulting from the higher level of capital stock come to predominate. Even if all the determinants of desired capital remain stationary at their new levels, gross investment is permanently increased by the higher levels of replacement associated with higher levels of capital.

From a quantitative point of view the tax measures we consider have substantially different impacts. The investment tax credit, essentially a subsidy to the purchase of equipment, has had a greater impact than any of the other changes in tax policy during the postwar period, especially after repeal of the Long amendment made it even more effective. The shortening of lifetimes used in calculating depreciation for tax purposes and the use of accelerated methods for depreciation have been very important determinants of levels of investment expenditure since 1954. Suspension of the investment tax credit and accelerated depreciation from late 1966 to early 1967 had an important restraining effect on the level of investment; if this suspension had been allowed to remain in force for fifteen months rather than five, the impact would have been substantially greater. Of all the tax measures, only the reduction of the corporate tax rate in 1964, in our view, has had little impact on the level of investment expenditures. The reason for this is that tax depreciation and economic depreciation were virtually equal by 1964 so that any change in the tax rate would have been neutral in its effects on the price of capital services. The much-acclaimed tax cut of 1964 affected investment, but its main direct impact was through the enhanced effectiveness of the investment tax credit; reduction in the tax rate had a small but clearly negative impact on the level of investment.

Notes

1. The effects of tax policy on investment behavior are analyzed from this point of view by, among others, E. Cary Brown (1955, 1962); Norman B. Ture (1963, esp. pp. 341–345); Sam B. Chase, Jr. (1962); Richard A. Musgrave (1963, pp. 53–54 and 117–129).

2. Paul A. Samuelson (1964) pp. 604–606.

3. The effects of changes in the corporate tax rate on the cost of capital is the subject of much controversy. Recent contributions to the discussion include those of Robert J. Gordon (1967a); Marian Krzyzaniak and Richard A. Musgrave (1963); and John G. Cragg, Arnold C. Harberger, and Peter Mieszkowski (1967).

4. Little is known about the effects of the rate of return on saving. Harberger (1971) assumes that changes in the rate of return leave saving unchanged. See Chap. 7.

5. Robert E. Hall and Dale W. Jorgenson (1967, 1969b).

6. These alternative points of view on the theory of optimal capital accumulation are described in more detail in Dale W. Jorgenson (1967).

7. William H. White (1956).

8. Negative results were reported in Jan Tinbergen (1939). Subsequently, similar results were reported in Charles F. Roos (1948); Charles F. Roos and Victor S. von Szeliski (1943); Lawrence R. Klein (1950, esp. pp. 14–40; 1951).

9. Robert Eisner (1965); W. H. Locke Anderson (1964); and John R. Meyer and Robert R. Glauber (1964). See also Dale W. Jorgenson, Jerald Hunter, and M. Ishag Nadiri (1970a).

10. The predictive performance of these alternative econometric models is compared in Dale W. Jorgenson, Jerald Hunter, and M. Ishag Nadiri (1970b).

11. Three hundred forty-five references, almost all presenting the results of econometric tests of the neoclassical theory of the firm, are listed in a recent survey of the econometric literature on cost and production functions. See A. A. Walters (1963).

12. Marc Nerlove (1967).

13. Here we assume that investment is fully reversible. A discussion of the relationship between the price of capital goods and the present value of future rentals where investment is irreversible may be found in Kenneth J. Arrow (1968).

14. A detailed derivation is given in Jorgenson (1967).

15. A direct subsidy at the rate k results in a cost of acquisition of investment goods $q(1 - k)$. With tax rate u and present value of depreciation z, the same formula is obtained for the rental price of capital as for the investment tax credit, $c = q(1 - k)$ $[(1 - u)\rho + \delta] \times (1 - uz)/(1 - u)$.

16. Similar results are given in E. Cary Brown (1948) and Samuelson (1964).

17. Similar results are given in Brown (1948); in Richard A. Musgrave (1959); and in Vernon L. Smith (1963).

18. For recent contributions to this controversy, see Gordon (1967a); Krzyzaniak and Musgrave (1963); Cragg, Harberger, and Kieszkowski (1967). Our assumption of "no shifting"—that is, the before-tax rate of return is unaffected by changes in the tax rate— is supported by the results reported by Gordon. Alternative assumptions are suggested by Cragg and others and by Krzyzaniak and Musgrave. None of these empirical results is based on a complete econometric model appropriate to a general equilibrium analysis of the incidence of the corporate income tax.

19. This is formula (7) in our earlier paper, Hall and Jorgenson (1967, p. 394).

20. See formula (8), *ibid.*

21. This result corrects an error in formula (9), *ibid.* Fortunately, this error did not affect any of the empirical results presented in that or the subsequent paper, Hall and Jorgenson (1969b).

22. Zvi Griliches (1967c, p. 285).

23. Kenneth J. Arrow, Hollis B. Chenery, B. S. Minhas, and Robert M. Solow (1961).

24. Griliches (1967c, p. 290).

25. *Ibid.*, p. 292.

26. *Ibid.*

27. *Ibid.*, p. 297.

28. Nerlove (1967).

29. Hall and Jorgenson (1967, 1969b).

30. For further discussion of this point, see Dale W. Jorgenson (1966).

31. Zvi Griliches (1967a).

32. Shirley Almon (1965).

33. Further details on properties of the least squares estimator are discussed in Jorgenson (1966, pp. 142–143).

34. James Durbin (1960).

35. See *ibid.*, pp. 150–153.

36. These unpublished data, collected by the U.S. Department of Commerce, Office of Business Economics, were kindly made available to us by Robert Wasson of the Office of Business Economics.

37. U.S. Department of Commerce, *The National Income and Product Accounts of the United States, 1929–1965* (1966).

38. Robert J. Gordon (1967b).

39. Our original estimate of the rate of growth of this bias was .0651 percent per year, or about one-third the bias for structures. See Hall and Jorgenson (1967).

40. U.S. Treasury Department, Bureau of Internal Revenue (1942).

41. See Jack J. Gottsegen (1967).

42. Depreciation under the sum-of-the-years-digits formula has a higher present value for the range of lifetimes and rates of return of interest for this study. See Hall and Jorgenson (1967, table 1, p. 395).

43. These estimates of the effective rate of the tax credit are based on data from tax returns for 1963. See U.S. Treasury Department, Internal Revenue Service (1968).

44. Dale W. Jorgenson and Zvi Griliches (1967).

45. U.S. Treasury Department Internal Revenue Service (1965).

46. See Griliches (1967a) and Edmond Malinvaud (1961).

47. For detailed discussion of this restriction and its use in estimating the parameter α, see Jorgenson (1966, pp. 135 and 147–148).

48. Dale W. Jorgenson and James A. Stephenson (1967a); Dale W. Jorgenson and Calvin D. Siebert (1968b).

49. Thomas Mayer (1960).

50. These are crude extrapolations of previous trends, modified by fragmentary data available in October 1967, the time of the computations.

51. U.S. Treasury Department, Internal Revenue Service (1962).

52. For further discussion of tax-neutral depreciation, see pp. 17–18 above and Brown (1948); Musgrave (1959); Smith (1963).

53. Policies under consideration during early 1966 and their potential impact on investment expenditures are discussed in Hall and Jorgenson (1969b).

54. *Ibid.*, and Hall and Jorgenson (1967).

3

Technology and Decision Rules in the Theory of Investment Behavior

Dale W. Jorgenson

3.1 Introduction

The theory of production—including the description of technology, the conditions for producer equilibrium, and the response of variables determined in the theory to changes in parameters—may be developed in a form that abstracts from specific interpretations, as in Hicks, Samuelson, and Debreu.[1] In the intertemporal theory of production, each commodity is distinguished by point of time. As an illustration, an hour of labor today and an hour of labor tomorrow are treated as distinct commodities. Given this interpretation, the intertemporal theory of producer behavior is formally analogous to the standard atemporal theory. This analogy has been developed extensively by Fisher, Lindahl, Hicks, and Malinvaud.[2]

The special character of the intertemporal theory of production arises from more detailed specifications of technology, permitting more precise characterization of producer behavior. The most important specialization of technology results from introduction of capital as a factor of production. Although the central concepts of capital theory—capital assets, capital services, and investment—are inessential to the development of the intertemporal theory of production, they provide additional structure that permits a much more detailed analysis of producer behavior.

First, in the theory of capital the service of a durable good at any point of time is a fixed proportion of the output of the same service at any other point of time. These proportions describe the relative efficiencies of a durable good of different ages. Second, the services of durable goods acquired at different points of time are perfect substitutes in production. Accordingly, the flow of capital services to the activity of production depends on the stock of capital. The assumptions of perfect complementarity and perfect substitution underlying the model of durable capital are highly restrictive, but the practical importance of this model is very great, as Lindahl and Malinvaud have pointed out.[3]

The special character of technology associated with capital as a factor of production results from the fact that production possibilities at each point of time depend only on the accumulated stock of investment goods at that point of time and are otherwise independent of past productive activity. We refer to this class of technologies as recursive; in recursive technologies production possibilities at any point of time may depend on accumulated stocks of the produced means of production, but are otherwise independent of past activity.

For recursive technologies the intertemporal theory of producer behavior may be radically simplified. Production and investment decisions at each point of time depend only on production possibilities at that point of time. Since production and investment decisions may depend on accumulated stocks of investment goods, we refer to the associated decision rules as recursive. For a recursive technology the objective of the firm may be interpreted as maximization of goodwill subject to initial capital stocks at each point of time. Recursive technologies and the associated decision rules provide the basis for optimal control theory.

In the classical theory of capital, as developed by Wicksell, Lindahl, and Malinvaud,[4] the installation of investment goods is assumed to be free of restriction. Any quantity of investment goods can be installed (or removed) at a given point of time. Under this assumption the possibilities for productive activity are independent of the accumulated stock of capital. This specialization of technology results in a further radical simplification of the intertemporal theory of producer behavior. The decisions of the producing unit at each point of time are independent of accumulated stocks; the intertemporal decision process can be decomposed into separate decisions taking place at distinct points of time. Accordingly, we refer to these technologies and the associated decision rules as decomposable. Under a decomposable technology the objective of the firm is simply to maximize profit at each point of time.

The notion of a decomposable technology was formalized by Malinvaud.[5] Decomposable technologies include the durable goods model of Walras, Åkerman, and Wicksell[6] and the inventory model underlying the Austrian theory of capital of Böhm-Bawerk and

Wicksell.[7] The notion of a decomposable decision rule was introduced by Malinvaud and interpreted as the consequence of maximization of profit at each point of time.[8]

3.2   Technology

We consider two alternative specifications of technology, both involving capital services as a factor of production. We retain the assumption that capital services from a durable good are perfectly complementary at different points of time. Further, we assume that the services of durable goods acquired at different points of time are perfect substitutes in production at any point of time. However, we do not retain the classical assumption that installation of durable goods is free of restriction. We first develop the theory of optimal capital accumulation with restriction on the installation of investment goods and then specialize the theory to the classical characterization of technology by eliminating this restriction.

Two types of restrictions on the installation of investment goods have been treated in the theory of investment behavior. First, the rate of installation of investment goods may be irreversible so that investment must be nonnegative. Optimal investment policy under this type of restriction has been analyzed in detail by Arrow and others.[9] Second, investment may be associated with the use of internal resources of the productive unit. Optimal policy under this type of restriction has been analyzed by Lucas, Uzawa, and others[10] as a formalization of the investment theory of Lerner,[11] and Eisner and Strotz.[12] We derive and characterize optimal investment policy under restrictions on the installation of investment goods including both irreversibility and the use of internal resources. Pontryagin's maximum principle provides a natural framework for unifying these disparate strands in the theory of investment.[13]

To simplify the presentation, we consider a description of technology involving only one product at any point of time, denoted $Q(t)$, and only one factor of production other than capital, say labor services, denoted $L(t)$. Finally, we assume that capital services are a factor of production; the quantity of capital services is denoted $K(t)$. The flow of labor services is measured in man-hours and the flow of capital services is measured in machine-hours. The intertemporal theory of producer behavior is easily extended to any number of products and factors of production.

The level of capital services provided to the productive process may be altered by investment activity. For *recursive* technologies this activity may be divided into two parts: the first external to the firm, representing the acquisition of investment goods, denoted $A(t)$; and the second internal to the firm, representing the installation of investment goods. The internal activities of the firm include the production of output and the installation of investment goods. We assume that capital is allocated between production and installation; the higher the rate of acquisition of investment goods, the larger the amount of capital that must be withheld from production. Flows of investment goods acquisition and installation are measured as the number of machines acquired or installed.

To formalize our description of recursive technologies, we first suppose that the set of production possibilities may be represented in the form,

$$Q(t) \leq F[K_F(t), L(t)], \quad Q(t) \geq 0, \quad K_F(t) \geq 0, \quad L(t) \geq 0, \qquad (3.1)$$

where F is the maximum level of output corresponding to the amount of capital input allocated to production $K_F(t)$ and the amount of labor input $L(t)$. We assume that output, capital input, and labor input are nonnegative and that the production process is characterized by free disposal. Any nonnegative level of production $Q(t)$ less than or equal to the maximum given by the production function F is feasible.

Similarly, we may represent the set of installation possibilities in the form,

$$A(t) \leq I[K_F(t), K_I(t)], \quad A(t) \geq 0, \quad K_I(t) \geq 0, \qquad (3.2)$$

where I is the maximum level of acquisition of investment goods corresponding to the amounts of capital input allocated to production $K_F(t)$ and to installation $K_I(t)$. We assume that acquisition of investment goods and capital input allocated to installation are nonnegative and that the installation process is characterized by free disposal. Any nonnegative level of acquisition $A(t)$ less than or equal to the maximum given by the installation function I is feasible. Finally, the total capital input available $K(t)$ is greater than or equal to the sum of capital input allocated to production and to installation:

$$K(t) \geqq K_F(t) + K_I(t).$$ (3.3)

The allocation of capital is also characterized by free disposal.

We assume that the production function F is twice differentiable and increasing, so that marginal products of labor and capital services are positive:

$$\frac{\partial F}{\partial K_F} > 0, \qquad \frac{\partial F}{\partial L} > 0.$$ (3.4)

Further, we assume that the production function is concave; production is characterized by nonincreasing returns and a decreasing marginal rate of substitution. The second-order derivatives satisfy the conditions,

$$\frac{\partial^2 F}{\partial K_F^2} < 0, \qquad \frac{\partial^2 F}{\partial L^2} < 0; \qquad \frac{\partial^2 F}{\partial K_F^2} \frac{\partial^2 F}{\partial L^2} \geqq \left(\frac{\partial^2 F}{\partial K_F \partial L} \right)^2.$$ (3.5)

If the last inequality is satisfied with strict equality, the production function is characterized by constant returns.

We assume that the installation function I is twice differentiable and increasing, so that marginal products of capital allocated to production and installation are positive:

$$\frac{\partial I}{\partial K_F} > 0, \qquad \frac{\partial I}{\partial K_I} > 0.$$ (3.6)

Further, we assume that the installation function is concave; installation is characterized by nonincreasing returns and a decreasing marginal rate of substitution. The second-order derivatives satisfy the conditions,

$$\frac{\partial^2 I}{\partial K_F^2} < 0, \qquad \frac{\partial^2 I}{\partial K_I^2} < 0; \qquad \frac{\partial^2 I}{\partial K_F^2} \frac{\partial^2 I}{\partial K_I^2} \geqq \left(\frac{\partial^2 I}{\partial K_F \partial K_I} \right)^2.$$ (3.7)

If the last inequality is satisfied with strict equality, the installation function is characterized by constant returns.

Our characterization of technology can be extended in a number of directions. First, the production and installation processes could be combined into an overall substitution law:

$G[Q(t),\ A(t),\ K(t),\ L(t)] = 0$.

Output and the acquisition of investment goods are joint products, and labor and capital services are factors of production. Under our assumption that production and installation are separable activities, the analysis is considerably simplified. Separable processes have been analyzed by Lucas, Uzawa, Gould, and Treadway.[14] Treadway had studied nonseparable processes.[15] Second, the installation process could depend on the rate of change of capital rather than the rate of investment.[16] Third, production and installation could be characterized by nonnegative and nondecreasing marginal products. The marginal rate of substitution of labor for capital input in production could be made nonincreasing, and the marginal rate of substitution of capital for installation could be made nonincreasing. All of these extensions would introduce inessential detail into our presentation. Only dropping the assumption of separability of the processes of production and installation produces qualitatively different results.

To simplify our presentation further, it is useful to add conditions that assure the existence of an interior solution to the usual first-order conditions for a maximum of profit in the absence of the internal installation process. For all positive K_F we assume that the marginal product of labor input has limits:

$$\lim_{L \to 0} \frac{\partial F}{\partial L} = +\infty, \qquad \lim_{L \to +\infty} \frac{\partial F}{\partial L} = 0; \qquad\qquad (3.8)$$

similarly, we assume that for all positive L,

$$\lim_{K_F \to 0} \frac{\partial F}{\partial K_F} = +\infty, \qquad \lim_{K_F \to +\infty} \frac{\partial F}{\partial K_F} = 0. \qquad\qquad (3.9)$$

We impose analogous conditions on the installation process, so that for all positive K_I we assume that the marginal product of capital input allocated to production has limits:

$$\lim_{K_F \to 0} \frac{\partial I}{\partial K_F} = +\infty, \qquad \lim_{K_F \to +\infty} \frac{\partial I}{\partial K_F} = 0; \qquad\qquad (3.10)$$

similarly, we assume that for all positive K_F,

$$\lim_{K_I \to 0} \frac{\partial I}{\partial K_I} = +\infty, \qquad \lim_{K_I \to +\infty} \frac{\partial I}{\partial K_I} = 0. \qquad (3.11)$$

For *decomposable* technologies the acquisition of investment goods is unconstrained. No capital is required for the installation of investment goods. The level of acquisition may be positive, negative, or zero. We can specialize the description of technology outlined above by eliminating the installation function and nonnegativity of the acquisition of investment goods (2) as constraints and by setting the value of capital allocated to installation K_I equal to zero. We retain the production function (1) as characterized by assumptions (4) and (5) as a constraint. Under this specialization our description of technology at each point of time reduces to the *classical* technology of the atemporal theory of production. Accordingly, we may refer to a description of technology with constraints on the acquisition of investment goods as *nonclassical*.

3.3 Objective Function

For intertemporal choice the objective of economic activity can be described as the selection of a most preferred consumption plan, subject to technology and to economic possibilities for transformation of the results of production into consumption. This optimization problem involves the selection of a production plan and a consumption plan. Given fixed prices, the optimization problem is recursive in structure. The productive unit, firm or industry, selects a production plan that maximizes its value. The resulting maximum value is then taken as given for the determination of an optimal consumption plan. The choice of a production plan is completely independent of the choice of a consumption plan. We may identify the selection of a production plan with the theory of producer behavior and the selection of a consumption plan with the theory of consumer behavior.

The intertemporal interpretation of the recursive structure of the problem of optimal consumption and production planning under fixed prices is due to Fisher.[17] Recursive decomposition of production and consumption planning is not specific to the intertemporal interpretation of atemporal economic theory, but is characteristic of economic decisions at the most abstract theoretical level, as Koopmans has emphasized.[18] The full implications of this recursive decomposition for intertemporal production planning have been appreciated only recently, largely as a consequence of the revival and extension of Fisher's analysis of the investment decision by Hirshleifer and Bailey.[19]

From one point of view the objective of maximizing the value of the firm is only one of many possible criteria for production and investment decisions.[20] Alternative criteria discussed in the literature include maximization of the average internal rate of return, maximization of the rate of return on capital owned by the firm, investment in any project with internal rate of return greater than the market rate of interest, and so on. None of these criteria can be derived as a necessary condition for selection of an optimal consumption plan under the conditions we have outlined. Hirshleifer has summarized the justification for Fisher's approach as follows:

Since Fisher, economists working in the theory of investment decision have tended to adopt a mechanical approach—some plumping for the use of this formula, some for that. From a Fisherian point of view, we can see that none of the formulas so far propounded is universally valid. Furthermore, even where the present-value rule, for example, is correct, few realize that its validity is conditional upon making certain associated financing decisions as the Fisherian analysis demonstrates. In short, the Fisherian approach permits us to define the range of applicability and the short-comings of all the proposed formulas—thus standing over against them as the general theoretical solution to the problem of investment decision under conditions of certainty.[21]

A basic difficulty with the usual intertemporal interpretation of the theory of production, as in Fisher,[22] is that transactions in present and all future commodities are viewed as taking place in the present, ostensibly requiring future markets for all commodities in all time periods. But are the specified future deliveries actually made or are contracts modified as a given future time point approaches the present? If the contracts are modified, why do individuals agree to contracts at the terms originally stipulated? Hicks has altered Fisher's interpretation by identifying future transactions with hypothetical plans that do not result in actual contracts. These plans are constructed in accord with expectations of future prices. Plans may be modified as expectations change.[23]

In the intertemporal interpretation of economic theory developed by Fisher and Hicks, a "horizon" is imposed on producers so that only a finite interval of time is considered. The imposition of a finite time horizon is inappropriate for analyzing the movement of an economic system through time. The selection of a production plan in the present involves decisions about the future based on maximization of the value of the producing unit in the present. To be consistent with future decisions, the present production plan must be based on the same technological and economic possibilities as future plans. If a finite horizon is imposed on present decisions, the horizon must remain fixed in time so that as time proceeds, the horizon becomes shorter and shorter, introducing a complete asymmetry between present and future decisions. To overcome this difficulty, it is useful to introduce an unlimited time horizon, as in Malinvaud's intertemporal interpretation of economic theory.[24]

In the absence of a time horizon, the value of the producing unit, industry or firm, at any point of time is the integral of the value of revenue less outlay on current account, less outlay on capital account over current and future points of time. Outlay on capital account includes costs of acquisition of investment goods. We will refer to the value of revenue less outlay on current account as the value of *cash flow* and the value of revenue less outlay on both current and capital account as *net cash flow,* defined by

$$p(t)C(t) = P_Q(t)Q(t) - p_L(t)L(t) - p_A(t)A(t),\tag{3.12}$$

where $p(t)$ is the present price of money or discount factor and $r(t)$ is the rate of interest:

$$p(t) = e^{-\int_0^t r(s)\,ds},$$

and $p_Q(t)$, $p_L(t)$, and $p_A(t)$ are present prices of output, labor services, acquisition of investment goods, respectively. To simplify the presentation, we assume that all present prices are positive. Interpreting cash flow in terms of future prices, we may write

$$C(t) = q_Q(t)Q(t) - q_L(t)L(t) - q_A(t)A(t),\tag{3.13}$$

where $p_Q(t) = p(t)q_Q(t)$, and so on.

The value of the producing unit at time s is the integral of the value of net cash flow from s forward, defined by

$$p(s)V(s) = \int_s^\infty p(t)C(t)\,dt.\tag{3.14}$$

The *present value* of the producing unit is its value in the present:

$$p(O)V(O) = \int_0^\infty p(t)C(t)\, dt, \tag{3.15}$$

of course, $p(O) = 1$, so that we may refer to $V(O)$ as present value. An obvious property of this objective function is that present value of a production plan is equal to the integral of the value of net cash flow from the present to some future time, say t, plus the present value of the producing unit at t.

Under recursive decomposition of production and consumption planning, the objective of the producing unit is to maximize its present value, subject to the past time path for capital accumulation. If the producing unit follows an optimal production and investment plan from the present to some future time, say t, the optimal plan from t forward maximizes the current present value at t, subject to the time path for accumulation of capital up to that point. Present and future decisions are *consistent* in the sense of Strotz.[25] The optimal production plan at each point of time may be generated by maximizing the current present value of the producing unit, subject to the past time path for capital accumulation.

Before deriving the optimal plan for production and investment, it is useful to analyze further the acquisition and replacement of investment goods. We may write the value of the producing unit at time s in the form,

$$\begin{aligned}
p(s)V(s) &= \int_s^\infty [\, p_Q(t)Q(t) - p_L(t)L(t) - p_A(t)A(t)]\, dt\,, \\
&= \int_s^\infty [\, p_Q(t)Q(t) - p_L(t)L(t)]\, dt \\
&\quad - \int_s^\infty p_A(t)A(t)\, dt\,,
\end{aligned}$$

provided, of course, that all present values are defined.

We may define the value of revenue less outlay on current account and the time rental value of capital services as the value of *profits*, defined by

$$p(t)P(t) = p_Q(t)Q(t) - p_L(t)L(t) - p_K(t)K(t). \tag{3.16}$$

The *goodwill* of the producing unit at time s is the integral of the value of profits from s forward, defined by

$$p(s)V^+(s) = \int_s^\infty p(t)P(t)\,dt\,. \tag{3.17}$$

The present value of goodwill of the producing unit is its value in the present:

$$p(O)V^+(O) = \int_0^\infty p(t)P(t)\,dt\,; \tag{3.18}$$

since $p(O) = 1$, we may refer to $V^+(O)$ as the *present value of goodwill*.

Returning to our expression for the value of the producing unit, we may write

$$
\begin{aligned}
p(s)V(s) &= \int_s^\infty [\,p_Q(t)Q(t) - p_L(t)L(t) - p_K(t)K(t)]\,dt \\
&\quad + \int_{-\infty}^s p_A(s,t)A(t)\,dt \\
&= p(s)V^+(s) + \int_{-\infty}^s p_A(s,t)A(t)\,dt\,.
\end{aligned} \tag{3.19}
$$

The value of the producing unit is equal to the value of goodwill plus the value of the firm's capital stock, where $p_A(s,t)$ is the present price of a capital good first acquired at time t. This formula for the value of the producing unit is due to Malinvaud.[26]

For exponential decline in efficiency we may write the value of capital stock in the form,

$$
\begin{aligned}
\int_s^\infty p_K(u) \int_{-\infty}^s A(t)e^{-\delta(u-t)}\,dt\,du\,, \\
= \int_s^\infty p_K(u)e^{-\delta(u-s)} \int_{-\infty}^s A(t)^{-\delta(s-t)}\,dt\,du\,, \\
= p_A(s)K(s)\,.
\end{aligned}
$$

The value of capital stock is equal to the acquisition price of capital goods multiplied by the quantity of capital. The value of the producing unit may be expressed in the form,

$$p(s)V(s) = p(s)V^+(s) + p_A(s)K(s)\,, \tag{3.20}$$

or in future prices,

$$V(s) = V^+(s) + q_A(s)K(s)\,. \tag{3.21}$$

3.4   Optimal Investment Policy

The objective of the producing unit, firm or industry, is to maximize
present value (3.15), defined as

$$V(O) = \int_0^\infty [\, p_Q(t)Q(t) - p_L(t)L(t) - p_A(t)A(t)]\, dt\,,$$

subject to the production function (3.1),

$$Q(t) \leqq F[K_F(t),\, L(t)]\,,$$

the installation function (3.2),

$$A(t) \leqq I[K_F(t),\, K_I(t)]\,,$$

and the identity for the allocation of capital (3.3),

$$K(t) \geqq K_F(t) + K_I(t)\,,$$

for nonnegative levels of output $Q(t)$, labor input $L(t)$, and acquisition
of investment goods $A(t)$, and nonnegative levels of capital for production $K_F(t)$ and for installation $K_I(t)$. To simplify the discussion, we
assume that the decline in relative efficiency of investment goods with
age is exponential,

$$K'(t) = A(t) - \delta K(t)\,,$$

so that current replacement requirements depend on the current level
of capital stock and are independent of past levels. Given the initial
level of capital stock $K(O)$, this is a problem in optimal control theory.
To characterize the optimal policy, we employ Pontryagin's maximum
principle.[27]

Interpreting the determination of investment policy as a problem in
control theory, we may identify output $Q(t)$, labor input $L(t)$, acquisition of investment goods $A(t)$, and capital allocated to production
$K_F(t)$ and installation $K_I(t)$ as control variables or instruments. Similarly, we may identify the level of capital stock $K(t)$ as a state variable
or target.[28] At this point we may rewrite the present value of the producing unit in terms of future prices:

$$V(O) = \int_0^\infty p(t)[q_Q(t)Q(t) - q_L(t)L(t) - q_A(t)A(t)]\, dt\,,$$

where the present value of money $p(t)$ serves as a discount factor.

To employ Pontryagin's maximum principle for the characterization of an optimal investment policy we introduce the Hamiltonian function,

$$p(t)\,\mathcal{H}(K; Q, L, A, K_F, K_I; \lambda_A; t) = p(t)\,(q_Q Q - q_L L - q_A A)$$
$$+ p(t)\lambda_A(t)(A - \delta K)\,, \tag{3.22}$$

where $\lambda_A(t)$ is a multiplier associated with the acquisition and installation of investment goods at time t. This multiplier represents the discounted value of all future increments in cash flow associated with an increment in investment at time t. We discount this multiplier to the present in order to facilitate its economic interpretation; future prices are discounted to the present in the same way. The multiplier $\lambda_A(t)$ represents the value of acquisition and installation of a unit of investment goods at time t; accordingly, we refer to this multiplier as the *shadow asset price of capital*. Given the shadow asset price of capital for the optimal investment policy, the Hamiltonian must be a maximum, subject to the production function, the installation function, and the identity for the allocation of capital.[29] To characterize maxima of the Hamiltonian, we employ the Kuhn-Tucker theorem of concave programming.[30]

By the Kuhn-Tucker theorem, maxima of the Hamiltonian subject to constraint for a given value of the multiplier $\lambda_A(t)$ correspond to saddlepoints of the Lagrangian function,

$$p(t)\,\mathcal{L}(K; Q, L, A, K_F, K_I; \lambda_A; \mu_Q, \mu_I, \mu_K; t)$$
$$= p(t)\mathcal{H} + p(t)\,\mu_Q(t)(Q(K_F, L) - Q) + p(t)\mu_I(t)(I(K_F, K_I) - A)$$
$$+ p(t)\mu_K(t)(K - K_F - K_I)\,. \tag{3.23}$$

The multiplier $p(t)\mu_Q(t)$ represents the increment in the value of the Hamiltonian associated with an increment in output at time t, holding levels of capital and labor input constant. Similarly, the multiplier $p(t)\mu_I(t)$ represents the increment in the value of the Hamiltonian associated with an increment in the installation of capital at time t, holding levels of capital for production and capital for installation constant. Finally, the multiplier $p(t)\mu_K(t)$ represents the increment in the value of the Hamiltonian associated with an increment in capital stock at time t. We refer to μ_Q as the *shadow price of output*, μ_I as the *shadow price of installation of investment goods*, and μ_K as the *shadow rental price of capital*. The multipliers $\{p\mu_Q, p\mu_I, p\mu_K\}$ are equal to the shadow prices $\{\mu_Q, \mu_I, \mu_K\}$, discounted to the present; this convention facilitates comparisons between the shadow prices and future market prices.

A necessary condition for an optimal investment policy is that at each point of time the shadow asset price of capital satisfies

$$
\lambda_A' = \lambda_A r - \frac{\partial \mathscr{L}}{\partial K} \tag{3.24}
$$
$$
= \lambda_A r + \lambda_A \delta - \mu_K .
$$

The shadow rental price of capital is equal to the shadow asset price of capital, multiplied by the sum of the rate of interest and the rate of depreciation, less the rate of change of the shadow asset price of capital,

$$
\mu_K = \lambda_A (r + \delta) - \lambda_A' .
$$

To characterize saddlepoints of the Lagrangian function $\mathscr{L}$ at each point of time, we first observe that the Hamiltonian function for investment policy is linear in the instruments $\{Q, L, A, K_F, K_I\}$. The identity for the allocation of capital is linear, and the production and installation functions are concave in these instruments. We conclude that for given values of capital K and the shadow asset price of capital λ_A, the objective function and the constraints are concave. Provided that for any set of shadow prices $\{\mu_Q, \mu_I, \mu_K\}$, nonnegative and not all zero, the constraint qualification,

$$
\mu_Q(F(K_F, L) - Q) + \mu_I(I(K_F, K_I) - A) + \mu_K(K - K_F - K_I) > 0 ,
$$

is satisfied for some set of instruments $\{Q, L, A, K_F, K_I\}$, any maximum of the Hamiltonian corresponds to a saddlepoint of the Lagrangian.[31] If output, capital, and investment goods are freely disposable, so that for some feasible investment policy,

$$
Q < F(K_F, L), \qquad A < I(K_F, K_I), \qquad K_I + K_F < K ,
$$

then the constraint qualification is satisfied.

For given values of capital K and the shadow asset price of capital λ_A, a saddlepoint of the Lagrangian function implies the differential inequalities,

$$\frac{\partial \mathcal{L}}{\partial \mu_Q} = F(K_F, L) - Q \geq 0,$$

$$\frac{\partial \mathcal{L}}{\partial \mu_I} = I(K_F, K_I) - A \geq 0,$$

$$\frac{\partial \mathcal{L}}{\partial \mu_K} = K - K_F - K_I \geq 0, \tag{3.25}$$

and the complementary slackness condition,

$$\mu_Q \frac{\partial \mathcal{L}}{\partial \mu_Q} + \mu_I \frac{\partial \mathcal{L}}{\partial \mu_I} + \mu_K \frac{\partial \mathcal{L}}{\partial \mu_K} = 0, \tag{3.26}$$

for nonnegative multipliers $\{\mu_Q, \mu_I, \mu_K\}$. Further, a saddlepoint of the Lagrangean implies the differential inequalities,

$$\frac{\partial \mathcal{L}}{\partial Q} = q_Q - \mu_Q \leq 0,$$

$$\frac{\partial \mathcal{L}}{\partial L} = -q_L + \mu_Q \frac{\partial F}{\partial L} \leq 0,$$

$$\frac{\partial \mathcal{L}}{\partial A} = -q_A + \lambda_A - \mu_I \leq 0,$$

$$\frac{\partial \mathcal{L}}{\partial K_F} = \mu_Q \frac{\partial F}{\partial K_F} + \mu_I \frac{\partial I}{\partial K_F} - \mu_K \leq 0,$$

$$\frac{\partial \mathcal{L}}{\partial K_I} = \mu_I \frac{\partial I}{\partial K_I} - \mu_K \leq 0; \tag{3.27}$$

and the complementary slackness condition,

$$Q \frac{\partial \mathcal{L}}{\partial Q} + L \frac{\partial \mathcal{L}}{\partial L} + A \frac{\partial \mathcal{L}}{\partial A} + K_F \frac{\partial \mathcal{L}}{\partial K_F} + K_I \frac{\partial \mathcal{L}}{\partial K_I} = 0, \tag{3.28}$$

for nonnegative instruments $\{Q, L, A, K_F, K_I\}$.[32]

3.5   Decision Rules

To characterize the decision rules associated with an optimal investment policy, we now proceed to a detailed analysis of the saddlepoint conditions—(3.25)–(3.28)—for the Lagrangian function (3.23). At each point of time we take the value of capital K and its shadow price λ_A as given by the optimal investment policy up to that point. From the differential inequality for output (3.27) we first observe that

$$\mu_Q \geqq q_Q > 0,$$

by our assumption that prices are positive. If the price of output is positive, the shadow price of output is positive, and free disposal of output does not pay. By complementary slackness (3.26) we may replace the inequality constraint (3.25) on output by the strict equality.

$$Q = F(K_F, L). \tag{3.29}$$

Second, for $\mu_Q > 0$ the differential inequality (3.27),

$$\mu_Q \frac{\partial F}{\partial L} \leqq q_L,$$

can be satisfied only if labor input is positive, $L > 0$. But this implies that output is positive, $Q > 0$. By complementary slackness (3.28), the inequalities we have considered up to this point become equalities;

$$q_Q = \mu_Q, \qquad q_Q \frac{\partial F}{\partial L} = q_L, \tag{3.30}$$

the shadow price of output is equal to its market price and the value of the marginal product of labor is equal to the wage rate.

Turning to the differential inequality (3.27) for capital allocated to production K_F, we observe that a positive price of output implies that the constraint,

$$q_Q \frac{\partial F}{\partial K_F} + \mu_I \frac{\partial I}{\partial K_F} \leqq \mu_K,$$

can be satisfied only if capital allocated to production is positive, $K_F > 0$. By complementary slackness (3.28) the inequality becomes an equality,

$$q_Q \frac{\partial F}{\partial K_F} + \mu_I \frac{\partial I}{\partial K_F} = \mu_K. \tag{3.31}$$

The value of the marginal product in both production and installation of capital allocated to production is equal to the shadow rental price of capital. The value in production is a market value, measured at the market price of output q_Q. The value in installation is an imputed value, measured at the shadow price of installation of investment goods μ_I. Since the shadow rental price of capital is positive, $\mu_K > 0$, complementary slackness (3.26) implies that installed capital is fully utilized,

$$K = K_F + K_I. \qquad (3.32)$$

Free disposal of capital does not pay.

At this point we must consider two cases. First, the shadow price of installation of investment goods μ_I may be zero. In this case no capital is allocated to installation, since

$$0 = \mu_I \frac{\partial I}{\partial K_I} < \mu_K, \qquad (3.33)$$

the value of the marginal product of capital allocated to installation is less than the shadow rental price of capital. All capital is allocated to production, and the acquisition of capital is zero. The shadow asset price of capital is less than or equal to its market acquisition price (3.27),

$$\lambda_A \leqq q_A.$$

Second, the price of installation of new investment goods may be positive, $\mu_I > 0$. In this case the differential inequality for capital allocated to installation (3.27) can be satisfied only if capital allocated to installation is positive, $K_I > 0$. By complementary slackness (3.28) this inequality becomes an equality,

$$\mu_I \frac{\partial I}{\partial K_I} = \mu_K; \qquad (3.34)$$

the value of the marginal product of capital allocated to installation is equal to the shadow rental price of capital. By complementary slackness (3.26), the constraint on the installation of capital (3.25) is satisfied with strict equality,

$$A = I(K_F, K_I). \qquad (3.35)$$

Free disposal of investment goods does not pay. Since levels of capital allocated to production and installation are both positive, acquisition of investment goods is positive. By complementary slackness (3.28),

$$\lambda_A = q_A + \mu_I,\tag{3.36}$$

the shadow asset price of capital is equal to the market price of acquisition plus the shadow price of installation.

We have presented necessary conditions for an optimal investment policy. To complete the characterization of an optimal policy, we employ a set of sufficient conditions consisting of the necessary conditions given above and the transversality conditions,

$$\lim_{t \to \infty} p(t)\lambda_A(t) \geqq 0, \qquad \lim_{t \to \infty} p(t)\lambda_A(t)K(t) = 0.\tag{3.37}$$

The first of these conditions states that the limiting value of the discounted shadow asset price of capital must be nonnegative. The second states that the limiting value of capital, evaluated at its discounted shadow asset price, must be equal to zero.[33] This condition requires, for example, that if the shadow price $\lambda_A(t)$ is constant, capital $K(t)$ is growing at a constant rate, and the rate of interest $r(t)$, equal to the rate of decline of the discount factor $p(t)$, is constant, then the rate of interest must exceed the rate of growth of capital. If there exists an investment policy that satisfies the differential equations for capital and its shadow asset price, the saddlepoint conditions for the Lagrangean at each point of time and the transversality conditions, then this policy is optimal.[34]

At any point of time, the target K and the multiplier λ_A are determined by the optimal investment policy up to that point; the values of these variables depend on the initial condition for capital and the terminal condition for the shadow asset prices derived from the transversality conditions. For given values of capital and its shadow asset price, a set of values for the instruments $\{Q, L, A, K_F, K_I\}$ and the Lagrange multipliers $\{\mu_Q, \mu_I, \mu_K\}$ are determined from the saddlepoint conditions for the Lagrangean function $p\mathscr{L}$. Given optimal values of the instruments and the Lagrange multipliers, optimal rates of change of capital and its shadow asset price are determined from the differential equations,

$$K' = A - \delta K, \qquad \lambda'_A = \lambda_A(r + \delta) - \mu_K.$$

The optimal production and investment plan at any point of time can be generated by maximizing the current present value of the productive unit, subject to technology and to the level of capital accumulated up to that point. The optimal plan depends on the level of capital and the value of the optimal shadow asset price of capital. This plan determines the level of investment and the rate of change of capital, together with the rate of change of the shadow asset price. The resulting decision rules are *recursive*, since they generate a new time path for capital and its shadow asset price and new decision rules of the same form.

The optimal investment plan for recursive technologies depends on the level of capital services required for the optimal production plan at each point of time and on replacement requirements. Replacement requirements depend only on the level of capital stock and are otherwise independent of the time path for capital accumulation if and only if the efficiency of investment goods declines exponentially with age. Under this condition decision rules for the optimal investment plan are *Markovian* in the sense that the current stock of capital contains all the information about past decisions that is relevant to the future. The optimal production and investment plan at any point of time depends on accumulated capital stock, but is otherwise independent of past production and investment decisions.

The acquisition of capital goods is unconstrained if no capital is required for the installation of investment goods, and the level of acquisition may be positive, negative, or zero. We first specialize the model outlined above by eliminating the installation function (3.2) as a constraint and setting the corresponding Lagrange multiplier μ_I, the shadow price of installation of investment goods, equal to zero. We retain the nonnegativity constraint on the level of acquisition; the resulting technology is recursive. If the level of acquisition is positive, the shadow asset price capital is equal to its market acquisition price (3.27),

$$\lambda_A = q_A .$$

The marginal productivity conditions (3.27) reduce to

$$q_Q \frac{\partial F}{\partial L} = q_L, \qquad q_Q \frac{\partial F}{\partial K} = q_K ,$$

where

$$q_K = q_A(r + \delta) - q'_A$$

is the market rental price of capital. The value of the marginal product of capital is equal to its market rental price, and the value of the marginal product of labor is equal to its market wage rate.

If the acquisition of investment goods is zero, the shadow asset price of capital is less than or equal to the market acquisition price (3.27),

$$\lambda_A \leqq q_A .$$

The marginal productivity condition for capital (3.27) becomes

$$q_Q \frac{\partial F}{\partial K} = \mu_K ,$$

where

$$\mu_K = \lambda_A(r + \delta) - \lambda'_A$$

is the shadow rental price of capital (3.26). The value of the marginal product of capital is equal to its shadow rental price; as before, the value of the marginal product of labor is equal to its market wage rate.

First, we conclude that at every point of time the necessary conditions for an optimal production plan of the atemporal theory of production are satisfied or the level of acquisition of investment goods is zero. If this level is zero, the marginal productivity condition for capital of atemporal theory is replaced by an analogous condition with the shadow rental price μ_K in place of the market rental price q_K. The resulting decision rules are recursive in the sense that the optimal plan depends on the level of capital and the value of the optimal shadow asset price of capital. This plan generates a new time path for capital and its shadow asset price and new decision rules of the same form. This model of investment policy has been analyzed in greater detail by Arrow.[35]

Second, we specialize the model outlined above by eliminating both the installation function and the nonnegativity constraint on the level of acquisition of investment goods (3.2). The resulting technology is decomposable in the sense that production possibilities at any point of time are independent of past productive activity, including accumulated stocks. The inequality constraint (3.27) relating the shadow asset price of capital to its market acquisition price becomes an equality,

$$\lambda_A = q_A,$$

so that the marginal productivity conditions reduce to the necessary conditions for an optimal production plan of the atemporal theory of production, as given above. The value of the marginal product of capital is equal to its market rental and the value of the marginal product of labor is equal to its market wage.

As before, the optimal production and investment plan at any point of time can be generated by maximizing the current present value of the productive unit at that point, subject to technology and the level of capital accumulated up to that point. Given the initial level of capital, this is equivalent to maximizing the current present value of goodwill at each point of time, subject to technology. For decomposable technologies there is no restriction on the acquisition of investment goods. The optimal production plan is independent of the past time path of capital accumulation. Production decisions at each point of time are independent of decisions at other points of time; investment decisions are related only through replacement requirements. The optimal production plan at any point of time can be generated by maximizing the current level of profit.

Profit depends on the price of output, the wage rate, and the rental price of capital services. The rental price of capital at each point of time depends on the current price and own rate of interest of investment goods if and only if the decline in relative efficiency of investment goods with age is exponential. In this case the decision rules that result from profit maximization are independent both of current capital stock and of all future prices and rates of interest. Current profit depends only on current prices of output, labor services, and investment goods, and the current own rate of interest on investment goods. Under these conditions decision rules associated with profit maximization are *myopic* in the sense of Strotz.[36] Myopic decision rules for durable goods with exponential decline in relative efficiency are derived from present value maximization by Haavelmo.[37]

Decision rules that result from maximizing current present value at each point of time are *decomposable* in the sense that they are independent of decision rules at other points of time. These are the usual decision rules of the atemporal theory of production. This model of investment policy has been analyzed in greater detail by Jorgenson.[38]

Decomposable decision rules associated with profit maximization at each point of time are derived from present value maximization by Malinvaud.[39] In earlier treatments of the durable goods model, for example by Walras,[40] the decomposable decision rule of marginal productivity theory had been employed without deriving it as an implication of present value maximization.

Notes

1. J. R. Hicks (1946); P. A. Samuelson (1947); and G. Debreu (1959).
2. I. Fisher (1961); E. Lindahl (1939); Hicks, *op. cit.*; Malinvaud (1953).
3. Lindahl, *op. cit.*; Malinvaud, *op. cit.*
4. K. Wicksell (1934a, esp. pp. 144–206); Lindahl, *op. cit.*; Malinvaud, *op. cit.*
5. Malinvaud, *op. cit.*
6. L. Walras (1954); G. Åkerman (1923); K. Wicksell (1934b).
7. E. R. Böhm von Bawerk (1891); and Wicksell (1934a, esp. pp. 144–206).
8. Malinvaud, *op. cit.*, p. 253.
9. See K. J. Arrow (1968, pp. 1–20, and the references given there).
10. R. Lucas (1967a); H. Uzawa (1969).
11. A. P. Lerner (1944).
12. R. Eisner and R. H. Strotz (1962, Section I, *The Theoretical Framework*, pp. 61–116).
13. L. S. Pontryagin, V. G. Boltyanskii, R. V. Gamkrelidze, and E. F. Mishchenko (1962).
14. Lucas, *op. cit.*; Uzawa, *op. cit.*; J. P. Gould (1968); and A. B. Treadway (1969a).
15. A. B. Treadway (1969b).
16. Treadway, *op. cit.*, employs the rate of change of capital; Lucas, *op. cit.*, and Gould, *op. cit.*, employ the rate of investment.
17. Fisher, *op. cit.*, p. 148.
18. T. C. Koopmans (1957, esp. pp. 16–21).
19. J. Hirshleifer (1958); M. J. Bailey (1959); and J. Hirshleifer (1970).
20. In a survey paper on the theory of capital Lutz remarks: "It is one of the surprising things about capital theory that no agreement seems to have been reached as to what the entrepreneur should maximize." F. A. Lutz (1961, p. 6).
21. J. Hirshleifer, *op. cit.*, p. 228.
22. Fisher, *op. cit.*, pp. 302–310.
23. Hicks, *op. cit.*, pp. 124–126, 202–226.
24. Malinvaud, *op. cit.*, pp. 242–251.
25. R. H. Strotz (1956).
26. Malinvaud, *op. cit.*, p. 253.
27. See note 4.
28. The terms "instruments" and "targets" are employed by J. Tinbergen (1956, pp. 3–10).
29. Our application of Pontryagin's maximum principle follows the exposition of K. J. Arrow and M. Kurz (1970, pp. 33–51).
30. H. W. Kuhn and A. W. Tucker (1950).
31. This form of the constraint qualification is employed by S. Karlin (1959, p. 201).
32. *Ibid.*, pp. 203–204.
33. Arrow and Kurz, *op.cit.*, pp. 43–51.
34. *Ibid.*, p. 49.
35. See note 9.

36. Strotz, *op. cit.*
37. T. Haavelmo, (1960a and b, esp. p. 163).
38. D. W. Jorgenson (1967).
39. Malinvaud, *op. cit.*, p. 253.
40. Walras, *op. cit.*, pp. 382–386.

4   The Economic Impact of Investment Incentives

Dale W. Jorgenson

4.1   Introduction

The purpose of this study is to assess the economic impact of changes in the taxation of business income for the purpose of stimulating investment expenditures. On January 11, 1971, President Richard M. Nixon announced a new system of regulations for calculating depreciation allowances for tax purposes, the Asset Depreciation Range System. The objectives of the ADR System, as stated by President Nixon, are: (1) to reduce unemployment, (2) to promote economic growth, (3) to strengthen the balance of payments, (4) to simplify depreciation provisions of the Internal Revenue Code. Walter Heller and Arthur Okun, former chairmen of the Council of Economic Advisers, have proposed re-institution of the investment tax credit in order to stimulate investment expenditures.

In this study we consider the economic impact of the ADR System and a comparable tax credit on unemployment, economic growth, and the balance of payments. In addition, we consider the impact on the level and composition of investment expenditures, including business investment and private housing. Finally, we consider the impact on inflation, credit conditions, and Federal government revenue. Given the basic objective of stimulating the economy the alternatives for fiscal policy are to increase government expenditure or to reduce taxes. Tax cuts may be aimed at stimulation of consumption or investment; among tax measures that stimulate investment, re-enactment of the investment tax credit and adoption of the ADR System are alternative policy measures. In these comments we focus on the economic impact of tax measures that stimulate investment. The consideration of tax measures to stimulate consumption or possible increases in expenditure is outside the scope of the impact study reported below.

We begin with a brief history of tax incentives for business investment in the United States during the postwar period. The principal
incentives are the adoption of accelerated depreciation in the Internal
Revenue Code of 1954, the reduction in initial asset lifetimes for calculating depreciation allowances over the period from 1954 to 1962, and
the adoption of the investment tax credit in 1962. The ADR System
represents a further reduction in lifetimes allowable for tax purposes
and additional acceleration by a "modified half-year" convention to
be described in detail below.

The economic impact of investment incentives adopted in the
United States during the postwar period has been analyzed exhaus-
tively by econometric methods.[1] The general conclusion of these
studies is that incentives have a considerable impact on the level of
investment, but that the investment process is governed by a substantial lag. The direct impact of a change in incentives requires between
one and two years to take effect. The "multiplier" effect of expenditures induced by a change in incentives requires even longer. In view
of these lags investment incentives are not a useful tool for short-run
economic stabilization.

Investment incentives do have a considerable long-run impact on
the rate of capital accumulation. It is notable that each of the major
changes in investment incentives in the postwar period—accelerated
depreciation in 1954 and shorter asset lifetimes and the investment tax
credit of 1962—was followed by an investment boom. The pattern of
these major investment booms is an increase in investment followed
by high levels of economic activity that induce further increase in
investment. The lag between the change in tax policy and the full
impact on investment expenditures is considerable.

Our conclusion is that the economic impact of the ADR System will
be to provide substantial stimulation for the level of investment and
the general level of economic activity. Relatively little of this impact
will be felt during the first year of the new system, 1971; the maximum impact on investment, gross national product, and unemployment will occur in 1974. The total impact will be similar to the
response of the economy to adoption of fiscal measures to stimulate
investment in 1954 and 1962 but somewhat smaller in magnitude.

4.2   Postwar Investment Incentives in the United States

Tax policies for stimulating investment expenditures by providing
incentives through tax credits and accelerated depreciation are a

permanent part of the fiscal policies of the United States and many other countries.[2] Major changes in investment incentives in the United States were made in 1954 with the adoption of accelerated depreciation, in 1962 with shortening of asset lifetimes for calculating depreciation allowances and adoption of the investment tax credit, and in 1969 with the repeal of the investment tax credit. All of these changes in investment incentives have had substantial economic impact.

Prior to the Internal Revenue Code of 1954 essentially only one depreciation formula was permitted for tax purposes, the straight-line formula. Under this formula depreciation allowances over the lifetime of an asset for tax purposes are constant at an annual rate equal to unity divided by the lifetime of the asset. Beginning in 1954 three depreciation formulas were allowed for tax purposes—straight-line, sum of the years' digits, and double declining balance. Both sum of the years' digits and double declining balance formulas begin with depreciation allowances substantially greater than the straight-line rate for the first year with the level declining over the life of the asset. These depreciation formulas are referred to as "accelerated" formulas since the depreciation allowances are accelerated in time.

The critical parameter in determining depreciation allowances for tax purposes is the period over which the asset is depreciated. In both straight-line formula and accelerated formulas, the initial depreciation allowance is inversely proportional to the period. From this it follows that a reduction in asset lifetime represents an acceleration of depreciation allowances and provides an added incentive to investment. Before 1954 asset lifetimes allowable for tax purposes were based essentially on *Bulletin F* of the Bureau of Internal Revenue, first issued before World War II. Beginning in 1954 lifetimes were gradually reduced by negotiations with individual taxpayers. An attempt was made to standardize lifetimes for equipment in the Depreciation Guidelines of 1962; these Guidelines represented a reduction of almost fifty percent in *Bulletin F* lifetimes.

In 1962, a new tax incentive for investment was introduced in the form of an investment tax credit for equipment. From an economic point of view the investment tax credit is a subsidy to the purchase of equipment. Instead of paying the subsidy directly to the purchaser, the Internal Revenue Service permitted the purchaser of equipment to reduce his tax payments by an amount proportional to the value of equipment purchases. At the initiation of the investment tax credit in 1962, the credit claimed by the taxpayer was deducted from the value of the asset used as a base for calculation of depreciation allowances.

In 1964, this provision of the tax credit, the Long Amendment to the original legislation, was repealed resulting in a further increase in investment incentives. In 1964, a general cut in personal and corporate income tax rates was introduced that reduced the corporate tax rate from fifty-two to forty-eight percent over a two-year period. In the ensuing rise in the general level of economic activity, investment incentives were dampened through temporary suspension of the investment tax credit from October 1966 to March 1967. In 1969, the investment tax credit was repealed. Both the initial suspension of the credit and its final repeal had the effect of reducing the level of investment activity from what it would otherwise have been.

4.3   The Economic Analysis of Investment Incentives

The range of possible fiscal policy measures for the control of investment activity is very considerable. To analyze and compare the impact of these alternative measures economists have developed the concept of a rental price of capital services.[3] In this approach to the analysis of investment incentives businesses are divided into two activities—an activity that rents capital, hires labor, buys materials, and sells output and an activity that buys capital goods and rents capital services. Although rented capital is an important part of many businesses, the separation of the activity of owning assets and the activity of renting them for productive purposes amount to putting all capital services onto a rental basis. This fiction has often been useful for analytical purposes, as in the conversion of home ownership to a rental basis for measuring housing services. This conversion is used in estimating U.S. gross national product.

Conversion of capital services to a rental basis requires representation of a complex tax and financial structure in a highly simplified manner. This representation is, nonetheless, capable of reducing the vast range of investment incentives, both those that have been adopted and those that are contemplated, to a common unit of account. This unit is the rental price for an asset associated with a given or proposed tax structure. Rental prices are like space rentals or equipment rentals and represent the cost of using an asset for a stipulated period of time.

An expression for the rental price, say c, useful in analyzing the impact of investment incentives in the following:

$$c = \frac{1 - k - uz}{1 - u} \, q \, (r + \delta).$$

In this formula u is the corporate tax rate, currently forty-eight percent. The parameter z is the present value of depreciation allowances, the value today of the stream of depreciation allowances resulting from the acquisition of one dollar's worth of an asset. Of course the value of depreciation allowances over the lifetime of an asset is one dollar. But the value today can be calculated by discounting future depreciation allowances back to the present. The present value of z is higher for accelerated depreciation formulas than for straight line. It is also higher for short asset lifetimes than for long lifetimes. Finally, the parameter k is the investment tax credit. Between 1962 and 1969 the tax credit was set at three percent for most utilities and seven percent for other businesses; with suspension during 1967–1968 and final repeal in 1969 the tax credit dropped to zero.

The remaining elements in the formula for the rental price of capital reflect economic forces outside the tax system. The variable q is the price of an investment good. As inflation proceeds this price rises. The variable r is the real rate of return after taxes. Finally, the parameter δ is the economic rate of depreciation, which may differ from the rate of depreciation for tax purposes.

In analyzing the impact of a change in tax incentives our method is, first, to translate the change in tax incentives into a change in the rental price. Adoption of accelerated depreciation formulas in 1954 resulted in an increase in the present value of depreciation allowances. For producer' durables the adoption of accelerated depreciation formulas raised the present value of depreciation allowances from 39.7 cents on a dollar of investment to 54.3 cents on a dollar, a very substantial change. This change had the effect of reducing the effective rental price of capital and providing an incentive to investment.

All of the changes in investment incentives we have discussed can be translated into a change in the rental price of capital services. Changes in depreciation formulas, asset lifetimes for tax purposes, and modifications in depreciation allowable during the year the asset is acquired can be translated into a change in the present value of depreciation allowances z. Changes in z in the investment tax credit k or the income tax rate u can be incorporated into the rental price of capital services c. The impact of the change in tax incentives can then be analyzed by tracing out the impact of the change in the rental price of capital services on the level of investment expenditures.

Our method can be applied directly to contemplated change in investment incentives such as the ADR System and the "modified half-year convention." Both of these changes in tax policy can be translated into a change in the present value of depreciation allowances. These changes result in further acceleration of depreciation allowances and a further increase in the present value of depreciation allowances claimed for tax purposes. An increase in present value of depreciation allowances results in a reduction in the rental price of capital and an addition to investment incentives.

The first step in tracing out the impact of a prospective change in investment incentives is to establish a benchmark representing the development of the economy in the absence of the policy change. In the impact study to be described below we take a five-year projection of the United States economy for the period 1971–1975 prepared by Data Resources, Inc., on the basis of the DRI econometric model. This projection includes the intermediate-range outlook for the overall level of economic activity and the level of employment along with the projected development of consumption and investment expenditures, prices, government activity, the balance of payments, and credit conditions.

The second step in our analysis is to develop an alternative five-year projection of the development of the economy assuming that a change in tax policy takes place and that other economic policies are adjusted so as to maintain the same general level of economic activity, but to provide for an increased level of business investment. Obviously, this implies a reduction in government and foreign purchases of goods and services, consumer expenditures, and other components of investment. We refer to the resulting change in investment as the direct impact of the change in investment incentives.

The third step in our analysis is to allow the change in investment expenditures to feed back through the economic system allowing the general level of economic activity to vary with the change in investment. The total impact of a change in investment incentives includes both the direct effect on business investment and induced effects on other expenditures, including further changes in the level of investment expenditures induced by changes in the general level of activity. These effects include changes in the level of unemployment, the level of consumption, the development of prices, the level of government receipts and the government deficit, the balance of payments, and credit conditions.

Assessment of the total impact of tax policy involves the interaction of business, government, and household receipts and expenditures. The full effects of this interaction require a considerable period of time to be worked out. To assess the full impact a detailed econometric model like the DRI system is indispensable. As a point of reference for measuring the impact in quantitative terms a projection of economic activity for at least five years is required.

4.4 Current Policy Alternatives

The Asset Depreciation Range System provides additional options for business in depreciating equipment for tax purposes. The essential changes are:

1) Guideline lifetimes for equipment are reduced by as much as twenty percent.

2) The reserve ratio test is abolished. Under this administrative provision of the Internal Revenue Service, lifetimes employed for tax purposes are tied to actual retirement experience. Lifetimes for equipment acceptable to the IRS are both longer and shorter than the depreciation Guidelines adopted in 1962. Shorter lifetimes must be justified by a reserve ratio test. Abolition of the reserve ratio test makes the likely impact of the new Guidelines equal to a twenty percent reduction in lifetimes relative to existing depreciation practices.

3) Depreciation allowances are governed by a "modified half-year convention." Under the current convention, assets acquired during any tax year receive approximately half the first year's depreciation allowance in the year of acquisition. Under the modified convention, assets receive approximately three-quarters of the first year's depreciation allowance.

In addition to these three changes, there are other provisions of the new regulations such as those relating to the treatment of repairs and retirements for tax purposes. In our impact study, we neglect these provisions of the proposed regulations in order to focus attention on how the reduction in Guideline lifetimes and the modified half-year convention act as incentives to undertake investment. To apply our method of analysis to these changes in incentives, we first compute the impact of each change on the present value of depreciation allowances. In 1970, the present value of depreciation allowances was 69.8 cents for a dollar of investment in producers' durable equipment. The modified half-year convention increases this present value to 71.5

cents per dollar. The twenty percent reduction in Guideline lifetimes increases the present value to 74.4 cents per dollar. Both changes together increase the present value to 76.2 cents per dollar of investment. The President's Task Force on Business Taxation has proposed a forty percent reduction in Guideline lifetimes for equipment.[4] This would result in a present value of depreciation allowances of 81.4 cents per dollar of investment.

For the purpose of stimulating investment in producers' durable equipment, an alternative policy change is re-enactment of the investment tax credit. To analyze the impact of an investment tax credit, we employ the same method of analysis as for accelerated depreciation allowances. An incentive to investment equivalent to the ADR System, including both reduction of lifetimes by twenty percent and a modified half-year convention, would be provided by an effective investment tax credit of .032. With a statutory tax credit of .7, the effective rate was .067 in 1969, the last year of the investment tax credit. Re-enactment of an investment tax credit at a statutory rate of .033 would be equivalent in incentive effect to adoption of the ADR System.

To assess the economic impact of the ADR System we consider the effects of the changes in tax policy on the rental price of capital. We then assess the direct impact of the change in rental price on the level of investment expenditures. Since this impact requires considerable time we trace out the direct impact of the change in tax policy over a five-year period beginning with 1971. We assume that the ADR System is adopted for all assets acquired on or after January 1, 1971. Finally, we assess the total impact of the ADR System by permitting the change in investment expenditures to feed back through the economic system. We then estimate the total impact of the change in tax policy on business investment, housing, prices, international trade, government revenue and the government deficit, credit conditions, and the overall level of economic activity and employment.

As a complement to our assessment of the impact of the ADR System we consider some alternative policies for increasing incentives to invest. Either of the two main provisions of the ADR System—twenty percent reduction in asset lifetimes and modified half-year convention—could be adopted separately. We analyze the direct impact of each of the two provisions by itself and compare the results with the impact of the two provisions together. Second, it would be possible to adopt shorter Guideline lifetimes for tax purposes, as recommended by the President's Task Force on Business Taxation. We consider the impact of a modified ADR System with lifetimes forty percent rather than twenty percent less for producers' durable equipment. Finally, an alternative policy for stimulating investment is to re-enact the investment tax credit. We consider the impact of investment tax credits of statutory rates of 0.033 and .07. The second measure represents a considerably greater investment incentive than the ADR System; the first is equivalent in incentive effect to the ADR System.

The main alternatives for economic policy to be compared are then:

1) the ADR System;
2) twenty percent reduction in Guideline lifetimes alone;
3) modified half-year provision alone;
4) modified ADR System with forty percent reduction in Guideline lifetimes;
5) investment tax credit, statutory rate of .033;
6) investment tax credit, statutory rate of .07.

We assess the direct impact of each of these six alternative policy measures.

It is possible to consider the total impact of any of the six policy measures listed above. The most important of these measures is the ADR System itself. As a basis for comparison, we also tabulate the total impact of investment credit with a statutory rate of .033, which has an equivalent incentive effect.

The first step in our analysis is to translate a given change in investment incentives into a corresponding change in the rental price of capital. The results are tabulated in table 4.1.

Table 4.1
Rental price of capital services 1971, first quarter

1. No change in investment incentives	.377
2. The ADR system	.359
3. Twenty percent reduction in lifetimes	.364
4. Modified half-year convention	.372
5. Modified ADR system	.345
6. Investment tax credit .033	.359
7. Investment tax credit .07	.339

4.5   Direct Impact

As a benchmark for the development of the U.S. economy in the absence of changes in investment incentives, we employ a five-year projection for the period 1971, first quarter, through 1975, fourth quarter. The projected development of the overall level of economic activity and the level of employment together with consumption and investment expenditures, prices, government activity, the balance of payments, and credit conditions are given in table 4.2. In this projection, expenditures on producers' durable equipment fall in proportion to output over the first two years of the period. During the remaining three years, producers' durables rise in proportion to output eventuating in a rise of investment relative to output over the five-year period.

In real terms, gross national product rises from a level of 721.3 billions of 1958 dollars in the fourth quarter of 1970 to 926.6 in the fourth quarter of 1975. The level of unemployment is projected to decline from 5.8 percent in the fourth quarter of 1970 to 4.4 percent in the fourth quarter of 1975. In making these projections of the overall level of economic activity and the rate of investment expenditures tax policy is assumed to remain as it was at the end of 1970, before the ADR System was announced. The projections serve as a starting point for assessing the impact of the ADR System and alternative policy measures for stimulating investment.

Given the benchmark provided by the DRI five-year projection of the U.S. economy, the next step in assessment of the impact of the ADR System is to assess the direct impact of the System on producers' durable equipment expenditures. We first trace out the effect of the ADR regulations on the rental price of equipment services. The results are given for the ADR System and for alternative policy measures in table 4.1 above. Next, we project the direct impact of the change in the rental price on the level of investment expenditures. For this purpose, we employ an investment equation fitted to the historical record for 1956 to 1970; this equation is described in detail in the Technical Appendix to these comments. The period for which we have fitted the equation includes the period of major impact of earlier changes in investment incentives. The proportion of variance in producers' durable equipment expenditures explained during the historical period, measured by R^2, is .9875. The average lag between changes in investment incentives and changes in the level of expenditures is 6.4 quarters.

Table 4.2
DRI central projection: 1971, first quarter to 1975, fourth quarter

71:1	71:2	71:3	71:4	72:1	72:2	72:3	72:4	73:1	73:2
73:3	73:4	74:1	74:2	74:3	74:4	75:1	75:2	75:3	75:4

Investment

Investment in private nonresidential structures, current $:

| 35.5 | 36.0 | 36.5 | 36.8 | 37.4 | 38.3 | 39.4 | 40.5 | 41.6 | 42.9 |
| 44.2 | 45.6 | 46.9 | 48.5 | 50.2 | 51.8 | 53.5 | 55.5 | 57.4 | 59.3 |

Investment in private, nonresidential structures, constant 58$:

| 22.2 | 22.2 | 22.2 | 22.1 | 22.2 | 22.4 | 22.7 | 23.0 | 23.3 | 23.8 |
| 24.2 | 24.6 | 25.0 | 25.5 | 26.0 | 26.4 | 26.9 | 27.5 | 28.0 | 28.6 |

Fixed private, nonresidential investment, current $:

| 102.9 | 103.1 | 104.2 | 104.8 | 123.8 | 107.7 | 110.6 | 113.9 | 117.2 | 120.5 |
| 127.0 | 130.2 | 133.5 | 137.3 | 141.3 | 145.2 | 149.2 | 153.5 | 157.6 | 161.8 |

Fixed private, nonresidential investment, constant 58$:

| 77.0 | 76.1 | 76.0 | 75.6 | 76.9 | 78.1 | 79.6 | 81.0 | 82.5 | 84.0 |
| 85.4 | 86.8 | 88.3 | 90.2 | 92.1 | 93.9 | 95.8 | 97.8 | 99.7 | 101.5 |

Investment in producers' durable equipment, current $:

| 67.4 | 67.0 | 67.7 | 68.0 | 70.2 | 72.3 | 74.6 | 76.7 | 78.9 | 80.9 |
| 82.8 | 84.6 | 86.6 | 88.8 | 91.1 | 93.4 | 95.7 | 98.0 | 100.2 | 102.5 |

Investment in producers' durable equipment, constant 58$:

| 54.7 | 53.9 | 53.8 | 53.5 | 54.7 | 55.7 | 56.9 | 58.0 | 59.2 | 60.3 |
| 61.3 | 62.3 | 63.4 | 64.7 | 66.1 | 67.5 | 68.8 | 70.3 | 71.6 | 73.0 |

Housing

Investment in residential structures, current $:

| 34.3 | 35.3 | 36.4 | 37.2 | 38.6 | 40.2 | 41.6 | 42.6 | 43.3 | 44.1 |
| 44.9 | 45.5 | 46.8 | 48.2 | 49.4 | 49.7 | 50.3 | 51.3 | 52.0 | 52.1 |

Investment in residential structures, constant 58$:

| 23.4 | 23.9 | 24.4 | 25.0 | 25.9 | ?6.8 | 27.4 | 28.0 | 28.4 | 28.7 |
| 28.8 | 29.2 | 29.9 | 30.5 | 30.8 | 30.9 | 31.2 | 31.4 | 31.4 | 31.4 |

Housing starts, private—total:

| 1.621 | 1.662 | 1.716 | 1.763 | 1.824 | 1.852 | 1.888 | 1.924 | 1.947 | 1.966 |
| 1.969 | 2.043 | 2.097 | 2.126 | 2.146 | 2.147 | 2.188 | 2.185 | 2.183 | 2.184 |

Prices

Consumer price index

| 1.384 | 1.396 | 1.410 | 1.420 | 1.427 | 1.440 | 1.455 | 1.465 | 1.473 | 1.486 |
| 1.500 | 1.511 | 1.519 | 1.533 | 1.547 | 1.559 | 1.568 | 1.582 | 1.598 | 1.609 |

Implicit price deflators for GNP

| 1.385 | 1.393 | 1.407 | 1.417 | 1.430 | 1.440 | 1.451 | 1.463 | 1.474 | 1.486 |
| 1.498 | 1.510 | 1.522 | 1.533 | 1.545 | 1.557 | 1.570 | 1.582 | 1.595 | 1.607 |

Implicit price deflators for private nonresidential structures

| 1.597 | 1.623 | 1.645 | 1.667 | 1.689 | 1.713 | 1.737 | 1.760 | 1.783 | 1.807 |
| 1.830 | 1.855 | 1.880 | 1.906 | 1.933 | 1.960 | 1.989 | 2.018 | 2.047 | 2.077 |

Implicit price deflators for fixed private non residential structures

| 1.337 | 1.355 | 1.371 | 1.387 | 1.401 | 1.417 | 1.432 | 1.447 | 1.460 | 1.474 |
| 1.487 | 1.499 | 1.511 | 1.523 | 1.535 | 1.546 | 1.558 | 1.570 | 1.582 | 1.593 |

Implicit price deflators for producers' durable equipment

| 1.231 | 1.245 | 1.258 | 1.271 | 1.284 | 1.298 | 1.311 | 1.323 | 1.333 | 1.343 |
| 1.351 | 1.359 | 1.366 | 1.372 | 1.378 | 1.384 | 1.389 | 1.395 | 1.399 | 1.404 |

Implicit price deflators for residential structures

| 1.464 | 1.479 | 1.491 | 1.487 | 1.488 | 1.503 | 1.520 | 1.520 | 1.524 | 1.540 |
| 1.557 | 1.558 | 1.565 | 1.583 | 1.604 | 1.607 | 1.615 | 1.635 | 1.656 | 1.659 |

Table 4.2
(continued)

| 71:1 | 71:2 | 71:3 | 71:4 | 72:1 | 72:2 | 72:3 | 72:4 | 73:1 | 73:2 |
| 73:3 | 73:4 | 74:1 | 74:2 | 74:3 | 74:4 | 75:1 | 75:2 | 75:3 | 75:4 |

Interest rates

Money rate, commercial paper, 4–6 months

| 6.11 | 6.05 | 6.17 | 6.28 | 6.32 | 6.38 | 6.54 | 6.56 | 6.74 | 6.84 |
| 6.77 | 6.68 | 6.58 | 6.56 | 6.62 | 6.64 | 6.63 | 6.59 | 6.56 | 6.54 |

Yield on U.S. government bonds, long term (10 years or more):

| 5.94 | 5.88 | 5.83 | 5.78 | 5.76 | 5.76 | 5.72 | 5.72 | 5.68 | 5.62 |
| 5.54 | 5.51 | 5.49 | 5.48 | 5.48 | 5.44 | 5.41 | 5.37 | 5.35 | 5.31 |

Yield on U.S. government bonds, short term (3 months):

| 5.03 | 5.13 | 5.26 | 5.34 | 5.36 | 5.42 | 5.61 | 5.54 | 5.82 | 5.80 |
| 5.70 | 5.61 | 5.52 | 5.54 | 5.62 | 5.60 | 5.60 | 5.54 | 5.53 | 5.52 |

Yield on Moody's AAA corporate bonds, seasoned

| 7.37 | 7.30 | 7.31 | 7.31 | 7.11 | 7.12 | 7.11 | 7.11 | 6.91 | 6.88 |
| 6.83 | 6.80 | 6.60 | 6.60 | 6.61 | 6.59 | 6.36 | 6.34 | 6.31 | 6.29 |

Yield on Moody's AAA corporate bonds, new issue:

| 7.74 | 7.66 | 7.60 | 7.54 | 7.49 | 7.41 | 7.36 | 7.32 | 7.31 | 7.23 |
| 7.16 | 7.09 | 7.06 | 7.04 | 7.03 | 6.95 | 6.88 | 6.81 | 6.75 | 6.68 |

Employment and GNP

Rate of unemployment—all civilian workers

| 5.9 | 5.7 | 5.6 | 5.7 | 5.6 | 5.3 | 5.1 | 5.1 | 5.0 | 4.9 |
| 4.8 | 4.8 | 4.8 | 4.6 | 4.5 | 4.5 | 4.5 | 4.5 | 4.4 | 4.4 |

GNP, current $

| 1018.3 | 1041.0 | 1054.4 | 1074.0 | 1105.8 | 1133.0 | 1157.2 | 1179.9 | 1204.5 | 1229.2 |
| 1253.0 | 1276.3 | 1304.1 | 1333.1 | 1359.5 | 1383.6 | 1409 | 1436.9 | 1463.1 | 1489.4 |

GNP, constant 58$

| 735.4 | 747.3 | 749.1 | 757.8 | 773.5 | 787.0 | 797.3 | 806.5 | 816.9 | 827.1 |
| 836.3 | 845.2 | 857.1 | 869.6 | 880.0 | 880.5 | 898.3 | 908.0 | 917.1 | 926.6 |

Government

Federal government receipts

| 204.7 | 210.4 | 212.2 | 216.8 | 221.1 | 228.0 | 233.7 | 238.8 | 243.3 | 249.1 |
| 254.5 | 259.8 | 256.8 | 264.0 | 270.2 | 275.6 | 281.1 | 287.4 | 293.5 | 299.5 |

Government deficit, Federal

| −12.7 | −7.7 | −11.7 | −9.6 | −15.9 | −10.8 | −7.4 | −4.8 | −8.2 | −6.2 |
| −4.3 | −2.7 | −11.4 | −8.2 | −5.9 | −2.8 | −4.5 | −1.7 | 0.3 | 2.4 |

Government deficit, state and local

| −1.0 | −2.0 | −0.2 | −0.7 | −0.1 | −0.1 | −0.1 | 0.0 | 0.5 | 0.7 |
| 0.5 | 0.6 | 0.6 | 1.0 | 1.2 | 0.7 | 1.0 | 0.6 | 0.9 | 1.2 |

International

Imports, current $

| 60.2 | 61.0 | 61.6 | 62.5 | 63.8 | 65.1 | 66.5 | 67.9 | 69.4 | 71.0 |
| 72.6 | 74.2 | 76.0 | 77.9 | 79.8 | 81.7 | 83.7 | 85.7 | 87.8 | 89.9 |

Imports, constant 58$

| 49.9 | 50.0 | 49.9 | 50.0 | 51.8 | 52.7 | 53.6 | 54.5 | 55.5 | 56.6 |
| 57.6 | 58.6 | 59.8 | 61.1 | 62.3 | 63.6 | 64.9 | 66.2 | 67.5 | 68.9 |

Exports, current $
same
same

Exports, constant 58$
same
same

In our investment equation, the level of investment in producers' durable equipment depends on the rental price of capital services, the price of output, and the level of output. We have described the rental price. We measure output as real gross national product in 1958 prices and its price as the implicit deflator for gross national product. To project the direct impact of the ADR regulations, we assume that gross national product and its implicit deflator develop as in the DRI five-year projection for 1971, first quarter, to 1975, fourth quarter. We alter the rental price of capital to reflect the change in investment incentives resulting from the ADR regulations. Our projections of the direct impact of alternative policy changes are carried out by the same method. The results for the ADR System and the five alternative policy measures we consider are given in table 4.3.

Table 4.3
Direct impact of changes in investment incentives on producers' durable equipment expenditures (billions of dollars, annual rates)

| 71:1 | 71:2 | 71:3 | 71:4 | 72:1 | 72:2 | 72:3 | 72:4 | 73:1 | 73:2 |
73:3	73:4	74:1	74:2	74:3	74:4	75:1	75:2	75:3	75:4

1. The ADR System

Current $

| 0.000 | 0.000 | 0.2707 | 0.7363 | 1.332 | 2.002 | 2.696 | 3.366 | 3.976 | 4.500 |
| 4.924 | 5.241 | 5.459 | 5.601 | 5.698 | 5.797 | 5.898 | 6.001 | 6.107 | 6.218 |

2. Twenty percent reduction in lifetimes

Current $

| 0.000 | 0.000 | 0.1920 | 0.5221 | 0.9445 | 1.420 | 1.912 | 2.387 | 2.819 | 3.191 |
| 3.491 | 3.716 | 3.871 | 3.972 | 4.040 | 4.110 | 4.182 | 4.255 | 4.330 | 4.407 |

Constant 58$

| 0.000 | 0.000 | 0.1526 | 0.4108 | 0.7355 | 1.094 | 1.458 | 1.805 | 2.115 | 2.377 |
| 2.584 | 2.735 | 2.835 | 2.894 | 2.931 | 2.970 | 3.010 | 3.051 | 3.094 | 3.139 |

3. Modified half-year convention

Current $

| 0.000 | 0.000 | 0.0694 | 0.1889 | 0.3417 | 0.5135 | 0.6915 | 0.8635 | 1.020 | 1.154 |
| 1.263 | 1.344 | 1.400 | 1.437 | 1.461 | 1.487 | 1.513 | 1.539 | 1.566 | 1.594 |

Constant 58$

| 0.000 | 0.000 | 0.0552 | 0.1486 | 0.2661 | 0.3957 | 0.5275 | 0.6528 | 0.7651 | 0.8598 |
| 0.9346 | 0.9893 | 1.025 | 1.047 | 1.060 | 1.074 | 1.089 | 1.104 | 1.119 | 1.135 |

4. Modified ADR system

Current $

| 0.000 | 0.000 | 0.5108 | 1.389 | 2.513 | 3.777 | 5.087 | 6.352 | 7.502 | 8.491 |
| 9.289 | 9.888 | 10.30 | 10.57 | 10.75 | 10.94 | 11.13 | 11.32 | 11.52 | 11.73 |

Constant 58$

| 0.000 | 0.000 | 0.4060 | 1.093 | 1.957 | 2.911 | 3.880 | 4.802 | 5.628 | 6.324 |
| 6.875 | 7.277 | 7.542 | 7.701 | 7.799 | 7.902 | 8.008 | 8.119 | 8.233 | 8.352 |

Table 4.3
(continued)

| 71:1 | 71:2 | 71:3 | 71:4 | 72:1 | 72:2 | 72:3 | 72:4 | 73:1 | 73:2 |
| 73:3 | 73:4 | 74:1 | 74:2 | 74:3 | 74:4 | 75:1 | 75:2 | 75:3 | 75:4 |

5. Investment tax credit .033

Current $

| 0.000 | 0.000 | 0.2707 | 0.7363 | 1.332 | 2.002 | 2.696 | 3.366 | 3.976 | 4.500 |
| 4.924 | 5.241 | 5.459 | 5.601 | 5.698 | 5.797 | 5.898 | 6.001 | 6.107 | 6.215 |

Constant 58$

| 0.000 | 0.000 | 0.2152 | 0.5793 | 1.037 | 1.543 | 2.057 | 2.545 | 2.983 | 3.352 |
| 3.644 | 3.857 | 3.997 | 4.082 | 4.133 | 4.188 | 4.244 | 4.303 | 4.364 | 4.427 |

6. Investment tax credit .07

Current $

| 0.000 | 0.000 | 0.6263 | 1.703 | 3.081 | 4.631 | 6.236 | 7.788 | 9.198 | 10.41 |
| 11.39 | 12.12 | 12.63 | 12.96 | 13.18 | 13.41 | 13.64 | 13.88 | 14.13 | 14.38 |

Constant 58$

| 0.000 | 0.000 | 0.4978 | 1.340 | 2.399 | 3.569 | 4.758 | 5.888 | 6.900 | 7.754 |
| 8.429 | 8.922 | 9.247 | 9.442 | 9.562 | 9.688 | 9.819 | 9.954 | 10.09 | 10.24 |

For our model of investment, no changes in producers' durables spending occur until the third quarter of 1971 for tax incentives that take effect on January 1, 1971. The direct impact of alternative policy measures is roughly proportional to the change in investment incentives. The ADR System is equivalent to a statutory investment tax credit of .033 in its direct impact. Adoption of either of the features of the ADR System—shorter lifetimes or the modified half-year convention—in the absence of the other feature would represent reduction in investment incentives. If lifetimes were reduced by forty percent rather than twenty percent, as in the modified ADR System we consider, the impact on investment is more substantial than the impact of the ADR System itself. Finally, a statutory investment tax credit of .07, the level that prevailed for the period 1962–1969, would constitute roughly double the investment incentive represented by the ADR System.

4.6   Total Impact

The final step in our assessment of the impact of the ADR System is to allow the projected direct impact on investment expenditures to feed back through the economic system, allowing the general level of economic activity to vary with the change in investment. Although this analysis could be carried out for all six of the alternative changes in tax incentives we consider, our study is limited to an assessment of the total impact of the ADR System and a statutory investment tax credit of .033, which provides a direct stimulus to investment expenditures comparable to that provided by the ADR System. For any of the alternative policies we have described above, a similar analysis of total impact could be made. Since these changes are either changes in depreciation rules or changes in the tax credit, the time pattern of the total impact will be similar to the total impacts we analyze here. Of course, the differences in total impact will be roughly proportional to the differences in direct impact.

The projected economic impact of the ADR System is given in table 4.4 for the period 1971, first quarter, to 1975, fourth quarter. The total impact of the ADR System is measured by the difference between expenditures on producers' durable equipment under the system and equipment in the absence of any change in depreciation rules. The total impact of the ADR system on equipment expenditures in constant prices of 1958 rises from zero in the first quarter of 1971 to a maximum of 5.3 billions in the last three quarters of 1974. The total impact on producers' durables in current prices rises from zero to a maximum of 7.7 billions in the last two quarters of 1974 and the first two quarters of 1975. These impacts are very substantial measured relative to the projected level of producers' durable equipment expenditures in the absence of the change. In current prices of 1975, the level of expenditures in the fourth quarter of 1975 is projected at 102.5 billions; in constant prices of 1958, this figure is 73.0 billions.

The total impact of the ADR System on the overall level of economic activity may be assessed by tracing out the effects on gross national product in current and constant prices. In constant prices of 1958, the projected impact rises from 0.1 billions in the first quarter of 1971 to a maximum of 8.9 billions in the last quarter of 1973 and the first quarter of 1974. In current prices, the impact rises to 20.7 billions in the fourth quarter of 1975. The total impact of the ADR System on the implicit deflator for gross national product rises from zero in the first two quarters of 1971 to .011 points on a base projection of 1.609 in the fourth quarter of 1975. This is less than one percent of the price level projected for 1975, fourth quarter, in the absence of a change in investment incentives.

The total impact of the ADR System on business investment, investment in residential housing, the overall level of economic activity and

Table 4.4
Total impact of the ADR proposal on the economy (net change from the DRI central projection)

71:1	71:2	71:3	71:4	72:1	72:2	72:3	72:4	73:1	73:2
73:3	73:4	74:1	74:2	74:3	74:4	75:1	75:2	75:3	75:4

Investment

Investment in private, nonresidential structures, current $

0.0	0.0	0.1	0.2	0.4	0.7	1.1	1.5	1.9	2.3
2.7	3.1	3.4	3.7	3.9	4.1	4.2	4.4	4.5	4.6

Investment in private, nonresidential structures, constant 58$

0.0	0.0	0.0	0.1	0.3	0.4	0.6	0.8	1.0	1.2
1.4	1.5	1.6	1.7	1.7	1.8	1.8	1.7	1.7	1.7

Fixed private, nonresidential investment, current $

0.0	0.1	0.5	1.2	2.2	3.4	4.6	5.9	7.2	8.3
9.3	10.1	10.8	11.2	11.5	11.8	12.0	12.1	12.1	12.2

Fixed private, nonresidential investment, constant 58$

0.0	0.1	0.4	0.9	1.6	2.4	3.2	4.1	4.9	5.5
6.1	6.5	6.8	6.9	7.0	7.0	7.0	6.9	6.8	6.7

Investment in producers' durable equipment, current $

0.0	0.1	0.4	1.0	1.8	2.6	3.5	4.4	5.3	6.0
6.6	7.1	7.4	7.6	7.7	7.7	7.7	7.7	7.7	7.6

Investment in producers' durable equipment, constant 58$

0.0	0.1	0.3	0.8	1.4	2.0	2.6	3.3	3.9	4.3
4.7	5.0	5.2	5.3	5.3	5.3	5.2	5.2	5.1	5.0

Housing

Investment in residential structures, current $

0.0	0.0	0.0	0.1	0.1	0.1	0.1	0.1	0.1	0.1
0.1	0.0	−0.1	−0.1	−0.2	−0.3	−0.4	−0.4	−0.4	−0.4

Investment in residential structures, constant 58$

0.0	0.0	0.0	0.0	0.0	0.0	0.0	0.0	0.0	0.0
−0.1	−0.2	−0.3	−0.3	−0.4	−0.5	−0.6	−0.6	−0.6	−0.6

Housing starts, private—total

0.001	0.002	0.003	0.004	0.004	0.004	0.003	0.001	−0.002	−0.007
−0.012	−0.019	−0.026	−0.034	−0.041	−0.047	−0.051	−0.053	−0.053	−0.049

Prices

Consumer price index

0.000	0.000	0.000	0.000	0.000	0.001	0.001	0.002	0.002	0.003
0.004	0.005	0.006	0.008	0.009	0.010	0.011	0.013	0.014	0.015

Implicit price deflators for GNP:

0.000	0.000	0.000	0.000	0.000	0.000	0.000	0.000	0.001	0.001
0.002	0.003	0.004	0.005	0.006	0.007	0.009	0.010	0.010	0.011

Implicit price deflators for private nonresidential structures

0.000	0.000	0.000	0.000	0.001	0.001	0.002	0.003	0.004	0.006
0.008	0.011	0.013	0.016	0.019	0.023	0.026	0.029	0.032	0.035

Table 4.4
(continued)

| 71:1 | 71:2 | 71:3 | 71:4 | 72:1 | 72:2 | 72:3 | 72:4 | 73:1 | 73:2 |
73:3	73:4	74:1	74:2	74:3	74:4	75:1	75:2	75:3	75:4

Implicit price deflators for fixed private nonresidential structures

| 0.000 | 0.000 | 0.000 | 0.000 | −0.001 | −0.001 | 0.000 | 0.000 | 0.001 | 0.002 |
| 0.003 | 0.004 | 0.005 | 0.007 | 0.008 | 0.009 | 0.011 | 0.012 | 0.013 | 0.014 |

Implicit price deflators for producers' durable equipment

| 0.000 | 0.000 | 0.000 | 0.000 | 0.000 | 0.001 | 0.001 | 0.002 | 0.002 | 0.003 |
| 0.003 | 0.004 | 0.004 | 0.005 | 0.006 | 0.006 | 0.006 | 0.007 | 0.007 | 0.007 |

Implicit price deflators for residential structures

| 0.000 | 0.000 | 0.000 | 0.000 | 0.001 | 0.002 | 0.002 | 0.003 | 0.005 | 0.006 |
| 0.008 | 0.010 | 0.011 | 0.013 | 0.015 | 0.016 | 0.018 | 0.019 | 0.020 | 0.021 |

Interest rates

Money rate, commercial paper, 4–6 months

| 0.00 | 0.00 | 0.00 | 0.02 | 0.04 | 0.06 | 0.09 | 0.12 | 0.19 | 0.23 |
| 0.23 | 0.23 | 0.24 | 0.25 | 0.25 | 0.25 | 0.25 | 0.25 | 0.25 | 0.24 |

Yield on U.S. government bonds long term (10 years or more)

| 0.00 | 0.00 | 0.00 | 0.01 | 0.01 | 0.02 | 0.02 | 0.03 | 0.04 | 0.05 |
| 0.06 | 0.07 | 0.08 | 0.09 | 0.10 | 0.11 | 0.12 | 0.13 | 0.14 | 0.15 |

Yield on U.S. government bonds short term (3 months)

| 0.00 | 0.00 | 0.01 | 0.02 | 0.04 | 0.06 | 0.09 | 0.11 | 0.20 | 0.21 |
| 0.20 | 0.20 | 0.21 | 0.21 | 0.21 | 0.21 | 0.21 | 0.21 | 0.21 | 0.20 |

Yield on Moody's AAA corporate bonds seasoned

| 0.00 | 0.00 | 0.00 | 0.01 | 0.01 | 0.02 | 0.03 | 0.04 | 0.05 | 0.06 |
| 0.08 | 0.09 | 0.11 | 0.12 | 0.13 | 0.15 | 0.16 | 0.17 | 0.18 | 0.19 |

Yield on Moody's AAA corporate bonds, new issue

| 0.00 | 0.00 | 0.00 | 0.01 | 0.02 | 0.03 | 0.04 | 0.06 | 0.08 | 0.10 |
| 0.12 | 0.14 | 0.16 | 0.18 | 0.20 | 0.22 | 0.23 | 0.25 | 0.26 | 0.27 |

Employment and GNP

Rate of unemployment—all civilian workers

| 0.0 | 0.0 | 0.0 | 0.0 | −0.1 | −0.1 | −0.2 | −0.2 | −0.3 | −0.3 |
| −0.3 | −0.3 | −0.3 | −0.3 | −0.3 | −0.3 | −0.3 | −0.3 | −0.3 | −0.2 |

GNP, current $

| 0.1 | 0.3 | 0.9 | 2.1 | 3.6 | 5.3 | 7.3 | 9.3 | 11.3 | 13.2 |
| 14.8 | 16.1 | 17.1 | 17.9 | 18.5 | 19.1 | 19.5 | 19.9 | 20.3 | 20.7 |

GNP, constant 58$

| 0.1 | 0.2 | 0.7 | 1.5 | 2.6 | 3.8 | 5.0 | 6.2 | 7.2 | 8.1 |
| 8.6 | 8.9 | 8.9 | 8.7 | 8.4 | 8.0 | 7.5 | 7.1 | 6.6 | 6.3 |

Government

Federal government receipts

| −2.5 | −2.5 | −2.4 | −2.2 | −1.7 | −1.2 | −0.7 | −0.2 | 0.3 | 0.7 |
| 1.0 | 1.3 | 1.4 | 1.4 | 1.4 | 1.4 | 1.3 | 1.2 | 1.1 | 1.0 |

Government deficit, Federal

| −2.5 | −2.5 | −2.4 | −2.2 | −1.6 | −1.1 | −0.5 | 0.0 | 0.5 | 1.0 |
| 1.4 | 1.6 | 1.8 | 1.8 | 1.8 | 1.7 | 1.7 | 1.5 | 1.4 | 1.3 |

Table 4.4
(continued)

| 71:1 | 71:2 | 71:3 | 71:4 | 72:1 | 72:2 | 72:3 | 72:4 | 73:1 | 73:2 |
73:3	73:4	74:1	74:2	74:3	74:4	75:1	75:2	75:3	75:4

Government deficit, state and local

| 0.0 | 0.0 | 0.0 | 0.1 | 0.1 | 0.2 | 0.2 | 0.2 | 0.3 | 0.3 |
| 0.3 | 0.3 | 0.2 | 0.2 | 0.2 | 0.1 | 0.1 | 0.1 | 0.1 | 0.1 |

International

Imports, current $

| 0.0 | 0.0 | 0.0 | 0.1 | 0.2 | 0.3 | 0.4 | 0.6 | 0.8 | 1.0 |
| 1.3 | 1.5 | 1.8 | 2.0 | 2.2 | 2.5 | 2.7 | 2.9 | 3.1 | 3.3 |

Imports, constant 58$

| 0.0 | 0.0 | 0.0 | 0.1 | 0.1 | 0.2 | 0.4 | 0.5 | 0.7 | 0.8 |
| 1.0 | 1.2 | 1.4 | 1.6 | 1.8 | 1.9 | 2.1 | 2.3 | 2.4 | 2.6 |

Exports, current $
same
same

Exports, constant 58$
same
same

employment, prices, credit conditions, government receipts and the government deficit, and the balance of payments are also given in table 4.4. The total impact of an investment tax credit at a statutory rate of 0.033 is given in table 4.5. These tables may be interpreted along the lines outlined above for the total impact on producers' durable equipment expenditures and the gross national product.

Table 4.5
Total impact of the tax credit proposal on the economy (net change from the DRI central projection)

| 71:1 | 71:2 | 71:3 | 71:4 | 72:1 | 72:2 | 72:3 | 72:4 | 73:1 | 73:2 |
73:3	73:4	74:1	74:2	74:3	74:4	75:1	75:2	75:3	75:4

Investment

Investment in private, nonresidential structures, current $

| 0.0 | 0.0 | 0.1 | 0.2 | 0.4 | 0.7 | 1.1 | 1.5 | 2.0 | 2.4 |
| 2.8 | 3.3 | 3.6 | 4.0 | 4.2 | 4.5 | 4.6 | 4.8 | 4.9 | 5.0 |

Investment in private, nonresidential structures, constant 58$

| 0.0 | 0.0 | 0.0 | 0.1 | 0.3 | 0.4 | 0.6 | 0.8 | 1.0 | 1.2 |
| 1.4 | 1.6 | 1.7 | 1.8 | 1.9 | 1.9 | 1.9 | 1.9 | 1.9 | 1.9 |

Fixed private, nonresidential investment, current $

| 0.0 | 0.1 | 0.5 | 1.2 | 2.2 | 3.4 | 4.7 | 6.1 | 7.5 | 8.8 |
| 9.9 | 10.9 | 11.6 | 12.2 | 12.7 | 13.0 | 13.2 | 13.3 | 13.4 | 13.4 |

Fixed private, nonresidential investment, constant 58$

| 0.0 | 0.1 | 0.4 | 0.9 | 1.6 | 2.4 | 3.3 | 4.2 | 5.1 | 5.8 |
| 6.5 | 7.0 | 7.4 | 7.6 | 7.7 | 7.7 | 7.7 | 7.6 | 7.5 | 7.4 |

Table 4.5
(continued)

71:1	71:2	71:3	71:4	72:1	72:2	72:3	72:4	73:1	73:2
73:3	73:4	74:1	74:2	74:3	74:4	75:1	75:2	75:3	75:4

Investment in producers' durable equipment, current $

0.0	0.1	0.4	1.0	1.8	2.6	3.6	4.6	5.5	6.3
7.0	7.6	8.0	8.3	8.4	8.5	8.5	8.5	8.5	8.4

Investment in producers' durable equipment, constant 58$

0.0	0.1	0.3	0.8	1.4	2.0	2.7	3.4	4.0	4.6
5.0	5.4	5.6	5.8	5.8	5.8	5.8	5.7	5.6	5.5

Housing

Investment in residential structures, current $

0.0	0.0	0.0	0.0	0.1	0.1	0.1	0.2	0.2	0.2
0.1	0.1	0.0	−0.1	−0.2	−0.3	−0.4	−0.4	−0.5	−0.4

Investment in residential structures, constant 58$

0.0	0.0	0.0	0.0	0.0	0.0	0.0	0.0	0.0	0.0
−0.1	−0.1	−0.2	−0.3	−0.4	−0.5	−0.6	−0.7	−0.7	−0.7

Housing starts, private—total

0.001	0.001	0.001	0.002	0.003	0.004	0.004	0.002	0.000	−0.004
−0.010	−0.017	−0.025	−0.034	−0.042	−0.049	−0.054	−0.058	−0.058	−0.056

Prices

Consumer price index

0.000	0.000	0.000	0.000	0.000	0.001	0.001	0.001	0.002	0.003
0.004	0.005	0.006	0.008	0.009	0.011	0.012	0.013	0.015	0.016

Implicit price deflators for GNP:

0.000	0.000	0.000	0.000	0.000	0.000	0.000	0.000	0.001	0.001
0.002	0.003	0.004	0.005	0.007	0.008	0.009	0.010	0.011	0.012

Implicit price deflators for private nonresidential structures

0.000	0.000	0.000	0.000	0.001	0.001	0.002	0.003	0.004	0.006
0.008	0.011	0.014	0.017	0.020	0.024	0.027	0.031	0.034	0.038

Implicit price deflators for fixed private nonresidential structures

0.000	0.000	0.000	0.000	−0.001	−0.001	0.000	0.000	0.001	0.002
0.003	0.004	0.005	0.007	0.008	0.010	0.011	0.013	0.014	0.015

Implicit price deflators for producers' durable equipment

0.000	0.000	0.000	0.000	0.000	0.001	0.001	0.002	0.002	0.003
0.003	0.004	0.005	0.005	0.006	0.006	0.007	0.007	0.008	0.008

Implicit price deflators for residential structures

0.000	0.000	0.000	0.000	0.001	0.001	0.002	0.003	0.005	0.006
0.008	0.010	0.012	0.014	0.016	0.017	0.019	0.020	0.022	0.022

Interest rates

Money rate, commercial paper, 4–6 months

0.00	0.00	0.00	0.02	0.03	0.06	0.09	0.12	0.19	0.23
0.24	0.24	0.25	0.26	0.27	0.27	0.27	0.27	0.27	0.27

Yield on U.S. government bonds long term (10 years or more)

0.00	0.00	0.00	0.00	0.01	0.01	0.02	0.03	0.04	0.05
0.06	0.07	0.08	0.10	0.11	0.12	0.13	0.14	0.15	0.16

Table 4.5
(continued)

71:1	71:2	71:3	71:4	72:1	72:2	72:3	72:4	73:1	73:2
73:3	73:4	74:1	74:2	74:3	74:4	75:1	75:2	75:3	75:4

Yield on U.S. government bonds short term (3 months)

0.00	0.00	0.01	0.02	0.04	0.06	0.09	0.11	0.20	0.21
0.21	0.21	0.22	0.23	0.23	0.23	0.23	0.23	0.23	0.22

Yield on Moody's AAA corporate bonds seasoned

0.00	0.00	0.00	0.01	0.01	0.02	0.03	0.04	0.05	0.06
0.08	0.09	0.11	0.13	0.14	0.16	0.17	0.18	0.19	0.20

Yield on Moody's AAA corporate bonds, new issue

0.00	0.00	0.00	0.01	0.02	0.03	0.04	0.06	0.08	0.10
0.12	0.14	0.17	0.19	0.21	0.23	0.25	0.27	0.28	0.29

Employment and GNP

Rate of unemployment—all civilian workers

0.0	0.0	0.0	0.0	−0.1	−0.1	−0.2	−0.2	−0.3	−0.3
−0.3	−0.4	−0.4	−0.4	−0.4	−0.3	−0.3	−0.3	−0.3	−0.3

GNP, current $

0.1	0.2	0.8	1.9	3.4	5.2	7.3	9.5	11.6	13.7
15.5	17.1	18.4	19.3	20.1	20.7	21.2	21.6	22.0	22.4

GNP, constant 58$

0.1	0.2	0.6	1.4	2.5	3.7	5.0	6.3	7.5	8.5
9.2	9.6	9.7	9.6	9.3	8.8	8.3	7.8	7.3	6.9

Government

Federal government receipts

−2.1	−2.0	−1.9	−1.5	−1.1	−0.7	0.0	0.4	1.0	1.5
1.9	2.2	2.5	2.6	2.6	2.6	2.5	2.5	2.4	2.3

Government deficit, Federal

−2.1	−2.0	−1.9	−1.5	−1.1	−0.6	0.1	0.6	1.2	1.8
2.3	2.6	2.9	3.0	3.0	3.0	2.9	2.9	2.7	2.7

Government deficit, state and local

0.0	0.0	0.0	0.1	0.1	0.1	0.2	0.2	0.3	0.3
0.3	0.3	0.3	0.2	0.2	0.2	0.2	0.1	0.1	0.2

International

Imports, current $

0.0	0.0	0.0	0.1	0.2	0.3	0.4	0.6	0.8	1.1
1.3	1.6	1.8	2.1	2.4	2.6	2.9	3.1	3.3	3.6

Imports, constant 58$

0.0	0.0	0.0	0.1	0.1	0.2	0.3	0.5	0.7	0.8
1.0	1.2	1.4	1.6	1.8	2.0	2.2	2.4	2.6	2.7

Exports, current $

same

same

Exports, constant 58$

same

same

4.7 Conclusion

Our overall conclusion from an assessment of the economic impact of the ADR System is that the effect on producers' durables spending is likely to be very substantial over the five-year period 1971–1975. The impact in real terms builds up slowly reaching a maximum in 1974; the impact in current prices continues to rise into later 1974 as prices go on rising in response to the higher level of activity. This pattern is comparable to the investment increases that followed the adoption of accelerated depreciation in 1954 and the Depreciation Guidelines and tax credit in 1962. Since the change in investment incentives associated with the adoption of the ADR System is smaller than in the two previous changes, the economic impact is more moderate.

Technical Appendix

The investment equation used in assessing the direct impact of investment incentives is:

$$I_t = 7.86678 + 0.00091 \frac{P_{t-2}}{c_{t-2}} Q_{t-1} + 0.00154 \frac{P_{t-3}}{c_{t-3}} Q_{t-2}$$

$$+ 0.00193 \frac{P_{t-4}}{c_{t-4}} Q_{t-3} + 0.00211 \frac{P_{t-5}}{c_{t-5}} Q_{t-4}$$

$$+ 0.00211 \frac{P_{t-6}}{c_{t-6}} Q_{t-5} + 0.00198 \frac{P_{t-7}}{c_{t-7}} Q_{t-6}$$

$$+ 0.00174 \frac{P_{t-8}}{c_{t-8}} Q_{t-7} + 0.00143 \frac{P_{t-9}}{c_{t-9}} Q_{t-8}$$

$$+ 0.00108 \frac{P_{t-10}}{c_{t-10}} Q_{t-9} + 0.00072 \frac{P_{t-11}}{c_{t-11}} Q_{t-10}$$

$$+ 0.00041 \frac{P_{t-12}}{c_{t-12}} Q_{t-11} + 0.00015 \frac{P_{t-13}}{c_{t-13}} Q_{t-12}$$

$$+ 0.06476 K_{t-1}$$

where I_t is Producers' Durable Equipment expenditures in constant prices of 1958, Q_t is Gross National Product in constant prices of 1958, K_t is Capital Stock, Producers' Durable equipment, in constant prices of 1958, P_t is the implicit deflator for Gross National Product, and c_t is the rental price of Producers' Durable equipment services. For this equation $\bar{R}^2$ is 0.9875, the Durbin-Watson ratio is 0.5812, and the average lag is 6.43089 quarters.

The rental price of capital services is:

$$c_t = \frac{1 - k_t - u_t z_t}{1 - u_t} \; q_t \; (r + \delta)$$

In this formula u_t is the statutory corporate income tax rate, z_t is the present value of depreciation allowances discounted at the annual discount rate of 0.10, k_t is the effective rate of the investment tax credit, q_t is the implicit deflator for Producers' Durable Equipment expenditures from the DRI five-year projection of the U.S. economy. The first evaluation assumed no change in investment incentives. The equation was next evaluated in the program MODSIM, using the same projections as before, but altering the investment incentives to provide projections of investment for each of the six alternative policies we consider. The difference between the results with no change in policy and the results for each change in tax incentives is tabulated as the direct impact of the policy change in table 4.3.

The final step in assessing total impact was to enter the DRI/MODEL program with the direct impact of each change in tax incentives as an add factor for investment in Producers' durable equipment expenditures in constant prices of 1958. Add factors for the change in capital consumption allowances were entered for the changes in depreciation rules. Add factors for the investment tax credit were entered for policy changes involving the tax credit. Capital consumption allowances are increased by a change in depreciation rules while tax receipts are reduced for either increased depreciation or an investment tax credit. The results of these five-year simulations of the DRI model are presented in tables 4.4 and 4.5.

The investment equation for Producers' Durable Equipment in the DRI model is similar in form to the equation given in this Appendix, but it is not suitable for the assessment of the impact of changes in depreciation rules. In this equation economic depreciation is treated as identical with the tax depreciation allowances. As an example, a twenty percent reduction in asset lifetimes would have two effects. The first is to lower the rental price of equipment capital and the second is to reduce the economic lifetime of equipment.

Notes

1. See Robert E. Hall and Dale W. Jorgenson (1971 and the references given there). See also: Hall and Jorgenson (1967, 1969a).

2. For a review and comparison of tax measures adopted in the U.S. and European countries see O. Eckstein and U. Tanzi (1964).

3. The effects of tax policy on investment behavior are analyzed by E. C. Brown (1955, 1962); by N. B. Ture (1963, esp. pp. 341–345); by S. B. Chase, Jr. (1962); and by R. A. Musgrave (1963, esp. pp. 53–54 and 117–129). Many other references could be given.

4. President's Task Force on Business Taxation, *Business Taxation*, September 1970.

5

The Economic Theory of Replacement and Depreciation

Dale W. Jorgenson

5.1 Introduction

The economic theory of production—including the description of technology, the conditions for producer equilibrium, and the response of variables determined in the theory to changes in parameters—may be developed in a form that abstracts from specific interpretations.[1] In the intertemporal theory of production each commodity is distinguished by point of time. As an illustration, an hour of labor today and an hour of labor tomorrow are treated as distinct commodities. Given this convention the intertemporal theory of producer behavior is formally analogous to the standard atemporal theory.[2]

The special character of the intertemporal theory of production arises from more detailed specifications of technology, permitting a more precise characterization of producer behavior. The most important specialization of technology results from the introduction of durable capital as a factor of production.[3] Although the central concepts of capital theory—capital assets, capital services and investment—are inessential to the development of the intertemporal theory of production, they provide additional structure that permits a much more detailed analysis of producer behavior.

To describe the durable goods model we begin with the relative efficiency of durable goods of different ages. At each point of time durable goods decline in efficiency, giving rise to needs for *replacement* in order to maintain productive capacity. For any given durable good the price of acquisition declines, reflecting the current decline in efficiency and the present value of future declines in efficiency; the decline in price is *depreciation* on the durable good.

The durable goods model is characterized by price-quantity dual-ity.[4] Capital stock corresponds to the acquisition price of investment goods, acquisition of investment goods corresponds to the time rental price of capital. Replacement corresponds to depreciation. In this paper we present the economic theory of replacement and its dual, the theory of depreciation. We then consider applications of the theory to the explanation of replacement investment and capital goods prices.

5.2   Replacement

5.2.1   Introduction

Characterization of the durable goods model of production begins with a description of the relative efficiency of durable goods of differ-ent ages. Replacement requirements are determined by losses in effi-ciency of existing durable goods as well as actual physical disappear-ance or retirement of capital goods. When a durable good is retired its relative efficiency drops to zero. To estimate replacement require-ments we must introduce an explicit description of decline in relative efficiency.

In the durable goods model the services provided by a given durable good at different points of time are proportional to each other. The proportions describing relative efficiency at different points of time depend only on the age of the durable good and not on the time the good is acquired.[5] In our description of technology we employ dis-crete time. In discrete time the *relative efficiency* of a durable good may be described by a sequence of nonnegative numbers[6]

$$d_0, d_1, \ldots.$$

We normalize initial relative efficiency at unity and assume that rel-ative efficiency is decreasing so that:

$$d_0 = 1, \qquad d_\tau - d_{\tau-1} \leqq 0 \qquad (\tau = 0, 1, \ldots).$$

We also assume that every capital good is eventually retired or scrapped so that relative efficiency declines to zero,

$$\lim_{\tau \to \infty} d_\tau = 0.$$

Replacement requirements are determined by declines in efficiency of previously acquired capital goods. The proportion of a given investment to be replaced during the τth period after its acquisition is equal to the decline in relative efficiency. We may refer to the decline in relative efficiency as the *mortality distribution* of a capital good, say m_τ, where:

$$m_\tau = - (d_\tau - d_{\tau-1}) \qquad (\tau = 1, 2, \ldots). \qquad (5.1)$$

By our assumption that relative efficiency is decreasing, the mortality distribution may be represented by a sequence of nonnegative numbers,

$$m_1, m_2, \ldots$$

where

$$\sum_{\tau=1}^{\infty} m_\tau = \sum_{\tau=1}^{\infty} (d_{\tau-1} - d_\tau) = d_0 = 1 .$$

Replacement requirements, say R_t, are a weighted average of past investments, say A_t

$$R_t = m_1 A_{t-1} + m_2 A_{t-2} + \ldots \qquad (5.2)$$

or, where S is the lag operator,

$$R_t = (m_1 S + m_2 S^2 + \ldots) A_t = m(S) A_t .$$

and $m(S)$ is a power series in the lag operator,

$$m(S) = m_1 S + m_2 S^2 + \ldots .$$

Capital stock at the end of the period, say K_t, is the sum of past investments, each weighted by its relative efficiency

$$K_t = \sum_{\tau=0}^{\infty} d_\tau A_{t-\tau} . \qquad (5.3)$$

Taking the first difference of this expression, we may write

$$K_t - K_{t-1} = A_t + \sum_{\tau=1}^{\infty} (d_\tau - d_{\tau-1})A_{t-\tau}$$
$$= A_t - \sum_{\tau=1}^{\infty} m_\tau A_{t-\tau}$$
$$= A_t - R_t \tag{5.4}$$

the change in capital stock in any period is equal to the aquisition of investment goods less replacement requirements.

Finally, we may express replacement requirements in terms of present and past net investments. First, we rewrite the expression for the change in capital stock in the form

$$K_t - K_{t-1} = A_t - m(S)A$$

so that

$$A_t = \frac{1}{1 - m(S)} [K_t - K_{t-1}]$$
$$= [1 + \delta(S)][K_t - K_{t-1}]$$
$$= [K_t - K_{t-1}] + \sum_{\tau=1}^{\infty} \delta_\tau [K_{t-\tau} - K_{t-\tau-1}] \tag{5.5}$$

where $\delta(S)$ is a power series in the lag operator. We may refer to the sequence of coefficients,

$$\delta_0, \delta_1, \ldots.$$

as the *replacement distribution*. Each coefficient δ_τ is *the rate of replacement* of a stock replaced τ periods after initial acquisition. The rate of replacement includes replacement of the initial investment and subsequent replacements of each succeeding replacement.

The sequence of replacement rates $\{\delta_\tau\}$ can be computed recursively from the sequence $\{m_\tau\}$ of mortality rates. The proportion of an initial investment replaced at time v and again at a later time $\tau > v$ is equal to $m_v \delta_{t-v}$. The proportion of the stock replaced at the τth period is the sum of proportions replaced first at periods 1, 2, . . . , and later at period τ; hence

$$\delta_\tau = m_1 \delta_{\tau-1} + m_2 \delta_{\tau-2} + \cdots + m_\tau \delta_0 \qquad (\tau = 1, 2, \ldots).$$

This equation is, of course, the *renewal equation* (Feller, 1957, pp. 290–293).

Since replacement requirements may be expressed in the form

$$R_t = \sum_{\tau=1}^{\infty} \delta_\tau [K_{t-\tau} - K_{t-\tau-1}]$$

the *average replacement rate* for capital stock at the beginning of the period

$$\hat{\delta} = \frac{R_t}{K_{t-1}} = \sum_{\tau=1}^{\infty} \delta_\tau \frac{[K_{t-\tau} - K_{t-\tau-1}]}{K_{t-1}} \tag{5.6}$$

is a weighted average of replacement rates with weights given by the relative proportions of net investments of each age in beginning of period capital stock.

To illustrate these relationships we take the relative efficiency distribution to be geometric

$$d_\tau = (1 - \delta)^\tau \qquad (\tau = 0, 1, \ldots).$$

Obviously, relative efficiency is initially moralized at unity, decreases and eventually declines to zero. The corresponding mortality distribution (5.1) is geometric since

$$m_\tau = d_{\tau-1} - d_\tau = (1 - \delta)^{\tau-1} - (1 - \delta)^\tau = \delta(1 - \delta)^{\tau-1}.$$

The coefficients of the mortality distribution are nonnegative and sum to unity.

Replacement requirements (5.2) are given by

$$R_t = \sum_{\tau=1}^{\infty} \delta(1 - \delta)^{\tau-1} A_{t-\tau}.$$

Capital stock at the end of the period (5.3) may be expressed as a weighted sum of past net investments,

$$K_t = \sum_{\tau=0}^{\infty} (1 - \delta)^\tau A_{t-\tau}$$

so that the change in capital stock (5.4) may be written

$$K_t - K_{t-1} = A_t - \sum_{\tau=1}^{\infty} \delta(1-\delta)^{\tau} A_{t-\tau}$$

$$= A_t - \delta K_{t-1} \, .$$

Replacement requirements are proportional to capital at the beginning of the period

$$R_t = \delta K_{t-1} \, .$$

Finally, the replacement distribution (5.5) takes the form

$$A_t = \frac{1}{1 - m(S)} (K_t - K_{t-1})$$

$$= \frac{1}{1 - \dfrac{\delta S}{1 - (1-\delta)S}} (K_t - K_{t-1})$$

$$= K_t - K_{t-1} + \sum_{\tau=1}^{\infty} \delta(K_{t-\tau} - K_{t-\tau-1}) \, .$$

The sequence of replacement rates $\{\delta_\tau\}$ and the average replacement rate $\hat{\delta}$ are constant and equal to δ. The average replacement rate is, of course, independent of the time path of past net investments.

A wide variety of retirement distributions have been found useful in describing the retirement or physical disappearance of capital goods.[7] Relatively little information is available on the decline in efficiency of existing capital goods.[8] In measuring capital stock net of replacement requirements, which include both retirement and decline in efficiency of existing capital goods, a smaller range of mortality distributions has been employed.[9] The geometric mortality distribution is among the distributions most commonly used in measuring capital stock.[10] A fundamental result of renewal theory is that the sequence of replacement rates $\{\delta_\tau\}$ tends to a constant value for almost any mortality distribution (5.1). The geometric mortality distribution, resulting in a constant rate of replacement of capital stock, may provide a useful approximation to replacement requirements for a broad class of mortality distributions. We turn now to estimation of replacement requirements for constant and growing (or declining) capital stock.

5.2.2 Single Investment, Constant Capital

An initial investment generates a set of replacements distributed over time and each replacement generates a new set of subsequent replacements. This process repeats itself indefinitely. Renewal theory shows that the distribution of replacements for such an infinite stream approaches a constant fraction of capital stock for (almost) any mortality distribution and for any initial age distribution of the capital stock. The result that replacement is a constant fraction of capital stock, which holds exactly for the geometric distribution, holds asymptotically for (almost) distribution. We verify this proposition in two stages: (a) considering a capital stock of fixed size; (b) extending the analysis to a growing (or declining) capital stock.

Consider a capital stock consisting of investments which are replaced over time according to the mortality distribution (a). Suppose that every investment is eventually replaced and that there is no integer greater than one such that replacements for a single investment can occur only at integral multiples of this integer. Then the proportion of capital stock replaced in any period approaches the inverse of the expected value of times to replacement as the age of the capital stock increases without limit.

The assumption that every investment is eventually replaced completely requires no loss of generality for the analysis of replacement demand. The restriction that there is no integer $\phi > 1$ such that replacements can occur only at integral multiples of ϕ, rules out purely periodic replacements. For a single initial investment with a fixed interval between replacements (the length of the interval being some integer greater than unity), the fraction of equipment replaced in each period is unity for integral multiples of the replacement interval and zero elsewhere. However, by taking the time period to be equal to the replacement interval, the conclusion holds as stated above.

To state the fundamental theorem of renewal theory formally, it is convenient to let

$$m_0 = 0, \qquad \delta_0 = 1. \tag{5.7}$$

If for the sequence $\{\delta_\tau\}$ there is an integer $\theta > 1$ such that the subsequence $\delta_\theta, \delta_{2\theta}, \ldots$ may be nonzero, but all δ_τ for $\tau \neq \theta, 2\theta, \ldots$ are zero, the sequence may be said to be periodic. The greatest θ with this property is called *period* of the sequence. Obviously, $\{\delta_\tau\}$ is periodic if and only if $\{m_\tau\}$ is periodic.

Let μ represent the expected value of the time to replacement. Then

$$\mu = \sum_{\tau=0}^{\infty} \tau\, m_{\tau} \qquad\qquad (5.8)$$

or where

$$m(\lambda) = \sum_{\tau=0}^{\infty} m_{\tau}\, \lambda^{\tau}$$

is the generating function of the sequence $\{m_{\tau}\}$

$$\mu = m'(1).$$

The main theorem may now be stated as follows. If the sequence $\{\delta_{\tau}\}$, representing the proportion of the total stock replaced in each period, is *not* periodic, and the sequence $\{m_{\tau}\}$, representing the distribution of replacements of the initial investment over time sums to unity, then

$$\delta_{\tau} \rightarrow \frac{1}{\mu} \qquad\qquad (5.9)$$

as $\tau \rightarrow \infty$.[11] To cover the case of periodic replacement, this theorem may be reformulated as follows. If the sequence $\{\delta_{\tau}\}$ has period θ and the sequence $\{m_{\tau}\}$ sums to unity, then

$$\delta_{\tau\theta} \rightarrow \frac{\theta}{\mu} \qquad\qquad (5.10)$$

for $\tau = 1, 2, \ldots$ and $\delta_{\tau} = 0$ otherwise.[12]

5.2.3   Multiple Investments, Constant Capital

These theorems are easily extended to an arbitrary distribution of the initial investment over time. Let the proportion of the initial investment completed at time τ be denoted ϕ_{τ}. The distribution of investments over time is described by a sequence of nonnegative numbers

$$\phi_0, \phi_1, \ldots \qquad\qquad (5.11)$$

where

$$\sum_{\tau=0}^{\infty} \phi_\tau = 1 \tag{5.12}$$

the entire amount of the investment is eventually completed. At this point we may drop the assumption that $\delta_0 = 1$, that is, that the entire capital stock is completed at period zero. Investment at any time is equal to new investment ϕ_τ, plus replacement investment; representing the sequence of investments by $\{\delta_\tau\}$ we have the following recursive relationships

$$\delta_0 = \phi_0$$
$$\delta_1 = \phi_1 + m_1 \delta_0 \tag{5.13}$$
$$\cdots$$
$$\delta_\tau = \phi_\tau + m_1 \delta_{\tau-1} + m_2 \delta_{\tau-2} + \cdots + m_\tau \delta_0 .$$

These relationships specialize to the preceding case when $\delta_0 = \phi_0 = 1$ and $\phi_\tau = 0$ for $\tau > 0$.

If μ is defined as above (5.8), the main theorem can be stated as follows. If the sequence $\{\delta_\tau\}$, representing investment as a proportion of total stock in each period, is *not* periodic, if the sequence $\{m_\tau\}$, representing the distribution of replacements of the initial investment over time sums to unity, and if the sequence $\{\phi_\tau\}$, representing the distribution of the initial investment over time also sums to unity, then

$$\delta_v \rightarrow \frac{\sum_{\tau=0}^{\infty} \phi_\tau}{\mu} = \frac{1}{\mu} \tag{5.14}$$

as $v \rightarrow \infty$. As before, if $\{\delta_\tau\}$ has period θ and the sequence $\{m_\tau\}$ sums to unity, then

$$\delta_{v\theta} \rightarrow \frac{\theta}{\mu} \sum_{\tau=0}^{\infty} \phi_\tau = \frac{\theta}{\mu} \tag{5.15}$$

for $v = 1, 2, \ldots$ and $\delta_\tau = 0$ otherwise (Feller, 1957, p. 294). The proportion of replacement investment in total investment approaches unity as $\tau \rightarrow \infty$, so that

$$\delta_\tau \rightarrow m_1 \delta_{\tau-1} + m_2 \delta_{\tau-2} + \cdots + \mu_\tau \delta_0$$

as $\tau \rightarrow \infty$. Hence statements (5.14) and (5.15) hold for the sequence of replacement investments.

5.2.4   Single Investment, Changing Capital

For a growing capital stock we adopt the convenient fiction that an initial investment is the progenitor of a infinite stream of new investments leading to the expansion of capacity. As an illustration, this model would include the situation considered by Domar (1953) and Eisner (1952) in which gross investment grows at a fixed percentage rate. As before, we represent the distribution of replacements over time by the sequence of nonnegative numbers

$m_0, m_1, \ldots$.

It is convenient to assume

$m_0 = 0$

and

$$\sum_{\tau = 1}^{\infty} m_\tau = 1$$

as before. We next represent the distribution of new investment by a sequence of nonnegative numbers

$\gamma_0, \gamma_1, \ldots$ (5.16)

where it is convenient to assume

$\gamma_0 = 0$ (5.17)

and, where $\gamma(\lambda)$ is the generating function of the sequence (5.16), that γ (5.1) is finite. The sum of the sequences $\{\mu_\tau\}$, $\{\gamma_\tau\}$ is represented by $\{\alpha_\tau\}$, where

$\alpha_\tau = m_\tau + \gamma_\tau$ $(\tau = 1, 2, \ldots)$.   (5.18)

For a constant capital stock the sequence representing gross investment approaches, as a limit, the sequence representing replacement investment. For a growing capital stock the difference between the two sequences does not converge to zero. Consequently, it is necessary to introduce sequences representing gross investment, replacement investment and investment for the expansion of capacity. First, we introduce a sequence representing gross investment as a proportion of initial capital stock. This sequence, denoted $\{\delta_\tau\}$, is computed recursively from the sequence $\{\alpha_\tau\}$, representing replacement and new investment as a proportion of any initial investment. The proportion of the initial capital stock invested at time v and again at a later time $\tau > v$ is equal to $\alpha_v \delta_{\tau - v}$. The proportion of the initial stock invested at the τth period is the sum of the proportions invested first at periods $1, 2, \ldots$ and later at period τ; hence

$$\delta_\tau = \alpha_1 \delta_{\tau - 1} + \alpha_2 \delta_{\tau - 2} + \cdots + \alpha_\tau \delta_0 . \tag{5.19}$$

As before, it is convenient to assume

$$\delta_0 = 1$$

in particular, $\alpha_\tau = \alpha_\tau \delta_0$. Equation (5.19) is, of course, the renewal equation. Unless the generating function for the sequence $\{\gamma_\tau\}$, $\gamma(\lambda)$, is zero at $\lambda = 1$, the sequence diverges.

Next, we introduce sequences representing replacement investment and investment for expansion of capacity as a proportion of initial capital stock. Let $\{\beta_\tau\}$ represent the sequence of replacement investments and $\{\kappa_\tau\}$ the sequence of investments for expansion of capacity. Then

$$\beta_\tau = m_1 \delta_{\tau - 1} + m_2 \delta_{\tau - 2} + \cdots + m_\tau \delta_0$$
$$\kappa_\tau = \gamma_1 \delta_{\tau - 1} + \gamma_2 \delta_{\tau - 2} + \cdots + \gamma_\tau \delta_0 \tag{5.20}$$

of course

$$\delta_\tau = \beta_\tau + \kappa_\tau .$$

That is, gross investment is the sum of replacement investment and investment for the expansion of capacity. Finally, we introduce a sequence representing current capital stock as a proportion of initial capital stock. Let $\{\varepsilon_\tau\}$ represent this sequence; then

$$\varepsilon_\tau = \delta_0 + \sum_{v = 0}^{\tau - 1} \kappa_v . \tag{5.21}$$

But $\varepsilon_0 = \delta_0$, so that

$$\varepsilon_\tau = \varepsilon_0 + \sum_{\nu=0}^{\tau-1} (\gamma_1 \, \delta_{\nu-1} + \gamma_2 \, \delta_{\nu-2} + \cdots + \gamma_\nu \, \delta_0).$$

Unless $\gamma(\lambda)$ is zero for $\lambda = 1$, each of the sequences $\{\beta_\tau\}$, $\{\kappa_\tau\}$ and $\{\varepsilon_\tau\}$ diverges.

The following discussion is based on the fundamental result of renewal theory that if $\gamma(1)$ is not zero and if the sequence $\{\alpha_\tau\}$ is not periodic, there exists a unique positive root, $\xi < 1$, of the equation

$$\alpha(\xi) = m(\xi) + \gamma(\xi) = 1 \tag{5.22}$$

where $\alpha(\lambda)$, $m(\lambda)$ and $\gamma(\lambda)$ are the generating functions of the sequences $\{\alpha_\tau\}$, $\{m_\tau\}$ and $\{\gamma_\tau\}$, such that

$$\delta_\tau \sim \frac{1}{\alpha'(\xi)} \, \xi^{-\tau} \tag{5.23}$$

where the sign $\sim$ indicates that the ratio of the two sides approaches unity as $\tau \to \infty$. Asymptotically, the sequence of gross investment $\{\delta_\tau\}$ grows at a rate $\xi^{-1} - 1$; this rate, defined as a root of equation (5.22), is nonnegative since the generating functions $m(\lambda)$, $\gamma(\lambda)$ have nonnegative coefficients; it is positive if and only if $\gamma(1) > 0$. The rate of growth, $\xi^{-1} - 1$, is unique since the function $\alpha(\xi)$ is monotone. We consider the sequences $\{\delta_\tau \xi^\tau\}$, $\{\alpha_\tau \xi^\tau\}$; since $\alpha(\xi) = 1$

$$\delta_\tau \xi^\tau \to \frac{1}{\alpha'(\xi)}$$

as $\tau \to \infty$, by (5.9) above. Hence

$$\delta_\tau \sim \frac{1}{\alpha'(\xi)} \, \xi^{-\tau}$$

as $\tau \to \infty$, as asserted.

As a consequence of the result (5.23) for the sequence of gross investments $\{\delta_\tau\}$, we have the following result for the sequence of replacement investments $\{\beta_\tau\}$

$$\beta_\tau \sim m_1 \frac{\xi^{-(\tau-1)}}{\alpha'(\xi)} + m_2 \frac{\xi^{-(\tau-2)}}{\alpha'(\xi)} + \cdots + m_\tau \frac{\xi^0}{\alpha'(\xi)} = \frac{1}{\alpha'(\xi)} \, (1/\xi) \sum_{\nu=1}^{\tau} m_\tau \xi^\tau$$

so that

$$\beta_\tau \backsim \frac{m(\xi)}{\alpha'(\xi)}\, \xi^{-\tau}. \qquad (5.24)$$

If gross investment grows at a rate $\xi^{-1} - 1$, replacement investment grows, asymptotically, at the same rate. This implies that replacement investment approaches a constant proportion of gross investment. This proportion is, of course, $m(\xi) \le 1$.

Similarly, for the sequence of investments for the expansion of capacity $\{\kappa_\tau\}$, we have the result

$$\kappa_\tau \backsim \frac{\gamma(\xi)}{\alpha'(\xi)}\, \xi^{-\tau} \qquad (5.25)$$

that is, investment for expansion grows at the same rate as gross investment and replacement investment, asymptotically. Investment for expansion of capacity approaches the proportion $\gamma(\xi)$ of gross investment.

Finally, the sequence $\{\varepsilon_\tau\}$, representing capital stock, takes the form

$$\varepsilon_\tau = \varepsilon_0 + \sum_{v=0}^{\tau-1} \kappa_v$$

$$= \varepsilon_0 + \sum_{v-0}^{\tau-1} \frac{\gamma(\zeta)}{\alpha'(\xi)}\, \xi^{-v}$$

$$= \varepsilon_0 + \frac{\gamma(\xi)}{\alpha'(\xi)} \sum_{v=0}^{\tau-1} \xi^{-v}$$

$$= \varepsilon_0 \frac{\gamma(\xi)}{\alpha'(\xi)} \frac{1-\xi^\tau}{(\xi^\tau)\,1-\xi}.$$

Hence

$$\varepsilon_\tau \backsim \frac{\xi\gamma(\xi)}{(1-\xi)\alpha'(\xi)}\, \xi^{-\tau} \qquad (5.26)$$

that is, capital stock grows at the same rate as gross investment.

We conclude that, for a growing capital stock, replacement investment approaches a constant proportion of capital stock

$$\frac{\beta_\tau}{\epsilon_\tau} \rightarrow \frac{\dfrac{m(\xi)}{\alpha'(\xi)}\xi^{-\tau}}{\dfrac{\gamma(\xi)}{(1-\xi)\alpha'(\xi)}\xi^{-\tau}} = \frac{(1-\xi)m(\xi)}{\xi\gamma(\xi)} \tag{5.27}$$

as $\tau \rightarrow \infty$. A similar expression may be derived for the limit of the proportion of investment for the expansion of capacity to capital stock

$$\frac{\kappa_\tau}{\epsilon_\tau} \rightarrow \frac{\dfrac{\gamma(\xi)}{\alpha'(\xi)}\xi^{-\tau}}{\dfrac{\xi\gamma(\xi)}{(1-\xi)\alpha'(\xi)}\xi^{-\tau}} = \frac{1}{\xi} - 1 \tag{5.28}$$

which is the rate of growth of capital stock. Since $0 < \xi \leq 1$, both the expressions (5.27) and (5.28) are nonnegative.

5.2.5 Multiple Investments, Changing Capital

These results are easily generalized to an arbitrary distribution of the initial investment over time. As before, we introduce the sequence of nonnegative numbers

$$\phi_0, \phi_1, \ldots$$

where ϕ_τ represents the proportion of the initial investment put in place at time τ. Condition (5.12) is satisfied as follows

$$\sum_{\tau=0}^{\infty} \phi_\tau = 1 .$$

The recursive relations (5.13) hold in the form

$$\delta_0 = \phi_0$$
$$\delta_1 = \phi_1 + \alpha_1\delta_0$$
$$\cdots$$
$$\delta_\tau = \phi_\tau + \alpha_1\delta_{\tau-1} + \alpha_2\delta_{\tau-2} + \cdots + \alpha_\tau\delta .$$

The fundamental result (5.23) takes the form

$$\delta_\tau \backsim \frac{\sum\limits_{v=0}^{\infty} \phi_v}{\alpha'(\xi)} \xi^{-\tau} = \frac{1}{\alpha'(\xi)} \xi^{-\tau}.$$

The sequence of new investments $\{\kappa_\tau\}$ is represented by

$$\kappa_\tau = \phi_\tau + \gamma_1 \delta_{\tau-1} + \gamma_2 \delta_{\tau-2} + \ldots + \gamma_\tau \delta_0. \tag{5.29}$$

Of course $\delta_0 = \phi_0$. The sequence $\{\varepsilon_\tau\}$, representing capital stock as a proportion of the initial investment, becomes

$$\varepsilon_\tau = \sum_{v=0}^{\tau-1} \phi_v + \sum_{v=0}^{\tau-1} (\gamma_1 \delta_{v-1} + \gamma_2 \delta_{v-2} + \cdots + \gamma_v \delta_0).$$

where $\sum_{v=0}^{\infty} \phi_v$ plays the role of ε_0, the remaining argument is essentially unchanged.

In conclusion, then, if the sequence $\{\alpha_\tau\}$ is periodic with period θ

$$\frac{\beta_{\theta\tau}}{\varepsilon_{\theta\tau}} \rightarrow \frac{(1-\xi)m(\xi)}{\xi\gamma(\xi)} \tag{5.30}$$

as $\tau \rightarrow \infty$ and $\beta_\tau/\varepsilon_\tau = 0$ for $\tau \neq 1\theta, 2\theta, \ldots$.

For illustrative purposes we consider the special case discussed by Domar (1953) and Eisner (1952) in which replacement investment is equal to gross investment v periods previous and gross investment grows at a constant rate. We choose the sequence $\{m_\tau\}$, $\{\gamma_\tau\}$ and $\{\phi_\tau\}$ as follows

$$m_0 = m_1 = \cdots = m_{v-1} = m_{v+1} = \cdots = 0$$

$$\gamma_0 = \gamma_1 = \cdots = \gamma_{v-1} = \gamma_{v+1} = \cdots = 0$$

and

$$m_v = 1$$

$$\gamma_v = (1+\gamma)^v - 1$$

where γ is the rate of growth of gross investment

$$\phi_\tau = \phi_{\tau-1}$$

for $\tau < v$ and

$\phi_\tau = 0$

for $\tau \geq v$. Finally

$$\phi_0 = \frac{1 + \gamma}{\sum\limits_{\tau = 1}^{v} (1 + \gamma)^\tau} \, .$$

Then, the asymptotic result (5.27) becomes

$$\frac{(1 - \xi)m(\xi)}{\gamma\,(\xi)} = \frac{\left(\dfrac{1}{1 + \gamma}\right)^v}{\{(1 + \gamma)^v - 1\}\left(\dfrac{1}{1 + \gamma}\right)^v}$$

$$= \frac{\gamma}{(1 + \gamma)^v - 1}$$

which holds exactly for $\tau \geq v$. Using methods based on renewal theory, it is a simple matter to derive replacement as a proportion of gross investment for *any* distribution of replacement over time.

5.3   Depreciation

5.3.1   Introduction

The durable goods model developed above is characterized by price-quantity duality. In this section we develop the depreciation model dual to the model of replacement developed in the preceding section. The price model relates the price of acquisition of investment goods to future time rental prices of capital input. It also relates changes in the acquisition price to the current time rental and current depreciation.

We begin presentation of the depreciation model by introducing an intertemporal price system. The *present price* of the ith commodity in period t, say p_{it}, is the present unit value of that commodity purchased in the present period for delivery in period t. We assume that present prices are positive and go to zero as time increases,

$$p_{it} > 0, \qquad \lim_{t \to \infty} p_{it} = 0 \, .$$

Similarly, the *future price* of the ith commodity in period t, say q_{it}, is the unit value of that commodity purchased in period t for delivery in that period.

The *rate of interest* (on money) is defined as

$$r_t = \frac{p_t - p_{t-1}}{p_t} \tag{5.31}$$

where p_t is the present price of money or the price of a bond maturing in period t so that $p_0 = 1$. The present price of money may be expressed in the form

$$p_t = \prod_{s=1}^{t} \frac{1}{1 + r_s}.$$

The present price of a commodity is the product of the future price and the present price of money

$$p_{i,t} = p_t q_{it} = \prod_{s=1}^{t} \frac{1}{1 + r_s} q_{it}.$$

By analogy with the rate of interest on money we may define the *own-rate of interest* on the ith commodity as

$$r_{it} = \frac{p_{i,t-1} - p_{it}}{p_{it}} \tag{5.32}$$

which is equivalent to

$$q_{it} r_{it} = q_{i,t-1} r_t - (q_{it} - q_{i,t-1})$$

the future price of the ith commodity in period t multiplied by the own-rate of interest on that commodity is equal to the money rate of interest multiplied by the future price of the commodity in period $t - 1$ plus the difference between the future price in period $t - 1$ and the price in period t.

5.3.2   Price-Quantity Duality

Capital stock is the sum of *past* acquisitions of capital goods weighted by their current *relative efficiency* given by the sequence $\{d_\tau\}$

$$K_t = \sum_{\tau=0}^{\infty} d_\tau A_{t-\tau}. \tag{5.33}$$

The price of acquisition of a capital good is the sum of *future* rental prices of capital services weighted by the relative efficiency of the capital good

$$p_{At} = \sum_{\tau=0}^{\infty} d_\tau p_{K,t+r+1} . \tag{5.34}$$

Replacement requirements are a weighted average of *past* investments with weights given by the *mortality distribution*

$$R_t = \sum_{t=1}^{\infty} m_\tau A_{t-\tau} . \tag{5.35}$$

Depreciation on a capital good p_{Dt} is a weighted average of *future* rental prices of capital services with weights given by the mortality distribution:

$$p_{Dt} = \sum_{\tau=1}^{\infty} m_\tau p_{K,t+\tau} . \tag{5.36}$$

Taking the first difference of the expression for the price of acquisition of a capital good

$$
\begin{aligned}
p_{At} - p_{A,t-1} &= - p_{Kt} - \sum_{\tau=1}^{\infty} (d_\tau - d_{\tau-1}) p_{K,t+\tau} \\
&= - p_{Kt} + \sum_{\tau=1}^{\infty} m_\tau p_{Kt+\tau} \\
&= - p_{Kt} + p_{Dt} .
\end{aligned}
\tag{5.37}
$$

The capital service price is equal to depreciation less the period-to-period change in the price of acquisition.

Finally, we may express the capital service price in terms of present and future changes in asset prices. First, we rewrite the expression for change in the asset price in the form

$$
\begin{aligned}
p_A - p_{A,t-1} &= - p_{Kt} + \sum_{\tau=1}^{\infty} m_\tau p_{K,t+\tau} \\
&= - p_{Kt} + \sum_{\tau=1}^{\infty} m_\tau T^\tau p_{Kt} \\
&= - p_{Kt} + m(T) p_{Kt}
\end{aligned}
$$

where T is the lead operator and $m(T)$ is a power series in the lead operator

$$m(T) = \sum_{\tau=1}^{\infty} m_\tau T^\tau \,.$$

Solving for the price of capital services, we obtain

$$p_{Kt} = \frac{1}{1 - m(T)} [\, p_{At} - p_{A,t-1}]$$

$$= - [1 + \delta(T)][\, p_{At} - p_{A,t-1}]$$

$$= - [\, p_{At} - p_{A,t-1}] - \sum_{\tau=1}^{\infty} \delta_\tau [\, p_{A,t+\tau} - p_{A,t+\tau-1}] \qquad (5.38)$$

where $\delta(T)$ is a power series in the lead operator. The sequence of coefficients $\{\delta_\tau\}$ is the *replacement distribution* and can be computed from the mortality distribution by means of the renewal equation (Feller, 1957).

Depreciation may be expressed in the form

$$p_{Dt} = - \sum_{\tau=1}^{\infty} \delta_\tau [\, p_{A,t+\tau} - p_{A,t+\tau-1}]$$

so that the *average depreciation rate* on the acquisition price of the capital good,

$$\bar{\delta} = \frac{p_{Dt}}{p_{At}} \qquad (5.39)$$

may be expressed as a weighted average of replacement rates,

$$\bar{\delta} = - \sum_{\tau=1}^{\infty} \delta_\tau \frac{[\, p_{A,t+\tau} - p_{A,t+\tau-1}]}{p_{At}}$$

or, alternatively,

$$= \sum_{\tau=1}^{\infty} \delta_\tau r_{A,t+\tau} \prod_{s=1}^{\tau-1} (1 - r_{A,t+s})$$

where

$$r_{At} = \frac{p_{At} - p_{A,t-1}}{p_{A,t-1}}$$

is the own-rate of interest on the acquisition of capital goods. The weights may be expressed in terms of changes in the forward acquisition prices of capital goods $\{p_{At}\}$.

The price of capital services may be expressed in the form

$$p_{Kt} = -[p_{At} - p_{A,t-1}] + \bar{\delta}p_{At}$$
$$= p_{At}[r_{At} + \bar{\delta}] \tag{5.40}$$

the capital service price is the product of the price of acquisition of investment gods and the sum of the current own-rate of interest on investment goods and the average depreciation rate. This expression for the capital service price is in terms of present prices. An analogous expression in terms of future prices is

$$q_{Kt} = q_{A,t-1}r_t + q_{At}\bar{\delta} - (q_{At} - q_{A,t-1})$$

where q_{Kt} is the future price of capital services, q_{At} is the future price of acquisition of investment goods and r_t is the rate of interest on money.

As before,[13] we illustrate these relationships by taking the relative efficiency distribution to be geometric,

$$d_\tau = (1 - \delta)^\tau \qquad (\tau = 0, 1, \ldots).$$

The mortality distribution is also geometric,

$$m_\tau = d_{\tau-1} - d_\tau = \delta(1 - \delta)^{\tau-1} \qquad (\tau = 1, 2, \ldots).$$

Finally, the replacement distribution is constant,

$$\delta_\tau = \delta \qquad (\tau = 1, 2, \ldots).$$

The price of acquisition of capital goods becomes

$$p_{At} = \sum_{\tau=0}^{\infty} (1 - \delta)^\tau p_{K,t+\tau+1}$$

depreciation may be expressed in the form

$$p_{Dt} = \sum_{\tau=1}^{\infty} \delta(1 - \delta)^{\tau-1} p_{K,t+\tau}$$

$$= \sum_{\tau=1}^{\infty} \delta(p_{A,t+\tau} - p_{A,t+\tau-1})$$
$$= \delta p_{A,t} \, .$$

The average depreciation rate p_{Dt}/p_{At} is a constant.

The capital service price may be expressed as:

$$p_{Kt} = p_{At}(r_{At} + \delta) \, .$$

The time rental of capital at any time depends only on the current price and own-rate of interest of capital goods and is independent of future prices; for arbitrarily given own-rates of interest geometric decline in efficiency is necessary and sufficient for independence of future prices. Alternatively, if the weights in the average depreciation rate are constant over time, the average rate is constant. In terms of future prices the time rental prices of capital services is

$$q_{Kt} = q_{A,t-1} r_t + q_{At}\delta - (q_{At} - q_{A,t-1})$$

for geometric decline in efficiency.

The replacement distribution $\{\delta_\tau\}$ enters the theory of investment behavior in two ways. First, the average rate of depreciation $\bar{\delta}$ entering the time rental price of capital services is a weighted average of replacement rates with weights determined by future own rates of interest on investment goods.[14] Second, the average rate of replacement $\hat{\delta}$ entering the determination of replacement requirements is a weighted average of replacement rates with weights determined by past net investment as a proportion of current capital stock. For the geometric mortality distribution replacement rates are constant and

$$\bar{\delta} = \hat{\delta} = \delta$$

where δ is the constant rate of replacement.

A fundamental result of renewal theory is that the sequence of replacement rates $\{\delta_\tau\}$ tends to a constant value for almost any mortality distribution (5.1). For the geometric mortality distribution the average rates of replacement, $\bar{\delta}$ and $\hat{\delta}$, are independent of future own-rates of interest or investment goods and of past net investments, respectively. For almost any mortality distribution these average rates of replacement are independent non-rates of interest on investments goods in the distant future and net investments in the distant past, since the sequence of replacement rates $\{\delta_\tau\}$ tends to a constant value as τ, the time elapsed since initial acquisition of an investment good, increases. The geometric distribution may be employed as an approximation to an arbitrary mortality distribution. The quality of this approximation depends on the speed of convergence of the sequence of replacement rates $\{\delta_\tau\}$ to a constant value and on the variation of weights that determine the average depreciation rate $\bar{\delta}$ and the average replacement rate $\hat{\delta}$. Even if the weights are constant, the average rates may be constant but unequal to each other.

5.4   Form of the Replacement Distribution

The geometric mortality distribution is very commonly employed in the estimation of replacement requirements in econometric studies of investment behavior. This distribution has been employed by Grunfeld in analyzing annual data on investment by individual firms and by Hickman in analyzing data on investment by industry groups (Grunfeld, 1960, Hickman, 1965). The geometric mortality distribution has also been extensively employed in measuring capital for social accounting purposes, as in Office of Business Economics capital goods studies (Grose, Rottenberg and Wasson, 1969). Although the geometric distribution may provide a useful approximation to an arbitrary mortality distribution in estimating replacement requirements, the validity of the approximation must be tested.

A direct test of the validity of the geometric approximation can be obtained from data on replacement investment and capital stock or from data on rental prices of capital goods and prices of used capital goods. Very little direct evidence is available on replacement requirements relative to the extensive evidence available on retirement of capital goods. As we have already emphasized, retirement is only part of the decline in efficiency that generates the mortality distribution. We now review the limited evidence on mortality distributions available from studies of replacement investment. Meyer and Kuh have studied the "echo effect" in analyzing data for individual firms (1957, pp. 91–100). An extreme form of the "echo effect" is associated with a periodic mortality distribution, resulting in a periodic distribution of replacements and periodic cycles of replacement investment.[15] A weaker form of the echo effect is associated with relatively high values of the replacement distribution at particular ages. This is the form of the echo effect tested by Meyer and Kuh. The age of a firm's capital equipment is measured by acumulated depreciation reserves divided by gross fixed assets at the beginning of the period. Firms are divided into fifteen industry groups within manufacturing, corresponding roughly to two-digit industries (Meyer and Kuh, 1957, pp. 209–232). The dependent variable is gross investment divided by gross fixed assets on the grounds ". . . that since replacement investment is included in gross investment the net impact of the echo effect should be ascertainable even when using gross investment as the dependent variable—although perhaps not as precisely as would be desirable" (Meyer and Kuh, 1957, p. 93).

Meyer and Kuh employ a profit model and a sales model to explain gross investment. In regressions for averages of annual data over the period 1946–1950 the age variable is significant in both models for only one industry group—Vehicles and Suppliers; age is significantly negative for this industry, suggesting high rates of replacement for low ages of capital goods (Meyer and Kuh, 1957, pp. 255–256). For other industry groups the age variable is both positive and negative with small negative values predominating. Age is significantly negative for Light Chemicals in the sales model but not in the profits model. The proportion of significant results—three out of thirty regressions—is not out of line with the null hypothesis that the echo effect plays no role in the determination of investment for individual firms. It may be noted that these results hold for the immediate postwar period, when the assumption of constant weights for the average replacement rate $\hat{\delta}$, based on a constant growth rate of capital stock, is least likely to hold. The validity of the geometric approximation evidenced in these data may be attributed to relatively rapid convergence of the sequence of replacement rates $\{\delta_\tau\}$ to a constant value.[16]

As alternative test of the validity of the geometric approximation has been proposed by Feldstein and Foot (1971). If data on replacement investment and capital stock are available separately, the geometric approximation may be tested by analyzing the ratio of replacement investment to capital stock. This variable is, of course, the average rate of replacement $\hat{\delta}$. The average replacement rate depends on the time path of past net investment; the geometric approximation may be tested by regressing the average replacement rate on lagged values of net investment divided by current capital stock. If the geometric approximation is appropriate, the average replacement rate is a constant and is independent of lagged values of net investment. Obviously, this test requires data on both replacement investment and capital stock; net investment can be calculated only by observing period-to-period changes in capital stock; the level of capital stock is required to compute the average replacement rate $\hat{\delta}$. Feldstein and Foot have obtained data on replacement investment from the McGraw-Hill survey. However, this survey does not provide the corresponding data on capital stock, so that a test of the geometric approximation cannot be carried out.

Feldstein and Foot compute average replacement rates using perpetual inventory estimates of capital stock for the manufacturing sector by the Department of Commerce (Grose, Rottenberg and Wasson, 1969). In these estimates a fixed mortality distribution is applied to past data on gross investment. Capital stock is a weighted sum of past acquisitions of investment goods with each acquisition weighted by its relative efficiency (5.3). Of course, the capital stock estimates imply a set of estimates of replacement investment; replacement investment is a weighted sum of past acquisitions with weights given by the mortality distribution (5.2). This set of estimates of replacement investment is, of course, distinct from the estimates of Feldstein and Foot, based on the McGraw-Hill survey. It would be possible to estimate a regression of the average replacement rate $\hat{\delta}$ implicit in the Department of Commerce estimates of capital stock on past net investments as a proportion of current capital stock with past net investments also derived from the Department of Commerce estimates of capital stock. However, this would result in a set of coefficients equal to the replacement rates implicit in the mortality distribution employed in the Department of Commerce perpetual inventory estimates. Regression of this type would provide no independent evidence on the mortality or replacement distributions.

Feldstein and Foot proceed with a statistical analysis of average replacement rates computed from McGraw-Hill survey estimates of replacement investment and Department of Commerce estimates of capital stock. Their first error is to employ Department of Commerce data on gross capital stock in estimating the average replacement rate $\hat{\delta}$ (Feldstein and Foot, 1971, p. 52). Gross capital stock is an unweighted sum of past gross investments; the average replacement rate is the ratio of replacement investment to a weighted sum of past gross investment with weights given by the relative efficiency of capital goods of different ages. Second, Feldstein and Foot regress the average replacement rate on variables such as cash flow and capacity utilization. If the decline in efficiency of capital goods depends on cash flow and relative utilization in each period, the perpetual inventory estimates of capital stock of the Department of Commerce are inappropriate. In the perpetual inventory method decline in relative efficiency is independent of time and also of variables that are functions of time, such as cash flow or capacity utilization. The relative efficiency of a capital good depends only on the age of the capital good and not on time or of the variables. The hypothesis that the average replacement rate depends on cash flow or capacity utilization contradicts the assumptions underlying the Department of Commerce perpetual inventory estimates of capital stock. Either the perpetual inventory method is valid and the average replacement rate depends on the proportion of past net investments in current capital stock or the average replacement rate depends on such variables as time, cash flow and capacity utilization and the perpetual inventory method is invalid. Feldstein and Foot use perpetual inventory estimates of capital stock in estimating the average replacement rate and regress the average replacement rate so estimated on cash flow and capacity utilization, which is self-contradictory.

We conclude that Feldstein and Foot have not successfully avoided the necessity for direct observation of both replacement investment and capital stock in studying the validity of the geometric approximation to the replacement distribution. The use of perpetual inventory estimates of capital stock implies that the average replacement rate calculated from an internally consistent body of data, replacement investment and capital stock estimated by the perpetual inventory method, depends only on the proportions of past net investments in current capital stock. Analysis of this relationship by statistical methods is superfluous since a regression of the average replacement rate on the ratios of past net investments to current capital stock will simply generate the replacement distribution implicit in the mortality distribution employed in the perpetual inventory method. Regressions of average replacement rates on variables such as cash flow or capacity utilization are self-contradictory. The conclusions of Feldstein and Foot, based on regressions of this type, are vitiated by this elementary error.

We have reviewed evidence on the mortality distribution from studies of replacement requirements. An alternative approach to the empirical study of mortality distributions is through the analysis of used equipment prices. Data on used equipment prices are limited to readily moveable assets. A study of price data for farm tractors is reported by Griliches (1960, pp. 181–210) and studies of price data for automobiles are presented by Cagan (1965) and Wykoff (1970). A much more intensive study of price data for pick-up trucks is given by Hall (1971a, pp. 240–271). Used equipment prices, like prices for acquisition of new equipment, are equal to the sum of future rental prices weighted by the relative efficiency of the capital good over its remaining lifetime. For equipment of age σ at time t, the acquisition price is

$$p^\sigma_{At} = \sum_{\tau=0}^{\infty} d_{\tau+\sigma} p_{K,t+\tau+1}. \tag{5.41}$$

For geometric decline in efficiency the acquisition prices decline geometrically with age, since

$$p^\sigma_{At} = \sum_{\tau=0}^{\infty} (1-\delta)^{\tau+\sigma} p_{K,t+\tau+1}$$

$$= (1-\delta)^\sigma \sum_{\tau=0}^{\infty} (1-\delta)^\tau p_{K,t+\tau+1}$$

$$= (1-\delta)^\sigma p_{At}.$$

We now review the evidence on decline in relative efficiency from data on used equipment prices.

Studies of prices of acquisition of new and used capital goods reveal a sharp drop between the price of new equipment and the price of used equipment. The obvious explanation is that prices of new equipment are "list" prices paid by relatively few purchases. The actual prices paid vary over a model year, declining as a new model year approaches; this variation is omitted from the observed list prices. The prices of used equipment are based on actual transactions and vary over the year.[17] From an examination of prices of used farm tractors ages one to thirteen for ten different points of time during the years 1937–1958, Griliches concludes: "The data point to a declining balance [geometric] depreciation model, with a rate somewhat higher in the 1930s than in the 1950s" (1960, p. 198). Wykoff's findings for used automobiles ages one to seven for five different points of time during the years 1950–1968, are similar: "After the first year cars do appear to decay exponentially [geometrically]" (1970, pp. 171–172). Cagan also finds that geometric depreciation provides a satisfactory approximation (1965, pp. 225–226).

Hall's study of pick-up trucks includes an estimate of the mortality distribution in a statistical model that also provides estimates of the time pattern of the price of acquisition of new capital goods, and an index of embodied technological change. The data are prices for secondhand pick-up trucks ages one to six for the years 1961–1967. Two makes of pick-up trucks, Ford and Chevrolet, are included in the study. Hall first fits a model of used equipment prices separately to data for both makes. He then tests the hypothesis that the two makes are perfect substitutes in the sense that prices of acquisition of new capital goods move in fixed proportion to each other. This hypothesis is accepted at a level of significance of 0.05. He then imposes this hypothesis and tests the hypothesis that the mortality distribution is the same for both makes. This hypothesis is also accepted at a level of significance of 0.05. He imposes these two hypotheses and tests the hypothesis that the index of embodied technical change is the same for both makes; again the hypothesis is accepted. Finally, he imposes the hypotheses that the prices of acquisition of the two makes are proportional, that the mortality distribution is the same for the two makes, and that the index of embodied technical change is the same for both makes, and tests the hypothesis that the mortality distribution is geometric. The critical value of F at a level of significance of 0.05 is 2.57; the compound value of F is 3.59. Hall also tests the hypothesis that the index of embodied technical change is geometric.

The statistical design employed by Hall is not the most natural one for the sequence of tests he carries out. Five hypotheses are tested on the same data, used equipment prices for Fords and Chevrolets, 1961–1967. A "nested" structure for all five would be: (a) the two makes are perfect substitutes, (b) the mortality distribution is the same for both makes, (c) the index of embodied technical change is the same for both makes, (d) the mortality distribution is geometric, (e) the index of embodied technical change is geometric. The level of significance for all five tests is, approximately, the sum of levels of significance at each stage. Controlling the overall level of significance, the probability of rejecting at least one hypothesis when it is true, at 0.05, the level of significance at each stage would be 0.01. Hall's statistical design differs in two respects from this proposed design. First, the hypothesis that the index of embodied technical change is geometric is tested out of sequence so that the associated test statistic is not distributed independently of test statistics for the other hypotheses. Second, a level of significance of 0.05 is used for each hypothesis, so that the overall length of significance is close to 0.25. Employing the nested design we obtain the results in table 5.1. Test statistics for each of the hypothesis and critical values for these statistics are given in the first part of this table.[18] Test statistics for the nested sequence of hypotheses outlined above are given in the second part of the table.

A second problem with Hall's test procedure arises from the assumption that errors for the two makes of pick-up trucks have the same variance and that these errors are distributed independently in each period. The residual variance for Chevrolets is 0.0006133; the variance for Fords is 0.0002991 or less than half that for Chevrolets. The covariance between error for the two makes is 0.0003315, so that the correlation is 0.774. Hall's assumption of equal variances and zero covariance for the two makes is clearly inconsistent with the evidence.

Table 5.1
Test statistics for Hall's study of pick-up trucks*

Calculated F-statistics		Critical values	
		0.05	0.01
Full F-tests			
Same p:	$F(7, 40) = 0.86$	2.25	3.12
Same D:	$F(5, 40) = 0.00$	2.45	3.51
Same b:	$F(10, 40) = 1.00$	2.07	2.80
Geom. D:	$F(8, 40) = 1.71$	2.18	2.99
Geom. b:	$F(20, 40) = 6.35$	1.84	2.37
Nested F-tests			
Same p:	$F(7, 40) = 0.86$	2.25	3.12
Same D:	$F(5, 47) = 0.50$	2.41	3.43
Same b:	$F(10, 52) = 0.79$	2.01	2.68
Geom. D:	$F(4, 62) = 3.66$	2.51	3.64
Geom. b:	$F(10, 66) = 13.73$	1.98	2.61

* The hypotheses tested are:
Same p: The two makes are perfect substitutes.
Same D: The mortality distribution is the same for both makes.
Same b: The index of embodied technical change is the same for both makes.
Geom. D: The mortality distribution is geometric.
Geom. b: The index of embodied technical change is geometric.

Table 5.2
Test statistics for Hall's study of pick-up trucks,
estimated variance-covariance matrix*

Calculated F-statistics		Critical values	
		0.05	0.01
Full F-tests			
Same p:	$F(7, 40) = 2.92$	2.25	3.12
Same D:	$F(5, 40) = 0.84$	2.45	3.51
Same b:	$F(10, 40) = 3.34$	2.07	2.80
Geom. D:	$F(8, 40) = 1.00$	2.18	2.99
Geom. b:	$F(20, 40) = 4.66$	1.84	2.37
Nested F-tests			
Same p:	$F(7, 40) = 2.92$	2.25	3.12
Same D:	$F(5, 47) = 1.30$	2.41	3.43
Same b:	$F(10, 52) = 1.99$	2.01	2.68
Geom. D:	$F(4, 62) = 0.92$	2.51	3.64
Geom. b:	$F(10, 66) = 4.78$	1.98	2.61

* The hypotheses tested are the same as those in table
5.1. The test statistics are distributed asymptotically
as F-ratios.

Test statistics for each of the hypotheses and critical values for these
statistics are given in table 5.2;[19] the format of this table is the same as
that for table 5.1. The results differ substantially from those of Hall.
First, at levels of significance of 0.01 for each stage the only hypothesis
rejected is that the index of embodied technical change is geometric.
At levels of significance of 0.05 or an overall level of significance of
0.25 for all five stages, the hypotheses that the makes are perfect substitutes would be rejected. Hall's conclusion is that ". . . the geometric
[mortality distribution] function is probably a reasonable approximation for many purposes. Certainly, there are no grounds for believing
that any very serious error has been committed by using a geometric
deterioration function in calculating capital stock" (Hall, 1971a). The
fitted relative efficiency sequence, normalizing on the value of the
function at age one year is $d_1 = 1.000$, $d_2 = 0.828$, $d_3 = 0.693$, $d_4 = 0.581$,
$d_5 = 0.475$, $d_6 = 0.381$ (Hall, 1971a). We conclude that Hall's data on
the mortality distribution for pick-up trucks supports the conclusions
of Cagan, Griliches and Wykoff for automobiles and farm tractors.
The geometric mortality distribution explains the behavior of used
equipment prices for all three types of capital goods.

5.5 Summary and Conclusion

In this paper we have presented the economic theory of replacement and its dual, the economic theory of depreciation. This theory is based on the durable goods model of capital, relating capital stock to past acquisitions of capital goods and changes in capital stock to current acquisitions and current replacement requirements. Replacement requirements are determined by losses in efficiency of existing capital goods as well as by retirements. Retirement represents the point at which efficiency declines to zero. A large body of evidence exists on the age of retirement of capital goods, but relatively little evidence is available on losses in efficiency of existing capital goods.

A fundamental result of renewal theory is that the replacement distribution corresponding to almost any morality distribution converges to a constant value. This result suggests the possibility of approximating replacement requirements and the time rental value of capital services by means of a geometric mortality distribution with constant replacement rate δ. For this approximation the average replacement rate determining replacement requirements $\hat{\delta}$ is constant and equal to the replacement rate δ. The usefulness of the geometric approximation depends on the speed of convergence of the replacement distribution to its constant asymptotic value and in variation in the weights that determine the average replacement rate $\hat{\delta}$.

The geometric mortality distribution has been employed for estimating replacement requirements in national wealth accounting and in econometric studies of investment behavior. Direct tests of the validity of this approximation have been made by Meyer and Kuh in analyzing replacement requirements. They find that replacement requirements as a proportion of capital stock are independent of the age of capital stock, an implication of the geometric mortality distribution.

The durable goods model that underlies our theory of replacement is characterized by price-quantity duality. The level of acquisition of capital goods is dual to the rental price of capital services. Capital stock is dual to the acquisition price of capital goods. Replacement requirements, a component of investment expenditures, are dual to depreciation, a component of the rental price of capital services. Beginning with the expression of the acquisition price of a capital good as the value of future capital services we derive a model of the time rental price of capital input. This model provides the basis for further empirical investigation of the form of the mortality distribution through analysis of data on used equipment prices.

The empirical evidence from studies of used equipment prices supports the findings of Meyer and Kuh from an analysis of replacement requirements.[20] The empirical evidence on the decline in efficiency of capital goods is limited to assets for which a secondhand market exists and to overall replacement requirements. This evidence is consistent with the geometric mortality distribution. The use of this distribution in econometric studies of investment behavior may also be justified as an approximation to an arbitrary mortality distribution.

Notes

1. See, for example, G. Debreu (1959), J. Hicks (1946) and P. A. Samuelson (1947).
2. This analogy has been developed extensively by I. Fisher (1961), J. Hicks (1946), E. Lindahl (1939) and E. Malinvaud (1953).
3. The durable goods model was developed by L. Walras (1954), G. Åkerman (1923) and K. Wicksell (1934b).
4. The dual to the durable goods model was developed by K. J. Arrow (1964) and R. E. Hall (1968), on the basis of earlier work by H. S. Hotelling (1925) and T. Haavelmo (1960a).
5. The assumption that relative efficiency depends only on the age of durable equipment is dropped by Hall (1968). Variations in efficiency among capital goods of the same age acquired at different times correspond to "embodied" technical change. Variations in efficiency among capital goods of the same age used at different times correspond to "disembodied" technical change. This terminology coincides with that of R. M. Solow (1960, pp. 89–104).
6. We assume that the proportions are nonrandom; for a treatment of the economic theory of replacement with random deterioration in efficiency, see Jorgenson, McCall and Radner (1967).
7. A relatively recent work on capital equipment is in Marston, Winfrey and Hempstead (1953). The classic work in the field is by Kurtz (1930) which provides other references.
8. See section 5.4 for a review of the evidence.
9. A representative study is the OBE Capital Goods Study; in this research straight-line and double declining balance methods are employed (Grose, Rottenberg and Wasson, 1969, pp. 46–52).
10. This distribution is employed by Y. Grunfeld (1960) for individual firms and by B. Hickman (1965) for industry groups.
11. See Feller (1957, p. 286, Theorem 3). Proof of this theorem is given on pp. 306–307.
12. See Feller (1957, p. 287, Theorem 4).
13. See section 5.2.1.
14. See formula (5.39), above.
15. See section 5.2.2.
16. See section 5.2.
17. This argument is developed by Griliches (1960, p. 198, fn. 32).
18. The empirical study reported in tables 5.1 and 5.2 was carried out by Rafael Weston.
19. See Note 11, above.
20. See Meyer and Kuh (1957).

6

Investment and Production: A Review

Dale W. Jorgenson

6.1 Introduction

In the past decade the econometric study of investment behavior has developed from empirical comparisons of alternative determinants of investment expenditures to increasingly explicit theories of producer behavior. As a consequence of these developments econometric studies of investment and production have become closely interrelated. In an earlier survey paper we considered the implications of econometric studies of investment for the theory of investment and production (Jorgenson, 1971a). In this paper we consider the implications of econometric studies of production for the theory. We focus attention on empirical studies of cross section and time-series data for manufacturing industries in the U.S.

The point of departure for the modern approach to the econometric study of investment has been the flexible accelerator model of Chenery and Koyck (Chenery, 1952; Koyck, 1954). In this model capital is adjusted toward its desired level by a constant proportion of the difference between desired and actual capital. Denoting the actual level of capital by K and the desired level by K^+, the flexible accelerator model can be written:

$$K_t - K_{t-1} = [1 - \lambda][K_t - K_{t-1}^+]. \qquad (6.1)$$

Alternatively, actual capital can be represented as a weighted average of all past levels of desired capital with geometrically declining weights:

$$K_t = [1 - \lambda] \sum_{\tau=0}^{\infty} \lambda^\tau K_{t-\tau}^+. \qquad (6.2)$$

These two forms of the flexible accelerator model are, of course, equivalent.

The flexible accelerator mechanism can be transformed into a complete theory of investment behavior by adding a specification of the desired level of capital and a model of replacement investment. The choice of a model of replacement is important since replacement investment predominates in total investment expenditures, at least at the aggregate level.[1] The geometric mortality distribution has been widely adopted for empirical work; for this distribution replacement is proportional to actual capital stock (Hickman, 1965; Jorgenson, 1963, 1965). Under this assumption the change in capital stock may be written

$$K_t - K_{t-1} = A_t - \delta K_{t-1}, \tag{6.3}$$

where A is gross investment and δ the rate of replacement. Combining the geometric model of replacement with the flexible accelerator model of net investment, we obtain a model of investment expenditures:

$$A_t = [1 - \lambda][K_t^+ - K_{t-1}] + \delta K_{t-1}. \tag{6.4}$$

In the economic theory of investment behavior the form of the optimal policy depends critically on the character of returns to scale. For diminishing returns the optimal policy determines an optimal long-run level of capital input and associated levels of output and labor input for any set of prices of output, labor input, and capital input. The optimal path for capital accumulation converges to the optimal values of output, capital input, and labor input (Treadway, 1969). For constant returns to scale the optimal policy determines an optimal rate of growth of capital and associated capital-output and labor-output ratios for any set of prices of output, labor input, and capital input (Lucas, 1967a; Uzawa, 1969). Both forms of the optimal policy for capital accumulation are associated with distributed lag functions for net investment based on the flexible accelerator of Chenery and Koyck.

The interpretation of the desired level of capital stock in a distributed lag investment function is very different under constant returns to scale and under diminishing returns. Under diminishing returns the desired level of capital is the long-run equilibrium level and depends on the prices of output, labor input, and capital input.

Under constant returns to scale there is no long-run equilibrium level of capital; desired capital is a perpetually moving target to which actual capital never converges. Failure to distinguish between these two alternative interpretations of desired capital has been an important source of confusion in theoretical studies of investment and in the interpretation of empirical work.[2]

Econometric models of investment behavior differ substantially in the determinants of desired capital. In the original form of the flexible accelerator model desired capital is proportional to output and the constant of proportionality or accelerator coefficient is determined by technology. This description of technology is consistent with the "fixed coefficients" productions function of Walras and Leontief (Walras, 1954; Leontief, 1951). The "fixed coefficients" production function is characterized by constant capital-output and labor-output coefficients and has constant returns to scale and elasticity of substitution zero. For this description of technology capacity utilization of output provides the only significant determinant of desired capital. The investment models of Bourneuf, Eisner, Evans, Hickman, and Kuh reduce to the flexible accelerator model of Chenery and Koyck with desired capital proportional to output.[3]

The empirical evidence now available from econometric studies of investment behavior strongly supports the hypothesis that real output is not the only significant determinant of desired capital. Profits, internal funds, or liquidity are highly correlated with output and do not play an independent role in the determination of investment expenditures (Jorgenson, 1971a, pp. 1130–1134). However, the cost of external finance is an important determinant of desired capital (Jorgenson, 1971a, pp. 1133–1134). The introduction of financial considerations together with variations in output necessitates substantial modification of the flexible accelerator model of Chenery and Koyck. Studies of investment by individual firms by Jorgenson and Siebert and studies of industry groups by Jorgenson and Stephenson embody a description of technology based on a Cobb-Douglas production function (Douglas, 1948; Wicksell, 1934a) with constant returns to scale and elasticity of substitution equal to unity.[4] For this description of technology the cost of capital plays an important role in the determination of investment.

Our primary objective in this survey is to review the empirical evidence on the description of technology appropriate for an econometric model of investment behavior. Given the description of technology the proper rule of output and the cost of capital as determinants of investment behavior can be assessed. Our second objective is to examine the empirical evidence on returns to scale in order to select an appropriate interpretation of desired capital in the theory of investment behavior. The evidence requires careful examination since increasing returns to scale cannot be excluded as a possible characterization of technology. Increasing returns imply the failure of the usual marginal conditions for an optimal production plan. Evidence of increasing returns must be based on direct estimation of the production function rather than relationships implied by the marginal conditions.

A complete description of technology for the theory of investment and production requires specification of the form of the production function and the character of returns to scale. A convenient framework for the description of technology is provided by the constant elasticity of substitution (CES) production function proposed by Arrow *et al.* (1961). This form of the production function has been extended to incorporate decreasing, constant, or increasing returns to scale by Dhrymes and Kmenta (Dhrymes, 1965; Kmenta, 1967). The CES production function can be written

$$Q = \gamma [\delta K^{-\rho} + (1 - \delta) L^{-\rho}]^{-v/\rho}, \tag{6.5}$$

where Q is output, L is labor input, γ is the efficiency parameter, δ the distribution parameter, ρ the substitution parameter, and v the scale parameter. The elasticity of substitution σ is equal to $1/1 + \rho$ (Allen, 1938, pp. 340–345). The scale parameter is the degree of homogeneity of the production function.[5]

As the substitution parameter ρ becomes infinite the CES production function approaches the "fixed coefficients" production function. As the substitution parameter goes to zero, the limiting production function is Cobb-Douglas in form. For these two limiting cases the elasticity of substitution is zero or unity, respectively. Under constant returns to scale, $v = 1$, the marginal conditions for producer equilibrium with no costs of adjustment are

$$\frac{\partial Q}{\partial L} = \gamma^{-\rho}(1 - \delta) \left(\frac{Q}{L} \right)^{1 + \rho} = \frac{q_L}{q_Q},$$

$$\frac{\partial Q}{\partial K} = \gamma^{-\rho}\delta \left(\frac{Q}{K} \right)^{1 + \rho} = \frac{q_K}{q_Q}, \tag{6.6}$$

where q_Q is the price of output, q_L the price of labor input, and q_K the price of capital input. With costs of adjustment, the second marginal condition is replaced by

$$\frac{\partial Q}{\partial K} = \frac{q_K}{q_Q} - \frac{q_K}{q_I}\frac{\partial Q}{\partial I}, \tag{6.7}$$

where $\partial Q/\partial I$ is the change in output with respect to investment and q_I is the price of investment goods.[6] In this form the marginal condition can be approximated by a distributed lag investment function.[7]

6.2   Form of the Production Function: Cross Sections

We turn next to an examination of the empirical evidence on the form of the production function. The original empirical study by Arrow *et al.* was based on internal cross sections of data on output and labor input for three-digit manufacturing industries. The major conclusions of this study are: (1) The elasticity of substitution is different from zero. (2) The elasticity of substitution is significantly below unity. The first of these conclusions holds for every industry group included in the original study. The record holds for only ten of 24 industry groups.[8] Fuchs has run regressions for the same groups, inserting a dummy variable to allow for differences in level of development among the countries included in the sample (Fuchs, 1963). The results confirm the first conclusion of Arrow *et al.* but not the second. For only two industry groups is the estimated elasticity of substitution significantly different from unity and in one of these it is significantly *above* unity. We conclude that the finding of Arrow *et al.* that the elasticity is less than unity results from a bias due to variations in labor quality of the price of output between developed and less developed countries.

We next review evidence on the elasticity of substitution from cross section studies for two-digit manufacturing industries in the U.S. The empirical literature through 1967 has been surveyed by Griliches, Lucas, and Nerlove.[9] We focus attention on empirical studies that have become available since 1967.[10] Important sources of bias in estimation of the elasticity of substitution in earlier studies have been removed in later ones. Discrepancies between alternative estimates from the same body of data have been traced to an error in reporting the results. Evidence has now accumulated that the elasticity of substitution can be estimated reliably from cross sections and from successive cross sections. The most important evidence of this type has been reported by Zarembka (1970, pp. 48–49).

Zarembka has estimated the elasticity of substitution for two separate cross sections of states for 1957 and 1958, taking into account possible serial correlation in the errors for the two periods. Data on labor input and wage rates are corrected for quality change, but the effects of differences in product prices or regional differences in efficiency appear as possible sources of serial correlation (Zarembka, 1970, p. 49). The estimated elasticities for the two periods and an F-ratio for a test of the hypothesis that the parameters are the same is given in columns (a), (b), and (c) of table 6.1. The estimated elasticities for the two periods are not significantly different for 11 of the 13 industries at a significance level of 0.025.

Proceeding conditionally on the hypothesis that elasticities of substitution are the same for the two years 1957 and 1958, Zarembka estimates the elasticity from data fo both years, again taking into account the possibility of serial correlation in errors for the two years. The results are presented in column (d) of table 6.1. For only two of the industry groups is the estimated elasticity of substitution significantly different from unity at a significance level of 0.025. The test statistic for this hypothesis and the F-ratio of column (c) are distributed independently since the two hypotheses are "nested." The overall level of significance for the two tests is, of course, 0.05. For all but one industry group the estimated elasticity is significantly different from zero, corroborating the results of Arrow *et al.* Zarembka concludes:

... that the elasticity of substitution does not in general depart significantly from unity. Therefore, the more complicated CES production function simplifies to the Cobb-Douglas. (Zarembka, 1970, p. 51.)

The results of Zarembka are for data on output and labor input for successive cross sections of states in 1957 and 1958. These data have also been analyzed by Griliches (1967a, pp. 290–294). The statistical model employed by Zarembka is similar to that of Griliches, except that Griliches maintains the hypothesis of equality of the elasticities of substitution for the two time periods, while Zarembka tests this hypothesis. Further, Zarembka's estimator is more efficient, since Griliches ignores constraints on the parameters of the model and estimates this model by ordinary least squares (Griliches, 1967c, pp. 291–294). Data for cross sections of states have been analyzed by

Table 6.1
Estimates of the elasticity of substitution for two-digit manufacturing
industries in the U.S., by Zarembka

Industry group	(a) 1957*	(b) 1958*	(c) F-ratio*	(d) Both years*
Food	0.96 (0.19)	1.01 (0.14)	0.12	1.01 (0.14)
Textile	0.79 (0.17)	0.91 (0.18)	0.73	0.84 (0.16)
Apparel	0.96 (0.21)	0.86 (0.18)	0.87	0.88 (0.19)
Furniture	1.13 (0.19)	1.07 (0.12)	0.11	1.08 (0.11)
Paper	0.88 (0.34)	0.72 (0.25)	0.40	0.77 (0.26)
Chemicals	1.15 (0.24)	0.92 (0.27)	2.88	1.11 (0.24)
Petroleum	1.06 (0.40)	0.31 (0.58)	3.18	1.00 (0.42)
Stone, clay, glass	0.77 (0.25)	0.64 (0.23)	0.48	0.70 (0.22)
Primary metals	1.17 (0.26)	1.81 (0.26)	12.26	1.43 (0.25)
Fabricated metals	0.59 (0.14)	0.67 (0.15)	0.35	0.63 (0.13)
Machinery, excluding electrical	1.36 (0.32)	1.13 (0.28)	0.93	1.22 (0.26)
Electrical machinery	0.63 (0.24)	0.21 (0.21)	5.89	0.38 (0.21)
Transportation equipment	1.49 (0.49)	1.47 (0.33)	0.01	1.46 (0.32)

* Source: Zarembka (1970), table 1, p. 50.

Bell and Minasian for 1957 and Dhrymes for 1958 (Bell, 1964;
Minasian, 1969; Dhrymes, 1965). Solow has estimated the elasticity of
substitution for a cross section of regions for 1956 (Solow, 1964,
pp. 101–128). The results of Bell, Griliches, Minasian, and Solow are
similar to those of Zarembka (Jorgenson, 1972, pp. 229–235). The
results originally reported by Dhrymes are described as based on a
regression of the output-labor ratio on the wage rate (Dhrymes, 1965,
pp. 357–358). Subsequently, Zarembka discovered that the reported
results are for a regression of the wage rate on the output-labor ratio.

The corrected version of Dhrymes' results is very similar to the results of Zarembka (Dhrymes and Zarembka, 1970, pp. 115–117).

Nerlove has compared the results of Minasian with the uncorrected version of Dhrymes' results as follows:

... results obtained by Dhrymes ... are based on logarithmic regressions of value, added per unit of labor on the wage rate across states in 1957. Even though these results appear to be based on substantially the same data (individual states, 1957) as those obtained by Minasian, it is clear ... that they differ very substantially from the corresponding estimates obtained by Minasian. For example, Minasian's estimate of σ for pulp, paper, and products is nearly eight times Dhrymes', while his estimate of σ for primary metal products is nearly ten times Dhrymes'. Conversely, Minasian's estimate for rubber products is double Dhrymes'. The only explanation for these gross differences appears to be slight variation in the basic series employed. (Nerlove, 1967, p. 74).

The correct explanation is more straightforward, namely that Dhrymes' reported results, as originally reported, are erroneous.

Griliches has compared his results with the original results reported by Dhrymes. In discussing this discrepancy Griliches reports that:

The major difference ... is in the definition of labor and the associated wage rate. Dhrymes defines labor as total employment and the associated "wage rate" as total payrolls/total employment. I define the "wage rate" as the average wage rate per hour of production workers (given by production worker wages/total man hours of production workers) and the associated "labor input" measure as total man hours in production worker hour equivalents. (Griliches, 1967b, p. 608.)

This difference is adduced as an explanation of the discrepancy between Griliches' results (for states in 1958) and Dhrymes' results (for states in 1957). Dhrymes' corrected results are closely comparable to those of Griliches. Neither the difference in concept nor the difference in time period results in substantial discrepancies between the two sets of results.

We conclude that evidence on the elasticity of substitution from cross sections for two-digit manufacturing industries in the U.S. is consistent with the Cobb-Douglas form of the production function. Estimated elasticities of substitution for cross sections of states in 1957 and 1958 by Zarembka, taking into account possible serial correlation in the residuals for the two years, are not significantly different from unity. These results are consistent with those of Bell, Dhrymes, and Minasian for cross sections of states for a given year, with those of

Griliches for successive cross sections, and with those of Solow for a cross section of regions. Second, this evidence is inconsistent with the "fixed coefficients" production function, that is, with constant capital-output and labor-output ratios. The empirical results support the conclusion of Arrow *et al.* that the elasticity of substitution is significantly different from zero.

6.3   Form of the Production Function: Time Series

The evidence on the form of the production function we have reviewed up to this point is based on cross sections for two-digit industries within manufacturing. We turn next to evidence based on time series. Ferguson has presented estimates of the elasticity of substitution from data on labor input and output for two-digit industries within U.S. manufacturing for the period 1949–1961 that are very similar to the cross section results (Ferguson, 1965). Lucas and McKinnon have reported estimates for these industries that are substantially lower than the cross section estimates (Lucas, 1969; McKinnon, 1962). Coen has given estimates of the elasticity of substitution for total manufacturing that are similar to those of Lucas and McKinnon (Coen, 1969). A careful investigation of possible sources of bias in time series estimates has been carried out by Berndt, using data on both labor and capital input (Berndt, 1976). We turn now to a review of the time series evidence presented by Berndt.

Berndt has compared five different methods for constructing estimates of the rental rate for capital services. The rental price for a depreciable asset is

$$q_{K,t} = \frac{1 - u_t z_t - k_t + y_t}{1 - u_t} \, [q_{a,t-1} r_t + q_{A,t} \delta - (q_{A,t} - q_{A,t-1})] + q_{A,t} \tau_t, \quad (6.8)$$

where $q_{A,t}$ is the asset price, r_t the after-tax cost of capital, and δ the rate of replacement. The tax structure is introduced through the variables u_t the corporate income tax rate, z_t the discounted value of depreciation allowances for tax purposes, k_t the rate of the investment tax credit, $y_t = k_t u_t z_t$, and τ_t the property tax rate. This form of the rental price for depreciable assets was developed by Christensen and Jorgenson, based on earlier work by Hall and Jorgenson (Christensen and Jorgenson, 1969). Berndt estimates the variables that appear in this formula separately for plan and equipment in U.S. total manufacturing, 1929–1968, and combines data for plant and equipment to obtain an estimate of the overall rental price of capital. He combines data for capital and labor to obtain a measure of output, corrected for technical change. This measure of output, like that of capital services, depends on the method for measuring the rental price of capital.

Alternative methods for measuring the price of capital services employed by Berndt are summarized in table 6.2. In the first set of estimates (A) all tax variables are set equal to zero, the before-tax and after-tax cost of capital is set equal to Moody's AAA bond yield, the capital gains term $q_{A,t} - q_{A,t-1}$ is ignored, and fixed weights are used to combine data for plant and equipment into an overall rental price of capital. In the second set of estimates (B) all tax variables are set equal to the statutory rates, except for the property tax rate, which is set equal to zero. The before-tax cost of capital is treated as constant at 20% per year, capital gains are ignored, and fixed weights are used to combine data for plant and equipment. In the third set of estimates (C) all tax variables are set equal to their effective rates and data for plant and equipment are combined by means of a Divisia index rather than a fixed weight index. In the fourth set of estimates (D) the before-tax cost of capital is set equal to its effective nominal rate. In the fifth set of estimates (E) the before-tax cost of capital is set equal to its effective real rate.

Moody's AAA bond rate has been employed as a measure of the cost of capital in Grunfeld's study of time series data on investment by

Table 6.2
Alternative procedures used to construct $q_K{}^*$

q_K index	Tax variables	Before-tax cost of capital	Capital gains	Aggregation procedure used to construct q_K
A	All zero	Moody AAA bond yield	Ignored	Fixed weights
B	Statutory rates except τ_t = zero	Constant 0.20	Ignored	Fixed weights
C	Effective rates	Constant 0.20	Ignored	Divisia index
D	Effective rates	Effective rates	Ignored	Divisia index
E	Effective rates	Effective rates	Included	Divisia index

* Source: Berndt (1976), table 1, p. 18.

individual firms and studies of time series on investment for industry groups by Evans and by Meyer and Glauber (Jorgenson, 1971a, pp. 1128–1129). This measure of the cost of capital is incorporated into the rental price of capital in Berndt's first method of estimation (A). The second method for estimation (B) used by Berndt corresponds very closely to the method employed by Coen in his studies of investment in U.S. manufacturing (Coen, 1969). The third, fourth, and fifth methods for estimation (C, D, E) provide successively better approximations to the price of capital services employed by Christensen and Jorgenson (1969). The third method incorporates effective rates rather than statutory rates of the tax variables; the fourth method measures the cost of capital in the same way as in the study by Christensen and Jorgenson but ignores capital gains; the fifth method incorporates capital gains.

Berndt has estimated the elasticity of substitution from six different regressions: (1) the regression of the output-capital ratio on the rental rate employed in Dhrymes' cross section study of industry groups and Coen's time series study for total manufacturing; (2) the regression of the output-labor ratio on the wage rate employed in the cross section studies of Arrow, Chenery, Minhas, and Solow, Bell, Dhrymes, Fuchs, Griliches, Minasian, Solow, and Zarembka, and the time series studies of Ferguson, Lucas, and McKinnon; (3) the regression of the capital-labor ratio on the wage rental ratio; (4) the reverse of regression (1), employed in the uncorrected version of Dhrymes' study of cross sections for industry groups; (5) the reverse of regression (2), also employed in the uncorrected version of Dhrymes' study; and (6) the reverse of (3), employed by Bell in a cross section study for industry groups (Bell, 1965). Berndt has estimated the parameters of each of these six regressions by ordinary least squares and by two-stage least squares. The results are given in table 6.3.

Berndt's results lead to the striking conclusion that time series estimates of the elasticity of substitution converge to unity as better methods of measurement are introduced and the method of ordinary least squares is replaced by two-stage least squares. Coen's estimate of the elasticity of substitution is 0.2 for U.S. total manufacturing. His estimate is based on the output-capital ratio and corresponds to regression B(1) in table 6.2. The estimate obtained for data constructed in the same manner as Coen's, using the method of ordinary least squares, is 0.269. Improving the data through better measurement of the variables determining the tax structure, capital gains,

Table 6.3
Estimates of the elasticity of substitution for U.S. manufacturing, 1929–1968, from data on capital and labor by Berndt*

Method of estimation:	OLS	OLS	OLS	OLS	OLS	2SLS
Data procedure:	A	B	C	D	E	E
Form						
1	−0.079	0.269	0.250	−0.441	0.967	1.148
	(0.202)	(0.149)	(0.156)	(0.035)	(0.082)	(0.098)
	0.004	0.079	0.063	0.805	0.185	0.757
	0.121	0.154	0.156	0.618	2.162	2.656
2	−0.651	0.024	−0.020	0.604	0.960	1.165
	(0.242)	(0.202)	(0.212)	(0.041)	(0.084)	(0.103)
	0.161	0.001	0.001	0.854	0.776	0.740
	0.148	0.166	0.168	0.934	2.119	2.668
3	−0.164	0.234	0.211	0.466	0.966	1.151
	(0.208)	(0.156)	(0.163)	(0.036)	(0.082)	(0.098)
	0.016	0.056	0.042	0.813	0.784	0.755
	0.125	0.156	0.158	0.669	2.160	2.663
4	−19.722	3.412	3.943	−0.548	1.231	1.233
	(50.493)	(1.892)	(2.459)	(0.043)	(0.103)	(0.108)
	0.004	0.079	0.063	0.805	0.785	0.785
	0.036	0.058	0.048	1.008	2.699	2.699
5	−4.056	64.655	−85.981	0.707	1.238	1.245
	(1.504)	(543.74)	(915.33)	(0.46)	(0.108)	(0.113)
	0.161	0.001	0.001	0.854	0.776	0.775
	0.066	0.051	0.043	1.203	2.705	2.705
6	−10.137	4.171	5.007	0.573	1.232	1.235
	(12.820)	(2.773)	(3.869)	(0.444)	(0.104)	(0.108)
	0.016	0.056	0.042	0.813	0.784	0.784
	0.036	0.055	0.046	1.044	2.704	2.704

* Source: Berndt (1976), table 2, p. 20. The first row of each subsection gives the estimated elasticity of substitution; the second row gives the estimated standard error; the third row gives the square of the correlation coefficient; the fourth gives the Durbin-Watson ratio.

and the cost of capital raises this estimate to 0.967. Shifting from the method of ordinary least squares employed by Coen to two-stage least squares raises the estimate to 1.148, which is not significantly different from unity. We conclude that Coen's estimate is the result of faulty data construction and an inappropriate method of estimation. For the sector of the economy he analyzes, total manufacturing, the hypothesis that the elasticity of substitution is equal to unity is entirely consistent with the evidence.

As a further check on the validity of alternative specifications, Berndt has estimated the elasticity of substitution separately for the periods 1929–1946 and 1947–1968. For methods of data construction other than those based on the methods of Christensen and Jorgenson, estimates of the elasticity of substitution for the two subperiods vary widely; for example, for the second version (B) of Berndt's results, based on Coen's methods of measurement, estimates of the elasticity of substitution are positive and significantly different from zero for the postwar period, while estimates for the prewar period are negative and significantly different from zero. However, for the final version (E) of Berndt's results, estimates of the elasticity of substitution are very similar, using either ordinary least squares or two-stage least squares methods of estimation. A formal test for the similarity of results for the two subperiods, 1929–1946 and 1947–1968, is given in table 6.4. Even for the relatively large level of significance of 0.05,

Table 6.4
F-ratios for a test of the hypothesis that the elasticity of substitution is the same for U.S. manufacturing, 1929–1946 and 1947–1968, from data on capital and labor by Berndt*

Form	Method of estimation	
	OLS	2 SLS
1	0.342	0.851
2	0.285	0.685
3	0.328	0.843
4	1.642	1.632
5	2.057	2.052
6	1.710	1.702

* Source: Berndt (1976), p. 25. Critical value of $F_{0.05}$ (2,36) is 3.254.

none of the test statistics falls in the critical region for a test of the hypothesis that the parameters are different for the two subperiods.

The alternative estimates of the elasticity of substitution presented by Berndt give results similar to those for the output-capital ratio we have reviewed. For example, the results for the output-labor ratio, regression (2), are insignificantly different from zero for methods of measurement similar to those of Coen. Elimination of errors in measurement and substitution of the method of two-stage least squares for ordinary least squares produces an estimated elasticity of substitution of 1.165, which is significantly different from zero and not significantly different from unity. This result, based on time series for U.S. total manufacturing, is comparable to results for cross sections of industry groups within manufacturing we have reviewed above. The conflict between cross section results and time series results of Lucas and McKinnon is eliminated when appropriate methods of measurement and estimation are employed.

Comparing Berndt's time series results for regression (1) with those for regression (2), we find that estimates of the elasticity of substitution from data on capital and output are similar to estimates from data on labor and output. This is inconsistent with Dhrymes' cross section results for the same regressions. One possible explanation of differences between estimates based on labor data and estimates based on capital data is easily discarded. In Dhrymes' cross section study the rental price of capital is measured by the ratio of property income to the quantity of capital. Random errors in measurement of the quantity of capital result in corresponding biases in the measured output-capital ratio and the measured rental rate; biases of this type would bias the estimated elasticity of substitution toward unity; only five of the 17 estimates from capital data are between unity and the corresponding estimates from labor data, which are unaffected by the bias due to errors in the measurement of capital.[11] This completes our review of time series and cross section evidence on the form of the production function, based on the hypothesis of constant returns to scale. We turn now to evidence on returns to scale.

6.4   Returns to Scale

Our next objective is to consider evidence on economies of scale from econometric studies of the production function. This evidence may be divided into two groups, estimates based on direct estimation of the production function and estimates based on the marginal conditions for labor and capital. The marginal conditions are appropriate for both constant and diminishing returns; for increasing returns these conditions are inappropriate since the corresponding second-order conditions are not satisfied. Evidence of increasing returns can be obtained only by direct estimation of the production function.

Estimates of the scale parameter of the CES production function by Zarembka, based on a second-order approximation to the function, are presented in table 6.5.[12] The second-order parameter is zero if the elasticity of substitution is unity. The statistical analysis proceeds in two stages. For each industry the hypothesis that the elasticity of substitution and the scale parameter are the same for the two years 1957 and 1958 is tested. Proceeding conditionally on the hypothesis that these parameters are the same, two hypotheses are tested: (1) that the scale parameter is equal to unity, and (2) that the elasticity of substitution is equal to unity. The hypothesis that the production functions are the same is rejected for only one industry group, Chemicals, at a level of significance of 0.025. In testing the remaining hypotheses Scheffé's S-method[13] is the appropriate statistical procedure. The two hypotheses are tested simultaneously at a level of significance of 0.025 by an appropriate choice of critical regions for each. The scale parameter is not significantly different from unity for any industry group; the elasticity of substitution is significantly different from unity for only one industry group, Furniture. The overall level of significance for the two sets of tests is 0.05, since the two sets of tests is 0.05, since the two sets of hypotheses are "nested" (Scheffé, 1959). The individual observations are establishment averages by state for each industry groups so that Zarembka's results are consistent with the hypothesis of constant returns to scale at the plant level.[14]

Estimates of the elasticity of substitution and the scale parameter based on the same second-order approximation in the logarithms of the variables have been made by Griliches for 1958 on the hypothesis that the production function is the same for all two-digit industries. Again employing Scheffé's S-method, the elasticity of substitution is not significantly different from unity, but the scale parameter is significantly different from unity (Griliches, 1967c, p. 297). Unfortunately, the hypothesis that distribution, efficiency, and scale parameters are the same for all industry groups is employed throughout Griliches' extensive studies of economies of scale at the plant level.[15] The maintained hypothesis is clearly in conflict with the empirical evidence,

Table 6.5
Estimates of the scale parameter and second-order parameter for two-digit manufacturing industries in the U.S., by Zarembka*

Industry group	(a) F-ratio	(b) Scale parameter	(c) Second-order parameter
Food	1.93	1.44 (0.07)	0.23 (0.21)
Textile	1.04	0.91 (0.04)	0.03 (0.13)
Apparel	0.04	0.88 (0.06)	−0.06 (0.07)
Furniture	0.11	0.90 (0.06)	−0.44 (0.12)
Paper	0.49	1.07 (0.03)	−0.02 (0.04)
Chemicals	6.30	1.01 (0.06)	0.00 (0.11)
Petroleum	0.82	1.11 (0.09)	0.02 (0.29)
Stone, clay, glass	2.02	0.96 (0.05)	0.00 (0.06)
Primary metals	1.18	1.05 (0.05)	0.12 (0.06)
Fabricated metals	1.65	0.98 (0.04)	−0.01 (0.06)
Machinery, excluding electrical	1.15	1.00 (0.07)	0.13 (0.08)
Electrical machinery	0.18	1.02 (0.05)	0.07 (0.08)
Transportation equipment	1.35	1.12 (0.04)	−0.02 (0.04)

* Source: Zarembka (1970), table 2, p. 52.

invalidating the conclusions based on the corresponding statistical model. Griliches' maintained hypothesis accounts for the conflict between his results and the evidence presented by Zarembka.

Another approach to simultaneous estimation of scale and substitution parameters has been suggested by Dhrymes. Reverting to the original form of the constant elasticity of substitution production function presented above,[16] the marginal condition for labor may be written

$$\frac{\partial Q}{\partial L} = v(1 - \delta)\, \gamma^{-\rho/v} Q^{(v+\rho)/v} L^{-(1+\rho)} = \frac{q_L}{q_Q}. \tag{6.9}$$

Since the relationship involves both the scale parameter v and the substitution parameter ρ, the two parameters can be estimated simultaneously. Dhrymes fits this relationship to data on labor input and output for two-digit industries for 1958. For all but one industry group the scale parameter is slightly greater than unity, invalidating the marginal conditions employed by Dhrymes to estimate the scale parameter.[17] Equality between the marginal product of labor and the real wage is not a necessary condition for profit maximization with increasing returns.

Dhrymes' model has been employed by Eisner and Nadiri in estimating the scale and substitution parameters from investment functions. Eisner and Nadiri employ a distributed lag function with changes in the logarithms of capital as a dependent variable and lagged values of these changes as independent variables. They did not test for serial correlation of the residuals; least squares estimates of the parameters of the distributed lag function corresponding to their model are inconsistent if the residuals are serially correlated.[18] The remaining variables in their model are seven lagged values of changes in the logarithms of output and the ratio of the price of output to the price of capital services. Bischoff has re-examined the results of Eisner and Nadiri, including eight lagged values of changes in the logarithms of output and the price ratio and introducing an autoregressive parameter to generalize the stochastic structure of the Eisner-Nadiri model. These two changes produce a substantial improvement in the goodness of fit of the model. Estimating the generalized model by maximum likelihood, Bischoff reduces the sum of squared residuals by more than 10%.[19]

Proceeding on the basis of the best-fitting specification of the lag structure, which generalizes that of Eisner and Nadiri, Bischoff has tested for the presence of serial correlation in the original Eisner-Nadiri lag specification. Bischoff finds that the residuals are serially correlated so that least squares estimates of the parameters of the distributed lag function conditional on the Eisner-Nadiri stochastic specification are inconsistent.[20] Bischoff has corrected this error and has tested the hypothesis that the elasticity of substitution and the scale parameter in the Eisner-Nadiri model are equal to unity. These hypotheses cannot be rejected. The critical value of the appropriate F-statistic is 3.27; the calculated value is 2.08, well inside the interval for acceptance of the null hypothesis.[21] This analysis is based on data employed in the original Eisner-Nadiri article.[22]

Bischoff has estimated the elasticity of substitution and scale parameter for a different set of data, consisting of quarterly observations on U.S. postwar investment in producers' durables. An autoregressive parameter is estimated together with the elasticity of substitution and the scale parameter. The results are given in table 6.6.[23] For the maximum likelihood estimate of the autoregressive parameter, the estimated value of $\hat{\sigma}$ is 1.0199 and the estimated value of $\hat{\sigma} + (1 - \hat{\sigma})/\hat{v}$ is 1.0294. The values appropriate for a Cobb-Douglas function with constant returns to scale are both unity. The hypothesis that the autoregressive parameter is equal to zero is consistent with the evidence presented in table 6.6. Employing this value of the autoregressive parameter as a maintained hypothesis the estimated value of $\hat{\sigma}$ is 1.0125 and the estimated value of $\hat{\sigma} + (1 - \hat{\sigma})/\hat{v}$ is 1.0277. Again testing the hypothesis that the elasticity of substitution and the

Table 6.6
Estimates of $\hat{\sigma}$, $\hat{\sigma} + (1 - \hat{\sigma})/\hat{v}$, and the autoregressive parameter by Bischoff*

(a) $\hat{\sigma}$	(b) $\hat{\sigma} + (1 - \hat{\sigma})/\hat{v}$	(c) Autoregressive parameter	(d) Sum of squared residuals
0.1139	0.8945	1.0	1.7251×10^{-4}
1.0125	1.0277	0.0	1.0002×10^{-4}
1.0199	1.0294	−0.1	0.9984×10^{-4}
1.0203	1.0320	−0.2	1.0067×10^{-4}

* Source: Bischoff (1969), table 3, p. 364.

scale parameter are equal to unity, Bischoff obtains an F-statistic of 0.419 with a critical value of 3.17.[24]

Bischoff's results provide strong support for the Cobb-Douglas form of the production function with constant returns to scale. For completeness Bischoff has also tested the hypothesis that the elasticity of substitution is equal to zero for data on equipment investment. Allowing the scale parameter to be estimated, the resulting F-statistic is 26.91 with a critical value of 4.02; maintaining the hypothesis of constant returns to scale the F-statistic is 18.88 with a critical value of 3.17.[25] These findings effectively demolish the main conclusion of Eisner and Nadiri, namely, "Results . . . are generally consistent with the implications of CES production functions with elasticities of substitution nearer zero than unity and, possibly, increasing returns to scale" (1968, p. 381). The empirical results reported by Eisner and Nadiri have been traced by Bischoff to errors in specification of the lag structure and in the stochastic specification. When these errors are corrected, the empirical results are consistent with values of unity for the elasticity of substitution and the scale parameter.[26]

6.5   Conclusion

Our objective in this paper has been to select an appropriate description of technology for the theory of investment and production. We have examined the empirical evidence from studies of manufacturing industries in the U.S. for the postwar period. We have taken a production function with constant elasticity of substitution and constant degree of returns to scale as a maintained hypothesis. The CES production function can be described by four parameters: the elasticity of substitution, the degree of returns to scale, the distribution parameter, and the efficiency parameter. Except for the efficiency parameter, all of the parameters are assumed to be constant for cross section or time-series observations. We have reviewed evidence based on direct estimation of the production function and evidence based on marginal productivity conditions for labor and capital. Our overall conclusion is that the elasticity of substitution and the degree of returns to scale can be taken to be equal to unity. For these values of the parameters the CES production function reduces to the Cobb-Douglas function with constant returns to scale.

The description of technology has important implications for the theory of investment and production. Under constant returns to scale the optimal policy for capital accumulation determines the rate of growth of capital and the labor-output and capital-output ratios corresponding to any set of prices of output and of labor and capital input. The marginal productivity condition for capital is incorporated into a distributed lag function determining investment expenditures. The desired level of capital is a perpetually moving target to which actual capital never converges. This characterization of optimal capital accumulation can be contrasted with the optimal policy under decreasing returns to scale. The distribution lag function determining investment depends on the long-run equilibrium demand for capital, which depends in turn on the prices of output and of labor and capital input. Under constant returns there exists no long-run equilibrium demand for capital as a function of prices.

The empirical evidence we have reviewed suggests that desired capital should be interpreted as a moving target rather than the long-run equilibrium value of capital. This interpretation is consistent with the neoclassical theory of investment behavior, employed extensively in econometric studies of investment expenditures.[27] In this theory the optimal policy for production and investment is described by an iterative process with output and employment determined by the marginal productivity condition for labor and the production function. Given output and employment, the desired level of capital is determined by the marginal productivity condition for capital; the actual level of capital is determined by a distributed lag investment function.[28] This policy is identical to that appropriate for a description of technology with production and installation subject to constant returns to scale. In econometric studies based on the neoclassical theory, the hypothesis that the elasticity of substitution is equal to unity has been employed.[29] This hypothesis is also consistent with the evidence we have reviewed.

The characterization of optimal investment policy has been the subject of considerable controversy in the econometric literature on investment. The problem is posed by Borch:

(1) Capital stock is taken as fixed, and the firm determines the optimal level of output. This is a very reasonable short-run assumption. (2) The output level determined under the first assumption is taken as fixed, and the optimal amount of capital stock is determined. This seems to be a rather doubtful assumption. . . . It seems natural to assume that intelligent management will

see more than one step ahead in this process and try to optimize output level and capital stock simultaneously. (Borch, 1963, p. 273).

The error in Borch's reasoning is that under constant returns to scale, the optimal program for capital accumulation involves selection of an optimal capital-output ratio followed by selection of an optimal rate of growth of capital. No matter how far ahead intelligent management can see, the optimal policy at each point in time may be described in this way. By suggesting that output and capital stock be optimized simultaneously, Borch assumes that optimal levels of output and capital exist so that returns to scale are decreasing. But this is contradicted by the empirical evidence we have reviewed.[30]

Borch's reasoning has been repeated and elaborated by Coen, Gould, Griliches, and Mundlak. Mundlak analyzes Koyck's flexible accelerator model, purporting "... to show how the use of current output as a measure of desired capital can lead to erroneous results."[31] Mundlak develops a model of the competitive firm as a basis for analyzing Koyck's distributed lag function. Long-run equilibrium for the model is characterized by optimal levels of output, labor, and capital input.[32] Mundlak assumes decreasing returns to scale; his analysis of Koyck's model presumes that long-run equilibrium is characterized by a supply function for output and demand functions for labor and capital input. Under constant returns to scale these supply and demand functions do not exist, so that Mundlak's analysis of Koyck's model is completely erroneous. This analysis is extended by Mundlak in developing a distributed lag investment model with desired capital a function of the ratios of input prices of output. While such a model would be appropriate under decreasing returns, the empirical evidence we have reviewed supports an assumption of constant returns. For this description of technology Mundlak's distributed lag investment model is inappropriate.

The arguments of Borch and Mundlak have been repeated by Griliches as part of a criticism of distributed lag investment models.

In particular, the use of output as an exogenous variable in the demand equation needs further justification. There is no problem in treating it econometrically as predetermined, but it is hard to accept the long-run notions of "desired" capital being conditional on current output. (Griliches, 1968a, p. 216).

Under constant returns the optimal policy is characterized by an optimal capital-output ratio and an optimal rate of growth of capital. The rate of growth of capital may be expressed as a function of the capital-output ratio. Alternatively, investment is determined by a distributed lag function that incorporates the marginal productivity of capital; under constant returns to scale the marginal product is a function of the capital-output ratio. A point of view similar to that of Griliches is expressed by Coen: "While output may be predetermined for the capital stock decision, it is not an exogenous variable for a profit maximizing firm. Like labor input and capital stock, output is a decision variable" (1969, p. 370). Coen is explicit in associating this point of view with decreasing returns to scale (1969, p. 375). The error in Coen's analysis of distributed lag investment models is that constant returns to scale are excluded as a possible description of technology. From the evidence we have reviewed, constant returns provides the characterization of technology most appropriate to the analysis of investment behavior.

The most elaborate presentation of the point of view of Borch, Coen, Griliches, and Mundlak on flexible accelerator models of investment has been given by Gould (1969). Gould's presentation is all the more remarkable in that it ostensibly relies on a theory of optimal capital accumulation. This theory is not used explicitly on the grounds that

Different adjustment mechanisms are derived when alternative assumptions are made about the form of the production function and the cost of adjustment function. We need not dwell here on the actual derivation of these alternative forms, since the main concern is not adjustment mechanism *per se* but rather what happens when past or current sales are used in the specification (of desired capital) instead of the correct long-run equilibrium value. (Gould, 1969).

The error in this line of reasoning is more transparent in Gould's presentation than in those of Borch, Coen, Griliches, and Mundlak. Alternative assumptions about the form of the production function are critical to Gould's analysis. Under constant returns no "correct" long-run equilibrium value of capital exists. All of Gould's conclusions, like those of Borch, Coen, Griliches, and Mundlak, are predicated on the existence of such a long-run equilibrium value of capital. These conclusions are irrelevant to distributed lag models of investment based on constant returns to scale.

Notes

1. Kuznets (1961), table 8, pp. 92–93; capital consumption has dominated gross capital formation for the economy as a whole since 1919.

2. See section 6.5.

3. Jorgenson (1971a), pp. 1113–1114 (Kuh), 1122–1124 (Evans), 1124–1125 (Eisner), 1125–1126 (Hickman), and 1126 (Bourneuf).

4. Jorgenson (1971a), pp. 1116–1117 (Jorgenson-Siebert) and 1126–1127 (Jorgenson-Stephenson).

5. $\lambda^\nu Q = \gamma[\delta(\lambda K)^{-\rho} + (1 - \delta)(\lambda L)^{-\rho}]^{-\nu/\rho}$.

6. Lucas (1967a), formula (9), p. 325.

7. For approximation under diminishing returns, see Lucas (1967b).

8. Arrow *et al.* (1961), table 2, p. 227.

9. Griliches (1967c), pp. 285–290; Lucas (1969), pp. 232–241; Nerlove (1967), passim.

10. An evaluation of earlier studies in the light of recent evidence is given by Jorgenson (1972).

11. Griliches (1967c), p. 287, fn. 28, presents an analysis of bias for errors in the measurement of labor; the analysis for capital is strictly analogous.

12. The approximation is given by Kmenta (1967): $\ln Q = \ln \gamma + \nu\delta \ln K + \nu(1 - \delta) \ln L - \rho\nu\delta(1 - \delta) (\ln K - \ln L)^2$.

13. Under the hypothesis that the elasticity of substitution is equal to one, the second-order parameter $\rho\nu\delta(1 - \delta)$ is equal to zero. For discussion of the S-method, see Scheffé (1959), pp. 66–72.

14. Similar results are reported for cross section data for three-digit industries within manufacturing by Zarembka and Chernicoff (1971), and for data on individual plants classified by four-digit industry within manufacturing by Klotz (1970).

15. Griliches (1968b), p. 155, argues: ". . . one of the major objections to [this] . . . study is its implicit assumption that the coefficients of 'thc' production function are the same for all two-digit industries. Such an objection is in part misdirected as far as the economies of scale and labor-quality measures are concerned since we are interested in estimating the *average* importance of these factors for *total* manufacturing." His estimates of the scale parameter with no allowance for variation in efficiency or distribution parameters across industries are appropriate averages only if industry dummy variables, associated with variations in efficiency parameters, and industry capital labor ratios, associated with variations in distributed parameters, are uncorrelated with industry employment, associated with the scale parameter. Otherwise, estimates of the scale parameter are biased and do not represent an appropriate average.

16. See formula (6.2) above.

17. Dhrymes (1965), table 2, p. 364.

18. Inconsistency of least squares is discussed by Griliches (1961, 1967b).

19. Bischoff (1969), table 1, p. 358; results labelled "c_1" are for the data employed by Eisner and Nadiri.

20. Bischoff (1969), p. 359; this erroneous specification is employed by Eisner (1969); Eisner's estimates are also inconsistent.

21. Bischoff (1969), table 2; results for model no. 9 provide the appropriate test.

22. Eisner and Nadiri (1968), p. 381. Eisner and Nadiri (1970) have subsequently employed the original Eisner-Nadiri specification in analyzing this same body of data, ignoring Bischoff's demonstration that this specification is inferior to the one employed by Bischoff.

23. Bischoff (1969), table 3, p. 364; results in table III-9 are with the constant term included in the regression.

24. Bischoff (1969), table 4, p. 365; results for model no. 9 provide the appropriate test.

25. Bischoff (1969), table 4, p. 365; results are for model no. 5.

26. Eisner has published a series of five articles attempting to support the conclusion of Eisner and Nadiri that the elasticity of substitution is equal to zero and that returns to scale are increasing. For an evaluation of this work, see Jorgenson (1972), pp. 244–245.

27. In addition to the references given in note 4 above, see: Jorgenson and Stephenson (1967a, 1969a); Hall and Jorgenson (1967, 1969, 1971a); Jorgenson and Siebert (1968a); and Jorgenson and Handel (1971).

28. See section 6.1.

29. See the references given in note 27 above.

30. See section 6.4.

31. Mundlak (1966), p. 51; the reference to Koyck is (1954).

32. Mundlak (1966); see also Mundlak (1967).

7   The Investment Tax Credit and Counter-Cyclical Policy

Roger H. Gordon and
Dale W. Jorgenson

7.1   Summary

The purpose of this study is to assess the impact of the investment tax credit for business purchases of producers' durable equipment over the period 1960–1985. We have divided this twenty-five year period into two subperiods, roughly from 1960 to the present and from now to 1985. For the first subperiod we base our evaluation of the investment tax credit on historical experience. For the second subperiod we assess the tax credit against the backdrop of a projection of the likely growth of the U.S. economy over the next decade.

Our evaluation of the investment tax credit is based on its contribution to the policy objectives of economic growth and stability. We measure the contribution of the tax credit to economic growth through its impact on increases in productive capacity. We measure the contribution of the tax credit to stability through its effectiveness in reducing the gap between actual level of output and the potential level of output determined by available productive capacity.

Our main conclusions are the following:

(1) Over the period from 1960 to now the investment tax credit has made an important contribution to economic growth. By the end of 1972 the productive capacity of the U.S. economy was more than five percent higher than it would have been in the absence of the credit.

(2) Removal of the investment tax credit at this time would result in a substantial slowdown of growth in productive capacity over the next decade. By 1985 capacity could be as much as ten percent below the level resulting from retention of the tax credit in its present form.

(3) During the period from 1960 to the present, the use of the investment tax credit as an instrument of counter-cyclical policy has been highly detrimental to economic stability. Of the five major changes in the investment tax credit since 1962, three were badly mistimed and two were correctly timed but in precisely the wrong direction.

(4) Over this same period a constant investment tax credit at a rate approximately double the current rate of seven percent would have been superior to the policy actually followed for both economic growth and economic stability.

(5) For the next decade the best rate of the investment tax credit for stabilization purposes would be roughly triple the current rate of seven percent. By 1985 the higher rate would increase productive capacity by almost thirty percent over the level that will result from the present tax credit.

Our overall conclusion is that economic growth rather than counter-cyclical stabilization should be the primary criterion for selecting the appropriate rate for the investment tax credit. To stimulate economic growth and enhance the performance of stabilization policy, much higher rates of the investment tax credit should be adopted. Changes in the rate of the investment tax credit should be less frequent than they have been in the past. There is no justification for a transfer of responsibilities for administration of the tax credit from the Congress to the Administration or to an independent agency, such as the Federal Reserve System.

7.2   Introduction

After much dispute the important role of the investment tax credit in stimulating investment expenditures has come to be widely appreciated in both business and academic communities. Indeed, the impact of investment incentives is so widely recognized that proposals have come forward for the use of investment incentives as a counter-cyclical device. One proposal of this type is to make the rate of the investment tax credit, now fixed at a statutory rate, flexible upwards or downwards, depending on the state of economic activity.

The case for a flexible investment tax credit relies heavily on a reduction of the "inside lag" in the administration of stabilization policy. The inside lag is the lag between recognition of the need for a change in policy and actual implementation of the change in policy.

Under a flexible investment tax credit the Congress would be asked to grant authority to the Administration to vary the rate of the investment tax credit within broad statutory limits, ranging in some proposals from four to fifteen percent.

Although a flexible investment tax credit could be administered in many ways, at least one specific proposal has been subjected to detailed analysis by the research staff of the Board of Governors of the Federal Reserve System at the direction of Chairman Arthur Burns. This proposal, referred to as the Business Investment Fund (BIF) system, has been analyzed by Pierce and Tinsley (1972) as part of a Federal Reserve Board Staff study of measures to stabilize housing investment.

As described by Pierce and Tinsley, the BIF proposal is equivalent to a flexible investment tax credit. Although Pierce and Tinsley consider a number of alternative possibilities, they finally propose to apply the BIF system to investment in producers' durables, to base the credit on expenditures rather than orders, and to administer the system through the Internal Revenue Service. In one important respect the BIF proposal differs from a tax credit: Responsibility for changes in the rate of the credit would be lodged with the Federal Reserve Board rather than the Congress.

Under the BIF system a unit BIF rate would be announced by the Federal Reserve Board. If the rate were positive, businesses would contribute a fraction of their current investment expenditures to the Business Investment Fund. If the rate were negative, businesses would receive a fraction of their investment expenditures from the Fund. Contribution rates would be set at negative levels to encourage investment and positive levels to discourage investment. Rather than balance income and outlay by the Fund, Pierce and Tinsley propose to aim at a zero net effect on investment from the policy over some stipulated period.

The BIF system could be used to achieve the same effects as a flexible investment tax credit by keeping the statutory rate of the investment credit at seven percent. Rates of contribution to the Business Investment Fund could be varied from plus three percent to minus eight percent to achieve an effect equivalent to a flexible tax credit ranging from four to fifteen percent.[1] From the point of view of businesses subject to the BIF system, contributions and payments from the Business Investment Fund could be regarded as an offset or an enhancement to the investment tax credit.

Pierce and Tinsley (1972, p. 354) indicate that among the advantages of the BIF system is that:

In both conceptual and operational detail, the BIF proposal is direct and uncomplicated. Unlike most new and untried schemes, it has the important properties that its quantitative effects can be estimated with some accuracy because the stabilization BIF rate can be readily inserted into the investment equations of existing econometric models. These models could be used to estimate the changes in the stabilization rate necessary to attain the optimal path for aggregate business investment.

In studying the role of investment incentives as a counter-cyclical policy we will focus on a flexible tax credit similar to the BIF system.

7.3   Impact of the Investment Tax Credit

Tax incentives for investment have been altered at frequent intervals by the Congress with a view toward stimulating or reducing the level of investment expenditures. The investment tax credit was originally introduced to stimulate investment in 1962. The effectiveness of the tax credit was increased substantially in 1964 with the repeal of the Long Amendment. The investment tax credit was suspended in 1966–1967 and repealed in 1969 in order to reduce the level of investment. The tax credit was re-enacted in 1971 to stimulate investment expenditures.

As a result of very extensive experience with econometric modeling of investment behavior, the general outlines of the response of investment to changes in tax policy are well established. Investment expenditures respond to a change in investment incentives after a lag of about two quarters. At first the response is limited to investment itself, but as the income generated by investment activity feeds through the economy, a multiplier effect drives down unemployment and drives up economic activity. The maximum impact of a change in investment incentives on the level of economic activity extends over a period from three to five years after the change in incentives takes place.

The most recent experience with this general sequence of events is the current investment boom. An increase in the level of investment expenditures was triggered by a very substantial change in investment incentives in early 1971. The investment tax credit for expenditures on producers' durables was restored at the statutory rate of seven percent. The Asset Depreciation Range (ADR) system for depreciation of equipment, adopted at almost the same time, reduced effective lifetimes of equipment up to twenty percent.

Expenditures on producers' durable equipment began to turn up as early as the third quarter of 1971, rising sharply over the following eighteen months to a level thirty percent above the level of investment in early 1971. The investment boom that began in 1971 and pushed the rate of unemployment to its lowest level since 1968, is now beginning to level off. Leading indicators of investment expenditures such as anticipations of investment and appropriations imply that investment will remain flat in real terms for the next year and then will begin to decline. The pattern repeats the experience of the period 1962–1965, when the level of investment rose to historic highs, following adoption of the investment tax credit and the 1962 guideline lifetimes for depreciation.

To assess the impact of the investment tax credit from the time of its introduction in 1962 until the present, we have compared the levels of investment, GNP, and the gap between actual and potential GNP, all in real terms, that actually occurred with the levels that would have occurred without the tax credit. Our results are presented in table 7.1. Estimates for the performance of the U.S. economy in the absence of the tax credit are derived through a simulation study, based on the DRI quarterly model of the U.S. economy, setting the effective rate of the tax credit equal to zero for the whole period.

We find that the introduction of the investment tax credit in 1962 increased investment expenditures by 7.7 percent after three years and 10.2 percent after five years over what they would have been without the credit. The stimulus to investment provided by the tax credit was weakened by the temporary suspension of the credit in 1966 and brought to an end by repeal of the credit in 1969. By mid-1971 investment was only 1.3 percent higher than it would have been if the tax credit had never been introduced. The reintroduction of the tax credit in 1971 set off a rise in investment that continued through the end of 1972, where our historical study ends.

The cumulative impact of the tax credit on investment over the period 1962–1972 resulted in a level of capital stock at the end of 1972 that was 5.5 percent higher than it would have without the credit. This is a very conservative estimate of the impact of the tax credit on economic growth since our period ends before the full impact of the investment incentives adopted in 1971 had been realized. The resulting increase in investment has continued up to the present and only

Table 7.1
Effect of the investment tax credit, 1962–1972 (billions of dollars)

	Historical data			Simulation with no tax credit		
Period	IPDE58	GNP58	Real GNP gap	IPDE58	GNP58	Real GNP gap
62:1	30.3	519.5	−31.5	30.3	519.5	−31.5
62:2	31.3	527.7	−28.1	31.3	527.7	−28.1
62:3	32.8	533.4	−27.2	32.7	533.2	−27.4
62:4	32.6	538.3	−27.1	32.3	537.7	−27.7
63:1	32.5	541.2	−29.4	31.9	540.1	−30.5
63:2	33.1	546.0	−29.9	32.3	544.4	−31.5
63:3	34.7	554.7	−26.5	33.6	552.5	−28.7
63:4	35.9	562.1	−24.5	34.5	559.3	−27.3
64:1	36.9	571.1	−20.9	35.2	567.8	−24.2
64:2	37.9	578.6	−18.9	36.0	574.9	−22.6
64:3	39.8	585.8	−17.2	37.6	581.5	−21.5
64:4	40.3	588.5	−20.1	37.7	583.4	−25.2
65:1	42.1	601.6	−12.6	39.1	595.7	−18.5
65:2	42.7	610.4	− 9.5	39.4	603.9	−16.0
65:3	45.0	622.5	− 3.1	41.3	615.4	−10.2
65:4	46.4	636.6	5.2	42.5	629.0	− 2.4
66:1	48.1	649.1	11.5	44.0	614.0	3.4
66:2	49.4	655.0	11.1	45.1	646.5	2.6
66:3	50.9	660.2	10.0	46.5	651.6	1.4
66:4	52.0	668.1	11.5	47.5	659.3	2.7
67:1	49.8	666.6	3.5	45.2	657.4	− 5.7
67:2	51.1	671.6	2.0	47.0	662.7	− 6.9
67:3	50.6	678.9	2.7	47.1	670.9	− 5.3
67:4	50.8	683.6	0.7	47.4	676.8	− 6.1
68:1	52.1	692.6	3.0	48.7	685.0	− 4.6
68:2	51.3	705.3	8.9	47.8	697.6	1.2
68:3	52.4	712.3	9.0	48.6	704.3	1.0
68:4	53.1	716.5	6.3	48.9	708.2	− 2.0
69:1	55.6	722.4	5.2	50.9	713.8	− 3.4
69:2	55.4	725.8	1.5	50.3	717.2	− 7.1
69:3	56.0	729.2	− 2.2	50.9	720.9	−10.5
69:4	56.3	725.1	−13.5	51.7	716.8	−21.8
70:1	54.4	721.2	−25.2	50.4	715.0	−31.4
70:2	54.3	722.1	−32.2	51.0	718.3	−36.1
70:3	55.1	727.2	−35.1	52.6	725.6	−36.7
70:4	50.4	719.3	−51.1	48.7	719.5	−50.9
71:1	51.9	735.1	−43.4	50.8	737.4	−41.1
71:2	52.9	740.4	−46.3	52.1	743.6	−43.1
71:3	53.2	746.9	−48.2	52.5	750.5	−44.6
71:4	56.3	759.0	−44.5	55.2	761.4	−42.1
72:1	58.4	768.0	−44.0	56.6	770.5	−41.5
72:2	59.5	785.6	−35.0	56.9	786.8	−33.8
72:3	60.7	796.7	−32.6	57.2	797.4	−31.9
72:4	64.3	812.3	−25.7	59.9	811.3	−26.7

now is investment beginning to level off. We conclude that adoption of the investment tax credit has been a substantial stimulus to the growth of productive capacity and to economic growth over the period 1962–1972.

To assess the validity of our procedures for estimating the impact of the investment tax credit we have compared our results with estimates for other studies in table 7.2. In the first column we present the results of our simulations of the impact of the tax credit on investment alone, not allowing for feedback through the rest of the economy. In the fifth column we present results that allow for feedback, employing the DRI quarterly model of the U.S. economy. When feedbacks of investment on the economy are taken into account our estimate of the impact of the investment tax credit is increased, but only slightly.

In columns two through four of table 7.2 we present the results of three other studies of the impact of the investment tax credit. Our

Table 7.2
Effect of the investment tax credit on producers' durables, investment, alternative estimates, 1962–1972 (billions of 1958 dollars)

Year	Gordon-Jorgenson	Bischoff[a]	Hall-Jorgenson[b]	Aaron et al.[c]	Gordon-Jorgenson full-effect[d]
1962	0.11	0.00	0.95	0.05	0.12
1963	0.94	0.22	2.16	0.56	1.00
1964	1.87	1.51	3.64	0.81	2.10
1965	2.96	3.04	3.80	1.28	3.48
1966	4.14	4.31	2.96	2.24	4.31
1967	3.74	—	2.64	3.00	3.91
1968	3.40	—	3.03	5.11	3.71
1969	4.82	—	—	5.06	4.89
1970	2.78	—	—	2.94	2.87
1971	0.91	—	—	2.53	0.93
1972	2.87	—	—	2.90	3.09

a. Bischoff (1971a, table 3–15, col. 5).

b. Hall and Jorgenson (1971a, table 2–7, cols. 7 and 10). Figures for 1969 and 1970 were omitted since the authors ignored the suspension of the tax credit in 1969 and 1970 in their calculations.

c. Aaron et al. (1973, table 3B, col. 2).

d. These figures allow for any feedbacks from the rest of the economy.

specification corresponds closely with that used by Hall and Jorgenson, but we have made several minor adjustments in specification and our estimation procedure is not the same. The main difference between the two sets of estimates is in the time shape of the response of investment to a change in the tax credit. Hall and Jorgenson suggest that the response is more rapid than our results indicate, but their estimate of the effect of the tax credit on the level of investment is very similar to ours.

After two years have elapsed our estimates of the impact of investment tax credit are very similar to the estimates presented by Bischoff. Aaron et al., have used an investment equation that is similar in form to that of Bischoff. However, they have kept the level of total investment constant, assuming that interest rate adjustments will result in an unchanged level of saving and, hence, of total investment in the U.S. economy. Increases in producers durables investment result in corresponding reductions in investment in residential and nonresidential structures. A comparison of their results with Bischoff's reveals the implications of their assumption that interest rates adjust to keep the overall level of investment unchanged.

Our overall conclusion is that estimates obtained from the three competing specifications—our own, Bischoff's and Hall and Jorgenson's—are similar in magnitude but somewhat different in time pattern. Our estimate of the time pattern of the impact of the tax credit on investment expenditures is closer to that of Bischoff than to the Hall-Jorgenson estimate. Second, the assumption of Aaron et al., that total investment remains unchanged in response to a change in the investment tax credit for producers' durable equipment, is not consistent with the results of our simulations with output and interest rate feedbacks. When both feedbacks are taken into account, total investment increases and the impact of tax incentives on producers' durables investment is greater than when these feedbacks are ignored.

The evidence from the current investment boom and the boom of 1962–1965 leaves no doubt that tax incentives have a powerful impact on investment expenditures. The proposed range of a flexible tax credit, say from four to fifteen percent, represents a difference in incentives to investors equal to the most substantial changes in investment incentives in historical experience. Variations in the level of investment expenditures of up to fifty percent within a two-year period could result from variations in the rate of the credit within the range of four to fifteen percent.

We have assessed the impact of this investment tax credit on economic growth during the period 1962–1972 and we have compared our results with those of other studies for the same period. We next turn to an evaluation of the contribution of the investment tax credit to economic stabilization. The estimates presented in table 7.1 reveal that the introduction of the investment tax credit accelerated the movement of the U.S. economy to full capacity output by the end of 1965. However, the growth of defense expenditures during the Vietnam War, superimposed on an already booming economy, resulted in production in excess of normal capacity.

The most recent historical experience bearing on the contribution of the investment tax credit to economic stabilization is the period 1969–1970. A number of measures to reduce inflationary pressure on the economy were adopted in early 1969. One measure that attracted little attention at the time was the repeal of the investment tax credit. The precipitous drop in Federal purchases of goods and services over the period 1969–1970, associated with de-escalation in Vietnam, was accompanied by a slowdown in private investment, resulting from elimination of the investment tax credit. The combined effect of these measures was to end the longest uninterrupted advance in economic activity since World War II.

The repeal of the Long Amendment in 1964 enhanced the stimulus to investment provided by the credit, but its maximum impact coincided with the Vietnam buildup, so that the effect of the Long Amendment was destabilizing. The temporary suspension of the investment tax credit in 1966 was almost two years too late. The suspension of the investment tax credit in 1969 was a change in policy in precisely the wrong direction for stabilization of the U.S. economy in the early 1970s. Reintroduction of the investment tax credit in 1971 was mistimed. We conclude that the use of the investment tax credit as an instrument of counter-cyclical policy over the period from 1960 to the present has been highly detrimental to economic stability. Similarly, reintroduction of the investment tax credit in 1967 was two years too soon.

Prevailing lags in the U.S. economy imply that the period of maximum response of investment expenditures to changes in the investment tax credit occur between three and five years after a change in the credit. If the course of the economy could be predicted with perfect certainty a flexible tax credit could be designed to stabilize investment expenditures. In fact, the course of the economy three to five years in the future is highly uncertain, so that the assumption of perfect foresight is completely unrealistic. Forecast errors can lead to serious miscalculations in the attempt to use investment as a counterweight to destabilizing influences from other sectors of the U.S. economy.

The U.S. economy is now entering a period of great uncertainty about future stability. The unemployment rate has risen sharply and most forecasts suggest that it is likely to go higher. In table 7.3 we attempt to extend our assessment of the contribution of the investment tax credit to stabilization, using a long-term projection of the U.S. economy based on the DRI quarterly econometric model. We first present estimates of investment, GNP, and the gap between actual and potential GNP, all in real terms, for the period 1974–1985 on the assumption that the investment tax credit continues at its present rate of seven percent. The real output of the U.S. economy is projected to be well below its potential throughout the period.

In table 7.3 we also present estimates of investment, GNP, and the difference between actual and potential GNP, all in real terms, assuming suspension of the investment tax credit. By 1985 investment will be 14.1 percent higher with the tax credit than without it and capital stock will be 9.8 percent higher. The contribution of the tax credit to economic growth during the next decade is estimated to be much greater than during the decade 1962–1972 since no suspensions of the credit, such as those that took place in 1966–1967 and 1969–1970, are included in our projections for the future. Our main conclusions are the following:

(1) Over the period from 1960 to now the investment tax credit has made an important contribution to economic growth. A very conservative estimate of this contribution is that by 1972 the productive capacity of the U.S. economy was more than five percent higher than it would have been in the absence of the credit.

(2) Over the next decade removal of the investment tax credit would result in a substantial slowdown of the growth in productive capacity and in a much wider gap between actual and potential GNP. By 1985 capacity would be 9.8 percent higher with the credit than without it. The gap between actual and potential GNP would be as much as 20 billion dollars larger in real terms without the credit.

(3) During the period from 1960 to the present, the use of the tax credit as an instrument of counter-cyclical policy has been highly

Table 7.3
Effect of the investment tax credit, 1974–1985 (billions of 1958 dollars)

Period	Seven percent tax credit			No tax credit		
	IPDE58	GNP58	GNP gap	IPDE58	GNP58	GNP gap
74:2	68.5	837.1	−45.9	68.5	837.1	−45.9
74:3	71.2	845.1	−46.2	71.2	845.1	−46.2
74:4	72.5	857.4	−42.3	71.8	856.4	−43.2
75:1	73.3	864.6	−43.8	71.6	862.1	−46.2
75:2	74.0	873.5	−43.6	71.2	869.2	−47.8
75:3	74.3	880.8	−45.1	70.5	874.7	−51.2
75:4	74.9	888.5	−46.3	70.0	880.6	−54.1
76:1	75.5	895.9	−48.1	69.9	886.6	−57.4
76:2	76.4	905.6	−47.7	70.1	895.4	−57.9
76:3	77.4	915.0	−47.6	70.9	904.4	−58.3
76:4	78.5	924.8	−47.4	71.8	913.9	−58.2
77:1	81.1	940.1	−41.6	74.2	929.1	−52.7
77:2	82.4	951.3	−40.1	75.3	940.1	−51.3
77:3	84.3	962.0	−39.2	77.0	950.4	−50.8
77:4	85.8	973.1	−37.9	78.4	961.1	−49.9
78:1	87.5	983.7	−31.1	79.9	971.2	−49.6
78:2	89.2	993.2	−37.3	81.4	980.0	−50.6
78:3	91.0	1002.8	−37.7	83.0	990.5	−50.0
78:4	92.8	1012.1	−38.4	84.6	1000.3	−50.2
79:1	94.5	1022.8	−37.5	86.1	1009.8	−50.5
79:2	95.9	1032.2	−38.0	87.4	1015.7	−54.5
79:3	97.5	1043.0	−37.2	87.7	1027.8	−52.5
79:4	98.8	1053.1	−37.3	89.8	1038.1	−52.3
80:1	100.0	1062.4	−37.9	90.9	1048.5	−51.8
80:2	101.7	1073.3	−37.0	92.3	1058.8	−51.6
80:3	103.5	1084.5	−36.0	93.9	1069.0	−51.5
80:4	105.2	1097.2	−33.5	95.4	1080.1	−50.6
81:1	106.7	1106.5	−34.3	96.6	1090.6	−50.2
81:2	108.3	1116.7	−34.2	98.0	1101.0	−49.1
81:3	109.7	1125.7	−35.4	99.2	1108.7	−52.4
81:4	111.2	1134.7	−36.7	100.4	1118.7	−52.7
82:1	112.8	1145.6	−36.2	101.8	1130.4	−51.4
82:2	114.4	1156.5	−35.8	103.1	1141.0	−51.3
82:3	116.0	1166.6	−36.3	104.4	1152.2	−50.7
82:4	117.1	1177.6	−36.0	105.3	1161.5	−52.1
83:1	118.3	1186.0	−38.3	106.3	1171.5	−52.9
83:2	120.0	1196.9	−38.3	107.7	1182.9	−52.4
83:3	121.9	1208.2	−38.0	109.2	1192.8	−53.4
83:4	123.7	1219.5	−37.8	110.7	1204.0	−53.3

Table 7.3
(continued)

	Seven percent tax credit			No tax credit		
Period	IPDE58	GNP58	GNP gap	IPDE58	GNP58	GNP gap
84:1	125.3	1234.4	−34.0	112.0	1216.7	−51.8
84:2	127.1	1246.4	−33.3	113.3	1227.6	−52.1
84:3	128.9	1257.1	−34.0	114.6	1238.2	−52.9
84:4	130.7	1267.3	−35.3	115.9	1249.9	−52.7
85:1	132.4	1278.7	−35.5	117.1	1259.2	−54.9
85:2	134.1	1290.6	−35.2	118.3	1271.2	−54.6
85:3	135.9	1302.8	−34.7	119.4	1282.1	−55.5
85:4	137.6	1313.8	−35.6	120.6	1292.9	−56.5

detrimental to economic stability. The repeal of the Long Amendment in 1964 and the suspension of the investment tax credit in 1969 took place at a time when the investment tax credit should have been changed, but in each case the change should have been in precisely the opposite direction. Suspension of the tax credit in 1966 and reintroduction of the credit in 1967 and 1971 were changes in the right direction, but each move was badly mistimed.

7.4   Alternative Investment Tax Credits

Up to this point we have confined our consideration of the impact of the investment tax credit to the actual policy from 1962–1972 and continuation of the current policy through 1985. We now turn our attention to alternative policies for the investment tax credit. Our first problem is to measure the impact of a given tax credit policy. We assume that the objective of stabilization policy is to minimize the gap between actual and potential GNP. Accordingly, a policy that results in a narrow gap is judged to be more effective than a policy that results in a wide gap.

The impact of a change in the investment tax credit on the U.S. economy is distributed over time. This impact reaches its maximum over a period from three to five years after the change in policy takes place. In our assessment of alternative investment tax credits we must take into account the whole time path of the economy that results from a given change in policy. For this purpose we must combine the gaps between actual and potential GNP for different periods to obtain a measure of the average gap over a given time interval. These measures of the average gap can then be compared for different policies.

We use two types of averages in making our policy assessments. First, we take the gap between actual and potential GNP in each period, square it, and average the results over all periods included in a given time interval. This procedure assures that positive gaps are not set off against negative gaps in appraising alternative policies. Deviations from potential GNP in both positive and negative directions are undesirable from the point of view of economic stabilization. This measure also gives greater weight to larger gaps. To convert our results into a form that is comparable with the GNP gap in a single time period we take the square root of our average of squared deviations, obtaining an average that we can call the *root mean squared GNP gap*. We also use a weighted average with weights declining at five percent per year to weight early time periods more heavily than later time periods.[2] We call the resulting average *weighted root squared GNP gap*.

We present average gaps between actual and potential GNP for various investment tax credit policies in table 7.4. We extend the period for consideration of alternative policies back to 1959 to allow for the possibility that introduction of the investment tax credit in 1962 was

Table 7.4
Summary statistics on the real GNP gap (billions of 1958 dollars)

	Period 59:2–72:4	
	Root mean squared error	Weighted root squared error
(1) Actual policy	27.6	27.7
(2) Constant policies		
(a) 0%	27.9	28.1
(b) 7% (62:1–72:4)	26.0	26.4
(c) 7% (59:2–72:4)	23.2	23.6
(d) 10%	21.5	21.9
(e) 13%	20.8	21.1
(f) 15%	20.9	21.1
(g) 20%	22.5	22.4
(3) Optimal "flexible" policies		
(a) Unlagged	17.1	17.8
(b) Lagged 2 qtrs.	18.3	18.7
(c) Lagged 4 qtrs.	19.7	19.9
(d) Lagged 6 qtrs.	21.2	21.1
(e) Lagged 8 qtrs.	22.5	22.1
(f) Lagged 10 qtrs.	23.6	23.0
(4) Alternative range		
0–7 (62:1–72:4)	25.5	26.1

not properly timed. Our average gap for the period from the second quarter of 1959 to the fourth quarter of 1972 was 27.6 billions of 1958 dollars for the root mean squared error and 27.7 billions for the weighted mean squared error. These averages are computed from the gaps for each period obtained from historical data on actual and potential GNP.

We next consider the gap that would have resulted from alternative policies for the investment tax credit. For each alternative policy we insert the corresponding rate of the investment tax credit into our investment equation and simulate the development of the U.S. economy, using the DRI quarterly econometric model. In the second section of table 7.4 we present the results for policies with a constant rate of the investment tax credit over the whole time period. First, we present the average gap associated with a constant rate of zero. The results are only slightly worse than those for the actual policy from the point of view of economic stabilization. This reflects our earlier finding that the use of the investment tax credit for stabilization purposes was highly detrimental to economic stability over the period 1962–1972.

The next two policies we analyze have a constant investment tax credit at the statutory rate of seven percent, first, over the period from the first quarter of 1962 to the fourth quarter of 1972 and, second, from the second quarter of 1959 to the fourth quarter of 1972. Both policies would have been an improvement over the historical policy. The average gap with introduction of the tax credit in 1962 is 1.9 billions per year below the historical policy; the average gap with introduction of the tax credit in 1959 is 4.4 billions per year. Both policies are assessed on the basis of the root mean squared gap criterion. We conclude that the credit should have been introduced several years before 1962, its actual date of introduction.

Confining further consideration to the period 1959–1972, we then compare alternative investment tax credit policies with fixed rates. By the root mean squared GNP gap criterion the best of these policies is associated with a rate of at least thirteen percent. By the weighted root mean squared GNP gap criterion the best policy would have been somewhere in the range of thirteen to fifteen percent. These policies would have reduced the GNP gap by an average of 6.8 billions of 1958 dollars for the root mean squared error criterion and 6.6 billions for the weighted root squared error criterion. We conclude that the best policy of this type for the period 1959–1972 would have required a rate of almost double the statutory rate of seven percent introduced in 1962.

We have considered alternative policies with constant investment tax credit over the period 1959–1972. We can also consider the best "flexible" policy over this period, allowing the rate of the tax credit to vary within the range four to fifteen percent, as in recent proposals. We first assume that the timing of the implementation of a flexible policy is perfect, that is, there is no delay in implementation of the optimal policy. Given likely errors in forecasting the future state of the economy three to five years after a change in policy, this is a highly unrealistic assumption that favors the adoption of a flexible policy. The actual changes in policy may be mistimed or even in the wrong direction, as in the policy changes over the period 1962–1972 reviewed in the preceding section.

The optimal flexible policy has a very simple form, given in table 7.5. For the time interval up to the second quarter of 1964 the investment tax credit is set at its maximum rate of fifteen percent. Beginning with the second quarter of 1964 the rate of the credit is reduced to its minimum rate of four percent. In the second quarter of 1969 the credit is increased to its maximum rate again and continues at this rate throughout the remainder of the period ending with the fourth quarter of 1972. Under the extremely optimistic assumption that the administration of this policy is perfectly timed, this policy reduces the GNP gap by 3.7 billions of 1958 dollars by the root mean squared gap criterion and 3.3 billions by the weighted root squared gap criterion.

For comparison we present an analysis of the optimal flexible tax credit policy with rates confined to the historical range of zero and seven percent. We set the rate equal to zero for the period before the first quarter of 1962 and retain the unrealistic assumption that there is no error in timing or direction in the implementation of the optimal policy. Under these assumptions the optimal policy would have been to suspend the investment tax credit from the first quarter of 1965 to the first quarter of 1968. This policy would have produced a very marginal gain over keeping the tax credit constant at a rate of seven percent for the whole period of 500 millions of 1958 dollars for the root mean squared gap criterion and 300 million dollars for the weighted root squared gap criterion.

Our first conclusion is that the investment tax credit should be changed *less* rather than *more* frequently. During the period 1962–1972 the credit was changed in 1964, 1966, 1967, 1969 and 1971. It should

Table 7.5
Optimal rates of the investment tax credit,
1959–1972 (percent)[a]

Date	Historical simulation error	Optimal 0–7 rates (1962–)	Actual tax credit rate
59:2	15.0	0.0	0.0
59:3	15.0	0.0	0.0
59:4	15.0	0.0	0.0
60:1	15.0	0.0	0.0
60:2	15.0	0.0	0.0
60:3	15.0	0.0	0.0
60:4	15.0	0.0	0.0
61:1	15.0	0.0	0.0
61:2	15.0	0.0	0.0
61:3	15.0	0.0	0.0
61:4	15.0	0.0	0.0
62:1	15.0	7.0	7.0
62:2	15.0	7.0	7.0
62:3	15.0	7.0	7.0
62:4	15.0	7.0	7.0
63:1	15.0	7.0	7.0
63:2	15.0	7.0	7.0
63:3	15.0	7.0	7.0
63:4	15.0	7.0	7.0
64:1	15.0	7.0	7.0
64:2	4.0	7.0	7.0
64:3	4.0	7.0	7.0
64:4	4.0	7.0	7.0
65:1	4.0	0.0	7.0
65:2	4.0	0.0	7.0
65:3	4.0	0.0	7.0
65:4	4.0	0.0	7.0
66:1	4.0	0.0	7.0
66:2	4.0	0.0	7.0
66:3	4.0	0.0	7.0
66:4	4.0	0.0	0.0
67:1	4.0	0.0	0.0
67:2	4.0	0.0	7.0
67:3	4.0	0.0	7.0
67:4	4.0	0.0	7.0
68:1	4.0	0.0	7.0
68:2	4.0	7.0	7.0
68:3	4.0	7.0	7.0
68:4	10.4	7.0	7.0

Table 7.5
(continued)

Date	Historical simulation error	Optimal 0–7 rates (1962–)	Actual tax credit rate
69:1	15.0	7.0	7.0
69:2	12.6	7.0	0.0
69:3	15.0	7.0	0.0
69:4	15.0	7.0	0.0
70:1	15.0	7.0	0.0
70:2	15.0	7.0	0.0
70:3	15.0	7.0	0.0
70:4	15.0	7.0	0.0
71:1	15.0	7.0	0.0
71:2	15.0	7.0	7.0
71:3	15.0	7.0	7.0
71:4	15.0	7.0	7.0
72:1	15.0	7.0	7.0
72:2	15.0	7.0	7.0
72:3	15.0	7.0	7.0
72:4	15.0	7.0	7.0

a. In all these simulations, a cost of five hundred million 1958 dollars was associated with changes in the effective tax credit rate.

have been changed only twice—in 1964 and 1969. Furthermore, it should have been decreased in 1964 and increased in 1969; the actual policy in those years was just the reverse. We must emphasize that our evaluation of the flexible tax credit makes the most optimistic possible assumption about the timing and direction of changes in the credit. It assumes that gross errors in the direction of policy change, such as those that took place in 1964 and 1969, would not have taken place. It also assumes that changes will be properly timed, while the suspension of the tax credit in 1966 and its restoration in 1971 lagged an average of almost ten quarters behind the appropriate times for a policy change. The reintroduction of the investment tax credit in 1967 led the appropriate time for a policy change by seven quarters.

Even on the most optimistic assumptions about the administration of a flexible policy, changes in the rate of the tax credit should be very infrequent. During the period from 1960 to the present the only occasion when a change in the rate would have contributed to stabilization was during the Vietnam War. During this period the Administration intentionally avoided alterations in fiscal policy during the initial military buildup. When the Administration finally recommended suspension of the tax credit in 1966, Congressional action was swift. We conclude that there is no justification for a transfer of responsibilities for administration of the tax credit from the Congress to the Administration or to an independent agency such as the Federal Reserve System.

We have assumed away the possibility of errors in timing and direction of the optimal flexible investment tax credit. Actual changes in the tax credit in the correct direction were delayed by ten quarters in 1966 and by nine quarters in 1971. We have evaluated the root mean squared gap criterion and the weighted root mean squared gap criterion for delays of two, four, six, eight and ten quarters in implementation of the optimal policy. By either criterion a lag of six quarters or more in implementation of the optimal policy results in a performance of stabilization policy that is comparable to the performance of the best policy with a constant rate of the tax credit. We must stress that this comparison is favorable to the flexible tax credit in that errors in the direction of policy changes are not taken into account.

We conclude that even on the basis of the optimistic assumption there are no errors in direction of policy changes in the administration of a flexible tax credit, policies with a constant tax credit outperform the best policies with a flexible rate of the tax credit, given the realities of delay in implementation of policy changes. During the period from 1960 to the present a policy with a constant rate of fifteen percent would have outperformed both the actual policy and a flexible policy with a range of four to fifteen percent with an average delay of ten quarters in implementation. A policy with a slightly lower constant rate of thirteen percent does even better.

To provide additional information about the performance of alternative investment tax credit policies we present investment, GNP, and the gap between actual and potential GNP, all in real terms, for the period 1959–1972 for three policies—the optimal flexible policy, the optimal policy lagged ten quarters, and the optimal policy with a fixed tax credit of thirteen percent—in table 7.6.

The results for the optimal flexible policy are based on the unrealistic assumption that all policy changes are perfectly timed and in the right direction. The tax credit under this policy ranges between four and fifteen percent with two major changes in the rate to coincide

Table 7.6
Effect of an optimal investment tax credit, 1959–1972

Date	Optimal policy lagged ten qtrs.			Optimal fixed rate policy (13 percent)			Optimal flexible policy		
	IPDE58	GNP58	Real GNP gap	IPDE58	GNP58	Real GNP gap	IPDE58	GNP58	Real GNP gap
59:2	28.1	479.9	−21.4	28.1	479.9	−21.4	28.1	479.9	−21.4
59:3	28.4	475.0	−30.6	28.4	475.0	−30.6	28.4	475.0	−30.6
59:4	29.3	481.6	−28.4	29.2	481.4	−28.6	29.3	481.6	−28.4
60:1	30.9	493.4	−21.0	30.6	492.9	−21.5	30.9	493.4	−21.0
60:2	33.5	495.4	−23.4	33.1	494.5	−24.3	33.5	495.4	−23.4
60:3	34.1	495.7	−27.6	33.4	494.4	−28.9	34.1	495.7	−27.6
60:4	34.5	494.6	−33.2	33.7	492.9	−34.9	34.5	495.6	−33.2
61:1	33.5	495.5	−36.9	32.5	493.4	−39.0	33.5	495.5	−36.9
61:2	34.1	507.0	−30.0	33.0	504.8	−32.2	34.1	507.0	−30.0
61:3	35.5	516.3	−25.3	34.3	513.9	−27.7	35.5	516.3	−25.3
61:4	36.8	526.8	−19.5	35.6	524.4	−21.9	36.8	526.8	−19.5
62:1	38.0	534.9	−16.1	35.8	532.4	−18.6	38.0	534.9	−16.1
62:2	39.2	543.7	−12.1	38.0	541.1	−14.7	39.2	543.7	−12.1
62:3	40.5	549.5	−11.1	39.2	546.9	−13.7	40.4	549.5	−11.1
62:4	39.9	554.1	−11.3	38.7	551.4	−14.0	39.9	554.1	−11.3
63:1	39.2	556.2	−14.4	38.1	553.6	−17.0	39.2	556.2	−14.4
63:2	39.3	559.9	−16.0	38.2	557.4	−18.5	39.3	559.9	−16.0
63:3	40.3	567.5	−13.7	39.2	565.2	−16.1	40.3	567.6	−13.7
63:4	40.9	573.7	−12.9	39.9	571.4	−15.2	40.9	573.7	−12.9

Table 7.6
(continued)

Date	Optimal policy lagged ten qtrs.			Optimal fixed rate policy (13 percent)			Optimal flexible policy		
	IPDE58	GNP58	Real GNP gap	IPDE58	GNP58	Real GNP gap	IPDE58	GNP58	Real GNP gap
64:1	41.5	581.6	-10.5	40.5	579.4	-12.6	41.5	581.5	-10.5
64:2	42.3	588.3	- 9.2	41.3	586.3	-11.3	42.3	588.3	- 9.2
64:3	44.3	595.6	- 7.4	43.3	593.5	- 9.5	44.3	595.6	- 7.4
64:4	45.0	598.7	- 9.9	43.9	596.5	-12.1	44.1	597.6	-11.1
65:1	47.1	612.6	- 1.6	45.9	610.1	- 4.1	45.1	609.4	- 4.8
65:2	48.1	622.1	2.2	46.8	619.2	- 0.7	44.9	616.4	- 3.5
65:3	50.8	634.8	9.2	49.3	631.7	6.1	46.3	626.4	0.8
65:4	52.6	649.7	18.3	51.0	646.3	14.9	46.9	638.7	7.3
66:1	54.6	662.4	24.8	53.0	658.7	21.1	48.0	649.4	11.8
66:2	56.1	668.7	24.8	54.4	665.0	21.1	48.8	654.4	10.5
66:3	57.9	674.2	24.0	56.1	670.4	20.2	50.2	659.3	9.1
66:4	59.2	682.3	25.7	57.4	678.5	21.9	51.3	667.1	10.5
67:1	57.3	681.3	18.2	55.4	677.5	14.4	49.1	665.6	2.5
67:2	58.4	686.4	16.8	57.4	683.7	14.1	50.9	671.2	1.6
67:3	57.5	693.3	17.1	57.8	692.5	16.3	51.2	679.5	3.3
67:4	56.8	697.3	14.4	58.4	699.1	16.2	51.6	685.5	2.4
68:1	57.0	702.9	13.3	60.0	707.0	17.4	53.1	693.5	4.0
68:2	55.1	713.2	16.8	59.3	720.5	24.1	52.4	706.4	10.0
68:3	55.1	717.7	14.4	60.5	727.9	24.6	53.5	713.3	10.0
68:4	55.0	719.1	8.9	61.1	731.5	21.3	54.0	716.3	6.1
69:1	57.0	723.1	5.9	63.4	736.8	19.6	56.1	721.4	4.2
69:2	56.4	723.9	- 0.4	63.2	739.3	15.0	56.4	724.5	0.2
69:3	57.0	726.3	- 5.1	64.0	742.1	10.7	58.4	729.1	- 2.3
69:4	57.8	721.5	-17.1	65.1	737.8	- 0.8	60.5	727.2	-11.4

Table 7.6
(continued)

Date	Optimal policy lagged ten qtrs.			Optimal fixed rate policy (13 percent)			Optimal flexible policy		
	IPDE58	GNP58	Real GNP gap	IPDE58	GNP58	Real GNP gap	IPDE58	GNP58	Real GNP gap
70:1	56.6	719.6	−26.8	64.0	737.0	− 9.4	60.9	727.4	−19.0
70:2	57.3	721.3	−33.0	64.8	738.8	−15.5	63.1	733.1	−21.3
70:3	59.0	727.5	−34.8	66.5	744.7	−17.6	66.0	742.5	−19.8
70:4	55.1	721.1	−49.3	62.6	738.1	−32.4	63.1	738.9	−31.5
71:1	57.4	737.5	−41.0	64.8	753.4	−25.1	65.8	756.1	−22.4
71:2	59.0	744.5	−42.2	66.4	758.4	−28.3	67.8	762.7	−24.0
71:3	59.7	751.1	−44.0	67.1	764.8	−30.3	68.9	770.1	−25.0
71:4	63.5	763.8	−39.7	70.3	776.4	−27.1	72.4	782.5	−21.0
72:1	66.8	774.4	−37.6	72.3	784.6	−27.4	74.6	791.5	−20.5
72:2	69.0	793.1	−27.6	73.3	800.7	−19.9	75.7	808.2	−12.4
72:3	71.6	807.2	−22.1	74.2	811.9	−17.4	76.8	819.9	− 9.4
72:4	76.6	825.2	−12.8	77.6	826.9	−11.1	80.3	835.5	− 2.5

with escalation and de-escalation of the Vietnam War. Our first conclusion is that this policy would have helped to alleviate the inflationary pressures of the Vietnam buildup, but that the policy by itself
would have been inadequate to close the gap between actual and
potential GNP during the Vietnam War or during the period before
1965 and after 1969 when the actual level of GNP was below potential
GNP.

The optimal policy, lagged ten quarters, is based on a more realistic
assumption about the timing of the investment tax credit, namely that
policy changes will lag behind the optimal time for changes in policy.
On the other hand, miscalculations such as policy changes in the
wrong direction in 1964 and 1969, are ruled out by assumption under
this policy. The results also give an optimistic view of the performance of a flexible policy. With a lag of ten quarters, the reduction of
the rate of the investment tax credit to four percent during the Vietnam War makes a relatively modest contribution to containing
inflationary pressures. The performance of this policy is also unsatisfactory during the recession of 1969–1970.

A constant investment tax credit of thirteen percent performs about
as well as the optimal tax policy lagged ten quarters through 1969.
For the period from 1969 to the present the policy with a constant rate
performs substantially better than the optimal policy lagged ten quarters or the actual policy. This is a reflection of the fact that under a
fixed tax credit the suspension of 1969 would have avoided altogether,
while the optimal policy lagged ten quarters requires an increase in
the tax credit from four to fifteen percent at about the same time as the
reintroduction of the actual investment tax credit at a rate of seven
percent in 1971.

Up to this point we have focused attention on the contribution of
the investment tax credit to economic stability. Our overall conclusion
is the same as in the preceding section, that the tax credit should be set
with economic growth rather than economic stabilization as the
primary criterion. We turn next to an evaluation of the alternative
policies from the point of view of their contribution to the growth of
productive capacity in the form of capital stock. We present capital
stocks resulting from alternative policies in table 7.7.

In general, we find that a higher rate of the investment tax credit for
a longer period of time results in a more rapid growth of productive
capacity. The constant investment tax credit at the optimal rate of thirteen percent would have resulted in a 17.0 percent increase in capital

Table 7.7
End-of-period (1972) capital stock under various tax credit
policies (billions of 1958 dollars)

	Capital stock	Percentage change from actual figure
(1) Actual policy	299.5	—
(2) Constant policies		
(a) 0%	283.9	−5.2
(b) 7% (62–72)	309.4	3.3
(c) 7% (59–72)	316.9	5.8
(d) 10%	333.2	11.2
(e) 13%	350.4	17.0
(f) 15%	362.3	21.0
(g) 20%	397.2	32.6
(3) Optimal policies		
(a) No lag	340.0	13.5
(b) Lagged 10 qtrs.	331.4	10.7

stock over the period 1959–1972. By contrast the optimal flexible tax credit within the range four to fifteen percent would have resulted in a 13.5 percent increase, while the optimal policy lagged ten quarters would have resulted in a 10.7 percent increase. Although the investment tax credit has little to contribute to stabilization policy, it can be an effective policy instrument for stimulating capital formation and the associated growth of productive capacity.

To evaluate alternative policies for the investment tax credit for the next decade we can perform a similar assessment of the effectiveness of these policies, using a forecast of U.S. economic growth for the next decade, based on the DRI quarterly econometric model. The optimal flexible investment tax credit with a range of four to fifteen percent in the rate of the tax credit would be to move immediately to a fifteen percent rate and to stay at that rate through 1985. This reflects the gap between actual and potential GNP that has emerged in the course of the year 1974 and seems likely to persist throughout the next decade. Even a constant twenty percent rate would not close the gap, so that any flexible policy with an upper bound below twenty percent would be optimized by simply setting the tax credit at its maximum rate for the next decade.

We compare the performance of alternative policies with constant rates in table 7.8. With a zero rate of the tax credit the GNP gap will average 52.0 billions of 1958 dollars by the root mean squared gap cri-

Table 7.8
Summary statistics on the real GNP gap (billions of 1958 dollars)

	Period 74:2–85:4	
	Root mean squared error	Weighted root squared error
(1) Constant policies		
(a) 0%	52.0	51.8
(b) 7%	39.0	39.6
(c) 10%	33.4	34.3
(d) 15%	23.8	25.3
(e) 20%	16.6	18.5
(f) 23%	15.3	17.0
(g) 25%	16.3	17.5
(2) Sample flexible policy		
(a) 25% (74–76),		
(b) 22% (77–82),		
(c) 20% (83–85)	13.8	15.6

terion and 51.8 billions by the weighted root squared error criterion. A constant fifteen percent rate would reduce the gap to 23.8 billions of 1958 dollars and 25.3 billions by the two criteria. The time pattern of GNP gaps resulting from tax credits of fifteen and twenty percent are given in table 7.9. The best rate for the tax credit under a policy with an unchanging rate is twenty-three percent by either criterion. This policy will reduce the gap to 15.3 billions of 1958 dollars by the root mean squared gap criterion and 17.0 billions by the weighted root square error criterion.

For comparison we have analyzed a flexible investment tax credit with a maximum rate of twenty-five percent. Under this policy the optimal rate would be the maximum for the period 1974–1976; the rate would be reduced to twenty-two percent over the period 1977–1982 and to twenty percent over the period 1983–1985. The time pattern of these policy changes is presented in greater detail in table 7.10. As in our previous analysis we have evaluated this policy on the assumption that there are no errors of direction and timing in the administration of policy changes. Even on these overly optimistic assumptions the gain in moving from the best policy with a constant rate to the best flexible policy is only 1.5 billions of 1958 dollars by the root mean squared error criterion and 1.4 billions by the weighted root squared error criterion. These gains are unlikely to be realized when delays

Table 7.9
Effect of an investment tax credit, 1974–1985 (billions of 1958 dollars)

	Constant fifteen percent rate			Constant twenty percent rate		
Period	IPDE58	GNP58	GNP gap	IPDE58	GNP58	GNP gap
74:2	68.5	837.1	−45.9	68.5	837.1	−45.9
74:3	71.2	845.1	−46.2	71.2	845.1	−46.2
74:4	73.6	858.7	−41.0	74.4	859.7	−40.0
75:1	75.7	868.0	−40.3	77.6	870.6	−37.7
75:2	77.9	879.4	−37.6	80.8	883.9	−33.1
75:3	79.7	889.4	−36.5	83.8	895.9	−29.9
75:4	81.7	899.5	−35.2	86.9	908.0	−26.8
76:1	83.6	908.9	−35.1	89.7	918.9	−25.1
76:2	85.2	920.0	−33.2	92.0	931.1	−22.2
76:3	86.6	930.1	−32.6	93.7	941.5	−21.1
76:4	88.0	940.2	−32.0	95.3	951.8	−20.3
77:1	90.0	955.8	−26.0	98.5	967.6	−14.1
77:2	92.5	967.3	−24.1	100.3	979.2	−12.2
77:3	94.6	978.4	−22.7	102.6	990.4	−10.8
77:4	96.4	990.1	−21.0	104.6	1002.1	−8.9
78:1	98.4	1001.1	−19.6	106.7	1013.3	−7.5
78:2	100.4	1011.3	−19.3	108.9	1023.5	−7.0
78:3	102.4	1021.5	−19.0	111.1	1033.9	−6.6
78:4	104.4	1032.2	−18.3	113.2	1044.8	−5.7
79:1	106.4	1041.5	−18.8	115.4	1054.3	−6.0
79:2	108.1	1051.1	−19.1	117.3	1064.3	−5.9
79:3	109.9	1061.3	−19.0	119.2	1074.8	−5.5
79:4	111.4	1071.9	−18.5	120.9	1085.5	−4.9
80:1	112.9	1082.3	−18.1	122.7	1095.8	−4.5
80:2	114.9	1092.9	−17.4	124.8	1106.3	−4.0
80:3	116.9	1104.0	−16.5	127.0	1117.2	−3.3
80:4	118.9	1115.5	−15.2	129.2	1128.7	−2.0
81:1	120.7	1126.2	−14.6	131.2	1139.1	−1.7
81:2	122.6	1137.4	−13.5	133.3	1150.0	−0.9
81:3	124.3	1147.1	−14.0	135.3	1159.3	−1.8
81:4	126.2	1156.5	−14.9	137.3	1168.6	−2.8
82:1	128.1	1167.1	−14.7	139.5	1179.4	−2.5
82:2	130.1	1177.9	−14.5	141.7	1190.3	−2.0
82:3	132.1	1188.3	−14.7	144.0	1200.8	−2.1
82:4	133.6	1198.6	−15.0	145.9	1211.4	−2.2
83:1	135.3	1208.3	−16.1	147.9	1221.3	−3.1
83:2	137.5	1218.0	−17.3	150.4	1231.2	−4.1
83:3	139.8	1228.8	−17.4	153.1	1242.2	−4.0
83:4	142.0	1240.7	−16.6	155.8	1254.3	−3.0

Table 7.9
(continued)

Period	Constant fifteen percent rate			Constant twenty percent rate		
	IPDE58	GNP58	GNP gap	IPDE58	GNP58	GNP gap
84:1	144.2	1253.2	−15.2	158.4	1266.9	−1.5
84:2	146.5	1265.1	−14.7	161.2	1278.7	−1.0
84:3	148.8	1276.0	−15.1	164.0	1289.6	−1.5
84:4	151.3	1287.2	−15.3	167.0	1300.9	−1.7
85:1	153.6	1299.2	−14.9	169.9	1312.8	−1.3
85:2	156.0	1312.4	−13.4	172.9	1326.0	0.2
85:3	158.5	1325.2	−12.3	176.0	1339.0	1.4
85:4	161.1	1337.2	−12.3	179.2	1351.2	1.7

Table 7.10
Real GNP gap under sample flexible policy, 1974–1985
(billions of 1958 dollars)

Date	Credit rate	GNP gap	Date	Credit rate	GNP gap
74:2	25.0	−45.9	80:2	22.0	−2.2
74:3	25.0	−46.2	80:3	22.0	−1.6
74:4	25.0	−38.8	80:4	22.0	−0.5
75:1	25.0	−34.7	81:1	22.0	−0.3
75:2	25.0	−27.8	81:2	22.0	0.3
75:3	25.0	−22.2	81:3	22.0	−0.6
75:4	25.0	−16.9	81:4	22.0	−1.5
76:1	25.0	−13.4	82:1	22.0	−1.5
76:2	25.0	−9.2	82:2	22.0	−1.0
76:3	25.0	−7.7	82:3	22.0	−0.4
76:4	25.0	−6.6	82:4	22.0	−0.0
77:1	22.0	−0.4	83:1	20.0	−0.6
77:2	22.0	1.5	83:2	20.0	−1.3
77:3	22.0	1.9	83:3	20.0	−1.4
77:4	22.0	2.3	83:4	20.0	−0.8
78:1	22.0	2.0	84:1	20.0	0.0
78:2	22.0	0.6	84:2	20.0	−0.1
78:3	22.0	−0.8	84:3	20.0	−1.0
78:4	22.0	−1.4	84:4	20.0	1.5
79:1	22.0	−2.8	85:1	20.0	−1.2
79:2	22.0	−3.1	85:2	20.0	0.7
79:3	22.0	−2.9	85:3	20.0	2.5
79:4	22.0	−2.5	85:4	20.0	3.4
80:1	22.0	−2.4			

and errors in the implementation of the best flexible policy are taken into account.

To evaluate the alternative policies from the point of view of their contribution to the growth of productive capacity, we present end of period capital stocks for each of the policies in table 7.11. Relative to a constant tax credit rate of seven percent, a rate of fifteen percent would produce a capital stock that is 12.5 percent higher by 1985; a twenty percent rate would produce a capital stock of 22.0 percent higher; and a twenty-three percent rate, judged as best by the criterion of its contribution to stabilization, would produce a level of capital stock that is 28.4 percent higher than the level associated with a rate of seven percent. By comparison the best flexible policy with a maximum rate of twenty-five percent would produce a capital stock in 1985 that is only 25.7 percent higher.

The main conclusions of our comparison of alternative investment tax credit policies are as follows:

(1) The best constant rate for the investment tax credit over the period from 1960 to the present would have been almost double the maximum statutory rate in force during the period of seven percent. A policy with a constant rate at the higher level would have been superior to the actual policy from the point of view of both economic growth and economic stability.

Table 7.11
End-of-period (1985) capital stock under various tax credit policies (billions of 1958 dollars)

	Capital stock	Percentage change from actual figure
(1) Constant policies		
(a) 0%	617.7	−8.9
(b) 7%	678.4	—
(c) 10%	707.9	4.3
(d) 15%	763.3	12.5
(e) 20%	827.6	22.0
(f) 23%	871.2	28.4
(g) 25%	902.7	33.1
(2) Sample flexible policy 25% (74–76), 22% (77–82), 20% (83–85)	852.7	25.7

(2) For the next decade the best rate of the investment tax credit for stabilization purposes would be roughly triple the current rate of seven percent. By 1985 the higher rate would increase productive capacity by almost thirty percent over the level that would result from the present tax credit.

7.5   Conclusion

Combining the results of our analysis of the investment tax credit for the period from 1960 to the present and from the present through 1985, we conclude that a much higher rate of the tax credit, possibly in the range of twenty to twenty-five percent, should have been adopted at the outset and continued for the indefinite future. During the Vietnam War fiscal policy should have been tightened substantially with the military buildup beginning in 1964 and relaxed considerably with the de-escalation in 1969. The tax credit could have been suspended for this period as part of such a change in fiscal policy, but the major burden of stabilization should have been imposed on instruments that have maximum effect in less than three to five years after their adoption.

We have demonstrated that the investment tax credit has a powerful impact on the level of capital formation and the growth of productive capacity. Impressed with these and similar results, proponents of a flexible investment tax credit have suggested that the rate of the tax credit should be changed more frequently and for this purpose that responsibility for changes in the rate should be transferred from the Congress to the Administration or to an independent agency such as the Federal Reserve System. Our results do not support this view. Errors in the direction and timing of the rate of the investment tax credit under the present system of Congressional control have nullified any contribution that the investment tax credit could have made to stabilization. These errors were the result of changes that were too frequent, misdirected and mistimed.

On the optimistic assumption that the administration of a flexible policy is free from errors of direction and timing only two changes would have taken place of the period from 1960 to the present, coinciding with the beginning and end of the Vietnam military buildup. The general direction of tax policy, as recommended by the Administration and enacted by the Congress, was in precisely the wrong direction during this period. There was little delay in Congressional implementation of Administration proposals in 1964 and 1969, so that the major burden of responsibility for the errors in policy cannot be attributed to the sluggishness of Congressional procedures for consideration of policy changes.

Our overall conclusion is that economic growth rather than counter-cyclical stabilization should be the primary criterion for selecting the appropriate rate for the investment tax credit. To stimulate economic growth and close the persistent gap between actual and potential GNP that characterizes the period 1960–1985, except for the Vietnam War, much higher rates of the investment tax credit would be required. Changes in the rate of the investment tax credit should be less frequent than they have been in the past. There is no justification for a transfer of responsibilities for administration of the tax credit from the Congress to the Administration or to an independent agency, such as the Federal Reserve System.

Appendix A: The Investment Equation

Our methodology for analyzing the economic impact of investment incentives is based on simulation studies of U.S. economic activity under alternative investment incentive programs. In a study completed in 1970 we combined the quarterly econometric model of Data Resources, Inc., with an econometric model of investment behavior originated by Hall and Jorgenson, in a study of tax policy and investment behavior.[3] This investment model and closely related models have been successfully employed in studies of the impact of investment incentives by the Brookings Institution, the Fund for Public Policy Research for the Joint Committee on Internal Revenue Taxation of the U.S. Congress, and by the Board of Governors of the Federal Reserve System.[4] To study the impact of a flexible tax credit on economic stabilization, we take our earlier study as a point of departure.[5]

In determining the impact of the tax credit on the economy, our first objective is to determine an appropriate specification of the investment equation. We attempted to bias the selection procedure in favor of a volatile policy by using an equation in which the tax credit entered strongly and with short lags. Specifically, we chose to restrict our specification search to the type of neoclassical specification associated with Hall and Jorgenson (1967). Since this theory is described in detail elsewhere, our description here will be brief.

In the neoclassical theory desired capital stock is a function of output and the relative prices of capital and output. The use of actual output is appropriate if the firm takes output as given or sets output equal to long run desired output in each period. We assume that the production function is Cobb-Douglas, so that a one percent change in the rental price of capital leads by assumption to a one percent change in desired capital. Evidence from production studies for cross sections and a sophisticated time series study by Bischoff (1971a) support this assumption.

Given the desired capital stock and the actual capital stock in any period, the theory postulates that orders and contracts are let so as to close the gap. By using desired capital stock, rather than its separate components in the analysis, we assume that the speeds of adjustment to all possible changes are the same.[6] In one test of this assumption on industry data, Picou and Waud (1973) found differences in the nature of the reaction times to various components of desired capital. Since they find no consistent pattern among industries, the cost in an aggregate study of assuming equal reaction times is small.

The estimated equation used in this study, resulting from the above procedure, is as follows,

$$IPDE = -9.656 + 0.0572*K + 0.00181*V + 0.00218*V(-1)$$
$$\quad (1.522) \ (0.0163) \quad (0.00071) \quad (0.00033)$$

$$+ 0.00233*V(-2) + 0.00228*V(-3) + 0.00202*V(-4)$$
$$\quad (0.00019) \qquad\quad (0.00031) \qquad\quad (0.00038)$$

$$+ 0.00156*V(-5) + 0.00088*V(-6).$$
$$\quad (0.00036) \qquad\quad (0.00023)$$

Here, $IPDE58$ is real investment in producer's durable equipment, K is gross, beginning of period, real capital stock of producer's durable equipment, and the proxy for desired capital stock is $V = PGNP$ $(-2)*GNP58(-1)/C(-2)$, where $PGNP$ is the GNP price deflator and C, the rental cost of capital, is specified below. A second degree Almon polynomial lag structure constrained to pass through zero after seven periods was used. The original Durbin-Watson statistic was 0.7554 so a first-order autocorrelation transform was used. The standard error before transformation was 1.31375, and afterwards 1.01489.

In our study, the cost of capital, C, was defined as

$$C = PIPDE * (0.138 + R * (1 - U)) * (1 - U * Z - TC$$
$$\quad + Y * Z * TC * U)/(1 - U).$$

Here, $PIPDE$ is the price deflator for investment in producer's durable equipment; 0.138 is the depreciation rate on producer's durable equipment as calculated by Christensen and Jorgenson (1969); U is the nominal corporate tax rate; R, the interest rate on new issues of Aaa corporate bonds; Z, the present discontinued value of depreciation allowances; TC, the effective tax credit rate; and Y, the constant one during those years in which the Long Amendment applies, and zero otherwise. A detailed justification for the use of these definitions is given below.

Our procedure for constructing a quarterly series on the rate of the investment tax credit assumes an initial learning lag, when the credit is first introduced, and a maximum constant effective rate for the rest of the period. The maximum rate was calculated to be 5.6 percent, only four-fifths of the nominal seven percent rate. In our optimal control study, we ignored learning lags and assumed a strict proportional relationship between the effective and nominal rates, regardless of the size of the credit rate. Alternate assumptions will produce slight changes in the effectiveness of the tax credit, but will have virtually no effect on its sensitivity to timing errors.

Theoretically, the effective rate on marginal investment rather than the average effective rate should be used, but our data allowed no means of testing for any difference between them. However, this theoretical fact makes our results applicable to some alternative proposals for use of the tax credit. For example, Eisner (1973) has suggested that the tax credit apply only to investment in excess of depreciation charges. Since the marginal rate will remain unchanged for most firms, only minor adjustments need be made in the relation between effective and nominal rates to apply our analysis to this case. Another proposal Eisner made was to change the tax credit to a subsidy so as to make it available to firms without a taxable profit in any given year. Again, this just changes the relation between the effective and the nominal rates.

Historically, the Long Amendment only applied to 1962 and 1963. Since it was introduced with the tax credit, in the analysis below we assumed that it applied to all periods prior to the end of 1963. The Long Amendment limits the marginal effectiveness of the tax credit. In the quarter in which the repeal of this amendment was effective, the sensitivity (the derivative) of the desired capital stock with respect to the tax credit rose seventy percent. If our analysis had ignored the Long Amendment, we would have found the tax credit much more effective during the early 1960s.

We turn now to a more detailed description on our specification of an econometric equation for producers' durable equipment investment. The basic theoretical structure is outlined by Hall and Jorgenson and will not be repeated here.[7] For reference in the following discussion, the cost of capital is expressed by $c = q(r + \delta) (1 - UZ - TC)/(1 - U)$, where q is the price index of producers' durables, δ is the depreciation rate, r the discount rate, U the corporate tax rate, Z the present value of depreciation allowances, and TC the tax credit rate.

Our current research has focused on determining the most appropriate time series corresponding to the variables used in the above expression for c. For the capital price index q, the depreciation rate δ, and Z, the present value of depreciation allowances, we employed the same data used in our earlier study, brought up to date. In particular, the depreciation rate was fixed at a yearly rate of 13.8 percent, the rate arrived at by Christensen and Jorgenson (1969). The present value of depreciation was constructed using figures from the Department of the Treasury on average lifetimes, and using the most attractive depreciation formula available at any particular date. Though this is theoretically sound, it still remains true that many firms were slow to take advantage of tax breaks when they first became available. No attempt was made to allow for this learning period. The discount rate used in this construction of Z was assumed to be a constant rate of 10 percent—this rate should be interpreted as the real rate of return on producers' durable equipment. The current price index for producers' durable equipment, $PIPDE$, was used for q, as demanded by the theoretical model.

When changes are expected in prices, the effect of capital gains must be included in the cost of capital. The problem is more general, applying also to the other policy parameters. We have so far been unsuccessful at constructing a measure of these expectations which produces reasonable results. For the policy parameters, an adaptive form for expectations in which expected future values for a variable are a weighted average of past values is unsatisfactory, since the level of a policy variable may not be smooth or follow any trend. Also, there may be advance announcements, or strong rumors available in the business community about policy changes. Our attempts to incorporate inflationary expectations will be discussed below.

In the case of the tax credit rate, we did try to make corrections for learning lags and variations in the rate applying to different sectors. In our earlier study, we estimated an average effective rate by using the nominal rate for each sector. We used the size of the sectors as weights for aggregation.[8] In particular, we tried to correct for differences in the rates applying to long-lived assets, public utilities, and trucks. In this study, we used the effective tax credit rate—the total tax credit claimed, normalized by the level of investment. Thus learning lags and variations in the rate among sectors are automatically included.

We faced several problems in estimating the effective rate of the tax credit. First, the data are annual, but claims are reported for the year in which they are made, not the year in which the investment took place. Firms have a variety of fiscal years, so that effects occurring during one calendar year will be reported during the next year approximately half the time. If a firm has insufficient profit during the year, it is allowed to report the claim up to five years later, at such time as it does have sufficient profit. We took the effective rate at the end of 1968 as the maximum effective rate and distributed other claims so that there was a linear increase (a learning lag) from the date of introduction of the tax credit until it reached this maximum rate, at which point it stabilized. For the 7 percent tax credit, the maximum effective rate was approximately 5.6 percent.

We faced a similar problem in deciding on the appropriate measurement of the corporate income tax rate. A nominal and an effective tax rate are both available. As long as all companies pay some tax, the nominal rate is justified theoretically, since this is the marginal tax rate affecting all changes in investment (tax deductions immediately caused by the investment are already included in the formulation of the cost of capital). In the process of estimating the equation, we tried both alternatives, and found the nominal rate to consistently produce slightly better results, as expected.

The main area for re-examination of our specification involved the rate of discount. In equilibrium this would equal the expected after-tax internal rate of return on a marginal investment, or the rate of time preference plus risk and liquidity premiums. Unfortunately, neither approach provides a constructive definition.[9] In our previous study, we assumed the rate of return remained constant over time, independent of changes in policy parameters. This amounted to an assumption of full corporate tax shifting, or of constant tax rates. However, within the period of estimation, the latter assumption is not too extreme, since the corporate rate remained within the interval (0.48, 0.528).

The approach we tried here in constructing a measure of the after-tax rate of return to capital is to use a borrowing rate for the firm, in particular the long-term Aaa corporate bond rate for new issues. Since interest payments are tax deductible, the net cost in terms of after tax profits of interest payments is $(1 - U) \cdot R$ with R being the bond rate. In a world of certainty and no transactions costs, maximization of profits implies that the net of tax borrowing rate $(1 - U) \cdot R$ will be equated with the marginal internal after-tax rate of return to capital. We employed yearly bond rate multiplied by $(1 - U)$ as a measure for r. The results from this specification were reported in the text of the paper.

For this specification, the lag coefficients were constrained to lie along a second degree polynomial going back seven periods beyond the initial two period lag. This was arrived at by a series of tests on alternative lag structures. Changing the degree or the length of the lag structure caused slight deterioration of the fit. The coefficient on the capital stock should be an estimate of the depreciation rate, yet the figure produced of 5.7 percent is significantly below the cross-sectional figure of 13.8 percent. The difference is statistically very significant, with a t-test of 4.97. When various attempts were made to constrain this coefficient to 13.8 percent, the quality of fit deteriorated, and the lag structure became very weak. For this reason, since our control study focused on the lag structure, we used the unconstrained version. In comparison with the above, when a constant discount rate was used, the estimated depreciation rate became significantly negative.

The above results ignore the effects of changes in inflationary expectations. Inflation causes capital gains to the owner of the machinery, but if the rise in prices is uniform, then, in real terms, nothing has changed. An exception would be the value of depreciation allowances, which are carried over time in nominal terms. This implies that a real, not a nominal, interest rate is appropriate—the discount rate should be insensitive to inflation. In the study by Feldstein and Eckstein (1970) of the corporate bond rate used above, a proxy for the expected inflation rate was developed, whose coefficient was very close to one. This rate can be approximated by a simple weighted average of past inflation rates for the preceding six years, with linearly declining weights. We tried subtracting this proxy for expected inflation from the post-tax interest rate, but found that substituting this real rate for the money rate caused marked deterioration of the fit,

with the standard error climbing to 1.49 and the estimated depreciation rate moving far off base to −11 percent, and the lag structure
taking on implausible shapes.[10]

An alternative approach in constructing the discount rate is to focus
on the portfolio choice of the investor between stocks and bonds.
Here, however, the simplifying assumptions must be truly heroic.
One possible model is as follows. The real after (personal) tax rate of
return on bonds, $(1 - t) \cdot R$, is equated with the rate of return on equities. This rate will be approximated by

$$
\frac{EARNINGS}{PRICE} \cdot \left(\frac{DIVIDENDS}{EARNINGS} (1 - t) \right.
$$

$$
\left. + \left(1 - \frac{DIVIDENDS}{EARNINGS} \right) \left(1 - \frac{t}{2} \right) \right) + \pi \left(1 - \frac{t}{2} \right).
$$

The justification for this formulation is that undistributed profits
amount in the eyes of the investor to capital gains, which are taxed at
half the normal marginal rate; inflationary expectations lead to
increases in stock prices above those caused by reinvestment; and
other capital gains, due to cyclical swings in the economy, are common to both equities and bonds, and have been assumed, in this gross
approximation, to cancel.

The rate of return on capital after corporate taxes is
$EARNINGS/K$ (K = capital stock). Solving for this rate gives

$$
\frac{EARNINGS}{K} = \left[R \cdot (1 - t) - \pi \left(1 - \frac{t}{2} \right) \right] \cdot \frac{PRICE}{K}
$$

$$
\cdot \left(1 - \frac{t}{2} - \frac{t}{2} \cdot \frac{DIVIDENDS}{EARNINGS} \right)^{-1}.
$$

As a representative case, we tried $t = 2/3$ and $DIVIDENDS/EARNINGS$
$= 1/2$. The value of the capital stock was assumed to be the sum of
the values of outstanding equity and corporate bonds. The debt-
capital ratio has been changing over time, but we assumed it constant
at 25 percent, its representative value during the mid-1960s (see Pechman, 1971). With these assumptions, the rate of return on capital can
be represented by $(R/2) - \pi$, that is, one-half the interest rate on new
issues of corporate bonds, less the inflation rate.

Because the corporate tax rate has been near 50 percent throughout
the period used, $R/2$ is virtually indistinguishable from $R \cdot (1 - U)$.

The estimation produced only trivial differences. As before, inclusion of an expected inflation term caused marked deterioration. The close correspondence to our previous measure is due partly to the particular parameter values chosen, but experimentation seems to indicate that the fractions do not change much for any reasonable choice of the parameters. This approach was explored merely to lend more credence to the use of the bond rate as a proxy for the rate of return to capital.

Appendix B: Optimization Procedures

To study the effectiveness of a flexible investment tax credit, we have analyzed stabilization policy during the period from the second quarter of 1959 until the end of 1972. We assume that Congress would permit flexible determination of the tax credit within the range of four to fifteen percent. Therefore, tax credit rates are constrained to lie within the specified bounds, but no further costs or constraints on the tax rates are used.[11] We then choose optimal tax credit rates, subject to these constraints, holding real Federal government expenditures constant, and all other policy variables at their actual historical values. The degree of improvement in the GNP gap resulting from a slight relaxation of these constraints was also measured. In addition, we calculate the optimal rates for the tax credit within the range zero to seven percent for comparison with actual historical policy.

In order to choose the optimal tax credit we must determine GNP for each quarter as a function of past values of the tax credit. The impact on GNP can come from changes either in investment on in the government deficit. From our investment equation, we can estimate the effects of changes in the tax credit on the level of investment over time. Through simulations of the U.S. economy, using the quarterly econometric model of Data Resources Inc., we also can calculate the effect of investment on GNP. The effect of changes in tax revenues on GNP, though small, were also derived through simulations of the model. Together, these figures allow us to calculate the impact on GNP of past changes in the values of tax credit. We assume the effects on GNP of tax credit changes occurring more than five years earlier could be neglected.

As examples of the figures resulting from this process, table 7.12 shows the impact on real GNP in the first quarter of 1964, and the first quarter of 1967, of a one percent change in the tax credit from its his-

Table 7.12
Change in GNP (millions of 1957 dollars) due to a one percent
change in the investment tax credit

	Length of lag (in periods)										
Date	0	1	2	3	4	5	6	7	8	9	10
64:1	7.9	14.0	73.8	118.4	144.0	149.2	135.5	109.1	73.2	25.1	9.5
67:1	10.4	17.8	138.8	226.6	274.8	287.1	264.8	215.8	146.9	57.5	21.7

Date	11	12	13	14	15	16	17	18	19	20
64:1	6.0	8.6	11.7	12.6	11.2	8.7	6.2	4.4	2.8	2.0
67:1	11.2	13.3	10.0	10.2	8.1	5.0	2.1	−0.1	−1.2	−1.4

torical value in any one of the preceding twenty quarters. For example, if the tax credit were raised by one percent just in the first quarter of 1963, then real GNP in the first quarter of 1964 would have been 144 million dollars higher. These figures change as the initial value of the tax credit and the initial state of the economy change. To create a linear approximation at any point, we assume that the impact of the initial one percent change of the tax credit from its given value is identical in size to the impact of any further change, within the bounds specified.

The procedure for calculating the optimal tax rates uses as a first step such a linear approximation around the historical values. This puts the problem in a standard framework, except for the inequality constraints, of a linear model with a quadratic loss function, one solution algorithm for which is found in Chow (1973). Due to approximation errors in the linear model, the resulting rates will not be truly optimal. So we took this point, made a new linear approximation, and reoptimized. This procedure was iterated until convergence. In essence, it is a Newton-Raphson solution procedure for a nonlinear model. The convergence point will satisfy the first-order conditions for a full optimum.

We turn now to a precise description of the procedure we used to apply optimal control techniques to the study of the investment tax credit. Our discussion assumes familiarity with Chow (1973). This nonlinear procedure amounts to solution by successive linear approximations, that is, the "optimal rates" resulting from each round are plugged back into the full model, and a new linear approximation is taken around this new point. The initial point is taken to be the historical position of the economy. We first describe how this linear approximation is made, then justify our treatment of inequality constraints and our nonlinear procedure.

(1)   Linear Approximation

With real GNP as the sole target, what is sought in a linear model is to predict the impact on GNP of changes in present and past tax credit rates. To start out, a particular simulation of the economy must be chosen from which changes would be measured. In the first iteration, this basis simulation was made using actual tax credit rates holding real government expenditures constant, and holding all other exogenous variables at their historical values. Lagged endogenous variables were generated in the course of the simulation. Next, impact multipliers were calculated for marginal credit rate changes on future values of real GNP. This was done separately for each period. Several simplifying assumptions were made at this stage in order to simplify this computation. In particular, the impact of marginal credit rate changes on investment were calculated analytically while the impact of investment changes on GNP were approximated numerically.[12] By use of this set of multipliers, one can express the change in GNP from the base simulation as a linear function of changes in past tax credit rates. Two examples of this are found in table 7.12. The approximation comes in assuming that the impact of large credit rate changes is proportional to that of small credit rate changes.

In order to introduce some uncertainty, it was assumed that the simulation error of the model, when calculated using actual exogenous variables, would be independent of any tax credit rate changes. By this assumption, the simulation error can be used as an additive disturbance. However, it is severely autocorrelated, so a first-order autocorrelation process was assumed and the appropriate transformation made. This now gives us the following equation,

$$y_t = A_t y_{t-1} + C_t x_t + b_t + \varepsilon_t,$$

where,

$$y_t = \begin{bmatrix} GNP_t^p \\ x_t \\ \vdots \\ x_{t-20} \end{bmatrix}, \quad A_t = \begin{bmatrix} \rho & \alpha_t^* & \cdots & \alpha_{21,t}^* \\ 0 & 0 & 0 & 0 \\ 0 & 1 & 0 & 0 \\ \vdots & & & \\ 0 & 0 & 1 & 0 \end{bmatrix},$$

$$C_t = \begin{bmatrix} a_{0t} \\ 1 \\ 0 \\ \vdots \\ 0 \end{bmatrix}, \quad b_t = \begin{bmatrix} GNP_t^s - \rho\, GNP_{t-1}^s \\ 0 \\ \vdots \\ 0 \end{bmatrix}, \quad \varepsilon_t = \begin{bmatrix} e_t \\ 0 \\ \vdots \end{bmatrix}.$$

Here, GNP_t^p is predicted GNP after changes in the tax credit, x_t is the change in the tax credit rate, ρ is the autocorrelation coefficient, GNP_t^s is the value for GNP produced by the base simulation, ε_t is the additive disturbance after the autocorrelation transformation, and

$$a_{it}^* = a_{it} - \rho a_{i-1,t-1}, \quad \text{with} \quad a_{it} = \delta GNP_t^s / \delta x_{t-i}.$$

In the nonlinear procedure, this additive disturbance was ignored until the last step, when it was introduced into the linear approximation made about the nonlinear solution to the fully deterministic model.

(2) Inequality Constraints

The basic loss function used consisted of the discontinued sum of squares of the real GNP gap—real GNP minus real potential GNP. No attempt was made to measure the impact of investment on potential GNP, so the procedure, in effect, stabilizes the economy about one arbitrary fixed path. In addition, quadratic costs could be put on the level or movements of the instruments in the standard framework. However, the explicit constraints produced by the suggested legislation make it preferable to use inequality constraints alone rather than costs in the objective function. Using such constraints causes a slight modification in eqs. (14) and (15) in Chow (1973). When a constraint is binding in any given period, the credit rate in that period is insensitive at the margin to changes in earlier conditions. Therefore, using Chow's notation, $x_t = G_t y_{t-1} + g_t$ simplifies to $x_t = \alpha_t$ where α_t is the bound. This change produces new versions of eqs. (14) and (15):

$$H_{t-1} = K_{t-1} + A_t' H_t A_t, \tag{14$'$}$$

$$h_{t-1} = K_{t-1} + A_t'(h_t - H_t(b_t + C_t \alpha_t)). \tag{15$'$}$$

Then for a set of values of the tax rate to be optimal, eqs. (14$'$) and (15$'$) ought to have replaced the original equations in the optimization procedure in all periods in which the tax turns out to be constrained.

An optimal set of tax rates must exist, since one is minimizing a continuous function on a compact set (due to the constraints), and any optimal point must satisfy the first-order conditions produced in Chow, with the above alterations. We conclude that we have found a set of rates satisfying the first-order conditions necessary for optimality if the periods in which the new eqs. (14′) and (15′) are used turn out to be identically equal to those periods in which the resulting rates must be constrained accordingly. As in the unconstrained case, second-order conditions must be checked in order to guarantee local optimality.

In our calculations, we again attempted to take advantage of the linear-quadratic model. The technique tried was to start out using the original procedure of Chow, but applying the constraints when working forwards from the initial conditions, when the tax rates were determined as functions of earlier tax rates and earlier values of GNP. Then in those periods in which the constraints were binding, the new equations were used in a second sweep through the optimization procedure. As noted before, if the same set of rates is produced in two successive iterations, it satisfies the first-order conditions, so the procedure was iterated until this occurred. Unfortunately, this occasionally would produce cycles. Attempts at trying different starting values were not very successful. This is why we used a slight cost on movement of tax credit, for using such a cost seemed to ease the problem of finding a solution. In this paper, we did not check second-order conditions, though several starting conditions were tried in order to confirm the solution reached.

(3)   Nonlinear Solution

In proceeding to a nonlinear solution, the optimal values produced from the initial linear approximation were used in a resimulation of the full model, still holding all other policy tools, including those of monetary policy, constant. From this new model, a new linear equation was constructed using the same method as before, and the linear-quadratic problem was resolved. The new solution gives the optimal change from the rates produced in the first solution. This procedure of reconstructing and resolving the linear model was iterated until convergence. The convergence point then satisfies the first-order conditions for a full optimum. To show this, we let *GAP* be the GNP gap from the previous iteration's simulation, and let

$$\Delta G_t = \sum_{i=0}^{20} \alpha_{ti}(c)\Delta c_{t-i}$$

be the change in GNP from the past simulation values due to changes in the tax credit rates c_t.[13] Here c is the vector containing all these rates. We have now made the coefficients a function of all the tax credit rates,[14] so this nonlinear equation is a boiled-down version of the full model. Our objective is now to minimize the following,[15]

$$\min_{c_t\ member\ C} \sum_t \left(\sum_{i=0}^{20} \alpha_{ti}(c)\Delta c_{t-i} - GAP_t \right)^2 = \sum_t \left(\sum_{i=0}^{20} \alpha_{ti}(c)\Delta c_{t-i} \right)^2$$

$$+ \sum_t GAP_t^2 - 2\sum_t GAP_t \sum_{i=0}^{20} \alpha_{ti}(c)\Delta c_{t-i}.$$

Maximizing with respect to c_τ now gives,[16]

$$\sum_{t=\tau}^{\tau+20} \left[\alpha_{t,t-\tau}\left(\sum_{i=0}^{20} \alpha_{ti}\Delta c_{t-i} - GAP_t \right) \right]$$

$$+ \sum_t \left(\sum_i \frac{\delta\alpha_{ti}}{\delta c_\tau} \Delta c_{t-i} \right)\left(\sum_{i=0}^{20} \alpha_{ti}\Delta c_{t-i} - GAP_t \right)$$

$$\begin{cases} = 0 \text{ if constraint nonbinding,} \\ \neq 0 \text{ if constraint binding.} \end{cases}$$

If the model were linear, then the terms involving derivatives of α would drop out. However, when $\Delta c_t = 0$, for all t, solves the linear model, it also solves the nonlinear model, since all terms involving the derivative of α are then multiplied by zero. (Note that here, the values of α used in the linear model are correct since they were derived at $\Delta c_t = 0$.) Thus, the fixed point of our procedure is a solution to the nonlinear control problem.

As noted above, no uncertainty was introduced in this nonlinear solution procedure. Optimal adjustments from the solution point to the nonlinear deterministic problem, made in reaction to additive disturbances, were calculated from the linear approximation around that solution point.

An extension of this procedure applicable to stochastic problems, where there is no learning about the coefficients, is described in Gordon (1974).

Notes

1. The two policies would not be quite equivalent, since contributions under the BIF system would not be dependent on positive profits, whereas they are under the tax credit.

2. The discount rate used was 5 percent; the results are insensitive to the rate of discount. The potential GNP figures used are those published by the Council of Economic Advisers. The DRI model does not allow for the feedback of investment into potential GNP, so this welfare function really stabilizes GNP around an arbitrary path—the historical values for potential GNP.

3. See Jorgenson (1971b) and Gordon and Jorgenson (1972). See also Hall and Jorgenson (1967; 1969a and b; and 1971).

4. See Bischoff (1971b), Aaron *et al.* (1973) and Craine *et al.* (1972).

5. See Jorgenson (1971b) and Gordon and Jorgenson (1972).

6. Technically, we assume that the reaction to output changes is systematically one period faster than the reaction to price changes.

7. See note 2 above.

8. See note 2 above.

9. A measure of the realized rate of return developed by Christensen and Jorgenson (1969) was tried, but did not perform as well as a constant rate.

10. The above assumes relative prices unchanged, since Feldstein and Eckstein used inflation of the consumer price index, whereas capital gains result from changes in prices of producers' durable equipment.

11. Sometimes a minor cost would be put on the movement of the credit rate to ease the computational requirements.

12. It was found that the impact of investment changed little over time, so that this set of multipliers was approximated by a linear interpolation between the multipliers for two representative periods, thus cutting down on the computational cost enormously.

13. The correction for autocorrelation is ignored at this stage, since the additive disturbance was dropped during the nonlinear solution process.

14. Technically, one would normally assume that the α_{ti} depend only on earlier, not all, credit rates. To simplify notation, this was not incorporated.

15. The set C is the closed interval for the rates specified by Congress.

16. If the period τ is less than twenty periods from the horizon, then the summations in the formula will be shortened accordingly.

8 Inflation-Proof Depreciation of Assets

*Alan J. Auerbach and
Dale W. Jorgenson*

Since 1973, while the U.S. economy has been suffering from unprecedented rates of inflation, capital formation has stagnated and economic growth has slowed considerably. A very important reason for the capital stagnation is the widening gap between economic depreciation and capital consumption allowances for tax purposes. As a result, businesses cannot recover the real costs of their investments in plant and equipment.

Growing misallocations of capital, caused by distortions in depreciation allowances under the tax system, have further diminished the contribution of capital to productivity growth. Inflation exerts a differential impact on assets with different useful lives; and the greater the inflation rate, the greater the distortions in depreciation among asset classes.

The system for capital recovery governed by tax law has developed through many liberalizations of depreciation formulas and lifetimes for tax purposes and through the investment tax credit. One motive for these changes was the need to bring capital consumption allowances into line with economic depreciation. Double-digit inflation in recent years, however, has undercut the effectiveness of these reforms, so that revision of the depreciation provisions of the tax code is again under serious consideration.

The most widely supported proposal for revision is the bill introduced in the last session of Congress by Representatives Barber B. Conable, Jr., and James R. Jones. The measure, widely endorsed by business groups and supported by nearly 300 of the 435 members of the House and 51 of the 100 members of the Senate, proposes a "10–5–3" method of capital recovery. Structures would be written off in ten years, long-lived equipment in five years, and short-lived equipment (such as light trucks and autos) in three years. The bill would retain the investment tax credit for equipment.

Laudable as it is in its simplicity and liberality, the 10–5–3 idea is not the best solution. We propose a better approach, based on the recovery of capital consumption during the year the asset is acquired. Hence depreciation allowances would be unaffected by inflation or by variations in the rate of inflation.

Our so-called first-year capital recovery system directly attacks the problem confronting tax policy-makers: to design an approach that can cope with high, moderate, and low degrees of inflation without the distortions resulting from the tax structure in use. The first-year system would greatly stimulate capital formation and enhance its impact on productivity and economic growth.

Admittedly, the 10–5–3 approach would give a substantial impetus to capital formation. Much of that effect, however, would still be dissipated through misallocations of the capital stock. The Conable-Jones proposal would widen, rather than narrow, the substantial differentials in tax burdens that classes of assets now bear.

In addition, these differentials would become more sensitive to variations in the rate of inflation. Subsidies of some types of assets would replace taxes under moderate inflation rates, and these subsidies would grow dramatically under low inflation rates.

In this article we describe the first-year capital recovery system and compare it with capital recovery under current tax law and under the Conable-Jones proposal. Then we analyze the macroeconomic impact of the first-year system by simulating the U.S. economy under the assumption that the structure will be phased in over the five-year period 1981–1985.

8.1   The First-Year System . . .

Under our proposal, taxpayers could deduct the present value of economic depreciation as an expense in arriving at income for tax purposes. To avoid inflation-caused deterioration in the value of capital consumption allowances, the present value of economic depreciation would be allowed as a deduction in the same year than an asset is acquired.

(To arrive at present value, future depreciation must, of course, be discounted back to the present. For example, the present value of one dollar's worth of investment in a long-lived asset such as a manufacturing plant might be 50 cents, while the present value of one dollar's worth of investment in a short-lived asset such as a pickup truck might be 75 cents.)

Capital consumption allowances would be described by a schedule of present values of economic depreciation for one dollar's worth of investment in each class of assets. We propose use of about 30 classes—perhaps 10 types of structures and 20 types of equipment. The whole arrangement could be described in terms of only 30 numbers.

Rather than, as now, choosing among a range of asset lifetimes and a number of depreciation formulas, taxpayers would simply apply the particular first-year capital recovery allowances to their purchases of depreciable plant and equipment. No purchase records would be necessary to substantiate allowances taken in a given year.

Many assets are sold before the end of their useful lives. To ensure efficient allocation of the existing capital stock, it is important to provide for capital recovery on used assets. Under current tax law, to arrive at a basis for resale the purchase price is reduced by the capital consumption allowances. If the proceeds from the sale exceed this basis, the taxpayer is subject to tax on the difference.

Under the first-year capital recovery system, a buyer of a used asset could deduct the present value of economic depreciation on it in the year of acquisition. The seller of a used asset would be subject to ordinary income tax on the same amount; this amount would always be less than the price of the asset. If purchasers and sellers have the same marginal tax rates, transactions in used assets would not affect federal revenue.[1]

Would the establishment of large deductions in the first year of investment encourage creation of tax shelters? Perhaps high-bracket taxpayers could purchase assets to take the deductions, then lease the assets to low-bracket taxpayers using them in production. Actually, the new procedure would, if anything, discourage such leasing schemes and other tax shelters based on capital recovery. While high-bracket buyers would obviously get a bigger deduction in the first year, they would lose all subsequent deductions. This is a trade-off similar to that faced by prospective low-bracket purchasers.

It is reasonable to assume that high-bracket individuals have a lower discount rate than others do, precisely because they must pay a higher rate of tax on capital income. Low-bracket investors, with a higher discount rate, would perceive the conversion of all future deductions to a single current deduction as generous. They would prefer to acquire assets directly instead of lease them from high-bracket individuals.

8.2   Administrative Aspects

The first-year system would greatly reduce the administrative burden imposed on taxpayers and tax authorities. Taxpayers could dispense with the cumbersome system of capital accounts for tax-reporting purposes. Since tax liabilities and deductions arising from transactions in new and used assets would depend only on the prices paid, taxpayers would not need to keep records of past transactions.

The results of a study for the Treasury Department in 1979 by Charles Hulten and Frank Wykoff demonstrate the feasibility of a system for capital recovery that covers structures and equipment by a uniform method.[2] Like the present approach, this method would be based on a system of asset classes, but they would be far fewer than those in the asset depreciation range (ADR) system used now.

The declining-balance method for estimating economic depreciation would be employed for all assets. The rate of decline of the price of assets with age could be estimated for each asset class on the basis of Hulten and Wykoff's methods. The real rate of return could be taken to be 4%.[3] Distortions caused by departures from perfect measurements of economic depreciation or the real rate of return would be very small compared with distortions under current tax law or 10–5–3.

Although the first-year system would not rely on data required for financial reporting, it could be integrated with a financial reporting procedure and thus lead to major simplification. At present, many taxpayers maintain separate sets of books of capital accounts for tax purposes and for financial reporting. Since the new system would not require capital accounts, one set could be eliminated.

Rather than require a system of vintage accounts, as in the ADR approach, the declining-balance method would oblige the taxpayer to maintain a single account for each asset class. Capital recovery would be a constant fraction of the undepreciated balance remaining from all previous expenditures on assets in that class.

If, in addition, some kind of reevaluation were necessary for financial reporting purposes, the undepreciated balance in each account could be revalued at the end of each accounting period. The basis would be the change in the acquisition prices of new assets during that period.

8.3 ... Against Two Others

To compare the first-year capital recovery system with that under existing law and with the 10–5–3 proposal, we have analyzed their impact on five representative classes of assets (see table 8.1). For each asset we give the tax lifetime embodied in current law and the economic depreciation rate as calculated in the Treasury Department study. We also give the proportion of nonresidential investment in 1974 for each asset class. Together these five assets accounted for about one-third of all investment that year.

To analyze the impact of changes in capital recovery provisions of the tax law after World War II, we calculated the effective tax rate for each class of assets.

As table 8.4 in the Appendix to this article shows, the effective tax rates for the five asset classes have varied widely since 1952, depending on the provisions of the tax code and the rate of inflation. The figures we use in our analysis represent the average tax rate for each new asset over its lifetime.

Table 8.2 compares the effective tax rates for the five classes of assets under current tax law, the Conable-Jones approach, and the first-year system. Because the effective tax rates under the first two systems depend on the degree of inflation, we calculated those rates at 6% and 12% inflation. The effective tax rate under the first-year system, of course, equals the statutory rate and is unaffected by inflation.

Current tax law imposes a greater tax burden on structures than equipment, so the allocation of the capital stock is biased toward the latter. More output could be produced from the existing capital stock by a shift in its composition from equipment toward structures.[4]

The most striking feature of the Conable-Jones proposal is the substantial reduction in effective tax rates for all assets. In fact, with either 6% or 12% inflation, the effective tax rates under 10–5–3 would fall below the 46% statutory rate. Conable-Jones, however, has a very undesirable feature: in a time of moderate inflation, such as a 6% rate, the combined effect of greatly accelerated depreciation and the investment tax credit would produce negative tax rates for construction machinery and general industrial equipment. Rather than tax income produced by the assets, the government would, in effect, pay taxpayers to hold them!

As table 8.2 indicates, the current system causes sizable distortions of economic depreciation, and the size depends on the inflation rate.

Table 8.1
Selected assets and their characteristics

Asset class	Type	Years of tax life[1]	Economic depreciation rate[2]	Percentage of 1974 nonresidential investment
Construction machinery	Equipment	5.5 (7.0*)	.172	2.8%
General industrial equipment	Equipment	8.6	.122	4.4
Trucks, buses, and trailers	Equipment	5.5 (7.0*)	.254	9.0
Industrial buildings	Structures	23.8	.036	5.2
Commercial buildings	Structures	31.8	.025	11.0

1. Equals guideline lives for structures and 80% of guideline lives for equipment, as legally permitted (* except where a lengthening of the tax lifetime is preferred in order to obtain a full investment tax credit).

2. Annual rates of decline in asset value with age, as estimated by Hulten and Wykoff.

Table 8.2
Effective tax rates under three capital recovery systems

Asset class	Current system*		Conable-Jones†		First-year
	6% inflation rate	12% inflation rate	6% inflation rate	12% inflation rate	
Construction machinery	.06	.34	−.23	.16	.46
General industrial equipment	.16	.36	−.17	.13	.46
Trucks, buses, and trailers	.09	.42	.22	.45	.46
Industrial buildings	.49	.53	.36	.43	.46
Commercial buildings	.48	.51	.32	.39	.46

Note: The real discount rate is assumed to be 4%.

* Assumes adoption of the double-declining balance method (equipment) or 150% declining balance method (structures), with optimal switchover to straight-line, plus a 10% investment tax credit on equipment.

† Assumes tax lives of five years (equipment) or ten years (structures), plus a 10% investment tax credit on equipment.

The Conable-Jones proposal would create greater gaps between capital consumption allowances and economic depreciation than under current law, and these gaps would be more sensitive to the rate of inflation.[5] Under the first-year capital recovery system, capital consumption allowances would equal economic depreciation under any degree of inflation.

8.4 Future Economic Impact

In view of the emphasis today on reducing the federal deficit to combat inflation, a critical issue in tax reform is the effect of a proposed change on the budget. To assess the macroeconomic impact of adoption of the first-year system and its impact on federal revenue, we simulated the U.S. economy under the assumption that the system had been adopted for tax years beginning in 1981. (We assumed that any shortfall would result in creation of additional government debt and that the Federal Reserve would not adjust monetary policy to accommodate a revenue loss.)

We supposed that the system would be phased in over five years. In the 1981 tax year, 20% of the value of assets acquired would be included, and 20% more in each subsequent year until 1985, when all capital assets installed would be included. This pattern coincides with those following the liberalization of depreciation allowances in 1954 and the shift to the ADR system in 1971.

The results of our simulation, using the Data Resources, Inc. (DRI) quarterly econometric model of the U.S. economy,[6] can be seen in table 8.3. The base line simulation, denoted B, traces the course of the economy without the first-year capital recovery system. The alternative simulation, denoted A, assumes adoption of the new approach and discontinuance of the investment tax credit. The difference between the two simulations, denoted D, shows the impact of the new procedure. We also give the difference in percentage terms.

As table 8.3 demonstrates, the new system provides a very substantial stimulus to capital formation. By 1985, real investment in equipment has grown by $6 billion and real investment in nonresidential structures by $9.1 billion. The greater stimulus to the latter is the result of removal of the distortions between capital consumption allowances and economic depreciation that exist under current law. (Although the system offers no particular incentive to owner-occupied

Table 8.3
Five-year impact of the new system (except for the
unemployment rate, figures in billions of dollars)

	1981	1982	1983	1984	1985
Gross national product*					
A	1430.5	1485.6	1537.0	1597.4	1648.7
B	1430.6	1487.1	1531.2	1582.8	1635.3
D	−0.1	−1.5	5.8	14.6	13.4
%	−0.0	−0.1	0.4	0.9	0.8
Investment, producers' durable equipment*					
A	97.6	94.4	94.8	101.2	107.8
B	97.8	98.9	98.2	99.1	101.8
D	−0.2	−4.5	−3.4	2.1	6.0
%	−0.2	−4.6	−3.5	2.1	5.9
Investment, nonresidential structures*					
A	47.1	47.7	50.6	54.9	59.2
B	47.0	46.7	47.1	48.4	50.1
D	0.1	1.0	3.5	6.5	9.1
%	0.2	2.1	7.4	13.4	18.2
Investment, residential structures*					
A	45.7	59.6	66.8	73.9	74.7
B	45.5	57.8	62.3	69.3	72.4
D	0.2	1.8	4.5	4.6	2.3
%	0.4	3.1	7.2	6.7	3.2
Unemployment rate					
A	8.0	7.7	7.4	6.9	6.5
B	8.0	7.7	7.5	7.2	6.8
D	0.0	0.0	−0.1	−0.3	−0.3
%	0.0	0.0	−0.8	−4.3	−4.4
Federal surplus					
A	1.0	14.5	10.2	22.6	21.1
B	−4.0	20.5	19.4	34.6	49.8
D	5.0	−6.0	−9.2	−12.0	−28.7
%	−123.8	−29.3	−47.4	−34.7	−57.6

Note: Based on DRI's six-year control simulation as of
April 26, 1980.
* 1972 dollars

housing, real investment in residential structures increases by $2.3 billion in the five years.)

DRI forecasts a declining but still high, unemployment rate through 1985. The first-year system, according to the simulation, would reduce the rate somewhat by 1984.

The stimulus to investment would increase the real gross national product by substantial amounts. The inflation rate, as measured by the GNP deflator (not shown in table 8.3), would rise by .2% per year by 1984.

As a result of adoption of the first-year system, the projected federal deficit for 1981 would be turned into a surplus—partly because of elimination of the investment tax credit. Thereafter the federal accounts would show surpluses with both simulations, but lower surpluses under the first-year system. The revenue loss during the five years would total $50.9 billion.

8.5   A Better Way

In considering measures to stimulate U.S. economic growth, policymakers should give top priority to the design of a new approach to capital recovery. Such an arrangement should bring capital consumption allowances into line with economic depreciation. It should also enhance the impact of capital formation on economic growth through more efficient allocation of capital.

The first-year capital recovery system would eliminate the differentials between economic depreciation and capital consumption allowances that have arisen under current law. These allowances would be unaffected by inflation or by variations in its rate. At little revenue loss to the federal government, the system would give capital formation a great boost. It would also improve the allocation of capital and maximize the contribution of capital formation to growth in productivity and economic activity.

The first-year approach could be implemented within the present framework of the Treasury Department. Simplification of the system would greatly ease the administrative burden on the tax authorities. Moreover, it would drastically reduce taxpayers' reporting requirements and permit easy integration with their financial reporting procedures.

Appendix

The effective tax rate represents that fraction of a project's gross income that goes toward corporate taxes. To obtain the number, we first calculated the gross rate of return an investment would have if the corporate tax rate were zero. We then calculated the net rate of return, taking account of corporate taxes and adjusting for capital consumption allowances and the investment tax credit. We subtracted the net rate of return from the gross rate of return and divided this difference by the gross rate to find the proportion of the gross return paid in taxes.

Table 8.4 presents the effective tax rates for all five classes of assets from 1952 through 1979. For purposes of comparison, we give the statutory rate on corporate income each year.

Table 8.4
Effective tax rates, 1952–1979

Year	Statutory tax rate	Construction machinery	General industrial equipment	Trucks, buses, and, trailers	Industrial buildings	Commercial buildings
1952	.52	.57	.59	.65	.51	.51
1953	.52	.57	.59	.65	.51	.51
1954	.52	.58	.60	.66	.52	.52
1955	.52	.58	.60	.66	.52	.52
1956	.52	.54	.57	.62	.49	.49
1957	.52	.54	.57	.62	.49	.49
1958	.52	.54	.57	.62	.50	.50
1959	.52	.55	.58	.63	.50	.50
1960	.52	.56	.58	.63	.51	.50
1961	.52	.54	.57	.62	.50	.50
1962	.52	.41	.43	.49	.49	.49
1963	.52	.40	.43	.49	.49	.49
1964	.52	.31	.34	.38	.48	.48
1965	.48	.26	.29	.34	.45	.45
1966	.48	.35	.38	.43	.46	.46
1967	.48	.37	.40	.45	.47	.47
1968	.48	.35	.38	.43	.48	.48
1969	.48	.53	.56	.61	.52	.51
1970	.48	.43	.44	.51	.53	.52
1971	.48	.35	.37	.42	.53	.52
1972	.48	.35	.37	.43	.53	.52
1973	.48	.39	.40	.47	.54	.53
1974	.48	.43	.44	.51	.55	.54

Table 8.4
(continued)

Year	Statutory tax rate	Construction machinery	General industrial equipment	Trucks, buses, and, trailers	Industrial buildings	Commercial buildings
1975	.48	.33	.36	.40	.56	.54
1976	.48	.34	.37	.42	.56	.54
1977	.48	.37	.39	.45	.56	.55
1978	.48	.36	.39	.44	.56	.55
1979	.46	.32	.35	.39	.54	.53

Note: Assumes the real discount rate to be 4% and the relevant inflation rate to be an unweighted five-year moving average of past inflation rates.

Before 1954 the effective tax rates for structures were in line with that statutory rate, while those for equipment far exceeded it. Inauguration of accelerated depreciation in 1954 changed the situation somewhat, but the effective tax rates for equipment remained above statutory rates until the adoption of the guideline lifetimes and the investment tax credit in 1962. The repeal of the Long Amendment in 1964 caused a further reduction in rates on equipment to levels well below the statutory rate.

As the pace of inflation quickened during the late 1960s, the effective tax rates on equipment rose gradually, until repeal of the investment tax credit in 1969 raised them to the pre-1962 levels. Similarly, inflation and restriction of accelerated depreciation on structures to the 150% declining-balance method after 1966 resulted in increases in the effective tax rates for structures to levels exceeding those before 1954.

Reinstitution of the investment tax credit for equipment in 1970, adoption of the asset depreciation range system in 1971, and the increase in the rate of the credit from 7% to 10% produced effective tax rates well below the statutory rate, even in the face of double-digit inflation in 1973 and again in 1979.

Notes

1. Here we are consistent with the principle of tax neutrality of exchanges of assets proposed by Gerard M. Brannon and Emil M. Sunley, Jr. (1976, p. 413).
2. Charles Hulten and Frank Wykoff (1979).
3. This rate is suggested in Barbara M. Fraumeni and Dale W. Jorgenson (1980).

4. For a treatment of capital investment biases under current tax law, see Alan J. Auerbach, (1979a, p. 621).

5. For further discussion of the Conable-Jones bill and other capital recovery systems, see Martin Feldstein (1981).

6. For a description of the model, see Otto Eckstein (1983).

9 Inflation and Corporate Capital Recovery

Dale W. Jorgenson and
Martin A. Sullivan

9.1 Introduction

The objective of this paper is to analyze the impact of inflation on capital recovery under the U.S. corporate income tax. Corporate tax payments depend on the statutory corporate tax rate. They also depend on capital consumption allowances, expensing of investments, investment tax credits, and the deductibility of interest. We refer to the tax rate actually paid as the effective tax rate. The common feature of tax systems leading to an efficient allocation of capital is that they result in the same effective tax rate for all assets.

One approach to the efficient allocation of capital among assets is to permit taxpayers to deduct the decline in the value of their assets with age in arriving at taxable income. The decline in the value of an asset with age is called economic depreciation. Economic depreciation can be measured by observing the profile of prices corresponding to assets of different ages at a given point of time. A system of capital recovery enabling taxpayers to deduct economic depreciation would lead to income as a base for taxation and to an effective tax rate equal to the statutory rate for all assets.

An alternative approach to the efficient allocation of capital among assets is to allow taxpayers to deduct the actual cost of acquisition of assets in arriving at taxable income. In this approach the acquisition of assets would be treated in precisely the same way as other business expenses. However, income from capital in the form of interest, dividends, or retained earnings would not be deducted from income for tax purposes. This would have the effects of shifting the base for taxation from income to consumption and reducing the effective income tax rate to zero.

Deducting economic depreciation and expensing the cost of acquisition of assets could be combined without sacrificing efficiency. For example, a certain proportion of the net acquisition cost of assets could be expensed, while the remainder could be recovered through capital consumption allowances equal to economic depreciation. Combinations of these systems could lead to any effective tax rate between zero and the statutory rax rate. Although there are many ways to design a tax system that would lead to the same effective tax rate for all assets, the level of the effective tax rate can differ widely between the alternative systems.

To analyze the impact of inflation on the U.S. corporate income tax we first determine the effective tax rate for each type of asset for each year of the postwar period 1946–1980. Throughout this period the system of capital recovery has been based on the historical cost of an asset. Cost of acquisition provides the basis for the investment tax credit as an offset to tax liability. Historical cost also provides the basis for capital consumption allowances as a deduction from income for tax purposes. Finally, interest payments are also treated as a deduction from income under U.S. law.

Our most surprising finding is that for currently anticipated rates of inflation, which are among the highest of the postwar period, U.S. tax law results in effective corporate tax rates that are well below the statutory rate. This is due to the liberalization of capital consumption allowances during the postwar period and, most importantly, to the introduction of the investment tax credit. We also find that an increase in the rate of inflation for any given set of tax provisions results in higher effective tax rates on all corporate assets, while a decrease results in lower effective tax rates.

Our second major finding is that differences in effective tax rates among assets under the U.S. corporate income tax are very substantial. Transfers of investment from lightly taxed assets to heavily taxed assets would result in large gains in future output with no sacrifice of consumption either now or in the future. Under current law the differences in effective tax rates among assets would increase with a decrease in the rate of inflation, thereby further reducing the efficiency of capital allocation.

We next consider the likely impact of two specific proposals for more rapid capital recovery:

1. The Reagan administration proposal, introduced by Congressmen Conable and Jones in 1979 and advanced in somewhat different form by President Reagan in 1981.

2. The Senate Finance Committee proposal, originally introduced by Senator Bentsen in 1980 and reintroduced by Senator Long in 1981.

The Reagan administration and Senate Finance Committee proposals involve accelerated capital recovery rather than economic depreciation or expensing of acquisition costs. More rapid recovery of the cost of acquiring assets would be permitted by substituting more generous formulas and shorter lifetimes for those employed under current law. In addition, the rate of the investment tax credit would be increased. The objective of these proposals is to reduce effective tax rates on all assets.

In addition to the two proposals listed above for revising tax provisions for capital recovery, we consider expensing the costs of acquisition of assets and deducting economic depreciation as potential approaches to capital recovery under the U.S. corporate income tax. For current law and for each of the two proposed changes, we determine the effective tax rate for each type of asset. Under economic depreciation the effective rate for all assets would be equal to the statutory tax rate, while under expensing the effective tax rate on all assets would be equal to zero.

We find that the U.S. corporate income tax provides capital consumption allowances for corporate investment as a whole that are in line with economic depreciation at currently anticipated rates of inflation. At these inflation rates the Reagan administration proposal would provide capital consumption allowances 33.6 percent in excess of economic depreciation. The Senate Finance Committee proposal would result in an excess of 27.5 percent.

At current rates of inflation the effective tax rate on new corporate investment under present law is 24 percent or a little over half the statutory rate of 46 percent, due mainly to the impact of the investment tax credit. The Senate Finance Committee proposals would reduce the effective tax rate on corporate investment to 13 percent or a little over one-fourth the statutory rate. Finally, the Reagan administration proposal would result in a negative effective tax rate for corporate investment.

Under the Reagan administration proposal the combination of very short asset lifetimes for tax purposes and an increase in the investment tax credit for some assets would imply that the corporate income tax would be replaced by a corporate income subsidy for depreciable assets. Tax deductions and credits for these assets would be available to "shelter" income from nondepreciable assets such as land, inventories, and financial claims. The negative effective tax rate under the Reagan proposal would rise to 46 percent at rates of inflation anticipated in 1966 and to 58 percent at rates of inflation anticipated in 1960.

The second issue we consider in analyzing the impact of inflation on capital recovery under present law and alternative proposals is differences in effective tax rates among assets. Under present U.S. tax law the difference between effective tax rates on equipment and structures is 16 percent at currently anticipated rates of inflation. Under the Reagan administration proposal this difference would widen to 36 percent. The gap for the Senate Finance Committee proposal would be 23 percent.

We conclude that differences in effective tax rates among assets under present U.S. tax law are substantial, even at the very high anticipated rates of inflation prevailing currently. These differences would increase with a decrease in the rate of inflation, reducing efficiency in the allocation of capital. The differences in effective rates would widen significantly under the Senate Finance Committee proposal and would widen even further under the Reagan administration proposal. Just as under present law, these gaps would increase with a decrease in the rate of inflation.

In closing, we outline an approach to the reform of capital recovery under the U.S. corporate income tax that would deal effectively with the problem of inflation. The first step would be to replace existing capital recovery allowances for tax purposes by a first year allowance, as proposed by Auerbach and Jorgenson (1980). The first year allowance would provide taxpayers with a deduction from income equal to the present value of economic depreciation on an asset over its lifetime.

The second step in reform of capital recovery would be to provide an investment tax credit proportional to the difference between the cost of acquisition of an asset and the first year allowance, as proposed by Brown (1981). By varying the proportion of the investment tax credit between zero and the statutory corporate tax rate, it would be possible to produce any effective tax rate between the statutory rate and zero. Since the first year allowance and the investment tax credit would be taken in the same year an asset is acquired, the resulting first year capital recovery system would make corporate capital recovery completely independent of the rate of inflation.

9.2 Theoretical Framework

To analyze the impact of inflation on capital recovery under U.S. tax law we begin by modeling the provisions of the law over the postwar period 1946–1980 and under changes in tax law proposed by the Reagan administration and the Senate Finance Committee. For simplicity we limit ourselves to the provisions of the corporate income tax. We introduce the characteristic features of the tax law into the annualized cost or rental value of each type of asset. For this purpose we employ the concept of rental value introduced by Jorgenson (1963, 1965) and further developed by Hall and Jorgenson (1967).[1]

Under U.S. tax law the rental price of capital services depends on the statutory tax rate, which we denote by u, the depreciation formula giving capital consumption allowances at time s on one dollar's worth of investment at time t, denoted by $D(s - t)$, and the rate of the investment tax credit, denoted k.[2] We can determine the values of these tax parameters for each type of assets for each year during the period 1946–1980 and for each of the proposed changes in tax law. Using the rental price of capital services, we can determine the effective tax rate corresponding to each set of tax parameters.

The rental price of capital services is defined, implicitly, by the equality between the cost of acquisition of an asset at time t, say $q(t)$, and the present value of future rentals after taxes. In the absence of taxation this equality can be written

$$q(t) = \int_{t}^{\infty} e^{-(r + \pi)(s - t)} e^{-\delta(s - t)} c(s) \, ds.$$

In this formula the rental price of capital services at time s, $c(s)$, is multiplied by the quantity of capital services at time s, $e^{-\delta(s - t)}$.

We assume that the quantity of capital services resulting from the acquisition of one unit of the capital asset at time t declines exponentially at the rate of economic depreciation δ. Hulten and Wykoff (1981a) have shown that exponential or geometric decline in the quantity of capital services provides a satisfactory approximation to actual patterns of decline.[3] The rental value at time s, $e^{-\delta(s - t)} c(s)$, is discounted by the factor $e^{-(r + \pi)(s - t)}$, where $\pi = \dot{q}/q$ is the rate of inflation in the price of assets and r is the rate of return corrected for inflation.

Differentiating both sides of the identity between the cost of acquisition of an asset and the present value of future rentals, we obtain

$$c = q(r + \delta).$$

The rental price is the product of the acquisition price and the sum of the rate of return corrected for inflation and the rate of depreciation. We can solve this expression for the rate of return, obtaining

$$r = \frac{c}{q} - \delta.$$

For productive efficiency in the allocation of capital, the addition to wealth generated by one dollar's worth of an asset must be the same for all assets. This addition to wealth is measured by the rate of return before correction for inflation, $r + \pi$.

In the presence of taxation the cost of acquisition of an asset is reduced by an offset to tax liability for the investment tax credit and by deductions from taxable income for capital consumption allowances. The acquisition cost after taxes is equal to the present value of future rentals after taxes. The investment tax credit, $kq(t)$, is a direct offset to tax liability and is not discounted. We can view capital consumption allowances as an offset to the cost of acquisition of an asset by introducing the present value of capital consumption allowances, say z:

$$z = \int_{t}^{\infty} e^{-[r(1 - u) + \pi](s - t)} D(t - s) \, ds$$

where $r(1 - u) + \pi$ is the after-tax discount rate.

Given the definition of the present value of capital consumption allowances, we can express the cost of acquisition of an asset at time t, net of the investment tax credit and the present value of tax deductions for capital consumption, as the present value of future rentals after taxes:

$$(1 - k - uz)q(t) = \int_{t}^{\infty} e^{-[r(1 - u) + \pi](s - t)} e^{-\delta(s - t)} (1 - u)c(s) \, ds.$$

Our final step in modeling the provisions for capital recovery under U.S. tax law is to determine the rental price of capital services as a function of the cost of acquisition of an asset $q(t)$, the rate of return r, and the tax parameters—k, u, and z. For this purpose we differentiate both sides of the equality between the cost of acquisition of an asset after taxes and the present value of future rentals after taxes, obtaining

$$c = \frac{1 - k - uz}{1 - u} qr[(1 - u) + \delta].$$

Efficiency in the allocation of capital requires that the addition to wealth generated by the acquisition of one dollar's worth of an asset, net of depreciation, is the same for all assets. This addition to wealth is measured by the social rate of return before correction for inflation, say $\rho + \pi$, where

$$\rho = \frac{c}{q} - \delta.$$

Maximization of private wealth requires that the addition to wealth generated by the acquisition of one dollar's worth of an asset, net of both depreciation and taxes, is the same for all assets. This addition to wealth is measured by the private rate of return before correction for inflation $r(1 - u) + \pi$.

To summarize the impact of U.S. tax law on capital recovery on the efficiency of capital allocation, we employ the effective tax rate, say e. Reducing the social rate of return by the effective tax rate results in the private rate of return after taxes:

$$(1 - e)\rho = (1 - u)r.$$

We can express the effective tax rate as a function of the private rate of return, the statutory tax rate, the investment tax credit, and the present value of capital consumption allowances:

$$e = 1 - \left(\frac{(1 - u)r}{\dfrac{1 - k - uz}{1 - u}[(1 - u)r + \delta] - \delta} \right).$$

Maximization of private wealth results in an efficient allocation of capital only if the effective rate is the same for all assets.[4]

If capital consumption allowances were equal to economic depreciation, the present value of these allowances would be given by

$$z = \int_{t}^{\infty} e^{-r(1-u)(t-s)} \delta e^{-\delta(t-s)} ds$$

$$= \frac{\delta}{r(1 - u) + \delta}.$$

If the investment tax credit were equal to zero, the effective tax rate for all assets would be equal to the statutory tax rate. Alternatively, if the acquisition of assets could be immediately expensed, the present value of capital consumption allowances would be equal to unity. Again, setting the investment tax credit equal to zero, the effective tax rate for all assets would be equal to zero. Expensing a proportion of the cost of acquisition of assets and recovering the remainder through economic depreciation could lead to any effective tax rate between zero and the statutory rate.[5]

9.3   Empirical Implementation

The measurement of effective tax rates under U.S. tax law requires data on economic depreciation, the after-tax rate of return, capital consumption allowances for tax purposes, and the investment tax credit. Hulten and Wykoff (1981b) have estimated rates of economic depreciation for all types of assets employed in the U.S. national income and product accounts. These rates of economic depreciation are based on an analysis of data on the prices of assets of different ages. Economic depreciation is measured by the decline in the value of an asset with age.

In table 9.1 we present a list of the assets employed in the U.S. national accounts, the corresponding economic depreciation rates estimated by Hulten and Wykoff, and the percentage of each asset in total corporate investment in 1978. The first 20 categories of assets are classified as producers' durable equipment, the next 14 are classified as nonresidential structures, and the last is residential structures. Economic depreciation rates for equipment range from 33.33 percent per year for automobiles to 6.60 percent per year for railroad equipment. Rates for structures range from 5.63 percent per year for mining, exploration, shafts, and wells to 1.30 percent per year for residential structures.

Hulten and Wykoff (1981b) have compared their estimates of rates of economic depreciation by type of asset with estimates employed since 1976 in the U.S. national income and product accounts.[6] We present average economic depreciation rates employed in the national accounts in table 9.1. The depreciation rates for producers' durable equipment obtained by Hulten and Wykoff are similar in the aggregate to those employed in the U.S. national accounts but differ for specific types of equipment. The economic depreciation rates for nonresidential structures estimated by Hulten and Wykoff are much lower than those employed in the U.S. national accounts. Estimates employed in the national accounts are based on studies of useful lives

Table 9.1
Asset categories and depreciation rates

Asset category	Hulten-Wykoff[a] Depreciation rate	BEA[a] Depreciation rate	Percentage[b] of 1978 Corporate investment
1 Furniture and fixtures	11.00	12.67	2.7
2 Fabricated metal products	9.17	10.12	1.7
3 Engines and turbines	7.86	8.88	0.7
4 Tractors	16.33	25.42	1.5
5 Agricultural machinery	9.71	10.94	0.2
6 Construction machinery	17.22	23.16	3.3
7 Mining and oilfield machinery	16.50	19.24	1.2
8 Metalworking machinery	12.25	12.78	3.5
9 Special industry machinery	10.31	11.61	2.9
10 General industrial equipment	12.25	13.20	4.1
11 Office, computing, and accounting machinery	27.29	25.69	4.7
12 Service industry machinery	16.50	18.60	1.8
13 Electrical machinery	11.79	12.51	10.4
14 Trucks, buses, and trailors	25.37	23.01	11.9
15 Autos	33.33	12.63	4.8
16 Aircraft	18.33	7.55	1.7
17 Ships and boats	7.50	8.37	0.8
18 Railroad equipment	6.60	16.97	1.7
19 Instruments	15.00	16.59	4.5
20 Other equipment	15.00	16.95	1.5
21 Industrial buildings	3.61	7.21	6.3
22 Commercial buildings	2.47	5.18	7.3
23 Religious buildings	1.88	3.55	0.0
24 Educational buildings	1.88	3.52	0.0
25 Hospital buildings	2.33	3.40	0.1
26 Other nonfarm buildings	4.54	6.00	0.4
27 Railroads	1.76	4.88	0.5
28 Telephone and telegraph facilities	3.33	6.35	2.8
29 Electric light and power	3.00	5.81	7.1
30 Gas	3.00	5.93	1.1
31 Other public utilities	4.50	7.75	0.3
32 Farm	2.37	5.88	0.1
33 Mining, exploration, shafts and wells	5.63	11.74	6.1
34 Other nonbuilding facilities	2.90	6.38	0.5
35 Residential	1.30	2.71	1.7

a. Bureau of Economic Analysis (BEA) rates are estimated by Hulten and Wykoff (1981b) to be those implicit in the National Income and Product Accounts. Both sets of rates are found in table 2 of their study, except categories 27, 28, 29, 30, 31, and 35. These were derived for this study by applying Hulten-Wykoff methodology to data disaggregated by type of asset.
b. Investment data for 34 nonresidential assets for farm, manufacturing, and nonfarm, nonmanufacturing sectors in current dollars from 1832 to 1978 were made available by John Musgrave of the Bureau of Economic Analysis. To derive corporate investment, the proportions of investment in each category of assets by corporations (also supplied by John Musgrave) were employed. Corporate residential investment was provided by Jerry Silverstein of the Bureau of Economic Analysis.

for tax purposes summarized in *Bulletin F* (1942), issued by the Internal Revenue Service, and on data on retirement of assets collected by Marston, Winfrey, and Hempstead (1953).

The first step in the estimation of effective tax rates under U.S. tax law is to measure the offset to the cost of acquisition of assets provided by capital consumption allowances. To measure this offset we require present values of these allowances over the lifetime of each asset. Capital consumption allowances for tax purposes depend on accounting formulas for allocating the historical cost of an asset over its lifetime. They also depend on useful lifetimes and salvage values for assets permitted for tax purposes. Although lifetimes, salvage values, and accounting formulas are provided by statute or by regulation, considerable discretion is permitted to individual taxpayers in the calculation of capital consumption allowances.

To summarize practices permitted by the Internal Revenue Service in calculating capital consumption allowances for tax purposes, we have developed a detailed simulation model for the generation of the capital consumption allowances actually claimed by corporations. This model incorporates information about lifetimes and salvage values of assets and accounting formulas permitted for tax purposes. In table 9.2 we present two sets of lifetimes by type of asset—*Bulletin F* lifetimes, introduced by the Internal Revenue Service in 1942, and *Guideline* lifetimes from the Asset Depreciation Range System introduced in 1971.

Considerable survey evidence is available about the accounting formulas actually employed by taxpayers in calculating corporate capital consumption allowances. We can combine this information with scattered evidence on lifetimes used for tax purposes and on the salvage values of assets. Finally, we can simulate the values of capital consumption allowances claimed for tax purposes on the basis of data on investment by type of asset. We have adjusted our estimates of accounting formulas, lifetimes, and salvage values employed for tax purposes to fit historical data on capital consumption allowances; additional details are given in the appendix to this paper. We present simulated capital consumption allowances and estimates of these allowances based on *Statistics of Income* in table 9.3.[7] We also present simulated and actual values of the percentage of capital consumption allowance calculated on the basis of straight-line accounting formulas.

The results of our simulation of capital consumption allowances actually claimed by U.S. corporations over the period 1946 to 1978 are

Table 9.2
Asset lifetimes for tax purposes

Asset category	Bulletin F[a] lifetime	Guideline[b] ADR midpoint lifetime
1 Furniture and fixtures	17.6	10.0
2 Fabricated metal products	21.2	12.5
3 Engines and turbines	24.7	15.6
4 Tractors	9.4	4.3
5 Agricultural machinery	20.0	10.0
6 Construction machinery	10.6	9.9
7 Mining and oilfield machinery	11.8	9.6
8 Metalworking machinery	18.8	12.7
9 Special industry machinery	18.8	12.7
10 General industrial equipment	16.5	12.3
11 Office, computing, and accounting machinery	9.4	10.0
12 Service industry machinery	11.8	10.3
13 Electrical machinery	16.5	12.4
14 Trucks, buses, and trailors	10.6	5.6
15 Autos	11.8	3.0
16 Aircraft	10.6	6.3
17 Ships and boats	25.9	18.0
18 Railroad equipment	29.4	15.0
19 Instruments	12.9	10.6
20 Other equipment	12.9	10.2
21 Industrial buildings	31.8	28.8
22 Commercial buildings	42.3	47.6
23 Religious buildings	56.5	48.0
24 Educational buildings	56.5	48.0
25 Hospital buildings	56.5	48.0
26 Other nonfarm buildings	36.5	30.9
27 Railroads	60.0	30.0
28 Telephone and telegraph facilities	31.8	27.0
29 Electric light and power	35.3	27.0
30 Gas	35.3	24.0
31 Other public utilities	30.6	22.0
32 Farm	44.7	25.0
33 Mining, exploration, shafts and wells	18.8	6.8
34 Other nonbuilding facilities	36.5	28.2
35 Residential	40.0	40.0

a. *Bulletin F* lifetimes are obtained from the capital stock study by the Bureau of Economic Analysis (1976).
b. Guideline ADR midpoint lifetimes were calculated in three stages: (1) Where possible, Guideline lives were applied directly to asset categories, (2) Using industry investment in each category, industry-specific lifetimes were weighted to obtain average asset lifetimes, (3) Investment not covered otherwise was assigned 65 percent of *Bulletin F* lifetimes, which the Treasury estimated to be equivalent to Guideline lifetimes on average.

Table 9.3
Simulated corporate capital consumption allowances, 1946–1978

Year	Corporate capital consumption allowances			Proportion of depreciation using straight-line	
	Simulated	Actual[a]	Difference (1)–(2)	Simulated	Actual[b]
1946	4.82	4.59	0.23	0.97	
1947	5.53	5.68	−0.14	0.95	
1948	6.49	6.82	−0.33	0.94	
1949	7.43	7.77	−0.34	0.94	
1950	8.37	8.50	−0.13	0.93	
1951	9.67	9.81	−0.14	0.93	
1952	11.24	11.10	0.14	0.93	
1953	12.92	12.79	0.13	0.92	
1954	14.84	14.50	0.34	0.89	0.89
1955	17.03	17.21	−0.19	0.82	0.81
1956	19.10	18.90	0.20	0.74	0.74
1957	20.97	20.90	0.07	0.68	0.70
1958	22.35	22.23	0.12	0.63	0.61
1959	23.64	23.62	0.02	0.58	0.58
1960	25.05	25.25	−0.20	0.54	0.53
1961	26.38	26.61	−0.23	0.50	0.50
1962	30.50	30.44	0.06	0.48	
1963	32.48	32.44	0.04	0.45	
1964	34.72	34.57	0.15	0.42	
1965	37.83	37.41	0.42	0.39	
1966	41.25	40.61	0.64	0.36	
1967	44.54	44.12	0.42	0.34	
1968	48.53	48.09	0.44	0.32	
1969	52.99	52.99	0.00	0.30	
1970	56.64	56.61	0.02	0.28	
1971	60.33	60.89	−0.55	0.27	
1972	66.15	67.88	−1.73	0.25	
1973	74.08	73.75	0.34	0.24	
1974	82.31	81.61	0.70	0.22	
1975	89.66	89.22	0.43	0.21	
1976	97.20	97.12	0.08	0.20	
1977	107.73	109.29	−1.56	0.19	
1978	122.26	119.81	2.46	0.17	

a. Corporate capital consumption allowances based on *Statistics of Income* for corporations were prepared by Jerry Silverstein of the Bureau of Economic Analysis for this study.
b. Proportions of corporate capital consumption allowances using the straight-line method are reported for the years 1954–1961 in the *Statistics of Income: Corporation Income Tax Returns*, 1959–1960, p. 7, table E, and 1961–1962, p. 6, table E.

Table 9.4
Tax parameters employed in simulation of corporate capital consumption allowances

Year	Average equipment lifetime	Average structures lifetime	Proportion of new investment using accelerated methods	Equipment salvage value as proportion of original cost
1930	11.80	25.67	0.00	0.08
1931	11.02	25.34	0.00	0.08
1932	11.07	24.14	0.00	0.08
1933	10.88	22.93	0.00	0.08
1934	15.72	33.18	0.00	0.10
1935	15.30	31.71	0.00	0.10
1936	15.71	32.27	0.00	0.10
1937	15.98	30.77	0.00	0.10
1938	15.00	30.13	0.00	0.10
1939	13.77	28.62	0.00	0.10
1940	14.32	28.67	0.00	0.10
1941	14.42	28.53	0.00	0.10
1942	15.65	28.68	0.00	0.10
1943	15.36	28.04	0.08	0.09
1944	14.81	27.34	0.08	0.09
1945	13.63	27.23	0.08	0.09
1946	13.16	28.14	0.08	0.09
1947	13.80	27.93	0.08	0.09
1948	13.64	28.12	0.08	0.09
1949	13.56	28.21	0.08	0.09
1950	13.11	27.80	0.08	0.09
1951	13.69	27.50	0.08	0.09
1952	13.72	27.09	0.09	0.09
1953	13.56	27.25	0.09	0.09
1954	13.32	27.18	0.30	0.06
1955	13.00	27.06	0.52	0.06
1956	13.33	27.59	0.52	0.06
1957	13.36	27.29	0.57	0.06
1958	12.99	27.47	0.65	0.06
1959	12.60	27.45	0.69	0.06
1960	12.65	27.38	0.70	0.06
1961	12.32	27.24	0.71	0.06
1962	11.73	27.27	0.71	0.05
1963	11.54	27.55	0.72	0.04
1964	11.44	27.48	0.72	0.03
1965	11.23	27.80	0.73	0.03
1966	11.09	27.59	0.73	0.03
1967	11.02	27.57	0.74	0.03
1968	10.43	27.39	0.75	0.03
1969	10.33	27.85	0.77	0.03

Table 9.4
(continued)

Year	Average equipment lifetime	Average structures lifetime	Proportion of new investment using accelerated methods	Equipment salvage value as proportion of original cost
1970	10.39	27.55	0.78	0.03
1971	9.66	28.09	0.80	0.01
1972	8.51	28.06	0.81	0.01
1973	8.40	27.83	0.82	0.01
1974	8.57	27.00	0.83	0.01
1975	8.71	25.23	0.84	0.01
1976	8.43	24.75	0.84	0.01
1977	7.78	24.58	0.85	0.01
1978	7.64	24.72	0.85	0.01

presented in table 9.4. Since these data include capital consumption allowances on assets acquired in earlier years, we have developed estimates of lifetimes and salvage values for assets and relative proportions of newly acquired assets depreciated by straight-line and accelerated methods back to 1930. We have assumed that depreciation practices before 1930 are the same as those that prevailed in that year. Our results include estimates of lifetimes used for tax purposes for all 35 types of assets listed in table 9.1. The results also include simulated percentages of capital consumption allowances calculated on the basis of accelerated methods. Finally, we present simulated salvage values as a proportion of the acquisition cost of equipment. Salvage values for structures are simulated at 1 percent of acquisition cost throughout the period.

Comparing the average lifetimes presented in table 9.4 with the statutory lifetimes presented in table 9.2, we observe that lifetimes used for structures have declined steadily over the postwar period. At the end of this period the lifetimes are closely comparable to those employed during the 1930s. By contrast the lifetimes used for equipment have declined dramatically over the postwar period after rising during the 1930s. Although accelerated methods for calculating capital consumption allowances were used before 1954, the proportion of assets treated by these methods jumped from 9 percent in 1953 to 30 percent in 1954 and 52 percent in 1955. Since that time the proportion of assets depreciated by accelerated methods has risen steadily to a level of 85 percent in 1978. Salvage values as a proportion of cost of acquisition of equipment rose from 8 percent in 1933 to 10 percent in 1934. Since that time this ratio has declined steadily, reaching the level of 1 percent in 1978.

Our simulation model of capital consumption provides estimates of lifetimes and salvage values of assets and accounting formulas employed by taxpayers for each year and for each of the 35 types of assets listed in table 9.1. To proceed with the calculation of present values of capital consumption allowances for new assets acquired in each year, we require appropriate discount factors to be applied to the capital consumption allowances permitted under U.S. law. The discount factors depend on after-tax rates of return, not adjusted for inflation, since capital consumption allowances were based on historical cost. If capital consumption allowances were based on replacement cost, the inflation in capital consumption allowances would precisely offset the inflation in the after-tax rate of return.

Since tax deductions for capital consumption are an obligation of the U.S. government, we have constructed discount factors for these allowances on the basis of yields on U.S. government securities. These yields have precisely the characteristics appropriate to the discounting of government obligations. Second, since tax deductions are calculated at historical cost of acquisition of assets, the discount factors should not be corrected for inflation. Yields on government obligations embody anticipations about inflation that are current at the time an investment is made. We present yields on government securities by maturity in table 9.5.

We have estimated present values of capital consumption allowances for tax purposes for each of the 35 types of assets presented in table 9.1. We have weighted these present values by actual investment by type of asset in table 9.6. The first column of this table gives the present value for capital consumption allowances for tax purposes under U.S. tax law for an investment of one dollar in each year of the postwar period 1946–1980. Table 9.6 also provides data for investment in equipment and structures separately. We can compare the present value of capital consumption allowances on assets acquired in each year with the present values of economic depreciation on these assets.

The first two columns in table 9.6 give the present values of capital consumption allowances for tax purposes and economic depreciation

Table 9.5
Yields on U.S. government securities by maturity, 1950–1980[a]

Year	1 yr.	2 yr.	3 yr.	4 yr.	5 yr.	7 yr.	10 yr.	20 yr.	30 yr.
1950	1.28	1.37	1.42	1.47	1.54	1.77	2.11	2.39	2.39
1951	1.70	1.83	1.90	1.96	2.03	2.18	2.41	2.60	2.60
1952	1.87	2.03	2.14	2.22	2.26	2.30	2.47	2.68	2.68
1953	2.13	2.32	2.42	2.50	2.57	2.61	2.78	2.92	3.25
1954	1.03	1.24	1.46	1.70	1.89	2.11	2.43	2.57	2.76
1955	1.97	2.27	2.42	2.51	2.58	2.64	2.72	2.83	2.95
1956	2.89	3.03	3.10	3.12	3.13	3.10	3.08	3.07	3.10
1957	3.48	3.58	3.63	3.64	3.63	3.59	3.54	3.45	3.44
1958	2.17	2.50	2.75	2.89	2.98	3.10	3.27	3.45	3.48
1959	3.80	4.10	4.21	4.26	4.26	4.23	4.13	4.12	4.08
1960	3.55	3.78	3.97	4.08	4.13	4.13	4.13	4.13	4.12
1961	2.89	3.23	3.46	3.61	3.69	3.75	3.84	3.90	3.94
1962	3.05	3.28	3.47	3.61	3.71	3.81	3.96	4.02	4.06
1963	3.29	3.45	3.61	3.72	3.80	3.83	3.98	4.06	4.07
1964	3.80	3.94	4.01	4.05	4.08	4.12	4.17	4.18	4.19
1965	4.07	4.11	4.15	4.17	4.20	4.22	4.25	4.23	4.22
1966	5.12	5.19	5.20	5.18	5.14	5.03	4.86	4.72	4.69
1967	4.77	4.87	4.94	4.98	5.00	5.00	4.97	4.93	4.90
1968	5.54	5.56	5.57	5.57	5.56	5.58	5.48	5.40	5.35
1969	6.95	6.90	6.85	6.78	6.73	6.63	6.46	6.25	6.17
1970	7.05	7.22	7.33	7.41	7.43	7.30	7.21	6.79	6.73
1971	4.89	5.22	5.56	5.78	5.96	6.14	6.11	6.01	6.00
1972	4.88	5.29	5.59	5.77	5.90	6.07	6.23	5.82	5.80
1973	7.24	6.85	6.78	6.78	6.76	6.74	6.73	6.97	6.99
1974	8.23	7.83	7.75	7.74	7.73	7.66	7.31	7.93	7.98
1975	6.65	7.18	7.36	7.47	7.61	7.72	7.42	8.04	8.21
1976	5.92	6.50	6.82	7.04	7.20	7.46	7.53	7.86	7.94
1977	5.94	6.30	6.55	6.77	6.91	7.11	7.36	7.62	7.68
1978	8.20	8.22	8.21	8.22	8.23	8.28	8.33	8.42	8.42
1979	10.54	9.99	9.57	9.47	9.40	9.37	9.34	9.24	9.20
1980	11.61	11.38	11.10	11.12	11.15	11.12	11.16	11.09	11.03

a. Source: Salomon Brothers, *Analytical Handbook of Yields and Yield Ratios.* These yields are used to construct discount factors for calculating the present value of depreciation allowances.

Table 9.6
Present values of corporate capital consumption allowances for tax purposes and economic depreciation on new investment, 1946–1980

	Total[a]			Equipment			Structures		
Year	Tax	Economic	Ratio (1)/(2)	Tax	Economic	Ratio (1)/(2)	Tax	Economic	Ratio (1)/(2)
1946	.767	.551	1.39	.795	.697	1.14	.730	.358	2.04
1947	.769	.569	1.35	.789	.687	1.15	.732	.359	2.04
1948	.769	.567	1.36	.791	.691	1.14	.732	.356	2.06
1949	.768	.564	1.36	.792	.697	1.14	.731	.354	2.07
1950	.773	.579	1.34	.795	.706	1.13	.734	.357	2.06
1951	.756	.568	1.33	.778	.689	1.13	.719	.362	1.99
1952	.752	.565	1.33	.774	.685	1.13	.716	.367	1.95
1953	.730	.566	1.29	.762	.691	1.10	.678	.363	1.87
1954	.784	.568	1.38	.817	.694	1.18	.730	.364	2.00
1955	.785	.575	1.36	.817	.700	1.17	.730	.364	2.01
1956	.768	.563	1.37	.802	.688	1.16	.713	.359	1.99
1957	.754	.564	1.34	.788	.687	1.15	.696	.357	1.95
1958	.761	.553	1.38	.802	.685	1.17	.698	.350	1.99
1959	.739	.572	1.29	.780	.697	1.12	.664	.349	1.91
1960	.738	.567	1.30	.780	.693	1.13	.663	.346	1.92
1961	.749	.561	1.34	.793	.694	1.14	.676	.341	1.98
1962	.756	.566	1.34	.806	.698	1.15	.671	.338	1.98
1963	.762	.565	1.35	.815	.697	1.17	.668	.334	2.00
1964	.764	.568	1.34	.819	.696	1.18	.663	.334	1.98
1965	.762	.568	1.34	.819	.697	1.18	.659	.336	1.96
1966	.745	.572	1.30	.803	.696	1.15	.636	.339	1.88
1967	.740	.571	1.29	.800	.696	1.15	.627	.340	1.84
1968	.732	.575	1.27	.797	.703	1.13	.609	.333	1.83
1969	.702	.570	1.23	.774	.702	1.10	.572	.331	1.73
1970	.667	.561	1.19	.756	.695	1.09	.516	.332	1.56
1971	.710	.564	1.26	.808	.702	1.15	.542	.328	1.65
1972	.728	.568	1.28	.827	.706	1.17	.552	.323	1.71
1973	.705	.572	1.23	.816	.709	1.15	.506	.324	1.56
1974	.688	.577	1.19	.799	.707	1.13	.484	.336	1.44
1975	.692	.579	1.19	.794	.703	1.13	.503	.351	1.43
1976	.705	.590	1.20	.801	.710	1.13	.518	.353	1.47
1977	.726	.598	1.21	.819	.716	1.14	.532	.352	1.51
1978	.699	.593	1.18	.802	.720	1.11	.504	.351	1.44
1979	.679	.593	1.15	.783	.720	1.09	.481	.351	1.37
1980	.645	.593	1.09	.753	.720	1.05	.438	.351	1.25

a. The present value of capital consumption allowances is represented as a proportion of the original cost of the asset. Total is a weighted average for all 35 categories of investment. Equipment is a weighted average on 20 types of equipment. Structures is a weighted average on 15 types of structures.

for all corporate investment. Capital consumption for tax purposes has exceeded economic depreciation in every year by amounts ranging from 39 percent in 1946 at the beginning of the postwar period to 9 percent in 1980 at the end of the period. We present similar comparisons for investment in equipment and structures in table 9.6. We find that the present value of capital consumption allowances has exceeded economic depreciation on equipment by amounts ranging from 5 to 18 percent. The present value of capital consumption allowances has exceeded economic depreciation on structures by amounts ranging from 107 percent at the beginning of the period to 25 percent in 1980.

We have compared present values of capital consumption allowances for tax purposes and economic depreciation in table 9.6. This comparison provides the appropriate measure of the impact of inflation on capital consumption allowances for new investment. A different perspective on the impact of inflation is provided by a comparison between capital consumption allowances claimed for tax purposes at historical and at replacement cost. We present such a comparison, based on our simulation model for generating capital consumption allowances, in table 9.7. For this purpose we employ simulated values of lifetimes and salvage values and relative proportions of assets depreciated by accelerated methods for all 35 types of assets listed in table 9.1.

Since the rate of inflation in the prices of assets has been positive throughout the postwar period, except for 1958 and 1961, capital consumption allowances at historical cost have always fallen short of capital consumption at replacement cost. Historical cost capital consumption declined from 73 percent of replacement cost in 1946 to a postwar low of 66 percent in 1948. As inflation slowed during the 1950s and early 1960s, historical cost capital consumption rose relative to replacement cost, reaching a peak of 90 percent in 1965. The increase in the rate of inflation in the later 1960s and early 1970s resulted in a sizeable decline in the historical cost capital consumption relative to replacement cost capital consumption, reaching a trough of 72 percent in 1975.

We have compared capital consumption allowances for tax purposes at historical and at replacement cost in table 9.7. We can provide an analogous comparison between economic depreciation at historical and at replacement cost. The results are given for each year of the period 1946–1978 in table 9.8. At the beginning of the post-

Table 9.7
The effect of inflation on corporate capital consumption allowances for tax purposes, 1946–1978

Year	Simulated corporate capital consumption allowances		Ratio (1)/(2)	Percentage change of investment price deflator[b]
	Historical cost	Replacement[a] cost		
1946	4.82	6.57	0.73	11.3
1947	5.53	8.22	0.67	18.4
1948	6.49	9.78	0.66	9.6
1949	7.43	10.72	0.69	2.2
1950	8.37	11.70	0.72	3.1
1951	9.67	14.09	0.69	7.6
1952	11.24	15.73	0.71	2.1
1953	12.92	17.26	0.75	1.3
1954	14.84	19.08	0.78	0.8
1955	17.03	21.14	0.81	2.2
1956	19.10	24.45	0.78	5.5
1957	20.97	26.97	0.78	3.8
1958	22.35	28.05	0.80	−0.1
1959	23.64	29.23	0.81	1.2
1960	25.05	30.34	0.83	0.5
1961	26.38	31.08	0.85	−0.4
1962	30.50	35.27	0.86	0.5
1963	32.48	36.90	0.88	0.2
1964	34.72	38.98	0.89	0.8
1965	37.83	42.12	0.90	1.5
1966	41.25	46.23	0.89	3.3
1967	44.54	50.34	0.88	3.3
1968	48.53	55.44	0.88	4.3
1969	52.99	61.48	0.86	5.8
1970	56.64	67.07	0.84	4.8
1971	60.33	72.84	0.83	5.2
1972	66.15	79.57	0.83	4.3
1973	74.08	88.93	0.83	6.0
1974	82.31	105.48	0.78	10.7
1975	89.66	123.92	0.72	12.8
1976	97.20	133.65	0.73	5.6
1977	107.73	145.66	0.74	7.7
1978	122.26	164.38	0.74	9.2

a. Capital consumption allowances at replacement cost were calculated by multiplying the allowances for all assets by the ratio of the price deflator in each year to the price deflator in the year the asset was acquired.
b. Implicit price deflators corresponding to our 35 categories of investment were taken from the National Income and Product Accounts.

Table 9.8
The effect of inflation on corporate economic depreciation, 1946–1978

Year	Corporate economic depreciation		Ratio (1)/(2)	Percentage change of investment price deflator[c]
	Historical cost[a]	Replacement cost[b]		
1946	5.47	7.24	0.76	11.3
1947	6.47	9.18	0.70	18.4
1948	7.71	11.03	0.70	9.6
1949	8.81	12.09	0.73	2.2
1950	9.81	13.09	0.75	3.1
1951	10.91	15.24	0.72	7.6
1952	11.93	16.21	0.74	2.1
1953	12.97	16.99	0.76	1.3
1954	14.04	17.84	0.79	0.8
1955	15.17	18.88	0.80	2.2
1956	16.48	21.36	0.77	5.5
1957	17.94	23.31	0.77	3.8
1958	19.11	24.14	0.79	−0.1
1959	20.26	25.17	0.80	1.2
1960	21.68	26.28	0.82	0.5
1961	22.93	26.94	0.85	−0.4
1962	24.10	27.73	0.87	0.5
1963	25.46	28.79	0.88	0.2
1964	27.21	30.46	0.89	0.8
1965	29.61	32.92	0.90	1.5
1966	32.61	36.44	0.89	3.3
1967	35.68	40.21	0.89	3.3
1968	38.98	44.45	0.88	4.3
1969	42.68	49.62	0.86	5.8
1970	45.89	54.59	0.84	4.8
1971	49.11	59.77	0.82	5.2
1972	53.04	64.82	0.82	4.3
1973	58.43	71.74	0.81	6.0
1974	64.27	84.81	0.76	10.7
1975	69.78	100.06	0.70	12.8
1976	75.48	108.99	0.69	5.6
1977	82.97	119.63	0.69	7.7
1978	92.75	135.05	0.69	9.2

a. Economic depreciation at historical cost is calculated by applying Hulten-Wykoff depreciation rates to historical cost of acquisition of assets.

b. Economic depreciation at replacement cost is calculated by multiplying depreciation at historical cost for all assets by the ratio of the price deflator for each year to the price deflator in the year the asset was acquired.

c. Implicit price deflators used correspond to our 35 categories of investment. Price deflators were taken from the National Income and Product Accounts.

war period historical cost depreciation was 76 percent of replacement cost depreciation. As a consequence of the rapid inflation in the prices of assets during the period 1946–1948, the ratio of historical cost depreciation to replacement cost depreciation fell to 70 percent of 1948. This ratio began to rise gradually after 1948 as the rate of inflation declined, reaching a peak during the period 1964–1966 of 90 percent. This peak resulted from relatively low rates of inflation in asset prices during the period 1958–1964.

Rates of inflation in asset prices began to increase after 1964; by 1966 the ratio of historical cost depreciation to replacement cost depreciation began to decrease and fell to the postwar low of 69 percent during the period 1975–1978. Comparing economic depreciation at historical and replacement cost in table 9.8 with capital consumption allowances in table 9.7, we find that the impact of inflation was very similar. High rates of inflation result in a cumulative divergence between historical and replacement cost capital consumption allowances. The pattern of divergence for economic depreciation is nearly identical.

The next step in our analysis of the impact of inflation on capital recovery under the U.S. corporate income tax is to compare the allowances claimed by U.S. corporations with economic depreciation at replacement cost. We find that capital consumption allowances were below economic depreciation from the beginning of the postwar period until 1962. The reduction in asset lifetimes allowed for tax purposes and the introduction of new accounting formulas for accelerated capital recovery in 1954 did not overcome the impact of rapid inflation during the early years of the postwar period. In 1962 the Depreciation Guidelines were introduced, making shorter lifetimes applicable to existing assets. As a consequence, capital consumption allowances for tax purposes overtook economic depreciation at replacement cost in 1962; the excess of capital consumption allowances over economic depreciation rose to 14 percent in 1965. With increased rates of inflation beginning in 1965, the ratio of capital consumption allowances to economic depreciation began to decline but remained above unity through 1973. In 1971 the Asset Depreciation Range System was introduced, further shortening lifetimes for tax purposes. Beginning in 1974 very high rates of inflation resulted in economic depreciation in excess of capital consumption allowances for tax purposes.

Our overall conclusion is that the present value of capital consumption allowances, based on expectations of inflation current at the time

of investment, have exceeded the present value of economic depreciation throughout the postwar period, as indicated in table 9.6. This is
the reverse of the relationship between capital consumption
allowances actually claimed by U.S. corporations and economic depreciation at replacement cost in table 9.9 for the years 1946–1961 and
1974–1978. The difference is accounted for by the fact that increases in
the rate of inflation have been entirely unanticipated.

Throughout the postwar period anticipated future inflation rates
have been close to current rates of inflation, as indicated by the term
structure of interest rates on U.S. government securities given in table
9.5. Actual inflation rates have risen steadily since 1965, thereby
exceeding the rates of inflation that were anticipated. As a consequence, the present value of capital consumption allowances at currently anticipated rates of inflation has exceeded the present value of
economic depreciation. Actual capital consumption allowances
claimed by U.S. corporations have fallen short of economic depreciation at replacement cost, except for the period 1962–1973.

The final step in our analysis of the impact of inflation on capital
recovery under U.S. tax law is to incorporate the offset to the cost of
acquisition of assets provided by the investment tax credit. The
investment tax credit was first adopted in 1962. It originally applied
to equipment and certain special purpose structures. Under the Long
amendment the credit was subtracted from the cost of acquisition of
assets in establishing the historical cost employed in calculating capital consumption allowances for tax purposes. This amendment was
repealed in 1964. The investment tax credit was suspended briefly in
1967–1978, abolished in 1969, and reinstituted in 1971. During the
period from 1962 to 1974 the definition of special purpose structures
was gradually broadened.

In 1975 the investment tax credit was made permanent; the statutory rate was raised from 7 to 10 percent for most assets and from 4 to
10 percent for public utility assets. The credit was made applicable to
a large proportion of structures as well as equipment. As much as 57
percent of the cost of acquisition of structures in 1975 was covered by
the investment tax credit. Effective rates of the investment tax credit
for all of the investment for equipment and structures separately are
given in table 9.10 for the period 1962 to 1980. These rates are based
on estimates of effective rates for each of the 34 types of assets presented in table 9.1. The effective rates by type of asset are weighted by
actual investment in each type of asset in each year to obtain averages
for equipment and structures.

Table 9.9
Corporate capital consumption allowances for tax purposes and economic depreciation, 1946–1978

Year	Actual corporate capital consumption allowances[a]	Replacement cost corporate economic depreciation[b]	Ratio (1)/(2)
1946	4.59	7.24	0.63
1947	5.68	9.18	0.62
1948	6.82	11.03	0.62
1949	7.77	12.09	0.64
1950	8.50	13.09	0.65
1951	9.81	15.24	0.64
1952	11.10	16.21	0.68
1953	12.79	16.99	0.75
1954	14.50	17.84	0.81
1955	17.21	18.88	0.91
1956	18.90	21.36	0.88
1957	20.90	23.31	0.90
1958	22.23	24.14	0.92
1959	23.62	25.17	0.94
1960	25.25	26.28	0.96
1961	26.61	26.94	0.99
1962	30.44	27.73	1.10
1963	32.44	28.79	1.13
1964	34.57	30.46	1.13
1965	37.41	32.92	1.14
1966	40.61	36.44	1.11
1967	44.12	40.21	1.10
1968	48.09	44.45	1.08
1969	52.99	49.62	1.07
1970	56.61	54.59	1.04
1971	60.89	59.77	1.02
1972	67.88	64.82	1.05
1973	73.75	71.74	1.03
1974	81.61	84.81	0.96
1975	89.22	100.06	0.89
1976	97.12	108.99	0.89
1977	109.29	119.63	0.91
1978	119.81	135.05	0.89

a. Corporate capital consumption allowances based on *Statistics of Income* for corporations were prepared by Jerry Silverstein of the Bureau of Economic Analysis for this study.
b. Economic depreciation at replacement cost is calculated by multiplying depreciation at historical cost for all assets by the ratio of the price deflator in each year to the price deflator in the year the asset was acquired.

Table 9.10
Effective rates of the investment tax credit, 1962–1980

	Investment tax credit[a]		
Year	Total	Equipment	Structures
1962	0.034	0.054	0.000
1963	0.036	0.055	0.002
1964	0.037	0.055	0.005
1965	0.037	0.056	0.003
1966	0.030	0.043	0.004
1967	0.033	0.046	0.009
1968	0.038	0.054	0.009
1969	0.011	0.015	0.002
1970	0.000	0.000	0.000
1971	0.028	0.040	0.007
1972	0.037	0.053	0.009
1973	0.037	0.052	0.009
1974	0.038	0.053	0.011
1975	0.062	0.074	0.040
1976	0.070	0.081	0.049
1977	0.069	0.079	0.048
1978	0.067	0.078	0.044
1979	0.067	0.078	0.044
1980	0.067	0.078	0.044

a. Effective rates of the investment tax credit are averages of effective rates calculated separately for each category of investment, based on methods developed independently by Corcoran (1979) and Jeremias (1979). Estimates of the amount of property covered by the investment credit are derived from *Statistics of Income.* The applicable statutory credit rates are weighted by these amounts in each category. Public utility property before 1975 and shorter-lived assets are eligible for only a fraction of the full rate. Effective rates are also less than the statutory rate due to considerable carryover. In certain years the credit was available only part of the year.

9.4   Capital Recovery During the Postwar Period

The objective of our analysis of capital recovery under U.S. tax law during the postwar period 1946–1980 is to estimate effective tax rates for equipment and structures acquired by U.S. corporations during this period. We recall from the discussion of section 9.1 that the investment tax credit is a direct offset against tax liability, while capital consumption allowances are a deduction from taxable income. The effective tax rate for an asset depends on the statutory tax rate, the effective rate of the investment tax credit, the present value of capital consumption allowances for tax purposes, the rate of economic depreciation, and the rate of return after taxes, corrected for inflation.

We present effective tax rates for all corporate investment for each year in the postwar period 1946–1980 in table 9.11. We also present effective tax rates for structures and for equipment separately. If capital consumption allowances were equal to economic depreciation and the investment tax credit were equal to zero for all assets, the effective tax rate would be the same for all assets and equal to the statutory rate. We present the statutory rate in table 9.11 as a basis for comparison with the effective tax rates under U.S. tax law. We find that the effective tax rate was below the statutory rate in every year. The ratio of the effective tax rate to the statutory rate is given in the final column of table 9.11.

We find that the ratio of the effective tax rate on corporate investment to the statutory rate fluctuated between 68 and 80 percent over the period from 1946 to 1961. When the investment tax credit was first adopted in 1962, the ratio of the effective tax rate to the statutory rate dropped to 55 percent in that year from 76 percent in 1961. When the investment tax credit was repealed in 1969 and 1970, the effective tax rate climbed to 78 percent of the statutory rate in 1969 and to 87 percent of the statutory rate in 1970. Reinstitution of the investment tax credit in 1971 reduced the effective tax rate to 60 percent of the statutory rate in that year and 48 percent in the following year. Liberalization of the investment tax credit in 1975 reduced the effective tax rate to 43 percent of the statutory rate. The effective tax rate fell to 12.8 percent in 1977 as the rate of inflation decreased and rose to 24.3 percent in 1980 as the rate of inflation increased.

Our first conclusion is that the effective tax rate under U.S. tax law has been below the statutory tax rate throughout the postwar period 1946–1980. The effect of inflation under any given set of tax provisions for capital recovery is to increase the effective tax rate. This occurs through an increase in the discount rates applied to future capital consumption allowances, as indicated in table 9.5. However, tax provisions have been revised at frequent intervals with major revisions in 1954, 1962, 1970, and 1975. The impact of these revisions has been to reduce effective tax rates very dramatically, especially in 1962 with the adoption of the investment tax credit and the Depreciation Guidelines and, in 1975, with the liberalization of the investment tax credit.

Table 9.11
Effective corporate tax rates, 1946–1980

	Effective corporate tax rate[a]			Statutory	Ratio
Year	Total	Equipment	Structures	tax rate	(1)/(4)
1946	0.258	0.301	0.202	0.380	0.680
1947	0.265	0.301	0.201	0.380	0.697
1948	0.264	0.302	0.200	0.380	0.696
1949	0.266	0.307	0.200	0.380	0.699
1950	0.303	0.346	0.226	0.420	0.720
1951	0.389	0.436	0.310	0.510	0.762
1952	0.398	0.445	0.322	0.520	0.766
1953	0.418	0.460	0.348	0.520	0.803
1954	0.366	0.400	0.312	0.520	0.704
1955	0.370	0.405	0.311	0.520	0.712
1956	0.379	0.411	0.325	0.520	0.728
1957	0.394	0.429	0.335	0.520	0.758
1958	0.377	0.408	0.330	0.520	0.725
1959	0.412	0.444	0.355	0.520	0.792
1960	0.411	0.442	0.356	0.520	0.790
1961	0.397	0.428	0.346	0.520	0.764
1962	0.285	0.250	0.345	0.520	0.548
1963	0.265	0.219	0.344	0.520	0.509
1964	0.237	0.189	0.324	0.500	0.474
1965	0.213	0.160	0.309	0.480	0.444
1966	0.274	0.247	0.324	0.480	0.570
1967	0.269	0.240	0.323	0.480	0.560
1968	0.259	0.221	0.330	0.480	0.539
1969	0.372	0.378	0.361	0.480	0.776
1970	0.416	0.429	0.394	0.480	0.867
1971	0.289	0.244	0.367	0.480	0.603
1972	0.229	0.157	0.357	0.480	0.478
1973	0.257	0.188	0.383	0.480	0.536
1974	0.281	0.221	0.394	0.480	0.586
1975	0.206	0.131	0.345	0.480	0.430
1976	0.161	0.081	0.320	0.480	0.336
1977	0.128	0.041	0.308	0.480	0.266
1978	0.180	0.099	0.335	0.480	0.376
1979	0.192	0.121	0.327	0.460	0.418
1980	0.243	0.185	0.352	0.460	0.528

a. Effective tax rates are weighted averages of effective tax rates calculated for each category of investment. An after-tax rate of return corrected for inflation of 0.0606 is used. This is equal to the average rate of return after corporate taxes in the 1946–1978 period, based on the results of Christensen and Jorgenson (1978). Present values of capital consumption allowances for tax purposes and economic depreciation correspond to those of table 9.6. Effective rates of the investment tax credit correspond to those of table 9.10.

Since the effective tax rate increases with the rate of inflation, a decrease in the rate of inflation to levels below those prevailing since 1973 would reduce the effective tax rate substantially. The decrease in the rates of inflation in the prices of assets from 12.8 percent in 1975 to 5.6 in 1976 and 7.7 in 1977 brought the effective tax rate down to a level of 16.1 percent in 1976 and 12.8 percent in 1977. These tax rates can be compared with the statutory rate of 48 percent in both years. The increases in the rate of inflation in 1978, 1979, and 1980 brought effective tax rates up to 18.0 percent in 1978, 19.2 percent in 1979, and 24.3 percent in 1980.

Our second conclusion is that the U.S. corporate income tax imposes significantly different effective tax rates on different assets, resulting in serious misallocations of capital. Effective tax rates for equipment and structures have been substantially different through the postwar period. Until 1962, effective tax rates for structures were below those of equipment by 8 to 12 percent. After the introduction of the investment tax credit in 1962, the effective tax rate on equipment fell below that of structures by 10 percent in that year. After the liberalization of the investment tax credit in 1975 the gap between effective tax rates for equipment and structures rose to 21 percent in that year and reached a maximum of 27 percent in 1977. Differences in tax rates among assets increase with a decrease in the rate of inflation, resulting in greater misallocations of capital.

Differences in effective tax rates among assets result in differences in social rates of return on these assets. The gap between social rates of return on equipment and structures creates the opportunity for gains in future output at no sacrifice of consumption either now or in the future. For any given asset the social rate of return ρ, corrected for inflation and for taxes paid at the effective tax rate e, is equal to the private rate of return r, corrected for inflation and for taxes paid at the statutory rate u:

$$(1 - e)\, \rho = (1 - u)\, r.$$

We can denote effective tax rates on equipment and structures by e_E and e_S; the corresponding difference in social rates of return, say ρ_E and ρ_S is given by

$$\rho_S - \rho_E = \left(\frac{1}{1 - e_S} - \frac{1}{1 - e_E} \right)(1 - u)\, r.$$

Considering the effective tax rates in 1977 of 4.1 percent for equipment and 30.8 percent for structures, we find that the difference in social rates of return is 2.44 percent. This implies that the social rate of return to the transfer of one dollar's worth of investment from equipment to structures in 1977 would have been 2.44 percent per year. This can be compared with the private rate of return of 6.06 percent per year for the postwar period as a whole. To gain perspective on the gap between social rates of return that existed in 1977 we can consider the value of an investment at this rate of return in 1946. By 1956 this investment, corrected for inflation, would have been worth $1.27. By 1966 the investment would have been worth $1.62. By 1976 the investment would have been worth $2.06 and by 1981 the investment would have been worth $2.33. The returns of $0.27 by 1956, $0.62 by 1966, $1.06 by 1976, and $1.33 by 1981 for each dollar's worth of investment correspond to costless increases in the national wealth that would be available for consumption or additional investment.

In table 9.12 we present estimates of effective tax rates for the 35 types of assets listed in table 9.1. We give these effective tax rates for six business cycle peak year during this period—1953, 1957, 1960, 1966, 1973, and 1979. The discount rates applied to future capital consumption allowances have increased steadily from peak to peak throughout the postwar period. For each type of assets we present the present value of capital consumption allowances for tax purposes, the effective rate of the investment tax credit, and the effective tax rate. Differences in effective tax rates are much greater among the 35 types of assets given in table 9.12 than between equipment and structures given in table 9.11.

The gap among effective tax rates for different assets in 1953 was a maximum for autos with an effective tax rate of 58 percent and a rate of 29 percent for mining and exploration structures, shafts and wells. The gap of 29 percent equals the maximum gap between equipment and structures for the postwar period. The gap between effective tax rates for these two assets was also a maximum for 1957 at 26 percent and for 1960 at 25 percent. By 1966 the maximum effective tax rate for any asset had shifted to hospital buildings at 39 percent. The gap between effective tax rates for hospitals and for mining and exploration structures, shafts and wells was only 21 percent. By 1973 the minimum effective tax rate, 7 percent had shifted to aircraft. The gap between effective tax rates for aircraft and for hospital buildings was 38 percent. The maximum gap rose to 46 percent in 1979, when the

Table 9.12
Effective corporate tax rate by type of asset, selected years: 1953, 1957

Asset	1953			1957		
	Present value	ITC	Effective tax rate	Present value	ITC	Effective tax rate
1	0.751	0.00	0.43	0.776	0.00	0.41
2	0.720	0.00	0.43	0.748	0.00	0.41
3	0.691	0.00	0.43	0.721	0.00	0.41
4	0.825	0.00	0.41	0.846	0.00	0.38
5	0.730	0.00	0.43	0.756	0.00	0.41
6	0.813	0.00	0.44	0.836	0.00	0.41
7	0.801	0.00	0.44	0.825	0.00	0.41
8	0.740	0.00	0.46	0.766	0.00	0.43
9	0.740	0.00	0.43	0.766	0.00	0.41
10	0.760	0.00	0.44	0.785	0.00	0.41
11	0.825	0.00	0.51	0.846	0.00	0.48
12	0.801	0.00	0.44	0.825	0.00	0.41
13	0.760	0.00	0.43	0.785	0.00	0.41
14	0.813	0.00	0.51	0.836	0.00	0.48
15	0.801	0.00	0.58	0.825	0.00	0.55
16	0.813	0.00	0.45	0.836	0.00	0.42
17	0.681	0.00	0.44	0.714	0.00	0.41
18	0.650	0.00	0.44	0.689	0.00	0.41
19	0.791	0.00	0.44	0.815	0.00	0.41
20	0.791	0.00	0.44	0.815	0.00	0.41
21	0.683	0.00	0.35	0.703	0.00	0.34
22	0.600	0.00	0.38	0.633	0.00	0.36
23	0.519	0.00	0.41	0.557	0.00	0.39
24	0.519	0.00	0.41	0.557	0.00	0.39
25	0.519	0.00	0.42	0.557	0.00	0.40
26	0.639	0.00	0.41	0.671	0.00	0.38
27	0.502	0.00	0.41	0.540	0.00	0.39
28	0.683	0.00	0.35	0.703	0.00	0.33
29	0.650	0.00	0.36	0.680	0.00	0.34
30	0.650	0.00	0.36	0.680	0.00	0.34
31	0.694	0.00	0.37	0.711	0.00	0.35
32	0.586	0.00	0.38	0.619	0.00	0.36
33	0.805	0.00	0.29	0.802	0.00	0.29
34	0.639	0.00	0.37	0.671	0.00	0.35
35	0.616	0.00	0.34	0.647	0.00	0.32

Table 9.12 (continued)
Effective corporate tax rate by type of asset, selected years: 1960, 1966

	1960			1966		
Asset	Present value	ITC	Effective tax rate	Present value	ITC	Effective tax rate
1	0.763	0.00	0.42	0.797	0.05	0.20
2	0.732	0.00	0.42	0.770	0.04	0.26
3	0.704	0.00	0.42	0.740	0.03	0.29
4	0.841	0.00	0.39	0.822	0.02	0.33
5	0.742	0.00	0.42	0.790	0.05	0.20
6	0.829	0.00	0.42	0.809	0.05	0.24
7	0.817	0.00	0.42	0.820	0.05	0.20
8	0.751	0.00	0.45	0.767	0.05	0.26
9	0.751	0.00	0.42	0.773	0.05	0.23
10	0.772	0.00	0.43	0.803	0.05	0.21
11	0.841	0.00	0.49	0.814	0.05	0.29
12	0.817	0.00	0.42	0.815	0.05	0.22
13	0.772	0.00	0.42	0.784	0.04	0.25
14	0.829	0.00	0.49	0.865	0.03	0.28
15	0.817	0.00	0.56	0.890	0.02	0.31
16	0.829	0.00	0.43	0.860	0.03	0.20
17	0.694	0.00	0.43	0.717	0.05	0.27
18	0.669	0.00	0.43	0.721	0.05	0.25
19	0.806	0.00	0.42	0.809	0.05	0.22
20	0.806	0.00	0.42	0.811	0.05	0.21
21	0.678	0.00	0.36	0.649	0.00	0.34
22	0.605	0.00	0.38	0.526	0.00	0.38
23	0.527	0.00	0.40	0.504	0.00	0.37
24	0.527	0.00	0.40	0.504	0.00	0.37
25	0.527	0.00	0.42	0.504	0.00	0.39
26	0.642	0.00	0.40	0.622	0.00	0.38
27	0.509	0.00	0.41	0.581	0.01	0.32
28	0.678	0.00	0.35	0.657	0.01	0.32
29	0.652	0.00	0.36	0.650	0.01	0.31
30	0.652	0.00	0.36	0.669	0.01	0.30
31	0.685	0.00	0.37	0.692	0.01	0.32
32	0.590	0.00	0.38	0.640	0.02	0.29
33	0.784	0.00	0.31	0.847	0.01	0.18
34	0.642	0.00	0.36	0.606	0.02	0.32
35	0.620	0.00	0.33	0.592	0.00	0.31

Table 9.12 (continued)
Effective corporate tax rate by type of asset, selected years: 1973, 1979

	1973			1979		
Asset	Present value	ITC	Effective tax rate	Present value	ITC	Effective tax rate
1	0.813	0.06	0.13	0.773	0.09	0.06
2	0.774	0.06	0.20	0.728	0.09	0.13
3	0.730	0.04	0.29	0.680	0.09	0.19
4	0.883	0.04	0.08	0.849	0.06	0.05
5	0.813	0.06	0.11	0.773	0.09	0.06
6	0.810	0.06	0.19	0.773	0.09	0.08
7	0.818	0.06	0.14	0.780	0.09	0.06
8	0.776	0.06	0.20	0.724	0.09	0.16
9	0.776	0.06	0.18	0.724	0.09	0.15
10	0.813	0.06	0.15	0.773	0.09	0.06
11	0.805	0.06	0.25	0.751	0.09	0.19
12	0.810	0.06	0.18	0.767	0.09	0.09
13	0.781	0.05	0.24	0.730	0.09	0.15
14	0.889	0.03	0.18	0.865	0.05	0.13
15	0.929	0.02	0.14	0.908	0.03	0.12
16	0.860	0.06	0.07	0.819	0.08	0.00
17	0.694	0.06	0.26	0.644	0.09	0.23
18	0.739	0.06	0.20	0.686	0.09	0.17
19	0.805	0.06	0.19	0.763	0.09	0.10
20	0.813	0.06	0.15	0.769	0.09	0.08
21	0.514	0.00	0.42	0.437	0.00	0.43
22	0.372	0.00	0.45	0.304	0.00	0.45
23	0.370	0.00	0.43	0.302	0.00	0.44
24	0.370	0.00	0.43	0.302	0.00	0.44
25	0.370	0.00	0.45	0.302	0.00	0.45
26	0.495	0.00	0.45	0.421	0.00	0.46
27	0.504	0.02	0.35	0.428	0.09	0.29
28	0.534	0.02	0.38	0.458	0.09	0.31
29	0.534	0.02	0.37	0.458	0.09	0.30
30	0.566	0.02	0.35	0.491	0.09	0.28
31	0.593	0.02	0.37	0.518	0.09	0.30
32	0.558	0.04	0.31	0.482	0.09	0.27
33	0.841	0.03	0.15	0.793	0.06	0.11
34	0.528	0.04	0.34	0.447	0.09	0.31
35	0.503	0.00	0.36	0.446	0.00	0.36

effective tax rate on aircraft dropped to zero and the rate on other non-farm buildings rose to 46 percent.

A difference between effective tax rates of 46 percent in 1979 corresponds to a difference between social rates of return of 5.16 percent. As before, it is useful to put the gap between social rates of return that existed in 1979 in perspective by considering the value of an investment at this rate of return beginning in 1946. The investment would have been worth $1.65 in 1956 and $2.74 in 1966, both corrected for inflation. By 1976 the value of the investment would have grown to $3.93, and by 1981 the investment would have grown to $4.94, again corrected for inflation. We conclude that the loss in efficiency of capital allocation due to differences in effective tax rates among assets in 1979 was very large. It is important to emphasize that gaps among social rates of return would increase with a decrease in the rate of inflation.

To measure the burden of taxation on individual industries and differences in tax burdens among industries we have calculated effective tax rates by industry for the 44 industries listed in table 9.13. For each industry we have compiled data on the composition of investment by type of asset for each year of the postwar period 1946–1980.[8] Using the relative proportions of investment among assets as weights we have calculated effective tax rates for equipment, structures, and total investment in each industry in each year. We present the results in table 9.14 for the business cycle peaks 1953, 1957, 1960, 1966, 1973, and 1979. Differences in effective tax rates among industries given in table 9.14 are less than differences in these rates among assets given in table 9.12. Effective tax rates for individual industries are essentially averages of rates for all assets with weights that differ among industries.

The maximum gap between effective tax rates for different industries in 1953 was between street railway, bus lines, and taxicab service, with an effective tax rate of 56 percent and crude petroleum and natural gas extraction with a rate of 32 percent. The gap between effective tax rates for these two industries was also a maximum for 1957 and 1960 at 19 percent in each year. By 1966 the maximum effective tax rate for any industry had shifted to finance, insurance, and real estate at 33 percent while the minimum rate had shifted to air transportation at 20 percent. By 1973 the maximum effective tax rate was for pipelines, except natural gas at 36 percent; the minimum was for air transportation at 8 percent. By 1979 the effective tax rate for air transportation had dropped to zero, while the effective tax rate for metal

Table 9.13
Industries

1.	Food and kindred products
2.	Tobacco manufacturers
3.	Textile mill products
4.	Apparel and other fabricated textile products
5.	Paper and allied products
6.	Printing, publishing, and allied industries
7.	Chemicals and allied products
8.	Petroleum and coal products
9.	Rubber and miscellaneous plastic products
10.	Leather and leather products
11.	Lumber and wood products, except furniture
12.	Furniture and fixtures
13.	Stone, clay, and glass products
14.	Primary metal industries
15.	Fabricated metal industries
16.	Machinery except electrical
17.	Electrical machinery, equipment, and supplies
18.	Transportation equipment, except motor vehicles, and ordnance
19.	Motor vehicles, and motor vehicle equipment
20.	Professional photographic equipment and watches
21.	Miscellaneous manufacturing industries
22.	Agricultural production
23.	Agricultural services, horticultural services, forestry and fisheries
24.	Metal mining
25.	Coal mining
26.	Crude petroleum and natural gas extraction
27.	Nonmetallic mining and quarrying, except fuel
28.	Construction
29.	Railroads and railway express service
30.	Street railway, bus lines and taxicab service
31.	Trucking service, warehousing and storage
32.	Water transportation
33.	Air transportation
34.	Pipelines, except natural gas
35.	Services incidental to transportation
36.	Telephone, telegraph, and miscellaneous communication services
37.	Radio broadcasting and television
38.	Electric utilities
39.	Gas utilities
40.	Water supply, sanitary services, and other utilities
41.	Wholesale trade
42.	Retail trade
43.	Finance, insurance and real estate
44.	Services

Table 9.14
Effective corporate tax rate by industry, selected years

Industry	1953[a]			1957[a]		
	Total	Equipment	Structures	Total	Equipment	Structures
1	0.43	0.46	0.36	0.41	0.43	0.34
2	0.43	0.45	0.37	0.41	0.42	0.34
3	0.42	0.44	0.36	0.40	0.42	0.34
4	0.44	0.46	0.36	0.42	0.43	0.34
5	0.42	0.44	0.35	0.40	0.42	0.34
6	0.42	0.45	0.36	0.40	0.43	0.34
7	0.42	0.45	0.35	0.40	0.42	0.34
8	0.39	0.45	0.35	0.37	0.42	0.34
9	0.44	0.46	0.35	0.41	0.43	0.34
10	0.43	0.45	0.36	0.41	0.42	0.34
11	0.43	0.46	0.35	0.42	0.44	0.34
12	0.43	0.47	0.35	0.40	0.44	0.34
13	0.43	0.46	0.36	0.40	0.43	0.34
14	0.42	0.45	0.35	0.40	0.42	0.34
15	0.43	0.46	0.35	0.41	0.43	0.34
16	0.43	0.47	0.36	0.40	0.43	0.34
17	0.43	0.46	0.36	0.40	0.43	0.34
18	0.42	0.47	0.36	0.39	0.43	0.34
19	0.45	0.47	0.36	0.42	0.43	0.34
20	0.43	0.47	0.35	0.40	0.44	0.34
21	0.44	0.47	0.36	0.40	0.43	0.34
22	0.46	0.47	0.38	0.43	0.43	0.36
23	0.46	0.47	0.38	0.43	0.43	0.36
24	0.42	0.44	0.41	0.38	0.41	0.37
25	0.44	0.44	0.38	0.40	0.41	0.35
26	0.32	0.45	0.29	0.33	0.42	0.31
27	0.44	0.44	0.39	0.41	0.42	0.36
28	0.45	0.45	0.39	0.43	0.43	0.36
29	0.43	0.44	0.41	0.41	0.41	0.39
30	0.56	0.56		0.52	0.52	
31	0.50	0.50		0.47	0.47	
32	0.44	0.44		0.41	0.41	
33	0.45	0.45		0.42	0.42	
34	0.38	0.43	0.37	0.35	0.41	0.35
35	0.49	0.49	0.38	0.46	0.46	0.36
36	0.40	0.43	0.35	0.38	0.41	0.33
37	0.43	0.43	0.41	0.40	0.41	0.37
38	0.39	0.44	0.36	0.37	0.41	0.34
39	0.37	0.44	0.36	0.34	0.41	0.34
40	0.37	0.44	0.37	0.35	0.41	0.35
41	0.46	0.47	0.38	0.43	0.44	0.36
42	0.46	0.47	0.38	0.43	0.44	0.36
43	0.38	0.49	0.38	0.36	0.46	0.36
44	0.46	0.48	0.39	0.43	0.44	0.37

Table 9.14 (continued)

Industry	1960[a]			1966[a]		
	Total	Equipment	Structures	Total	Equipment	Structures
1	0.43	0.45	0.36	0.27	0.24	0.34
2	0.41	0.44	0.36	0.26	0.22	0.34
3	0.42	0.43	0.36	0.26	0.24	0.34
4	0.42	0.44	0.36	0.27	0.24	0.34
5	0.42	0.43	0.36	0.25	0.24	0.34
6	0.41	0.44	0.36	0.28	0.24	0.34
7	0.42	0.43	0.36	0.26	0.24	0.34
8	0.38	0.44	0.36	0.30	0.25	0.34
9	0.43	0.45	0.36	0.26	0.25	0.34
10	0.42	0.44	0.36	0.27	0.24	0.34
11	0.43	0.45	0.36	0.28	0.26	0.34
12	0.42	0.45	0.36	0.28	0.25	0.34
13	0.42	0.44	0.36	0.27	0.25	0.34
14	0.42	0.44	0.36	0.26	0.24	0.34
15	0.43	0.45	0.36	0.27	0.25	0.34
16	0.43	0.45	0.36	0.28	0.26	0.34
17	0.42	0.44	0.36	0.27	0.25	0.34
18	0.42	0.45	0.36	0.28	0.25	0.34
19	0.43	0.45	0.36	0.27	0.25	0.34
20	0.43	0.45	0.36	0.29	0.26	0.34
21	0.43	0.45	0.36	0.28	0.25	0.34
22	0.44	0.44	0.38	0.26	0.26	0.29
23	0.44	0.44	0.38	0.26	0.26	0.29
24	0.40	0.42	0.39	0.32	0.22	0.35
25	0.41	0.42	0.36	0.23	0.22	0.32
26	0.35	0.43	0.34	0.26	0.22	0.26
27	0.42	0.43	0.38	0.24	0.22	0.36
28	0.44	0.44	0.38	0.24	0.24	0.38
29	0.43	0.43	0.41	0.25	0.25	0.32
30	0.54	0.54	0.36	0.29	0.29	0.34
31	0.47	0.47	0.36	0.27	0.27	0.34
32	0.43	0.43		0.27	0.27	
33	0.43	0.43	0.38	0.20	0.20	0.38
34	0.37	0.42	0.37	0.32	0.27	0.32
35	0.47	0.47	0.38	0.27	0.26	0.38
36	0.39	0.42	0.35	0.27	0.25	0.32
37	0.41	0.42	0.40	0.30	0.25	0.38
38	0.38	0.42	0.36	0.29	0.25	0.31
39	0.36	0.42	0.36	0.30	0.25	0.30
40	0.36	0.42	0.36	0.32	0.25	0.32
41	0.44	0.45	0.38	0.26	0.24	0.38
42	0.43	0.45	0.38	0.28	0.24	0.38
43	0.38	0.47	0.38	0.34	0.26	0.37
44	0.43	0.45	0.38	0.28	0.24	0.38

Table 9.14 (continued)

Industry	1973[a]			1979		
	Total	Equipment	Structures	Total	Equipment	Structures
1	0.24	0.18	0.42	0.20	0.12	0.43
2	0.26	0.16	0.42	0.15	0.09	0.43
3	0.23	0.19	0.42	0.19	0.14	0.43
4	0.26	0.19	0.42	0.23	0.14	0.43
5	0.22	0.19	0.42	0.16	0.13	0.43
6	0.23	0.18	0.42	0.19	0.14	0.43
7	0.23	0.19	0.42	0.17	0.12	0.43
8	0.29	0.20	0.42	0.26	0.13	0.43
9	0.24	0.19	0.42	0.20	0.14	0.43
10	0.26	0.19	0.42	0.24	0.15	0.43
11	0.23	0.18	0.42	0.18	0.12	0.43
12	0.28	0.18	0.42	0.24	0.13	0.43
13	0.23	0.18	0.42	0.18	0.12	0.43
14	0.23	0.19	0.42	0.18	0.13	0.43
15	0.24	0.19	0.42	0.21	0.14	0.43
16	0.25	0.20	0.42	0.22	0.15	0.43
17	0.25	0.21	0.42	0.20	0.14	0.43
18	0.26	0.19	0.42	0.21	0.13	0.43
19	0.22	0.19	0.42	0.16	0.13	0.43
20	0.27	0.20	0.42	0.22	0.15	0.43
21	0.26	0.19	0.42	0.22	0.14	0.43
22	0.14	0.12	0.31	0.08	0.07	0.27
23	0.13	0.12	0.31	0.08	0.07	0.27
24	0.34	0.18	0.43	0.30	0.07	0.42
25	0.20	0.17	0.35	0.10	0.07	0.32
26	0.28	0.17	0.28	0.12	0.07	0.13
27	0.19	0.17	0.44	0.09	0.07	0.44
28	0.19	0.18	0.45	0.10	0.08	0.44
29	0.21	0.20	0.35	0.18	0.17	0.29
30	0.16	0.16	0.42	0.13	0.12	0.43
31	0.18	0.18	0.42	0.13	0.13	0.43
32	0.26	0.26		0.23	0.23	0.43
33	0.08	0.08	0.45	0.00	0.00	0.45
34	0.36	0.22	0.37	0.29	0.13	0.30
35	0.19	0.18	0.45	0.13	0.12	0.45
36	0.28	0.23	0.38	0.19	0.15	0.31
37	0.32	0.24	0.45	0.25	0.15	0.46
38	0.32	0.22	0.37	0.23	0.13	0.30
39	0.34	0.22	0.35	0.25	0.13	0.28
40	0.34	0.22	0.34	0.30	0.13	0.31
41	0.21	0.17	0.45	0.15	0.11	0.45
42	0.28	0.17	0.45	0.23	0.11	0.45
43	0.31	0.20	0.44	0.24	0.13	0.44
44	0.26	0.18	0.45	0.18	0.10	0.45

a. Absence of effective tax rates for structures implies that there was no investment in structures in the corresponding industry.

mining and water supply, sanitary services, and other utilities was a maximum among industries at 30 percent.

Our analysis of effective tax rates by type of asset and by industry corroborates the conclusions we reached on the basis of effective tax rates for U.S. corporations as a whole. Only one industry—street railways, bus lines, and taxicab service in 1953 and 1960—has had effective tax rates in excess of the statutory tax rate for any year in the postwar period. Similarly, only one asset—autos in 1953, 1957, and 1960—had an effective tax rate in excess of the statutory rate. For all other industries and all other assets the effective tax rates under U.S. law have been below the statutory tax rate throughout the postwar period. The impact of tax revisions has been to reduce effective tax rates very dramatically for all assets and all industries. However, effective tax rates under current law increase with a decrease in the rate of inflation.

Our analysis of differences in effective tax rates among types of assets and among industries reveals larger differences than those between equipment and structures for all U.S. corporations. Differences between effective tax rates correspond to gaps between social rates of return among assets and industries. These gaps present opportunities for costless increases in the national wealth that would be available for consumption or additional investment. The gaps are very large, indicating that there is a substantial loss in efficiency in the allocation of capital under U.S. tax law. It is important to reiterate that differences in effective tax rates among assets and industries would increase with a decrease in the rate of inflation.

9.5 Proposed Systems for Capital Recovery

The objective of our analysis of alternative systems for capital recovery under U.S. tax law is to estimate effective tax rates for assets acquired by U.S. corporations in the future. We consider the provisions of current law as a starting point for a comparison between alternative systems. We also consider two specific alternatives under consideration by the Congress—the Reagan administration proposal and the Senate Finance Committee proposal.[9] Finally, we consider expensing of the costs of acquisition of assets and the deduction of economic depreciation from income for tax purposes as possible approaches to capital recovery under U.S. law.

The present value of capital consumption allowances under immediate expensing of acquisition costs of assets is equal to unity for all assets. We have estimated present values of capital consumption allowances for tax purposes for each of the 35 types of assets presented in table 9.1 under current law and under each of the three alternative proposals we have listed above. We have also estimated the present value of economic depreciation on the basis of data on the rate of depreciation and the after-tax rate of return, corrected for inflation. For current law, for the two alternative proposals, and for economic depreciation, we have weighted the present values of actual investment to obtain average present values for equipment, structures, and total investment. We present the results of our calculations in table 9.15.

Under present U.S. tax law and under the two alternative proposals for more rapid capital recovery, capital consumption allowances are based on the historical cost of acquisition of an asset. We have calculated present values of these allowances under currently anticipated rates of inflation, based on the term structure for government securities for 1980 given in table 9.5. Since anticipated rates of inflation may be higher or lower in the future, we have also calculated present values under anticipated rates of inflation for 1960, 1966, and 1973–all of which involved lower anticipated rates of inflation than 1980. We have also added 4 percent to the yields on government securities for 1980 to obtain hypothetical values of anticipated rates of inflation that are higher than those in 1980.

In characterizing provisions for capital recovery under present law we have assumed that asset lifetimes, scrap values, and accounting formulas for tax purposes will remain the same as those for 1980. We find that at currently anticipated rates of inflation, present law provides capital consumption for tax purposes that exceeds economic depreciation by 7.6 percent. The excess over economic depreciation would rise to 22.3 percent at anticipated rates of inflation of 1973, to 31.4 percent at rates for 1966, and to 35.1 percent at rates for 1960. If anticipated rates of inflation were to increase by 4 percent over currently anticipated rates, the present value of capital consumption allowances for tax purposes would drop below economic depreciation by only 2.6 percent. Our first conclusion is that present law provides capital consumption allowances for corporate investment as a whole that are in line with economic depreciation at currently anticipated rates of inflation.

We next compare the two proposals for more rapid capital recovery introduced in Congress with present law. Under currently anticipated

Table 9.15
Present values of corporate capital consumption allowances for tax purposes on new investment

Discount factors	Policy	Present values equipment	Structures	Total	Ratio tax to economic	Yield on 10-year security
1960	Current	.886	.641	.801	1.351	4.13
	Reagan	.941	.823	.900	1.518	4.13
	Senate	.941	.760	.879	1.482	4.13
1966	Current	.867	.611	.779	1.314	4.86
	Reagan	.927	.803	.885	1.492	4.86
	Senate	.927	.735	.861	1.452	4.86
1973	Current	.831	.525	.725	1.223	6.73
	Reagan	.907	.758	.855	1.442	6.73
	Senate	.907	.669	.825	1.391	6.73
1980	Current	.754	.418	.638	1.076	11.16
	Reagan	.856	.672	.792	1.336	11.16
	Senate	.857	.563	.756	1.275	11.16
1980	Current	.696	.352	.578	.974	15.16
Plus four	Reagan	.815	.610	.745	1.256	15.16
percent	Senate	.819	.492	.706	1.191	15.16

rates of inflation we find that present values of capital consumption allowances would be 27.5 percent in excess of economic depreciation under the Senate Finance Committee proposal and 33.6 percent in excess under the Reagan administration proposal. Under lower anticipated rates of inflation the excess of capital consumption allowances over economic depreciation would rise substantially, reaching 51.8 percent of economic depreciation under the Reagan proposal for anticipated rates of inflation in 1960. At higher anticipated rates of inflation both proposals would result in capital consumption allowances that are greater than economic depreciation.

To calculate effective tax rates under present law and the two alternative proposals, we combine information on the offset to tax liability provided by the investment tax credit with the value of capital consumption allowances as a deduction from taxable income. The effective tax rate for an asset also depends on the statutory tax rate, the rate of economic depreciation, and the rate of return after taxes, corrected for inflation. We present effective tax rates for equipment, structures, and total investment under current law and each of the two alternative proposals in table 9.16. At this point it may be useful to recall that the effective tax rate for all assets under economic depreciation is equal to the statutory rate of 46 percent, while the effective tax rate

Table 9.16
Effective corporate tax rates on new investment

| Discount factors | Policy | Corporate tax rate | | | Ratio of effective rate to Rate |
		Equipment	Structures	Total	
1960	Current	−0.22	0.20	−0.08	−0.172
	Reagan	−0.88	−0.01	−0.58	−1.267
	Senate	−0.25	0.11	−0.13	−0.277
1966	Current	−0.14	0.22	−0.02	−0.033
	Reagan	−0.71	0.02	−0.46	−1.004
	Senate	−0.19	0.13	−0.08	−0.170
1973	Current	−0.01	0.28	0.09	0.200
	Reagan	−0.52	0.07	−0.31	−0.684
	Senate	−0.10	0.19	0.00	−0.006
1980	Current	0.19	0.35	0.24	0.528
	Reagan	−0.20	0.16	−0.07	−0.161
	Senate	0.05	0.28	0.13	0.275
1980 plus four percent	Current	0.29	0.39	0.32	0.702
	Reagan	−0.03	0.22	0.06	0.121
	Senate	0.14	0.32	0.20	0.440

with immediate expensing of the cost of acquisition of assets is equal to zero. As before, we have calculated effective tax rates under alternative assumptions about anticipated future rates of inflation.

At currently anticipated rates of inflation the effective tax rate under present law for corporate investment as a whole is 24 percent. This is a little over half the statutory tax rate of 46 percent. The Senate Finance Committee proposal would reduce the effective tax rate on corporate investment to 13 percent. This would represent a little over one-fourth of the statutory rate. Finally, the Reagan administration proposal would result in a negative effective tax rate for corporate investment. The combination of a very short asset lifetimes for tax purposes and an increase in the investment tax credit for some assets would imply that the corporate income tax would be replaced by a corporate income subsidy for depreciable assets. Tax deductions and credits for these assets would be available to "shelter" income from nondepreciable assets such as land, inventories, and financial claims.

If anticipated inflation rates were to increase as much as 4 percent relative to those that prevail currently, the Reagan administration proposal would result in a slightly positive effective tax rate. The effective tax rate under current law would rise to 32 percent, while the Senate proposal would result in effective tax rates of 20 percent. If anticipated inflation rates were to drop to those prevailing in 1973, the effective tax rate under the Reagan administration proposal would be a negative 31 percent. The resulting "shelter" for income from nondepreciable assets could be sufficient to reduce receipts from the corporate income tax to zero. The negative effective tax rate under the Reagan administration proposal would rise to 46 percent at 1966 anticipated rates of inflation and to 58 percent at 1960 anticipated rates of inflation.

Present U.S. corporate income tax law would result in an effective tax rate of 9 percent at 1973 anticipated rates of inflation, a negative 2 percent at rates of 1966 and a negative 8 percent at rates of 1960. The Senate Finance Committee proposal would result in a zero effective tax rate at 1973 anticipated rates of inflation; this would fall to negative levels at 1960 and 1966 rates, reaching a negative 13 percent at 1960 rates. Our overall conclusion is that current law and both alternative proposals would replace the corporate income tax by a corporate income subsidy at anticipated rates of inflation comparable to those that prevailed in 1960 and 1966, while the Reagan administration proposal would replace the corporate income tax by a corporate income subsidy at current inflation rates or at 1973 rates.

The second issue we consider in comparing alternative systems for capital recovery under the corporate income tax is the differences in effective tax rates among assets. Gaps among effective tax rates result in an inefficient allocation of capital among assets. Under present law the difference between effective tax rates on equipment and structures at currently anticipated rates of inflation is 16 percent. Under the Reagan administration proposal this difference would widen to 36 percent. The gap for the Senate Finance Committee proposal would be 23 percent.

The gap between effective tax rates on equipment and structures under present U.S. law would widen to 29 percent at 1973 anticipated rates of inflation, 36 percent at 1966 rates, and 42 percent at 1960 rates. Under the Reagan administration proposal the gap would widen to 59 percent at 1973 anticipated rates of inflation, 73 percent at 1966 rates, and 87 percent at 1960 rates. As before, we find it useful to translate this gap into the corresponding gap between social rates of return. For rates of inflation anticipated in 1960 the Reagan administration proposal would result in a difference in social rates of return to investment in equipment and structures of 2.78 percent. This can be compared with the average private rate of return of 6.06 for the postwar period.

Our overall conclusion is that differences in effective tax rates among assets under present U.S. tax law are substantial, even at the very high anticipated rates of inflation prevailing currently. These differences increase with a decrease in anticipated rates of inflation, reducing efficiency in the allocation of capital. The differences in effective tax rates would widen significantly under the Senate Finance Committee proposal and would widen even further under the Reagan administration proposal. Just as under present law, these gaps would increase with a decrease in anticipated rates of inflation.

We next provide additional detail on effective tax rates by type of asset under present law and the two alternative proposals. For this purpose we have calculated effective tax rates for all 35 assets listed in table 9.1 at currently anticipated rates of inflation. We give the present value of capital consumption allowances, the effective rate of the tax credit, and the effective tax rate for each asset in table 9.17. Under present law effective tax rates range from 48 percent for other nonfarm buildings to 8 percent for aircraft. Under the Reagan administration proposal the gap ranges from 36 percent for commercial buildings to a negative 32 percent for office, computing, and accounting machinery. The gap for the Senate Finance Committee proposal ranges from 41 percent for other nonfarm buildings to 2 percent for agricultural machinery.

Similarly, we provide additional detail on effective tax rates by industry under present law and the two alternative proposals. For this purpose we have calculated effective tax rates for all 44 industries listed in table 9.13 at currently anticipated rates of inflation. We give effective tax rates on equipment, structures, and total investment for each industry in table 9.18. Under present law the effective tax rates range from 35.2 percent for metal mining to 8.8 percent for air transportation. Under the Reagan administration proposal effective tax rates would be negative for 33 industries and small but positive for the remaining 11 industries. Effective subsidy rates range up to 25.4 percent for trucking service, warehousing, and storage. Under the Senate Finance Committee proposal all effective tax rates are positive and less than 27.4 percent.

Our analysis of effective tax rates by type of asset and by industry under present law and under the two alternative proposals corroborates the conclusions we reached on the basis of effective tax rates for

Table 9.17
Effective corporate tax rates by asset: Present law

Asset	Lifetime	Present discounted value	Investment tax credit	Effective corporate tax rate
1	7.8	0.743	0.09	0.12
2	9.8	0.692	0.09	0.19
3	12.2	0.639	0.09	0.24
4	5.0	0.828	0.06	0.11
5	7.8	0.743	0.09	0.11
6	7.8	0.743	0.09	0.16
7	7.5	0.750	0.09	0.14
8	10.0	0.687	0.09	0.22
9	10.0	0.687	0.09	0.21
10	7.8	0.743	0.09	0.13
11	8.9	0.718	0.09	0.28
12	8.1	0.735	0.09	0.17
13	9.7	0.694	0.09	0.21
14	4.4	0.846	0.05	0.19
15	3.0	0.897	0.03	0.16
16	6.0	0.794	0.08	0.08
17	14.1	0.601	0.09	0.27
18	11.8	0.646	0.09	0.21
19	8.3	0.731	0.09	0.17
20	8.0	0.738	0.09	0.16
21	25.3	0.389	0.00	0.45
22	41.8	0.264	0.00	0.47
23	42.1	0.262	0.00	0.45
24	42.1	0.262	0.00	0.45
25	42.1	0.262	0.00	0.47
26	27.1	0.373	0.00	0.48
27	26.3	0.380	0.09	0.32
28	23.7	0.409	0.09	0.34
29	23.7	0.409	0.09	0.33
30	21.1	0.441	0.09	0.31
31	19.3	0.468	0.09	0.33
32	21.9	0.432	0.09	0.30
33	6.0	0.765	0.06	0.14
34	24.7	0.399	0.09	0.34
35	24.8	0.398	0.00	0.38

Table 9.17 (continued)
Effective corporate tax rates by asset: Reagan proposal

Asset	Lifetime	Present discounted value	Investment tax credit	Effective corporate tax rate
1	5.0	0.851	0.09	−0.14
2	5.0	0.851	0.09	−0.12
3	5.0	0.851	0.09	−0.11
4	5.0	0.851	0.09	−0.19
5	5.0	0.851	0.09	−0.13
6	5.0	0.851	0.09	−0.20
7	5.0	0.851	0.09	−0.19
8	5.0	0.851	0.09	−0.15
9	5.0	0.851	0.09	−0.13
10	5.0	0.851	0.09	−0.15
11	5.0	0.851	0.09	−0.32
12	5.0	0.851	0.09	−0.19
13	5.0	0.851	0.09	−0.15
14	5.0	0.851	0.09	−0.29
15	3.0	0.913	0.06	−0.23
16	5.0	0.851	0.09	−0.21
17	5.0	0.851	0.09	−0.11
18	5.0	0.851	0.09	−0.10
19	5.0	0.851	0.09	−0.18
20	5.0	0.851	0.09	−0.18
21	10.0	0.727	0.00	0.27
22	15.0	0.529	0.00	0.36
23	10.0	0.727	0.00	0.23
24	10.0	0.727	0.00	0.23
25	10.0	0.727	0.00	0.24
26	10.0	0.727	0.00	0.29
27	10.0	0.727	0.09	0.07
28	10.0	0.727	0.09	0.09
29	10.0	0.727	0.09	0.09
30	10.0	0.727	0.09	0.09
31	10.0	0.727	0.09	0.10
32	10.0	0.727	0.09	0.08
33	5.0	0.851	0.09	−0.09
34	10.0	0.727	0.09	0.08
35	18.0	0.472	0.00	0.35

Table 9.17 (continued)
Effective corporate tax rates by asset: Senate Finance Committee proposal

Asset	Lifetime	Present discounted value	Investment tax credit	Effective corporate tax rate
1	4.0	0.866	0.06	0.03
2	7.0	0.774	0.09	0.05
3	10.0	0.692	0.09	0.17
4	4.0	0.866	0.06	0.04
5	2.0	0.942	0.02	0.02
6	2.0	0.942	0.02	0.03
7	4.0	0.866	0.06	0.04
8	7.0	0.774	0.09	0.06
9	7.0	0.774	0.09	0.06
10	4.0	0.866	0.06	0.03
11	4.0	0.866	0.06	0.06
12	4.0	0.866	0.06	0.04
13	7.0	0.774	0.09	0.06
14	2.0	0.942	0.02	0.04
15	2.0	0.942	0.02	0.04
16	4.0	0.866	0.06	0.05
17	10.0	0.692	0.09	0.17
18	7.0	0.774	0.09	0.04
19	4.0	0.866	0.06	0.04
20	4.0	0.866	0.06	0.04
21	15.0	0.539	0.00	0.39
22	15.0	0.539	0.00	0.36
23	15.0	0.539	0.00	0.34
24	15.0	0.539	0.00	0.34
25	15.0	0.539	0.00	0.35
26	15.0	0.539	0.00	0.41
27	15.0	0.539	0.09	0.22
28	15.8	0.526	0.09	0.27
29	15.8	0.526	0.09	0.26
30	15.8	0.526	0.09	0.26
31	15.8	0.526	0.09	0.29
32	15.0	0.539	0.09	0.24
33	4.0	0.845	0.06	0.05
34	15.0	0.539	0.09	0.25
35	20.0	0.420	0.00	0.37

Table 9.18
Effective corporate tax rates by industry: Present law

Industry	Equipment	Structures	Total
1	0.187	0.450	0.256
2	0.149	0.450	0.207
3	0.204	0.450	0.244
4	0.197	0.450	0.273
5	0.195	0.450	0.223
6	0.197	0.450	0.246
7	0.181	0.450	0.223
8	0.189	0.450	0.302
9	0.206	0.450	0.254
10	0.207	0.450	0.284
11	0.181	0.450	0.235
12	0.191	0.450	0.283
13	0.179	0.450	0.234
14	0.190	0.450	0.235
15	0.200	0.450	0.261
16	0.208	0.450	0.271
17	0.204	0.450	0.255
18	0.183	0.450	0.256
19	0.194	0.450	0.214
20	0.209	0.450	0.269
21	0.198	0.450	0.273
22	0.141	0.300	0.152
23	0.141	0.300	0.152
24	0.163	0.454	0.352
25	0.147	0.351	0.176
26	0.150	0.272	0.264
27	0.152	0.458	0.170
28	0.161	0.464	0.174
29	0.210	0.320	0.219
30	0.172	0.450	0.173
31	0.178	0.450	0.183
32	0.270	0.450	0.270
33	0.087	0.470	0.088
34	0.217	0.330	0.321
35	0.187	0.470	0.195
36	0.209	0.340	0.241
37	0.210	0.478	0.301
38	0.205	0.330	0.281
39	0.205	0.310	0.290
40	0.205	0.340	0.335
41	0.172	0.470	0.212
42	0.172	0.470	0.278
43	0.212	0.458	0.298
44	0.183	0.467	0.248

Table 9.18 (continued)
Effective corporate tax rates by industry: Reagan proposal

Industry	Equipment	Structures	Total
1	−0.167	0.270	−0.051
2	−0.156	0.270	−0.074
3	−0.139	0.270	−0.072
4	−0.146	0.270	−0.021
5	−0.142	0.270	−0.096
6	−0.138	0.270	−0.059
7	−0.148	0.270	−0.083
8	−0.169	0.270	0.021
9	−0.150	0.270	−0.067
10	−0.135	0.270	−0.006
11	−0.217	0.270	−0.121
12	−0.139	0.270	0.006
13	−0.190	0.270	−0.097
14	−0.153	0.270	−0.080
15	−0.149	0.270	−0.047
16	−0.159	0.270	−0.048
17	−0.156	0.270	−0.067
18	−0.148	0.270	−0.033
19	−0.159	0.270	−0.125
20	−0.165	0.270	−0.057
21	−0.158	0.270	0.032
22	−0.144	0.080	−0.129
23	−0.144	0.080	−0.129
24	−0.180	0.271	0.114
25	−0.190	0.100	−0.150
26	−0.180	0.067	0.052
27	−0.188	0.304	−0.158
28	−0.191	0.329	−0.169
29	−0.100	0.070	−0.086
30	0.054	0.270	0.055
31	−0.263	0.270	−0.254
32	−0.110	0.270	−0.110
33	−0.207	0.360	−0.205
34	−0.142	0.100	0.080
35	−0.256	0.360	−0.239
36	−0.152	0.090	−0.093
37	−0.150	0.298	0.002
38	−0.146	0.090	−0.003
39	−0.146	0.090	0.045
40	−0.146	0.080	0.071
41	−0.140	0.360	−0.073
42	−0.140	0.360	0.037
43	−0.168	0.333	0.007
44	−0.136	0.332	−0.030

Table 9.18 (continued)
Effective corporate tax rates by industry: Senate Finance
Committee proposal

Industry	Equipment	Structures	Total
1	0.047	0.390	0.138
2	0.035	0.390	0.103
3	0.056	0.390	0.111
4	0.052	0.390	0.154
5	0.055	0.390	0.092
6	0.052	0.390	0.118
7	0.048	0.390	0.101
8	0.051	0.390	0.198
9	0.055	0.390	0.121
10	0.056	0.390	0.162
11	0.044	0.390	0.113
12	0.049	0.390	0.170
13	0.043	0.390	0.113
14	0.050	0.390	0.109
15	0.052	0.390	0.135
16	0.053	0.390	0.141
17	0.053	0.390	0.123
18	0.050	0.390	0.143
19	0.049	0.390	0.076
20	0.052	0.390	0.137
21	0.050	0.390	0.151
22	0.037	0.240	0.051
23	0.037	0.240	0.051
24	0.045	0.385	0.267
25	0.038	0.262	0.069
26	0.041	0.186	0.178
27	0.040	0.374	0.060
28	0.034	0.363	0.048
29	0.040	0.220	0.054
30	0.040	0.390	0.041
31	0.038	0.390	0.044
32	0.170	0.390	0.170
33	0.050	0.360	0.051
34	0.093	0.290	0.274
35	0.041	0.360	0.050
36	0.059	0.270	0.111
37	0.060	0.404	0.177
38	0.070	0.260	0.185
39	0.070	0.260	0.224
40	0.070	0.250	0.243
41	0.042	0.360	0.084
42	0.042	0.360	0.155
43	0.049	0.350	0.154
44	0.047	0.359	0.118

all U.S. corporations. At currently anticipated rates of inflation the effective tax rate under present law exceeds the statutory rate of 46 percent only for commercial buildings, hospital buildings, and other nonfarm buildings. Effective tax rates under present law are as low as 8 percent for aircraft. The highest effective tax rate for any industry is 35.2 percent for metal mining. Even at the very high anticipated rates of inflation prevailing currently, liberalization of tax provisions for capital recovery during the postwar period has been sufficient to keep effective tax rates well below the statutory rate for all industries. Levels of effective tax rates would decrease for all assets and all industries under either of the alternative proposals.

Differences in effective tax rates among assets and among industries are very substantial under current law. As before, these differences correspond to gaps between social rates of return among assets and industries. These gaps represent opportunities to increase national wealth with no sacrifice in consumption either now or in the future. These gaps would widen significantly under the Reagan administration proposal and would narrow slightly under the Senate Finance Committee proposal. We can emphasize the fact that effective tax rates would decrease with a decrease in anticipated rates of inflation, while differences in effective tax rates among assets and among industries would increase with a decrease in the rate of inflation.

9.6 Conclusions

Our first major conclusion is that inflation has had a dramatic impact on capital recovery under the U.S. corporate income tax. For a given set of tax provisions, an increase in the rate of inflation reduces the present value of capital consumption allowances as an offset to the cost of acquisition of assets. The effective rate of taxation increases with an increase in the rate of inflation and decreases with a decrease in the rate of inflation. It is important to emphasize both the impact of higher inflation rates and the impact of lower inflation rates. An important objective of current economic policy is to reduce the rate of inflation. If this objective were to be realized, effective tax rates under present U.S. law would decline substantially, reaching the level of only 8 percent for U.S. corporations as a whole at anticipated rates of inflation like those prevailing as recently as 1973.

Our second major conclusion is that a decrease in the rate of inflation under present U.S. law increases the gaps among effective tax

rates for different assets and different industries. At currently anticipated rates of inflation these gaps are substantial, but they would
widen significantly with a decrease in the rate of inflation. Differences
in effective tax rates among assets correspond to differences in social
rates of return to investment in these assets. By transferring investment from lightly taxed assets to more heavily taxed assets it is possible to increase the national wealth with no sacrifice in present or
future consumption. Opportunities for costless increases in the
national wealth would increase considerably with a decrease in the
rate of inflation.

While effective tax rates in the United States are currently among
the lowest of the postwar period, proposals for further reduction in
these rates are under consideration by the Congress. Even with a 4
percent increase in the anticipated rate of inflation over the unprecedented prevailing levels, the Reagan administration proposal would
result in replacing the corporate income tax by a corporate income
subsidy with a negative effective tax rate for U.S. corporations as a
whole. At currently prevailing rates of inflation the Reagan administration proposal would generate huge offsets to the cost of acquisition
of depreciable assets through the investment tax credit and deductions
of capital consumption allowances for tax purposes. These offsets
would be sufficient to exhaust the income generated by investments in
depreciable assets and would spill over to provide "shelter" for
income from nondepreciable assets such as land, inventories, and
financial claims.

A second consequence of the adoption of the Reagan administration proposal for capital recovery under U.S. tax law would be a substantial widening of gaps among effective tax rates for different assets
and different industries. This would very significantly worsen the
efficiency of capital allocation and would reduce the level of productivity for the U.S. economy. Under current law and under both alternative proposals we have considered, the gaps among effective tax
rates would increase as rates of inflation decrease. Under these policies a successful anti-inflation program would worsen the efficiency of
capital allocation.

Our analysis of the impact of inflation on capital recovery under
U.S. tax law also provides an answer to the obvious question arising
from current pressures for more rapid capital recovery. If effective tax
rates on new investment have fallen, why are investors and policy
makers convinced that they have risen? The first part of the answer to

this question is that effective tax rates have risen since the postwar low of 1977, when rates of inflation in asset prices had fallen to 5.6 percent in 1976 and 7.7 percent in 1977. These rates of inflation can be compared with the level of 12.8 percent in 1975 at the time of the most recent change in tax provisions for capital recovery. However, while rates of inflation were at double-digit levels in 1980, the Reagan administration is projecting a rapid decline in rates of inflation.

A second part of the explanation for the perception that effective tax rates are currently high, while our analysis has shown that they are currently low, is the nature of offsets to tax liability. While the tax-payer receives the investment tax credit as an offset to tax liability in the year an asset is acquired, capital consumption allowances are a deduction from income and are distributed over the useful life of the asset by means of accounting formulas. In effect, the taxpayer receives a claim on future tax deductions that is analogous to a government bond. Unfortunately, the value of this claim, like the value of a government bond, drops with increases in anticipated rates of inflation. Anticipated rates of inflation have jumped almost 4 percent since 1975 and holders of depreciable assets, like holders of government bonds, have suffered drastic capital losses.

If the Reagan administration's anti-inflation program is successful, both holders of government bonds and holders of claims for future tax deductions on depreciable assets will experience capital gains that will offset capital losses under the Carter administration in the late 1970s. These capital gains will occur even with no changes in tax provisions for capital recovery. Effective tax rates will decline to very modest levels and may even become negative under current U.S. tax law. Unfortunately, this decline will be distributed very unevenly among assets and among industries. As a consequence, the efficiency of capital allocation will fall, undercutting future productivity.

The impact of the Reagan administration tax proposals will depend critically on the success of the administration's anti-inflation policy. Even if anticipated rates of inflation were to increase by 4 percent, the effective tax rate on new investment under the Reagan administration proposal for capital recovery would still be negative. However, substantial gaps in effective tax rates among assets and among industries would remain, resulting in a drag on productivity. If the Reagan anti-inflation program were to have no impact at all, the effective tax rate for the corporate sector would be negative, resulting in the replacement of the corporate income tax by a corporate income subsidy for investment in depreciable assets. If the Reagan anti-inflation program were to achieve its stated objective of reducing rates of inflation below those that prevailed in 1973, holders of depreciable assets would enjoy huge capital gains on capital consumption allowances still to be claimed on their existing assets. They would also receive substantial subsidies on new investments.

Our overall conclusion is that policies for corporate income taxation that deal effectively with the impact of inflation cannot be based on accelerated capital recovery. As we have seen, variations in the rate of inflation are an important part of the problem facing policy makers. Neither the Reagan administration proposal nor the Senate Finance Committee proposal is capable of coping with these variations. The Senate Finance Committee proposal would succeed in lowering the effective tax rates for different assets and different industries. However, the impact of this proposal, like the impact of the Reagan administration proposal, would be strongly dependent on the rate of inflation that actually occurs.

In closing we can briefly outline two possible approaches to the reform of provisions for capital recovery under the U.S. corporate income tax that would deal effectively with the problem of inflation. First, immediate expensing of the cost of acquisition of assets would result in a zero effective tax rate on income from all depreciable assets, whatever the rate of inflation. While immediate expensing would amount to the elimination of the corporate income tax, this proposal is superior to alternative proposals that would replace the tax by a corporate income subsidy. Policy makers who are optimistic about the success of anti-inflation measures and advocate the elimination of the corporate income tax should regard present high rates of inflation as the last great opportunity to shift to immediate expensing. As rates of inflation decline, subsidies to investment in specific assets through the tax structure will arise. Each such subsidy will generate a political constituency that will act as an obstacle to the introduction of immediate expensing.

A second pathway to the reform of capital recovery provisions of U.S. tax law is more closely related to current tax provisions and preserves flexibility in the selection of an appropriate level for the effective tax rate. The first step in tax reform would be to replace existing capital consumption allowances for tax purposes by a first year allowance, as proposed by Auerbach and Jorgenson (1980). This would completely eliminate the problems that result from forcing holders of depreciable assets to hold claims on the government in the form of future tax deductions that can appreciate or depreciate like government bonds. Since this proposal is equivalent to deducting economic depreciation, it has the unfortunate consequence of increasing the effective tax rate to the statutory rate.

The second step in tax reform would be to provide an investment tax credit that is proportional to the difference between the cost of acquisition of an asset and the first year allowance, as proposed by Brown (1981). By varying the proportion between zero and the statutory tax rate, it would be possible to produce any effective tax rate between the statutory rate and zero. Since the Brown investment tax credit, like the Auerbach-Jorgenson first year allowance, would be taken in the same year an asset is acquired, it would create no claims on the government that are subject to capital gains and losses with changes in the rate of inflation. The resulting first year capital recovery system would preserve the existing features of U.S. tax law— capital consumption allowances as a deduction from taxable income and the investment tax credit as an offset to tax liability.

As an illustration of a system for capital recovery under U.S. tax law based on the first year capital recovery system, we present in table 9.19 the first year allowances for all 35 types of assets listed in table 9.1. These first year allowances are based on a discount rate after taxes of 6 percent. We also present tax credits on these assets that would produce effective tax rates on all assets of zero, half the current statutory tax rate of 46 percent, and the statutory tax rate itself. Investment tax credits would range from 35 percent on residential structures to 7 percent on autos at an effective tax rate of zero for all assets. For an effective tax rate of 23 percent, which is comparable to present law at currently anticipated rates of inflation, investment tax credits would range from 19 percent on residential structures to 4 percent on autos.

The first year capital recovery system, as we have outlined it, would preserve the simplicity of the Auerbach-Jorgenson proposal. Existing provisions of the tax code on capital recovery could be replaced by a simple table like table 9.19, giving the first year allowances and the investment tax credits permitted by law. As under immediate expensing of assets, tax deductions and tax credits would depend only on current transactions in assets and would not require a cumbersome system of vintage accounts for auditing and verification. The main advantage of the first year system over immediate

Table 9.19
First year capital recovery system

Asset	First year allowance	Investment tax credit at various effective tax rates		
		Zero	.23	.46
1	0.645	0.16	0.08	0.00
2	0.602	0.18	0.09	0.00
3	0.565	0.20	0.10	0.00
4	0.729	0.12	0.06	0.00
5	0.616	0.18	0.09	0.00
6	0.740	0.12	0.06	0.00
7	0.731	0.12	0.06	0.00
8	0.669	0.15	0.08	0.00
9	0.630	0.17	0.09	0.00
10	0.669	0.15	0.08	0.00
11	0.818	0.08	0.04	0.00
12	0.731	0.12	0.06	0.00
13	0.660	0.16	0.08	0.00
14	0.807	0.09	0.04	0.00
15	0.846	0.07	0.04	0.00
16	0.752	0.11	0.06	0.00
17	0.553	0.21	0.10	0.00
18	0.521	0.22	0.11	0.00
19	0.712	0.13	0.07	0.00
20	0.712	0.13	0.07	0.00
21	0.373	0.29	0.14	0.00
22	0.290	0.33	0.16	0.00
23	0.237	0.35	0.18	0.00
24	0.237	0.35	0.18	0.00
25	0.278	0.33	0.17	0.00
26	0.428	0.26	0.13	0.00
27	0.225	0.36	0.18	0.00
28	0.355	0.30	0.15	0.00
29	0.331	0.31	0.15	0.00
30	0.331	0.31	0.15	0.00
31	0.426	0.26	0.13	0.00
32	0.281	0.33	0.13	0.00
33	0.482	0.24	0.17	0.00
34	0.324	0.31	0.12	0.00
35	0.173	0.38	0.19	0.00

expensing is the possibility of setting effective tax rates at levels other than zero.

Appendix

In this appendix we describe the methodology we have used to simulate practices permitted by the Internal Revenue Service in calculating capital consumption allowances for tax purposes. Our control total is based on capital consumption allowances claimed by U.S. corporations on their income tax returns. Our depreciable base is a time series of corporate investment disaggregated by the types of assets listed in table 9.1. Our objective is to estimate tax parameters by reconciling the depreciable base with reported depreciation. These parameters allow us to calculate effective tax rates in the historical period covered by our study, as well as to compare tax rates under present practices to those under proposed systems for capital recovery.

Our approach parallels an earlier study by Allan Young (1968), but contains additional detail on capital consumption practices. It should be noted that Young's study was not designed for estimating tax parameters, but for calculating capital consumption allowances to measure profits. This does not require the level of detail we have employed. The results of our simulation of reported capital consumption allowances show that we have significantly improved and extended Young's approach.[10]

We use a simulation model based on a system of closed-end vintage accounts. In each year we open a new set of accounts equal to the number of categories of depreciable investment. In general, gross investment in each asset class minus estimated salvage value serves as the depreciable base.[11] Current year investment is used for equipment investment; since capital consumption allowances on an asset are allowed only when it is put in use, structures investment, which is measured as it is put into place, is lagged one-half year to approximate the lag from the emplacement of capital to the beginning of the depreciation period.[12] Each asset account is divided into two subaccounts, one for accelerated depreciation and one for straight-line depreciation.

As a particular vintage of an asset ages, annual depreciation deductions are added together until accumulated depreciation equals the base. At this point the account is terminated and no asset is depreciated below its salvage value. In a model with two depreciation methods 20 categories of investment with an average lifetime of 10 years would result in approximately 400 active vintage accounts in the aggregate calculation.

Straight-line depreciation allowances are calculated by multiplying the straight-line rate of depreciation, that is, the inverse of the assigned lifetime, by the straight-line base. For accelerated depreciation, we multiply the straight-line rate by an appropriate constant and again by the declining base. Unlike the straight-line method, the base is reduced annually by the amount of capital consumption.[13] The constant, sometimes called the declining balance rate, corresponds to the type of declining balance (i.e., 2.0 for double declining balance, 1.5 for 150 percent declining balance).

Our starting point for parameterizing depreciation is the history of tax depreciation regulations promulgated by Congress and administered by the Internal Revenue Service.[14] Depreciation entered the tax code in 1909 in order to calculate income for tax purposes. Straight-line was the accepted method for calculating depreciation, but little is known about tax lifetimes, except that taxpayers were given considerable freedom of choice. This changed abruptly in 1934 with the revenue requirements of the New Deal. To achieve a desired 25 percent reduction in depreciation allowances, Treasury Decision 4422 was issued, shifting the burden of proving reasonableness of depreciation from the IRS to the taxpayer.

Tax lifetimes listed in the third edition of *Bulletin F* (1942) were generally longer than those provided in the 1931 edition and were probably indicative of the tough stance taken by the Treasury after 1934. Nevertheless, shorter lives were permitted under special facts and circumstances. In light of the long lifetimes suggested in *Bulletin F*, it is not surprising that controversy often arose between taxpayers and the IRS. Tax lifetimes are known to have decreased considerably below *Bulletin F* levels by the early 1950s, if not sooner.[15] The burden of proof of reasonableness was shifted from the taxpayer back to the IRS in 1953.

A notable exception to standard depreciation practices during the period was the special provision for 60-month amortization of defense-related facilities. Certificates of necessity for such practices were issued during World War II and the years around the Korean War. This provision had its greatest effect in 1945 when a statute allowed all remaining undepreciated balances to be written off in that year. This increased depreciation allowances an estimated $1.7 billion from a total of $4.3 billion.[16]

In 1954 the more generous double declining balance and sum-of-the-years'-digits methods were made available to all taxpayers for new investments. Although a small, but no negligible, amount of investment had been depreciated with the units-of-production method before 1954 and although 150 percent declining balance had been allowed since 1946, it was not until 1954 that the widespread use of the straight-line method began to decline significantly. The decline was not rapid; even in 1961, 50 percent of all depreciation deductions were calculated by the straight-line formula.[17]

The most far-reaching change in the taxation of income from capital occurred in 1962 with the introduction of the investment tax credit for equipment and certain qualifying structures. At the same time the Treasury issued Revenue Proclamation 62-21 which set forth "Guideline" lifetimes which were 30 to 40 percent shorter on average than *Bulletin F* lives.[18] There is considerable evidence that lifetimes on new investment at this time were already at the level prescribed by the Guidelines.[19] The large immediate impact of the Guidelines on the level of depreciation allowances was due to the inclusion of existing as well as new assets under the system. In the long run, the Guidelines increased depreciation allowances through a general relaxation of all depreciation rules:

A central objective of the new procedure is to facilitate the adoption of depreciable lives even shorter than those set forth in the Guidelines, or even shorter than those currently in use, provided only that certain standards are met and subsequent replacement practices are reasonably consistent with tax lives claimed.[20]

The "certain standards" took the form of the reserve ratio test. However, after a three-year grace period and subsequent extensions, the reserve ratio test was never adopted. Its relative complexity would have made it difficult to administer. However, it was generally believed that the requirements of the test would not be met by a large percentage of taxpayers, suggesting tax lifetimes lower than the Guideline lives.

In 1962 and 1963, the depreciable base of assets was reduced by the amount of the investment tax credit. The repeal of the Long amendment in 1964 removed this requirement and made depreciation allowances even more generous. The only significant reversal in the trend toward greater acceleration of allowances since 1934 occurred with the Tax Reform Act of 1969. This law limited all real estate signed into contract after July 24, 1969, to 150 percent declining balance depreciation.

In 1971, the same year the investment tax credit was reenacted after its suspension of nearly two years, the Asset Depreciation Range (ADR) System was introduced by the Treasury. This new system allowed taxpayers to adopt lifetimes generally 20 percent above or below their Guideline levels. Although most longer-lived assets used the lower limit, some shorter-lived assets moved upward within their range to take better advantage of the graduated rate of the investment tax credit.[21] Like the Guidelines, ADR was intended primarily for equipment, but had provision for special purpose structures.[22]

The ADR was intended to simplify depreciation accounting but actually proved quite complex, and only the largest corporations could comply with its detailed accounting requirements. However, it is believed that smaller firms, less subject to audit, have informally adopted the lower limit ADR lives.[23] The last major change in the tax code occurred in 1975 when the rate of investment tax credit was increased from 4 to 10 percent for public utility property and from 7 to 10 percent for other eligible property.

A striking feature of the history of tax depreciation is the slowly evolving liberalization of actual practices in contrast to the abrupt changes in regulations. In the case of tax lifetimes, the change in practices have to some degree effectively preceded the changes in rules. On the other hand, in the case of depreciation methods, adoption of accelerated depreciation took place gradually after it was first made generally available in 1954.

The tremendous growth of corporate tax depreciation allowances from the approximate figures of $4.6 billion in 1946 to $25.3 billion in 1960 to $119.8 billion in 1978 is attributable to four factors: (1) the growth of real investment in durable goods; (2) the rising price level of these goods; (3) successive liberalizations of depreciation rules; and (4) the increasing adoption over time by taxpayers of more liberal depreciation practices. We would expect a drift towards shorter lifetimes, more accelerated methods, and lower salvage values as taxpayers became more familiar with the tax code.

In our simulation model, the growth of real investment and the rising price level for investment goods are accounted for by use of a current dollar investment series as the depreciable base. All changes in the tax law mentioned above are incorporated as well. Th timing of their adoption into practice, before or after change in IRS regulations as appropriate in each case, is an issue often ignored. This issue is directly addressed by calibrating simulated capital consumption allowances to actual allowances claimed by U.S. corporations.

It should be noted that data on new corporate investment would not adequately describe the depreciable base over the simulation period unless adjustment was made for the sale of used assets at prices higher than their depreciable value. The only significant data available on used asset investment is from the *Census of Manufactures*. We adjust for resale of assets by constructing a used asset investment series based on percentages of used asset investment to total investment reported in the *Census of Manufactures*. For the years 1947, 1954, 1958, 1963, 1967, 1972 and 1977, the respective percentages are 9.6, 4.4, 5.2, 5.8, 4.3, 5.1, and 5.7. These percentages are scaled upward by a factor of 1.4 to take into account the larger proportion of used asset investment in nonmanufacturing industries apparent from *Statistics of Income* data on used asset investment eligible for the investment tax credit.[24] In our simulation, we create a separate set of accounts for used assets and depreciate them according to IRS rules for used assets. We assume that the undepreciated bases of original owners are 30 percent of resale value and accordingly scale down used asset investment by a factor of 0.70.

The results of our simulation are presented in table 9.3 and show a close fit of simulated to actual allowances. The parameters used to calculate simulated allowances are summarized in table 9.4. These results are now examined and checked for reasonableness on the basis of available information on capital consumption practices.

Weighted averages of assumed lifetimes of new equipment and plant used in the simulation appear in columns 2 and 3 of table 9.4. All pre-1962 tax lifetimes for our 35 classes of assets are changed uniformly as percentages of *Bulletin F* lifetimes.[25] Before 1934, all assets are depreciated at two-thirds their *Bulletin F* lifetimes. In 1934, these percentages are increased to 94 percent and then decreased to 84 percent by 1944 and then to 81 percent by 1958.

According to 1962 *Statistics of Income*, $9.2 billion, or 30 percent of all depreciation taken was under the Guidelines. This we approximated by applying the Guidelines to 26 percent of the total depreciable basis. It is assumed that all investment depreciated under the Guidelines applied to new and existing assets. Thus, there is a sharp increase in allowances in 1962 and no corresponding change in depreciation methods or tax lifetimes for new investment. Corcoran (1979) and Vasquez (1974) report in independent studies that no considerable decrease in lifetimes on new assets occurred in 1962. The present simulation achieves a large increase in 1962 allowances by applying the Guidelines to a fraction of all vintages, not just the latest vintage, and thus considerably increases the depreciation rate of older vintages with longer tax lifetimes.

From 1962 to 1971 it was assumed that the amount of the capital stock depreciated under the Guidelines increased in even increments each year from approximately 26 to 100 percent. At the same time, lifetimes on new assets decreased by about 10 percent. For 1971 and after, only Guideline-ADR midpoint lives are used to calculate depreciation. Lifetimes of certain short-lived assets were adjusted upward if they were eligible for a larger investment tax credit by doing so.

Vasquez (1974) reports a 14 percent decrease in tax lifetimes from 1970 to 1971. In our simulation, the decrease was only about 8 percent. This anomaly is probably explained by a survey sample heavily biased with ADR electors who had most to gain by the change in tax rules. Based on our estimates of Guideline-ADR midpoint lives, average lifetimes on new investment decreased sharply from 93.7 percent of their midpoint values in 1971 to 83.5 percent in 1972, to 78.5 percent by 1978.

Our results are consistent with a relatively small population of large corporations electing the ADR system quite early, followed by more gradual elections of lower ADR range lives by smaller corporations. Small corporations could less easily comply with the ADR's complex accounting requirements. In our simulation the average lifetimes of equipment are as low as they effectively can be in the ADR range by 1978, given upward adjustments of certain assets to take full advantage of the investment tax credit.

Our average equipment lifetime in 1976 was equal to 8.43, or 82 percent of our estimate of our average Guideline-ADR midpoint lifetime. Unpublished Treasury data on the amounts of investment in each ADR class in 1976 allow us to obtain an alternative estimate.[26] The Treasury data derived estimate gives a 9.13 ADR midpoint, which translates our figure 8.43 to 92 percent of the ADR midpoint. This suggests our assumed Guideline-ADR is too high, but much of this can be explained by the fact that Guideline-ADR lifetimes are adjusted upward to take advantage of the investment tax credit.[27]

The amount of new investment using accelerated depreciation is reported in column 4 of table 9.6. In contrast to Young's study, where all pre-1954 vintage investment was assumed to be straight-line, *Statistics of Income* data show that 7 percent of depreciation of pre-1954 vintage investment deducted in 1959 was calculated by accelerated depreciation methods.[28] To approximate depreciation methods before 1954, percentages of 1.5 declining balance were included that allowed us to duplicate the 1959 figure on depreciation of pre-1954 investment.

Following the lead of Young (1968) and Wales (1966), we take advantage of the similarity between double declining balance and sum-of-the-years'-digits methods and assume all accelerated depreciation after 1954 is double declining balance. In order to terminate the accelerated depreciation vintage accounts, an optimal switchover to straight-line is employed. *Statistics of Income* reports percentages of depreciation taken under different methods for the years 1954 to 1961.[29] This is probably our most reliable data source on which to base our parameterization. The close approximation of these figures in our simulation to the actual figures shown in the last two columns of table 9.5 gives added credibility to the results. In addition, our 1971 estimate of a new investment with accelerated depreciation of 80 percent is compatible with the 81.7 percent figure reported by Vasquez.[30]

Survey results of salvage value as a percentage of original cost on buildings were reported in a Treasury study[31] and were generally found to be about 1 percent; accordingly, this value was used for salvage of structures in our simulation. Unfortunately, data on the salvage value of equipment are not available. However, we do make inferences about salvage values for purposes of our simulation.

Combining the two facts that the double declining balance method of depreciation is more generous than the sum-of-the-years'-digits method only in the case of nonnegligible salvage value[32] and that double declining balance was much more widely used historically than sum-of-the-years'-digits, it is probable that salvage value was significant for some assets. Informal discussions with IRS field agents suggest figures on average between 5 and 10 percent.

Although the IRS code states explicitly that no asset may be depreciated below its salvage value, certain provisions in the code do effectively lower salvage value estimated for tax purposes. For property acquired after October 16, 1962, taxpayers were allowed to decrease salvage values by up to 10 percent. Therefore, a salvage at 15 percent could be lowered to 5 percent, and for assets with salvage values of less than 10 percent, no salvage value need be considered. In 1971, ADR electors were granted an additional 10 percent reduction in salvage value. Our assumed salvage values for equipment presented in column 5 of table 9.6 reflect these changes in law as well as the shifts in burden of proof of reasonableness to the taxpayer in 1934 and back to the IRS in 1953.

We conclude that the simulated depreciation parameters summarized in table 9.3 are close approximations of actual practices used by U.S. corporations and can replace more highly simplified assumptions often employed in models of the corporate income tax. Furthermore, by comparing these parameters with those of proposed policy alternatives, more accurate estimates of the likely impact of policy changes can be made.

Notes

1. The rental value of capital is employed in econometric studies of corporate investment behavior by Jorgenson and Siebert (1968a,b, 1972). This concept is also used in econometric studies by Jorgenson and Stephenson (1967a,b, 1969a) and by Hall and Jorgenson (1969a, 1971). See also: Bischoff (1971a) and Coen (1971). Econometric studies of investment behavior are surveyed by Jorgenson (1971a) and Hall (1977).

2. A history of provisions for capital recovery is given by Pechman (1977), Gravelle (1979), and Jeremias (1979). See the appendix for a detailed discussion of our methodology for incorporating these provisions into the rental price of capital services.

3. For detailed discussion of geometric approximation, see Hulten and Wykoff (1980, 1981a,b). References to the literature are given by Hulten and Wykoff (1981b). Additional details on the economic theory of depreciation are provided by Jorgenson (1973).

4. Taxation and efficient capital allocation is discussed by Samuelson (1964), Auerbach (1979a,b), Bradford (1980, 1981a) and Hall (1981).

5. Combinations of expensing and economic depreciation are analyzed by Auerbach (1979a), Harberger (1980), and Bradford (1981a).

6. Estimates of economic depreciation employed in the U.S. national accounts are discussed by Young and Musgrave (1980). These estimates are employed in a study of the U.S. corporate income tax by Feldstein and Summers (1979). See Gravelle (1980c) for a detailed critique of the Feldstein-Summers study and the reply by Feldstein and Summers (1980).

7. We are indebted to Jerry Silverstein of the Bureau of Economic Analysis for preparing these estimates for this study.

8. For each industry composition of investment by type of asset for each year was determined by a biproportional matrix model described by Bacharach (1965). Elements of the initial matrix are based on asset weights reported in Bureau of Economic Analysis (1975).

9. Alternative legislative proposals have been analyzed by Feldstein (1981), Gravelle (1980a,b) and Leape (1980).

10. Depreciation practices are known to differ significantly across industries. This is illustrated in tables 16 and 17 of a report for the U.S. Treasury by Vasquez (1974), and also in a statistical study by Wales (1966) that estimates rates of adoption of accelerated depreciation for two-digit manufacturing industries. Estimates of practices by industries, similar to our aggregate simulation, could be made with more disaggregated IRS-based data and the corresponding investment series.

11. There are some exceptions. Salvage value is removed from the depreciable base when determining allowances with the straight-line and sum-of-the-years' digits methods, but not in the case of the declining balance method, although the account still may not be reduced below its salvage value. The Long amendment, effective in 1962 and 1963, removed the amount of the investment tax credit from the depreciable base.

12. An extensive survey study by Thomas Mayer (1960) examined lags between the start of construction and completion and found the weighted average to be 15 months. If capital is installed evenly during this lag, the average lag between installment and starting depreciation is seven and one-half months.

13. Throughout our simulation we use a half-year convention which embodies the assumption that taxpayers begin taking depreciation on their new assets at midyear. This is implemented by dividing our depreciation rates in half the first year of an asset's life.

14. The following history of depreciation practices summarizes relevant details found in Gravelle (1979), Pechman (1977), Young (1968), and various issues of the *Statistics of Income: Corporation Income Tax Returns*.

15. See Young (1968, p. 20).

16. Young (1968, pp. 20, 23).

17. *Statistics of Income: Corporation Income Tax Returns*, 1961–1962, p. 6, table E.

18. Although it is widely believed that the new Guidelines as well as the investment tax credit applied only to equipment, there was allowance for certain structures. The Guidelines include "special-purpose structures which are an integral part of the production process and which, under normal practices, are replaced contemporaneously, with the equipment they house. . . . Special-purpose structure shall be classified with the equipment they house, support, or serve." (U.S. Treasury Dept. (1962), p. 12.) A considerable amount of investment classified as structures in NIPA falls into this category. Probably an increasing share of NIPA structures investment adopted considerably shorter tax lifetimes under this provision, as is evidenced by an increasing share of structures investment qualified for the investment tax credit, which has a similar eligibility rule.

19. Corcoran (1979) and Vasquez (1974) reach this conclusion independently.

20. U.S. Treasury Department (1962, p. 1).

21. Since 1971, the investment tax credit has been fully effective for assets with lifetimes over 6 years, two-thirds effective with lifetimes of 5 to 6, and one-third effective with lifetimes of 3 to 4. The movements within the range for shorter-lived assets are illustrated in an internal Office of Industrial Economics memo kindly provided by Dennis Cox, deputy director of the Office of Industrial Economics. From a nonrandom sample of approximately 2,000 taxpayers in 1973, we find, for example, that 90 percent of investment in automobiles were depreciated at the ADR midpoint and, therefore, become eligible for an investment tax credit. With aircraft, 76 percent were assigned 7 year lifetimes, the upper limit of the ADR, making such investments eligible for the full tax credit.

22. For instance, under ADR nuclear power plants were allowed to shorten their lifetimes from 20 to 16 years.

23. This was brought to our attention by Dennis Cox.

24. *Statistics of Income: Corporation Income Tax Returns*, 1974, p. 128, table 19, and 1975, p. 118, table 16.

25. *Bulletin F* and Guideline-ADR midpoint lifetimes are shown in table 9.4.

26. Kindly provided by William Sutton on the staff of Joint Committee on Taxation.

27. Tax lifetimes for asset categories 4, 15, 16, and 17, which make up 19 percent of corporate investment were adjusted upward to take advantage of the investment tax credit.

28. *Statistics of Income: Corporation Income Tax Returns*, 1959–1960, p. 7, table F.

29. *Statistics of Income: Corporation Income Tax Returns*, 1959–1960, p. 7, table E and 1961–1962, p. 6, table E.

30. Vasquez (1974, p. 36, table 16).

31. U.S. Treasury Department (1975, tables 23A, 23B).

32. For elaboration, see Myers (1960).

10 The Efficiency of Capital Allocation

*Dale W. Jorgenson and
Kun-Young Yun*

In this paper we present an intertemporal general equilibrium model of the U.S. economy. The purpose of this model is to analyze the efficiency of capital allocation. We have implemented our model econometrically for annual data covering the period 1955–1980. The model encompasses the critical features of U.S. tax laws applicable to income from capital. Equilibrium is determined by market clearing conditions for consumption and investment goods and for capital and labor services in each time period. Under perfect foresight, there exists a unique balanced growth equilibrium corresponding to any stationary tax policy.

10.1 Introduction

An intertemporal general equilibrium model of the U.S. economy is presented in this paper. The purpose of this model is to analyze the efficiency of capital allocation. The model is kindred in spirit to the model of the Swedish economy developed by Ragnar Bentzel (1978). We have implemented our model econometrically for annual data on the United States, covering the period 1955–1980.

Our general equilibrium model employs a description of technology based on capital as a factor of production. The central concepts of capital theory—capital assets, capital services and investment—are inessential to the development of intertemporal production theory. However, these concepts provide additional structure that greatly facilitates the implementation of our econometric model of producer behavior.[1]

We have further simplified the representation of technology by assuming that capital is perfectly malleable. The process of capital accumulation results in a single stock of capital at each point of time. This capital is allocated among alternative uses so as to equalize after tax rates of return. The U.S. tax structure affects capital allocation through the taxation of income from capital, the taxation of investment goods production, and the taxation of property.[2]

To facilitate the implementation of our econometric model of consumer behavior, we have simplified the description of preferences. Our model is based on the preferences of a single infinitely lived consumer. This rules out distributional considerations in the modeling of consumer behavior.[3] To further simplify the description of preferences we endow the infinitely lived consumer with perfect foresight about future prices.

Our intertemporal general equilibrium of the U.S. economy balances supplies and demands for all products and factors of production. Equilibrium at each point of time links the past and the future through markets for investment goods and capital services. Capital assets are accumulated as a result of past investments, net of replacement requirements. The price of acquisition of an asset is equal to the present value of future capital services, including depreciation.

In section 10.2 we undertake the construction of an econometric general equilibrium model of the U.S. economy. This model encompasses the critical features of U.S. tax laws applicable to income from capital. We distinguish among four commodity groups—consumption and investment goods and capital and labor services. We ignore costs of adjustment for capital stock, so that capital services are perfectly malleable.

We develop econometric models of the business and household sectors of the U.S. economy, based on the methodology presented by Jorgenson (1983, 1984). The business sector produces consumption and investment goods from inputs of labor services and the services of noncorporate and corporate assets. At a second stage the business sector allocates the value of noncorporate and corporate capital inputs between the services of long-lived and short-lived assets.

Our econometric model of the household sector is based on an intertemporal utility function that is additive in levels of full consumption in all time periods. Full consumption is an aggregate of the consumption of goods, household capital services, and leisure time. The household sector allocates the value of household capital between the services of long-lived and short-lived assets at a second stage.

In section 10.3 we define an intertemporal equilibrium of the U.S. economy. Equilibrium is determined by market clearing conditions for consumption and investment goods and for capital and labor services in each time period. In addition, the time path of consumption must satisfy the conditions for intertemporal optimality of the house-hold sector, assuming perfect foresight. Finally, the time path of investment must satisfy requirements for capital accumulation by the business and household sectors.

The government sector raises revenue through taxes on income from capital and labor services, sales taxes on the production of con-sumption and investment goods and property taxes. This revenue is used to finance purchases of consumption and investment goods and labor services. In addition, government revenue finances transfers to the household sector and government enterprises employ labor ser-vices and produce consumption goods.

Under perfect foresight there exists a unique balanced growth equi-librium of the U.S. economy corresponding to any stationary tax pol-icy. In balanced growth equilibrium the quantities of all commodities grow at a rate that is equal to the rate of growth of the time endow-ment of the household sector. Our model determines only relative prices and these prices are stationary in balanced growth equilibrium.[4]

In section 10.4 we provide a brief summary of our model. We con-clude with an outline of future research on the effects of tax policy on the efficiency of capital allocation.

10.2   Technology and Preferences

Our objective is to construct an intertemporal general equilibrium model of the U.S. economy. The distinctive feature of our model is that we employ econometric methods for estimating the unknown parameters that characterize technology and preferences. The result-ing econometric model encompasses the restrictions implied by eco-nomic theories of producer and consumer behavior.

To estimate the unknown parameters of our econometric models of the business and household sectors, we have constructed a system of national accounts for the United States, covering the period 1955–1980. These accounts are based on the accounting system origi-nated by Christensen and Jorgenson (1973) and further developed by Jorgenson (1980) and Jorgenson and Sullivan (1981). This system of accounts includes income and expenditure accounts for the business and household sectors in both current and constant prices.

Our system of national accounts includes expenditures by the busi-ness sector on capital services, disaggregated between noncorporate and corporate capital services. Within each of these categories the demand for capital services is further broken down between the services of long-lived and short-lived assets. This system also includes expenditures by the household sector on capital services, broken down between the services of long-lived and short-lived assets. The prices of capital services incorporate parameters that describe the U.S. tax structure.

Commodities. In our general equilibrium model we distinguish among four separate commodity groups. We employ the following notation for the commodity groups included in the model:

C private national consumption, excluding household capital services

I private national investment, including investment in consumers' durables

K private national capital stock, including the stock of household capital

L labor services.

Our concepts of consumption and investment correspond closely to the concepts employed in the U.S. National Income and Product Accounts. An important difference between our accounts and the official U.S. national accounts is in the treatment of consumers' durables. Purchases of consumers' durables are included in investment and excluded from consumption in our accounts. The capital stock includes stocks of consumers' durables.

A complete system of notation includes quantities of consumption and investment goods, labor services, and capital services in each of the three sectors of the economy—household, noncorporate and corporate:

CE supply of consumption goods by government enterprise
CG government purchase of consumption goods
CS supply of consumption goods by private enterprise
F full consumption
HD household capital services
HL household capital services from long-lived assets
HS household capital services from short-lived assets
IG government purchases of investment goods
IS supply of investment goods by private enterprise
K capital stock
KD capital services

LD   private enterprise purchases of labor services

LE   government enterprise purchases of labor services

LG   general government purchases of labor services

LH   time endowment

LJ   leisure time

LU   unemployment

MD   noncorporate capital services

ML   noncorporate capital services from long-lived assets

MS   noncorporate capital services from short-lived assets

QD   corporate capital services

QL   corporate capital services from long-lived assets

QS   corporate capital services from short-lived assets.

To denote prices we simply place a *P* before the corresponding symbol for quantity. For example *PC* denotes the price paid by the household sector for consumption goods.

Business Sector. We next present an econometric model for the business sector.[5] This model is based on a labor requirements function, giving labor input as a function of outputs of consumption and investment goods and inputs of noncorporate and corporate capital services. Required labor input also depends on time as an index of the level of technology. Producer equilibrium under constant returns to scale implies the existence of a price function, giving the price of labor input as a function of the prices of the two outputs, capital inputs and time. The price function must be homogeneous of degree one, nondecreasing, and convex in the prices of outputs and inputs.

In addition, we assume that the price function is homothetically separable in the prices of capital services from long-lived and short-lived assets in the noncorporate and corporate sectors. Under homothetic separability our model of producer behavior is based on a two-stage allocation process.[6] In the first stage the value of labor input is allocated among consumption and investment goods outputs and noncorporate and corporate capital inputs. In the second stage the value of each of these capital inputs is allocated between long-lived and short-lived assets.

To represent the first stage of our model of production for the business sector we require some additional notation. We first define the shares of outputs and inputs in the value of labor input by:

$$v_C = \frac{PCS \cdot CS}{PLD \cdot LD} \; , \; v_I = \frac{PIS \cdot IS}{PLD \cdot LD} \; , \; v_M = -\frac{PMD \cdot MD}{PLD \cdot LD} \; ,$$

$$v_Q = -\frac{PQD \cdot QD}{PLD \cdot LD} \; .$$

Outputs are valued in producers' prices, while inputs are valued in purchasers' prices. In addition, we require the notation:

$v = (v_C, v_I, v_M, v_Q)$ — vector of value shares

$\ln P = (\ln PCS, \ln PIS, \ln PMD, \ln PQD)$ — vector of logarithms of price of outputs and inputs

T — time as an index of technology.

We assume that the business sector allocates the shares of outputs and inputs in the value of labor input in accord with the price function:

$$\ln PLD = \ln P' \, \alpha_P + \alpha_T \cdot T + \frac{1}{2} \ln P' B_{PP} \ln P$$

$$+ \ln P' \, \beta_{PT} \cdot T + \frac{1}{2} \beta_{TT} \cdot T^2. \tag{10.1}$$

The price of labor input is a transcendental or, more specifically, exponential function of the logarithms of the prices of outputs and inputs. We refer to this form as the transcendental logarithmic price function or, more simply, the translog price function, indicating the role of the variables that enter the price function.[7] In this representation the scalars $\{\alpha_T, \beta_{TT}\}$, the vectors $\{\alpha_P, \beta_{PT}\}$, and the matrix B_{PP} are constant parameters.

The value shares can be expressed in terms of the logarithmic derivatives of the price function with respect to the logarithms of the prices of outputs and inputs:

$$v = \frac{\partial \ln PLD}{\partial \ln P} \; . \tag{10.2}$$

Applying this relationship to the translog price function, we obtain the system of value shares:

$$v = \alpha_P + B_{PP} \ln P + \beta_{PT} \cdot T. \tag{10.3}$$

Similarly, we can introduce the rate of growth of labor efficiency as a measure of technical change. We can define this measure as the rate of growth of the price of labor input with respect to time, holding the prices of outputs and inputs constant:

$$v_T = \frac{\partial \ln PLD}{\partial T} .$$

(10.4)

For the translog price function this relationship takes the form:

$$v_T = \alpha_T + \beta_{PT} \ln P + \beta_{TT} \cdot T.$$

(10.5)

To assure the existence of a balanced growth equilibrium for our intertemporal general equilibrium model we impose the condition that technical change must be Harrod-neutral. This implies that the parameters β_{PT} and β_{TT} are equal to zero. Under Harrod-neutral technical change we can redefine labor input in terms of efficiency units, so that the price function (10.1) can be represented in a form that is invariant with respect to time. For this purpose we can introduce the price of labor input measured in efficiency units, say PLD^*:

$$PLD^* = e^{-\alpha_T \cdot T} PLD.$$

(10.6)

The first stage of our model of production for the business sector consists of a system of equations giving the shares of outputs and input in the value of labor input and the rate of growth of labor efficiency as functions of relative prices and time. To formulate an econometric model we add a stochastic component to these equations. Since the rate of growth of labor efficiency is not directly observable, we consider a form of the model with autocorrelated disturbances. We then transform the data to eliminate autocorrelation.

In our intertemporal general equilibrium model the prices of outputs and inputs are endogenous variables. We estimate the unknown parameters of our model by methods appropriate for systems of nonlinear simultaneous equations, using instrumental variables that can be taken as exogenous to the model. A list of these instrumental variables is given in the Appendix to this paper. Estimates of the unknown parameters of our econometric model of production are obtained by the method of nonlinear three stage least squares introduced by Jorgenson and Laffont (1974).

We estimate the unknown parameters of our econometric model of production under the restrictions implied by Harrod-neutrality. In addition, we require that the parameters satisfy restrictions associated with summability—the condition that the value shares sum to unity—homogeneity of degree zero of the value shares and convexity of the price function in the prices of outputs and inputs, and symmetry of the matrix of parameters B_{PP}. Estimates of the parameters satisfying these restrictions are given in table 10.1.

The second stage of our model of production for the business sector consists of two submodels that allocate the values of noncorporate and corporate capital inputs between the services of long-lived and short-lived assets. We can denote the shares of the services of these two classes of assets in the values of capital input in the two sectors by:

$$v_{ML} = \frac{PML \cdot ML}{PMD \cdot MD}, \quad v_{MS} = \frac{PMS \cdot MS}{PMD \cdot MD}, \quad v_{QL} = \frac{PQL \cdot QL}{PQD \cdot QD},$$
$$v_{QS} = \frac{PQS \cdot QS}{PQD \cdot QD}.$$

As before, we find it convenient to employ vector notation:

$v_M = (v_{ML}, v_{MS})$ — vector of value shares in noncorporate capital input

$v_Q = (v_{QL}, v_{QS})$ — vector of value shares in corporate capital input

ln PM = (ln PML, ln PMS) — vector of logarithms of prices of capital inputs in the noncorporate sector

ln PQ = (ln PQL, ln PQS) — vector of logarithms of prices of capital inputs in the corporate sector.

We assume that the noncorporate and corporate sectors allocate the shares of long-lived and short-lived assets in the value of capital input in accord with the translog price functions:

$$\ln PMD = \ln PM' \alpha_{PM} + \frac{1}{2} \ln PM' B_{PM} \ln PM, \tag{10.7}$$

$$\ln PQD = \ln PQ' \alpha_{PQ} + \frac{1}{2} \ln PQ' B_{PQ} \ln PQ.$$

The value shares can be expressed in terms of the logarithmic derivatives of the price functions:

$$v_M = \alpha_{PM} + B_{PM} \ln PM, \tag{10.8}$$

$$v_Q = \alpha_{PQ} + B_{PQ} \ln PQ.$$

Table 10.1
Econometric model of producer behavior

Parameter	Estimate	Standard error
First stage submodel:		
α_C	0.884742	0.006072
α_I	0.518735	0.004920
α_M	−0.104489	0.003262
α_Q	−0.298989	0.003004
α_T	0.008883	0.011245
β_{CC}	0.821256	0.148522
β_{CI}	−0.744423	0.106604
β_{CM}	−0.084895	0.032768
β_{CQ}	0.008062	0.046366
β_{II}	0.457081	0.084859
β_{IM}	0.085760	0.025879
β_{IQ}	0.201583	0.029072
β_{MM}	0.011334	0.016599
β_{MQ}	−0.012200	0.013489
β_{QQ}	−0.197445	0.021768
Noncorporate capital submodel:		
α_S^M	0.185966	0.023888
β_{SS}^M	0.066618	0.022573
Corporate capital submodel:		
α_S^Q	0.381647	0.014020
β_{SS}^Q	0.019961	0.031542

In our intertemporal general equilibrium model the prices of capital inputs are endogenous variables. We estimate the unknown parameters of the second stage of our model of production by the method of nonlinear three stage least squares, using the instrumental variables listed in the Appendix. We impose the restrictions associated with summability, homogeneity of degree zero of the value shares and concavity of the price functions in the prices of long-lived and short-lived capital inputs, and symmetry of the matrices B_{PM} and B_{PQ}. Estimates of the parameters satisfying these restrictions are given in table 10.1.

Household Sector. Our model of the household sector can be divided between intertemporal and atemporal stages. At the intertemporal stage we assume that the household allocates full wealth among time periods in accord with the linear logarithmic intertemporal utility function:[8]

$$U = \sum_{t=0}^{\infty} \left(\frac{1+n}{1+\alpha} \right)^t \ln \frac{F_t}{P_t}, \tag{10.9}$$

where P is the population, n is the rate of population growth and α is the rate of time preference.

Full wealth is defined as:

$$WF = \sum_{t=0}^{\infty} \frac{PF_t \cdot F_t}{\prod_{s=0}^{t}(1+\rho_s)}, \tag{10.10}$$

where ρ_s is the nominal private rate of return after all taxes. Under the optimal intertemporal consumption plan the growth rate of full consumption is given by:

$$\frac{F_t}{F_{t-1}} = \frac{PF_{t-1}}{PF_t} \cdot \frac{(1+\rho_t)(1+n)}{1+\alpha}. \tag{10.11}$$

To represent the atemporal stage of our model for the household sector, we first introduce the shares of consumption goods, household capital services, and leisure in the value of full consumption and the shares of the services of long-lived and short-lived assets in household capital services:

$$v_C = \frac{PC \cdot C}{PF \cdot F}, \quad v_{HD} = \frac{PHD \cdot HD}{PF \cdot F}, \quad v_{LJ} = \frac{PLJ \cdot LJ}{PF \cdot F};$$

$$v_{HL} = \frac{PHL \cdot HL}{PHD \cdot HD}, \qquad v_{HS} = \frac{PHS \cdot HS}{PHD \cdot HD}.$$

As before, we find it convenient to employ vector notation:

$v_D = (v_C, v_{HD}, v_{LJ})$ — vector of value shares in full consumption

$v_H = (v_{HL}, v_{HS})$ — vector of value shares of household capital input

$\ln PD = (\ln PC, \ln PHD, \ln PLJ^*)$ — vector of logarithms of prices of consumption goods, household capital services and leisure; note that the price of leisure is defined in terms of labor measured in efficiency units

$\ln PH = (\ln PHL, \ln PHS)$ — vector of logarithms of prices of capital inputs in the household sector.

We assume that the household sector allocates the shares of consumption goods, household capital services and leisure in the value of full consumption in accord with the translog price index for full consumption:

$$\ln PF = \ln PD' \alpha_{PD} + \frac{1}{2} \ln PD' B_{PD} \ln PD. \tag{10.12}$$

Similarly, we assume that the household sector allocates the shares of long-lived and short-lived assets in the value of capital input in accord with the translog price index:

$$\ln PHD = \ln PH' \alpha_{PH} + \frac{1}{2} \ln PH' B_{PH} \ln PH. \tag{10.13}$$

The corresponding value shares can be expressed in terms of the logarithmic derivatives of the price functions:

$$v_D = \alpha_{PD} + B_{PD} \ln PD,$$
$$v_H = \alpha_{PH} + B_{PH} \ln PH. \tag{10.14}$$

We treat the prices of consumption goods, household capital services, and leisure and the prices of the services of long-lived and short-lived assets as endogenous variables. We estimate the unknown parameters of our atemporal model of consumption by the method of nonlinear three stage least squares. We impose the restrictions associated with summability, homogeneity of degree zero of the value shares and concavity of the price functions, and symmetry of the

Table 10.2
Econometric model of consumer behavior

Parameter	Estimate	Standard error
First stage submodel:		
α_C^D	0.188050	0.0011947
α_H^D	0.065590	0.0008922
α_L^D	0.746360	0.0009875
β_{CC}^D	0.096676	0.0129081
β_{CH}^D	−0.004293	0.0083668
β_{CL}^D	−0.092382	0.0114209
β_{HH}^D	0.050133	0.0028803
β_{HL}^D	−0.045840	0.0055592
β_{LL}^D	0.138222	0.0133601
Household capital submodel:		
α_S^D	0.504489	0.011362
β_{SS}^D	0.076729	0.009713

matrices of parameters B_{PD} and B_{PH}. Estimates of the parameters satisfying these restrictions are given in table 10.2.

10.3   General Equilibrium Model

The purpose of this section is to outline a general equilibrium model of the U.S. economy that incorporates the econometric models of business and household sectors that we have presented in the preceding section. In each time period we determine prices so as to clear markets for consumption and investment goods and for capital and labor services. Under the assumption of perfect foresight the sequence of such prices must also satisfy the conditions for an intertemporal equilibrium of the U.S. economy.

The behavioral equations of our model include supply functions for consumption and investment goods and demand functions for capital and labor services by the business sector. The behavioral equations also include a supply function for labor services and demand functions for consumption goods and capital services by the household sector. The government sector raises revenue by taxation, purchases consumption goods, investment goods, and labor services, and transfers part of its revenues to the household sector.

In the following section we employ our intertemporal general equilibrium model to simulate the U.S. economy under alternative tax policies. We first compute the equilibrium time path or the U.S. economy corresponding to each alternative policy. We then measure the level of potential economic welfare along each time path by means of an intertemporal social welfare function. Finally, we convert differences in levels of potential welfare among different time paths into equivalent variations in the level of U.S. national wealth.[9]

Market Equilibrium.   Our model incorporates markets for each of the four commodity groups—consumption and investment goods and capital and labor services. Supply and demand for consumption goods are equal, so that:

$$CS + CE = C + CG. \tag{10.15}$$

Similarly, supply and demand for investment good are equal, so that:

$$IS = I + IG. \tag{10.16}$$

The accumulation of capital is determined by an identity between capital stock at the end of each period the sum of beginning of period capital stock and investment net of replacement:

$$K = AI \cdot I + (1 - U)K(-1), \tag{10.17}$$

where AI converts investment into the sum of the change in capital stock and replacement and U is the replacement rate. The supply of capital services from the household sector is proportional to beginning of period capital stock:

$$KD = AK \cdot K(-1), \tag{10.18}$$

where AK converts capital stock at the beginning of the period into a flow of capital services.

For simplicity we have assumed that there are no costs of adjustment for capital stock, so that capital services are perfectly malleable. The supply of capital services is equal to the sum of capital input demands by the household, noncorporate, and corporate sectors:

$$KD = HL + HS + ML + MS + QL + QS. \tag{10.19}$$

Under this assumption the prices of the six different types of capital services are proportional to each other.

We take the rate of unemployment to be exogenous, so that labor supply is equal to the sum of labor demands by private enterprises, government enterprises, and general government, plus unemployment:

$$L = LD + LE + LG + LU. \tag{10.20}$$

In each time period the time endowment is equal to the sum of labor supply by the household sector and its demand for leisure:

$$LH = L + LJ. \tag{10.21}$$

Government. We have described markets for each of the four commodity groups included in our intertemporal general equilibrium model. We next outline the generation of government revenue through sales taxes on consumption and investment goods, income taxes on capital and labor services, and property taxes. We have outlined the tax structure for income from capital in section 10.1, so that we focus attention in this section on sales and taxes on labor income. We also consider the role of government enterprises and the allocation of government expenditure.

Government revenues from sales taxes on consumption goods, say RC, are generated by the identity:

$$RC = TC \cdot PCS \cdot CS, \tag{10.22}$$

where TC is the effective tax rate on the output of consumption goods at producers' prices. The prices paid by consumers differ from the prices received by producers, due to sales taxes:

$$PC = (1 + TC) PCS. \tag{10.23}$$

Similarly, government revenues from sales taxes on investment goods, say RI, are generated by the identity:

$$RI = TI \cdot PIS \cdot IS, \tag{10.24}$$

where TI is the effective tax rate on investment goods. The prices paid by investors differ from the prices received by producers:

$$PI = (1 + TI)\, PIS. \tag{10.25}$$

To model property taxes and the taxation of income from capital we first generate the revenue from taxation of property in the household, noncorporate, and corporate sectors by applying effective tax rates to the values of beginning of period capital stocks in all three sectors. The tax base for the corporate income tax is equal to the value of corporate capital services, less the sum of property taxes, capital consumption allowances, and interest expenses at the corporate level. Corporate tax liability is equal to the effective corporate tax rate applied to the corporate tax base, less the value of the investment tax credit at the corporate level.

To model the taxation of capital income through the individual income tax we first define an appropriate tax base. This tax base includes dividends and interest distributed by corporations and a proportion of retained earnings. Retained earnings generate accrued capital gains on holdings of corporate equity. The individual tax base for income from capital also includes the value of noncorporate capital services, less the sum of property taxes, capital consumption allowances, and interest expenses at the noncorporate level, and plus a proportion of capital gains accrued on noncorporate property.

Finally, the individual tax base for income from capital is reduced by property taxes and interest expenses and increased by a proportion of capital gains on household property. Individual tax liability for income from capital is equal to an effective tax rate applied to the tax base, less the value of the investment tax credit at the noncorporate level. We generate the revenue from wealth taxation through estate and gift taxes by applying an effective tax rate to the value of capital stock held by household, noncorporate, and corporate sectors.

To model the taxation of labor income through the individual income tax we generate the revenue from the labor income tax, say RL, through the identity:

$$RL = TL \cdot PL(L - LU), \tag{10.26}$$

where TL is the average effective tax rate on labor income. We define the corresponding marginal effective tax rate, say TM, through the equations:

$$TL = \lambda_0 + \frac{1}{2}\lambda_1 PL(L - LU),$$
$$TM = \lambda_0 + \lambda_1 PL(L - LU). \tag{10.27}$$

We choose the parameters λ_0 and λ_1 so as to approximate the taxation of labor income under the individual income tax.[10] The price of leisure differs from the wages paid by producers:

$$PLJ = (1 - TM)PL. \tag{10.28}$$

We assume that nontax payments are a constant fraction, say TT, of labor income:

$$RT = TT \cdot PL(L - LU), \tag{10.29}$$

where RT is nontax payments.

We assume that government enterprises employ a fixed proportion, say SLE, of total labor supply:

$$LE = SLE \cdot L. \tag{10.30}$$

Similarly, we assume that government enterprises produce a fixed proportion, say SCE, of the supply of consumption goods by private enterprises:

$$CE = SCE \cdot CS. \tag{10.31}$$

The surplus of government enterprises, say RE, is generated from the identity:

$$RE = PC \cdot CE - PL \cdot LE. \tag{10.32}$$

Government revenue is the sum of taxes on the supply of consumption and investment goods by the business sector and the supply of labor and capital services by the household sector, plus nontax payments and the surplus of government enterprises. To generate government expenditures on goods and services and expenditures on transfer payments other than social insurance funds, say EL, we assume that each of these expenditures is proportional to total government outlays on all these categories of expenditure:

$$PC \cdot CG = SCG \cdot E,$$
$$PI \cdot IG = SIG \cdot E,$$
$$PL \cdot LG = SLG \cdot E,$$
$$EL = SEL \cdot E. \tag{10.33}$$

In these identities the proportions of government outlays E for the four categories of expenditure are SCG, SIG, SLG and SEL. Finally,

government outlays are equal to government revenues plus an exogenously given variable that functions like a lump sum tax.

Intertemporal Equilibrium.   Under the assumption of perfect foresight the intertemporal equilibrium path of the economy must satisfy
the market clearing conditions for consumption and investment
goods—(10.15) and (10.16)—and for capital and labor services—(10.19)–(10.21). In addition, the time path of full consumption
must satisfy the condition (10.11) for intertemporal optimality. Finally,
the time path of the capital stock must satisfy the condition (10.17)
relating changes in capital stock to investment net of replacement.

Under the assumptions of constant returns to scale in production,
homotheticity in consumption, and Harrod-neutral technical change,
there exists a unique balanced growth equilibrium corresponding to
any stationary tax policy. In this equilibrium all quantities grow at the
rate $(1 + \alpha_H) (1 + n) - 1$, where α_H is the rate of technical change:

$$\alpha_H = e^{\alpha_T} - 1.$$

Similarly, all prices grow at the exogenously given inflation rate π.

In the absence of inflation the price of full consumption is stationary in balanced growth equilibrium, so that the nominal private rate
of return can be expressed in terms of the rate of time preference and
the rate of technical change:

$$1 + \rho = (1 + \alpha)(1 + \alpha_H). \tag{10.34}$$

With a constant rate of inflation at the rate π, the nominal private rate
of return in balanced growth equilibrium takes the form:

$$(1 + \rho) = (1 + \alpha)(1 + \alpha_H)(1 + \pi). \tag{10.35}$$

We conclude that the private rate of return corrected for inflation
depends only on the rate of time preference and the rate of technical
change.

We can represent the equilibrium time path in schematic form as in
figure 10.1. In this figure, full consumption per unit of labor in efficiency units is denoted F and capital per unit of labor, also in efficiency units, is denoted K. If an economy with a stationary time
endowment is initially in equilibrium at the point A and a change in
tax policy moves the equilibrium to the point E, there exists a unique
transition path to the new equilibrium. In this illustration the new
balanced growth equilibrium is associated with a higher level of capi-

tal intensity, so that the rate of return rises and the level of full consumption falls to the point B. The capital intensity of the economy at the point B is precisely the same as at the point A, before the change in tax policy.

The drop in consumption associated with a higher rate of return results in an increase in the rate of growth of capital stock. As the economy moves along the transition path to the new equilibrium at E, the rate of return corrected for inflation falls toward the balanced growth equilibrium rate $(1 + \alpha)(1 + \alpha_H) - 1$, which is independent of tax policy. The level of full consumption rises with the fall in the rate of return and the rise in capital stock. In the limit, full consumption and capital stock reach the new balanced growth equilibrium at point E.

Under the assumption of perfect foresight our procedure for computing an intertemporal equilibrium can be divided into two steps. The first step is to calculate the unique balanced growth equilibrium

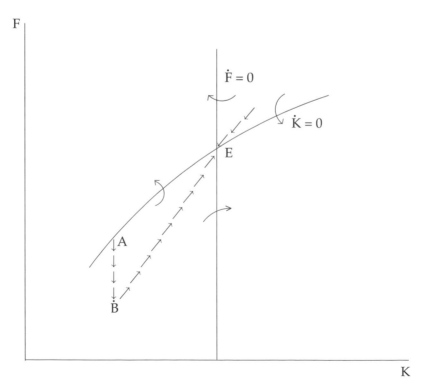

Figure 10.1
Equilibrium time path

associated with a given tax policy. Under the assumptions of constant returns to scale in production, homothetic preferences, and Harrod-neutral technical change the quantities of consumption and investment goods and of capital and labor services that characterize an equilibrium are homogeneous of degree one in the time endowment. We can scale these quantities relative to the time endowment.

Similarly, the demand and supply functions by the business and household sectors for all commodity groups included in our model are homogeneous of degree zero in the prices. Furthermore, all financial magnitudes, including the tax bases for sales, income, and property taxes, are homogeneous of degree one in the prices. Accordingly, we can express all prices relative to a numeraire commodity. We take the price of labor services in efficiency units as the numeraire and express all prices and financial magnitude relative to this price.

Given the balanced growth equilibrium of the economy as at point E, the second step in computing an intertemporal equilibrium is to select an appropriate initial level of full consumption, as at the point B. The main difficulty in this second step arises from the fact that the unique transition path to balanced growth equilibrium is unstable, so that errors in the initial level of full consumption are quickly magnified. We employ the multiple shooting technique described by Lipton, Poterba, Sachs and Summers (1982) in calculating the transition path.

Up to this point we have considered the intertemporal utility functions (10.9) as a representation of household preferences. In evaluating alternative tax policies we can interpret this function as an intertemporal social welfare function. The time path of full consumption is determined as part of the intertemporal equilibrium of the U.S. economy corresponding to each tax policy. We associate a level of social welfare, say U, with each policy. This level of social welfare can be calculated from the time path of full consumption per capita.

To evaluate the impact of alternative tax policies, we find it useful to express changes in social welfare in terms of changes in full wealth WF. We first consider the time path of the price of full consumption associated with current tax policy. We define *money metric social welfare* at the difference between the full wealth required to attain the level of social welfare after the policy change and the wealth required to attain the level of welfare before the change, both evaluated at prices before the change in policy.

If money metric social welfare is positive, social welfare is increased by the policy change; otherwise, the level of social welfare is decreased or left unaffected. Since we employ a model of household behavior based on a single infinitely lived consumer, our measure of social welfare excludes all distributional considerations. As a consequence, we provide measures of potential gains in social welfare associated with alternative tax policies. Measures of the actual gains in social welfare would require the incorporation of changes in the distribution of welfare among individuals.[11]

10.4   Conclusion

In this paper we have constructed an intertemporal general equilibrium model of the U.S. economy. The purpose of this model is to provide a quantitative measure of the loss in potential economic welfare in the United States due to inefficiency in the allocation of capital. Although general equilibrium techniques are widely utilized in modeling the impact of tax policy,[12] our approach embodies two distinctive features. First, we have simplified the representation of preferences by endowing the household sector with perfect foresight. This implies that market clearing prices at each point of time incorporate the present and future impact of changes in tax policy.

Our approach to general equilibrium modeling of the tax policy is also distinctive in describing technology and preferences by means of econometric models. These models incorporate all of the restrictions implied by economic theories of producer and consumer behavior. These include absence of money illusion or homogeneity of degree zero in prices, summability of budget shares to unity, symmetry of the appropriate Slutsky matrices, and curvature conditions that imply upward sloping supply functions and downward sloping demand functions.

Econometric methods appropriate for general equilibrium modeling require the estimation of parameters within systems of nonlinear simultaneous equations. Furthermore, economic theories of producer and consumer behavior imply equality and inequality restrictions that must be incorporated into the estimation process. These restrictions arise within individual equations and across equations and are highly nonlinear.

Although our approach to modeling the impact of tax policy appears to be promising, the research required to exploit this approach is just beginning. Perhaps the most important direction for future research is to extend our approach to a model with overlapping generations.[13] As Barro (1974) has demonstrated, such a model can be represented by means of a single infinitely lived consumer only under very stringent conditions on preferences and bequest motives. Our econometric methodology can be extended to incorporate differences in preferences among consumers along the lines suggested by Jorgenson (1984).

We have emphasized that our evaluation of alternative tax policies has excluded equity considerations. Our intertemporal social welfare function is defined on the time path of full consumption at the aggregate level. Aggregate full consumption can be interpreted as a measure of potential economic welfare, following Bentzel's (1970) pioneering approach to the analysis of income distributions. The actual level of welfare can be evaluated by the techniques of Jorgenson and Slesnick (1984), utilizing information on the distribution of individual welfare derived from an econometric model of the household sector.

Our next objective is to analyze the impact of U.S. tax policy on the efficiency of capital allocation. In a sequel[14] to this paper, we consider the extensive changes in policy that were introduced by the Reagan Administration in 1981 and 1982. We plan to compare capital allocation under the Reagan policy with allocation under tax policy prevailing in 1980 before the policy change. We also plan to consider alternative approaches to tax reform.

Appendix: List of Instrumental Variables

I1: constant (a vector of 1s)
I2: effective tax rate, labor services
I3: effective tax rate, imports
I4: time available (excluding time necessary for personal maintenance)
I5: domestic population (including armed forces overseas)
I6: implicit deflator, supply of labor services
I7: implicit deflator, general government purchases of labor services
I8: government transfer payments other than social insurance funds, less personal transfer payments to foreigners, less personal non-tax payments
I9: private national wealth
I10: $I4*(1 + 0.020224)**I14$
I11: value of imports
I12: price of consumption goods, imports
I13: $I6/(1 + 0.020224)**I14$
I14: time (T = 0 in 1972)

Notes

1. Intertemporal production theory is discussed by e.g. Fisher (1930), Hicks (1946), Lindahl (1939) and Malinvaud (1953). Classic references on capital theory are Åkerman (1923), Walras (1954) and Wicksell (1934b).

2. The taxation of income from capital in the United States is discussed in detail in King and Fullerton (1984, Chapter 6, pp. 193–267). This volume also contains descriptions of capital taxation in Sweden, the United Kingdom and West Germany and international comparisons.

3. Distributional considerations are employed in modeling intertemporal preferences by Bentzel and Berg (1983) and in modeling atemporal preferences by Jorgenson, Lau and Stoker (1980, 1981, 1982).

4. Intertemporal general equilibrium models of the impact of tax policy under perfect foresight are presented by Chamley (1981), Hall (1971a), Sinn (1981) and Turnovsky (1982).

5. The methodology for modeling produced behavior outlined in this section is presented in detail by Jorgenson (1983, 1984).

6. Two-stage allocation is discussed by Blackorby, Primont and Russell (1978, esp. pp. 103–216). They provide references to the literature.

7. The translog price function was introduced by Christensen, Jorgenson and Lau (1971, 1973). The translog indirect utility function that underlies the model of the household sector presented below was introduced by Christensen, Jorgenson and Lau (1975).

8. The properties of intertemporally additive utility functions are discussed by Arrow and Kurz (1970).

9. Equivalent variations in income or total expenditure were introduced as measures of economic welfare by Hicks (1942). Equivalent variations in wealth provide an exact measure of economic welfare that is analogous to the equivalent variations in total expenditure given by Jorgenson, Lau and Stoker (1981, 1982).

10. We employ the estimates of marginal tax rates under the individual income tax compiled by Barro and Sahasakul (1983).

11. Measures of social welfare incorporating inequality in the distribution of individual welfare are given by Jorgenson and Slesnick (1984).

12. See e.g. the studies contained in the collection edited by Feldstein (1983); a survey of general equilibrium modeling of tax policy has been provided by Fullerton, Henderson and Shoven (1984).

13. General equilibrium models with overlapping generations have been applied to the analysis of tax policy under perfect foresight by Auerbach and Kotlikoff (1983) and Auerbach, Kotlikoff and Skinner (1983).

14. Jorgenson and Yun (1986b) "Tax Policy and Capital Allocation," in *The Scandinavian Journal of Economics*, Vol. 88, No. 2: with a comment by Karl G. Jungenfelt.

11

Tax Policy and Capital Allocation

Dale W. Jorgenson and Kun-Young Yun

11.1   Introduction

The purpose of this paper is to analyze the impact of U.S. tax policy on the efficiency of capital allocation. To achieve this objective we employ an intertemporal general equilibrium model of the U.S. economy. This model is kindred in spirit to the model of the Swedish economy developed by Ragnar Bentzel (1978). We have implemented our model econometrically for annual data on the United States, covering the period 1955–1980.

Our general equilibrium model employs a description of technology based on capital as a factor of production. The central concepts of capital theory—capital assets, capital services, and investment—are inessential to the development of intertemporal production theory. However, these concepts provide additional structure that greatly facilitates the implementation of our econometric model of producer behavior.[1]

We have further simplified the representation of technology by assuming that capital is perfectly malleable. The process of capital accumulation results in a single stock of capital at each point of time. This capital is allocated among alternative uses so as to equalize after tax rates of return. The U.S. tax structure affects capital allocation through the taxation of income from capital, the taxation of investment goods production, and the taxation of property.[2]

To facilitate the implementation of our econometric model of consumer behavior, we have simplified the description of preferences. Our model is based on the preferences of a single infinitely lived consumer. This rules out distributional considerations in the modeling of consumer behavior.[3] To further simplify the description of preferences we endow the infinitely lived consumer with perfect foresight about future prices.

Our intertemporal general equilibrium of the U.S. economy balances supplies and demands for all products and factors of production. Equilibrium at each point of time links the past and the future through markets for investment goods and capital services. Capital assets are accumulated as a result of past investments, net of replacement requirements. The price of acquisition of an asset is equal to the present value of future capital services, including depreciation.

We begin the paper by presenting a detailed model of the provisions of U.S. tax law that are applicable to income from capital in section 11.2. This model is based on the rental price of capital services introduced by Jorgenson (1963). We incorporate the tax structure into the rental price by requiring that the acquisition cost of an asset after taxes is equal to the present value of future after tax rentals.

In modeling the taxation of income from capital in the U.S., it is essential to distinguish among assets held in different sectors, as emphasized by Harberger (1962). Income from capital held in the corporate sector is subject to taxation at both corporate and individual levels. Income from noncorporate capital is taxed only at the individual level, while income from household sector is not taxed at either level.

U.S. tax law provides for recovery of the costs of acquisition of assets through capital consumption allowances and an investment tax credit. Differences in provisions for capital recovery have resulted in important discrepancies in the tax treatment of income from different types of assets. In representing the U.S. tax structure we distinguish between long-lived and short-lived assets within each sector of the economy.

In section 11.3 we undertake the construction of an econometric general equilibrium model of the U.S. economy. This model encompasses the features of the tax structure outlined in section 11.2. We distinguish among four commodity groups—consumption and investment goods and capital and labor services. We ignore costs of adjustment for capital stock, so that capital services are perfectly malleable.

We develop econometric models of the business and household sectors of the U.S. economy, based on the methodology presented by Jorgenson (1983, 1984). The business sector produces consumption and investment goods from inputs of labor services and the services of noncorporate and corporate assets. At a second stage the business sector allocates the value of noncorporate and corporate capital inputs between the services of long-lived and short-lived assets.

Our econometric model of the household sector is based on an intertemporal utlity function that is additive in levels of full consumption in all time periods. Full consumption is an aggregate of the consumption of goods, household capital services, and leisure time. The household sector allocates the value of household capital between the services of long-lived and short-lived assets at a second stage.

In section 11.4 we define an intertemporal equilibrium of the U.S. economy. Equilibrium is determined by market clearing conditions for consumption and investment goods and for capital and labor services in each time period. In addition, the time path of consumption must satisfy the conditions for intertemporal optimality of the household sector, assuming perfect foresight. Finally, the time path of investment must satisfy requirements for capital accumulation by the business and household sectors.

The government sector raises revenue through taxes on income from capital and labor services, sales taxes on the production of consumption and investment goods, and property taxes. This revenue is used to finance purchases of consumption and investment goods and labor services. In addition, government revenue finances transfers to the household sector and government enterprises employ labor services and produce consumption goods.

Under perfect foresight there exists a unique balanced growth equilibrium of the U.S. economy corresponding to any stationary tax policy. In balanced growth equilibrium the quantities of all commodities grow at a rate that is equal to the rate of growth of the time endowment of the household sector. Our model determines only relative prices and these prices are stationary in balanced growth equilibrium.[4]

In section 11.5 we employ the intertemporal equilibrium paths of the U.S. economy corresponding to alternative tax policies to evaluate proposals for tax reform. Given a change in tax policy, there is a unique transition path to the balanced growth equilibrium corresponding to the new policy. To evaluate each tax reform proposal we interpret the level of utility associated with the time path of full consumption as a measure of social welfare.

As a basis for analyzing the impact of changes in tax policy, we first consider the future growth of the U.S. economy under current tax policy. We then convert the differences in levels of social welfare associated with alternative tax policies into equivalent changes in U.S.

national wealth. These changes in wealth provide a money measure of the social welfare associated with alternative tax policies.

As alternatives to current tax policy we first consider the policy prevailing in 1980, prior to the substantial changes introduced under the Reagan Administration. We then consider proposals for further tax reform. These proposals include changes in existing tax provisions to achieve greater neutrality in the treatment of different assets. They also include replacement of direct taxes on income from capital by indirect taxes on consumption.[5]

In section 11.6 we provide a brief summary of our major findings. We find that replacement of taxes on income from capital by a consumption tax would produce dramatic gains in potential social welfare in the United States. We conclude with an outline of future research on tax policy and capital allocation. This research includes a detailed study of the incidence of the U.S. tax system and the development of optimal tax policies for the United States.

11.2   Tax Policy

Our first objective is to model the provisions of U.S. tax law that are applicable to income from capital. We introduce the characteristic features of the tax law into the annualized cost or rental price of each type of asset. For this purpose we employ the concept of rental price originated by Jorgenson (1963, 1965, 1967) and further developed by Hall and Jorgenson (1967, 1969a, 1971a).

To summarize the impact of U.S. tax law on income from capital we introduce the notion of an effective tax rate for each type of asset.[6] Maximization of private wealth results in an efficient allocation of capital only if the effective tax rate is the same for all assets. Discrepancies in the tax treatment of different types of assets result in sizable obstacles to efficient capital allocation. Elimination of these discrepancies would require major reforms in the U.S. tax system.

In order to consider the impact of alternative tax reforms we construct a general equilibrium model of the U.S. economy that encompasses the critical features of U.S. tax policy. For this purpose we present econometric models of the business and household sectors of the U.S. economy in section 11.3. We incorporate these models into an intertemporal general equilibrium model in section 11.4. We apply the resulting model to the evaluation of specific proposals for the tax reform in section 11.5.

11.2.1   Rental Price

The rental price of capital services is defined, implicitly, by equality between the cost of acquisition of one unit of an asset at time t, say $q(t)$, and the present value of future rentals from that asset. In the absence of taxation this equality can be written:

$$q(t) = \int_t^\infty e^{-\rho(s-t)} e^{-\delta(s-t)} c(s) \, ds. \tag{11.1}$$

In this formula the rental price of capital services at time s, $c(s)$, is multiplied by the quantity of capital services at time s, $e^{-\delta(s-t)}$. The rental value at time s, $e^{-\delta(s-t)} c(s)$, is discounted at the nominal rate of return ρ.

We have assumed that the quantity of capital services resulting from the acquisition of one unit of an asset at time t declines exponentially at the rate of economic depreciation δ.[7] Differentiating both sides of the equality between the cost of acquisition and the present value of future rentals, we obtain:

$$c = q(\rho - \pi + \delta), \tag{11.2}$$

where $\pi = \dot{q}/q$ is the rate of inflation in the price of assets and ρ π is the rate of return corrected for inflation.

The rental price of an asset is the product of the acquisition price and an annualization factor. This factor is the sum of the rate of return corrected for inflation and the rate of depreciation. We can solve the expression (11.2) for the annualization factor, obtaining:

$$\frac{c}{q} = \rho - \pi + \delta. \tag{11.3}$$

The acquisition cost q, the inflation rate π, and the depreciation rate δ may differ among assets. Efficiency in the allocation of capital requires that the addition to wealth generated by one dollar's worth of investment must be the same for all assets. This addition is measured by the nominal rate of return ρ.

In order to represent the effect of the U.S. tax structure on capital allocation we distinguish among assets held in the household, noncorporate, and corporate sectors. Capital held in the household sector is subject to property taxes, but income from household property is not taxed at either individual or corporate levels. Income from noncorporate capital is subject to the individual income tax, while both individual and corporate income taxes are levied on income from corporate capital. Corporate and noncorporate capital are also subject to property taxes.

In representing the impact of U.S. tax law we also distinguish between long-lived and short-lived assets. Depreciable assets in the noncorporate and corporate sectors generate capital consumption allowances that can be treated as an expense for tax purposes. Since 1962 producers' durable equipment has been eligible for an investment tax credit that can be deducted from tax liability. These provisions have resulted in important differences in the tax treatment of income from different types of assets within the noncorporate and corporate sectors.

11.2.2   U.S. Tax Law

In order to represent the characteristic features of U.S. tax law for income from capital we require the following notation:

c_h, c_m, c_q — rental prices of capital services in the household (h), noncorporate (m) and corporate (q) sectors.

i — nominal interest rate.

k — rate of investment tax credit.

r_h, r_m, r_q — rates of return, corrected for inflation, in the household, noncorporate, and corporate sectors.

u_k, u_q — rates of taxation of income from capital at the individual (k) and corporate (q) levels.

z_m, z_q — present values of capital consumption allowances in the noncorporate and corporate sectors.

u_h^p, u_m^p, u_q^p — rates of taxation of property held in the household, noncorporate, and corporate sectors.

β_h, β_m, β_q — ratios of debt to the value of assets held in the household, noncorporate, and corporate sectors.

γ_h, γ_m, γ_q — ratios of tax rates on accrued capital gains to tax rates on ordinary income in the household, noncorporate, and corporate sectors.

ρ — rate of dividend payout in the corporate sector.

We first consider the rental price of assets held in the household sector. Income from these assets is not subject to tax, but property taxes are treated as an expense for tax purposes at the individual level. Interest payments on debt required to finance household capital—for example, mortgage payments on owner-occupied housing—are also treated as an expense. Finally, realized capital gains on household property are taxable at capital gains rates, except for gains on owner-occupied housing that are reinvested. Tax liabilities on accrued capital gains can be deferred until realization. In addition, the basis for an asset is written up to its value at the death of the owner. All of these tax provisions reduce the effective tax rate on accrued capital gains.

We can express the features of U.S. tax law that apply to income from household capital in terms of the annualization factor that converts the cost of acquisition of an asset q into a rental price c_h:

$$\frac{c_h}{q} = r_h + \delta + (1 - u_k)u_h^p. \tag{11.4}$$

We assume that the household sector has a maximum debt capacity and that the ratio of debt to the value of capital at replacement cost β_h is maintained at this maximum to take advantage of the tax deductibility of interest rates. Under this assumption the household rate of return r_h is a weighted average of rates of return to equity and debt on household assets, corrected for inflation:

$$r_h = (1 - \beta_h)[\rho - (1 - \gamma_h u_k)\pi] + \beta_h[(1 - u_k)i - \pi]. \tag{11.5}$$

Similarly, we can represent the features of U.S. tax law applicable to noncorporate income by means of an annualization factor. The cost of acquisition of an asset by the noncorporate sector is offset by an investment tax credit k that reduces tax liability. We can view capital consumption allowances as an additional offset by introducing the present value of these allowances:

$$z_m = \int_t^\infty e^{-(1 - u_k)i(s - t)}D(s - t) \, ds. \tag{11.6}$$

In this formula the level of capital consumption allowances at time s on one dollar's worth of investment at time t is denoted $D(s - t)$. We discount capital consumption allowances at the nominal interest rate,

allowing for tax deductibility of interest expense at the individual
level.

The acquisition cost of an asset after taxes $(1 - k - u_k z_m)q$ is equal to
the present value of future rentals after individual income taxes
$(1 - u_k)(c_m - u_m^p q)$, so that the annualization factor for assets held in
the noncorporate sector takes the form:

$$\frac{c_m}{q} = \frac{1 - k - u_k z_m}{1 - u_k}(r_m + \delta) + u_m^p. \tag{11.7}$$

As before, we assume that the ratio of debt to the value of capital at
replacement cost β_m is fixed. Under this assumption the noncorporate
rate of return r_m is a weighted average of rates of return to equity and
debt on noncorporate assets, corrected for inflation:

$$r_m = (1 - \beta_m)[\rho - (1 - \gamma_m u_k)\pi] + \beta_m[(1 - u_k)i - \pi].$$

Finally, we can represent the impact of U.S. tax law on corporate
income in terms of an annualization factor. In the corporate sector the
cost of acquisition of an asset is reduced by the investment tax credit k
and the corporate tax rate u_q multiplied by the present value of capital
consumption on allowances z_q. We discount capital consumption
allowances at the nominal interest rate, allowing for tax deductibility
of interest expense at the corporate level. The acquisition cost after
taxes $(1 - k - u_q z_q)q$ is equal to the present value of future rentals after
corporate income taxes $(1 - u_q)(c_q - u_q^p q)$, so that the annualization
factor takes the form:

$$\frac{c_q}{q} = \frac{1 - k - u_q z_q}{1 - u_q}(r_q + \delta) + u_q^p. \tag{11.8}$$

In the literature on corporate income taxation the rate of return r_q is
subject to two alternative and, unfortunately, conflicting interpretations.[8] The "traditional" view, which we adopt, is that the marginal
source of equity finance in the corporate sector is the issuing of new
shares. The acquisition cost of assets after taxes must be equal to the
increase in the value of the outstanding shares.

We assume that dividends are a fixed proportion ϕ of corporate
income available for investment after economic depreciation at the
rate δ and, as before, that the ratio of debt to the value of capital at
replacement cost β_q is fixed. Under these assumptions the corporate

rate of return r_q is a weighted average of rates of return to equity and debt on corporate assets, corrected for inflation:

$$r_q = (1 - \beta_q) \frac{[\rho - (1 - \gamma_q u_k)\pi]}{1 - \theta u_k} + \beta_q [(1 - u_q)i - \pi]. \tag{11.9}$$

In this formula θu_k is the effective tax rate at the individual level on income to holders of corporate equity; the parameter θ takes the form:

$$\theta = \phi + (1 - \phi)\gamma_q.$$

The alternative or "new" view of the corporate rate of return is that the marginal source of equity finance in the corporate sector is retained earnings. In the traditional view the corporate firm can reduce the effective tax rate at the individual level on income to holders of corporate equity by increasing retained earnings and reducing dividend payments. In fact, from this point of view there is no reason to pay dividends.

Shareholders are indifferent between dividends and retained earnings in the new view. However, on this view the corporate firm would serve the interests of its shareholders by liquidating assets and repurchasing its outstanding shares. We conclude that neither view provides a completely satisfactory explanation of corporate financial policy. Our analysis of the impact of U.S. tax policy on capital allocation could easily be modified to incorporate the new view rather than the traditional view of the corporate rate of return.

11.2.3   Capital Allocation

Maximization of private wealth requires that the addition to wealth generated by the acquisition of one dollar's worth of investment, net of depreciation and taxes, is the same for all assets. This addition to wealth is measured by the private rate of return before correction for inflation ρ. Efficient allocation of capital requires that the addition to wealth generated by the acquisition of one dollar's worth of an asset, net of depreciation, is the same for all assets. This addition is measured by the social rate of return before correction for inflation, say $\sigma + \pi$, where:

$$\sigma = \frac{c}{q} - \delta. \tag{11.10}$$

Since assets held in different sectors differ enormously in tax treatment under the individual and corporate income taxes, we would expect to find that U.S. tax law presents formidable barriers to the efficient allocation of capital. In addition, the tax rules for capital recovery within a sector, including the investment tax credit and capital consumption allowances, differ drastically among different types of assets, giving rise to further obstacles to efficient allocation.

To summarize the impact of U.S. tax law on income from capital, we find it useful to employ the notion of an effective tax rate, say e. The effective tax rate is defined by the reduction in the social rate of return σ that results in the private rate of return after taxes, corrected for inflation:

$$(1 - e)\,\sigma = \rho - \pi. \tag{11.11}$$

We can express the effective tax rate on income generated from assets held in the household sector, say e_h, in terms of the household rate of return, the rate of taxation on income from capital at the personal level, and the rate of taxation on household property:

$$e_h = 1 - \frac{\rho - \pi}{r_h + (1 - u_k)u_h^p}. \tag{11.12}$$

The effective tax rate on income generated from assets held in the noncorporate sector, say e_m, depends on the noncorporate rate of return, the rate of taxation of capital income at the individual level, and the rate of taxation on noncorporate property. The effective tax rate depends on provisions for capital recovery through the investment tax credit and capital consumption allowances:

$$e_m = 1 - \frac{\rho - \pi}{\dfrac{1 - k - u_k z_m}{1 - u_k}(r_m + \delta) + u_m^p - \delta}. \tag{11.13}$$

This rate depends on the rate of depreciation δ. It also depends on the rate of inflation.

The effective tax rate on income from corporate assets, say e_q, is analogous to the rate for noncorporate income. The rate of taxation of capital income at the corporate level, the rate of taxation of corporate property, and the corporate rate of return replace the corresponding noncorporate rates:

$$e_q = 1 - \frac{\rho - \pi}{\dfrac{1 - k - u_q z_q}{1 - u_q} (r_q + \delta) + u_q^p - \delta} . \tag{11.14}$$

As before, the effective tax rate depends on the rate of depreciation and the rate of inflation.

Maximization of private wealth results in an efficient allocation of capital only if the effective tax rate is the same for all assets. For a given rate of inflation this could be achieved through a system of first-year capital recovery allowances, as proposed by Auerbach and Jorgenson (1980). These allowances would replace the offsets to the cost of acquisition of assets provided by the present value of capital consumption allowances in the noncorporate sector $u_k z_m$ and the corporate sector $u_q z_q$. Alternatively, equality among effective tax rates could be achieved through a system of investment tax credits, as proposed by Brown (1981).

Unfortunately, neither the system of first-year capital recovery allowances nor the system of investment tax credits eliminates the dependence of effective tax rates on the rate of inflation. Tax deductibility of interest expense and the response of nominal interest rates to changes in the rate of inflation provide additional channels for inflation to alter effective tax rates.[9] In addition, first-year capital recovery allowances or investment tax credits would have to cover income from household capital as well as income from corporate and noncorporate capital.

Finally, intertemporal efficiency in the allocation of capital requires that the social rate of return σ is equal to the private rate of return after taxes, corrected for inflation. Under this condition all effective tax rates must be equal to zero. For example, the revenue now raised by individual and corporate income taxes and by taxation of property could be replaced by a consumption-base value added tax or a payroll tax.

A consumption-base tax could be implemented by altering the treatment of investment expenditures and interest expense at the individual and corporate levels. Investment expenditures could be treated as an expense and tax deductions for interest expenses could be eliminated. Property taxes could be treated as an offset to tax liability at the individual level. A variation on this approach would be to abolish the corporate income tax and to apply consumption tax rules to income from investments at the individual level. In effect, no taxes would be levied on returns to investment so long as they are reinvested.[10]

11.3   Technology and Preferences

Our next objective is to construct a general equilibrium model of the U.S. economy that encompasses the provisions of tax policy described in the preceding section. A distinctive feature of our model is that we employ econometric methods for estimating the unknown parameters that characterize technology and preferences. The resulting econometric model encompasses the restrictions implied by economic theories of producer and consumer behavior.

To estimate the unknown parameters of our econometric models of the business and household sectors, we have constructed a system of national accounts for the United States, covering the period 1955–1980. These accounts are based on the accounting system originated by Christensen and Jorgenson (1973) and further developed by Jorgenson (1980) and Jorgenson and Sullivan (1981). This system of accounts includes income and expenditure accounts for the business and household sectors in both current and constant prices.

Our system of national accounts includes expenditures by the business sector on capital services, disaggregated between noncorporate and corporate capital services. Within each of these categories the demand for capital services is further broken down between the services of long-lived and short-lived assets. This system also includes expenditures by the household sector on capital services, broken down between the services of long-lived and short-lived assets. The prices of capital services incorporate parameters that describe the U.S. tax structure.

11.3.1   Commodities

In our general equilibrium model we distinguish among four separate commodity groups. We employ the following notation for the commodity groups included in the model:

C — private national consumption, excluding household capital services.

I — private national investment, including investment in consumers' durables

K — private national capital stock, including the stock of household capital

L — labor services.

Our concepts of consumption and investment correspond closely to the concepts employed in the U.S. National Income and Product Accounts. An important difference between our accounts and the official U.S. national accounts is in the treatment of consumers' durables. Purchases of consumers' durables are included in investment and excluded from consumption in our accounts. The capital stock includes stocks of consumers' durables.

A complete system of notation includes quantities of consumption and investment goods, labor services, and capital services in each of the three sectors of the economy—household, noncorporate, and corporate:

CE — supply of consumption goods by government enterprise

CG — government purchases of consumption goods

CS — supply of consumption goods by private enterprise

F — full consumption

HD — household capital services

HL — household capital services from long-lived assets

HS — household capital services from short-lived assets

IG — government purchases of investment goods

IS — supply of investment goods by private enterprise

K — capital stock

KD — capital services

LD — private enterprise purchases of labor services

LE — government enterprise purchases of labor services

LG — general government purchases of labor services

LH — time endowment

LJ — leisure time

LU — unemployment

MD — noncorporate capital services

ML — noncorporate capital services from long-lived assets

MS — noncorporate capital services from short-lived assets

QD— corporate capital services

QL — corporate capital services from long-lived assets

QS — corporate capital services from short-lived assets.

To denote prices we simply place a *P* before the corresponding symbol for quantity. For example *PC* denotes the price paid by the household sector for consumption goods.

11.3.2   Business Sector

We next present an econometric model for the business sector.[11] This model is based on a labor requirements function, giving labor input as a function of outputs of consumption and investment goods and inputs of noncorporate and corporate capital services. Required labor input also depends on time as an index of the level of technology. Producer equilibrium under constant returns to scale implies the existence of a price function, giving the price of labor input as a function of the prices of the two outputs, capital inputs, and time. The price function must be homogeneous of degree one, nondecreasing, and convex in the prices of outputs and inputs.

In addition, we assume that the price function is homothetically separable in the prices of capital services from long-lived and short-lived assets in the noncorporate and corporate sectors. Under homothetic separability our model of producer behavior is based on a two-stage allocation process.[12] In the first stage the value of labor input is allocated among consumption and investment goods outputs and noncorporate and corporate capital inputs. In the second stage the value of each of these capital inputs is allocated between long-lived and short-lived assets.

To represent the first stage of our model of production for the business sector we require some additional notation. We first define the shares of outputs and inputs in the value of labor input by:

$$v_C = \frac{PCS \cdot CS}{PLD \cdot LD}, \; v_I = \frac{PIS \cdot IS}{PLD \cdot LD}, \; v_M = \frac{PMD \cdot MD}{PLD \cdot LD}, \; v_Q = -\frac{PQD \cdot QD}{PLD \cdot LD}.$$

Outputs are valued in producers' prices, while inputs are valued in purchasers' prices. In addition, we require the notation:

$v = (v_C, v_I, v_M, v_Q)$ — vector of value shares

$\ln P = (\ln PCS, \ln PIS, \ln PMD, \ln PQD)$ — vector of logarithms of price of outputs and inputs.

T — time as an index of technology.

We assume that the business sector allocates the shares of outputs and inputs in the value of labor input in accord with the price function:

$$\ln PLD = \ln P' \, \alpha_p + \alpha_T \cdot T + \frac{1}{2} \ln P' \, B_{PP} \ln P$$

$$+ \ln P' \, \beta_{PT} \cdot T + \frac{1}{2} \beta_{TT} \cdot T^2. \tag{11.15}$$

The price of labor input is a transcendental or, more specifically, exponential function of the logarithms of the prices of outputs and inputs. We refer to this form as the transcendental logarithmic price function or, more simply, the translog price function, indicating the role of the variables that enter the price function.[13] In this representation the scalars $\{\alpha_T, \beta_{TT}\}$, the vectors $\{\alpha_P, \beta_{PT}\}$, and the matrix B_{PP} are constant parameters.

The value shares can be expressed in terms of the logarithmic derivatives of the price function with respect to the logarithms of the prices of outputs and inputs:

$$v = \frac{\partial \ln PLD}{\partial \ln P}. \tag{11.16}$$

Applying this relationship to the translog price function, we obtain the system of value shares:

$$v = \alpha_P + B_{PP} \ln P + \beta_{PT} \cdot T. \tag{11.17}$$

Similarly, we can introduce the rate of growth of labor efficiency as a measure of technical change. We can define this measure as the rate of growth of the price of labor input with respect to time, holding the prices of outputs and inputs constant:

$$v_T = \frac{\partial \ln PLD}{\partial T}. \tag{11.18}$$

For the translog price function this relationship takes the form:

$$v_T = \alpha_T + \beta_{PT} \ln P + \beta_{TT} \cdot T. \tag{11.19}$$

To assure the existence of a balanced growth equilibrium for our intertemporal general equilibrium model we impose the condition that technical change must be Harrod-neutral. This implies that the parameters β_{PT} and β_{TT} are equal to zero. Under Harrod-neutral technical change we can redefine labor input in terms of efficiency units, so that the price function (11.15) can be represented in a form that is invariant with respect to time. For this purpose we can introduce the price of labor input measured in efficiency units, say PLD^*:

$$PLD^* = e^{-\alpha_T T} \, PLD. \tag{11.20}$$

The first stage of our model of production for the business sector consists of a system of equations giving the shares of outputs and inputs in the value of labor input and the rate of growth of labor efficiency as functions of relative prices and time. To formulate an econometric model we add a stochastic component to these equations. Since the rate of growth of labor efficiency is not directly observable, we consider a form of the model with autocorrelated disturbances. We then transform the data to eliminate autocorrelation.

In our intertemporal general equilibrium model the prices of outputs and inputs are endogenous variables. We estimate the unknown parameters of our model by methods appropriate for systems of nonlinear simultaneous equations, using instrumental variables that can be taken as exogenous to the model. A list of these intrumental variables is given in the Appendix to this paper. Estimates of the unknown parameters of our econometric model of production are obtained by the method of nonlinear three stage least squares introduced by Jorgenson and Laffont (1974).

We estimate the unknown parameters of our econometric model of production under the restrictions implied by Harrod-neutrality. In addition, we require that the parameters satisfy restrictions associated with summability—the condition that the value shares sum to unity— homogeneity of degree zero of the value shares and convexity of the price function in the prices of outputs and inputs, and symmetry of the matrix of parameters B_{PP}. Estimates of the parameters satisfying these restrictions are given in table 11.1.

The second stage of our model of production for the business sector consists of two submodels that allocate the values of noncorporate and corporate capital inputs between the services of long-lived and short-lived assets. We can denote the shares of the services of these

Table 11.1
Econometric model of producer behavior

Parameter	Estimate	Standard error
First stage submodel:		
α_C	0.884742	0.006072
α_I	0.518735	0.004920
α_M	−0.104489	0.003262
α_Q	−0.298989	0.003004
α_T	0.008883	0.011245
β_{CC}	0.821256	0.148522
β_{CI}	−0.744423	0.106604
β_{CM}	−0.084895	0.032768
β_{CQ}	0.008062	0.046366
β_{II}	0.457081	0.084859
β_{IM}	0.085760	0.025879
β_{IQ}	0.201583	0.029072
β_{MM}	0.011334	0.016599
β_{MQ}	−0.012200	0.013489
β_{QQ}	−0.197445	0.021768
Noncorporate capital submodel:		
α_S^M	0.185966	0.023888
β_{SS}^M	0.066618	0.022573
Corporate capital submodel:		
α_S^Q	0.381647	0.014020
β_{SS}^Q	0.019961	0.031542

two classes of assets in the values of capital input in the two sectors by:

$$v_{ML} = \frac{PML \cdot ML}{PMD \cdot MD}, \quad v_{MS} = \frac{PMS \cdot MS}{PMD \cdot MD}, \quad v_{QL} = \frac{PQL \cdot QL}{PQD \cdot QD},$$

$$v_{QS} = \frac{PQS \cdot QS}{PQD \cdot QD}.$$

As before, we find it convenient to employ vector notation:

$v_M = (v_{ML}, v_{MS})$ — vector of value shares in noncorporate capital input

$v_Q = (v_{QL}, v_{QS})$ — vector of value shares in corporate capital input

$\ln PM = (\ln PML, \ln PMS)$ — vector of logarithms of prices of capital inputs in the noncorporate sector

$\ln PQ = (\ln PQL, \ln PQS)$ — vector of logarithms of prices of capital inputs in the corporate sector.

We assume that the noncorporate and corporate sectors allocate the shares of long-lived and short-lived assets in the value of capital input in accord with the translog price functions:

$$\ln PMD = \ln PM' \alpha_{PM} + \frac{1}{2} \ln PM' B_{PM} \ln PM,$$

$$\ln PQD = \ln PQ' \alpha_{PQ} + \frac{1}{2} \ln PQ' B_{PQ} \ln PQ. \tag{11.21}$$

The value shares can be expressed in terms of the logarithmic derivatives of the price functions:

$$v_M = \alpha_{PM} + B_{PM} \ln PM,$$

$$v_Q = \alpha_{PQ} + B_{PQ} \ln PQ. \tag{11.22}$$

In our intertemporal general equilibrium model the prices of capital inputs are endogenous variables. We estimate the unknown parameters of the second stage of our model of production by the method of nonlinear three stage least squares, using the instrumental variables listed in the Appendix. We impose the restrictions associated with summability, homogeneity of degree zero of the value shares and concavity of the price functions in the prices of long-lived and short-lived capital inputs, and symmetry of the matrices B_{PM} and B_{PQ}. Estimates of the parameters satisfying these restrictions are given in table 11.1.

11.3.3 Household Sector

Our model of the household sector can be divided between intertemporal and atemporal stages. At the intertemporal stage we assume that the household allocates full wealth among time periods in accord with the linear logarithmic intertemporal utility function:[14]

$$U = \sum_{t=0}^{\infty} \left(\frac{1+n}{1+\alpha}\right)^t \ln \frac{F_t}{P_t}, \tag{11.23}$$

where P is the population, n is the rate of population growth and α is the rate of time preference.

Full wealth is defined as:

$$WF = \sum_{t=0}^{\infty} \frac{PF_t \cdot F_t}{\prod_{s=0}^{t}(1+\rho_s)}, \tag{11.24}$$

where ρ_s is the nominal private rate of return after all taxes. Under the optimal intertemporal consumption plan the growth rate of full consumption is given by:

$$\frac{F_t}{F_{t-1}} = \frac{PF_{t-1}}{PF_t} \cdot \frac{(1+\rho_t)(1+n)}{1+\alpha}. \tag{11.25}$$

To represent the atemporal stage of our model for the household sector, we first introduce the shares of consumption goods, household capital services, and leisure in the value of full consumption and the shares of the services of long-lived and short-lived assets in household capital services:

$$v_C = \frac{PC \cdot C}{PF \cdot F}, \quad v_{HD} = \frac{PHD \cdot HD}{PF \cdot F}, \quad v_{LJ} = \frac{PLJ \cdot LJ}{PF \cdot F};$$

$$v_{HL} = \frac{PHL \cdot HL}{PHD \cdot HD}, \quad v_{HS} = \frac{PHS \cdot HS}{PHD \cdot HD}.$$

As before, we find it convenient to employ vector notation:

$v_D = (v_C, v_{HD}, v_{LJ})$ — vector of value shares in full consumption

$v_H = (v_{HL}, v_{HS})$ — vector of value shares of household capital input

$\ln PD = (\ln PC, \ln PHD, \ln PLJ^*)$ — vector of logarithms of prices of consumption goods, household capital services and leisure;

note that the price of leisure is defined in terms of labor measured in efficiency units.

ln PH = (ln PHL, ln PHS) — vector of logarithms of prices of capital
inputs in the household sector.

We assume that the household sector allocates the shares of consumption goods, household capital services and leisure in the value of
full consumption in accord with the translog price index for full consumption:

$$\ln PF = \ln PD' \alpha_{PD} + \frac{1}{2} \ln PD' B_{PD} \ln PD. \tag{11.26}$$

Similarly, we assume that the household sector allocates the shares of
long-lived and short-lived assets in the value of capital input in accord
with the translog price index:

$$\ln PHD = \ln PH' \alpha_{PH} + \frac{1}{2} \ln PH' B_{PH} \ln PH. \tag{11.27}$$

The corresponding value shares can be expressed in terms of the logarithmic derivatives of the price functions:

$$v_D = \alpha_{PD} + B_{PD} \ln PD,$$
$$v_H = \alpha_{PH} + B_{PH} \ln PH. \tag{11.28}$$

We treat the prices of consumption goods, household capital services, and leisure and the prices of the services of long-lived and
short-lived assets as endogenous variables. We estimate the unknown
parameters of our atemporal model of consumption by the method of
nonlinear three stage least squares. We impose the restrictions associated with summability, homogeneity of degree zero of the value
shares and concavity of the price functions, and symmetry of the
matrices of parameters B_{PD} and B_{PH}. Estimates of the parameters satisfying these restrictions are given in table 11.2.

11.4   General Equilibrium Model

The purpose of this section is to outline a general equilibrium model
of the U.S. economy that incorporates the econometric models of business and household sectors that we have presented in the preceding
section. In each time period we determine prices so as to clear

Table 11.2
Econometric model of consumer behavior

Parameter	Estimate	Standard error
First stage submodel:		
α_C^D	0.188050	0.0011947
α_H^D	0.065590	0.0008922
α_L^D	0.746360	0.0009875
β_{CC}^D	0.096676	0.0129081
β_{CH}^D	−0.004293	0.0083668
β_{CL}^D	−0.092382	0.0114209
β_{HH}^D	0.050133	0.0028803
β_{HL}^D	−0.045840	0.0055592
β_{LL}^D	0.138222	0.0133601
Household capital submodel:		
α_S^D	0.504489	0.011362
β_{SS}^D	0.076729	0.009713

markets for consumption and investment goods and for capital and labor services. Under the assumption of perfect foresight the sequence of such prices must also satisfy the conditions for an intertemporal equilibrium of the U.S. economy.

The behavioral equations of our model include supply functions for consumption and investment goods and demand functions for capital and labor services by the business sector. The behavioral equations also include a supply function for labor services and demand functions for consumption goods and capital services by the household sector. The government sector raises revenue by taxation, purchases consumption goods, investment goods, and labor services, and transfers part of its revenues to the household sector.

In the following section we employ our intertemporal general equilibrium model to simulate the U.S. economy under alternative tax policies. We first compute the equilibrium time path of the U.S. economy corresponding to each alternative policy. We then measure the level of potential economic welfare along each time path by means of an intertemporal social welfare function. Finally, we convert differences in levels of potential welfare among different time paths into equivalent variations in the level of U.S. national wealth.[15]

11.4.1   Market Equilibrium

Our model incorporates markets for each of the four commodity groups—consumption and investment goods and capital and labor services. Supply and demand for consumption goods are equal, so that:

$$CS + CE = C + CG. \tag{11.29}$$

Similarly, supply and demand for investment good are equal, so that:

$$IS = I + IG. \tag{11.30}$$

The accumulation of capital is determined by an identity between capital stock at the end of each period the sum of beginning of period capital stock and investment net of replacement:

$$K = AI \cdot I + (1 - U)K(-1), \tag{11.31}$$

where AI converts investment into the sum of the change in capital stock and replacement and U is the replacement rate. The supply of capital services from the household sector is proportional to beginning of period capital stock:

$$KD = AK \cdot K(-1), \tag{11.32}$$

where AK converts capital stock at the beginning of the period into a flow of capital services.

For simplicity we have assumed that there are no costs of adjustment for capital stock, so that capital services are perfectly malleable. The supply of capital services is equal to the sum of capital input demands by the household, noncorporate, and corporate sectors:

$$KD = HL + HS + ML + MS + QL + QS. \tag{11.33}$$

Under this assumption the prices of the six different types of capital services are proportional to each other.

We take the rate of unemployment to be exogenous, so that labor supply is equal to the sum of labor demands by private enterprises, government enterprises, and general government, plus unemployment:

$$L = LD + LE + LG + LU. \tag{11.34}$$

In each time period the time endowment is equal to the sum of labor supply by the household sector and its demand for leisure:

$$LH = L + LJ. \tag{11.35}$$

11.4.2 Government

We have described markets for each of the four commodity groups included in our intertemporal general equilibrium model. We next outline the generation of government revenue through sales taxes on consumption and investment goods, income taxes on capital and labor services, and property taxes. We have presented the tax structure for income from capital in section 11.2, so that we focus attention in this section on sales taxes and taxes on labor income. We also consider the role of government enterprises and the allocation of government expenditure.

Government revenues from sales taxes on consumption goods, say RC, are generated by the identity:

$$RC = TC \cdot PCS \cdot CS, \tag{11.36}$$

where TC is the effective tax rate on the output of consumption goods at producers' prices. The prices paid by consumers differ from the prices received by producers, due to sales taxes:

$$PC = (1 + TC) PCS. \tag{11.37}$$

Similarly, government revenues from sales taxes on investment goods, say RI, are generated by the identity:

$$RI = TI \cdot PIS \cdot IS, \tag{11.38}$$

where TI is the effective tax rate on investment goods. The prices paid by investors differ from the prices received by producers:

$$PI = (1 + TI) PIS. \tag{11.39}$$

To model property taxes and the taxation of income from capital we first generate the revenue from taxation of property in the household, noncorporate, and corporate sectors by applying effective tax rates to the values of beginning of period capital stocks in all three sectors. The tax base for the corporate income tax is equal to the value of corporate capital services, less the sum of property taxes, capital consumption allowances, and interest expenses at the corporate level. Corporate tax liability is equal to the effective corporate tax rate applied to the corporate tax base, less the value of the investment tax credit at the corporate level.

To model the taxation of capital income through the individual income tax we first define an appropriate tax base. This tax base includes dividends and interest distributed by corporations and a proportion of retained earnings. Retained earnings generate accrued capital gains on holdings of corporate equity. The individual tax base for income from capital also includes the value of noncorporate capital services, less the sum of property taxes, capital consumption allowances, and interest expenses at the noncorporate level, and plus a proportion of capital gains accrued on noncorporate property.

Finally, the individual tax base for income from capital is reduced by property taxes and interest expenses and increased by a proportion of capital gains on household property. Individual tax liability for income from capital is equal to an effective tax rate applied to the tax base, less the value of the investment tax credit at the noncorporate level. We generate the revenue from wealth taxation through estate and gift taxes by applying an effective tax rate to the value of capital stock held by household, noncorporate, and corporate sectors.

To model the taxation of labor income through the individual income tax we generate the revenue from the labor income tax, say RL, through the identity:

$$RL = TL \cdot PL(L - LU), \tag{11.40}$$

where TL is the average effective tax rate on labor income. We define the corresponding marginal effective tax rate, say TM, through the equations:

$$TL = \lambda_0 + \frac{1}{2}\lambda_1 PL(L - LU),$$

$$TM = \lambda_0 + \lambda_1 PL(L - LU). \tag{11.41}$$

We choose the parameters λ_0 and λ_1 so as to approximate the taxation of labor income under the individual income tax.[16] The price of leisure differs from the wages paid by producers:

$$PLJ = (1 - TM)PL. \tag{11.42}$$

We assume that nontax payments are a constant fraction, say TT, of labor income:

$$RT = TT \cdot PL(L - LU), \tag{11.43}$$

where RT is nontax payments.

We assume that government enterprises employ a fixed proportion, say SLE, of total labor supply:

$$LE = SLE \cdot L. \tag{11.44}$$

Similarly, we assume that government enterprises produce a fixed proportion, say SCE, of the supply of consumption goods by private enterprises:

$$CE = SCE \cdot CS. \tag{11.45}$$

The surplus of government enterprises, say RE, is generated from the identity:

$$RE = PC \cdot CE - PL \cdot LE. \tag{11.46}$$

Government revenue is the sum of taxes on the supply of consumption and investment goods by the business sector and the supply of labor and capital services by the household sector, plus nontax payments and the surplus of government enterprises. To generate government expenditures on goods and services and expenditures on transfer payments other than social insurance funds, say EL, we assume that each of these expenditures is proportional to total government outlays on all these categories of expenditure:

$$PC \cdot CG = SCG \cdot E,$$
$$PI \cdot IG = SIG \cdot E,$$
$$PL \cdot LG = SLG \cdot E,$$
$$EL = SEL \cdot E. \tag{11.47}$$

In these identities the proportions of government outlays E for the four categories of expenditure are *SCG*, *SIG*, *SLG* and *SEL*. Finally, government outlays are equal to government revenues plus an exogenously given variable that functions like a lump sum tax.

11.4.3   Intertemporal Equilibrium

Under the assumption of perfect foresight the intertemporal equilibrium path of the economy must satisfy the market clearing conditions for consumption and investment goods—(11.29) and (11.30)—and for capital and labor services—(11.32), (11.33), and (11.34). In addition, the time path of full consumption must satisfy the condition (11.25) for intertemporal optimality. Finally, the time path of the capital stock must satisfy the condition (11.31) relating changes in capital stock to investment net of replacement.

Under the assumptions of constant returns to scale in production, homotheticity in consumption, and Harrod-neutral technical change, there exists a unique balanced growth equilibrium corresponding to any stationary tax policy. In this equilibrium all quantities grow at the rate $(1 + \alpha_H)(1 + n) - 1$, where α_H is the rate of technical change:

$$\alpha_H = e^{\alpha_T} - 1.$$

Similarly, all prices grow at the exogenously given inflation rate π.

In the absence of inflation the price of full consumption is stationary in balanced growth equilibrium, so that the nominal private rate of return can be expressed in terms of the rate of time preference and the rate of technical change:

$$1 + \rho = (1 + \alpha)(1 + \alpha_H). \tag{11.48}$$

With a constant rate of inflation at the rate π, the nominal private rate of return in balanced growth equilibrium takes the form:

$$(1 + \rho) = (1 + \alpha)(1 + \alpha_H)(1 + \pi). \tag{11.49}$$

We conclude that the private rate of return corrected for inflation depends only on the rate of time preference and the rate of technical change.

We can represent the equilibrium time path in schematic form as in figure 11.1. In this figure, full consumption per unit of labor in efficiency units is denoted F and capital per unit of labor, also in efficiency units, is denoted K. If an economy with a stationary time endowment is initially in equilibrium at the point A and a change in tax policy moves the equilibrium to the point E, there exists a unique transition path to the new equilibrium. In this illustration the new balanced growth equilibrium is associated with a higher level of capital intensity, so that the rate of return rises and the level of full consumption falls to the point B. The capital intensity of the economy at the point B is precisely the same as at the point A, before the change in tax policy.

The drop in consumption associated with a higher rate of return results in an increase in the rate of growth of capital stock. As the economy moves along the transition path to the new equilibrium at E, the rate of return corrected for inflation falls toward the balanced growth equilibrium rate $(1 + \alpha)(1 + \alpha_H) - 1$, which is independent of tax policy. The level of full consumption rises with the fall in the rate of return and the rise in capital stock. In the limit, full consumption

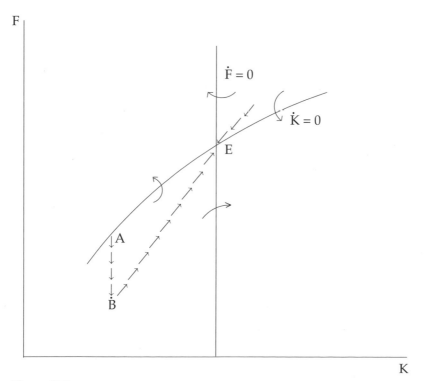

Figure 11.1
Equilibrium time path

and capital stock reach the new balanced growth equilibrium at the point E.

Under the assumption of perfect foresight our procedure for computing an intertemporal equilibrium can be divided into two steps. The first step is to calculate the unique balanced growth equilibrium associated with a given tax policy. Under the assumptions of constant returns to scale in production, homothetic preferences, and Harrod-neutral technical change the quantities of consumption and investment goods and of capital and labor services that characterize an equilibrium are homogeneous of degree one in the time endowment. We can scale these quantities relative to the time endowment.

Similarly, the demand and supply functions by the business and household sectors for all commodity groups included in our model are homogeneous of degree zero in the prices. Furthermore, all financial magnitudes, including the tax bases for sales, income, and property taxes, are homogeneous of degree one in the prices. Accordingly, we can express all prices relative to a numeraire commodity. We take the price of labor services in efficiency units as the numeraire and express all prices and financial magnitude relative to this price.

Given the balanced growth equilibrium of the economy as at the point E, the second step in computing an intertemporal equilibrium is to select an appropriate initial level of full consumption, as at the point B. The main difficulty in this second step arises from the fact that the unique transition path to balanced growth equilibrium is unstable, so that errors in the initial level of full consumption are quickly magnified. We employ the multiple shooting technique described by Lipton, Poterba, Sachs and Summers (1982) in calculating the transition path.

Up to this point we have considered the intertemporal utility functions (11.23) as a representation of household preferences. In evaluating alternative tax policies we can interpret this function as an intertemporal social welfare function. The time path of full consumption is determined as part of the intertemporal equilibrium of the U.S. economy corresponding to each tax policy. We associate a level of social welfare, say U, with each policy. This level of social welfare can be calculated from the time path of full consumption per capita.

In evaluating alternative tax policies we first consider the future growth of the U.S. economy under current tax policy. For this purpose we give values of the parameters that describe the composition of government expenditures and the role of government enterprises in table 11.3. We also present parameters that describe current tax policy

Table 11.3
Simulation parameters

Composition Parameters:

1. Government expenditures

$SCG = 0.24$	share of consumption goods
$SIC = 0.19$	share of investment goods
$SLG = 0.46$	share of labor services
$SEL = 0.11$	share of transfer payments

2. Labor services

$SLU = 0.055$	natural rate of unemployment
$SLE = 0.0175$	share of labor used by government enterprise

3. Consumption goods

$SCE = 0.03$	share of output by government enterprise

Tax Parameters:

λ_0	$= -0.0523$	intercept of the marginal labor tax rate schedule
λ_1	$= 0.000341$	slope of the marginal labor tax rate schedule
TC	$= 0.06058$	sales tax on consumption goods
TI	$= 0.06058$	sales tax on investment goods
u_q	$= 0.46$	corporate income tax
u_k	$= 0.40472$	individual capital income tax
u_h^p	$= 0.01095$	household property tax
u_m^p	$= 0.01034$	noncorporate property tax
u_q^p	$= 0.01422$	corporate property tax
TT	$= 0.01613$	nontax payments
TW	$= 0.00107$	wealth tax

Note: λ_0 and λ_1 are set to yield $TL = 0.12584$ and $TM = 0.304$ in 1980.

Rates of Economic Depreciation

1. Underlying economic depreciation rates

Consumer durables	0.200
Producer durable equipment	0.138
Nonresidential structures	0.056
Residential structures	0.039
Inventories and land	0.000

2. Economic depreciation rates

Corporate

Short-lived Assets	0.1380
Long-lived Assets	0.0269

Noncorporate

Short-lived Assets	0.1380
Long-lived Assets	0.0155

Household

Short-lived Assets	0.0199
Long-lived Assets	0.0296

Table 11.3
(continued)

Relative Prices of Assets and Other Constants

1. Relative prices of assets (1980 values)

PK(1) = 1.0
PK(2) = 2.40254/1.68700
PK(3) = 1.0
PK(4) = 2.60406/1.68700
PK(5) = 1.56385/1.68700
PK(6) = 2.39406/1.68700

2. Other constants

Total time endowment (in 1980)	4675.0
Long-run private rate of return	0.027
Rate of technical change	0.00888
Rate of population growth	0.01
Rate of inflation	0.06
Effective proportion of after-corporate-tax Income included in individual tax base	0.55
Debt/capital ratio	0.25

Note: The rate of economic depreciation for PDE is comparable with Hulten-Wykoff estimates. However, those for long-lived assets are rather high compared with Hulten-Wykoff and Jorgenson-Sullivan estimates. See Jorgenson and Sullivan (1981), table 1, p. 179.

in this table, together with rates of economic depreciation for the six classes of assets that are distinguished in our model. Finally, we give the other parameters required for simulation of the U.S. economy by means of our intertemporal general equilibrium model.

We have estimated parameters that describe technology in the business sector and preferences within each time period in the household sector. The remaining unknown parameters, the rate of time preference α, describes intertemporal preferences in the household sector. We set this parameter so that the rate of return (11.21) is consistent with the capital stock available in 1980 at a six percent inflation rate. This implies that the 1980 capital stock is in balanced growth equilibrium, corresponding to the tax policy prevailing in that year. This equilibrium is associated with a private rate of return, corrected for inflation, of 2.7 percent per year.

For the reference case we project government expenditure on goods and services and transfers to be 26 percent of net private national income. For the tax parameters given in table 11.3, this produces a differences between revenue and expenditure amounting to less than one half of the percent of total government spending. For alternative tax policies we set government expenditures at the same level as in the reference case and adjust tax revenues to cover the shortfall or over-run. A lump sum tax adjustment corresponds to a change in the difference between expenditures and revenue. A sales tax adjustment requires changes in the sales tax rates TC and TI. Finally, we adjust labor taxes by changing the parameter λ_0 in (11.41), which alters both average and marginal effective tax rates.

To evaluate the impact of alternative tax policies, we find it useful to express changes in social welfare in terms of changes in full wealth WF. We first consider the time path of the price of full consumption associated with current tax policy. We define *money metric social welfare* as the difference between the full wealth required to attain the level of social welfare after the policy change and the wealth required to attain the level of welfare before the change, both evaluated at prices before the change in policy.

If money metric social welfare is positive, social welfare is increased by the policy change; otherwise, the level of social welfare is decreased or left unaffected. Since we employ a model of household behavior based on a single infinitely lived consumer, our measure of social welfare excludes all distributional considerations. As a consequence, we provide measures of potential gains in social welfare associated with alternative tax policies. Measures of the actual gains in social welfare would require the incorporation of changes in the distribution of welfare among individuals.[17]

11.5 Tax Reform

Our final objective is to evaluate the impact of alternative policies for taxation of property and taxation of income from capital on potential economic welfare in the United States. In the preceding section we have outlined an intertemporal general equilibrium model of the U.S. economy appropriate for this purpose. In this section we employ this model to simulate the U.S. economy under alternative tax policies. We evaluate the consequences of these policies, using an intertemporal social welfare function.

We begin our analysis of alternative tax policies by considering the future growth of the U.S. economy under current tax policy. As a basis for comparison we consider the tax policy that prevailed until the end of 1980. Tax rates and rules for capital cost recovery were altered substantially during 1981 and 1982—the first two years of the Reagan Administration. We find that the Reagan tax program increased potential U.S. economic welfare by 3.5 to 4 percent of the 1980 private national wealth.

We conclude our evaluation of alternative U.S. tax policies by considering the impact of further tax reforms. At one extreme we consider a shift from direct taxation of income from capital to indirect taxation of consumption. As alternative to a thorough-going reform along these lines, we consider measures to reduce the discrepancies in the tax treatment of assets of different types. We find that a shift to a consumption tax would produce dramatic gains in potential U.S. economic welfare. These gains would amount to 26 to 27 percent of the 1980 private national wealth.

11.5.1   Reagan Tax Program

Under the Reagan Administration the U.S. Congress has enacted two major pieces of tax legislation. The first is the Economic Recovery Tax Act (ERTA) of 1981.[18] This Act introduced a program of multi-year tax cuts, intended to provide incentives ". . . to work, save, and invest, consistent with the goal of eliminating the Federal budget deficit by 1984." The second is the Tax Equity and Fiscal Responsibility Act (TEFRA) of 1982.[19] This Act substantially reduced the tax cuts embodied in the 1981 legislation.

The Economic Recovery Tax Act of 1981 included an Accelerated Cost Recovery System (ACRS) for recovering the cost of investments through tax deductions. Under ACRS the cost of investment in structures can be recovered through capital consumption allowances extending over fifteen years. Most investments in producers' durable equipment can be recovered over five years; however, short-lived assets such as automobiles can be recovered over three years and long-lived assets such as public utility equipment can be recovered over ten or fifteen years.

Prior to the 1981 Tax Act investment cost recovery was permitted under the Asset Depreciation Range System (ADRS). Under ADRS capital consumption allowances were tied to estimates of useful lifetimes for different classes of assets. In addition, an investment tax credit was permitted for producers' durable equipment. A ten percent tax credit was allowed for assets with a useful life of seven or more years; two-thirds of this credit was allowed for assets with a 5–6 year life and one-third for assets with a 3–4 year life.

Under the 1981 Tax Act assets eligible for cost recovery over 5, 10, and 15 years were made eligible for a ten percent investment tax credit. Sixty percent of the tax credit was allowed for assets eligible for three year cost recovery. In addition to accelerated cost recovery and a liberalized investment tax credit, the 1981 legislation reduced individual income tax rates and introduced "safe harbor" leasing rules.

The 1981 Tax Act provided for three sets of capital consumption schedules. The first was to be applied to assets placed in service during 1981–1984. A second, more accelerated, schedule was to be applied to assets placed in service in 1985 and a third schedule—with even greater acceleration—to assets placed in service in later years. The Tax Equity and Fiscal Responsibility Act of 1982 repealed the second and final acceleration of capital cost recovery. In addition, investment costs to be recovered through capital consumption allowances were reduced by fifty percent of the investment tax credit. Finally, the safe harbor leasing rules were repealed as of January 1, 1984.

We can summarize the differences between the Reagan tax program and the previous tax policy in terms of the investment tax credit and the present value of capital consumption allowances. In table 11.4 we present these tax parameters for noncorporate and corporate sectors and for long-lived and short-lived assets. The present value of capital consumption allowances depends on the rate of inflation under both the Reagan program and previous policy. We present tax parameters for three different rates of inflation—zero, six, and ten percent. Overall, income from business assets receives much more favorable treatment under the Reagan program than under previous tax policy.

To assess the impact of the Reagan tax program we have simulated the U.S. economy under this program and under the previous policy. We consider three alternative methods for offsetting the loss in tax revenue. The first is a lump sum tax adjustment, simulated by replacing transfer payments by taxes. Although lump sum tax adjustment is purely hypothetical, it is useful as a measure of the effects of tax distortions. We also consider replacing lost revenue by increases in taxes on labor income or increases in sales taxes.

We take the Reagan tax program with an inflation rate of six percent per year as the reference case. With a lump sum tax adjustment to offset the revenue loss under the Reagan program, we find that the

Table 11.4
Tax parameters

Previous Policy:

1. Investment tax credit

Noncorporate		Corporate	
Long	Short	Long	Short
0.0085	0.0928	0.0196	0.0928

2. Present value of capital consumption allowances

	Noncorporate		Corporate	
Rate of inflation	Long	Short	Long	Short
0	0.3571	0.9321	0.4007	0.9321
6	0.2589	0.8348	0.2909	0.8348
10	0.2174	0.7809	0.2457	0.7809

Reagan Program:

1. Investment tax credit

Noncorporate		Corporate	
Long	Short	Long	Short
0.0092	0.0972	0.0213	0.0972

2. Present value of capital consumption allowances

	Noncorporate		Corporate	
Rate of inflation	Long	Short	Long	Short
0	0.3939	0.9204	0.4412	0.9204
6	0.3320	0.8638	0.3741	0.86.38
10	0.2999	0.8298	0.3392	0.8298

gain in potential welfare under this program amounts to $542 billions of 1980 dollars. With distortionary taxes to offset the revenue loss the potential welfare gains are considerably reduced. With an increase in taxes on labor income the welfare gain is $328 billions while an increase in sales taxes reduces the gain to $295 billions.

11.5.2   Further Tax Reform

Although the potential welfare impact of the Reagan tax program is positive, there are at least three areas for potential improvement in the efficiency of capital allocation. The first is through reduction in tax distortions due to differences in capital cost recovery for long-lived and short-lived assets.[20] The second is through reduction in distortions due to differential taxation of income from capital held in household, noncorporate and corporate sectors.[21] The third is through reduction in the gap between social and private rates of return resulting from "double taxation" of saving.[22]

Under the first year capital recovery system (FYCRS) proposed by Auerbach and Jorgenson (1980), capital consumption allowances over the lifetime of an asset would be replaced by a first year allowance that would be treated as an expense in the year an asset is placed in service. By selecting appropriate first year allowances for each asset, effective tax rates could be equalized. Alternatively, these tax rates could be equalized through the system of investment tax credits proposed by Brown (1981). Combining first year capital recovery and Brown's system of tax credits, the effective tax rate of all assets could be made to vary from the statutory rate to zero.

At least since Harberger (1966) economists have considered a variety of alternative approaches to equalizing taxes among sectors of the U.S. economy. These alternatives include outright abolition of the corporate income tax and the integration of corporate and individual income taxes. Under integration both dividends and retained earnings by corporations would be treated as income at the individual level. Of course, full integration would also require the imputation of income from household capital. This imputed income would be taxed along with income from noncorporate and corporate business at the individual level.

The elimination of the gap between social and private rates of return would require the abolition of property taxes and taxes on capital income. The whole burden of taxation would be shifted to consumption and to labor income. This could be achieved by eliminating taxes on property and capital income and the corresponding tax deductions and tax credits. Alternatively, all investment expenditures could be treated as an expense in calculating income for tax purposes and interest deductions could be abolished. Under either of these approaches all interasset and intersectoral tax distortions would be eliminated.

In order to evaluate the potential welfare impact of further tax reforms, we have simulated the U.S. economy under each tax policy. As before, we treat the Reagan tax program with six percent inflation as the reference case. First, we estimate the welfare impact of eliminating differences in effective tax rates between long-lived and short-lived assets within the noncorporate and corporate sectors. We set the steady state effective tax rate for each asset equal to the average of the effective tax rates within each sector in the reference case. This leaves differences in effective tax rates between sectors unchanged.

Second, we estimate the potential welfare impact of eliminating distortions due to differences in effective tax rates between the noncorporate and corporate sectors. We set the steady state effective tax rate for each asset equal to the average of effective tax rates in the two sectors in the reference case. This leaves differences in effective tax rates between assets unaffected. This is not equivalent to integration of the corporate and individual income taxes under existing tax rules. Integration would reduce taxation of corporate income to the level of taxation of noncorporate income.

We can combine the effects of equalizing interasset and intersectoral effective tax rates by setting these rates equal to the steady state average for all assets in the noncorporate and corporate sectors. This could be achieved through integration of individual and corporate income taxes and through the imposition of rules for capital recovery like those in FYCRS that would result in equal effective tax rates. For comparison we also present a simulation based on integration with existing tax rules. In this simulation noncorporate income is treated in the same way as corporate income for tax purposes.

Finally, we can simulate the impact of applying consumption tax rules to investment expenditures in the noncorporate and corporate sectors. We first consider expensing of investment and abolishing tax deductions for interest expenses with no changes in sales taxes applied to investment goods. We then consider the combination of expensing with the elimination of sales taxes on investment goods.

Under either of these tax policies the effective tax rates on long-lived and short-lived assets in the noncorporate and corporate sectors are set equal to zero.

The tax parameters employed in our simulations are presented in table 11.5. For the reference case—the Reagan tax program under six percent inflation—we present the investment tax credit, the present value of depreciation allowances, the rate of depreciation, and the rental price of capital services. For the reference case and the five alternative policies we present the social rate of return and the effective tax rate for long-lived and short-lived assets in the corporate and noncorporate sectors.

11.5.3   Potential Economic Welfare

In table 11.6 we give our estimates of the impact of alternative tax reforms on potential economic welfare. Our simulations of the U.S. economy show that policies with effective tax rates for all assets equal to zero dominate all other tax reforms. Under lump sum tax adjustment the expensing of investment expenditures and the elimination of sales taxes on investment goods result in a potential welfare gain of $3,599 billions of 1980 dollars. This is the equivalent of more than 43 percent of the U.S. private national wealth in 1980. The potential welfare gain dwarfs the gain from the Reagan tax program. With lump sum tax adjustment the Reagan program yields potential welfare gains of only $542 billions of 1980 dollars or less than one-sixth the gain from eliminating all taxes on capital income and investment goods.

With tax adjustments through increases in labor income or sales taxes, the reduction in tax distortions in the allocation of capital are partly offset by the addition in tax distortions in the allocation of labor services and consumption goods. The welfare gain from elimination of taxes on income from capital and on investment goods is reduced to $1893 billions of 1980 dollars under labor income tax adjustment and $1724 bilions under sales tax adjustment. By comparison welfare gains from expensing of investment alone are $2156 billions under labor income tax adjustment and $2208 billions under sales tax adjustment.

Expensing of investment with labor income tax adjustment would require an increase in average (and marginal) rates of labor income taxes of 6.34 percent, while sales tax adjustment would require an

Table 11.5
Balanced growth tax parameters

Class of assets	Investment tax credit rate	Capital consumption allowances	Economic depreciation rate	Annualization factor
	Reference case			
Noncorporate				
Long	0.0092	0.3320	0.0155	0.0638
Short	0.0972	0.8638	0.1380	0.1550
Corporate				
Long	0.0213	0.3741	0.0269	0.0945
Short	0.0972	0.8638	0.1380	0.1631

	Social rate of return	Effective tax rate	Social rate of return	Effective tax rate
	1. Reference case		2. No interasset tax differences	
Noncorporate				
Long	0.0483	0.4408	0.0450	0.3999
Short	0.0170	−0.5855	0.0450	0.3999
Corporate				
Long	0.0675	0.6001	0.0560	0.5174
Short	0.0251	−0.0740	0.0560	0.5174

	Social rate of return	Effective tax rate	Social rate of return	Effective tax rate
	3. No intersector tax differences		4. No intratemporal tax differences	
Noncorporate				
Long	0.0594	0.5457	0.0519	0.4797
Short	0.0236	−0.1422	0.0519	0.4797
Corporate				
Long	0.0594	0.5457	0.0519	0.4797
Short	0.0236	−0.1422	0.0519	0.4797

	Social rate of return	Effective tax rate	Social rate of return	Effective tax rate
	5. Corporate tax integration		6. Consumption tax rules on capital income	
Noncorporate				
Long	0.0483	0.4408	0.0270	0.0000
Short	0.0170	−0.5855	0.0270	0.0000
Corporate				
Long	0.0483	0.4408	0.0270	0.0000
Short	0.0170	−0.5855	0.0270	0.0000

Table 11.6
Potential economic welfare (billions of 1980 dollars)

1. Lump sum tax adjustment

No interasset tax differences	815.0
No intersector tax differences	−232.0
No intratemporal tax differences	633.8
Corporate tax integration	1174.3
Consumption tax rules on capital income	3428.5
Consumption tax equivalent	3598.8

2. Labor income tax adjustment

No interasset tax differences	899.9
No intersector tax differences	−259.2
No intratemporal tax differences	674.0
Corporate tax integration	654.0
Consumption tax rules on capital income	2156.1
Consumption tax equivalent	1892.5

3. Sales tax adjustment

No interasset tax differences	909.5
No intersector tax differences	−259.2
No intratemporal tax differences	678.7
Corporate tax integration	623.1
Consumption tax rules on capital income	2208.4
Consumption tax equivalent	1723.5

increase in the sales tax rate of 7.15 percent. Even with distorting tax increases to offset revenue losses, the expensing of investment would produce dramatic gains in potential welfare. These gains would amount to 26 to 27 percent of the 1980 U.S. private national wealth. By comparison the Reagan tax program produces gains of only 3.5 to 4 percent of the private national wealth.

We can briefly summarize the remaining results presented in table 11.5: Almost half the benefits of expensing investment could be obtained by equalizing effective tax rates on assets within the noncorporate and corporate sectors. This could be achieved by adoption of a version of the First Year Capital Recovery System. Surprisingly, elimination of differences in effective tax rates on long-lived and short-lived assets between the noncorporate and corporate sectors reduces potential welfare gains relative to the Reagan tax program. Equalizing effective tax rates on all assets and corporate tax integration produce about the same gains in potential welfare. These gains are approximately one-third the benefits of a shift to expensing investment.

11.6   Conclusion

We have summarized the impact of provisions of the U.S. tax law that are applicable to income from capital by means of effective tax rates. A necessary condition for efficient allocation of capital within each time period is that effective tax rates are the same for all assets. Discrepancies in the tax treatment of income from different types of assets held in different sectors of the U.S. economy give rise to substantial barriers to efficient allocation.

In table 11.5 above we have presented effective tax rates for long-lived and short-lived assets in the noncorporate and corporate sectors at a six percent rate of inflation. These rates vary from sixty percent on long-lived assets in the corporate sector to a negative 59 percent on short-lived assets in the noncorporate sector. These startling gaps in effective tax rates are associated with the effects of the corporate income tax and with differences in provisions for capital recovery between long-lived and short-lived assets.

We have constructed an intertemporal general equilibrium model of the U.S. economy in order to provide a quantitative measure of the loss in potential economic welfare in the United States due to inefficiency in the allocation of capital. Although general equilibrium techniques are widely utilized in modeling the impact of tax policy,[23] our approach embodies two distinctive features. First, we have simplified the representation of preferences by endowing the household sector with perfect foresight. This implies that market clearing prices at each point of time incorporate the present and future impact of changes in tax policy.

Our approach to general equilibrium modeling of tax policy is also distinctive in describing technology and preferences by means of econometric models. These models incorporate all of the restrictions implied by economic theories of producer and consumer behavior. These include absence of money illusion or homogeneity of degree zero in prices, summability of budget shares to unity, symmetry of the appropriate Slutsky matrices, and curvature conditions that imply upward sloping supply functions and downward sloping demand functions.

Econometric methods appropriate for general equilibrium modeling require the estimation of parameters within systems of nonlinear simultaneous equations. Furthermore, economic theories of producer and consumer behavior imply equality and inequality restrictions that must be incorporated into the estimation process. These restrictions arise within individual equations and across equations and are highly nonlinear.

Given the novel elements in our approach to general equilibrium modeling, it is not surprising that our analysis of alternative tax policies produces some interesting new results. The most striking of these results in the dramatic gain in potential economic welfare associated with a shift from direct taxation of income from capital to indirect taxation through a consumption-base tax. Such a shift has attracted the attention of tax reformers in Sweden, the United Kingdom, and the United States. We have provided new quantitative evidence supporting these efforts at reform.

Although our approach to modeling the impact of tax policy appears to be promising, the research required to exploit this approach is just beginning. Perhaps the most important direction for future research is to extend our approach to a model with overlapping generations.[24] As Barro (1974) has demonstrated, such a model can be represented by means of a single infinitely lived consumer only under very stringent conditions on preferences and bequest motives. Our econometric methodology can be extended to incorporate differences in preferences among consumers along the lines suggested by Jorgenson (1984).

We have emphasized that our evaluation of alternative tax policies has excluded equity considerations. Our intertemporal social welfare function is defined on the time path of full consumption at the aggregate level. Aggregate full consumption can be interpreted as a measure of potential economic welfare, following Bentzel's (1970) pioneering approach to the analysis of income distributions. The actual level of welfare can be evaluated by the techniques of Jorgenson and Slesnick (1984), utilizing information on the distribution of individual welfare derived from an econometric model of the household sector.

Our evaluation of tax reform has left at least two directions for future applications of our existing intertemporal general equilibrium model. The first is to the analysis of tax incidence.[25] We have evaluated the impact of tax policy in terms of potential economic welfare, but we can also study the impact on rates of remuneration of factors of production, shares of different sectors in the composition of capital input, present versus future consumption, and so on. A second direction for future applications is the development of optimal tax policies for the United States along the lines proposed by Diamond and Mirrless.[26]

Appendix: List of Instrumental Variables

I1:   constant (a vector of 1s)
I2:   effective tax rate, labor services
I3:   effective tax rate, imports
I4:   time available (excluding time necessary for personal mainte-
      nance)
I5:   domestic population (including armed forces overseas)
I6:   implicit deflator, supply of labor services
I7:   implicit deflator, general government purchases of labor services
I8:   government transfer payments other than social insurance
      funds, less personal transfer payments to foreigners, less per-
      sonal non-tax payments
I9:   private national wealth
I10: $I4*(1 + 0.020224)**I14$
I11: value of imports
I12: price of consumption goods, imports
I13: $I6/(1 + 0.020224)**I14$
I14: time (T = 0 in 1972)

Notes

1. Intertemporal production theory is discussed, for example, by Fisher (1930), Hicks (1946), Lindahl (1939) and Malinvaud (1953). Classic references on capital theory are Åkerman (1923), Walras (1954) and Wicksell (1934b).

2. The taxation of income from capital in the United States is discussed in detail in King and Fullerton (1984), Chapter 6, pp. 193–267. This volume also contains descriptions of capital taxation in Sweden, the United Kingdom and West Germany and international comparisons.

3. Distributional considerations are employed in modeling intertemporal preferences by Bentzel and Berg (1983) and in modeling atemporal preferences by Jorgenson, Lau and Stoker (1980, 1981, 1982).

4. Intertemporal general equilibrium models of the impact of tax policy under perfect foresight are presented by Chamley (1981), Hall (1971b), Sinn (1981) and Turnovsky (1982).

5. A shift from direct to indirect taxation has been advocated for the United States by the U.S. Treasury (1977). Similar tax reforms have been proposed by Sweden by the Royal Commission on Taxation (Lodin, 1976) and for the United Kingdom by the Meade Committee (1978).

6. Effective tax rates are discussed by King and Fullerton *et al.* (1984), especially Chapters 2 and 7, pp. 7–30 and 268–302. See also: Papers by Bradford (1981b), Fullerton (1981 *et al.*), Gravelle (1981), Hall (1981), and Jorgenson and Sullivan (1981), and Hulten and Wykoff (1981b).

7. Hulten and Wykoff (1981b) have shown that exponential or geometric decline in the quantity of capital services provides a satisfactory approximation to actual patterns of decline.

8. The "traditional" and the "new" view are compared by Poterba and Summers (1983). The new view was introduced by Auerbach (1979c), Bradford (1981b), and King (1977). Stiglitz (1976) has presented a third view, based on debt as the marginal source of funds for investment. On this view tax policy has no impact on capital allocation, since interest is expense and tax deductible.

9. We have also ignored an important complexity in the practical application of these systems, namely, that the marginal tax rate on capital income at the individual level u_k may differ among taxpayers.

10. Alternative approaches to implementing a consumption-base tax in the United States are discussed in detail by the U.S. Treasury (1977).

11. The methodology for modeling producer behavior outlined in this section is presented in detail by Jorgenson (1983, 1984).

12. Two-stage allocation is discussed by Blackorby, Primont and Russell (1978, esp. pp. 103–216). They provide references to the literature.

13. The translog price function was introduced by Christensen, Jorgenson and Lau (1971, 1973). The translog indirect utility function that underlies the model of the household sector presented below was introduced by Christensen, Jorgenson and Lau (1975).

14. The properties of intertemporally additive utility functions are discussed by Arrow and Kurz (1970).

15. Equivalent variations in income or total expenditure were introduced as measures of economic welfare by Hicks (1942). Equivalent variations in wealth provide an exact measure of economic welfare that is analogous to the equivalent variations in total expenditure given by Jorgenson, Lau and Stoker (1981, 1982).

16. We employ the estimates of marginal tax rates under the individual income tax compiled by Barro and Sahasakul (1983).

17. Measures of social welfare incorporating inequality in the distribution of individual welfare are given by Jorgenson and Slesnick (1984).

18. See: Joint Committee on Taxation (1981).

19. See: Joint Committee on Taxation (1982).

20. Tax distortions due to differences in the tax treatment of different types of assets are discussed by Abel (1981), Auerbach (1979c), and the papers in Hulten and Wykoff (1981b) cited in note 6, above.

21. Tax distortions due to differences in the tax treatment of assets held in different sectors are discussed by Harberger (1966), Shoven and Whalley (1972), and Shoven (1976), among others. The literature on the Harberger approach is reviewed by McClure (1976). The impact of corporate tax integration is evaluated by Fullerton, King, Shoven, and Whalley (1981).

22. Tax distortions due to "double taxation" of saving are discussed by Diamond (1970), Feldstein (1978), and Levhari and Sheshinski (1972).

23. See, for example, the studies contained in the collection edited by Feldstein (1983); a survey of general equilibrium modeling of tax policy has been provided by Fullerton, Henderson, and Shoven (1984).

24. General equilibrium models with overlapping generations have been applied to the analysis of tax policy under perfect foresight by Auerbach and Kotlikoff (1983) and Auerbach, Kotlikoff, and Skinner (1983).

25. A very detailed general equilibrium analysis of tax incidence in the United States is given by Ballard, Shoven and Whalley (1983).

26. See, for example, Diamond (1973), Diamond and Mirrlees (1971a, b) and Mirrlees (1971, 1976).

12

Tax Reform and U.S. Economic Growth

Dale W. Jorgenson and
Kun-Young Yun

In this chapter we evaluate the impact of the Tax Reform Act of 1986 on U.S. economic growth. We first calculate effective tax rates on income from capital employed in corporate, noncorporate, and household sectors. We then project the future growth of the U.S. economy with and without the 1986 tax reform. We find that much of the potential gain in welfare was dissipated through failure to index the income tax base for inflation. The most promising avenue for future reform is to include income from household assets in the tax base, while reducing tax rates on business income.

12.1   Introduction

The purpose of this chapter is to evaluate the impact of the Tax Reform Act of 1986 on U.S. economic growth.[1] Major tax legislation such as the 1986 Tax Act can produce substantial alterations in the rate of capital accumulation and the allocation of capital among sectors and types of assets. An assessment of the impact of tax reform depends not only on the changes in tax policy but also on the elasticities of substitution along all the relevant margins. The intertemporal margin, involving the allocation of resources between present and future consumption, is essential to the evaluation of the consequences of a tax reform involving changes in the the treatment of income from capital. We conclude that a fully dynamic model of the U.S. economy is required in assessing the impact of the tax reform on economic welfare.

Harberger (1962, 1966) has argued that the U.S. tax system leads to a loss in efficiency since it fails to impose a uniform tax rate on income from capital in competing economic activities. There have been wide gaps between the rates of return on investment before and after taxes for assets employed in different sectors and differing in durability. However, the efficient use of capital requires a uniform tax rate only under the restrictive assumption that the allocation of capital is separable from the allocation of other resources in production and consumption. In a more general setting, uniform treatment of income from capital is neither necessary nor sufficient for efficient resource allocation.[2]

Harberger's analysis of the impact of tax policy on the efficiency of capital allocation is limited to the allocation of a given capital stock.[3] However, saving behavior may be affected by changes in tax policy, so that the capital stock must be determined endogenously in order to assess the economic impact of tax reform.[4] In addition, the notion of efficient resource allocation must be extended to encompass intertemporal allocation. The elimination of tax distortions in the intertemporal allocation of resources requires that income from capital should not be taxed at all. Taxes on capital income could be replaced by taxes on labor income. Alternatively, income taxes could be replaced by taxes on consumption.[5]

The argument for eliminating capital income taxes ignores the fact that distortions in resource allocation resulting from these taxes must be replaced by other tax induced distortions. For example, the taxation of labor income has important implications for economic efficiency through its effects on the choice between labor and leisure. Labor income accounts for roughly sixty percent of U.S. private national income and a very substantial proportion of U.S. tax revenues. It is well established that, even though the price elasticity of labor supply is very low, there is a substantial substitution effect that is similar in magnitude but opposite in sign to the income effect of a change in the wage rate.[6] It is the substitution effect, not the total price effect, that is relevant to the impact of a tax on labor income on economic efficiency.

In order to evaluate the economic impact of the 1986 tax reform, we employ a dynamic general equilibrium model. This model provides a highly schematic representation of the U.S. economy. A single representative producer employs capital and labor services to produce outputs of consumption and investment goods. By modeling the substitution between consumption and investment goods in production, we are able to introduce costs of adjustment in the response of investment to changes in tax policy. We have simplified the representation of technology in the model by introducing a single stock of capital at each point of time. This capital is perfectly malleable and is allocated so as to equalize after-tax rates of return to equity in the corporate, noncorporate, and household sectors.

Our model also incorporates a representative consumer that supplies labor services, demands consumption goods, and makes choices between consumption and saving. This model of consumer behavior is based on an intertemporally additive utility function that depends on levels of full consumption in all time periods. Full consumption is an aggregate of consumption goods, household capital services, and leisure. To simplify the representation of preferences, we endow the representative consumer with an infinite lifetime and perfect foresight about future prices. We have fitted econometric models of producer and consumer behavior to data for the U.S. economy covering the period 1947–1986.[7]

The government sector of the U.S. economy raises revenues through taxes on income from capital and labor services. Corporate capital income is taxed at both corporate and individual levels, noncorporate capital income is taxed only at the individual level, and household capital income is not taxed at either level. In addition, the government sector imposes sales taxes on the production of consumption and investment goods and property taxes on assets held by the business and household sectors. Taxes insert wedges between demand and supply prices for investment and consumption goods and for capital and labor services. These tax wedges distort private decisions and lead to losses in efficiency.

In our model the equilibrium of the U.S. economy is characterized by an intertemporal price system that clears the markets for all four commodity groups included in the model: labor and capital services and consumption and investment goods. Equilibrium at each point of time links the past and the future through markets for investment goods and capital services. Assets are accumulated as a result of past investments, while the prices of assets must equal the present values of future capital services. The time path of consumption must satisfy the conditions for intertemporal optimality of the household sector under perfect foresight.[8] Similarly, the time path of investment must satisfy requirements for the accumulation of assets by both business and household sectors.

In order to evaluate alternative tax policies, we first consider the intertemporal equilibrium associated with each policy. Under perfect foresight there is a unique transition path to balanced growth equilibrium for any tax policy and any initial level of capital. The growth path of the U.S. economy consists of a plan for consumption of goods and leisure at every point of time by the representative consumer and a plan for production of investment and consumption goods from capital and labor services at every point of time by the representative producer. These plans are brought into consistency by the intertemporal price system.

Associated with each tax policy and the corresponding intertemporal equilibrium is a level of welfare for the representative consumer. This level of welfare can be interpreted as a measure of economic efficiency corresponding to the potential level of welfare for society as a whole. The actual level of welfare also depends on the distribution of welfare among consuming units. To evaluate changes in tax policy in terms of efficiency, we translate changes in potential welfare into an equivalent variation in private national wealth. We first consider the time path of the price of full consumption associated with current tax policy. We then evaluate the difference in wealth required to attain levels of potential welfare before and after the change in tax policy at prices prevailing before the change.

This chapter is organized as follows. In section 12.2, we summarize the 1986 tax reform in terms of changes in tax rates, the treatment of deductions from income for tax purposes, the availability of tax credits, and provisions for indexing taxable income for inflation. We also summarize proposals for tax reform that figured prominently in the debate leading up to the 1986 Tax Act. We consider proposals advanced by the Department of the Treasury and by President Ronald Reagan in detail, since these proposals were instrumental in shaping the final legislation. The starting point for our discussion of the alternative proposals is the tax law in existence prior to the 1986 reform. A number of important features of the pre-existing tax law can be traced to tax reforms in the early 1980s.

In section 12.3, we analyze the tax burdens on capital income under four alternative tax policy regimes: the tax law in existence before the 1986 tax reform, the Treasury proposal, the President's proposal, and the Tax Reform Act of 1986. We utilize the concept of an effective tax rate, which summarizes statutory tax rates and provisions of tax law that affect the definition of taxable income. We also employ the notion of a tax wedge, defined in terms of differences in tax burdens imposed on different forms of income. Tax wedges represent gaps between the marginal products of different types of assets. These gaps are useful indicators of the likely impact of substitutions among different kinds of capital induced by changes in tax policy.

In section 12.4 of the chapter we analyze the impact of each of the alternative tax policies on U.S. economic growth. We evaluate the effects of changes in tax policy on economic efficiency by measuring the corresponding changes in potential economic welfare. The reference level of welfare, which serves as the basis of comparison among alternative tax policies, is the level attainable by the U.S. economy under the tax law in effect prior to the 1986 tax reform. We also analyze losses in efficiency associated with tax wedges among different kinds of capital income. These tax wedges are the consequences of the corporate and personal income taxes, property taxes, and sales taxes on investment goods.

Section 12.5 provides a summary of the chapter and presents our main conclusions. We find that much of the potential gain in welfare from the 1986 tax reform was dissipated through failure to index the income tax base for inflation. At rates of inflation near zero the loss is not substantial. However, at moderate rates of inflation, such as those prevailing for the past decade, the loss is highly significant. Second, the greatest welfare gains would have resulted from incorporating the income from household assets into the tax base, while reducing tax rates on income from business assets. The potential welfare gains from an income-based tax system, reconstructed along these lines, would have exceeded those from a consumption-based system.

12.2 Tax Reform

When the Reagan Administration took office in 1981, there was widespread concern about the slowdown in U.S. economic growth. Tax reform proposals by the Administration received overwhelming support from the Congress with the enactment of the Economic Recovery Tax Act (ERTA) of 1981.[9] The 1981 Tax Act combined sizable enhancements in investment incentives with substantial reductions in statutory tax rates for individuals and corporations. These reductions created the prospect of rising federal deficits. Only one year later the Congress passed the Tax Equity and Fiscal Responsibility Act of 1982 (TEFRA), which repealed the provisions of the 1981 Act for phasing in a more accelerated cost recovery system for property placed in service after 1985 and reduced the capital cost to be amortized over the lifetime of an asset.

The tax reforms of the early 1980s substantially reduced the burden of taxation on capital income. However, these reforms also introduced important nonneutralities in the taxation of income from different sources. Differences in the tax treatment of different types of assets gave rise to concerns in Congress about the fairness of the tax system and the impact of tax-induced distortions on the efficiency of capital allocation. In the State of the Union Address in January 1984, President Reagan announced that he had requested a plan for further tax reform from the Department of the Treasury, setting off a lengthy debate that resulted in the enactment of the Tax Reform Act of 1986.

In describing the key features of the 1986 tax reform, we find it useful to begin with a description of the pre-existing tax law in order to provide a basis for comparison. The main provisions of the 1986 Tax Act went into effect on January 1, 1987. However, the investment tax credit was repealed for assets acquired after December 31, 1985. We refer to the pre-existing tax law as the Tax Law of 1985, since it remained in force until the end of calendar 1985. To provide additional perspective on the objectives of the 1986 tax reform, we also characterize two alternative tax reform proposals presented by the Department of the Treasury and the President.

12.2.1   The 1985 Tax Law

We summarize the statutory tax rates under the 1985 Tax Law, the Treasury and President's proposals, and the 1986 Tax Act in table 12.1. The first column in table 12.1 gives average marginal tax rates for different types of income under the 1985 Tax Law for zero, six, and 10 percent annual inflation rates. The tax rate on each type of income is a weighted average of marginal tax rates paid by taxpayers in all income tax brackets. Average tax rates on different types of income reflect differences in the distribution of each type of income over the tax brackets. We present rates for income in the form of dividends and other distributions on corporate and noncorporate equity, capital gains accruing on corporate and noncorporate equity, and interest on corporate, noncorporate, household, and government debt.[10]

We also give the average marginal tax rate on labor income, the average marginal tax rate on income under the corporate income tax, and the average tax rate under the individual income tax. All tax rates include taxes levied at both federal and state and local levels and take into account the deductibility of state and local taxes at the federal level. In projecting U.S. economic growth under the 1986 Tax Law we take the average marginal tax rates on each type of income and the

Table 12.1
Tax rates

1. Average marginal tax rates of individual capital income

	1985 law (1)	Treasury proposal (2)	President's proposal (3)	1986 act (4)
	A. 0 percent inflation			
Individual income accruing to:				
Corporate equity	.2555	.2261	.2240	.2029
Noncorporate equity	.2934	.2427	.2572	.2494
Capital gains accruing to:				
Corporate equity	.0303	.0596	.0325	.0562
Noncorporate equity	.0293	.0607	.0322	.0624
Interest income accruing to:				
Corporate debt	.1533	.1452	.1532	.1285
Noncorporate debt	.1971	.1805	.1912	.1670
Household debt	.2717	.2252	.2387	.2310
Government debt	.2205	.1868	.1970	.1852
	B. 6 percent annual inflation			
Individual income accruing to:				
Corporate equity	.2559	.2261	.2240	.2033
Noncorporate equity	.2934	.2427	.2572	.2494
Capital gains accruing to:				
Corporate equity	.0303	.0596	.0600	.0562
Noncorporate equity	.0293	.0607	.0643	.0624
Interest income accruing to:				
Corporate debt	.1730	.1452	.1532	.1434
Noncorporate debt	.2151	.1805	.1912	.1807
Household debt	.2722	.2252	.2387	.2314
Government debt	.2260	.1868	.1970	.1894
	C. 10 percent annual inflation			
Individual income accruing to:				
Corporate equity	.2560	.2261	.2240	.2034
Noncorporate equity	.2934	.2427	.2572	.2494
Capital gains accruing to:				
Corporate equity	.0303	.0596	.0600	.0562
Noncorporate equity	.0293	.0607	.0643	.0624
Interest income accruing to:				
Corporate debt	.1806	.1452	.1532	.1492
Noncorporate debt	.2222	.1805	.1912	.1861
Household debt	.2724	.2252	.2387	.2315
Government debt	.2282	.1868	.1970	.1910

Table 12.1
(continued)

2. Marginal tax rates of labor income, corporate
income, and average personal tax rates

	1985 law (1)	Treasury proposal (2)	President's proposal (3)	1986 act (4)
Labor income	.2967	.2512	.2536	.2517
Corporate income[1]	.5084	.4006	.4006	.3847
Individual income[2]	.1315	.1203	.1223	.1233

3. Tax rates held constant across the alternative tax policies

Property tax rate:	
Corporate assets	.0100
Noncorporate assets	.0096
Household assets	.0100
Sales tax rate:	
Consumption goods	.0579
Investment goods	.0579
Personal nontax rate	.0229
Effective rate of wealth taxation	.0006

Note — Individual income accruing to household equity is equal to income accruing to noncorporate equity. Capital Gains accruing to household equity are equal to zero.
1. Includes federal plus state and local taxes.
2. The Treasury proposal, the president's proposal, and the 1986 Tax Reform Act are assumed to reduce the average tax rate of individual income by 8.5 percent, 7.0 percent, and 6.2 percent, respectively.

average individual income tax rate as fixed. Tax revenues received by the government are generated by applying these tax rates to streams of income generated endogenously within our model of U.S. economic growth.

We summarize the definition of income for tax purposes under the 1985 Tax Law in table 12.2. The first section describes the provisions for indexing the tax base for inflation. The 1985 Tax Law included no provisions of this type. The second section of table 12.2 describes provisions for deductibility of capital income. Dividends paid were not deductible from corporate income for tax purposes under the 1985 Tax Law. However, 85 percent of corporate dividends received were excluded from corporate income. The inside buildup of life insurance companies was not taxed under the 1985 Tax Law. Household interest

Table 12.2
Indexing and deduction of capital income

	1985 law (1)	Treasury proposal (2)	President's proposal (3)	1986 act (4)
		1. Indexing		
Long-term capital gains[1]	0.0	1.0	$0.0\ (1.0)^2$	0.0
Interest income and interest expenses, corporate and noncorporate sectors[1]	0.0	INF/(.06 + INF)	0.0	0.0
Household interest payments	0.0	0.0	0.0	0.0
		2. Deduction of capital income		
Dividends paid for corporate tax purposes	0.0	0.5	0.1	0.0
Intercorporate dividends received	0.85	0.50	0.90	0.80
Fraction of accrual-based taxation of life insurance company's inside buildup	0.0	1.0	1.0	0.0
Household interest expenses	1.0	1.0	1.0	1.0
Fraction of long-term capital gains taxed as ordinary income	0.4	1.0	$0.5\ (1.0)^2$	1.0
		3. Deduction of state and local taxes		
Income taxes	1.0	0.0	0.0	1.0
Other corporate taxes	1.0	1.0	1.0	1.0
Other noncorporate taxes	1.0	1.0	1.0	1.0
Other household taxes	1.0	0.0	0.0	1.0

1. Equals 1.0 for complete indexing.
2. Beginning in 1991, instead of excluding 50 percent of long-term capital gains, taxpayers have the option of 100 percent inclusion and complete indexing. We assume that if inflation is higher than 6 percent, taxpayers choose indexing.

expenses were fully deductible from income at the personal level. Only 40 percent of capital gains were included in income for tax purposes. Finally, all state and local taxes were deductible from income for tax purposes, as indicated in the third section of table 12.2.

In table 12.3, we present economic depreciation rates for each of fifty-one classes of assets distinguished in the U.S. national income and product accounts. We also give statutory rates of the investment tax credit and tax lifetimes under the 1985 Tax Law, the Treasury and

Table 12.3
Tax lives, investment tax credit, and economic rate of depreciation

Asset	Depreciation rate	Investment tax credit 1985	Economic lifetime	1985 law	Treasury proposal	President's proposal	1986 act
Household furniture and fixtures	.138	.10	12.0	5.0	17.0	7.0	5.0
Other furniture	.118	.10	14.0	5.0	17.0	7.0	7.0
Fabricated metal products	.092	.10	18.0	5.0	17.0	7.0	7.0
Steam engines and turbines	.052	.10	32.0	10.0	25.0	10.0	15.0
Internal combustion engines	.206	.10	8.0	10.0	25.0	10.0	10.0
Farm tractors	.145	.10	9.0	5.0	12.0	6.0	7.0
Construction tractors	.163	.10	8.0	5.0	12.0	6.0	5.0
Agricultural machinery	.118	.10	14.0	5.0	17.0	7.0	7.0
Construction machinery	.172	.10	10.0	5.0	12.0	6.0	5.0
Mining and oil field machinery	.150	.10	11.0	5.0	12.0	6.0	7.0
Metalwork machinery	.123	.09	16.0	5.0	17.0	7.0	5.0
Special industrial machinery	.103	.10	16.0	5.0	17.0	7.0	7.0
General industrial machinery	.123	.10	16.0	5.0	17.0	7.0	7.0
Office and computing machinery	.273	.10	8.0	5.0	8.0	5.0	5.0
Service industry machinery	.165	.10	10.0	5.0	12.0	6.0	5.0
Communication equipment	.110	.10	15.0	7.0	17.0	7.0	10.0
Electrical transmission	.050	.10	33.0	7.0	17.0	7.0	10.0
Household appliances	.165	.10	10.0	5.0	17.0	7.0	5.0
Other electrical equipment	.183	.10	9.0	5.0	17.0	7.0	5.0
Trucks, buses, and truck trailers	.254	.07	9.0	5.0	8.0	5.0	5.0
Autos	.333	.06	10.0	3.0	5.0	4.0	5.0
Aircraft	.183	.10	16.0	5.0	12.0	6.0	7.0
Ships and boats	.061	.10	27.0	5.0	25.0	10.0	10.0
Railroad equipment	.055	.10	30.0	5.0	25.0	7.0	7.0
Instruments	.135	.10	12.0	7.0	12.0	6.0	7.0

Table 12.3 (continued)

Asset	Depreciation rate	Investment tax credit 1985	Economic lifetime	1985 law	Treasury proposal	President's proposal	1986 act
Photocopy and related equipment	.180	.10	9.0	5.0	12.0	6.0	5.0
Other nonresidential equipment	.147	.10	11.0	5.0	12.0	6.0	5.0
Industrial buildings	.036	.03	31.0	19.0	63.0	28.0	31.5
Mobile offices	.056	.00	16.0	19.0	63.0	28.0	31.5
Office buildings	.025	.00	36.0	19.0	63.0	28.0	31.5
Commercial warehouses	.022	.00	40.0	19.0	63.0	28.0	31.5
Other commercial buildings	.026	.07	34.0	19.0	17.0	7.0	15.0
Religious buildings	.019	.00	48.0	19.0	63.0	28.0	31.5
Educational buildings	.019	.00	48.0	19.0	63.0	28.0	31.5
Hospital and institutional buildings	.023	.00	48.0	19.0	63.0	28.0	31.5
Hotels and motels	.025	.00	32.0	19.0	63.0	28.0	31.5
Amusement and recreational buildings	.047	.10	30.0	10.0	17.0	7.0	15.0
Other nonfarm buildings	.037	.00	38.0	19.0	63.0	28.0	31.5
Railroad structures	.017	.10	54.0	5.0	38.0	10.0	7.0
Telephone and telegraph structures	.023	.08	40.0	10.0	38.0	10.0	15.0
Electric light and power structures	.023	.10	40.0	15.0	38.0	10.0	20.0
Gas structures	.023	.06	40.0	10.0	38.0	10.0	20.0
Local transit	.045	.10	38.0	5.0	38.0	10.0	5.0
Petroleum pipelines	.045	.10	40.0	5.0	38.0	10.0	15.0
Farm structures	.024	.00	38.0	19.0	63.0	28.0	20.0
Petroleum and natural gas	.056	.10	16.0	5.0	38.0	7.0	7.0
Other mining exploration	.056	.10	16.0	5.0	38.0	7.0	7.0
Other nonresidential structures	.023	.00	40.0	19.0	63.0	28.0	31.5
Railroad replacement track	.024	.10	38.0	5.0	38.0	10.0	7.0
Nuclear fuel	.250	.10	6.0	5.0	12.0	6.0	7.0
Residential structures	.013	.00	—	19.0	63.0	28.0	27.5

President's proposals, and the Tax Reform Act of 1986.[11] In panel 1 of table 12.4 we present average rates of the investment tax credit and present values of capital consumption allowances for short-lived and long-lived business assets under the 1985 Tax Law. Short-lived assets include all types of producers' durable equipment employed in the business sector. Long-lived assets include residential and nonresidential structures, land, and inventories.

12.2.2   The Treasury Proposal

In November 1984 the Treasury Department presented a tax reform plan that became known as the Treasury proposal. A principal objective of the Treasury plan was to reduce statutory tax rates at both individual and corporate levels. However, the Treasury plan was intended to be "revenue neutral," that is, to produce the same revenue as the existing tax system.[12] Lower statutory tax rates were to be offset by eliminating a wide range of tax preferences, greatly broadening the tax base. In addition, the plan had the objective of introducing greater neutrality in the tax treatment of different types of assets. The Treasury proposed to offset the decreased progressivity of the rate structure by curtailing tax preferences heavily used by high-income taxpayers. The tax burden for low-income earners was to be reduced through increased personal exemptions and zero bracket amounts for household heads.

Under the 1985 Tax Law the rate structure for the individual income tax consisted of fourteen separate tax brackets with statutory tax rates ranging from 11–50 percent of taxable income. Corporate income was taxed under a graduated rate structure with a top rate of 46 percent. The Treasury plan proposed to replace the fourteen individual income tax brackets with three broader brackets. Individual income was to be taxed at statutory rates of 15, 25 and 35 percent. The reduction of statutory income tax rates was expected to lower the average marginal tax rate of individuals by 20 percent and the average individual tax rate by 8.5 percent.

Column 2 of table 12.1 shows the effects of the Treasury plan on average marginal tax rates. Under the central assumption of six percent inflation, the average marginal tax rate on income from equity would have been reduced by 11.6 percent—from 25.59 to 22.61 percent—and the corresponding average marginal tax rate on interest from corporate bonds would have been reduced by 16.1 percent—

Table 12.4
Investment tax credit and tax deduction of depreciation allowances

Annual rate of inflation	Corporate		Noncorporate	
	short	long	short	long
		1. 1985 law		
		A. Investment tax credit		
0 precent	.0945	.0423	.0954	.0056
6 precent	.0944	.0426	.0953	.0057
10 precent	.0944	.0427	.0953	.0057
		B. Present value of capital consumption allowances		
0 precent	.9223	.6347	.9204	.5529
6 precent	.8755	.5569	.8714	.4609
10 precent	.8469	.5156	.8416	.4143
		2. Treasury proposal		
		A. Investment tax credit		
0 precent	.0000	.0000	.0000	.0000
6 precent	.0000	.0000	.0000	.0000
10 precent	.0000	.0000	.0000	.0000
		B. Present value of capital consumption allowances		
0 precent	.8926	.4997	.8981	.3960
6 precent	.9194	.5479	.9237	.4441
10 precent	.9275	.5647	.9313	.4610
		3. President's proposal		
		A. Investment tax credit		
0 precent	.0000	.0000	.0000	.0000
6 precent	.0000	.0000	.0000	.0000
10 precent	.0000	.0000	.0000	.0000
		B. Present value of capital consumption allowances		
0 precent	.9471	.6142	.9490	.4843
6 precent	1.0059	.7320	1.0058	.6487
10 precent	1.0452	.8283	1.0437	.7925
		4. Tax act of 1986		
		A. Investment tax credit		
0 precent	.0000	.0000	.0000	.0000
6 precent	.0000	.0000	.0000	.0000
10 precent	.0000	.0000	.0000	.0000
		B. Present value of capital consumption allowances		
0 precent	.9472	.5929	.9515	.4861
6 precent	.8714	.4626	.8807	.3407
10 precent	.8281	.4058	.8397	.2807

from 17.30 to 14.52 percent. Finally, the average marginal tax rate on labor income would have been reduced by 15.3 percent—from 29.67 to 25.12 percent. These reductions in average marginal tax rates would have been offset by broadening the definition of taxable income at both individual and corporate levels in order to achieve revenue neutrality.

Under the Treasury proposal the tax base would have been broadened by wholesale elimination of tax preferences for individuals and corporations. For example, the deduction for state and local income taxes would have been repealed and other state and local taxes would have been deductible only to the extent that they were incurred in income-generating activity, as indicated in table 12.2. Property taxes on owner-occupied residential real estate would not have been deductible. Other proposed changes included the taxation of unemployment compensation, curtailment of the tax deductions for mortgage and other personal interest expenses, elimination of accelerated capital cost recovery, abolition of the investment tax credit, taxation of interest on private-purpose municipal bonds, accrual basis taxation of earnings on life insurance policies, recovery of intangible drilling costs in the production of petroleum and natural gas through amortization rather than immediate expensing, and many others.

The Treasury proposal included extensive provisions for indexing income and deductions from income for tax purposes for inflation. This proposal would have retained the indexing of tax brackets, personal exemptions, and zero bracket amounts from the 1981 Tax Act to prevent the upward creep of tax brackets as a consequence of inflation. In addition, the proposal would have indexed capital gains, interest expenses, interest income, first in, first out (FIFO) inventory accounting, and capital cost recovery.[13] Prior to the tax reform of 1986, 60 percent of net capital gains were excluded from income. With the indexing of capital gains, this exclusion could no longer be justified as an adjustment for inflation and would have been eliminated.

In order to provide relief from multiple taxation of dividend income, the Treasury proposal would have allowed 50 percent of dividends to be deducted from corporate income, as defined for tax purposes. The proposal would have eliminated multiple taxation for intercorporate dividends by excluding 50 percent of dividends received by corporations from taxable income. About 40–50 percent of corporate profits after taxes are distributed to the shareholders in the form of dividends, so that these provisions would have significantly reduced the tax burden on corporate equity. Column 2 of table 12.2 summarizes the key features of the Treasury proposal.

Utilization of the economic concept of income as the base for income taxation requires that capital cost recovery must coincide with economic depreciation. To achieve this objective the Treasury proposal would have classified producers' durable equipment into five categories and structures into two categories by economic lifetime. In addition, the Treasury proposal would have indexed capital cost recovery for inflation. Panels 1 and 2 of table 12.4 show that at a high rate of inflation capital cost recovery under the Treasury proposal would have been more favorable than under the 1985 Tax Law for both short-lived and long-lived assets; the reverse is true at a low rate of inflation.[14]

12.2.3   The President's Proposal

The Treasury tax reform plan resulted in a great public outcry, especially among taxpayers whose tax liabilities would have been adversely affected by the elimination of tax preferences. However, the rate reductions in the proposal attracted widespread approval and considerable public support. The Reagan administration did not endorse the Treasury plan, but set the Treasury staff to work on a revised proposal, duly delivered in May 1985.[15] The second Treasury tax reform plan was endorsed by the administration and become known as the President's proposal.

The President's proposal would have followed the Treasury proposal by taxing individual income in only three tax brackets with statutory rates of 15, 25, and 35 percent. The President's proposal would also have raised personal exemptions and zero bracket amounts in order to compensate low-income taxpayers for the loss in progressivity of the tax structure. The President's proposal would have maintained the favorable treatment of long-term capital gains under the 1985 Tax Law, but would have reduced the proportion of capital gains excluded from income from 60 to 50 percent. In addition, beginning in 1991 taxpayers would have had the option of electing exclusion of 50 percent of capital gains from income for tax purposes or 100 percent inclusion of capital gains with complete indexing.

Under the President's proposal the corporate tax rate would have been graduated up to a top rate of 33 percent and corporate capital gains would have been taxed at a lower rate of 28 percent, as under the 1985 Tax Law. Column 3 of table 12.1 shows the impact of the proposal on average marginal tax rates. These changes would have lowered the average marginal tax rates at the individual level by 19 percent and the average individual tax rate by seven percent. We find that average marginal tax rates under the Treasury and President's proposals are similar, except that the tax rates on interest and labor income would have been slightly higher under the President's proposal.[16]

Like the Treasury proposal, the President's proposal was intended to produce the same tax revenue as the 1985 Tax Law. In order to offset the sharply lower statutory tax rates, the tax base would have been broadened by curtailing or eliminating tax preferences at both individual and corporate levels. In addition, many preferences favoring high-income taxpayers would have been limited or abolished on grounds of fairness. Important changes in the list of tax preferences would have included the repeal of the investment tax credit, repeal of the deductibility of state and local income taxes, and accrual-based taxation of earnings on life insurance policies, as indicated in table 12.2.

Unlike the Treasury proposal, however, the President's proposal would not have indexed interest income and expenses. When combined with the option of indexing capital gains, this feature of the proposal would have reduced the cost of capital for projects with debt financing. Another implication of the deduction of nominal interest expenses is apparent in panel 3 of table 12.4. The present value of capital consumption allowances for short-lived assets is slightly greater than unity when inflation is 6 or 10 percent per year, since the after-tax real interest rate becomes negative above a certain inflation rate.[17] The present value for long-lived assets in panel 3 of table 12.4 is smaller than unity only because this category includes land and inventories as well as depreciable assets.

In order to alleviate multiple taxation of income from corporate equity, the President's proposal would have allowed a deduction of 10 percent of dividends paid from corporate income. Double taxation of intercorporate dividends would have been eliminated by excluding 90 percent of dividends received by corporations from taxable income. The President's proposal would have had the same effect as the Treasury proposal on the double taxation of intercorporate dividends, but would have had less impact on double taxation at corporate and individual levels. Column 3 of table 12.2 summarizes the specific provisions of the President's proposal pertaining to taxation of income from capital.

12.2.4 The Tax Reform Act of 1986

The lengthy debate over tax reform was brought to a conclusion on October 22, 1986, by enactment of the Tax Reform Act of 1986.[18] The main provisions of the new tax law took effect on January 1, 1987. The 1986 Tax Act preserved many features of the Treasury and President's proposals. The final legislation resulted in sharply lower tax rates for both individuals and corporations. The highest statutory tax rate for individuals was lowered from 50 to 28 percent.[19] The corresponding rate for corporations was lowered from 46 to 34 percent. The substantial reductions in tax rates were offset by sharp cutbacks in tax preferences for both individuals and corporations.

Column 4 of table 12.1 shows that the tax reform reduced average marginal tax rates on various types of income in approximately the same proportion as the Treasury and President's proposals. For example, at an annual rate of inflation of six percent, the average marginal tax rate on individual income from equity was reduced by 20.6 percent—from 25.59 to 20.33—and the average marginal tax rate on interest income from corporate debt was reduced by 17.1 percent—from 17.30 to 14.34 percent. The reduction in the corporate income tax rate by 24.3 percent—from 50.84 to 38.47 percent—is even more dramatic. By contrast the average marginal tax rate on labor income was reduced by only 15.2 percent—from 29.67 to 25.17 percent.

The magnitude of the 1986 reductions in statutory tax rates for individuals and corporations is very large. It is not surprising that the base for income taxation at both individual and corporate levels had to be broadened very substantially in order to achieve revenue neutrality. Under the 1985 Tax Law, individuals, estates, and trusts were eligible for a 60 percent exclusion of realized net capital gains from taxable income. Corporations were taxed on capital gains at a rate of 28 percent, which was lower than the statutory corporate tax rate. Under the Tax Reform Act of 1986, the 60 percent exclusion of capital gains from taxable income at the individual level was repealed. All corporate capital gains, whether long-term or short-term, are taxed at the statutory corporate tax rate.

In spite of the reduction in the individual income tax rates, the accrual-based average marginal tax rate on capital gains increased from 3.03 percent under the 1985 Tax Law to 5.62 percent under the Tax Reform Act of 1986. The 1986 tax reform did not include a provision for excluding dividend payments from corporate income. In addition, the deductibility of dividends received by corporations was reduced from 85 to 80 percent. This change mainly affects the tax burden on corporate equity owned through life insurance and other insurance companies and has little impact on the overall tax burden on corporate equity.

The Tax Reform Act of 1986 also repealed the 10 percent investment tax credit for property placed in service after December 31, 1985. Since the credit was applicable mainly to investments in short-lived business assets, it had been a major source of nonneutralities in the taxation of income from different types of assets. Panel 4 of table 12.4 shows the differential impact of the investment tax credit on the cost of capital for short-lived and long-lived assets in the corporate and noncorporate sectors. Under the 1985 Tax Law the average rate of the investment tax credit in the corporate sector was 9.44 percent for short-lived assets and 4.26 percent for long-lived assets.[20] The repeal of the investment tax credit has substantially reduced differences in the tax treatment of different types of assets.

Table 12.4 shows that the Tax Reform Act of 1986 increased the present value of capital consumption allowances for short-lived corporate assets at low or moderate rates of inflation and reduced the present value for high rates of inflation. This reflects the repeal of investment tax credit, since the basis of capital cost recovery was reduced by 50 percent of the investment tax credit under the 1985 Tax Law.[21] Capital cost recovery was made less rapid for producers' durable equipment, primarily through longer tax lifetimes. For structures, the adoption of longer tax lives works in the same direction, reducing the present value of capital cost recovery.

12.3   Effective Tax Rates

The tax burden on capital income can be summarized by means of effective marginal tax rates on income from each type of assets. An effective tax rate represents the complex provisions of tax law in terms of a single *ad valorem* rate. This tax rate is based on the social rate of return, defined as income per dollar of capital, adjusted for inflation and depreciation but not for taxes. This social rate of return can be compared with the corresponding private rate of return, which excludes all tax liabilities at both corporate and individual levels. The effective tax rate is defined as the difference between the social and private rates of return, divided by the social rate of return.[22]

To describe the Tax Reform Act of 1986, the pre-existing 1985 Tax Law, and the alternative reform proposals presented by the Treasury and the President, we utilize effective tax rates for capital income from three different legal forms of organization—corporate, noncorporate, and household—and from short-lived and long-lived assets. We also present tax wedges among different types of assets, defined as differences between social rates of return on these assets. We give tax wedges for transfers between asset categories within a sector, between sectors, and between the present and the future. We refer to these as interasset, intersectoral, and intertemporal tax wedges. The interasset and intersectoral wedges correspond to differences between marginal products of different types of assets.

In generating effective marginal tax rates and tax wedges we have employed parameters describing alternative tax laws and tax reform proposals from tables 12.1–12.3. In addition, we have set the values of parameters describing the financial structure of each sector, the corporate after-tax rate of return to corporate equity, and the rate of interest at corresponding averages for the 1967–1986 period. We assume that nominal after-tax rates of return to equity are the same for all sectors and debt/equity ratios are the same for all assets with each sector. Property tax rates are set at 1986 levels. Finally, we have assumed that an increase in the rate of inflation raises the nominal rate of interest point for point.[23]

12.3.1   The 1985 Tax Law

We present effective tax rates under the 1985 Tax Law in table 12.5. With a six percent rate of inflation, these rates were 2.4 percent for short-lived assets and 44.4 percent for long-lived assets in the corporate sector. The difference in social rates of return between the two asset classes was 4.0 percent. Transferring one dollar's worth of capital from short-lived to long-lived assets would have increased the national income in perpetuity by four cents per year with no additional investment. This is a very substantial tax wedge, comparable in magnitude to the private rate of return, suggesting that the potential gains from tax reform were very large. These gains approached one

Table 12.5
Effective tax rates and the distortionary impacts of capital income taxation: 1985 law

Sector	Short-lived assets			Long-lived assets			All assets		
	social rate of return	gap	effective tax rate	social rate of return	gap	effective tax rate	social rate of return	gap	effective tax rate
1. 0 percent inflation									
Corporate	.049	−.007	−.133	.094	.039	.410	.080	.025	.308
Noncorporate	.044	−.011	−.257	.076	.021	.272	.074	.018	.251
Household	.058	.007	.119	.058	.007	.119	.058	.007	.119
2. 6 percent inflation									
Corporate	.053	.001	.024	.094	.042	.444	.081	.029	.359
Noncorporate	.045	−.007	−.152	.075	.023	.312	.073	.021	.293
Household	.052	.007	.127	.052	.007	.127	.052	.007	.127
3. 10 percent inflation									
Corporate	.056	.006	.110	.093	.043	.461	.082	.032	.387
Noncorporate	.045	−.004	−.085	.074	.025	.337	.072	.023	.319
Household	.048	.006	.133	.048	.006	.133	.048	.006	.133

Tax wedges

Inflation	Interasset (short-long)		Intersector (short and long)					
	corporate	noncorporate	corporate-noncorporate		corporate-household		noncorporate-household	
			short	long	short	long	short	long
0 percent	−.045	−.032	.005	.018	−.008	.036	−.014	.018
6 percent	−.040	−.030	.009	.019	.002	.042	−.007	.023
10 percent	−.037	−.029	.011	.019	.009	.045	−.002	.026

dollar for each dollar transferred as a consequence of a change in tax policy.

The provisions of tax law interact with the rate of inflation in determining the tax burden on capital income. First, a higher rate of inflation reduced the present value of capital cost recovery under the 1985 Tax Law since cost recovery was not indexed against the impact of inflation. Second, taxation of nominal interest income, coupled with tax deductibility of nominal interest expenses, reduced the tax burden as the rate of inflation increased. For corporate and noncorporate assets the firm's marginal tax rate for the deduction of interest expenses was higher than the individual's marginal tax rate on interest income. On balance the tax burden on corporate and noncorporate assets increased with the rate of inflation.[24] As the rate of inflation rose, the tax burden on short-lived assets increased faster than that on long-lived assets. As a consequence the interasset tax wedge declined with the rate of inflation.

Under the 1985 Tax Law, assets in the noncorporate sector had lower tax burdens than corresponding assets in the corporate sector. Table 12.5 shows that the effective marginal tax rates for short-lived and long-lived assets were -15.2 and 31.2 percent, respectively. These rates were substantially lower than the corresponding rates in the corporate sector. The interasset tax wedge between short-lived and the long-lived assets was 3.0 percentage points. Although this tax wedge was smaller than that in the corporate sector, the interasset tax wedge in the noncorporate sector suggests substantial opportunities for potential gains from tax reform.

A striking feature of effective tax rates in the noncorporate sector under the 1985 Tax Law is that the effective tax rate on short-lived assets was negative. The provisions for capital cost recovery and the investment tax credit were so favorable that the tax system, in effect, provided subsidies to noncorporate investment in short-lived assets. These subsidies took the form of "tax shelter" that could be used to reduce tax liabilities on other types of income. The effects of inflation on the tax burdens and the interasset tax wedge in the noncorporate sector was similar to those in the corporate sector. Inflation increased the tax burden on capital income and reduced the interrasset tax wedge.

The value of capital services of household assets, such as the rental equivalent of owner-occupied housing or the services of consumers' durables, was not included in taxable income under the 1985 Tax Law.

However, effective tax rates on household assets were affected by provisions of the individual income tax since payments for personal and mortgage interest were deductible and interest income from the debt claims on household assets was taxable. Like the assets in the corporate and noncorporate sectors, household assets were also subject to property taxes. Table 12.5 shows that the effective tax rate on household assets was 12.7 percent with six percent inflation. This rate increased slightly with inflation. Since the income from household assets was not taxable, there was no interasset tax wedge in the household sector.

Table 12.5 shows intersectoral tax wedges under the 1985 Tax Law for short-lived and long-lived assets. When the rate of inflation was six percent per year, the intersectoral tax wedge between the corporate and noncorporate sectors was 0.9 percent for the short-lived assets and 1.9 percent for long-lived assets. The wedges between the noncorporate and household sectors were -0.7 percent for short-lived assets and 2.3 percent for long-lived assets. The wedges between the corporate and household sectors were 0.2 percent for short-lived assets and 4.2 percent for long-lived assets. Unlike the interasset tax wedges, the intersectoral tax wedges tended to increase with the rate of inflation since the tax burden of corporate assets increased faster than that of noncorporate assets, which in turn increased faster than that of household assets.

12.3.2   The Treasury Proposal

Effective marginal tax rates on business assets under the Treasury proposal are given in table 12.6. These rates are similar to those under the 1985 Tax Law. A comparison of tables 12.5 and 12.6 reveals that at six percent inflation the Treasury proposal would have slightly reduced the effective marginal tax rate from 35.9 to 35.1 percent for corporate assets and from 29.3 to 27.1 percent for noncorporate assets. Since the 1985 Tax Law did not index taxable income and tax deductions, the Treasury proposal would have increased the tax burden at a lower rate of inflation, but would have decreased it at a higher inflation rate.

The effective marginal tax rates under the Treasury proposal reflect the combined effects of the repeal of investment tax credit, the introduction of economic depreciation, lowering of statutory tax rates, and indexing of interest income, interest expenses, and capital gains. Of the many tax policy changes in the Treasury proposal, the repeal of

Table 12.6
Effective tax rates and the distortionary impacts of capital income taxation: Treasury proposal

Sector	Short-lived assets			Long-lived assets			All assets		
	social rate of return	gap	effective tax rate	social rate of return	gap	effective tax rate	social rate of return	gap	effective tax rate
	1. 0 percent inflation								
Corporate	.080	.025	.310	.091	.036	.397	.088	.033	.373
Noncorporate	.071	.016	.224	.077	.022	.284	.076	.021	.280
Household	.060	.009	.156	.060	.009	.156	.060	.009	.156
	2. 6 percent inflation								
Corporate	.076	.021	.280	.088	.033	.379	.085	.030	.351
Noncorporate	.069	.014	.207	.075	.021	.275	.075	.020	.271
Household	.060	.009	.157	.060	.009	.157	.060	.009	.157
	3. 10 percent inflation								
Corporate	.075	.020	.271	.087	.033	.373	.084	.029	.345
Noncorporate	.068	.014	.203	.075	.020	.272	.074	.020	.268
Household	.059	.009	.158	.059	.009	.158	.059	.009	.158

Tax wedges

Inflation	Interasset (short-long)		Intersector (short and long)					
	corporate	noncorporate	corporate-noncorporate		corporate-household		nonorporate-household	
			short	long	short	long	short	long
0 percent	-.011	-.006	.009	.015	.020	.031	.010	.016
6 percent	-.012	-.006	.007	.013	.017	.029	.009	.016
10 percent	-.012	-.007	.007	.013	.016	.028	.009	.016

investment tax credit would have had the greatest impact on effective tax rates on income from capital. Since short-lived business assets received the most important benefits from the investment tax credit under the 1985 Tax Law, the increase in the tax burden on short-lived assets under the Treasury proposal would have been most marked.

The objectives of the Treasury proposal were to reduce tax wedges among different forms of investment and insulate the tax structure from the impact of inflation. We find that the Treasury proposal would have reduced interasset tax wedges substantially. Under the 1985 Tax Law with six percent inflation, the tax wedges between short-lived and long-lived assets were 4.0 percent in the corporate sector and 3.0 percent in the noncorporate sector. They would have been reduced to only 1.2 percent and 0.6 percent, respectively, under the Treasury proposal. To the extent that the welfare cost of a tax distortion increases with the tax wedge, reductions in the interasset tax wedges of this magnitude would have significantly improved the efficiency of capital allocation within each sector.

Second, the Treasury proposal would have substantially reduced the intersectoral tax wedges for long-lived assets, in part because of the elimination of property tax deductions, but would have had mixed effects for short-lived assets. The impact of the proposal on intersectoral tax wedges for short-lived assets would have depended on the rate of inflation. The Treasury proposal would have been relatively ineffective in eliminating the substantial intersectoral tax wedges for long-lived assets under the 1985 Tax Law, since long-lived assets would have borne a heavier tax burden than the short-lived assets under the proposal. In addition, corporate assets would have been more heavily taxed than noncorporate assets, which, in turn, would have been more heavily taxed than household assets.

Third, the repeal of investment tax credit would have increased the tax burden roughly as much as as the reduction of the statutory tax rates would have decreased it at a six percent rate of inflation. The average effective tax rate for the entire corporate sector would have changed only from 35.9 percent to 35.1 percent and the intertemporal tax wedge would have increased slightly from 2.9 percent to 3.0 percent. The effect of the repeal of investment tax credit is seen most clearly in the case of the short-lived business assets. At a six percent rate of inflation, the effective tax rate on short-lived corporate assets would have increased from 2.4 percent under the 1985 law to 28.0 percent under the Treasury proposal and the intertemporal tax wedge would have increased from 0.1 percent to 2.1 percent. The pattern is reversed for long-lived assets, since the intertemporal tax wedges would have been smaller under the Treasury proposal.

Finally, the Treasury proposal would have reduced the impact of inflation on the tax burden on capital income by defining taxable income to approximate economic income more closely. In fact, the tax burden would have declined with inflation, due to incomplete indexing of interest payments.[25] To the extent that interest is not completely indexed, inflation tends to increase the after-tax real interest rate and reduce the present value of capital consumption allowances, even if tax depreciation is completely indexed against inflation. On the other hand, incomplete indexing reduces the cost of debt financing. Table 12.6 indicates that the result of these two opposing effects would have been to reduce the marginal tax burden of capital with higher rates of inflation.

12.3.3   The President's Proposal

We summarize effective tax rates under the President's proposal in table 12.7. Overall, the effects of the President's proposal would have been similar to those of the Treasury proposal. The tax burden on income from capital would have increased at a low rate of inflation and decreased at a high rate. The interasset tax wedges in the corporate and noncorporate sectors would have been reduced; the intersectoral tax wedges of long-lived assets would also have been reduced, but effects on the tax wedges for the short-lived assets would have been mixed. However, a careful comparison of tables 12.6 and 12.7 reveals a number of subtle differences between the Treasury and President's proposals, many of which are attributable to differences in the impact of inflation on the tax system.

With no inflation the President's proposal would have been more favorable to investment, since it would have retained accelerated schedules for capital cost recovery. At six or 10 percent inflation rates, the President's proposal would have been even more favorable to investment, since the indexing of capital consumption allowances would have been coupled with the deduction of nominal interest expenses. This would have increased the present value of capital consumption allowances at higher rates of inflation. In addition, inflation would have lowered the tax burden on capital as a consequence of the tax deductibility of nominal interest expenses. The value of the result-

Table 12.7
Effective tax rates and the distortionary impacts of capital income taxation: President's proposal

Sector	Short-lived assets			Long-lived assets			All assets		
	social rate of return	gap	effective tax rate	social rate of return	gap	effective tax rate	social rate of return	gap	effective tax rate
				1. 0 percent inflation					
Corporate	.077	.021	.271	.091	.034	.381	.086	.030	.351
Noncorporate	.069	.013	.187	.077	.021	.273	.076	.020	.268
Household	.061	.009	.154	.061	.009	.154	.061	.009	.154
				2. 6 percent inflation					
Corporate	.066	.012	.182	.080	.026	.330	.076	.022	.290
Noncorporate	.061	.008	.134	.070	.016	.235	.069	.016	.229
Household	.056	.009	.162	.056	.009	.162	.056	.009	.162
				3. 10 percent inflation					
Corporate	.058	.005	.091	.073	.020	.271	.068	.015	.224
Noncorporate	.057	.005	.089	.065	.013	.196	.064	.012	.190
Household	.053	.009	.167	.053	.009	.167	.053	.009	.167

Table 12.7
(continued)

Tax wedges

Inflation	Interasset (short-long)		Intersector (short and long)					
	corporate	noncorporate	corporate-noncorporate		corporate-household		noncorporate-household	
			short	long	short	long	short	long
0 percent	−.014	−.008	.008	.014	.016	.029	.008	.016
6 percent	−.014	−.008	.004	.011	.010	.024	.005	.013
10 percent	−.014	−.008	.001	.008	.005	.019	.004	.011

ing deductions would have been greater than the additional tax liabilities resulting from the taxation of nominal interest income at the individual level. Similar reasoning can be applied to explain the decline of the intersectoral tax wedges with inflation.

Under the 1985 Tax Law and the Tax Reform Act of 1986 capital cost recovery is not indexed for inflation, so that an increase in the inflation rate adds to the tax burden on income from capital. Under the Treasury proposal, the recovery of capital cost would have been indexed and interest would have been indexed incompletely. There would have been a slight tendency for the tax burden on capital income to decline with inflation. This tendency would have been strengthened under the President's proposal, since capital cost recovery would have been indexed, while interest deductions would not. Tables 12.6 and 12.7 show that the President's proposal would have narrowed the intersectoral tax wedges relative to the Treasury proposal. By contrast the Treasury proposal would have had uniformly smaller interasset tax wedges.

12.3.4   The Tax Reform Act of 1986

Since the Tax Reform Act of 1986 embraced many of the ideas contained in the Treasury and President's proposals, the impact of the tax reform on effective tax rates and tax wedges is similar to that of the two proposals. Table 12.8 shows that the repeal of the investment tax credit more than offset the reduction in the statutory tax rates, so that the overall tax burden on income from capital is increased. Despite the acceleration of capital cost recovery and lower marginal tax rates, the impact of repeal of the investment tax credit is most evident in the increase of the tax burden on short-lived business assets. At six percent inflation, the Tax Reform Act of 1986 imposes an effective tax rate on short-lived assets of 38.2 percent in the corporate sector and 28.2 percent in the noncorporate sector, while the corresponding tax rates were 2.4 percent and -15.2 percent under the 1985 Tax Law.

For long-lived assets, effective tax rates were not much affected by tax reform. The effects of lower tax rates were approximately offset by the combined effects of the longer cost recovery period and the repeal of the investment tax credit. At six percent inflation, the interasset tax wedges in the corporate and noncorporate sectors are only 1.0 percent and 0.6 percent, while the corresponding figures were 4.0 percent and 3.0 percent, respectively, under the 1985 Tax Law. Table 12.8 shows

Table 12.8
Effective tax rates and the distortionary impacts of capital income taxation: 1986 Tax Reform Act

Sector	Short-lived assets			Long-lived assets			All assets		
	social rate of return	gap	effective tax rate	social rate of return	gap	effective tax rate	social rate of return	gap	effective tax rate
	1. 0 percent inflation								
Corporate	.078	.022	.279	.092	.036	.390	.087	.031	.360
Noncorporate	.068	.012	.182	.076	.020	.268	.075	.020	.262
Household	.059	.007	.125	.059	.007	.125	.059	.007	.125
	2. 6 percent inflation								
Corporate	.084	.032	.382	.094	.042	.449	.091	.039	.430
Noncorporate	.071	.020	.282	.077	.026	.335	.076	.025	.332
Household	.052	.007	.135	.052	.007	.135	.052	.007	.135
	3. 10 percent inflation								
Corporate	.087	.038	.439	.093	.045	.478	.091	.043	.467
Noncorporate	.073	.025	.342	.077	.029	.373	.076	.028	.371
Household	.048	.007	.143	.048	.007	.143	.048	.007	.143

Table 12.8
(continued)

Tax wedges

Inflation	Interasset (short-long)		Intersector (short and long)					
	corporate	noncorporate	corporate-noncorporate		corporate-household		nonporate-household	
			short	long	short	long	short	long
0 percent	−.014	−.008	.009	.016	.019	.033	.009	.017
6 percent	−.010	−.006	.012	.017	.031	.041	.019	.025
10 percent	−.006	−.004	.014	.017	.039	.045	.025	.029

that the effective tax rates on household assets were essentially unaffected by the reform, since the difference between the average marginal tax rates on equity and debt claims was almost unchanged and property taxes remained the same.

Overall, the tax burden on the income from capital was increased by the 1986 tax reform. As a consequence, the intertemporal tax wedges are larger and the efficiency of intertemporal resource allocation was adversely affected. On the other hand, the interasset tax wedges were considerably reduced and the efficiency of interasset capital allocation was enhanced. At six percent inflation intersectoral wedges were increased for short-lived assets and decreased for long-lived assets.

The 1986 tax reform did not incorporate the indexing of capital income taxation provided in the Treasury proposal. The impacts of inflation on effective tax rates and tax wedges under the Tax Reform Act of 1986 are similar to those under the 1985 Tax Law. The tax burden on income from capital increases with inflation. Since the tax burden on short-lived assets rises faster than that on long-lived assets, interasset tax wedges decline with the rate of inflation. The tax burden on corporate assets increases faster than that on noncorporate assets, which in turn increases faster than that on household assets, so that intersectoral tax wedges increase with the rate of inflation.

12.4 Economic Growth

In this section we estimate the impact of alternative tax policies—the Treasury proposal, the President's proposal, and the Tax Reform Act of 1986—on U.S. economic growth. We evaluate the effect of each of the alternative tax reform proposals by comparing the resulting level of welfare with that attainable under the "base case" given by the 1985 Tax Law. Since effective tax rates and tax wedges depend on the rate of inflation, we consider three alternative rates of inflation—zero, six, and 10 percent. In these comparisons we impose the requirement that the revenue and expenditure of the government sector are the same as in the base case.

We consider four alternative methods for adjusting tax revenues in order to keep the budgetary position of the government sector the same as in the base case. The first method is to increase or decrease government revenues by means of a "lump-sum" tax or subsidy. We model a lump-sum tax by altering the budget constraint facing the representative consumer. A tax results in a contraction of the budget available to the consumer and a corresponding increase in government revenue. Similarly, a subsidy expands the budget available to the consumer and decreases government revenue. A lump-sum tax or subsidy does not distort decisions in the household or business sectors of the economy by altering the tax wedges facing the representative consumer or the representative producer.

We also consider three methods for adjusting government revenues that involve changes in tax-induced distortions. These include proportional adjustments to labor income taxes, sales taxes on investment and consumption goods, and taxes on income from both capital and labor. The labor income tax adjustment affects the tax rate for labor services, the sales tax adjustment affects the tax rates for consumption and investment goods, and the income tax adjustment affects the tax rates for both capital and labor services. By considering all three methods we are able to assess the sensitivity of the welfare rankings of alternative tax policies to changes in the constraints imposed by the requirement of revenue neutrality.

12.4.1   The Impact of Tax Reform

We summarize the results of our simulations of U.S. economic growth under alternative tax policies in table 12.9. An important conclusion we can draw from table 12.9 is that the Treasury proposal, the President's proposal and the Tax Reform Act of 1986 all improve potential economic welfare substantially. In our central case with six percent inflation and a lump-sum tax adjustment, the President's proposal would have generated a welfare gain of $2,452.2 billion, while the Treasury proposal would have generated a gain of $1,907.6 billion. However, the welfare gain associated with the Tax Reform Act of 1986 is only $448.4 billion.[26]

With no change in government expenditures, the Tax Reform Act of 1986 results in more revenue than is necessary to keep the government in the same budgetary position as under the 1985 Tax Law. In order to leave government revenue the same under the two tax policies, tax revenues must be rebated to the household sector. Replacing the lump-sum tax adjustment with a distortionary tax adjustment lowers the rates of the distortionary taxes involved and improves the perfor-

Table 12.9
Welfare effects of tax reform (billions of 1987 dollars)

Revenue adjustment	1985 tax law	Treasury proposal	President's proposal	1986 tax act
	0 percent inflation			
Lump-sum tax	724.0	1,489.6	1,691.4	1,561.8
Labor income tax	478.2	1,468.8	1,642.4	1,565.0
Sales tax	400.3	1,452.9	1,614.6	1,558.7
Individual income tax	374.5	1,456.1	1,619.1	1,563.1
	6 percent inflation			
Lump-sum tax	0.0	1,907.6	2,452.2	448.4
Labor income tax	0.0	1,711.4	2,170.4	746.9
Sales tax	0.0	1,600.1	2,104.9	901.2
Individual income tax	0.0	1,595.8	2,007.9	999.4
	10 percent inflation			
Lump-sum tax	−477.1	2,060.4	3,015.6	−200.8
Labor income tax	−333.7	1,791.6	2,584.7	267.3
Sales tax	−285.2	1,623.5	2,356.4	517.0
Individual income tax	−221.9	1,604.8	2,353.1	748.6

Note—The 1987 national wealth (beginning of the year) and the gross national product were $15,920.2 billion and $4,488.5 billion.

mance of the economy under the 1986 tax reform. By contrast, the Treasury and the President's proposals would have resulted in less revenue than the 1985 Tax Law. The welfare gains would have been smaller under the distortionary tax adjustments than under the lump-sum tax adjustment.

Another perspective on the economic impact of the alternative tax reform proposals is provided by a comparison of the welfare gains from tax reform with private national wealth. The nominal value of the U.S. private national wealth at the beginning of 1987 was $15,920.2 billion. Making use of this figure, we estimate that the welfare gains from the Treasury and the President's proposals would have been equivalent to increases of 12.0 and 15.4 percent, respectively, of U.S. private national wealth in 1987.[27] The welfare gain from the Tax Reform Act of 1986 is equivalent to an increase of only 2.8 percent of the national wealth.

Under distortionary tax adjustments the welfare gains would have been somewhat smaller for the President's proposal and slightly smaller for the Treasury proposal. The gains are substantially larger for the 1986 Tax Reform Act. However, these gains are not sensitive to the differences among the distortionary tax adjustments.[28] If we consider a sales tax adjustment with a six percent inflation rate, the welfare gains would have been $1,600.1 billion for the Treasury proposal and $2,014.9 billion for the President's proposal. These gains would have totaled 10.1 and 12.3 percent of the U.S. private national wealth in 1987. The corresponding welfare gain is $901.2 billion for the Tax Reform Act of 1986. This is equivalent to 5.7 percent of the national wealth.

Table 12.9 also shows how the welfare effects of alternative tax reforms would be affected by the rate of inflation. It is useful to focus on lump-sum tax adjustments since distortionary tax adjustments result in reallocations of resources due to substitutions as well as changes in the rate of inflation. Economic welfare would have increased with higher inflation under the Treasury and President's proposals. On the other hand, welfare declines with inflation under the 1985 Tax Law and the Tax Reform Act of 1986. The reason is that the tax burden on capital income would have been reduced with higher inflation under the two proposals, while inflation increases the tax burden on capital income under the 1985 Tax Law and the Tax Reform Act of 1986.

An increase in the rate of inflation from zero to six percent is sufficient to alter the welfare ranking between the Treasury proposal and the Tax Reform Act of 1986. The welfare gains from the 1986 tax reform are substantially attenuated at a six percent inflation rate. At a ten percent inflation rate these gains are further reduced. Our first conclusion is that potential gains in welfare from the 1986 reform are largely dissipated at moderate rates of inflation, such as those that have prevailed for the past decade. Insulating the U.S. tax system from the impact of inflation should retain high priority in future deliberations about tax reform.

12.4.2   Alternative Approaches to Tax Reform

We have measured the impact of the Tax Reform Act of 1986 on economic welfare, employing the 1985 Tax Law as a basis for comparison. We have also assessed the potential impact of the Treasury and President's tax reform proposals. We next consider alternative approaches to tax reform based on the elimination of tax wedges among different types of assets. As before, the growth path of the U.S. economy under the 1985 Tax Law is taken as a basis for comparison. We measure the potential gains in economic welfare from changes in tax policy by comparing the resulting levels of welfare with those corresponding to the 1985 Tax Law.

For the purposes of this analysis we find it useful to distinguish between atemporal and intertemporal tax wedges. The elimination of an atemporal tax wedge requires that the social rates of return on the corresponding assets are equalized within a given time period. We eliminate atemporal tax wedges among assets by equalizing the corresponding social rates of return at a weighted average of these rates of return, where stocks of assets are used as weights. More precisely, we equalize social rates of return associated with balanced growth equilibrium under the 1985 Tax Law, using the balanced growth proportions of assets as weights.

To model the integration of the corporate and individual income taxes we set the social rates of return on corporate assets equal to those on the corresponding noncorporate assets. This procedure does not affect the private rates of return in the two sectors, so that effective tax rates are not equalized between the sectors. The private rates of return on assets in different sectors differ for two reasons. The first is that debt/asset ratios differ across sectors. The second is that average marginal tax rates on individual income vary from sector to sector, because of the differences in the distribution of asset ownership among taxpayers in different income tax brackets.

We consider the elimination of five sets of tax wedges: (1) interasset tax wedges within the corporate and noncorporate sectors; (2) intersectoral tax wedges between assets of the same type held in the corporate and noncorporate sectors; (3) intersectoral tax wedges among assets of the same type held in the business and household sectors, where the business sector includes both corporate and noncorporate business; (4) all atemporal tax wedges in the business sector;

and (5) all atemporal tax wedges in the business and the household sectors. We also consider (6) the integration of corporate and noncorporate taxes.

Elimination of an intertemporal tax wedge requires equalizing the social and private rates of return, so that the effective tax rate on the corresponding assets is reduced to zero. We consider two possible approaches to eliminating intertemporal tax distortions. First, we consider (7) the elimination of intertemporal tax wedges resulting from income and property taxes. This leaves the sales tax on investment goods at its level in the base case, while reducing the effective tax rate on capital income to zero. Second, we eliminate the tax burden on capital altogether by (8) removing the sales tax on investment goods as well as taxes on income from capital and property taxes. These two approaches correspond to alternative implementations of consumption tax rules for the taxation of capital income.

We summarize the sums of the investment tax credit and the present value of tax deductions for capital cost recovery that result in the elimination of tax wedges among different classes of assets in table 12.10. Panel A represents the base case, corresponding to 1985 Tax Law. Panel B represents the elimination of interasset tax wedges within the corporate and noncorporate sectors. This can be achieved by setting the sums of the investment tax credit and the present value of tax deductions for capital cost recovery at the values specified in the table. The social rates of return and the effective tax rates must be the same for short-lived and long-lived assets within each sector, since the private rate of return is the same for all assets within the sector. After interasset wedges are eliminated, the intersectoral and intertemporal tax wedges remain.

In panel C we eliminate the intersectoral tax wedges between assets in the corporate and noncorporate sectors by equalizing social rates of return on short-lived assets in the two sectors. Similarly, we equalize social rates of return on long-lived assets. After the intersectoral tax wedges within the business sector are removed, the interasset tax wedges and intersectoral wedges between the business and household sectors still remain. In panel D we also eliminate the intersectoral tax wedges between business and household sectors. This approach to tax reform eliminates all the intersectoral tax wedges, but creates an interasset tax wedge in the household sector where none existed before the change in tax policy. There are interasset tax wedges in the corporate and noncorporate sectors as well.

Table 12.10
Elimination of tax wedges: 1985 tax law

1. Capital stock in the steady state of the reference case (%)

Corporate		Nonorporate		Household	
short	long	short	long	short	long
.0893	.2563	.0185	.2580	.0909	.2870

2. Removal of capital income tax distortions

Class of assets	Social rate of return	Effective tax rate	ITC + T · Z[1]
	A. 1985 tax law		
Corporate:			
Short	.0518	.0229	.5395
Long	.0914	.4460	.3257
Nonorporate:			
Short	.0433	−.1544	.3510
Long	.0731	.3152	.1409
Household:			
Short	.0503	.1301	.0000
Long	.0503	.1301	.0000
	B. No within-sector interasset wedges		
Corporate:			
Short	.0812	.3762	.4652
Long	.0812	.3762	.3942
Nonorporate:			
Short	.0711	.2960	.2552
Long	.0711	.2960	.1641
Household:			
Short	.0503	.1301	.0000
Long	.0503	.1301	.0000
	C. No intersector wedges: business assets		
Corporate:			
Short	.0504	−.0052	.5432
Long	.0822	.3840	.3873
Nonorporate:			
Short	.0504	.0068	.3267
Long	.0822	.3913	.0341
Household:			
Short	.0503	.1301	.0000
Long	.0503	.1301	.0000

Table 12.10
(continued)

Class of assets	Social rate of return	Effective tax rate	ITC + T · Z[1]
	D. No intersector wedges: all sectors		
Corporate:			
Short	.0503	−.0062	.5433
Long	.0708	.2844	.4639
Nonorporate:			
Short	.0503	.0058	.3268
Long	.0708	.2930	.1677
Household:			
Short	.0503	.1311	−.0002
Long	.0708	.3821	−.3766
	E. No tax wedges: all assets, business sector		
Corporate:			
Short	.0767	.3397	.4766
Long	.0767	.3397	.4243
Nonorporate:			
Short	.0767	.3476	.2358
Long	.0767	.3476	.0985
Household:			
Short	.0503	.1301	.0000
Long	.0503	.1301	.0000
	F. No tax wedges: all assets, all sectors		
Corporate:			
Short	.0667	.2408	.5019
Long	.0667	.2408	.4911
Nonorporate:			
Short	.0667	.2499	.2703
Long	.0667	.2499	.2152
Household:			
Short	.0667	.3444	−.0666
Long	.0667	.3444	−.3020

Table 12.10
(concluded)

Class of assets	Social rate of return	Effective tax rate	ITC + T · Z[1]
	G. Corporate tax integration: apply noncorporate social rates of return to corporate assets		
Corporate:			
Short	.0433	−.1684	.5610
Long	.0731	.3069	.4486
Nonorporate:			
Short	.0433	−.1544	.3510
Long	.0731	.3152	.1409
Household:			
Short	.0503	.1301	.0000
Long	.0503	.1301	.0000
	H. Zero effective tax rates		
Corporate:			
Short	.0506	.0000	.5425
Long	.0506	.0000	.5986
Nonorporate:			
Short	.0500	.0000	.3279
Long	.0500	.0000	.4100
Household:			
Short	.0437	.0000	.0265
Long	.0437	.0000	.1202

Note—Steady-state allocation of capital in the base case is used as the weights. The annual rate of inflation is assumed to be 6 percent.
1. Equals investment tax credit plus the tax rate at the firm level times the present value of capital consumption allowances.

In panel E we eliminate both the interasset and intersectoral tax wedges in the business sector. Conceptually, the tax reforms represented in panel E are a combination of the reforms represented in panels B and C. In panel F all the atemporal tax wedges are eliminated, so that the only remaining sources of tax distortions are the intertemporal tax wedges. In panel G, we eliminate the intersectoral tax wedges between corporate and noncorporate sectors by setting the social rates of return on corporate assets equal to the corresponding rates on noncorporate assets. The substantial reduction in tax revenue can be offset by a lump-sum tax or by proportional adjustments in the labor income tax, sales tax, or individual income tax. Finally, in panel H all the intertemporal tax wedges are eliminated and the social and private rates of return are equalized for all assets.

12.4.3   Welfare Impacts

We summarize the welfare impacts of the eight hypothetical tax reform proposals in table 12.11. Beginning with lump-sum tax adjustments, we find that the welfare gain from elimination of interasset tax wedges that existed under the 1985 Tax Law would have been $443.9 billion. The elimination of intersectoral tax wedges between assets in the corporate and noncorporate sectors yields welfare losses instead of gains. Given Harberger's (1966) analysis of the impact of the corporate income tax, this is a rather surprising result. The elimination of a tax wedge would usually be expected to increase the efficiency of resource allocation and improve the level of economic welfare. However, the demand for capital services is much more elastic in the noncorporate sector than in the corporate sector. Equalizing the social rates of return between the corporate and noncorporate assets reduces the total demand for the business capital services.

The third change in tax policy analyzed in table 12.11 is the elimination of intersectoral tax wedges between household and business sectors. The results suggest that there would have been a very large potential welfare gain from this change in tax policy under the 1985 Tax Law. The estimated gain is $2,262.6 billion at a six percent rate of inflation. Given the substantial tax wedges between business and household assets under the 1985 Tax Law, this result is not surprising. For example, the intersectoral tax wedges for short-lived assets were 0.2 percent between the corporate and household sectors and −0.7

percent between the noncorporate and household sectors. The corresponding figures for long-lived assets were 4.2 percent and 2.3 percent, respectively.

The welfare gain from eliminating the interasset and intersectoral wedges among business assets is estimated to be only $326.4 billion under the 1985 Tax Law. The welfare gain from eliminating all the atemporal tax wedges in the private sector of the U.S. economy is estimated to be $2,663.7 billion. This gain is much larger than the welfare gain resulting from elimination of interasset distortions within each sector and somewhat larger than that resulting from elimination of intersectoral tax distortions for all sectors. In view of the relative magnitude of these effects, we can attribute most of the welfare gain to elimination of intersectoral tax wedges between business and household assets.

The sixth change in tax policy we consider is the elimination of intersectoral tax wedges between assets in the corporate and noncorporate sectors. For this purpose we set social rates of return on corporate assets equal to the corresponding rates of return on noncorporate assets under the 1985 Tax Law. The effective tax burden on corporate assets is unambiguously reduced by this hypothetical change in tax policy. The estimated welfare gain from this change in tax policy is $1,313.1 billion. The gain is about half of that attainable by eliminating all intersectoral tax wedges.

In the six changes in tax policy we have considered up to this point, we have focused attention on the distortionary impact of atemporal tax wedges. We next consider the elimination of intertemporal tax wedges by setting effective tax rates on all types of income from capital equal to zero. We find that the elimination of intertemporal tax wedges would have generated huge welfare gains under lump-sum tax adjustment. If sales taxes on investment goods were also abolished, the welfare gain would become even larger. Taking the 1985 Tax Law as the base case, the welfare gain from removing intertemporal tax wedges on all assets would have been $3,853.9 billion. The elimination of the sales taxes on investment goods would have produced a gain of $4,128.1 billion.

The magnitudes of welfare gains from elimination of the intertemporal tax wedges under distortionary tax adjustments presented in table 12.11 are substantially lower than those under lump-sum tax adjustment. The changes in marginal tax rates required to offset revenue losses can generate significant subsitution effects. The welfare effects resulting from the elimination of intertemporal tax wedges, as given in table 12.11, are also sensitive to the choice among distortionary tax adjustments, since the required increase in tax revenue is so large.

If a proposed tax reform is roughly revenue neutral, so that the magnitude of the required adjustment in tax revenue is small, the welfare ranking of alternative policy changes does not depend on the method for adjusting tax revenue. For a change in tax policy that involves substantial rate cuts with no compensating enhancement of tax revenues through base broadening, the welfare measures under the lump-sum tax adjustment can be interpreted as upper bounds of the welfare gains that can be achieved. Any realistic tax reform involving revenue adjustment through changes in distortionary taxes would result in welfare gains well below those attainable under the hypothetical lump-sum tax adjustment.

The fact that the estimated welfare gains from the elimination of the intertemporal tax wedges is in the range of four trillion dollars suggests that the potential welfare gain from replacing the current system of income taxes with consumption-based taxes would be very large indeed. However, the welfare gains would be reduced by approximately half under the more realistic assumption that revenue losses are offset by distortionary tax adjustments. These welfare gains are still impressive.

Our second conclusion is that the consequences in reductions of intertemporal tax wedges associated with consumption-based taxation must be carefully weighed against possible worsening of atemporal resource allocation as a consequence of distortions associated with increased taxes on consumption. An idealized income tax with income from household assets incorporated into the tax base would have permitted substantial reductions in tax rates on income from business assets. Such a tax would have produced greater potential gains in welfare than an idealized consumption tax, with the 1985 Tax Law taken as a starting point. Harberger's case for uniform tax rates on all types of capital income is strengthened by this finding, provided that uniform treatment is not limited to income from business assets.

12.5 Conclusion

The Tax Reform Act of 1986 increases the effective marginal tax burden on income from capital at any positive inflation rate. Nonetheless, the change in economic welfare relative to the 1985 Tax Law is positive. The 1986 Tax Act improves the efficiency of atemporal resource allocation sufficiently to offset the negative impact of greater effective tax rates on capital income. Higher rates of inflation result in a marked reduction in the welfare gains from the 1986 tax reform. For example, we estimate that the welfare gain is $448.4 billion at a six percent rate of inflation, which amounts to 2.8 percent of U.S. private national wealth in 1987. The 1986 Tax Act substantially reduces interasset tax wedges within the business sector, so that potential welfare gains from further reductions are small.

An important feature of the Treasury and President's proposals is that the tax base would have been largely indexed against inflation. By contrast, the tax burden on income from capital under the Tax Reform Act of 1986 increases significantly with the rate of inflation. While the gains from the 1986 Tax Act are comparable to those of under the Treasury and President's proposals at inflation rates near zero, the gains under the two proposals are much greater at moderate or high rates of inflation. For example, the President's proposal would have resulted in a welfare gain of $2,452.2 billion dollars at a six percent inflation rate, which dwarfs the corresponding gain from the Tax Reform Act of 1986.

However, the largest welfare gains from tax reform would have been obtained by transferring part of the tax burden on business capital to household capital. There are obviously important political obstacles to such a transfer. Limitations on the deductibility of mortgage interest and elimination of the tax deductibility of state and local property taxes were included in the Treasury proposal. However, only very modest restrictions on the deductibility of mortgage interest survived into the 1986 tax reform legislation. The welfare gain from a tax policy that treats all forms of capital income symmetrically would have been $2,663.7 billion at a six percent inflation rate. This exceeds the gain from the 1986 Tax Act by $2,215.3 billion and outranks the gains from both the Treasury and President's proposals.

An alternative approach to equalizing the tax burdens between business and household assets would have been to replace the 1985 Tax Law with a tax system based on consumption. At a six percent inflation rate the welfare gain from shifting to a consumption-based tax system from a system primarily based on income would have been much larger than the gain from the Tax Reform Act of 1986. This conclusion holds for any of the alternative methods we have considered for maintaining government revenue at same level as under the 1985 Tax Law. The prospective revenue losses associated with elimination of capital income taxation would have required large increases in distortionary taxes. However, the resulting welfare losses would have been outweighed by gains in efficiency from eliminating capital income taxes.

Our overall conclusion is that indexing the U.S. tax system should receive high priority in future tax reforms. Although potential gains in welfare from the Tax Reform Act of 1986 are substantial, these gains are sharply diminished at moderate rates of inflation. The Treasury and President's proposals can provide important guidance in the practical implementation of indexing schemes. A properly indexed tax system based on income may be superior to a system based on consumption, provided that income from household assets is included in the tax base and all assets are taxed at a uniform rate. This is a second important priority for future tax reforms.

Notes

1. A detailed description of the Tax Reform Act of 1986 is given by the Joint Committee on Taxation (1986). The economic impact of the 1986 tax reform has been analyzed by the Office of Tax Analysis of the U.S. Department of the Treasury (1987) and in the symposium edited by Henry Aaron (1987).
2. For example, in section 12.4 below we find that the equalization of tax rates on corporate and noncorporate capital considered by Harberger (1966) actually reduces efficiency. However, we show that symmetrical tax treatment of income from business and household assets is a very promising avenue for future reform.
3. An alternative to the Harberger model, focusing on the incidence of the corporate income tax, is presented by Gravelle and Kotlikoff (1989). Harberger's general equilibrium approach to the analysis of tax policy has been greatly further developed by Ballard, Fullerton, Shoven, and Whalley (1985). The economic impact of the Tax Reform Act of 1986 has been analyzed, with an extension of this model, by Fullerton, Henderson, and Mackie (1987). A recent survey of the literature on applied general equilibrium models for tax policy analysis is provided by Whalley (1988).
4. The literature on the effect of taxation on saving is reviewed by Sandmo (1985) and Summers (1984). The impact of the Tax Reform Act of 1986 on saving behavior is analyzed by Hausman and Poterba (1987).
5. Proposals for the implementation of a consumption tax in the United States are discussed by the U.S. Department of the Treasury (1977), Hall and Rabushka (1983), and Bradford (1986). Arguments against a consumption tax are presented by the U.S. Department of the Treasury (1984, vol. 3).

6. The elasticity of labor supply and its implications for tax policy are discussed by Hausman (1981, 1985). The impact of the Tax Reform Act of 1986 on labor supply is analyzed by Hausman and Poterba (1987).

7. See Jorgenson and Yun (1986a) for a discussion of the model and Jorgenson and Yun (1986b) for an application to earlier changes in tax policy. The results presented in these papers are based on econometric models fitted to data covering the period 1955–1980. Alternative approaches to dynamic general equilibrium modeling of U.S. tax policy are presented by Auerbach and Kotlikoff (1987) and Goulder and Summers (1989).

8. Perfect foresight models of tax incidence have been presented by Hall (1971b), Chamley (1981), Judd (1987), Sinn (1987) and many others.

9. We have analyzed the impact of the 1981 Tax Act on U.S. economic growth in a previous paper (Jorgenson and Yun, 1986b, esp. pp. 365–370).

10. These tax rates are based on detailed simulations of the Office of Tax Analysis Individual Income Tax Model presented by Cilke and Wyscarver (1987).

11. The statutory rates of the investment tax credit and the tax lifetimes are based on the estimates of Fullerton, Gillette, and Mackie (1987).

12. See U.S. Department of the Treasury (1984). The Treasury plan and its relationship to the Tax Reform Act of 1986 are discussed in detail by McLure and Zodrow (1987).

13. Deduction of mortgage and other personal interest would not have been indexed under the Treasury proposal. Indexing of interest income and interest expenses would have been based on the assumptions that the real interest rate is constant at six percent per year and that inflation raises the rate of inflation point for point. To the extent that the real rate of interest deviates from six percent, the indexing would have been incomplete.

14. In this calculation, we have assumed that inflation rate increases the nominal interest rate point for point. Thus, the after-tax real interest rate would have declined with inflation and the present value of capital consumption allowances would have increased with inflation under the Treasury proposal.

15. The provisions of the Treasury proposal, the President's proposal, and the 1985 Tax Law are compared in U.S. Department of the Treasury (1985, pp. 26–30, Chart 18).

16. In table 12.1 we assume that the taxpayers would elect to be taxed on real capital gains when inflation is zero and 50 percent of nominal capital gains when inflation is six or 10 percent.

17. Under our assumption that an increase in the rate of inflation would result in a point-for-point increase in the nominal rate of interest, the after-tax real interest rate is $(1 - TQ)(i_0 + \pi) - \pi$, where i_0 is the real interest rate, π is the rate of inflation, and TQ is the corporate tax rate. The after-tax real interest rate is negative for an inflation rate above $(1 - TQ)i_0 / TQ$.

18. The Tax Reform Act of 1986 is described by the Joint Committee on Taxation (1986). The economic impact of the 1986 tax reform is discussed in detail by Musgrave (1987) and Pechman (1987). An illuminating account of the tax reform debate is presented by Birnbaum and Murray (1987).

19. Due to the phasing out of the 15 percent tax bracket and the personal and dependents' exemptions for high-income taxpayers, the top marginal rate is as high as 33 percent for certain ranges of taxable income. Statutory tax rates under the 1986 Tax Act were higher for the transitional year 1987.

20. If capital cost recovery coincides with economic depreciation, equality of effective tax rates requires that the investment tax credit must be greater for long-lived assets than for short-lived assets, since short-lived assets can take the credit more frequently.

21. If we adjust the present value of capital consumption allowances by increasing the basis for capital cost recovery to 100 percent, we find that the tax reform reduced the present value of capital cost recovery for short-lived assets. To adjust capital consump-

tion allowances under the 1985 Tax Law for the effect of the provision reducing the basis of capital cost recovery by 50 percent of the investment tax credit, we can multiply the present value of capital cost recovery in table 12.4 under 1985 law by $1/(1-0.5 \text{ ITC})$, where ITC is the rate of investment tax credit in the same table. For example, when the annual rate of inflation is zero, the adjusted present value of capital cost recovery for a short-lived corporate asset is $0.9223/(1-0.5\times0.0944) = 0.9680$, which is larger than the corresponding value, 0.9472, under the Tax Reform Act of 1986.

22. The definition of effective tax rates is discussed in more detail in our earlier paper (Jorgenson and Yun, 1986b, pp. 357–364). The effective tax rates presented below are based on the "traditional view" of corporate finance discussed by Poterba and Summers (1983). Effective tax rates at the corporate level have compared for Germany, Sweden, the United Kingdom and the United States for the year 1980 by King and Fullerton (1984). These effective tax rates are based on the so-called "new view" of corporate finance. The literature on the new view is surveyed by Auerbach (1983). Auerbach (1987) presents effective tax rates based on the new view for different types of assets within the corporate sector under the Tax Reform Act of 1986. Fullerton, Gillette, and Mackie (1987) give effective tax rates under the 1986 Tax Act for both views of corporate finance. These effective tax rates differ, due to the fact that the 1986 Tax Act raises the statutory tax rate on capital gains and lowers corporate and individual tax rates.

23. The validity of our assumption that the debt/equity ratio is the same for all assets within each sector is debated by Gordon, Hines, and Summers (1987) and Gravelle (1987). Our assumption that the nominal interest rate before taxes increases point for point with inflation is consistent with the results of Summers (1983). King and Fullerton (1984) employ the alternative assumption that the nominal interest rate after taxes increases point for point with inflation. Ballentine (1987) lists a number of other important features of the 1986 Tax Act that are not modeled in effective tax rate calculations, such as those we present below and those given by Fullerton, Gillette, and Mackie (1987, pp. 165–167). They provide an assessment of the sensitivity of their results to these omissions.

24. Another mechanism, which we do not model, is that firms using the first-in-first-out (FIFO) inventory accounting method overstate their profits and hence their taxable income when inflation is positive.

25. We assume that the real interest rate is 3.57 percent as opposed to the six percent used in the proposal. Under our assumptions interest income and expenses would have been incompletely indexed and inflation would have had an impact on effective tax rates.

26. These welfare gains are measured in 1987 dollars.

27. In interpreting these comparisons in terms of the U.S. private national wealth, it is useful to bear in mind that the private national wealth includes only nonhuman wealth, while the welfare gains from tax reform accrue to the owners of nonhuman capital and also to recipients of labor income, which can be regarded as a return to human capital.

28. This does not imply that the distortionary effects of the taxes used for revenue adjustments are similar. Rather it reflects the fact that the size of the required revenue adjustments is not large enough to produce sizable differences.

13

The Excess Burden of Taxation in the U.S.

*Dale W. Jorgenson and
Kun-Young Yun*

13.1   Introduction

The purpose of this paper is to measure the excess burden of taxation in the United States. Excess burden is one of the the central concepts in public finance. This concept is employed in the cost-benefit analysis of public expenditure; the benefits of a program are balanced against the costs of raising tax revenue to finance it. The concept also plays an important role in optimal taxation, where the government meets given revenue requirements by choosing taxes so as to maximize social welfare. In both applications it is necessary to measure the social cost of raising tax revenue.[1]

The government sector of the U.S. economy raises revenues through taxes on income from capital and labor services. Corporate capital income is taxed at both corporate and individual levels, noncorporate capital income is taxed only at the individual level, and household capital income is not taxed at either level. In addition, the government sector imposes sales taxes on the production of consumption and investment goods and property taxes on assets held by the business and household sectors. Taxes insert wedges between demand and supply prices for investment and consumption goods and for capital and labor services. These tax wedges distort private decisions and lead to losses in efficiency.

In measuring the excess burden of taxation in the U.S., we use a hypothetical nondistorting tax system as a standard. In this tax system all revenue is raised by means of a lump sum levy that does not distort private decisions and involves no loss in efficiency. Our most important conclusion is that the excess burden imposed on the U.S. economy by the current tax system is very large. The welfare loss is equivalent to 18 percent of government tax revenue. Each dollar of tax revenue costs the private sector a dollar of foregone expenditure and an average loss in efficiency due to tax induced distortions of 18 cents. Our estimate is based on the *average excess burden*. This is the gain in efficiency that would result from replacing the U.S. tax system by a lump sum levy.

The concept of efficiency loss relevant to tax reform is the *marginal excess burden*. The marginal excess burden of the U.S. tax system is defined in terms of the efficiency loss per dollar for the last dollar of revenue raised. We find the cost of raising a dollar of government tax revenue at the margin is 39.1 cents. In addition, there are large differences in marginal excess burdens among different types of taxes. For example, the marginal efficiency cost of raising a dollar of government revenue for taxes on capital income at the individual level is 101.7 cents for each dollar of revenue. Since marginal excess burdens must be equalized for an optimal tax system, this is an indication of important opportunities for gains in efficiency from future tax reform.[2]

In order to measure the average and marginal excess burdens of taxation, we employ a dynamic general equilibrium model of the U.S. economy.[3] In this highly schematic representation of the U.S. economy, a single representative producer employs capital and labor services to produce outputs of consumption and investment goods. We have simplified the representation of technology in the model by introducing a single stock of capital at each point of time. This capital is perfectly malleable and allocated so as to equalize after-tax rates of return to equity in the corporate, noncorporate, and household sectors. By modeling the substitution between consumption and investment goods, we introduce costs of adjustment in the response of investment to changes in tax policy.[4]

Our model includes a representative consumer who supplies labor services, demands consumption goods, and allocates income between consumption and saving. This model of consumer behavior is based on an intertemporally additive utility function that depends on levels of full consumption in all time periods. Full consumption is an aggregate of consumption goods, household capital services, and leisure. To simplify the representation of preferences, we endow the representative consumer with an infinite lifetime and perfect foresight about future prices and rates of return.[5] We have fitted econometric models of producer and consumer behavior to data for the U.S. economy covering the period 1947–1986.

In our model of the U.S. economy, equilibrium is characterized by an intertemporal price system. This price system clears the markets for all four commodity groups included in the model—labor and capital services and consumption and investment goods. Equilibrium at each point of time links the past and the future through markets for investment goods and capital services. Assets are accumulated as a result of past investments, while the prices of assets must be equal the present values of future capital services. The time path of full consumption must satisfy the conditions for intertemporal optimality of the household sector under perfect foresight.

In order to measure the excess burden of taxation in the United States, we first consider the intertemporal equilibrium associated with a reference tax policy. In this paper we consider the excess burden of taxation for tax policies that prevailed before and after the Tax Reform Act of 1986. We refer to the tax policy before the 1986 reform as the 1985 Tax Law, since this policy remained in force until the end of calendar year 1985.[6] Under perfect foresight there is a unique transition path to balanced growth equilibrium for any tax policy and any initial level of capital. The growth path of the U.S. economy consists of a plan for consumption of goods and leisure at every point of time by the representative consumer and a plan for production of investment and consumption goods from capital and labor services at every point of time by the representative producer. These plans are brought into consistency by the intertemporal price system.

Associated with the reference tax policy and the corresponding intertemporal equilibrium is a level of welfare for the representative consumer. This can be interpreted as a measure of economic efficiency, corresponding to the potential level of welfare for society as a whole. The actual level of welfare also depends on the distribution of welfare among consuming units. To measure the excess burden of taxation we substitute a nondistorting tax for all or part of the reference tax system. We then consider the level of welfare associated with this alternative tax system. We evaluate the excess burden of taxation in terms of the difference in wealth required to attain levels of potential welfare before and after the tax substitution.

This paper is organized as follows: In section 13.2 we present an analytical framework for comparison of alternative tax policies. This framework is based on our model of consumer behavior. Using the intertemporal welfare function for the representative consumer and the corresponding budget constraint, we derive an intertemporal expenditure function. This expenditure function gives the wealth required to achieve a given level of consumer welfare as a function of future prices and rates of return. We then define an intertemporal counterpart of Hicks's equivalent variation.[7] This can be interpreted as a money metric of the difference in levels of consumer welfare between the reference tax policy and the alternative tax policy.

In section 13.3 we apply our analytical framework to the 1985 Tax Law and the Tax Reform Act of 1986. For this purpose we hold government expenditure, the government deficit, and net foreign investment constant. We then measure the excess burden of taxation for each of the major programs included in the U.S. tax system. We also consider the excess burden of the tax system as a whole. For this purpose we simulate the growth of the U.S. economy under each of the two reference tax policies and alternative policies incorporating a nondistorting tax. We then compare these tax policies by means of the equivalent variation in wealth.

In section 13.4 we summarize our main results. We find the U.S. tax system imposes a very substantial excess burden on the economy. However, the average burden was substantially reduced by the Tax Reform Act of 1986. Second, we find that marginal excess burdens differ substantially among alternative tax programs, both before and after the 1986 tax reform. This suggests important opportunities still remain for gains in efficiency from future tax reform.

13.2 Analytical Framework

We represent the household sector by a representative consumer who takes prices and rates of return as given. We also assume that the representative consumer has an infinite time horizon and is endowed with perfect foresight. The assumption of an infinite time horizon can be interpreted as a way of explaining intergenerational transfers of wealth through bequests.[8] This assumption appears to be a viable alternative to the life-cycle theory in modeling consumer behavior.[9] Finally, we assume that the services provided by the government sector enter the utility function of the consumer in an additively separable manner. This implies that the marginal utility of private consumption is independent of the level of public consumption.

To represent our model of consumer behavior we introduce the following notation:

F_t — full consumption per capita with population measured in
   efficiency units
PF_t — price of full consumption per capita
n — rate of population growth
μ — rate of Harrod-neutral productivity growth.
ρ — nominal private rate of return.

In our model of consumer behavior the representative consumer
maximizes the *intertemporal welfare function*:

$$V = \frac{1}{(1-\sigma)} \sum_{t=0}^{\infty} \left(\frac{1+n}{1+\gamma}\right)^t U_t^{1-\sigma} \qquad (13.1)$$

where σ is the inverse of the intertemporal elasticity of substitution
and γ is the subjective rate of time preference. These two parameters
describe the preferences of the representative consumer. The
intertemporal welfare function is a discounted sum of products of
total population, which grows at the constant rate *n*, and per capita
atemporal welfare functions U_t $(t = 0, 1, \dots)$. These welfare functions
depend on full consumption per capita F_t with population measured
in efficiency units:

$$U_t = F_t (1+\mu)^t, \quad (t = 0, 1, \dots). \qquad (13.2)$$

In this expression the term $(1+\mu)^t$, involving the rate of Harrod-
neutral productivity growth μ, converts the population from efficiency
units to natural units.

The representative consumer maximizes the welfare function (13.1),
subject to the *intertemporal budget constraint*:

$$W = \sum_{t=0}^{\infty} \frac{PF_t \, F_t \, (1+\mu)^t \, (1+n)^t}{\prod_{s=0}^{t}(1+\rho_s)}, \qquad (13.3)$$

where *W* is full wealth. Full wealth is the present value of full consumption over the whole future of the U.S. economy. The current
value of full consumption is discounted at the nominal private rate of
return ρ.

The intertemporal welfare function *V* is additively separable in the
atemporal welfare functions U_t $(t = 0, 1, \dots)$. These functions depend
on the consumption of leisure, consumption goods, and capital services in each period, so that we can divide the representative con-

sumer's optimization problem into two stages. In the first stage, the consumer allocates full wealth among consumption levels of different time periods. In the second stage, the consumer allocates full consumption among leisure, consumption goods, and household capital services in each period.

The necessary conditions for a maximum of the intertemporal utility function, subject to the constraint on full wealth, are given by the discrete time Euler equation:

$$\frac{F_t}{F_{t-1}} = \left[\frac{PF_{t-1}}{PF_t} \cdot \frac{1 + \rho_t}{(1 + \gamma)(1 + \mu)^\sigma} \right]^{\frac{1}{\sigma}}, \quad (t = 1, 2, \dots). \tag{13.4}$$

Equation (13.4) describes the optimal time path of full consumption, given the sequence of prices of full consumption and nominal rates of return. We refer this equation as the *transition equation* for full consumption. The growth rate of full consumption is uniquely determined by the transition equation, so that we only need to determine the level of full consumption in any one period in order to find the whole optimal time path.

In a steady state with no inflation, the level of full consumption per capita with population measured in efficiency units is constant. Therefore, the only private nominal rate of return consistent with the steady state, say $\tilde{\rho}$, is

$$\tilde{\rho} = (1 + \gamma)(1 + \mu)^\sigma - 1. \tag{13.5}$$

This rate of return depends on the rate of Harrod-neutral productivity growth and the parameters of the intertemporal welfare function, but is independent of tax policy.

We denote the rate of inflation in the price of full consumption by π_t, where:

$$\pi_t = \frac{PF_t}{PF_{t-1}} - 1, \quad (t = 1, 2, \dots).$$

In a steady state with a constant rate of inflation, say $\tilde{\pi}$, the nominal private rate of return is:

$$\tilde{\rho} = (1 + \gamma)(1 + \mu)^\sigma(1 + \tilde{\pi}) - 1. \tag{13.6}$$

If we denote the real private rate of return by r_t, where:

$$r_t = \frac{PF_{t-1}}{PF_t} (1 + \rho_t) - 1, \quad (t = 1, 2, \dots),$$

the steady state real private rate of return, say $\tilde{r}$, is:

$$\tilde{r} = (1 + \gamma)(1 + \mu)^\sigma - 1 . \tag{13.7}$$

This rate of return is independent of tax policy and the rate of inflation.

The transition equation for full consumption implies that if the real private rate of return exceeds the steady-state rate of return, full consumption rises; conversely, if the rate of return is below its steady-state value, full consumption falls. To show this we take the logarithm of both sides of the transition equation, obtaining:

$$\ln \frac{F_t}{F_{t-1}} = \frac{1}{\sigma} [\ln (1 + r) - \ln(1 + \tilde{r})] . \tag{13.8}$$

To a first-order approximation, the growth rate of full consumption is proportional to the difference between the real private rate of return and its steady-state value.[10] The constant of proportionality is the intertemporal elasticity of substitution $1/\sigma$. The greater this elasticity, the more rapidly full consumption approaches its steady-state level.

In order to evaluate alternative tax policies, we compare the levels of social welfare associated with these policies. We can translate welfare comparisons into monetary terms by introducing the intertemporal counterpart of Hicks's equivalent variation. For this purpose, we express the full wealth required to achieve a given level of intertemporal welfare in terms of the time path of future prices of full consumption and rates of return. Since full wealth is the present value of full consumption over the whole future of the U.S. economy, we refer to this expression as the *intertemporal expenditure function*. Using this expenditure function, we can express differences in welfare in terms of differences in wealth.

To derive the intertemporal expenditure function we first express the time path of full consumption in terms of the initial level and future real private rates of return:

$$\frac{F_t}{F_0} = \prod_{s=0}^{t} \left[\frac{1 + r_s}{(1 + \gamma)(1 + \mu)^\sigma} \right]^{\frac{1}{\sigma}} , \quad (t = 1, 2, \dots) . \tag{13.9}$$

Using this expression, we can write the intertemporal welfare function as:

$$V = \frac{F_0^{1-\sigma}}{1-\sigma} D \, , \tag{13.10}$$

where:

$$D \equiv \sum_{t=0}^{\infty} \left[\frac{1+n}{(1+\gamma)^{\frac{1}{\sigma}}} \right]^t \prod_{s=0}^{t} (1+r_s)^{\frac{1-\sigma}{\sigma}} \, .$$

The function D summarizes the effect of all future prices and rates of return on the initial level of full consumption F_0 associated with a given level of welfare V.

Since the optimal time path for full consumption must satisfy the intertemporal budget constraint, we can express the initial level of full consumption in terms of full wealth and all future real private rates of return:

$$F_0 = \frac{W}{PF_0} \frac{1}{D} \, .$$

Combining this expression with the intertemporal welfare function (13.10) and solving for full wealth, we obtain the intertemporal expenditure function, say $W(PF, D, V)$, where:

$$W(PF, D, V) = PF_0 \left[\frac{(1-\sigma) V}{D^{\sigma}} \right]^{\frac{1}{1-\sigma}} \, . \tag{13.11}$$

We employ the intertemporal expenditure function to provide a money metric of differences in levels of welfare associated with alternative tax policies. For this purpose we first calculate the solution to our dynamic general equilibrium model of the U.S. economy for the reference tax policy. We denote the resulting prices and discount rates by PF_0 and D_0 and the corresponding level of welfare by V_0. We then solve the model for an alternative tax policy and denote the resulting level of welfare by V_1. Finally, we calculate the *equivalent variation in full wealth*, say ΔW, where:

$$\Delta W = W(PF_0, D_0, V_1) - W(PF_0, D_0, V_0)$$
$$= W(PF_0, D_0, V_1) - W_0 \ . \tag{13.12}$$

The equivalent variation in full wealth (13.12) is the wealth required to attain the welfare associated with the alternative tax policy at prices of the reference policy $W(PF_0, D_0, V_1)$ less the wealth for the reference policy W_0. In calculating the excess burden associated with the U.S. tax system, we consider two reference policies—the 1985 Tax Law and the Tax Reform Act of 1986. The alternative policies involve replacing distorting taxes by nondistorting taxes. If the equivalent variation is positive, a change in policy produces a gain in welfare; otherwise, the policy change results in a welfare loss. The equivalent variations in full wealth enable us to rank the reference policy and any number of alternative policies in terms of a money metric of the corresponding welfare levels.

In order to measure the efficiency cost associated with tax-induced distortions in private decisions, we replace distorting taxes by a lump-sum levy. We express the gain in welfare in terms of the equivalent variation in wealth (13.12). We find it useful to compare this excess burden with the present value of the tax revenue generated from the lump sum tax. For this purpose we add the time path of the lump-sum levy to the time path of full consumption under the reference tax policy. We then evaluate the level of welfare associated with the composite time path consisting of the lump-sum tax and full consumption. We obtain a monetary equivalent of this level of welfare by evaluating the intertemporal expenditure function at prices and rates of return of the reference tax policy. The difference between this level of wealth and the wealth of the reference policy W_0 is the present value of the lump-sum tax in terms of full consumption.

More formally, we can express the difference in levels of intertemporal welfare between a reference tax policy and an alternative policy with a lump-sum tax in terms of the equivalent variation (13.12). Similarly, we can express the present value of the time path of the lump-sum tax as the equivalent variation:

$$T = W(PF_0, D_0, V_2) - W_0 \ , \tag{13.13}$$

where V_2 is the welfare corresponding to the composite time path of the lump-sum tax and full consumption under the reference tax policy.

Finally, we define the *average efficiency cost*, say *AEC*, imposed on the U.S. economy by the taxes we have replaced by a lump-sum levy, as follows:

$$AEC = \frac{\Delta W}{T} , \tag{13.14}$$

where ΔW and T are defined by (13.12) and (13.13), respectively. This is the ratio of the gain in welfare achieved by replacing distorting taxes by a nondistorting tax to the corresponding tax revenue. Both the welfare gain and the tax revenue are expressed in terms of the prices and rates of return of the reference tax policy. Similarly, we can define the *marginal efficiency cost*, say *MEC*, as follows:

$$MEC = \frac{\Delta (\Delta W)}{\Delta T} . \tag{13.15}$$

This is the ratio of the incremental gain in welfare achieved by replacing distorting taxes by a nondistorting tax to the incremental tax revenue.

Obviously, there are many different ways of expressing the average and marginal excess burdens of the U.S. tax system. An alternative approach has been proposed by Ballard, Fullerton, Shoven and Whalley (1985, Chap. 7). This approach is based on the difference between present values of time paths of full consumption associated with alternative tax policies. Although there are important similarities between comparisons of present values of full consumption and comparisons of full wealth by means of the intertemporal expenditure function, these two approaches do not coincide. Only comparisons based on the expenditure function provide a money metric of differences in intertemporal welfare.

The first proposal of Ballard *et al.*, is to calculate the present value of differences in full consumption at prices of the reference tax policy. This amounts to replacing the present value of the full consumption $W(PF_0, D_0, V_1)$ required for the level of welfare under the alternative tax policy (13.12) with the present value of the time path of full consumption associated with that policy. Since the representative consumer minimizes the present value of the full consumption required to attain any level of welfare, this overstates welfare gains and understates welfare losses. The second proposal of Ballard *et al.*, is to calculate the present value of differences in full consumption at prices of the alternative tax policy. This measure understates welfare gains and overstates welfare losses and has the added disadvantage of producing welfare comparisons among alternative tax policies that are intransitive.

13.3   Efficiency Costs of Taxation

The welfare level of the U.S. economy depends on both private and public consumption. Since we have assumed that the intertemporal welfare function is additively separable in these two components of consumption, we did not include public consumption in the welfare function (13.1) for private consumption. When we compare the performance of the U.S. economy under alternative tax policies, it is essential to fix the size and composition of government spending, so that welfare derived from public consumption is held constant. For this purpose we introduce a welfare function for public consumption.

We assume that the allocation of total government expenditures in any time period, net of interest payments on government debt, is based on a linear logarithmic welfare function. This implies that shares of consumption goods, investment goods, labor services, transfer payments to U.S. citizens, and transfer payments to foreigners are unaffected by changes in the corresponding prices. Under the reference policy, we set the steady-state level of government spending at a fixed fraction of private national income. Along the transition path, the level of government spending is determined by the sum of tax revenue and the government deficit. When we solve the model under alternative tax policies, we set the level of public consumption in each period at the same value as under the reference policy.

On the revenue side of the government budget, there are two alternative sources of income—tax revenues and borrowing from the public. The government budget constraint requires that the present value of government spending be equal to the present value of government receipts plus the net worth of the government sector. In our model tax and debt financing are not equivalent. Barro's (1974) Ricardian equivalence theorem fails to hold, since taxes distort private decisions. To take account of this aspect of the revenue side of the government budget, we hold the time path of the government deficit for the reference tax policy constant for all alternative tax policies.

Our model of the U.S. economy achieves a steady state within about 35 years after a change in tax policy. We assume the level of government debt reaches its steady-state value in 35 years after introduction of a new policy. We close the gap between the initial and the steady-state levels of government debt by reducing the gap at an annual rate equal to 1/35 of the gap at the beginning of the transition path. Since the time paths of government spending and the government budget deficit are fixed at the levels of the reference tax policy, tax revenue must be adjusted to meet the government budget constraint under the alternative policies.

Trade with the rest of the world sector need not be balanced in our model of the U.S. economy. From the viewpoint of an individual, it does not matter whether a given amount of saving is invested domestically or abroad. However, for the economy as a whole it does make a difference for at least two reasons. First, capital employed abroad does not generate corporate tax revenue. Second, this capital does not affect domestic output. Therefore, we control the time path of claims on the rest of the world in the same way as the time path of government debt. To keep the trade deficit on a time path implied by claims on the rest of the world for the reference tax policy, we adjust net exports of consumption and investment goods and labor services for the alternative policies.

It is worth noting that there is no reason to believe that the actual levels of the government budget deficit and net foreign investment will follow the paths we have employed in simulating the reference tax policies. The purpose of controlling government budget deficit and the deficit of the rest of the world sector is to eliminate the effects of changes in government budget policy or trade policy on consumer welfare, so that we can concentrate on the effects of tax policy changes. The accuracy of our projections of the future time paths of the two deficits is a secondary consideration.

In this section, we estimate the efficiency costs for various parts of the U.S. tax system under the 1985 Tax Law and the Tax Reform Act of 1986. For this purpose, we carry out alternative simulations of the U.S. economy under reductions of tax rates for the following nine components of the U.S. tax system: (1) the corporate income tax; (2) capital income taxes at the individual level, including taxes levied on noncorporate capital income and taxes on individual capital income originating in the corporate sector; (3) property taxes on corporate, noncorporate, and household assets; (4) capital income taxes at both corporate and individual levels; (5) labor income taxes; (6) capital and labor income taxes; (7) the individual income tax; (8) sales taxes on consumption and investment goods; and (9) all taxes.

In each simulation we reduce the tax rates and evaluate the average efficiency cost (AEC) and marginal efficiency cost (MEC) generated by tax distortions. When the corporate income tax is reduced, we also reduce the tax credits on corporate investment in the same proportion. Similarly, when the capital income tax at the individual level is reduced, we reduce the tax credits on noncorporate investment. We consider 11 points between the reference tax policy and the alternative tax policy in which the relevant tax rates are reduced to zero. The excess burdens are evaluated with tax rates reduced by 5, 10, 20, . . . , 90, and 100 percent. Except for the first two points, which are only five percentage points apart, the points for measuring the excess burdens are ten percentage points apart. The first two intervals are shorter, so that we can measure the efficiency cost of each tax program more precisely at rates prevailing under the reference tax policy.

In the first set of simulations, we evaluate the efficiency cost of all nine components of the U.S. tax system under the 1985 Tax Law. Each of the alternative tax policies for evaluation of the excess burdens is obtained by lowering the average and marginal rates of the relevant taxes and replacing the lost revenue by a lump-sum levy. For each alternative policy, the average efficiency cost is defined relative to the tax revenue replaced by the lump-sum tax. We consider the growth of the U.S. economy with the 1985 Tax Law as the reference tax policy. The present value T of the lump sum tax is evaluated along the corresponding time path of full consumption, as indicated in equation (13.13).

Table 13.1 presents the average and marginal efficiency costs of the various components of the U.S. tax system under the 1985 Tax Law. We begin by considering the marginal and average efficiency costs at the tax rates prevailing under the 1985 law. The first column of table 13.1 shows the marginal efficiency cost (MEC) for all taxes is 0.460 when these taxes are increased from 95 to 100 percent of their 1985 levels. If the government increases all taxes in the same proportion, the burden imposed on the U.S. economy in excess of the tax revenue raised is 47.2 cents per dollar of revenue. Since this efficiency cost is measured relative to the 1985 Tax Law as the reference tax policy, the estimated marginal and average efficiency costs are the same.

Next, we consider the results presented in the last column of table 13.1. This column gives the efficiency loss when tax revenue is raised by increasing all taxes in the same proportion from zero to ten percent of the 1985 levels. For all taxes that make up the U.S. tax system the

Table 13.1
Efficiency cost of U.S. tax revenues: 1985 Tax Law

Tax bases			Reduction in tax rates (%)										
		5	10	20	30	40	50	60	70	80	90	100
1. Corporate income	MEC	.842	.786	.719	.647	.594	.551	.516	.492	.467	.451	.440
	AEC	.842	.815	.770	.734	.706	.683	.665	.650	.637	.627	.619
2. Ind. cap. income	MEC	1.128	1.103	1.061	1.016	.969	.926	.885	.845	.810	.774	.740
	AEC	1.128	1.116	1.089	1.065	1.042	1.020	.999	.979	.960	.941	.923
3. Property value	MEC	.186	.183	.181	.176	.173	.169	.166	.161	.157	.154	.149
	AEC	.186	.185	.183	.181	.179	.177	.175	.173	.171	.169	.167
4. All cap. income	MEC	.975	.913	.848	.773	.714	.669	.631	.601	.574	.554	.537
	AEC	.975	.945	.898	.860	.828	.802	.779	.760	.744	.729	.717
5. Labor income	MEC	.488	.457	.414	.365	.322	.285	.259	.230	.209	.194	.184
	AEC	.488	.473	.444	.418	.394	.373	.355	.338	.323	.310	.299
6. 1 + 2 + 5 = 4 + 5	MEC	.651	.593	.519	.434	.361	.299	.246	.200	.161	.128	.102
	AEC	.651	.622	.572	.528	.489	.455	.424	.397	.372	.350	.331
7. Ind. income	MEC	.616	.573	.515	.445	.383	.327	.278	.235	.196	.163	.135
	AEC	.616	.595	.555	.519	.486	.456	.428	.402	.379	.358	.339
8. Sales value	MEC	.260	.256	.252	.245	.239	.232	.227	.220	.215	.209	.203
	AEC	.260	.258	.255	.251	.248	.245	.242	.239	.236	.233	.230
9. All tax bases	MEC	.472	.424	.361	.286	.223	.169	.125	.090	.069	.055	.045
	AEC	.472	.449	.405	.367	.333	.304	.277	.255	.237	.224	.214

marginal efficiency cost (MEC) drops to 0.045, which implies that the efficiency cost is only 4.5 cents per dollar of tax revenue. However, the average efficiency cost (AEC) is 0.214, so that the loss in efficiency from all distorting taxes is 21.4 cents per dollar of tax revenue. This is the difference in wealth corresponding to differences in welfare between the growth of the U.S. economy under the 1985 Tax Law and economic growth with all tax revenue obtained from a nondistorting lump-sum levy.

For all the taxes we consider in table 13.1, the marginal efficiency cost (MEC) declines with the size of the tax revenue replaced by a lump-sum levy. This cost is lower than the average efficiency cost (AEC), except for the first tax reduction in each set of simulations. The average efficiency cost drops much less precipitously than the marginal efficiency cost. This corresponds to the standard result of partial equilibrium analysis of tax policy that total welfare cost increases more than in proportion to the increase in the tax rate. We conclude that the efficiency cost of the U.S. tax system is rising at a rapidly increasing rate as we approach tax rates like those actually prevailing in the 1985 Tax Law. From this finding we would anticipate considerable gains in efficiency from the reductions in marginal tax rates embodied in the Tax Reform Act of 1986.

From the efficiency costs rates presented in the first column of table 13.1 we can see that the 1985 Tax Law placed excessive reliance on income taxes. Marginal and average efficiency costs for all income taxes on capital and labor income at both corporate and individual levels are given in the sixth panel of table 13.1. The marginal efficiency cost of these taxes at rates prevailing in the 1985 Tax Law is 0.651, so that a proportional change in these taxes from 95 to 100 percent of the 1985 levels costs 63.1 cents for each dollar of tax revenue raised. By contrast, marginal efficiency costs of property taxes in the third panel and sales taxes in the eighth panel are only 0.186 and 0.260, respectively. The loss in efficiency at rates prevailing under the 1985 law was 18.6 cents per dollar of property tax revenue and 26.0 cents per dollar of sales tax revenue. A shift from income taxes toward sales and property taxes would have considerably reduced the overall excess burden of the U.S. tax system.

A third conclusion from the results given in table 13.1 is that the allocation of income taxes under the 1985 Tax Law between capital and labor income and between corporate and individual income led to further losses in efficiency. Capital income taxes in the fourth panel of table 13.1 had a marginal efficiency cost of 0.975, so that the efficiency loss for each dollar of revenue raised by taxing capital income was 97.5 cents. By contrast, the marginal efficiency cost of labor income taxes was only 0.488, leading to a loss in efficiency of 48.8 cents for each dollar of labor income tax revenue. Gains in efficiency could have been achieved by substituting taxes on labor income for taxes on capital income. At the other extreme, the marginal efficiency cost of all income taxes at ten percent of the rates under the 1985 Tax Law was only 0.102 or 10.2 cents per dollar of tax revenue, while the costs of capital and labor income taxes were 0.537 and 0.184 or 53.7 cents and 18.4 cents per dollar of tax revenue. These results illustrate the fact that the marginal efficiency costs of mutually exclusive sets of taxes are not additive, so that combining the results of partial equilibrium measures of tax distortions can be grossly misleading.

The results given in table 13.1 show that the allocation of taxes on capital income between corporate and income levels was far from optimal. The marginal efficiency cost of taxes on capital income at the individual level was 1.128, so that the efficiency losses for each dollar of revenue raised actually exceeded a dollar. At this margin, the cost of each dollar of tax revenue was one dollar removed from the private sector plus one dollar and thirteen cents of loss in efficiency due to tax distortions. For the corporate income tax the marginal efficiency cost was 0.842, so that the excess burden of taxation for each additional dollar of corporate tax revenue was 84.2 cents. There would have been a gain in efficiency from transferring part of the burden of taxation on capital income from the individual to the corporate level.

We have carried out a parallel set of simulations to estimate the average and marginal efficiency costs of the various components of the U.S. tax system under the Tax Reform Act of 1986. The results are summarized in table 13.2. Overall, we find that this tax reform significantly reduced the average and marginal efficiency costs of taxation. An important exception is sales taxes, where the estimated efficiency costs are slightly higher. Beginning with the average and marginal efficiency costs of the whole U.S. tax system in the ninth panel of table 13.2, we find that that the marginal efficiency cost at rates prevailing under the 1986 tax act was 0.391, so that the loss in efficiency for each dollar of tax revenue raised was 39.1 cents. This is a considerable reduction from the loss in efficiency under the 1985 Tax Law and reflects the drastic decline in marginal tax rates under the 1986 tax reform. The average efficiency cost for the whole tax system fell to

Table 13.2
Efficiency cost of U.S. tax revenues: Tax Reform Act of 1986

Tax bases		Reduction in tax rates (%)										
		5	10	20	30	40	50	60	70	80	90	100
1. Corporate income	MEC	.448	.435	.418	.397	.379	.363	.348	.334	.322	.310	.301
	AEC	.448	.442	.431	.421	.412	.404	.397	.391	.384	.379	.374
2. Ind. cap. income	MEC	1.017	.989	.951	.904	.853	.812	.767	.727	.688	.650	.613
	AEC	1.017	1.003	.977	.953	.928	.906	.884	.863	.842	.822	.803
3. Property value	MEC	.176	.174	.171	.168	.164	.160	.157	.153	.149	.145	.142
	AEC	.176	.175	.173	.171	.169	.168	.166	.164	.162	.160	.158
4. All cap. income	MEC	.675	.650	.616	.573	.533	.498	.466	.435	.407	.382	.359
	AEC	.675	.663	.640	.619	.600	.582	.566	.551	.537	.524	.512
5. Labor income	MEC	.376	.358	.333	.303	.276	.253	.237	.216	.201	.190	.183
	AEC	.376	.367	.350	.334	.320	.307	.296	.285	.275	.266	.259
6. 1 + 2 + 5 = 4 + 5	MEC	.497	.462	.414	.355	.301	.254	.212	.175	.142	.114	.091
	AEC	.497	.480	.448	.418	.391	.366	.343	.323	.304	.287	.271
7. Ind. income	MEC	.520	.490	.449	.396	.349	.305	.265	.229	.196	.167	.140
	AEC	.520	.505	.477	.451	.426	.403	.381	.361	.342	.325	.308
8. Sales value	MEC	.262	.259	.254	.249	.242	.236	.230	.224	.218	.211	.205
	AEC	.262	.261	.257	.254	.251	.248	.245	.242	.239	.236	.232
9. All tax bases	MEC	.391	.356	.308	.249	.197	.151	.113	.082	.063	.048	.040
	AEC	.391	.374	.342	.312	.285	.260	.238	.220	.204	.190	.180

0.180, so that replacing all taxes by a lump-sum levy would have increased consumer welfare by an average of 18 cents per dollar of tax revenue.

The Tax Reform Act of 1986 did not successfully address the issue of excessive reliance of the U.S. tax system on income taxes. The marginal efficiency cost of sales taxes given in the eighth panel of table 13.2 was .262 after the reform, while the cost of property taxes given in the third panel was 0.176. By contrast, the marginal efficiency cost of all income taxes given in the sixth panel of table 13.2 was 0.497. The efficiency losses were 49.7 cents per dollar of income tax revenue, only 17.6 cents per dollar of property tax revenue, and only 26.2 cents per dollar of sales tax revenue. A substantial increase in efficiency could have been realized by reducing income taxes rates and increasing the rates of sales and property taxes. Similarly, the structure of the income tax itself remained out of balance with marginal efficiency costs of labor income taxes at 0.376, individual capital income taxes at 1.017, and corporate income taxes at 0.448. Gains in efficiency could have been realized by further reductions in marginal tax rates on individual and corporate taxes on capital income and increases in marginal tax rates on labor income.

Our overall conclusion is that the Tax Reform Act of 1986 led to improvements in efficiency, mainly through reductions in marginal income tax rates. However, the basic structural defects in the U.S. tax system were unaffected by the tax reform. The U.S. tax system relies much too heavily on income taxes, relative to sales and property taxes. Since income taxes are used almost exclusively at the federal level, while sales and property taxes are employed at the state and local level, one way to achieve better balance among these tax programs would be to shift the tax burden from the federal to the state and local level. Within the income tax at both federal and state and local levels there is excessive reliance on taxes on capital income at the individual level. Taxes on capital income at both corporate and individual levels are too burdensome, relative to taxes on labor income.

13.4   Conclusion

At this point we find it useful to compare our estimates of average and marginal efficiency costs with those obtained in other studies. Table 13.3 summarizes important features of previous studies of the U.S. tax system and the estimates of efficiency costs obtained in these

Table 13.3
Comparison with other studies

Author(s)	Key features	Central results
Browning (1976)	partial equilibrium model, tax on labor (U.S.)	MEC = 0.09 – 0.16
Stuart (1984)	simple static general equilibrium model, tax on labor (U.S.)	MEC = 0.207
Hausman (1981)[1]	partial equilibrium model, tax on labor (U.S.)	AEC = 0.221 for prime-age male, 0.184 for wives
Ballard, Shoven, and Whalley (1985a,b)	dynamic general equilibrium model, U.S. tax system (1973)	MEC = 0.332, AEC = 0.238 for the tax system
Hansson and Stuart (1985)	two-sector static general equilibrium model, taxes on capital and labor (Sweden, MTL = 0.7)	MEC = 0.69 – 1.29
Jorgenson and Yun (1990)[2]	dynamic general equilibrium model, U.S. tax system (1985 law)	MEC = 0.460, AEC = 0.212 for the tax system MEC = 0.482, AEC = 0.295 for tax on labor

1. Quoted from Hausman (1985).
2. The MEC and AEC also appear in columns 1 and 11, respectively, of table 13.1.

studies. In this table the average efficiency cost (AEC) from our study refers to the average efficiency cost resulting from the total revenue raised by each tax from column 11 of table 13.1. The marginal efficiency cost (MEC) is the cost at tax rates close to those that actually prevailed under the 1985 Tax Law from the first column of table 13.1.

Browning (1976) and Hausman (1981) have employed partial equilibrium methods to estimate the efficiency cost of the taxes on labor in the United States Hausman estimates only the average efficiency cost. Stuart (1984) employs a static general equilibrium model to estimate the marginal efficiency cost of taxes on labor income in the U.S. Finally, Ballard, Shoven and Whalley (1985a,b) use a general equilibrium model to estimate both marginal and average efficiency costs of various components of the U.S. tax system. Compared with the results

Table 13.4
Comparison with Ballard–Shoven–Whalley

Author(s)	Taxes	MEC	AEC
	all taxes	0.332	0.238
	capital taxes at industry level	0.463	0.335
Ballard, Shoven,	labor taxes at industry level	0.230	0.145
and Whalley	consumer sales taxes	0.388	0.208
(1985a,b)	sales taxes on commodities other		
	than alcohol, tobacco, and gasoline	0.115	0.087
	income taxes	0.314	0.374
	output taxes	0.279	0.194
	all taxes	0.460	0.212
	corporate income tax	0.838	0.614
Jorgenson and	capital income taxes,		
Yun (1990)	individual & corporate	0.924	0.674
	property taxes	0.174	0.158
	labor income tax	0.482	0.295
	sales tax	0.256	0.228
	individual income tax	0.598	0.333

of Browning (1976), Hausman (1981), and Stuart (1984), our estimates of the average efficiency cost and the marginal efficiency cost of taxes on labor income are much higher.

We present a more extensive comparison between the results of our study and those of Ballard, Shoven, and Whalley (1985a,b) in table 13.4. Both studies employ very detailed general equilibrium models of the U.S. economy. Table 13.4 compares our results with the central estimates of the average and marginal efficiency costs obtained by Ballard, Shoven, and Whalley. Overall, our estimates of the efficiency costs of U.S. taxes are much higher than those of Ballard, Shoven, and Whalley. In particular our estimates for taxes on capital income are almost twice as large. For example, our estimate of the marginal and average efficiency costs of the corporate income tax are 0.842 and 0.614, respectively, while their estimates are only 0.463 and 0.355. Their estimates are based on capital taxes at industry level, which include corporate taxes, corporate franchise taxes, and property taxes on business capital. The differences in the efficiency costs appear to be even larger when taxes on capital income are broadened to include both the corporate income tax and taxes on capital income at the individual level. In this case, our estimates of the marginal and average efficiency costs are 0.975 and 0.674, respectively.

The only tax program for which Ballard, Shoven, and Whalley obtain higher estimates of the marginal efficiency cost is sales taxes. Their estimates of the welfare costs of labor taxes at industry level are not comparable with our results, since they define labor income taxes to include social security taxes and contributions to unemployment insurance and workman's compensation. Our labor income tax represents only the portion of the individual income tax attributable to labor income. For the individual income tax, our estimate of the marginal efficiency cost of taxes on labor income is almost twice as large. A surprising feature of their estimates is that the average efficiency cost is higher than the marginal efficiency cost.

Although Ballard, Shoven, and Whalley employ a general equilibrium model of the U.S. economy, there are many differences between their approach and ours. The most important difference between the two studies appears to be in the representation of the tax system. They treat the corporate income tax as an *ad valorem* tax on capital inputs. This ignores the critical differences in marginal rates of taxation among different types of assets. Their results show that differences in the taxation of income in different industries is not an important source of loss in efficiency in the U.S. tax system. In Jorgenson and Yun (1990), we have shown that differences in taxation between short-lived and long-lived assets and among assets held in the corporate, noncorporate, and household sectors are very significant sources of efficiency loss.

Ballard, Shoven, and Whalley do not distinguish between average and marginal tax rates and represent the individual income tax by a linear tax schedule. By contrast, we distinguish between average and marginal tax rates for both corporate and individual income taxes. We distinguish the average and marginal tax rates at the corporate level by recognizing the difference between the effective marginal tax rates and the statutory rates. At the individual level, we model the average income tax rates as a part of the revenue generating mechanism while the marginal tax rates are used in determining the relative prices at the margins of resource allocation. We have separate average tax rates for labor income and capital income and marginal tax rates for labor income, dividends, noncorporate equity income, interest income originating from the corporate, noncorporate, and household sectors, capital gains, and the marginal tax rates of the household equity owners.

We conclude that the results of our study differ substantially from those of other studies. These differences are primarily a consequence of our very detailed representation of the U.S. tax system. Our study also differs from the studies summarized in table 13.3 in selecting parameter values by econometric methods. These parameter values reflect responses by producers and consumers to the tax wedges we have modeled in our representation of the tax system. We also incorporate both backward-looking dynamics, relating capital services to past streams of investment, and forward-looking dynamics, requiring that prices of assets are determined by expectations about future capital service prices. Not surprisingly, these differences in methodology lead to different empirical results for the marginal and average efficiency costs of the U.S. tax system. For the most part our estimates of marginal efficiency costs are much higher than those obtained in other studies.

In this paper, we have estimated the efficiency costs of various portions of the U.S. tax system under the 1985 Tax Law and the Tax Reform Act of 1986. We find that the marginal efficiency costs of taxation under both tax laws are very substantial. The main effect of the Tax Reform Act of 1986 was to lower marginal income tax very significantly. This undoubtedly reduced the excess burden of taxation in the United States. However, this tax reform did not address the significant structural defects of the U.S. tax system. The most important of these is the excessive reliance on income taxes as a source of revenue and imbalances among corporate income taxes and individual taxes on labor and capital income. As a consequence, large potential gains in efficiency remain as an objective for future tax reforms.

Notes

1. Important progress has been made in measuring the excess burden of the U.S. tax system, beginning with the work of Harberger (1966). Recent contributions include Shoven (1976), Stuart (1984), Ballard, Shoven, and Whalley (1985a,b), Ballard (1988), and Auerbach (1989a). An excellent survey is presented by Auerbach (1985).
2. See Diamond and Mirrlees (1971a,b) and Stiglitz and Dasgupta (1971). A survey of optimal tax theory is given by Auerbach (1985).
3. See Jorgenson and Yun (1986a) for a detailed discussion of the model. The results presented in that paper are based on econometric models fitted to data for the period 1955–1980. Alternative approaches to dynamic general equilibrium modeling of U.S. tax policy are presented by Auerbach and Kotlikoff (1987) and Goulder and Summers (1989).
4. For alternative approaches to costs of adjustment, see Summers (1981) and Auerbach (1989b).
5. Perfect foresight models of tax incidence have been presented by Hall (1971a), Chamley (1981), Judd (1987), Sinn (1987), Lucas (1990), and many others.

6. Detailed descriptions of the 1985 Tax Law and the Tax Reform Act of 1986 are given in Jorgenson and Yun (1990). In that paper we have utilized our dynamic general equilibrium model of the U.S. economy to assess the impact on U.S. economic growth of tax reform proposals leading up to the 1986 tax act. A detailed survey of alternative appraisals of the 1986 reform is presented by Henderson (1990). In Jorgenson and Yun (1986b) we used an earlier version of our model analyze the tax reform of 1981.

7. See Hicks (1942). The expenditure function has been utilized in measuring the excess burden of taxation by Diamond and McFadden (1974) and Kay (1980).

8. Barro (1974) has provided a rationale for the infinite horizon representative consumer model in terms of intergenerational altruism. Intergenerational altruism has implications very different from those of the life-cycle theory, based on a finite lifetime for each consumer. Examples of these implications are distortions in intertemporal consumption by a Social Security tax, considered by Feldstein (1974), the burden of national debt analyzed by Barro (1974), and dynamic tax reform and intergenerational distribution of the tax burden studied by Auerbach and Kotlikoff (1987) and Auerbach (1989a).

9. For example, Kotlikoff and Summers (1981) have suggested that life-cycle saving accounts for only a small fraction of the total saving, so that a significant fraction of saving is motivated by bequests.

10. Chamley (1981) derives this formula in a continuous time framework with a single good and fixed labor supply.

References

Aaron, Henry J. 1987. Symposium on Tax Reform. *Journal of Economic Perspectives* 1 (Summer): 7–10.

Aaron, Henry J., R.S. Russek Jr., and N.M. Singer. 1973. Tax Changes and the Composition of Fixed Investment: An Aggregative Simulation. In *A Study Conducted to Inform the Joint Committee on Internal Revenue Taxation, U.S. Congress, as to the Impact of the Tax Reform Act of 1969 on Investment in Housing,* March 1973, 31–52.

Abel, Andrew B. 1981. Taxes, Inflation, and the Durability of Capital. *Journal of Political Economy* 89, no. 3 (June): 548–560.

Åkerman, Gustaf. 1923. *Realkapital und Kapitalzins.* Stockholm: Centraltrycheriet.

Allen, Roy George Douglas. 1938. *Mathematical Analysis for Economists.* London: Macmillan.

Almon, Shirley. 1965. The Distributed Lag Between Capital Appropriations and Expenditures. *Econometrica* 33, no. 1 (January): 178–196.

Anderson, William Henry Locke. 1964. *Corporate Finance and Fixed Investment, an Econometric Study.* Boston, MA: Division of Research, Graduate School of Business Administration, Harvard University.

Arrow, Kenneth J. 1964. Optimal Capital Policy, the Cost of Capital, and Myopic Decision Rules. *Annals of the Institute of Statistical Mathematics* 16, nos. 1–2: 21–30.

———. 1968. Optimal Capital Policy with Irreversible Investments. In *Value, Capital, and Growth,* Papers in Honor of Sir John Hicks, ed. James N. Wolfe, 1–19. Chicago, IL: Aldine Publishing Company.

Arrow, Kenneth J., Hollis B. Chenery, Bagicha S. Minhas, and Robert M. Solow. 1961. Capital-Labor Substitution and Economic Efficiency. *Review of Economics and Statistics* 43, no. 3 (August): 225–250.

Arrow, Kenneth J., and Mordecai Kurz. 1970. *Public Investment, the Rate of Return, and Optimal Fiscal Policy.* Baltimore, MD: Johns Hopkins University Press.

Atkinson, Anthony B., and Joseph E. Stiglitz. 1980. *Lectures on Public Economics.* Cambridge, MA: The MIT Press.

Auerbach, Alan J. 1979a. Inflation and the Choice of Asset Life. *Journal of Political Economy* 89 (June): 621–638.

———. 1979b. The Optimal Taxation of Heterogeneous Capital. *Quarterly Journal of Economics* 93, no. 4 (November): 589–612.

———. 1979c. Wealth Maximization and the Cost of Capital. *Quarterly Journal of Economics* 93, no. 3 (August): 433–446.

———. 1983. Taxation, Corporate Financial Policy, and the Cost of Capital. *Journal of Economic Literature* 21 (September): 905–940.

———. 1985. The Theory of Excess Burden and Optimal Taxation. In *Handbook of Public Economics*, vol. 1, eds. Alan J. Auerbach and Martin S. Feldstein, 61–127. Amsterdam: North-Holland.

———. 1987. The Tax Reform Act of 1986 and the Cost of Capital. *Journal of Economic Perspectives* 1 (Summer): 73–86.

———. 1989a. The Deadweight Loss from 'Nonneutral' Taxation. *Journal of Public Economics* 40, no. 1 (October): 1–36.

———. 1989b. Tax Reform and Adjustment Costs: The Impact on Investment and Market Value. *International Economic Review* 30, no. 4 (November): 939–962.

Auerbach, Alan J., and Dale W. Jorgenson. 1980. Inflation-Proof Depreciation of Assets. *Harvard Business Review* 58, no. 5 (September-October): 113–118.

Auerbach, Alan J., and Lawrence J. Kotlikoff. 1983. National Savings, Economic Welfare, and the Structure of Taxation. In *Behavioral Simulation Models in Tax Policy Analysis*, ed. Martin S. Feldstein, 459–493. Chicago, IL: University of Chicago Press.

———. 1987. *Dynamic Fiscal Policy.* Cambridge: Cambridge University Press.

Auerbach, Alan J., Lawrence J. Kotlikoff, and Jonathan Skinner. 1983. Efficiency Gains from Dynamic Tax Reform. *International Economic Review* 24, no. 1 (February): 81–100.

Bacharach, Michael. 1965. Estimating Nonnegative Matrices from Marginal Data. *International Economic Review* 6, no. 3 (September): 294–310.

Bailey, Martin J. 1959. Formal Criteria for Investment Decisions. *Journal of Political Economy* 67 (October): 476–488.

Ballard, Charles L. 1988. The Marginal Efficiency Cost of Redistribution. *American Economic Review* 78, no. 5 (December): 1019–1033.

Ballard, Charles L., Don Fullerton, John B. Shoven, and John Whalley. 1985. *A General Equilibrium Model for Tax Policy Evaluation.* Chicago, IL: University of Chicago Press.

Ballard, Charles L., John B. Shoven, and John Whalley. 1982. The Welfare

Cost of Distortions in the United States Tax System: A General Equilibrium Approach. Working Paper No. 1043. Cambridge, MA: National Bureau of Economic Research.

———. 1985a. General Equilibrium Computations of the Marginal Welfare Costs of Taxes in the United States. *American Economic Review* 75, no. 1 (March): 128–138.

———. 1985b. The Total Welfare Cost of the United States Tax System: A General Equilibrium Approach. *National Tax Journal* 38, no. 2 (June): 125–140.

Ballentine, J. Gregory. 1987. The impact of Fundamental Tax Reform on the Allocation of Resources: Comment. In *The Effects of Taxation on Capital Accumulation*, ed. Martin S. Feldstein, 437–443. Chicago, IL: University of Chicago Press.

Barro, Robert J. 1974. Are Government Bonds Net Wealth? *Journal of Political Economy* 82, no. 6 (November-December): 1095–1117.

Barro, Robert J., and C. Sahasakul. 1983. Measuring the Average Marginal Tax Rate from the Individual Income Tax. Working Paper No. 1060. Cambridge, MA: National Bureau of Economic Research.

Bell, Frederick W. 1964. The Role of Capital-Labor Substitution in the Economic Adjustment of an Industry Across Regions. *Southern Economic Journal* 31, no. 2 (October) : 123–131.

———. 1965. A Note on the Empirical Estimation of the CES Production Function with the Use of Capital Data. *Review of Economics and Statistics* 47, no. 3 (August): 328–330.

Bentzel, Ragnar. 1970. The Social Significance of Income Distribution Statistics. *Review of Income and Wealth*, ser. 16, no. 3 (September): 253–264.

———. 1978. A Vintage Model of Swedish Economic Growth from 1870 to 1975. In *The Importance of Technology and the Permanence of Structure in Industrial Growth*, eds. B. Carlsson, G. Eliasson, and Mohammed Ishaq Nadiri, 13–50. Stockholm: Industrial Institute for Economic and Social Research.

Bentzel, Ragnar, and Lennart Berg. 1983. The Role of Demographic Factors as a Determinant of Savings in Sweden. In *The Determinants of National Saving and Wealth*, eds. Franco Modigliani and R. Hemming, 152–179. London: Macmillan.

Berndt, Ernst R. 1976. Reconciling Alternative Estimates of the Elasticity of Substitution. *Review of Economics and Statistics* 58, no. 1: 59–68.

Birnbaum, Jeffrey H., and Alan S. Murray. 1987. *Showdown at Gucci Gulch. Lawmakers, Lobbyists, and the Unlikely Triumph of Tax Reform*. New York, NY: Random House.

Bischoff, Charles W. 1969. Hypothesis Testing and the Demand for Capital Goods. *Review of Economics and Statistics* 51, no. 3 (August): 354–368.

———. 1971a. The Effect of Alternative Lag Distributions. In *Tax Incentives and Capital Spending*, ed. Gary Fromm, 61–130. Washington, DC: Brookings Institution.

———. 1971b. The Outlook for Investment in Plant and Equipment. *Brookings Paper on Economic Activity* 3: 735–753.

Blackorby, Charles, Daniel Primont, and Robert R. Russell. 1978. *Duality, Separability, and Functional Structure.* Amsterdam, North-Holland.

Böhm von Bawerk, Eugen R. 1891. *The Positive Theory of Capital*, trans. W. Smart. London: Macmillan.

Borch, Karl. 1963. Topics in Economic Theory: Discussion. *American Economic Review* 53, no. 2 (May): 269–274.

Bradford, David F. 1980. The Economics of Tax Policy Toward Savings. In *The Government and Capital Formation*, ed. George von Furstenberg, 11–71. Cambridge, MA: Ballinger.

———. 1981a. Issues in the Design of Saving and Investment Incentives. In *Depreciation, Inflation, and the Taxation of Income from Capital*, ed. Charles R. Hulten, 13–47. Washington, DC: The Urban Institute Press.

———. 1981b. The Incidence and Allocation Effects of a Tax on Corporate Distribution. *Journal of Public Economics* 15, no. 1 (February): 1–22.

———. 1986. *Untangling the Income Tax.* Cambridge, MA: Harvard University Press.

Brannon, Gerard M., and Emil M. Sunley, Jr. 1976. The 'Recapture' of Excess Tax Depreciation on the Sale of Real Estate. *National Tax Journal* 29, no. 9 (December): 413–421.

Brown, Edgar Cary. 1948. Business-Income Taxation and Investment Incentives. In *Income, Employment and Public Policy: Essays in Honor of Alvin H. Hausen.* W.W. Norton.

———. 1955. The New Depreciation Policy Under the Income Tax: An Economic Analysis. *National Tax Journal* 8 (March): 81–98.

———. 1962. Tax Incentives for Investment. *American Economic Review* 52 (May): 335–345.

———. 1981. The 'Net' Versus the 'Gross' Investment Tax Credit. *Depreciation, Inflation, and the Taxation of Income from Capital*, ed. Charles R. Hulten, 133–4. Washington, DC: The Urban Institute.

Bureau of the Census. 1972. *Census of Manufactures.* Washington, DC: United States Government Printing Office.

———. 1977. *Census of Manufactures.* Washington, DC: United States Government Printing Office.

Bureau of Economic Analysis. 1975. *Interindustry Transactions in New Structures and Equipment, 1963 and 1967.* Supplement to the Survey of Current Business. Washington, DC: U.S. Department of Commerce.

————. 1976. *Fixed Nonresidential Business and Residential Capital in the United Sates, 1925–1975.* PB-253 725. Washington, DC: U.S. Department of Commerce, National Technical Information Service.

Cagan, Phillip. 1965. Measuring Quality Changes and the Purchasing Power of Money: An Exploratory Study of Automobiles. *National Banking Review* 3 (December): 217–236.

Chamley, Christophe. 1981. The Welfare Cost of Capital Income Taxation in a Growing Economy. *Journal of Political Economy* 89, no. 3 (June): 468–496.

Chase, Samuel B., Jr. 1962. Tax Credits for Investment Spending. *National Tax Journal* 15 (March): 32–52.

Chenery, Hollis B. 1952. Overcapacity and the Acceleration Principle. *Econometrica* 20, no. 1 (January): 1–28.

Chirinko, Robert S., and Robert Eisner. 1983. Tax Policy and Investment in Major U.S. Macroeconometric Models. *Journal of Public Economics* 20, no. 2 (March): 139–166.

Chow, Gregory C. 1973. Problems of Economic Policy from the Viewpoint of Optimal Control. *American Economic Review* 63, no. 5: 825–837.

Christensen, Laurits R., and Dale W. Jorgenson, 1969. The Measurement of U.S. Real Capital Input, 1929–1967. *Review of Income and Wealth*, ser. 15, no. 4 (December): 293–320.

————. 1973. Measuring Economic Performance in the Private Sector. In *The Measurement of Economic and Social Performance*, ed. Milton Moss, 233–351. New York, NY: Columbia University Press.

————. 1978. U.S. Input, Output, Saving and Wealth, 1929–1977. Cambridge, MA: Harvard Institute for Economic Research (December).

Christensen, Laurits R., Dale W. Jorgenson, and Lawrence J. Lau. 1971. The Transcendental Logarithmic Production Function. *Econometrica* 39, no. 4 (July): 255–256.

————. 1973. Transcendental Logarithmic Production Frontiers. *Review of Economics and Statistics* 55, no. 1 (February): 28–45.

————. 1975. Transcendental Logarithmic Utility Functions. *American Economic Review* 65, no. 3 (June): 367–383.

Cilke, James M., and Roy A. Wyscarver. 1987. The Individual Income Tax Simulation Model. In *Compendium of Tax Research 1987*, U.S. Department of the Treasury. Washington, DC: U.S. Government Printing Office.

Coen, Robert M. 1969. Tax Policy and Investment Behavior: Comment. *The American Economic Review* 59, no. 3 (June): 370–379.

————. 1971. The Effect of Cash Flow on the Speed of Adjustment. In *Tax Incentives and Capital Spending*, ed. Gary Fromm, 131–196. Washington, DC: The Brookings Institution.

Commerce Clearing House. 1962. *New Tax Rules on Business Assets*. Chicago, IL: Commerce Clearing House.

―――. 1978. *The 1978 Depreciation Guide*. Chicago, IL: Commerce Clearing House.

Corcoran, Patrick J. 1979. Inflation, Taxes, and the Composition of Business Investment. *Federal Reserve Bank of New York Quarterly Review* 4, no. 3 (Autumn); 13–24.

Cragg, John, G., Arnold C. Harberger, and Peter Mieszkowski. 1967. Empirical Evidence on the Incidence of the Corporation Income Tax. *Journal of Political Economy* 75 (December): 811–821.

Craine, R., J.A. Stephenson, and P.A. Tinsley. 1972. Some Evidence on a Fiscal Instrument to Alter Business Investment. In *Federal Reserve Staff Study, Ways to Moderate Fluctuations in Housing Construction*, 110–126. Washington, DC: Federal Reserve.

Dacy, Douglas C. 1964. A Price and Productivity Index for a Nonhomogeneous Product. *Journal of the American Statistical Association* 59 (June): 469–480.

Davidson, Sidney, and D.F. Drake. 1961. Capital Budgeting and the "Best" Tax Depreciation Method. *Journal of Business University of Chicago* 34 (October): 442–452.

―――. 1964. The "Best" Tax Depreciation Method — 1964. *Journal of Business University of Chicago* 37 (July): 258–260.

Debreu, Gerard. 1959. *The Theory of Value*. New York, NY: John Wiley and Sons.

Dhrymes, Phoebus J. 1965. Some Extensions and Tests for the CES Class of Production Functions. *Review of Economics and Statistics* 47, no. 4 (November): 357–366.

Dhrymes, Phoebus J., and Zarembka, Paul. 1970. Elasticities of Substitution for Two-Digit Manufacturing Industries: A Correction. *Review of Economics and Statistics* 52, no. 1 (February): 115–117.

Diamond, Peter A. 1970. Incidence of an Interest Income Tax. *Journal of Economic Theory* 2, no. 3 (September): 211–224.

―――. 1973. Taxation and Public Production in a Growing Setting. In *Models of Economic Growth*, eds. J.A. Mirrlees and N.H. Stern, 215–235. London: Macmillan.

Diamond, Peter A., and Daniel L. McFadden. 1974. Some Uses of the Expenditure Function in Public Finance. *Journal of Public Economics* 3, no. 1 (February): 3–22.

Diamond, Peter A., and J.A. Mirrlees 1971a. Optimal Taxation and Public Production I: Production Efficiency. *American Economic Review* 61, no. 1 (March): 8–27.

————. 1971b. Optimal Taxation and Public Production II: Tax Rules. *American Economic Review* 61, no. 3, June, pp. 261–78.

Domar, Evsey D. 1953. Depreciation, Replacement and Growth. *Economic Journal* 63 (March): 1–32.

Douglas, Paul H. 1948. Are There Laws of Production? *The American Economic Review* 38, no. 1 (March): 1–41.

Durbin, J. 1960. Estimation of Parameters in Time-Series Regression Models. *Journal of the Royal Statistical Society* 22, ser. B, no. 1: 139–153.

Eckstein, Otto. 1962. Tax Problems: Discussion. *American Economic Review* 52 (May): 351–352.

————. 1964. The 'Best' Tax Depreciation Method—1964. *Journal of Business University of Chicago* 34 (October): 442–452.

————. 1983. *The DRI Model of the U.S. Economy.* New York: McGraw-Hill.

Eckstein, Otto, and U. Tanzi. 1964. Comparison of European and United States Tax Structures and Growth Implications. In *The Role of Direct and Indirect Taxes in the Federal Revenues System,* 217–285. Princeton, NJ: National Bureau of Economic Research and The Brookings Institution.

Eisner, Robert. 1952. Depreciation Allowances, Replacement Requirements and Growth. *American Economic Review* 62 (December): 820–831.

————. 1965. Realization of Investment Anticipations. In *The Brookings Quarterly Econometric Model of the United States,* eds. James S. Duesenberry, Gary Fromm, Lawrence R. Klein, and Edwin Kuh, 93–128. Chicago, IL: Rand McNally.

————. 1969. Investment and the Frustrations of Econometricians. *American Economic Review* 59, no. 2 (May): 50–64.

————. 1973. Tax Incentives for Investment. *National Tax Journal* 26, no. 3: 397–401.

Eisner, Robert, and Mohammed Ishaq Nadiri. 1968. Investment Behavior and the Neoclassical Theory. *Review of Economics and Statistics* 50, no. 3 (August): 369–382.

————. 1970. Neoclassical Theory of Investment Behavior: A Comment. *Review of Economics and Statistics* 52, no. 2 (May): 216–222.

Eisner, Robert, and Robert H. Strotz. 1963. Determinants of Business Investment. In *Impacts of Monetary Policy,* Commission on Money and Credit, eds. D.B. Suits *et al.,* 60–333. Englewood Cliffs, NJ: Prentice-Hall.

Fair, Ray C., and John B. Taylor. 1983. Solution and Maximum Likelihood Estimation of Dynamic Nonlinear Rational Expectations Models. *Econometrica* 51, no. 4 (July): 1169–1185.

Feldstein, Martin S. 1974. Social Security, Induced Retirement, and Aggregate Capital Accumulation. *Journal of Political Economy* 82, no. 5 (September/October): 905–926.

————. 1978. The Welfare Cost of Capital Income Taxation. *Journal of Political Economy* 86, no. 2, pt. 2 (April): S29–S51.

————. 1981. Adjusting Depreciation in an Inflationary Economy: Indexing Versus Acceleration. *National Tax Journal* 34, no. 1 (March).

————. 1983. *Inflation, Tax Rules, and Capital Formation.* Chicago, IL: University of Chicago Press.

————, ed. 1983. *Behavioral Simulation Methods in Tax Policy Analysis.* Chicago, IL: University of Chicago Press.

Feldstein, Martin S., and Otto Eckstein. 1970. The Fundamental Determinants of the Interest Rate. *Review of Economics and Statistics* 52, no. 4 (November): 363–375.

Feldstein, Martin S., and D.K. Foot. 1971. The Other Half of Gross Investment: Replacement and Modernization Expenditures. *Review of Economics and Statistics* 53, no. 1 (February): 49–58.

Feldstein, Martin S., Jerry Green, and Eytan Sheshinski. 1978. Inflation and Taxes in a Growing Economy with Debt and Equity Finance. *Journal of Political Economy* 86, no. 2, part 2 (April): S53–70.

Feldstein, Martin S., and Lawrence H. Summers. 1979. Inflation and the Taxation of Capital Income in The Corporate Sector. *National Tax Journal* 32, no. 4 (December): 445–470.

————. 1980. Inflation and the Taxation of Capital Income in the Corporate Sector: Reply. *National Tax Journal* 33, no. 4 (December): 485–488.

Feller, W. 1957. *An Introduction to Probability Theory and Its Applications,* vol. I, 2nd edition. New York, NY: John Wiley and Sons.

Ferguson, Charles E. 1965. Time-Series Production Functions and Technological Progress in American Manufacturing Industry. *Journal of Political Economy* 73, no. 2 (April): 135–147.

Fisher, Irving. 1961. *The Theory of Interest.* New York: Augustus M. Kelley (1st ed., 1930).

Fraumeni, Barbara M., and Dale W. Jorgenson. 1980. The Role of Capital in U.S. Economic Growth, 1948–76. In *Capital, Efficiency and Growth,* ed. George M. von Furstenberg, 9–250. Cambridge, MA: Ballinger.

Fuchs, Victor. 1963. Capital-Labor Substitution: A Note. *Review of Economics and Statistics* 45, no. 4 (November): 436–438.

Fullerton, Don. 1987. The Indexation of Interest, Depreciation, and Capital Gains and Tax Reform in the United States. *Journal of Public Economics* 32, no. 1 (February): 25–52.

Fullerton, Don, Robert Gillette, and James Mackie. 1987. Investment Incentives under the Tax Reform Act of 1986. In *Compendium of Tax Research 1987,* 131–171. U.S. Department of the Treasury. Washington, DC: U.S. Government Printing Office.

Fullerton, Don, and Yolanda K. Henderson. 1989a. A Disaggregate Equilibrium Model of Distortions among Assets, Sectors, and Industries. *International Economic Review* 30, no. 2 (May): 391–414.

———. 1989b. The Marginal Excess Burden of Different Capital Instruments. *Review of Economics and Statistics* 71, no. 3 (August): 435–442.

Fullerton, Don, Yolanda K. Henderson, and James Mackie. 1987. Investment Allocation and Growth under the Tax Reform Act of 1986. In *Compendium of Tax Research 1987*, 173–201. U.S. Department of the Treasury. Washington, DC: U.S. Government Printing Office.

Fullerton, Don, Yolanda K. Henderson, and John B. Shoven. 1984. A Comparison of Methodologies in Empirical General Equilibrium Models of Taxation. In *Applied General Equilibrium Analysis*, eds. H. Scarf and John B. Shoven, 367–410. Cambridge: Cambridge University Press.

Fullerton, Don, Mervyn A. King, John B. Shoven, and John Whalley. 1981. Corporate Tax Integration in the United States: A General Equilibrium Approach. *American Economic Review* 71, no. 4 (September): 677–691.

Gordon, Robert J. 1967a. The Incidence of the Corporation Income Tax in U.S. Manufacturing, 1925–62. *American Economic Review* 57 (September): 731–758.

———. 1967b. *Problems in the Measurement of Real Investment in the U.S. Private Economy*. Ph.D. Dissertation, Cambridge, MA: Massachusetts Institute of Technology,

Gordon, Roger H. 1974. The Investment Tax Credit as a Supplementary Discretionary Stabilization Tool. Paper presented at the Third NBER Stochastic Control Conference, May 29, 1974.

Gordon, Roger H., James R. Hines Jr., and Lawrence H. Summers. 1987. Notes on the Tax Treatment of Structures. In *The Effects of Taxation on Capital Accumulation*, ed. Martin S. Feldstein, 223–254. Chicago, IL: University of Chicago Press.

Gordon, Roger H., and Dale W. Jorgenson. 1972. Investment Incentives in the 1971 Tax Bill. *Business Economics* 7, no. 3: 7–13.

Gottsegen, Jack J. 1967. Revised Estimates of GNP by Major Industries. *Survey of Current Business* 47 (April): 18–24.

Gould, John P. 1968. Adjustment Costs in the Theory of Investment of the Firm. *Review of Economic Studies* 35 (January): 47–55.

———. 1969. The Use of Endogenous Variables in Dynamic Models of Investment. *Quarterly Journal of Economics* 83(4), no. 333 (November): 580–599.

Goulder, Lawrence H., and Lawrence H. Summers. 1989. Tax Policy, Asset Prices, and Growth: A General Equilibrium Analysis. *Journal of Public Economics* 38, no. 3 (April): 265–296.

Gravelle, Jane G. 1979. The Capital Cost Recovery System and the Corporate Income Tax. Report no. 79–230E (November). Washington, DC: Congressional Research Service.

————. 1980a. The Capital Cost Recovery Act: An Economic Analysis of 10–5–3 Depreciation. Report no. 80–29E (January). Washington, DC: Congressional Research Service.

————. 1980b. Depreciation Policy Options. Report no. 80–182E (October). Washington, DC: Congressional Research Service

————. 1980c. Inflation and the Taxation of Capital Income in the Corporate Sector: A Comment. *National Tax Journal* 33, no. 4, (December): 473–483.

————. 1984. Assessing Structural Tax Revision with Macroeconomic Models. Washington, DC: Congressional Research Service, Report 85–645E.

————. 1987. Tax Policy and Rental Housing: An Economic Analysis. Washington, DC: Congressional Research Service.

Gravelle, Jane G., and Laurence J. Kotlikoff. 1989. The Incidence and Efficiency Costs of Corporate Taxation when Corporate and Noncorporate Firms Produce the Same Good. *Journal of Political Economy* 97, no. 1 (August): 749–780.

Griliches, Zvi. 1960. The Demand for Durable Input: U.S. Farm Tractors in the United States, 1921–57. In *The Demand for Durable Goods*, ed. Arnold C. Harberger, 181–207. Chicago, IL: University of Chicago Press.

————. 1961. A Note on Serial Correlation Bias in Estimates of Distributed Lags. *Econometrica* 29, no. 1 (January): 65–73.

————. 1967a. Distributed Lags: A Survey. *Econometrica* 35, no. 1 (January): 16–49.

————. 1967b. More on CES Production Functions. *Review of Economics and Statistics* 49, no. 4 (November): 608–610.

————. 1967c. Production Functions in Manufacturing: Some Preliminary Results. In *The Theory and Empirical Analysis of Production*, ed. Murray Brown, 275–322. NBER Studies in Income and Wealth, vol. 31. New York, NY: Columbia University Press.

————. 1968a. The Brookings Model Volume: A Review Article. *Review of Economics and Statistics* 50, no. 2 (May): 215–234.

————. 1968b. Production Functions in Manufacturing: Some Additional Results. *Southern Economic Journal* 35, no. 2 (October): 151–156.

Griliches, Zvi, and Dale W. Jorgenson. 1966. Sources of Measured Productivity Change: Capital Input. *American Economic Review* 56, no. 2 (May): 50–61.

Grose, Lawrence, Irving Rottenberg, and Robert Wasson. 1969. New Estimates of Fixed Business Capital in the United States. *Survey of Current Business* 69 (February): 46–52.

Grunfeld, Yehuda. 1960. The Determinants of Corporate Investment. In *The Demand for Durable Goods*, ed. Arnold C. Harberger, 211–266. Chicago, IL: University of Chicago Press.

Haavelmo, Trygve. 1960a. *A Study in the Theory of Investment*. Chicago, IL: University of Chicago Press.

————. 1960b. The Individual Producer's Demand for Capital. In *A Study in the Theory of Investment*, Chapter 28, 161–170. Chicago, IL: University of Chicago Press.

Hall, Robert E. 1968. Technical Change and Capital from the Point of View of the Dual. *Review of Economic Studies* 35 (January): 35–46.

————. 1971a. The Measurement of Quality Changes from Vintage Price Data. In *Price Indexes and Quality Change*, ed. Zvi Griliches, 240–271. Cambridge, MA: Harvard University Press.

————. 1971b. The Dynamic Effects of Fiscal Policy in an Economy with Foresight. *Review of Economic Studies* 38(2), no. 114 (April): 229–244.

————. 1977. Investment, Interest Rates, and the Effects of Stabilization Policies. In *Brookings Papers on Economic Activity*, 61–122.

————. 1981. Tax Treatment of Depreciation, Capital Gains, and Interest in an Inflationary Economy. In *Depreciation, Inflation, and the Taxation of Income from Capital*, ed. Charles R. Hulten, 149–167. Washington, DC: The Urban Institute Press.

Hall, Robert E., and Dale W. Jorgenson. 1967. Tax Policy and Investment Behavior. *American Economic Review* 57, no. 3 (June): 391–414.

————. 1969a. Tax Policy and Investment Behavior: Reply and Further Results. *The American Economic Review* 59, no. 3 (June): 388–401.

————. 1969b. The Role of Taxation in Stabilizing Private Investment, In *Policy Makers and Model Builders, Cases and Concepts*, ed. Vincent P. Rock, 73–96. New York: Gordon and Breach.

————. 1971. Application of the Theory of Optimum Capital Accumulation. In *Tax Incentives and Capital Spending*, ed. Gary Fromm, 9–60. Washington, DC: Brookings Institution.

Hall, Robert E., and Alvin Rabushka. 1983. *Low Tax, Simple Tax, Flat Tax*. New York, NY: McGraw-Hill.

Harberger, Arnold C. (ed.) 1960. *The Demand for Durable Goods*. Chicago, IL: University of Chicago Press.

————. 1962. The Incidence of the Corporation Tax. *Journal of Political Economy* 70, no. 3 (June): 215–240.

————. 1966. Efficiency Effects of Taxes on Income from Capital. *Effects of Corporation Income Tax*, ed. Martin Krzyzaniak, 107–117. Detroit, MI: Wayne State University Press.

————. 1971. Chapter 7. In *Tax Incentives and Capital Spending*, ed. Gary Fromm. Washington, DC: Brookings Institution.

————. 1980. Tax Neutrality in Investment Incentives. In *The Economics of*

Taxation, eds. Henry J. Aaron and Michael J. Boskin, 299–313. Washington, DC: The Brookings Institution.

Hausman, Jerry A. 1981. Labor Supply. In *How Taxes Affect Economic Behavior*, eds. Henry J. Aaron and Joseph A. Pechman, 213–263. Washington, DC: The Brookings Institution.

————. 1985. Taxes and Labor Supply. In *Handbook of Public Economics*, Vol. 1, eds. Alan J. Auerbach and Martin S. Feldstein. Amsterdam: North-Holland.

Hausman, Jerry A., and James M. Poterba. 1987. Household Behavior and the Tax Reform Act of 1986. *Journal of Economic Perspectives* 1 (Summer): 101–119.

Henderson, Yolanda K. 1991. Applications of General Equilibrium Models to the 1986 Tax Reform Act in the United States. *de Economist* 139, no. 2: 147–168.

Hickman, B.G. 1965. *Investment Demand and U.S. Economic Growth*. Washington, DC: The Brookings Institution.

Hicks, John R. 1942. Consumers' Surplus and Index Numbers. *Review of Economic Studies* 9, no. 2 (Summer): 126–137.

————. 1946. *Value and Capital*, 2nd ed. Oxford: Oxford University Press.

Hirshleifer, Jack. 1958. On the Theory of the Optimal Investment Decision. *Journal of Political Economy* 66 (August): 329–352; reprinted in *The Management of Corporate Capital*, ed. E. Solomon, 205–228. Glencoe: The Free Press, 1959.

————. 1970. *Investment, Interest, and Capital*. Englewood Cliffs, NJ: Prentice Hall.

Hotelling, Harold S. (ed.) 1925. A General Mathematical Theory of Depreciation. *Journal of the American Statistical Association* 20 (September): 340–353.

Hulten, Charles R. 1981. *Depreciation, Inflation, and the Taxation of Income from Capital*. Washington, DC: The Urban Institute Press.

Hulten, Charles R., James W. Robertson, and Frank C. Wykoff. 1989. Energy, Obsolescence, and the Productivity Slowdown. In *Technology and Capital Formation*, eds. Dale W. Jorgenson and Ralph Landau, 225–258. Cambridge, MA: The MIT Press.

Hulten, Charles R., and Frank C. Wykoff. 1979. Tax and Economic Depreciation of Machinery and Equipment: A Theoretical and Empirical Appraisal. *Report to the Office of Tax Analysis*. U.S. Department of Treasury.

————. 1980. Economic Depreciation and the Taxation of Structures in U.S. Manufacturing Industries: Empirical Analysis. In *The Measurement of Capital*, 83–109. Chicago, IL: University of Chicago Press.

————. 1981a. The Estimation of Economic Depreciation Using Vintage Asset Prices: An Application of the Box-Cox Power Transformation. *Journal of Econometrics* 15, no. 3 (April): 367–396.

————. 1981b. The Measurement of Economic Depreciation. In *Depreciation, Inflation, and the Taxation of Income from Capital*, ed. Charles R. Hulten, 81–125. Washington, DC: The Urban Institute.

Jaszi, George, Robert Wasson, and Lawrence Grose. 1962. Expansion of Fixed Business Capital in the United States. *Survey of Current Business* 42 (November): 9–18.

Jeremias, Ronald A. 1979. Dead-Weight Loss from Tax-Induced Distortion of Capital Mix. Ph.D. Dissertation, Virginia Polytechnic Institute and State University.

Joint Committee on Taxation. 1981. *General Explanation of the Economic Recovery Tax Act of 1981*. Washington, DC: U.S. Congress.

———. 1982. General Explanation of the Revenue Provisions of the Tax Equity and Fiscal Responsibility Act of 1982. Washington, DC: U.S. Congress.

———. 1986. *Summary of Conference Agreement on H.R. 3838 (Tax Reform Act of 1986)*. Washington, DC: U.S. Government Printing Office.

Jorgenson, Dale W. 1963. Capital Theory and Investment Behavior. *American Economic Review* 53, no. 2 (May): 247–259.

———. 1965. Anticipations and Investment Behavior. In *The Brookings Quarterly Econometric Model of the United States*, eds. James S. Duesenberry, Edwin Kuh, Gary Fromm, and Lawrence R. Klein, 35–92. Chicago, IL: Rand McNally.

———. 1966. Rational Distributed Lag Functions. *Econometrica* 34, no. 1 (January): 135–149.

———. 1967. The Theory of Investment Behavior. In *Determinants of Investment Behavior*, ed. Robert Ferber, 129–156. New York: National Bureau of Economic Research.

———. 1971a. Econometric Studies of Investment Behavior: A Review. *Journal of Economic Literature* 9, no. 4 (December): 1111–1147.

———. 1971b. The Economic Impact of Investment Incentives. In *Long-term Economic Implications of Current Tax and Spending Proposals*, Joint Economic Committee, Congress of the United States, 92nd Congress, First Session, May 1971, 176–192.

———. 1972. Investment Behavior and the Production Function. *The Bell Journal of Economics and Management Science* 3, no. 1 (Spring): 220–251.

———. 1973. The Economic Theory of Replacement and Depreciation. In *Econometrics and Econometric Theory*, ed. W. Sellekaerts, 189–221. New York, NY: MacMillan.

Jorgenson, Dale W. 1979a. Statement. In *Tax Restructuring Act of 1979*, Committee on Ways and Means, 62–76. Washington, DC: Ninety-Second Congress, First Session.

——— 1979b. Statement. In *Tax Cut Proposals*, Part 2, Committee on Finance, 349–378. Washington, DC: Ninety-Sixth Congress, Second Session.

———. 1980. Accounting for Capital. In *Capital Efficiency and Growth*, ed. George von Furstenberg, 251–319. Cambridge, MA: Ballinger.

————. 1983. Modeling Production for General Equilibrium Analysis. *Scandinavian Journal of Economics* 85, no. 2: 101–112.

————. 1984. Econometric Methods for Applied General Equilibrium Analysis. In *Applied General Equilibrium Analysis*, eds. H. Scarf and John Shoven, 139–203. Cambridge, Cambridge University Press.

————. 1989. Capital as a Factor of Production. In *Technology and Capital Formation*, eds., Dale W. Jorgenson and Ralph Landau, 1–35. Cambridge, MA: The MIT Press.

————. 1993. Introduction and Summary. In *Tax Reform and the Cost of Capital: An International Comparison*, eds. Dale W. Jorgenson and Ralph Landau, 1–56. Washington, DC: The Brookings Institution.

————. 1995. *Productivity, Volume 1: Postwar U.S. Economic Growth.* Cambridge, MA: The MIT Press.

Jorgenson, Dale W., Frank M. Gollop, and Barbara M. Fraumeni. 1987. *Productivity and U.S. Economic Growth.* Cambridge, MA: Harvard University Press.

Jorgenson, Dale W., and Zvi Griliches. 1967. The Explanation of Productivity Change. *Review of Economic Studies* 34, no. 99 (July): 249–280.

Jorgenson, Dale W., and S.S. Handel. 1971. Investment Behavior in U.S. Regulated Industries. *The Bell Journal of Economics and Management Science* 2, no. 1 (Spring): 213–264.

Jorgenson, Dale W., Jerald Hunter, and Mohammed Ishaq Nadiri. 1970a. A Comparison of Alternative Econometric Models of Quarterly Investment Behavior. *Econometrica* 38, no. 2 (March): 187–212.

————. 1970b. The Predictive Performance of Econometric Models of Quarterly Investment Behavior. *Econometrica* 38, no. 2 (March): 213–224.

Jorgenson, Dale W., and Jean-Jacques Laffont. 1974. Efficient Estimation of Nonlinear Simultaneous Equations with Additive Disturbances. *Annals of Social and Economic Measurement* 3, no. 4 (October): 615–640.

Jorgenson, Dale W., and Ralph Landau, eds. 1989. *Technology and Capital Formation.* Cambridge, MA: The MIT Press.

Jorgenson, Dale W., Lawrence J. Lau, and Thomas M. Stoker. 1980. Welfare Comparison and Exact Aggregation. *American Economic Review* 70, no. 2 (May): 268–272.

————. 1981. Aggregate Consumer and Individual Welfare. *Macroeconomic Analysis*, eds. D. Currie, R. Nobay, and D. Peel, 35–61. London: Croom-Helm.

————. 1982. The Transcendental Logarithmic Model of Aggregate Consumer Behavior. *Advances in Econometrics*, Vol. I, eds. Robert L. Basmann and G. Rhodes, 97–238. Greenwich: JAI Press.

Jorgenson, Dale W., J.J. McCall, and R. Radner. 1967. *Optimal Replacement Policy.* Amsterdam: North-Holland.

Jorgenson, Dale W., and Calvin D. Siebert. 1968a. A Comparison of Alternative Theories of Corporate Investment Behavior. *American Economic Review* 58, no. 4 (September): 681–712.

————. 1968b. Optimal Capital Accumulation and Corporate Investment Behavior. *Journal of Political Economy* 76, no. 6 (November/December): 1123–1151.

————. 1972. An Empirical Evaluation of Alternative Theories of Corporate Investment. In *Problems and Issues in Current Econometric Practice*, ed. K. Brunner, 155–218. Columbus, OH: Ohio State University.

Jorgenson, Dale W., and D.T. Slesnick. 1984. Aggregate Consumer Behavior and the Measurement of Inequality. *Review of Economic Studies* 51(3), no. 166 (July): 369–392.

Jorgenson, Dale W., and J.A. Stephenson. 1967a. The Time Structure of Investment Behavior in U.S. Manufacturing, 1947–1960. *Review of Economics and Statistics* 49, no. 1 (February), 16–27.

————. 1967b. Investment Behavior in U.S. Manufacturing, 1947–1960. *Econometrica* 35, no. 2 (April): 169–220.

————. 1969a. Anticipations and Investment Behavior in U.S. Manufacturing, 1947–1960. *Journal of the American Statistical Association* 64, no. 325 (March): 67–89.

————. 1969b. Issues in the Development of the Neo-Classical Theory of Investment Behavior. *Review of Economics and Statistics* 51, no. 3 (August): 346–353.

Jorgenson, Dale W., and Martin A. Sullivan. 1981. Inflation and Corporate Capital Recovery. In *Depreciation, Inflation, and the Taxation of Income from Capital*, ed. Charles R. Hulten, 171–237, 311–313. Washington, DC: The Urban Institute.

Jorgenson, Dale W., and Kun-Young Yun. 1986a. The Efficiency of Capital Allocation. *Scandinavian Journal of Economics* 88, no. 1: 85–107.

————. 1986b. Tax Policy and Capital Allocation. *Scandinavian Journal of Economics* 88, no. 2: 355–377.

————. 1990. Tax Reform and U.S. Economic Growth. *Journal of Political Economy* 98, no. 5 (part 2, October): S151–S193.

————. 1991. *Tax Reform and the Cost of Capital.* New York, NY: Oxford University Press.

Judd, Kenneth L. 1987. The Welfare Cost of Factor Taxation in a Perfect-Foresight Model. *Journal of Political Economy* 95, no. 4 (August): 675–709.

Karlin, S. 1959. *Mathematical Methods and Theory in Games, Programming and Economics.* Reading, MA: Addison-Wesley.

Kay, J.A. 1980. The Deadweight Loss from a Tax System. *Journal of Public Economics* 13, no. 1 (February): 111–119.

King, Mervyn A. 1977. *Public Policy and the Corporation.* London: Chapman and Hall.

King, Mervyn A., and Don Fullerton. 1984. *The Taxation of Income from Capital: A Comparative Study of the United States, the United Kingdom, Sweden, and West Germany.* Chicago, IL: University of Chicago Press.

Klein, Lawrence R. 1950. *Economic Fluctuations in the United States, 1921–1941.* Cowles Commission for Research in Economics, Monograph No. 11. New York, NY: John Wiley and Sons.

————. 1951. Studies in Investment Behavior. In *Conference on Business Cycles,* Universities-National Bureau Conference Series, no. 2, 233–303. New York, NY: Columbia University Press for the National Bureau of Economic Research.

Klotz, B.P. 1970. *Productivity Analysis in Manufacturing Plants.* BLS Staff Paper 3, U.S. Department of Labor.

Kmenta, Jan. 1967. On Estimation of the CES Production Function. *International Economic Review* 8, no. 2 (June): 180–189.

Koopmans, Tjalling C. 1957. Allocation of Resources and the Price System. In *Three Essays on the State of Economic Science,* ed. Tjalling C. Koopmans, 1–126. New York, NY: McGraw Hill.

Kotlikoff, Laurence J., and Lawrence H. Summers. 1981. The Role of Intergenerational Transfers in Capital Accumulation. *Journal of Political Economy* 89, no. 4 (August): 706–732.

Koyck, Leendert M. 1954. *Distributed Lags and Investment Analysis.* Amsterdam: North-Holland.

Krzyzaniak, Marian, and Richard A. Musgrave. 1963. *The Shifting of the Corporation Income Tax: An Empirical Study of its Short-run Effect upon the Rate of Return.* Baltimore, MD: John Hopkins Press.

Kuhn, H.W., and A.W. Tucker. 1950. Nonlinear Programming. In *Proceedings of the Second Berkeley Symposium on Mathematical Statistics and Probability,* ed. J. Neyman, 481–492. Berkeley, CA: University of California Press.

Kurtz, E.B. 1930. *Life Expectancy of Physical Property Based on Mortality Laws.* New York, NY: Ronald Press.

Kuznets, Simon. 1961. *Capital in the American Economy: Its Formation and Financing.* Princeton, NJ: Princeton University Press.

Leape, Jonathan. 1980. Tax Incentives and Capital Formation. Washington, DC: U.S. House of Representatives, Committee on Ways and Means.

Leontief, Wassily W. 1951. *The Structure of the American Economy, 1919–1939,* 2nd ed. New York, NY: Oxford University Press.

Lerner, Abba P. 1944. Capital, Investment, and Interest. In *The Economics of Control,* Chapter 25, 323–345. New York, NY: The Macmillan Company.

Levhari, David, and Eytan Sheshinski. 1972. Lifetime Excess Burden of a Tax. *Journal of Political Economy* 80, no. 1 (January-February): 139–147.

Lindahl, Erik. 1939. The Place of Capital in the Theory of Prices. In *Studies in the Theory of Money and Capital*, ed. E. Lindahl. London: Allen and Unwin.

Lipton, David, James M. Poterba, Jeffrey Sachs, and Lawrence H. Summers. 1982. Multiple Shooting in Rational Expectations Models. *Econometrica* 50, no. 5 (September): 1329–1333.

Lodin, S.O. 1976. *Progressive Expenditure Tax — An Alternative?* Stockholm: LiberForlag.

Lucas, Robert E. 1967a. Adjustment Costs and the Theory of Supply. *Journal of Political Economics* 75, no. 4 (August): 321–334.

———. 1967b. Optimal Investment Policy and the Flexible Accelerator. *International Economic Review* 8 (February): 78–85.

———. 1969. Labor-Capital Substitution in U.S. Manufacturing. *The Taxation of Income from Capital*, eds. Arnold C. Harberger and M.J. Bailey, 223–274. Washington, DC: The Brookings Institution.

———. 1976. Econometric Policy Evaluation: A Critique. In *The Phillips Curve and Labor Markets*, eds. Karl Brunner and Allan H. Meltzer, 19–46. Amsterdam, North-Holland.

———. 1990. Supply-Side Economics: An Analytical Review. *Oxford Economic Papers* 42, no. 3 (August): 293–316.

Lutz, Friedrich A. 1961. The Essentials of Capital Theory. In *The Theory of Capital*, eds. Friedrich A. Lutz and D. Hague, 3–17. London: Macmillan.

Malinvaud, Edmond. 1953. Capital Accumulation and the Efficient Allocation of Resources. *Econometrica* 21, no. 2 (April): 233–268.

———. 1961. Estimation et Prévision dans les Modèles Economiques Autoregressifs. *Revue de l'Institut International de Statistique* 29, no. 2: 1–32.

Marston, Anson, Robley Winfrey, and John C. Hempstead. 1953. *Engineering Evaluation and Depreciation*, 2nd ed. New York, NY: McGraw-Hill.

Mayer, Thomas. 1960. Plant and Equipment Lead Times. *Journal of Business* 33, no. 2 (April): 127–132.

McLure, Charles E. 1975. General Equilibrium Incidence Analysis: The Harberger Model after Ten Years. *Journal of Public Economics* 4, no. 2 (February) 125–161.

McLure, Charles E., and George R. Zodrow. 1987. Treasury I and the Tax Reform Act of 1986: The Economics and Politics of Tax Reform. *Journal of Economic Perspectives* 1 (Summer): 37–58.

McKinnon, R.I. 1962. Wages, Capital Costs, and Employment in Manufacturing: A Model Applied to 1947–1958 U.S. Data. *Econometrica* 30, no. 3 (July): 501–21.

Meade, James Edward. 1978. *The Structure and Reform of Direct Taxation: Report of a Committee Chaired by Professor James Edward Meade.* London: Allen and Unwin.

Meyer, John R., and Robert R. Glauber. 1964. *Investment Decisions, Economic Forecasting and Public Policy.* Boston, MA: Division of Research, Graduate School of Business Administration, Harvard University.

Meyer, John R., and Edwin Kuh. 1957. *The Investment Decision: An Empirical Study.* Cambridge, MA: Harvard University Press.

Minasian, Jora R. 1961. Elasticities of Substitution and Constant-Output Demand Curves for Labor. *Journal of Political Economy* 69, no. 3 (June): 261–270.

Mirrlees, J.A. 1971. An Exploration in the Theory of Optimal Income Taxation. *Review of Economic Studies* 38(2), no. 114 (April): 175–208.

――――. 1976. Optimal Tax Theory: A Synthesis. *Journal of Public Economics* 6, no. 4 (November): 327–358.

Mundlak, Yair. 1966. On the Microeconomic Theory of Distributed Lags. *Review of Economics and Statistics* 48, no. 1 (February): 51–60.

――――. 1967. Long-Run Coefficients and Distributed Lag Analysis: A Reformulation. *Econometrica* 35, no. 2 (April): 278–293.

Musgrave, Richard A. 1959. Tax Deductibility of Economic Depreciation to Insure Invariant Valuations. *The Theory of Public Finance.* New York, NY: McGraw-Hill.

――――. 1963. Effects of Tax Policy on Private Capital Formation. In *Fiscal and Debt Management Policies,* Commission on Money and Credit, 45–142. Englewood Cliffs, NJ: Prentice-Hall.

――――. 1987. Short of Euphoria. *Journal of Economic Perspectives* 1 (Summer): 59–71.

Myers, John H. 1960. The Influence of Salvage Value Upon the Choice of Tax Depreciation Methods. *The Accounting Review* 35, no. 4 (October): 598–602.

Nerlove, Marc. 1967. Recent Empirical Studies of the CES and Related Production Functions. In *The Theory and Empirical Analysis of Production,* ed. Murray Brown, 55–122. NBER Studies in Income and Wealth, Vol. 32. New York, NY: Columbia University Press for the National Bureau of Economics.

Office of Industrial Economics. 1975. Business Building Statistics. Washington, DC: U.S. Department of the Treasury (August).

Pechman, Joseph A. 1971. *Federal Tax Policy,* 2nd ed. 115. New York, NY: W. Norton.

――――. 1977. *Federal Tax Policy,* 3rd ed. Washington, DC: The Brookings Institution.

――――. 1987. Tax Reform: Theory and Practice. *Journal of Economic Pespectives* 1 (Summer): 11–28.

Picou, G.C., and Roger N. Waud. 1973. The Cost of Capital, the Desired Capital Stock, and a Variable Investment Tax Credit as a Stabilization Tool. Special Studies Paper No. 37. Washington, DC: Federal Reserve Board.

Pierce, J.L., and P.A. Tinsley. 1972. A Proposal for a Policy Instrument to Affect Business Investment. In Federal Reserve Staff Study, *Ways to Moderate Fluctuations in Housing Construction*, 345–354. Washington, DC: Federal Reserve.

Pontryagin, Lev S., V.G. Boltyanskii, R.V. Gamkrelidze, and E.F. Mishchenko. 1962. *The Mathematical Theory of Optimal Processes*, trans. K.N. Trirogoff. New York, NY: Interscience Publishers.

Poterba, James M., and Lawrence H. Summers. 1983. Dividend Taxes, Corporate Investment, and 'Q'. *Journal of Public Economics* 22, no. 2 (November): 135–167.

President's Task Force on Business Taxation. 1970. *Business Taxation* (September).

Roos, Charles F. 1948. The Demand for Investment Goods. *American Economic Review* 38 (May), 311–320.

———. 1955. Survey of Economic Forecasting Techniques. *Econometrica* 23 (October): 363–395.

Roos, Charles F., and Victor S. von Szeliski. 1943. The Demand for Durable Goods. *Econometrica* 11 (April): 97–122.

Salomon Brothers. *Analytical Handbook of Yields and Yield Ratio*.

Samuelson, Paul A. 1947. *Foundations of Economic Analysis*. Cambridge, MA: Harvard University Press.

———. 1964. Tax Deductibility of Economic Depreciation to Insure Invariant Valuations. *Journal of Political Economy* 72 (December): 604–606.

Sandmo, Agnar. 1985. The Effects of Taxation on Savings and Risk Taking. In *Handbook of Public Economics*, vol. 1, eds. Alan J. Auerbach and Martin S. Feldstein, 265–311. Amsterdam: North-Holland.

Scheffé, H. 1959. *The Analysis of Variance*. New York: John Wiley and Sons.

Shoven, John B. 1976. The Incidence and Efficiency Effects of Taxes on Income from Capital. *Journal of Political Economy* 84, no. 6 (December):1261–1284.

Shoven, John B., and John Whalley. 1972. A General Equilibrium Calculation of the Effects of Differential Taxation of Income from Capital in the U.S. *Journal of Public Economics* 1, no. 3/4 (November): 281–321.

Sinn, Hans-Werner. 1981. Capital Income Taxation, Depreciation Allowances and Economic Growth: A Perfect-Foresight General Equilibrium Model. *Zeitschrift für Nationalökonomie* 41, nos. 3–4: 295–305.

———. 1987. *Capital Income Taxation and Resource Allocation*. Amsterdam: North-Holland.

———. 1991. Taxation and the Cost of Capital: The 'Old' View, the 'New' View, and Another View. In *Tax Policy and the Economy*, vol. 5, ed. David Bradford, 25–54. Cambridge, MA: The MIT Press.

Smith, Vernon L. 1963. Tax Depreciation Policy and Investment Theory. *International Economic Review* 4 (January): 80–91.

Solow, Robert M. 1960. Investment and Technical Progress. In *Mathematical Methods in the Social Sciences, 1959*, eds. Kenneth J. Arrow, Samuel Karlin, and Patrick Suppes, 89–104. Stanford, CA: Stanford University Press.

———. 1964. Capital, Labor, and Income in Manufacturing. In *The Behavior of Income Shares*, 101–128. NBER Studies in Income and Wealth, Vol. 27. Princeton, NJ: Princeton University Press for the National Bureau of Economics.

Stiglitz, Joe E. 1976. The Corporation Tax. *Journal of Public Economics* 5, Nos. 3–4 (April-May): 303–311.

Stiglitz, Joe E., and P.S. Dasgupta. 1971. Differential Taxation, Public Goods and Economic Efficiency. *Review of Economic Studies* 38(2), no. 114 (April): 151–174.

Strotz, Robert H. 1956. Myopia and Inconsistency in Dynamic Utility Maximization. *Review of Economic Studies* 23 (January): 165–180.

Stuart, Charles. 1984. Welfare Costs Per Dollar of Additional Tax Revenue in the United States. *American Economic Review* 74, no. 3 (June): 352–362.

Summers, Lawrence H. 1981. Capital Taxation and Accumulation in a Life-Cycle Growth Model. *American Economic Review* 71, no. 4 (September): 533–544.

———. 1983. The Nonadjustment of Nominal Interest Rates: A Study of the Fisher Effect. In *Macroeconomics, Prices and Quantities: Essays in Memory of Arthur M. Okun*, ed. James Tobin, 204–241. Washington, DC: The Brookings Institution.

———. 1984. The After-Tax Rate of Return Affects Private Savings. *American Economic Review* 74, no. 2 (May): 249–253.

Tinbergen, Jan. 1939. *Statistical Testing of Business Cycle Theories, Vol. I: A Method and its Application to Investment Activity*. Geneva: League of Nations.

———. 1956. *Economic Policy: Principles and Design*, 3–10. Amsterdam: North-Holland.

Treadway, Arthur B. 1969a. On Rational Entrepreneurial Behaviour and the Demand for Investment. *Review of Economic Studies* 36(2), no. 106 (April): 227–239.

———. 1969b. On a Dynamic Theory of the Competitive Firm and its Implications for Propositions in Static Theory. Unpublished manuscript, April, 62 pp.

Ture, Norman B. 1963. Tax Reform: Depreciation Problems. *American Economic Review* 53, no. 2 (May): 334–353.

Turnovsky, Stephen J. 1982. The Incidence of Taxes: A Dynamic Macroeconomic Analysis. *Journal of Public Economics* 18, no. 2 (July): 161–194.

U.S. Department of Commerce. 1958. Office of Business Economics. *U.S. Income and Output.*

――――. 1959. Office of Business Economics. *Survey of Current Business,* and subsequent issues.

――――. 1966. Office of Business Economics, *The National Income and Product Accounts of the United States, 1929–1965, Statistical Tables.*

U.S. Department of the Treasury. 1977. *Blueprints for Basic Tax Reform.* Washington, DC: U.S. Government Printing Office.

――――. 1984. *Tax Reform for Simplicity, Fairness, and Economic Growth,* 3 vols. Washington, DC: U.S. Government Printing Office.

――――. 1985. *The President's Tax Proposals to the Congress for Fairness, Growth, and Simplicity.* Washington, DC: U.S. Government Printing Office.

――――. 1987. *Compendium of Tax Research 1987.* Washington, DC: U.S. Government Printing Office.

U.S. Department of the Treasury, Bureau of Internal Revenue. 1942. Income Tax Depreciation and Obsolescence Estimated Useful Lives and Depreciation Rates. Bulletin F (Revised Jan. 1942).

U.S. Department of the Treasury, Internal Revenue Service. 1959. Supplementary Depreciation Data from Corporate Returns. *Statistics of Income.*

――――. 1962. Depreciation Guidelines and Rules. Pub. 456 (July): 7–62.

――――. 1965. *Statistics of Income — 1959: Supplementary Depreciation Data from Corporation Income Tax Returns, with Special Appendix — Depreciation Methods and Amortization Data, 1954 through 1961* (June).

――――. 1968. *Statistics of Income — 1963, Corporation Income Tax Returns.*

U.S. Department of the Treasury, Office of Tax Analysis. 1962. Release, July 10.

Uzawa, Hirofumi. 1969. Time Preference and the Penrose Effect in a Two-Class Model of Economic Growth. *Journal of Political Economics* 77, no. 4 (July-August): 628–652.

Vasquez, Thomas. 1974. The Effects of the Asset Depreciation Range System on Depreciation Practices. Office of Tax Analysis Paper no. 1 (May). Washington, DC: U.S. Department of the Treasury.

Wales, Terrence J. 1966. Estimation of an Accelerated Depreciation Learning Function. *Journal of the American Statistical Association* 61, no. 316 (December): 995–1009.

Walras, L. 1954. *Elements of Pure Economics.* Translated by W. Jaffé. Homewood, IL: Richard D. Irwin, Inc.

Walters, Alan A. 1963. Production and Cost Functions: An Econometric Survey. *Econometrica* 31, nos. 1–2 (January–April): 1–66.

Whalley, John. 1988. Lessons from General Equilibrium Models. In *Uneasy Compromise: Problems of a Hybrid Income-Consumption Tax*, eds. Henry J. Aaron, Harvey Galper, and Joseph A. Pechman, 15–50. Washington, DC: The Brookings Institution.

White, William H. 1956. Interest Inelasticity of Investment Demand — The Case from Business Attitude Surveys Reexamined. *American Economic Review* 46 (September): 565–587.

Wicksell, Knut. 1934a. The Theory of Production and Distribution. In *Lectures on Political Economy*, translated by E. Classen, vol. I, part II, 144–206. London: Routledge and Kegan Paul (first published in Swedish, 1923).

———. 1934b. A Mathematical Analysis of Dr. Åkerman's Problem. In *Lectures on Political Economy*, ed. L. Robbins, trans. E. Classen, vol. I, 274–299. London: Routledge and Kegan Paul.

Wykoff, Frank C. 1970. Capital Depreciation in the Postwar Period: Automobiles. *Review of Economics and Statistics* 52, no. 2 (May): 168–172.

Young, Allan H. 1968. Alternative Estimates of Corporate Depreciation and Profits: Part I. *Survey of Current Business* 48, no. 4 (April): 17–28.

Young, Allan H., and John C. Musgrave. 1980. Estimation of Capital Stock in the United States. In *The Measurement of Capital*, ed. Dan Usher, 23–58. Chicago, IL: University of Chicago Press.

Zarembka, P. 1970. On the Empirical Relevance of the CES Production Function. *Review of Economics and Statistics* 52, no. 1 (February): 47–53.

Zarembka, P., and H. Chernicoff. 1971. Further Results on the Empirical Relevance of the CES Production Function. *Review of Economics and Statistics* 53, no. 1 (February): 106–110.

Index